JOHN CONSTANTINE
HELLBLAZER
original sins

JAMIE DELANO
WRITER

JOHN RIDGWAY
ALFREDO ALCALA
ARTISTS

LOVERN KINDZIERSKI
COLORIST

ANNIE HALFACREE
TODD KLEIN
JOHN COSTANZA
LETTERERS

DAVE MCKEAN
COVERS

DC COMICS

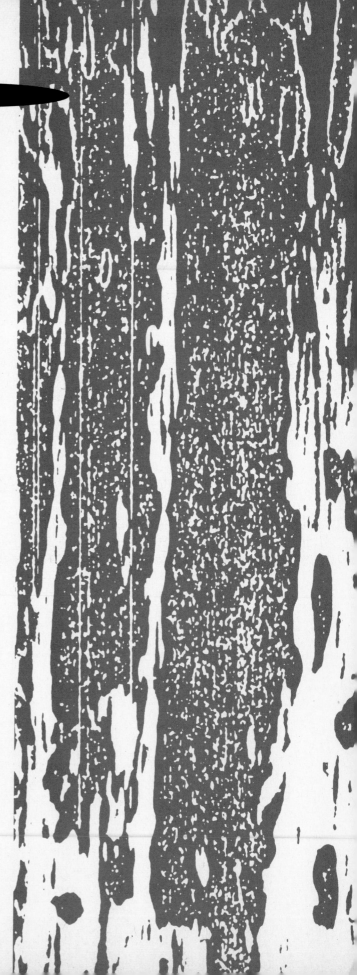

JOHN CONSTANTINE
HELLBLAZER: ORIGINAL SINS
Published by DC Comics. Cover and compilation
copyright © 1992.
All Rights Reserved.

Originally published in single magazine form
as HELLBLAZER #1-9.
Copyright © 1987, 1988 DC Comics. All Rights
Reserved. All characters, their distinctive likenesses
and related indicia featured in this publication are
trademarks of DC Comics.
The stories, characters, and incidents featured in
this publication are entirely fictional.
DC Comics
1700 Broadway
New York, NY 10019
DC Comics. A division of Warner Bros.
- A Time Warner Entertainment Company.
Printed in Canada.
Third Printing.
ISBN: 1-56389-052-6

Pages 179, 180, 181
Brett Ewins and Jim McCarthy
Artists.

Cover illustration by Dave McKean.

INTRODUCTION

n writing this introduction, a mild sense of *déjà vu* is unavoidable.

As it was back in 1987, when I began work on the stories contained in this volume, it is election year in both the U.K. and the U.S.A. Over here, it appears that some of the Thatcherite "vultures" may be coming home to roost—or at least to hover patiently over the disabled and whining Tory body-politic. It would be nice to think that Bush and his Republican reptiles might similarly be forced back under their stones. Perhaps such an occurrence would be a tiny encouragement, indicating a minute turbulence of conscience disturbing the blank stare of our culture's self-righteous myopia.

'Trouble is, it is probably too late to make any difference. The planet's immune system is still going to reject us if we don't ease up immediately, and the democratic left has no more desire for revolutionary change to our suicidal consumerist life-styles than does the right.

My personal response to the state of our civilisation has been to acquire a boat to live on. Then, when the oceans rise, I shall be able to sail cheerfully about, sneering at the capitalists marooned on their skyscraper-islands in the flooded financial districts of the northern hemisphere, basking contentedly in the solar radiation pouring, unfiltered, down upon a sterile ocean from a pure blue ozone-hole.

Late news: The right retains power in the U.K. No wheels on our wagon, now.

I had begun to think that perhaps the popularity of the horror genre during the last decade was in some way a product of the hellish zeitgeist of the 90's and that maybe the concerns of the 1990's would call for a more forward-looking, radical-evolutionary response from fiction. No such luck. Greed and self-interest prevail and our collective subconscious will continue to squirm and extrude guilty nightmares in response.

So fill up your inkwells with blood, chaps. Sharpen your bone stylus and stretch your human-skin vellum. If you thought you saw a lightening of the sky, it was but a false dawn, or a reactor fire somewhere just over the horizon.

These stories are the first nine in a currently continuing monthly comic-book series published by DC Comics under the title, HELLBLAZER. They detail the adventurings of one John Constantine, an insouciant, somewhat amoral occult dabbler and "psychic detective" with a British working-class background.

John Constantine first strolled into the repertory of comic-book characters as a creation of Alan Moore during his tenure on THE SAGA OF THE SWAMP THING. The cruel wit and elusive personality with which Moore imbued the character proved popular with readers and it was decided by the publishers that a series featuring John Constantine in his own right would be a viable proposition. I was approached by editor Karen Berger to provide scripts for John Ridgway to visualize. I could not refuse.

These stories are the result of that initial collaboration. Subject, as they are, to the constraints imposed by the necessity of feeding a voracious monthly publishing schedule, there are imperfections but, re-reading them now, I am far less embarrassed than I feared I might be.

Problems often arise when comic-book series are collected in one volume. Most of these can be laid at the door of "continuity." By this I mean the tradition amongst comic-book publishers to suppose that their diverse casts of characters contemporaneously occupy a "shared Universe." This concept obviously provides for the practice of allowing the story-lines of individual stories to "cross-over" with those of other related series. This may be fun for marketing executives and devoted comics aficionados but, in my personal experience, can be tedious for creators and casual, or selective, readers.

As you may have guessed, a cross-over is involved in the later stories in this volume. It arose as a result of the desire of Rick Veitch, who took over the scripting and drawing of SWAMP THING with the departure of Alan Moore, to develop a story-line which included a role for John Constantine before he was aware that Constantine was to "star" in his own new series.

The role for which Rick, a creator whom I admire, had destined Constantine was one which coincided well with my own concept of the character and which, in addition, provided me with a potential method of reconciling my own story-line. I therefore did not find it difficult to cooperate.

It is possible to read and, I hope, enjoy these nine stories without any knowledge of the details of Constantine's involvement with The Swamp Thing.

However, I feel that the unexplained appearance of The Swamp Thing, growing out of Constantine's box of duty-free cigarettes, is a somewhat unsatisfactory conclusion to the volume.

It may therefore help you to resolve the strands of the story if you know that: a) The Swamp Thing is a plant elemental who can animate any organic matter; b) He has a human wife; c) They want to have a "baby"; d) In order to accomplish this, Swamp Thing has realised that he requires a human body that, animated by him, will provide him with a biological means of impregnating his wife. The Swamp Thing has elected John Constantine to be this surrogate. Constantine is unaware of this.

Meanwhile...Constantine's balancing act between the Resurrection Crusade and the Damnation Army has gone a bit out of kilter. He has managed to thwart the messianic plans of the Resurrection Crusaders, but this leaves the equally reprehensible Damnation Army with an advantage that he must redress.

Aware of the demon Nergal's prophecy (detailed in "Intensive Care"), Constantine independently concludes that this might be fulfilled if he offers his sexual services to The Swamp Thing, with whom he is uneasily familiar; thus accomplishing the birth of the offspring who will represent "a conjunction between nature and super-nature..." He is ruminating upon the possibility of contacting The Swamp Thing and embroiling him in this plan when The Swamp Thing "coincidentally" materialises in front of him.

There, that was relatively painless, wasn't it? I'm sure everything will make perfect sense now.

It only remains for me to thank everybody concerned in the creation of these fictions, particularly Karen Berger, whose gentle hand on the tiller is always much appreciated and to wish you, the reader, as much dubious pleasure in their reading as I gained from their writing.

Just remember, as Constantine points out, "There's more than one road to Hell."

See you there.

Jamie Delano
April 1992
Afloat on the Grand Union Canal, Northamptonshire.

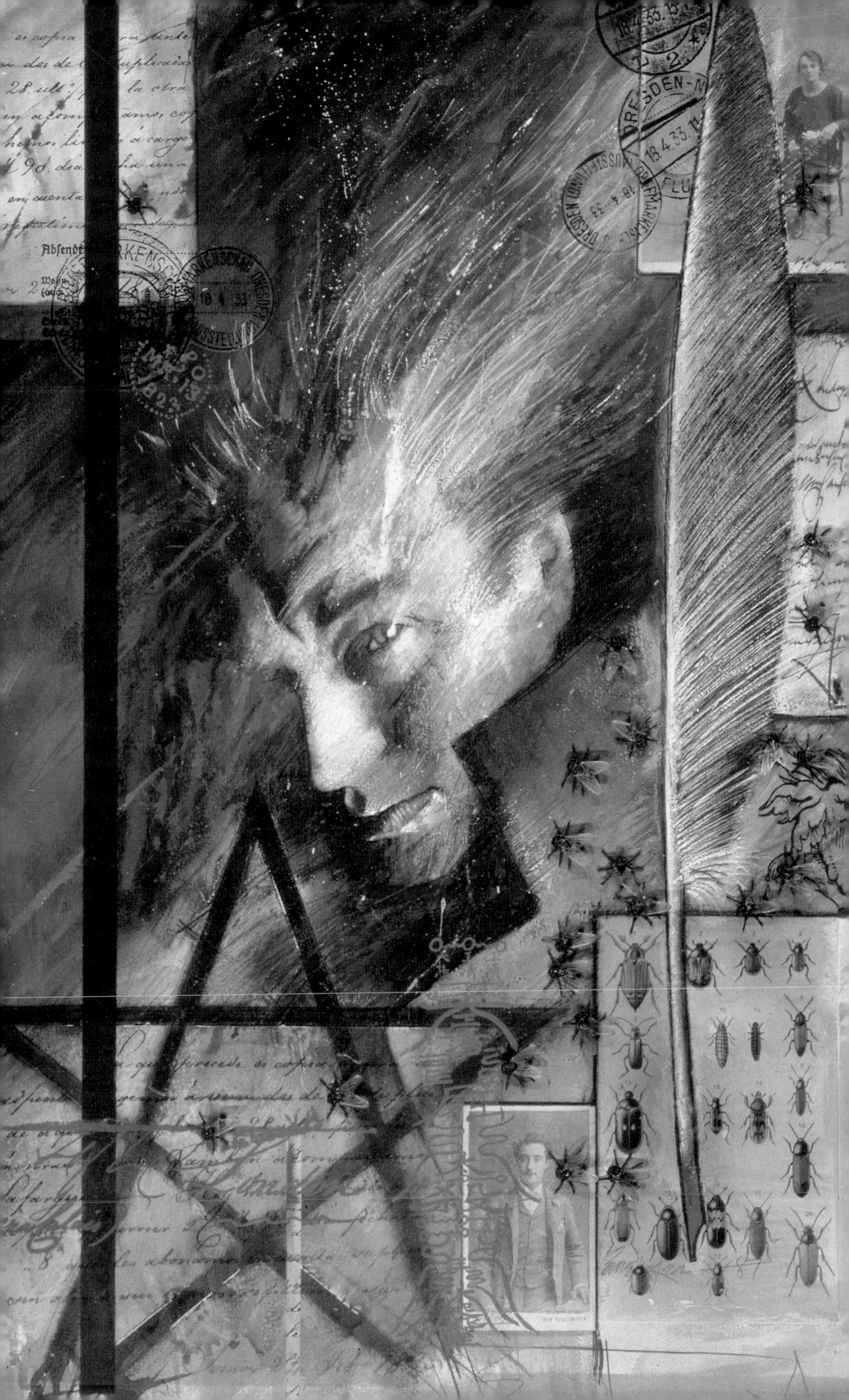
DRESDEN-N
18.4.33

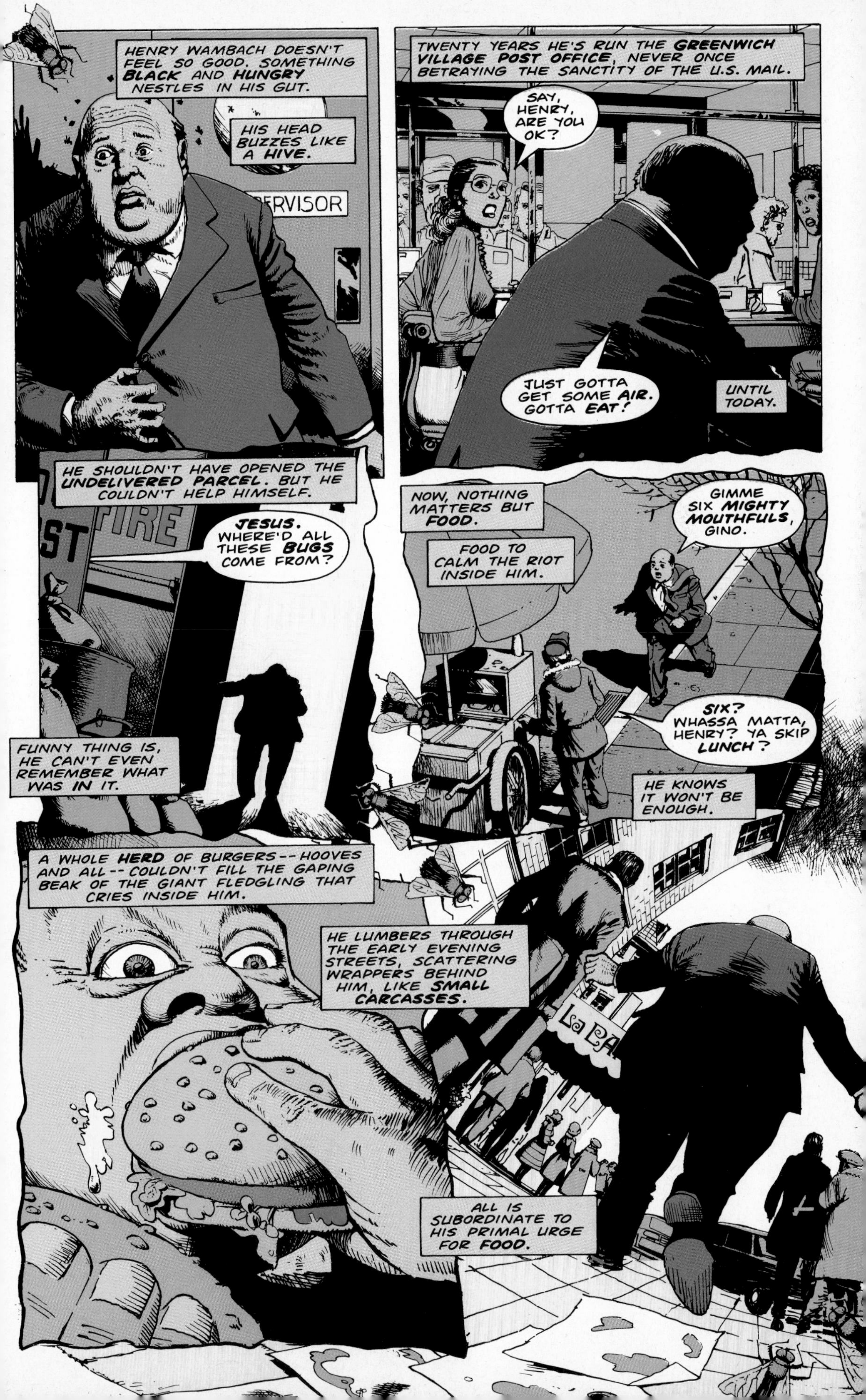
HENRY WAMBACH DOESN'T FEEL SO GOOD. SOMETHING BLACK AND HUNGRY NESTLES IN HIS GUT.
HIS HEAD BUZZES LIKE A HIVE.
ERVISOR
TWENTY YEARS HE'S RUN THE GREENWICH VILLAGE POST OFFICE, NEVER ONCE BETRAYING THE SANCTITY OF THE U.S. MAIL.
SAY, HENRY, ARE YOU OK?
JUST GOTTA GET SOME AIR. GOTTA EAT!
UNTIL TODAY.
HE SHOULDN'T HAVE OPENED THE UNDELIVERED PARCEL. BUT HE COULDN'T HELP HIMSELF.
JESUS. WHERE'D ALL THESE BUGS COME FROM?
FIRE
FUNNY THING IS, HE CAN'T EVEN REMEMBER WHAT WAS IN IT.
NOW, NOTHING MATTERS BUT FOOD.
FOOD TO CALM THE RIOT INSIDE HIM.
GIMME SIX MIGHTY MOUTHFULS, GINO.
SIX? WHASSA MATTA, HENRY? YA SKIP LUNCH?
HE KNOWS IT WON'T BE ENOUGH.
A WHOLE HERD OF BURGERS -- HOOVES AND ALL -- COULDN'T FILL THE GAPING BEAK OF THE GIANT FLEDGLING THAT CRIES INSIDE HIM.
HE LUMBERS THROUGH THE EARLY EVENING STREETS, SCATTERING WRAPPERS BEHIND HIM, LIKE SMALL CARCASSES.
ALL IS SUBORDINATE TO HIS PRIMAL URGE FOR FOOD.

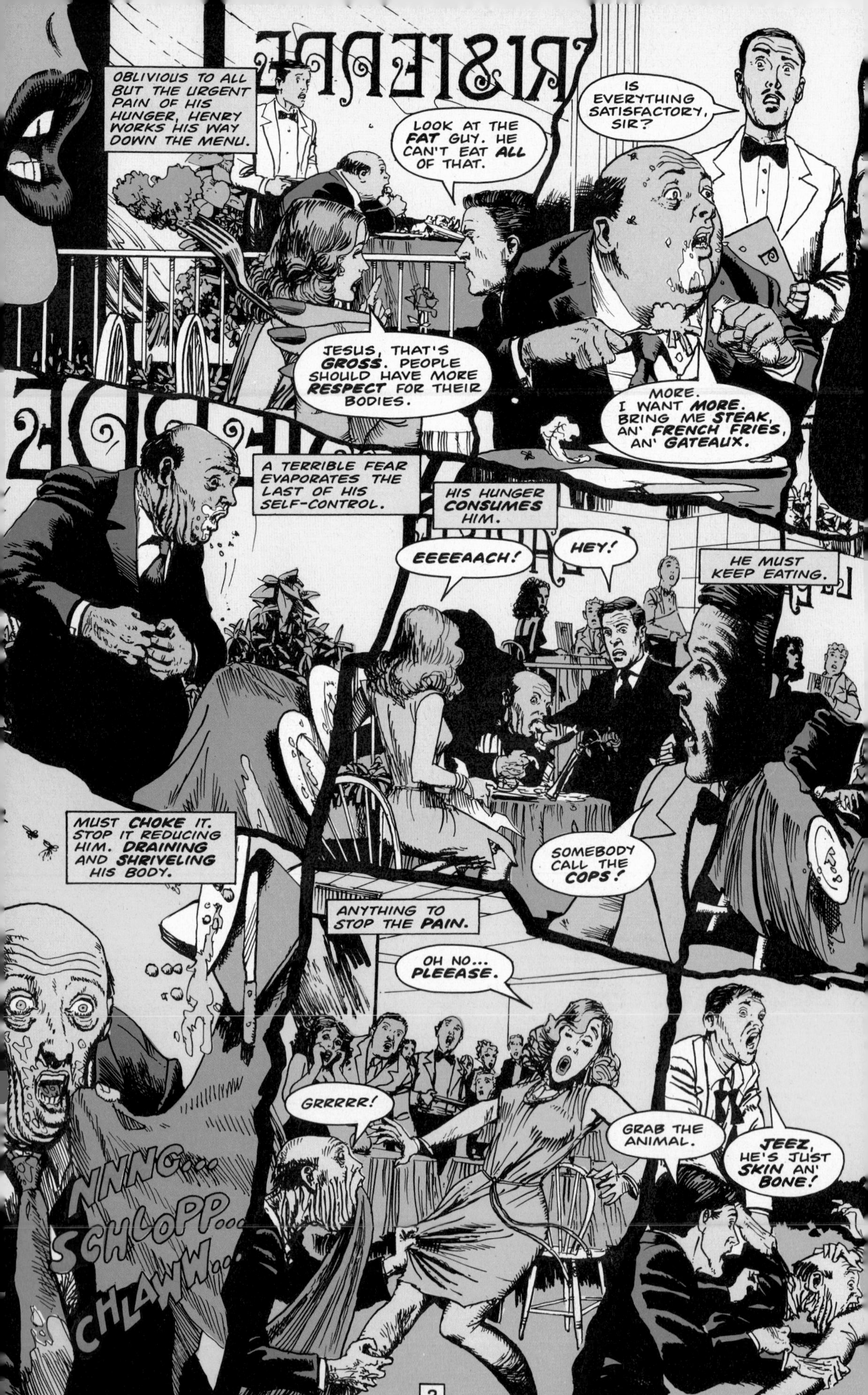
OBLIVIOUS TO ALL BUT THE URGENT PAIN OF HIS HUNGER, HENRY WORKS HIS WAY DOWN THE MENU.
LOOK AT THE FAT GUY. HE CAN'T EAT ALL OF THAT.
IS EVERYTHING SATISFACTORY, SIR?
JESUS, THAT'S GROSS. PEOPLE SHOULD HAVE MORE RESPECT FOR THEIR BODIES.
MORE. I WANT MORE. BRING ME STEAK, AN' FRENCH FRIES, AN' GATEAUX.
A TERRIBLE FEAR EVAPORATES THE LAST OF HIS SELF-CONTROL.
HIS HUNGER CONSUMES HIM.
EEEEAACH!
HEY!
HE MUST KEEP EATING.
MUST CHOKE IT. STOP IT REDUCING HIM. DRAINING AND SHRIVELING HIS BODY.
SOMEBODY CALL THE COPS!
ANYTHING TO STOP THE PAIN.
OH NO... PLEEASE.
GRRRRR!
GRAB THE ANIMAL.
JEEZ, HE'S JUST SKIN AN' BONE!
NNNG...
SCHLOPP...
CHLAWW...

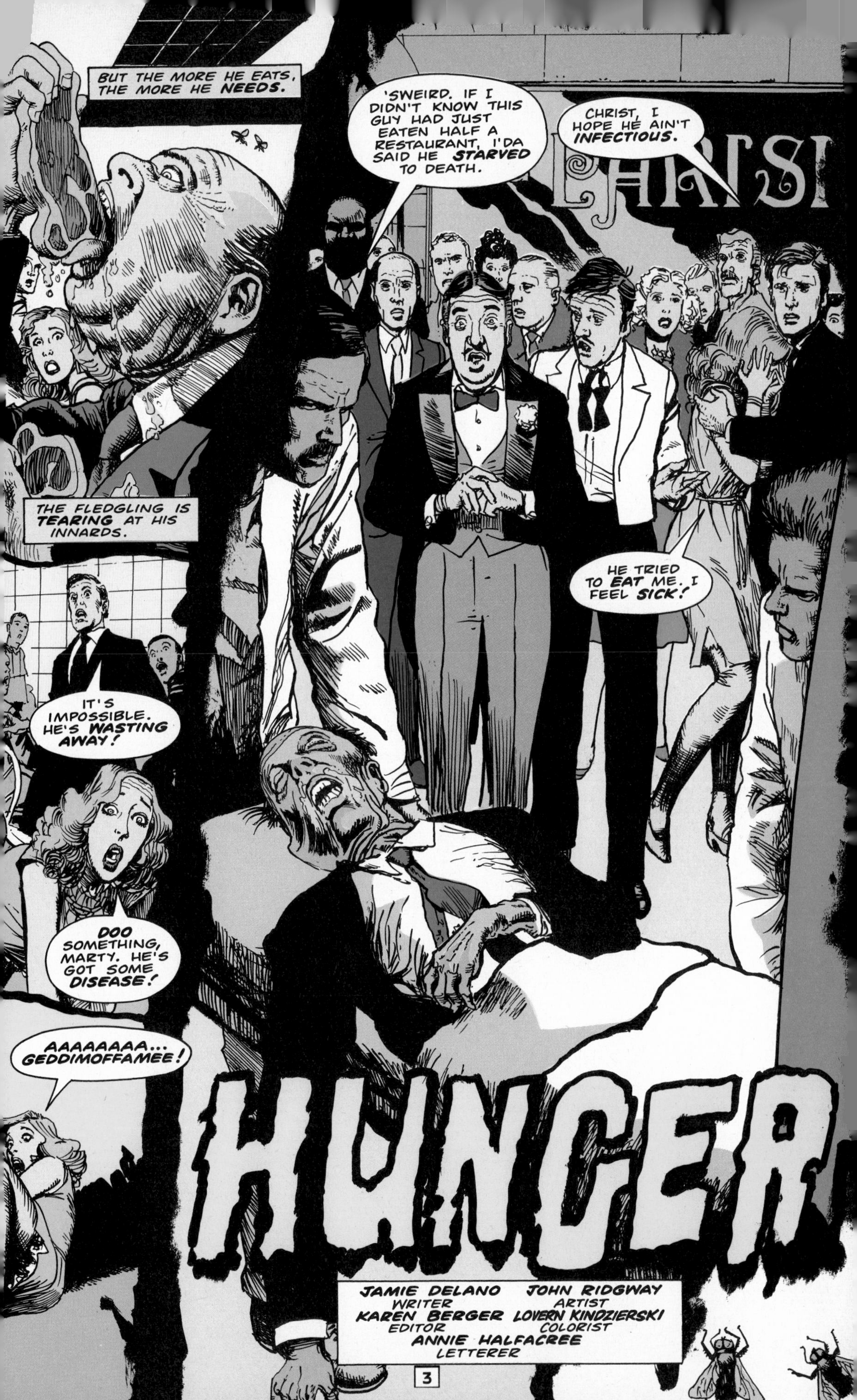
BUT THE MORE HE EATS, THE MORE HE NEEDS.
'SWEIRD. IF I DIDN'T KNOW THIS GUY HAD JUST EATEN HALF A RESTAURANT, I'DA SAID HE STARVED TO DEATH.
CHRIST, I HOPE HE AIN'T INFECTIOUS.
CHRISI
THE FLEDGLING IS TEARING AT HIS INNARDS.
HE TRIED TO EAT ME. I FEEL SICK!
IT'S IMPOSSIBLE. HE'S WASTING AWAY!
DOO SOMETHING, MARTY. HE'S GOT SOME DISEASE!
AAAAAAAA... GEDDIMOFFAMEE!
HUNGER
JAMIE DELANO WRITER
JOHN RIDGWAY ARTIST
KAREN BERGER EDITOR
LOVERN KINDZIERSKI COLORIST
ANNIE HALFACREE LETTERER

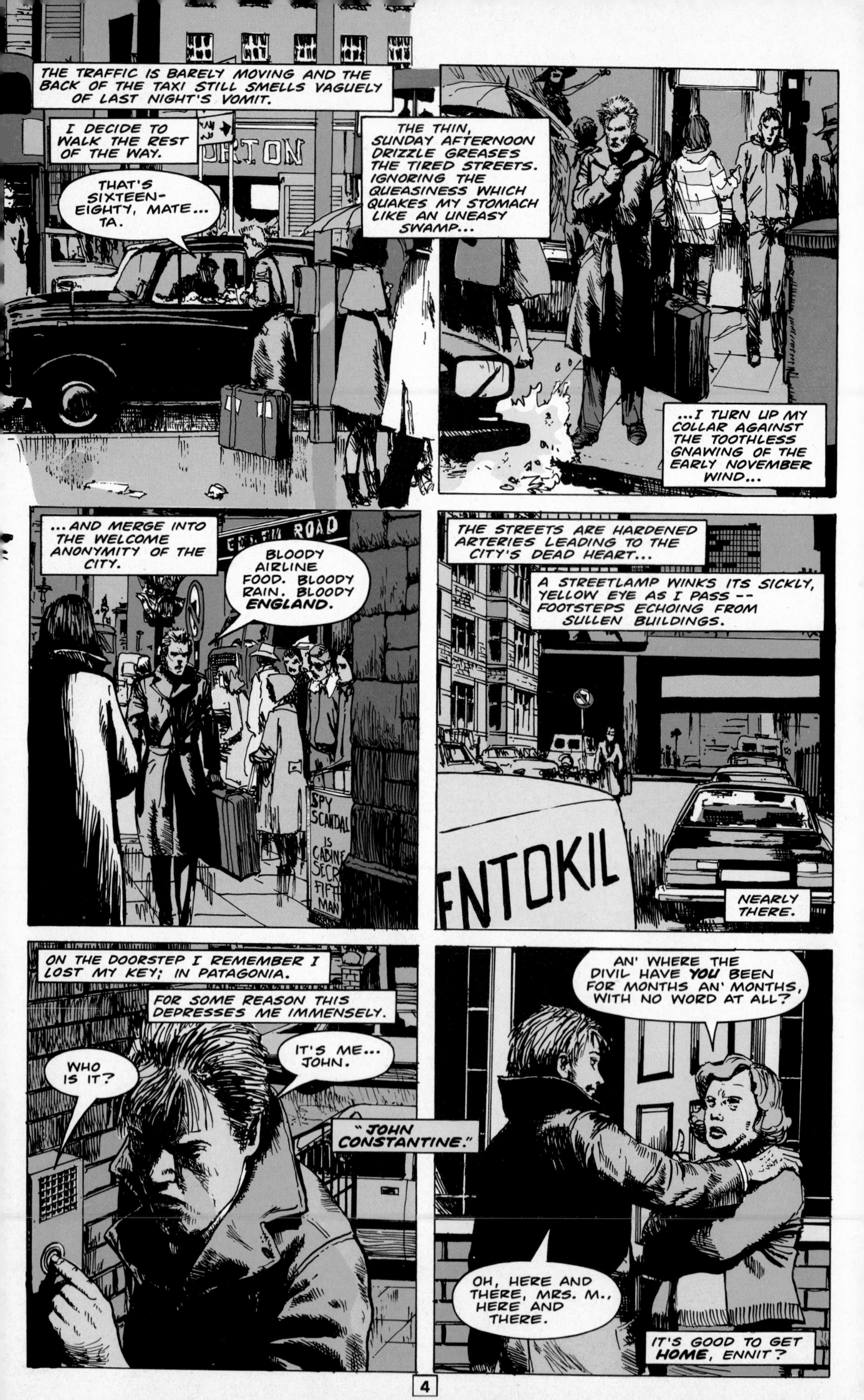
THE TRAFFIC IS BARELY MOVING AND THE BACK OF THE TAXI STILL SMELLS VAGUELY OF LAST NIGHT'S VOMIT.
I DECIDE TO WALK THE REST OF THE WAY.
THAT'S SIXTEEN-EIGHTY, MATE... TA.
THE THIN, SUNDAY AFTERNOON DRIZZLE GREASES THE TIRED STREETS. IGNORING THE QUEASINESS WHICH QUAKES MY STOMACH LIKE AN UNEASY SWAMP...
...I TURN UP MY COLLAR AGAINST THE TOOTHLESS GNAWING OF THE EARLY NOVEMBER WIND...
...AND MERGE INTO THE WELCOME ANONYMITY OF THE CITY.
BLOODY AIRLINE FOOD. BLOODY RAIN. BLOODY ENGLAND.
SPY SCANDAL IS CABINE SECR FIFTH MAN
THE STREETS ARE HARDENED ARTERIES LEADING TO THE CITY'S DEAD HEART...
A STREETLAMP WINKS ITS SICKLY, YELLOW EYE AS I PASS -- FOOTSTEPS ECHOING FROM SULLEN BUILDINGS.
ENTOKIL
NEARLY THERE.
ON THE DOORSTEP I REMEMBER I LOST MY KEY; IN PATAGONIA.
FOR SOME REASON THIS DEPRESSES ME IMMENSELY.
WHO IS IT?
IT'S ME... JOHN.
"JOHN CONSTANTINE."
AN' WHERE THE DIVIL HAVE YOU BEEN FOR MONTHS AN' MONTHS, WITH NO WORD AT ALL?
OH, HERE AND THERE, MRS. M., HERE AND THERE.
IT'S GOOD TO GET HOME, ENNIT?

A FAMILIAR CLAUSTROPHOBIA ENVELOPS ME. AN AROMA OF MINGLED GREEN AND BROWN-- *STEWED CABBAGE* AND *FURNITURE POLISH.*

JUST A MINUTE, M' BOY.

I'VE GOT A *BONE* T' PICK WITH YOU.

NOT *NOW,* MRS. M. THERE'S A *LUV.* I'M A BIT *KNACKERED.*

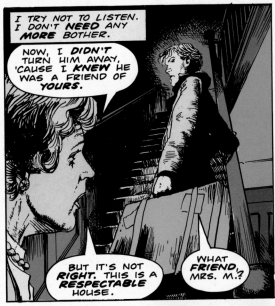

I TRY NOT TO LISTEN. I DON'T *NEED* ANY *MORE* BOTHER.

NOW, I *DIDN'T* TURN HIM AWAY, 'CAUSE I *KNEW* HE WAS A FRIEND OF *YOURS.*

BUT IT'S NOT *RIGHT.* THIS IS A *RESPECTABLE* HOUSE.

WHAT *FRIEND,* MRS. M.?

ALL I WANT TO DO IS *SLEEP.*

THAT *DRUGGY* ONE. *LESTER,* OR *GARY,* I FORGET. IN A *TERRIBLE* STATE HE WAS. COME BARGING IN HERE WANTING YOU.

CHRIST-- IS HE STILL HERE?

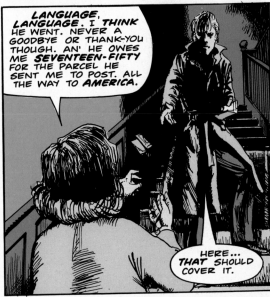

LANGUAGE, LANGUAGE. I *THINK* HE WENT. NEVER A GOODBYE OR THANK-YOU THOUGH. AN' HE OWES ME *SEVENTEEN-FIFTY* FOR THE PARCEL HE SENT ME TO POST. ALL THE WAY TO *AMERICA.*

HERE... *THAT* SHOULD COVER IT.

AS IF I HAVEN'T GOT *ENOUGH* ON M' PLATE WITH THE RUDDY *INSECTS.*

SHE MUTTERS OFF TO TORTURE MORE VEGETABLES IN HER FOUL KITCHEN.

INSECTS, EH? THAT EXPLAINS THE *RENTOKIL VAN.*

I CLIMB THE THREADBARE STAIRS. A SENSE OF *DREAD* CLIMBS WITH ME.

GARY LESTER.

WHAT DID *THAT* MESSED-UP BASTARD WANT WITH ME? HE WAS NEVER *ANYTHING* BUT...

... *BAD NEWS.*

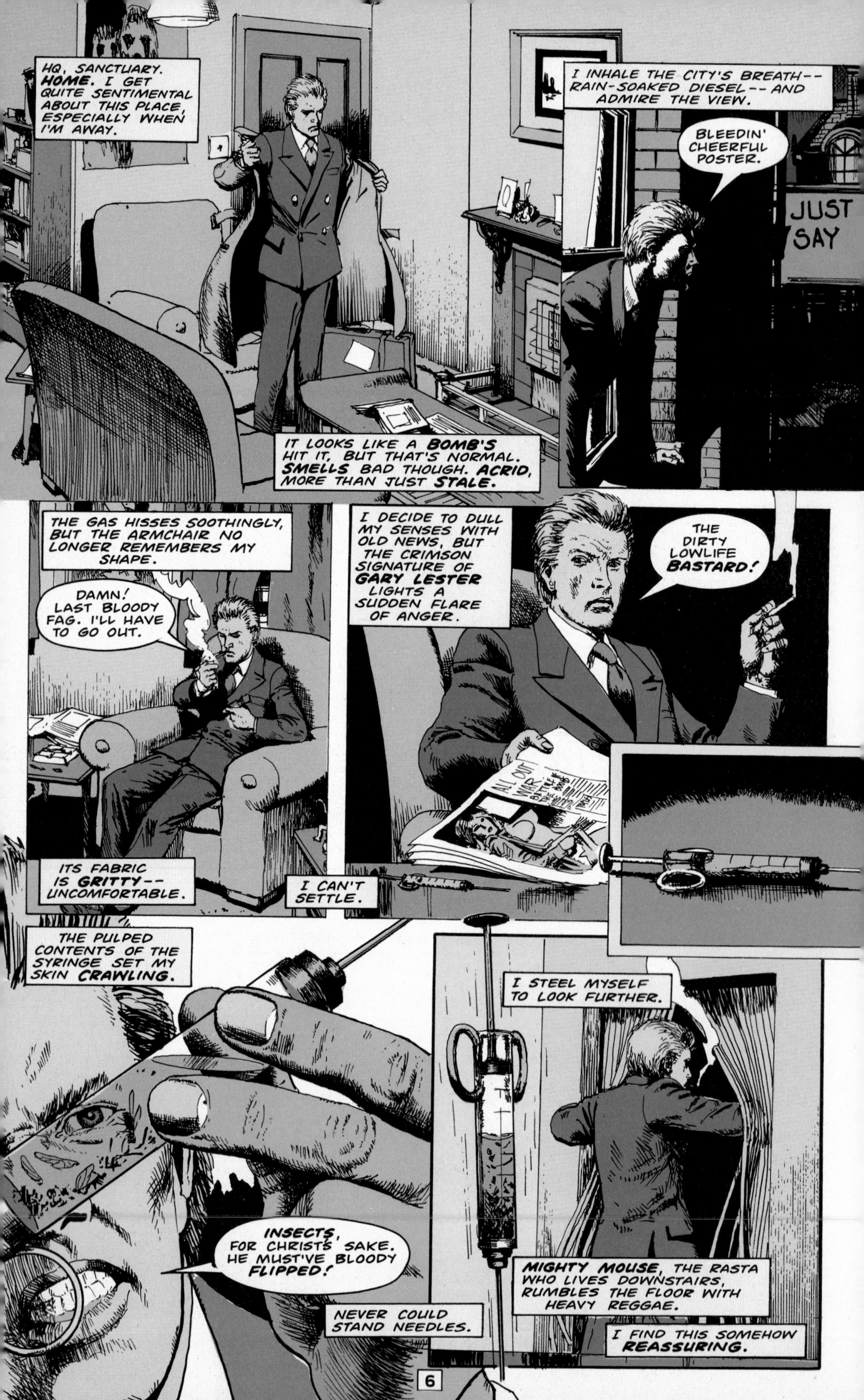
HQ, SANCTUARY. HOME. I GET QUITE SENTIMENTAL ABOUT THIS PLACE, ESPECIALLY WHEN I'M AWAY.
IT LOOKS LIKE A BOMB'S HIT IT, BUT THAT'S NORMAL. SMELLS BAD THOUGH. ACRID, MORE THAN JUST STALE.
I INHALE THE CITY'S BREATH-- RAIN-SOAKED DIESEL-- AND ADMIRE THE VIEW.
BLEEDIN' CHEERFUL POSTER.
JUST SAY
THE GAS HISSES SOOTHINGLY, BUT THE ARMCHAIR NO LONGER REMEMBERS MY SHAPE.
DAMN! LAST BLOODY FAG. I'LL HAVE TO GO OUT.
ITS FABRIC IS GRITTY-- UNCOMFORTABLE.
I DECIDE TO DULL MY SENSES WITH OLD NEWS, BUT THE CRIMSON SIGNATURE OF GARY LESTER LIGHTS A SUDDEN FLARE OF ANGER.
THE DIRTY LOWLIFE BASTARD!
ALL OUT WAR
I CAN'T SETTLE.
THE PULPED CONTENTS OF THE SYRINGE SET MY SKIN CRAWLING.
INSECTS, FOR CHRIST'S SAKE. HE MUST'VE BLOODY FLIPPED!
NEVER COULD STAND NEEDLES.
I STEEL MYSELF TO LOOK FURTHER.
MIGHTY MOUSE, THE RASTA WHO LIVES DOWNSTAIRS, RUMBLES THE FLOOR WITH HEAVY REGGAE.
I FIND THIS SOMEHOW REASSURING.

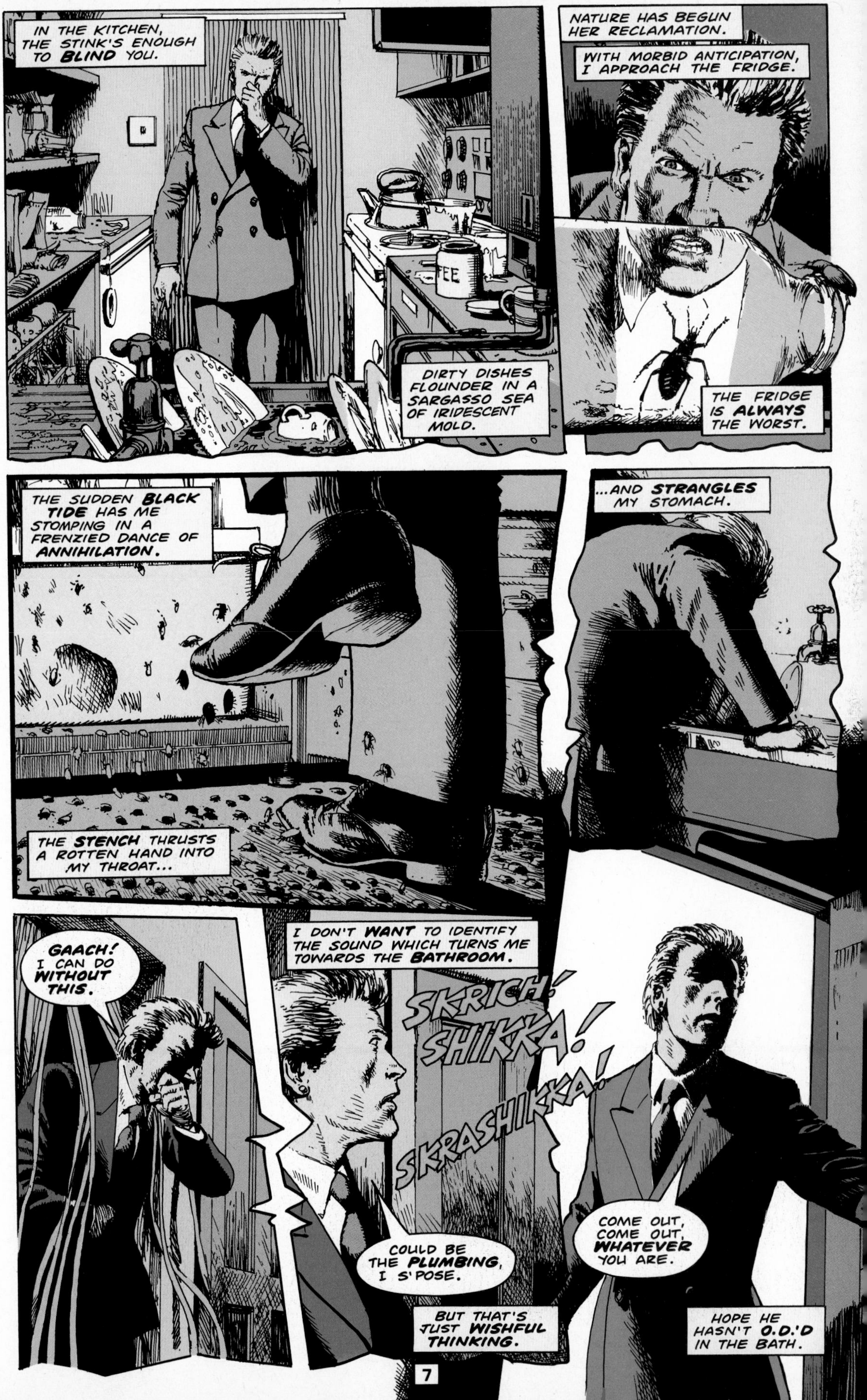
IN THE KITCHEN, THE STINK'S ENOUGH TO BLIND YOU.
FEE
DIRTY DISHES FLOUNDER IN A SARGASSO SEA OF IRIDESCENT MOLD.
NATURE HAS BEGUN HER RECLAMATION.
WITH MORBID ANTICIPATION, I APPROACH THE FRIDGE.
THE FRIDGE IS ALWAYS THE WORST.
THE SUDDEN BLACK TIDE HAS ME STOMPING IN A FRENZIED DANCE OF ANNIHILATION.
THE STENCH THRUSTS A ROTTEN HAND INTO MY THROAT...
...AND STRANGLES MY STOMACH.
GAACH! I CAN DO WITHOUT THIS.
I DON'T WANT TO IDENTIFY THE SOUND WHICH TURNS ME TOWARDS THE BATHROOM.
SKRICH! SHIKKA! SKRASHIKKA!
COULD BE THE PLUMBING, I S'POSE.
BUT THAT'S JUST WISHFUL THINKING.
COME OUT, COME OUT, WHATEVER YOU ARE.
HOPE HE HASN'T O.D.'D IN THE BATH.

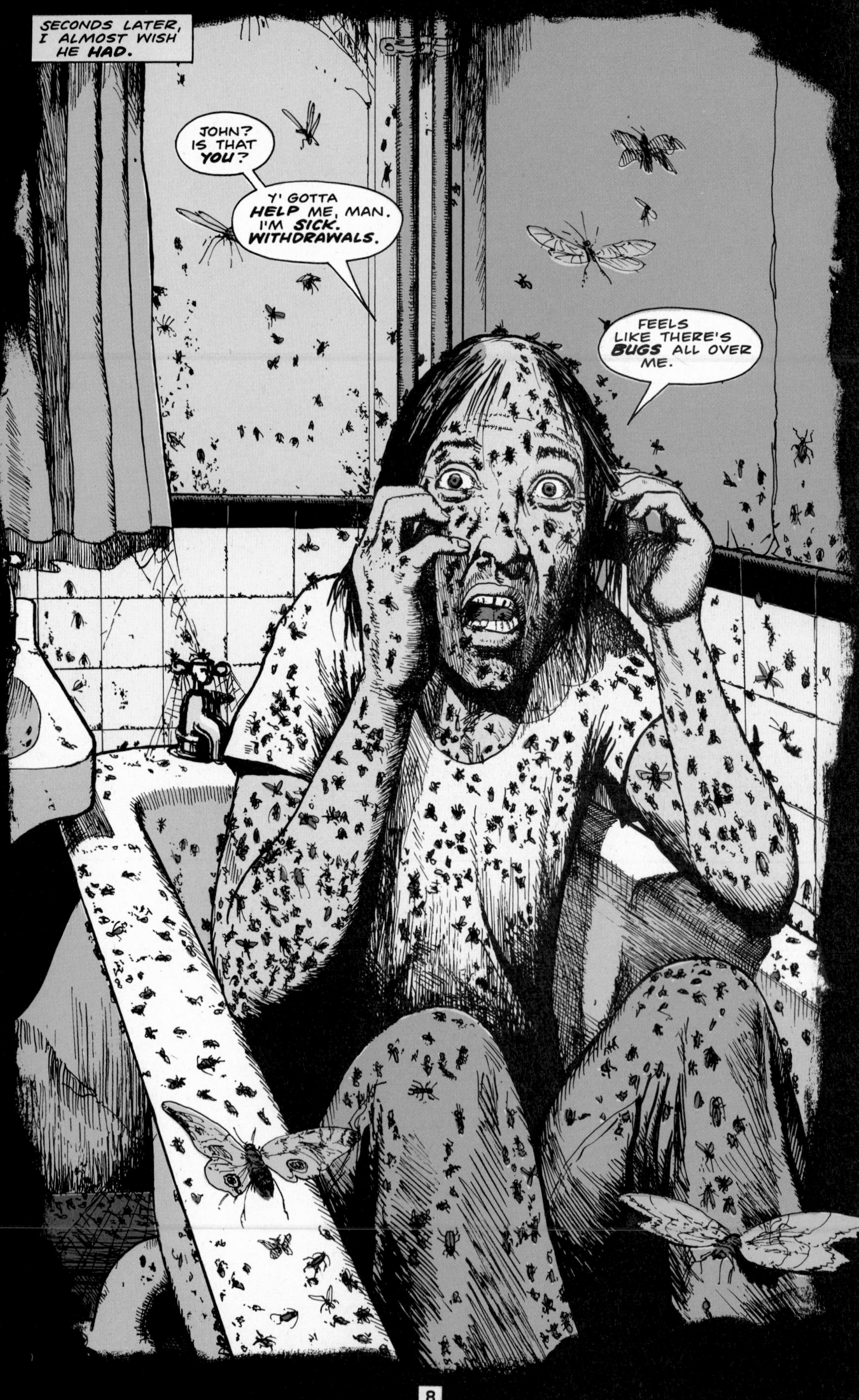
SECONDS LATER, I ALMOST WISH HE HAD.
JOHN? IS THAT YOU?
Y' GOTTA HELP ME, MAN. I'M SICK. WITHDRAWALS.
FEELS LIKE THERE'S BUGS ALL OVER ME.

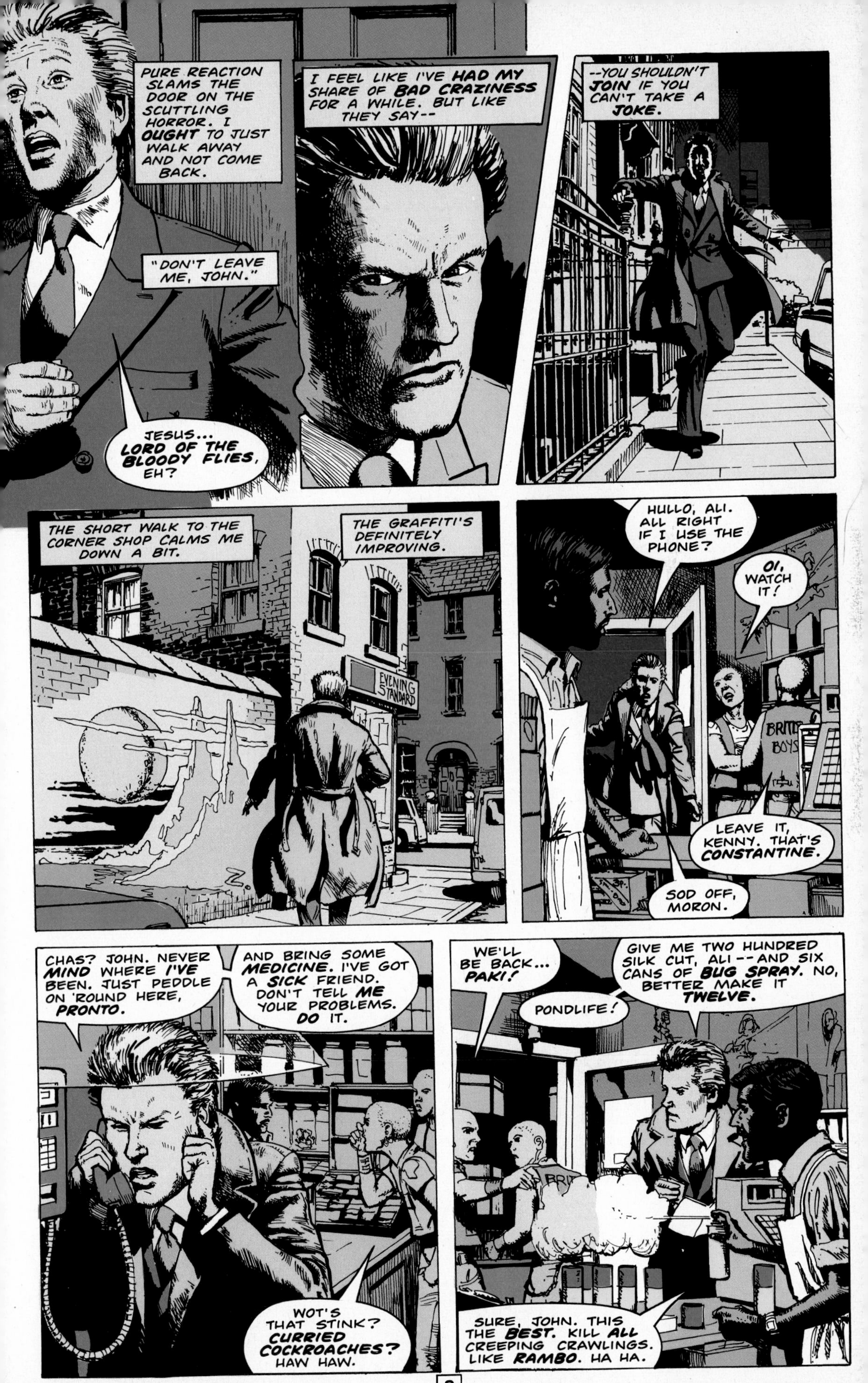
PURE REACTION SLAMS THE DOOR ON THE SCUTTLING HORROR. I OUGHT TO JUST WALK AWAY AND NOT COME BACK.
"DON'T LEAVE ME, JOHN."
JESUS... LORD OF THE BLOODY FLIES, EH?
I FEEL LIKE I'VE HAD MY SHARE OF BAD CRAZINESS FOR A WHILE. BUT LIKE THEY SAY--
--YOU SHOULDN'T JOIN IF YOU CAN'T TAKE A JOKE.
THE SHORT WALK TO THE CORNER SHOP CALMS ME DOWN A BIT.
THE GRAFFITI'S DEFINITELY IMPROVING.
EVENING STANDARD
HULLO, ALI. ALL RIGHT IF I USE THE PHONE?
OI, WATCH IT!
BRIT BOYS
LEAVE IT, KENNY. THAT'S CONSTANTINE.
SOD OFF, MORON.
CHAS? JOHN. NEVER MIND WHERE I'VE BEEN. JUST PEDDLE ON 'ROUND HERE, PRONTO.
AND BRING SOME MEDICINE. I'VE GOT A SICK FRIEND. DON'T TELL ME YOUR PROBLEMS. DO IT.
WOT'S THAT STINK? CURRIED COCKROACHES? HAW HAW.
WE'LL BE BACK... PAKI!
PONDLIFE!
GIVE ME TWO HUNDRED SILK CUT, ALI--AND SIX CANS OF BUG SPRAY. NO, BETTER MAKE IT TWELVE.
SURE, JOHN. THIS THE BEST. KILL ALL CREEPING CRAWLINGS. LIKE RAMBO. HA HA.

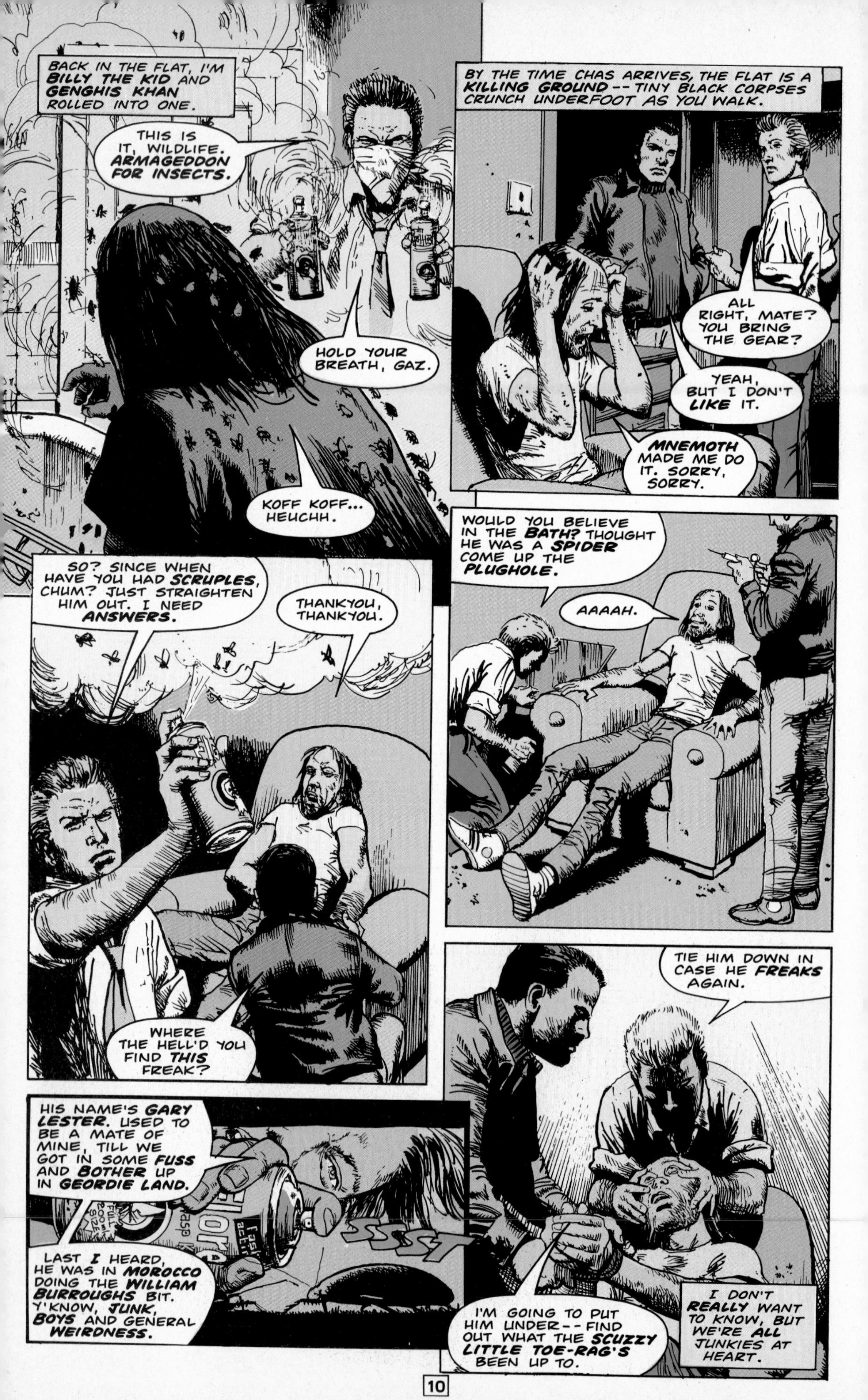
BACK IN THE FLAT, I'M BILLY THE KID AND GENGHIS KHAN ROLLED INTO ONE.
THIS IS IT, WILDLIFE. ARMAGEDDON FOR INSECTS.
HOLD YOUR BREATH, GAZ.
KOFF KOFF... HEUCHH.
BY THE TIME CHAS ARRIVES, THE FLAT IS A KILLING GROUND -- TINY BLACK CORPSES CRUNCH UNDERFOOT AS YOU WALK.
ALL RIGHT, MATE? YOU BRING THE GEAR?
YEAH, BUT I DON'T LIKE IT.
MNEMOTH MADE ME DO IT. SORRY, SORRY.
SO? SINCE WHEN HAVE YOU HAD SCRUPLES, CHUM? JUST STRAIGHTEN HIM OUT. I NEED ANSWERS.
THANKYOU, THANKYOU.
WHERE THE HELL'D YOU FIND THIS FREAK?
WOULD YOU BELIEVE IN THE BATH? THOUGHT HE WAS A SPIDER COME UP THE PLUGHOLE.
AAAAH.
HIS NAME'S GARY LESTER. USED TO BE A MATE OF MINE, TILL WE GOT IN SOME FUSS AND BOTHER UP IN GEORDIE LAND.
SSST
LAST I HEARD, HE WAS IN MOROCCO DOING THE WILLIAM BURROUGHS BIT. Y'KNOW, JUNK, BOYS AND GENERAL WEIRDNESS.
TIE HIM DOWN IN CASE HE FREAKS AGAIN.
I'M GOING TO PUT HIM UNDER-- FIND OUT WHAT THE SCUZZY LITTLE TOE-RAG'S BEEN UP TO.
I DON'T REALLY WANT TO KNOW, BUT WE'RE ALL JUNKIES AT HEART.

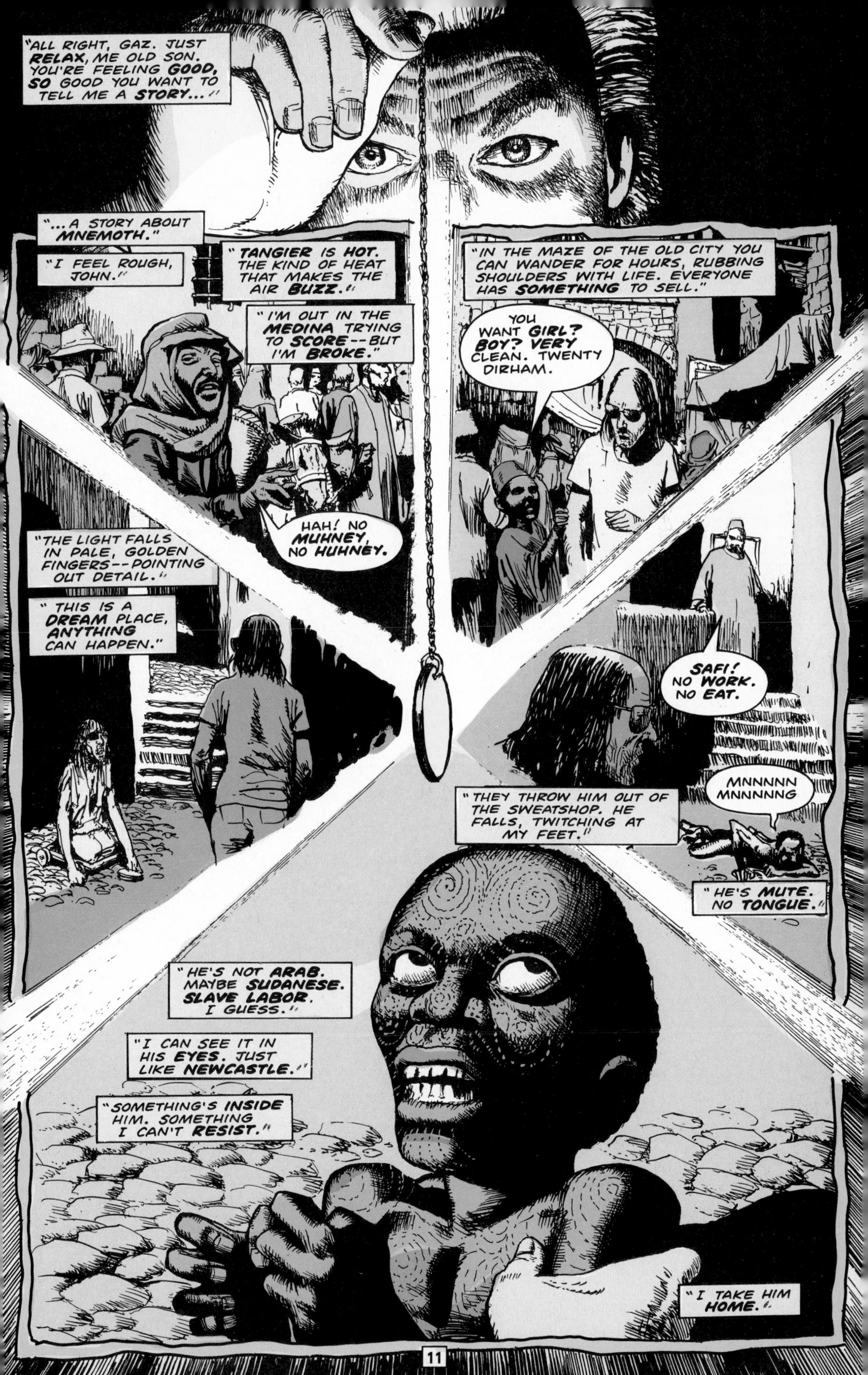

"ALL RIGHT, GAZ. JUST RELAX, ME OLD SON. YOU'RE FEELING GOOD, SO GOOD YOU WANT TO TELL ME A STORY..."
"...A STORY ABOUT MNEMOTH."
"I FEEL ROUGH, JOHN."
"TANGIER IS HOT. THE KIND OF HEAT THAT MAKES THE AIR BUZZ."
"I'M OUT IN THE MEDINA TRYING TO SCORE--BUT I'M BROKE."
HAH! NO MUHNEY, NO HUHNEY.
"IN THE MAZE OF THE OLD CITY YOU CAN WANDER FOR HOURS, RUBBING SHOULDERS WITH LIFE. EVERYONE HAS SOMETHING TO SELL."
YOU WANT GIRL? BOY? VERY CLEAN. TWENTY DIRHAM.
"THE LIGHT FALLS IN PALE, GOLDEN FINGERS--POINTING OUT DETAIL."
"THIS IS A DREAM PLACE, ANYTHING CAN HAPPEN."
SAFI! NO WORK. NO EAT.
MNNNNN MNNNNNG
"THEY THROW HIM OUT OF THE SWEATSHOP. HE FALLS, TWITCHING AT MY FEET."
"HE'S MUTE. NO TONGUE."
"HE'S NOT ARAB. MAYBE SUDANESE. SLAVE LABOR. I GUESS."
"I CAN SEE IT IN HIS EYES. JUST LIKE NEWCASTLE."
"SOMETHING'S INSIDE HIM. SOMETHING I CAN'T RESIST."
"I TAKE HIM HOME."

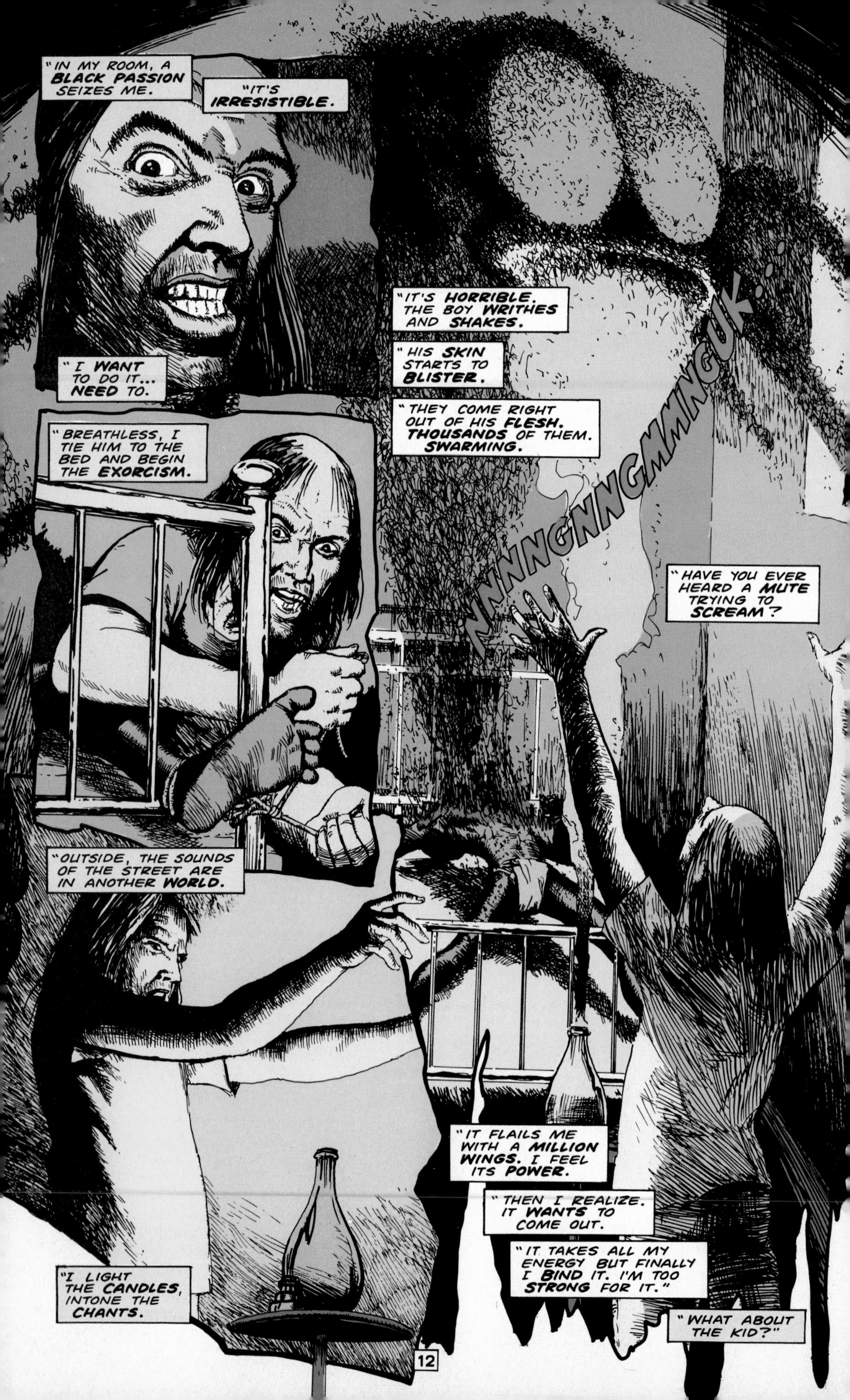
"IN MY ROOM, A BLACK PASSION SEIZES ME.
"IT'S IRRESISTIBLE.
"I WANT TO DO IT... NEED TO.
"BREATHLESS, I TIE HIM TO THE BED AND BEGIN THE EXORCISM.
"OUTSIDE, THE SOUNDS OF THE STREET ARE IN ANOTHER WORLD.
"I LIGHT THE CANDLES, INTONE THE CHANTS.
"IT'S HORRIBLE. THE BOY WRITHES AND SHAKES.
"HIS SKIN STARTS TO BLISTER.
"THEY COME RIGHT OUT OF HIS FLESH. THOUSANDS OF THEM. SWARMING.
NNNNGNNGMMNGUK...
"HAVE YOU EVER HEARD A MUTE TRYING TO SCREAM?
"IT FLAILS ME WITH A MILLION WINGS. I FEEL ITS POWER.
"THEN I REALIZE. IT WANTS TO COME OUT.
"IT TAKES ALL MY ENERGY BUT FINALLY I BIND IT. I'M TOO STRONG FOR IT."
"WHAT ABOUT THE KID?"

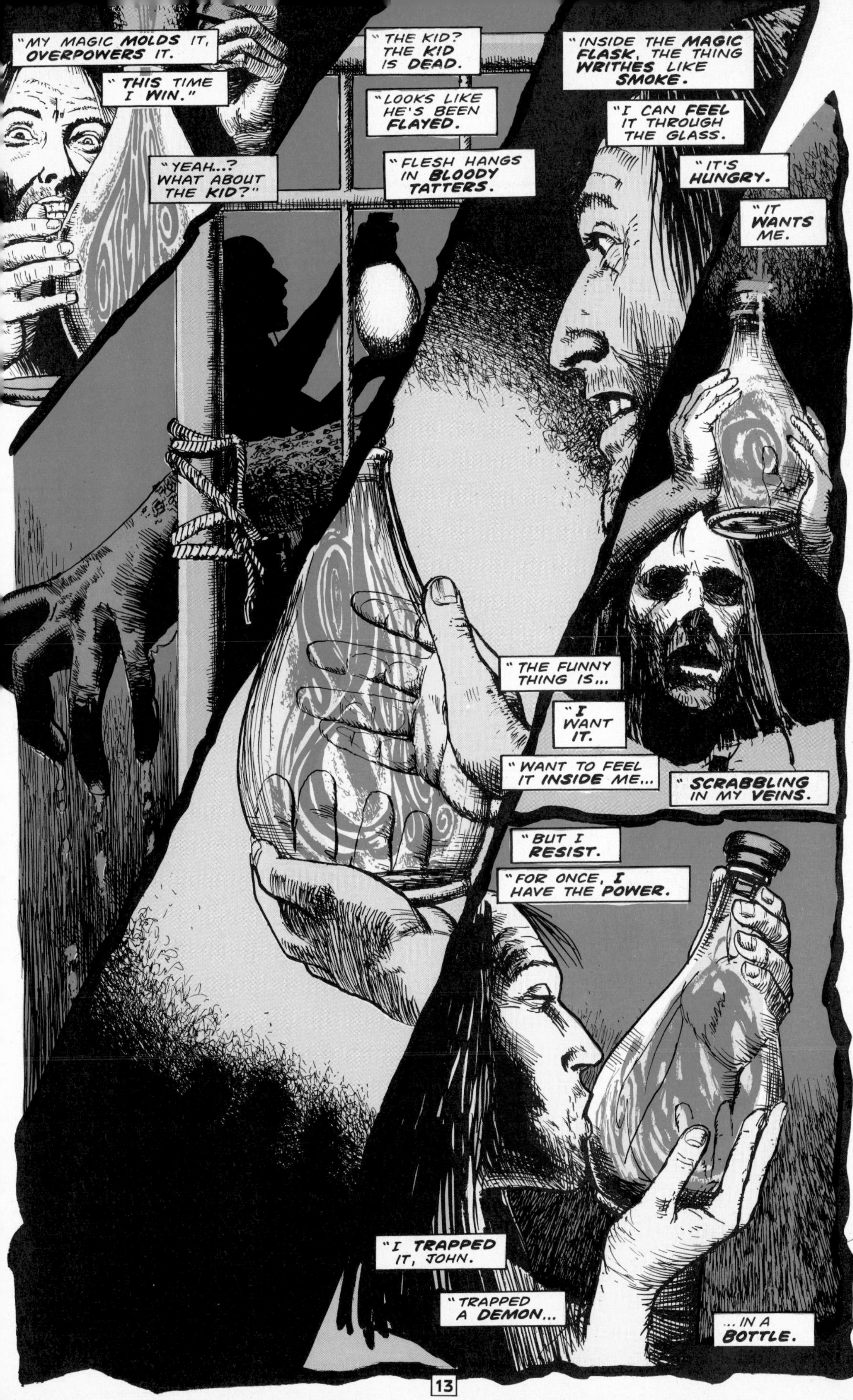
"MY MAGIC MOLDS IT, OVERPOWERS IT.
"THIS TIME I WIN."
"YEAH...? WHAT ABOUT THE KID?"
"THE KID? THE KID IS DEAD.
"LOOKS LIKE HE'S BEEN FLAYED.
"FLESH HANGS IN BLOODY TATTERS.
"INSIDE THE MAGIC FLASK, THE THING WRITHES LIKE SMOKE.
"I CAN FEEL IT THROUGH THE GLASS.
"IT'S HUNGRY.
"IT WANTS ME.
"THE FUNNY THING IS...
"I WANT IT.
"WANT TO FEEL IT INSIDE ME...
"SCRABBLING IN MY VEINS.
"BUT I RESIST.
"FOR ONCE, I HAVE THE POWER.
"I TRAPPED IT, JOHN.
"TRAPPED A DEMON...
...IN A BOTTLE.

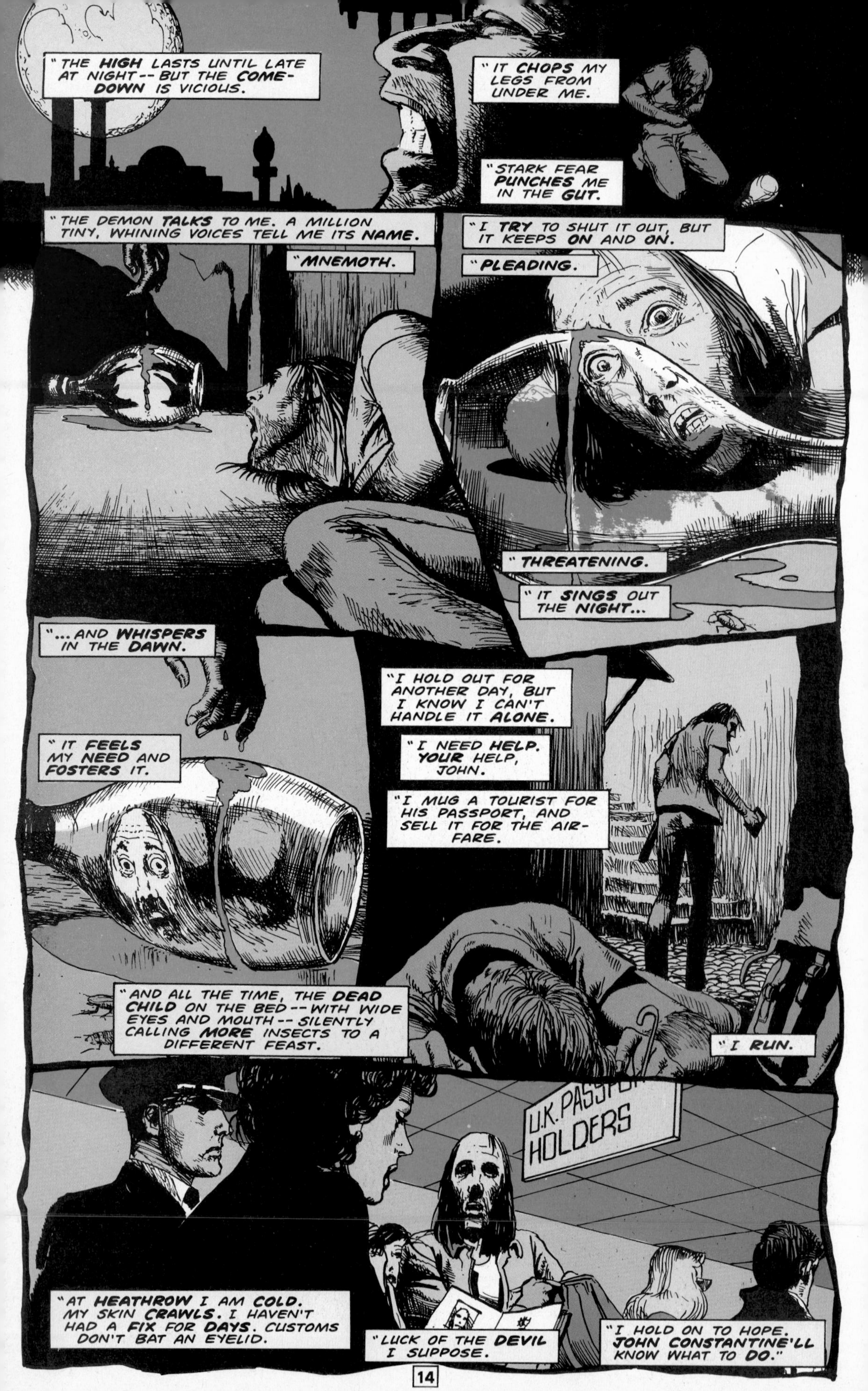
"THE HIGH LASTS UNTIL LATE AT NIGHT -- BUT THE COME-DOWN IS VICIOUS.
"IT CHOPS MY LEGS FROM UNDER ME.
"STARK FEAR PUNCHES ME IN THE GUT.
"THE DEMON TALKS TO ME. A MILLION TINY, WHINING VOICES TELL ME ITS NAME.
"MNEMOTH.
"I TRY TO SHUT IT OUT, BUT IT KEEPS ON AND ON.
"PLEADING.
"THREATENING.
"IT SINGS OUT THE NIGHT...
"...AND WHISPERS IN THE DAWN.
"IT FEELS MY NEED AND FOSTERS IT.
"I HOLD OUT FOR ANOTHER DAY, BUT I KNOW I CAN'T HANDLE IT ALONE.
"I NEED HELP. YOUR HELP, JOHN.
"I MUG A TOURIST FOR HIS PASSPORT, AND SELL IT FOR THE AIR-FARE.
"AND ALL THE TIME, THE DEAD CHILD ON THE BED -- WITH WIDE EYES AND MOUTH -- SILENTLY CALLING MORE INSECTS TO A DIFFERENT FEAST.
"I RUN.
HOLDERS
"AT HEATHROW I AM COLD. MY SKIN CRAWLS. I HAVEN'T HAD A FIX FOR DAYS. CUSTOMS DON'T BAT AN EYELID.
"LUCK OF THE DEVIL I SUPPOSE.
"I HOLD ON TO HOPE. JOHN CONSTANTINE'LL KNOW WHAT TO DO."

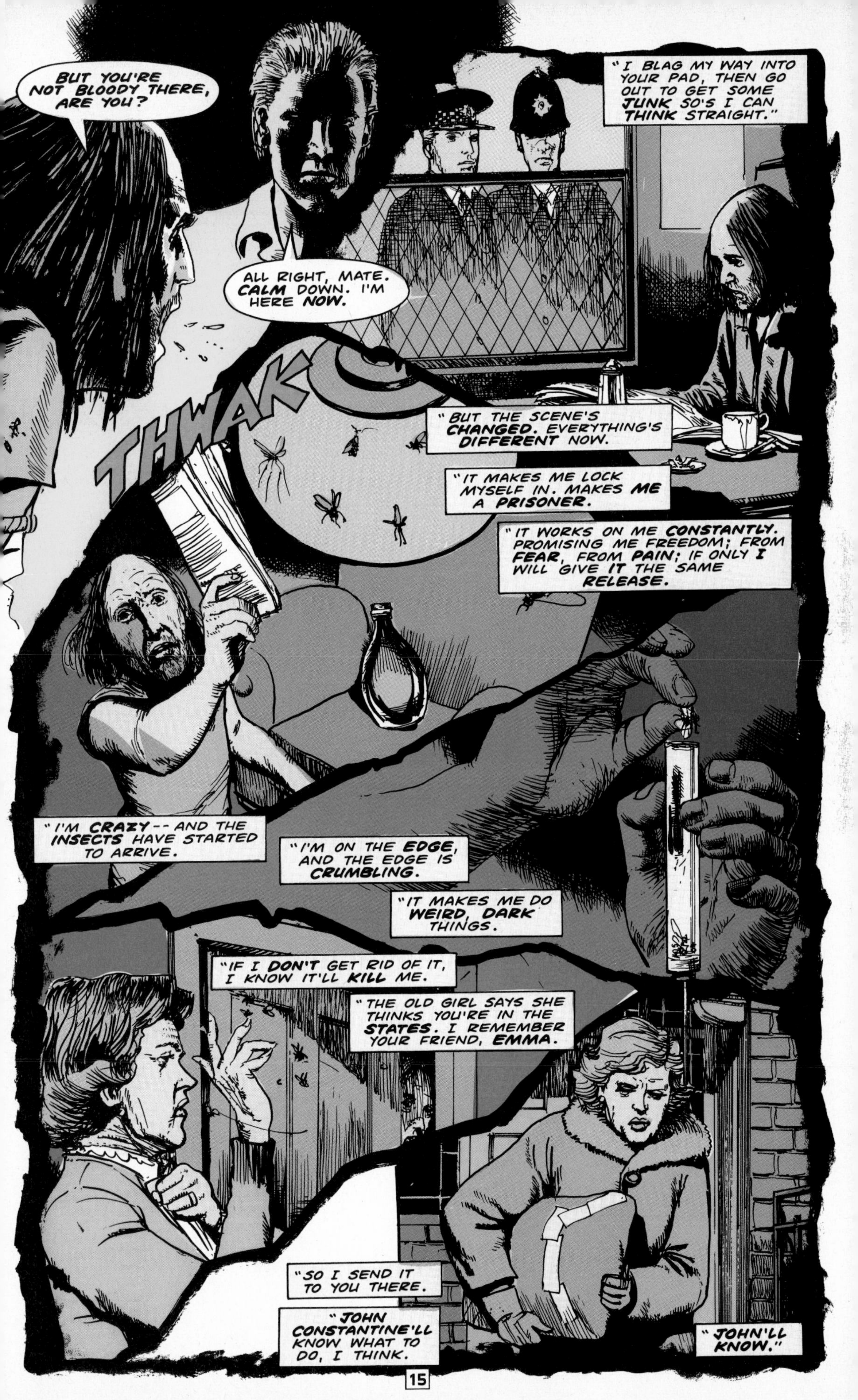
BUT YOU'RE NOT BLOODY THERE, ARE YOU?
ALL RIGHT, MATE. CALM DOWN. I'M HERE NOW.
"I BLAG MY WAY INTO YOUR PAD, THEN GO OUT TO GET SOME JUNK SO'S I CAN THINK STRAIGHT."
THWAK
"BUT THE SCENE'S CHANGED. EVERYTHING'S DIFFERENT NOW.
"IT MAKES ME LOCK MYSELF IN. MAKES ME A PRISONER.
"IT WORKS ON ME CONSTANTLY. PROMISING ME FREEDOM; FROM FEAR, FROM PAIN; IF ONLY I WILL GIVE IT THE SAME RELEASE.
"I'M CRAZY-- AND THE INSECTS HAVE STARTED TO ARRIVE.
"I'M ON THE EDGE, AND THE EDGE IS CRUMBLING.
"IT MAKES ME DO WEIRD, DARK THINGS.
"IF I DON'T GET RID OF IT, I KNOW IT'LL KILL ME.
"THE OLD GIRL SAYS SHE THINKS YOU'RE IN THE STATES. I REMEMBER YOUR FRIEND, EMMA.
"SO I SEND IT TO YOU THERE.
"JOHN CONSTANTINE'LL KNOW WHAT TO DO, I THINK.
"JOHN'LL KNOW."

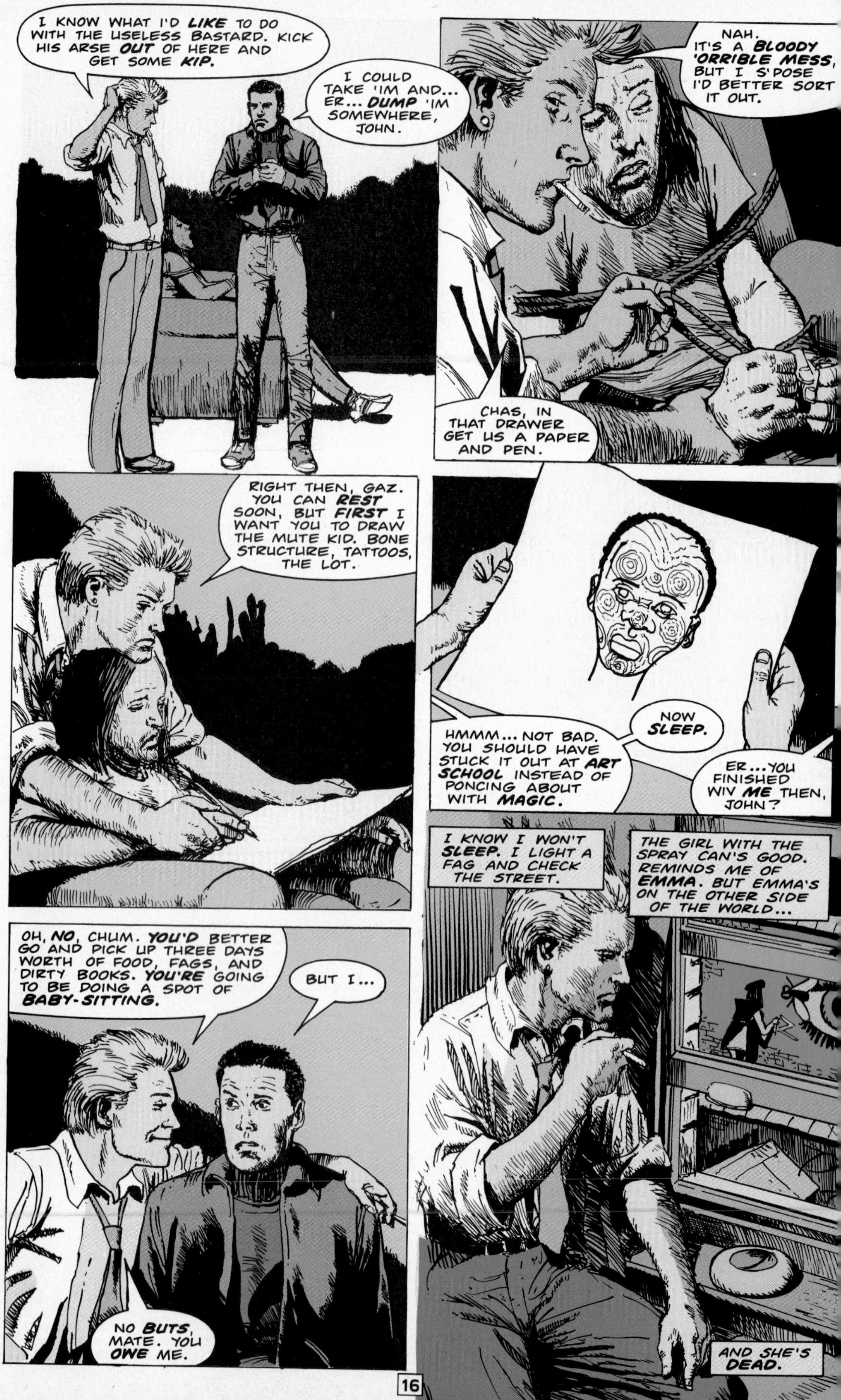
I KNOW WHAT I'D LIKE TO DO WITH THE USELESS BASTARD. KICK HIS ARSE OUT OF HERE AND GET SOME KIP.
I COULD TAKE 'IM AND... ER... DUMP 'IM SOMEWHERE, JOHN.
NAH. IT'S A BLOODY 'ORRIBLE MESS, BUT I S'POSE I'D BETTER SORT IT OUT.
CHAS, IN THAT DRAWER GET US A PAPER AND PEN.
RIGHT THEN, GAZ. YOU CAN REST SOON, BUT FIRST I WANT YOU TO DRAW THE MUTE KID. BONE STRUCTURE, TATTOOS, THE LOT.
HMMM... NOT BAD. YOU SHOULD HAVE STUCK IT OUT AT ART SCHOOL INSTEAD OF PONCING ABOUT WITH MAGIC.
NOW SLEEP.
ER... YOU FINISHED WIV ME THEN, JOHN?
OH, NO, CHUM. YOU'D BETTER GO AND PICK UP THREE DAYS WORTH OF FOOD, FAGS, AND DIRTY BOOKS. YOU'RE GOING TO BE DOING A SPOT OF BABY-SITTING.
BUT I...
NO BUTS, MATE. YOU OWE ME.
I KNOW I WON'T SLEEP. I LIGHT A FAG AND CHECK THE STREET.
THE GIRL WITH THE SPRAY CAN'S GOOD. REMINDS ME OF EMMA. BUT EMMA'S ON THE OTHER SIDE OF THE WORLD...
AND SHE'S DEAD.

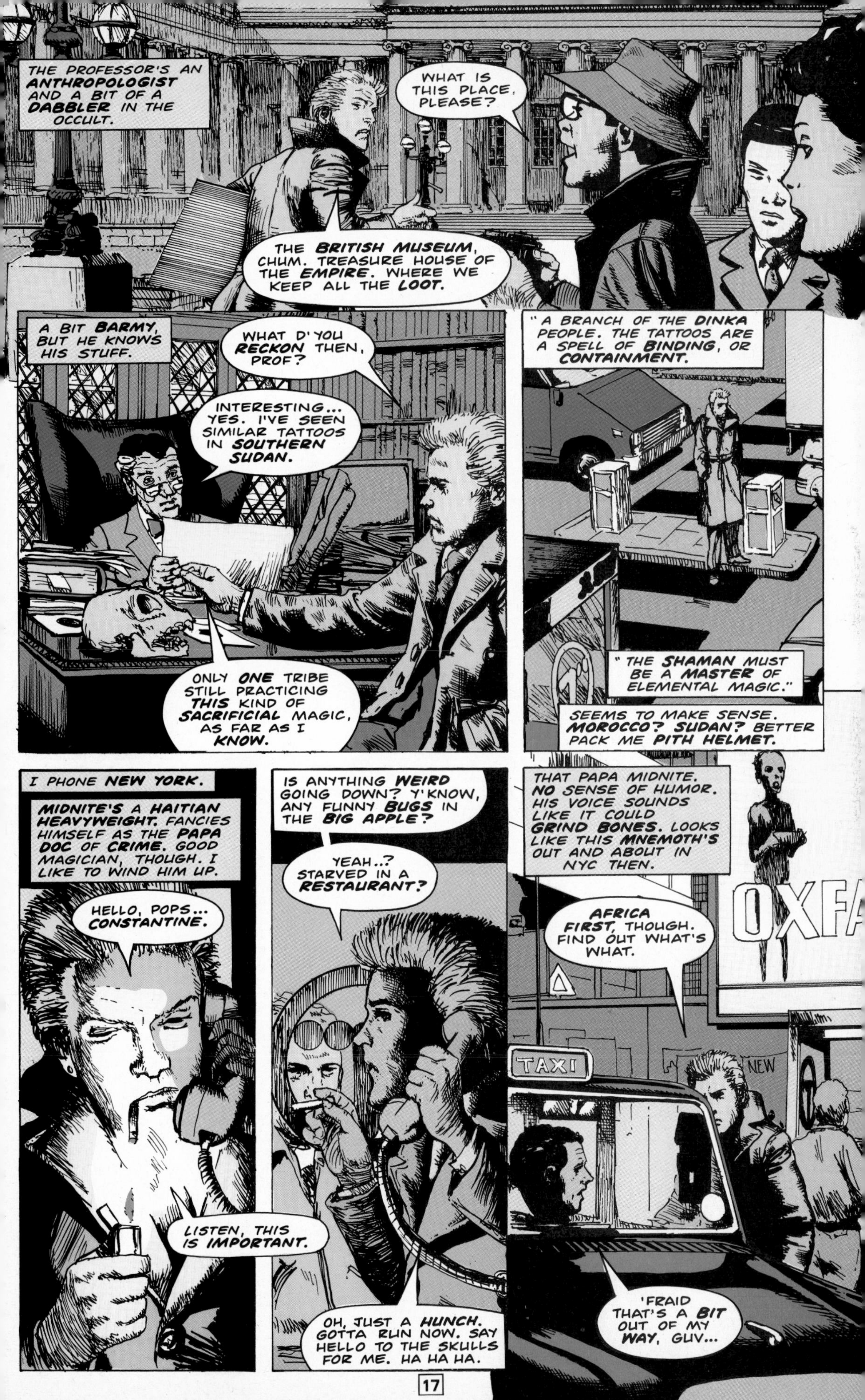
THE PROFESSOR'S AN ANTHROPOLOGIST AND A BIT OF A DABBLER IN THE OCCULT.
WHAT IS THIS PLACE, PLEASE?
THE BRITISH MUSEUM, CHUM. TREASURE HOUSE OF THE EMPIRE. WHERE WE KEEP ALL THE LOOT.
A BIT BARMY, BUT HE KNOWS HIS STUFF.
WHAT D'YOU RECKON THEN, PROF?
INTERESTING... YES. I'VE SEEN SIMILAR TATTOOS IN SOUTHERN SUDAN.
ONLY ONE TRIBE STILL PRACTICING THIS KIND OF SACRIFICIAL MAGIC, AS FAR AS I KNOW.
"A BRANCH OF THE DINKA PEOPLE. THE TATTOOS ARE A SPELL OF BINDING, OR CONTAINMENT.
"THE SHAMAN MUST BE A MASTER OF ELEMENTAL MAGIC."
SEEMS TO MAKE SENSE. MOROCCO? SUDAN? BETTER PACK ME PITH HELMET.
I PHONE NEW YORK.
MIDNITE'S A HAITIAN HEAVYWEIGHT. FANCIES HIMSELF AS THE PAPA DOC OF CRIME. GOOD MAGICIAN, THOUGH. I LIKE TO WIND HIM UP.
HELLO, POPS... CONSTANTINE.
LISTEN, THIS IS IMPORTANT.
IS ANYTHING WEIRD GOING DOWN? Y'KNOW, ANY FUNNY BUGS IN THE BIG APPLE?
YEAH..? STARVED IN A RESTAURANT?
OH, JUST A HUNCH. GOTTA RUN NOW. SAY HELLO TO THE SKULLS FOR ME. HA HA HA.
THAT PAPA MIDNITE. NO SENSE OF HUMOR. HIS VOICE SOUNDS LIKE IT COULD GRIND BONES. LOOKS LIKE THIS MNEMOTH'S OUT AND ABOUT IN NYC THEN.
OXFA
AFRICA FIRST, THOUGH. FIND OUT WHAT'S WHAT.
TAXI
NEW
'FRAID THAT'S A BIT OUT OF MY WAY, GUV...

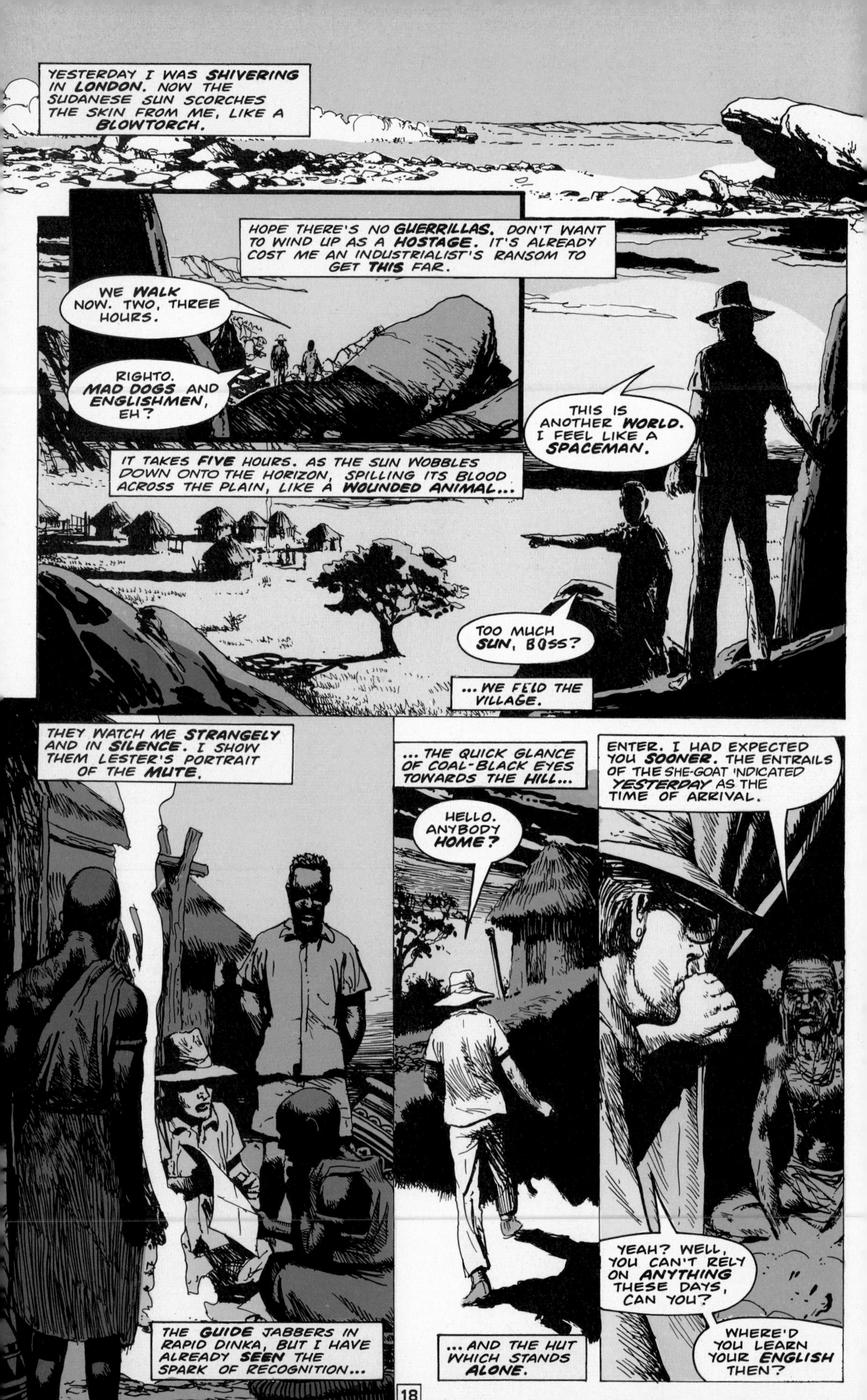
YESTERDAY I WAS SHIVERING IN LONDON. NOW THE SUDANESE SUN SCORCHES THE SKIN FROM ME, LIKE A BLOWTORCH.
HOPE THERE'S NO GUERRILLAS. DON'T WANT TO WIND UP AS A HOSTAGE. IT'S ALREADY COST ME AN INDUSTRIALIST'S RANSOM TO GET THIS FAR.
WE WALK NOW. TWO, THREE HOURS.
RIGHTO. MAD DOGS AND ENGLISHMEN, EH?
IT TAKES FIVE HOURS. AS THE SUN WOBBLES DOWN ONTO THE HORIZON, SPILLING ITS BLOOD ACROSS THE PLAIN, LIKE A WOUNDED ANIMAL...
THIS IS ANOTHER WORLD. I FEEL LIKE A SPACEMAN.
TOO MUCH SUN, BOSS?
...WE FIND THE VILLAGE.
THEY WATCH ME STRANGELY AND IN SILENCE. I SHOW THEM LESTER'S PORTRAIT OF THE MUTE.
THE GUIDE JABBERS IN RAPID DINKA, BUT I HAVE ALREADY SEEN THE SPARK OF RECOGNITION...
...THE QUICK GLANCE OF COAL-BLACK EYES TOWARDS THE HILL...
HELLO. ANYBODY HOME?
...AND THE HUT WHICH STANDS ALONE.
ENTER. I HAD EXPECTED YOU SOONER. THE ENTRAILS OF THE SHE-GOAT INDICATED YESTERDAY AS THE TIME OF ARRIVAL.
YEAH? WELL, YOU CAN'T RELY ON ANYTHING THESE DAYS, CAN YOU?
WHERE'D YOU LEARN YOUR ENGLISH THEN?

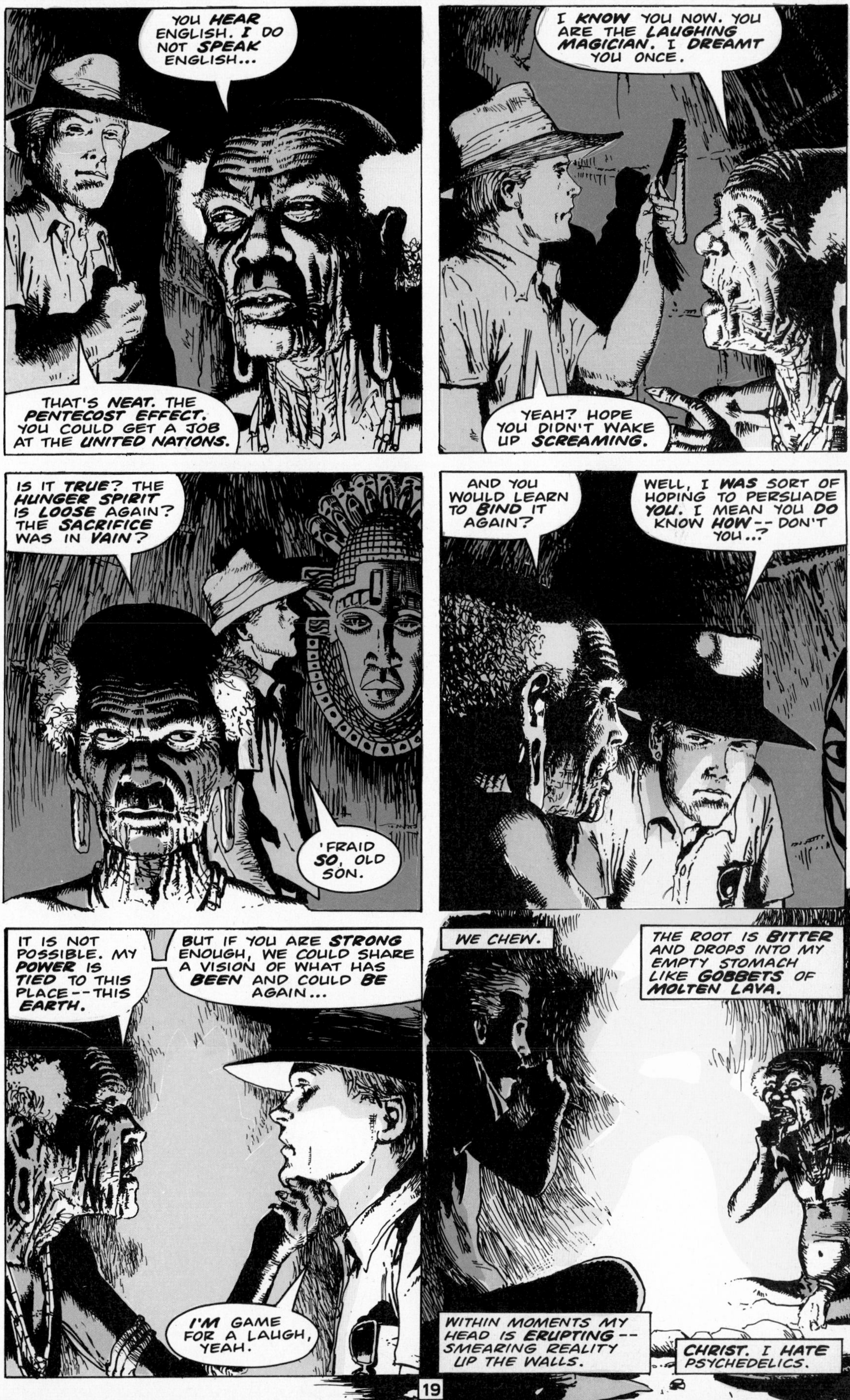
YOU HEAR ENGLISH. I DO NOT SPEAK ENGLISH...
THAT'S NEAT. THE PENTECOST EFFECT. YOU COULD GET A JOB AT THE UNITED NATIONS.
I KNOW YOU NOW. YOU ARE THE LAUGHING MAGICIAN. I DREAMT YOU ONCE.
YEAH? HOPE YOU DIDN'T WAKE UP SCREAMING.
IS IT TRUE? THE HUNGER SPIRIT IS LOOSE AGAIN? THE SACRIFICE WAS IN VAIN?
'FRAID SO, OLD SON.
AND YOU WOULD LEARN TO BIND IT AGAIN?
WELL, I WAS SORT OF HOPING TO PERSUADE YOU. I MEAN YOU DO KNOW HOW-- DON'T YOU..?
IT IS NOT POSSIBLE. MY POWER IS TIED TO THIS PLACE--THIS EARTH.
BUT IF YOU ARE STRONG ENOUGH, WE COULD SHARE A VISION OF WHAT HAS BEEN AND COULD BE AGAIN...
I'M GAME FOR A LAUGH, YEAH.
WE CHEW.
THE ROOT IS BITTER AND DROPS INTO MY EMPTY STOMACH LIKE GOBBETS OF MOLTEN LAVA.
WITHIN MOMENTS MY HEAD IS ERUPTING-- SMEARING REALITY UP THE WALLS.
CHRIST. I HATE PSYCHEDELICS.

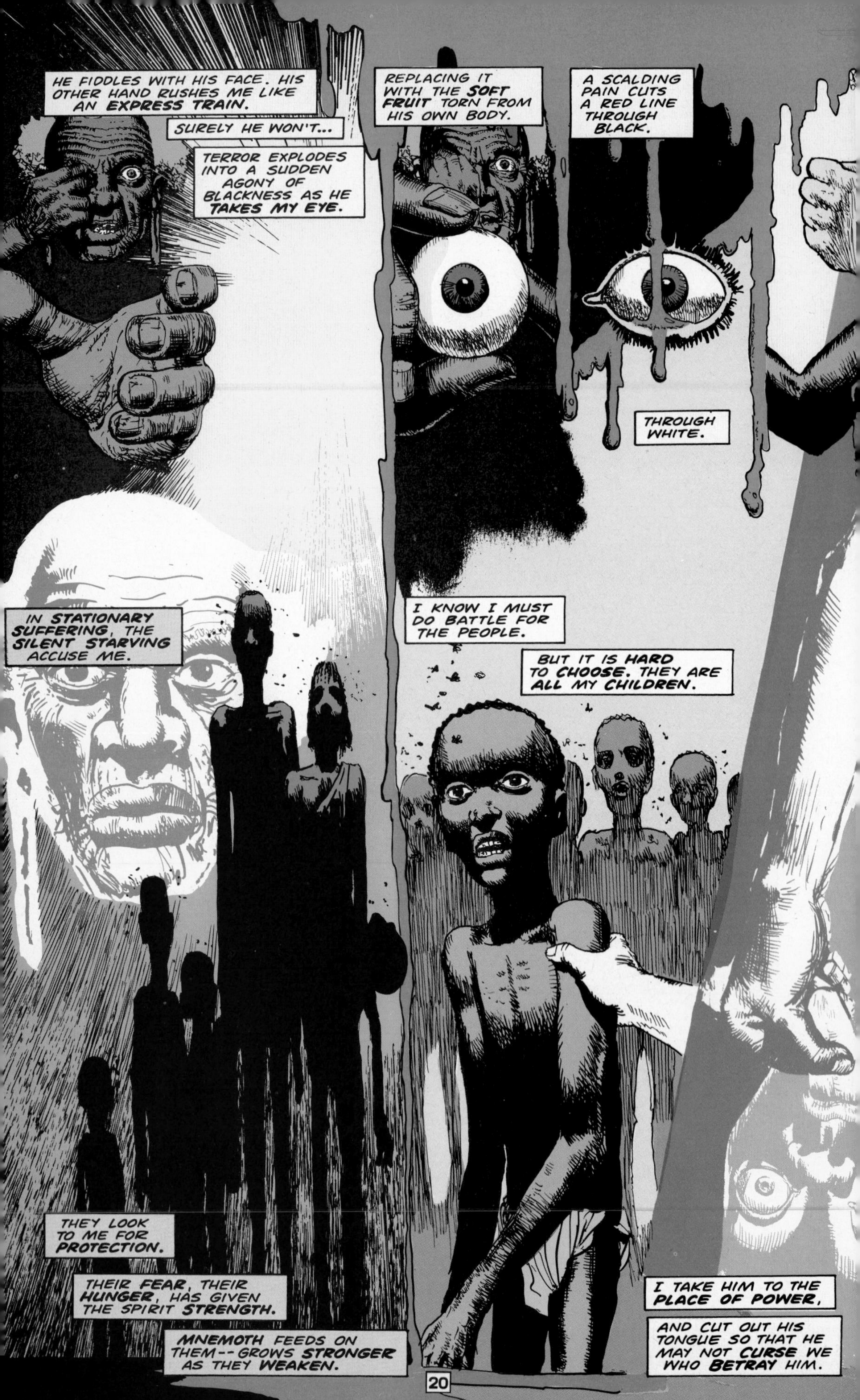
HE FIDDLES WITH HIS FACE. HIS OTHER HAND RUSHES ME LIKE AN EXPRESS TRAIN.
SURELY HE WON'T...
TERROR EXPLODES INTO A SUDDEN AGONY OF BLACKNESS AS HE TAKES MY EYE.
REPLACING IT WITH THE SOFT FRUIT TORN FROM HIS OWN BODY.
A SCALDING PAIN CUTS A RED LINE THROUGH BLACK.
THROUGH WHITE.
IN STATIONARY SUFFERING, THE SILENT STARVING ACCUSE ME.
THEY LOOK TO ME FOR PROTECTION.
THEIR FEAR, THEIR HUNGER, HAS GIVEN THE SPIRIT STRENGTH.
MNEMOTH FEEDS ON THEM--GROWS STRONGER AS THEY WEAKEN.
I KNOW I MUST DO BATTLE FOR THE PEOPLE.
BUT IT IS HARD TO CHOOSE. THEY ARE ALL MY CHILDREN.
I TAKE HIM TO THE PLACE OF POWER,
AND CUT OUT HIS TONGUE SO THAT HE MAY NOT CURSE WE WHO BETRAY HIM.

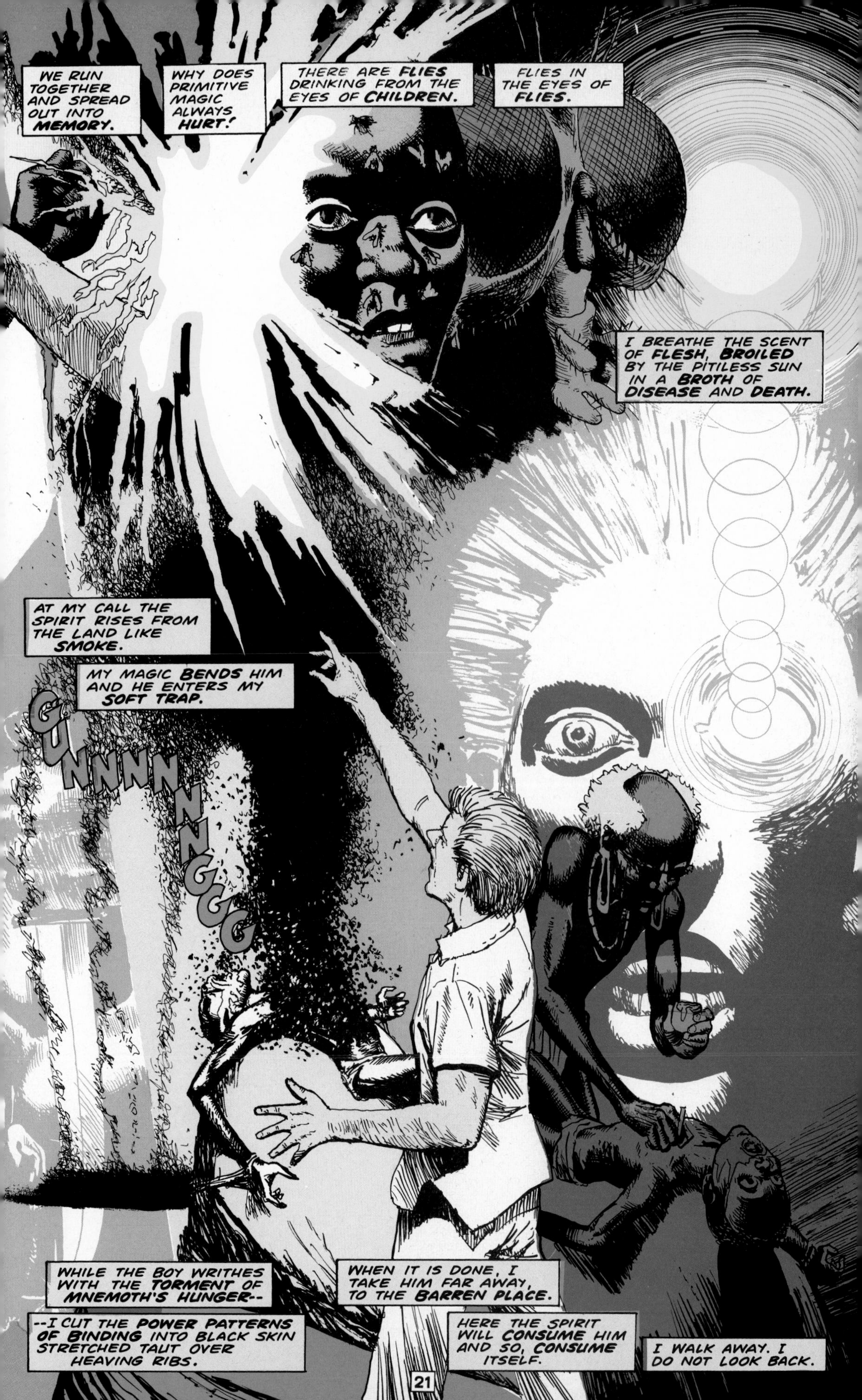
WE RUN TOGETHER AND SPREAD OUT INTO MEMORY.
WHY DOES PRIMITIVE MAGIC ALWAYS HURT!
THERE ARE FLIES DRINKING FROM THE EYES OF CHILDREN.
FLIES IN THE EYES OF FLIES.
I BREATHE THE SCENT OF FLESH, BROILED BY THE PITILESS SUN IN A BROTH OF DISEASE AND DEATH.
AT MY CALL THE SPIRIT RISES FROM THE LAND LIKE SMOKE.
MY MAGIC BENDS HIM AND HE ENTERS MY SOFT TRAP.
GUNNNNNNNGGG
WHILE THE BOY WRITHES WITH THE TORMENT OF MNEMOTH'S HUNGER--
--I CUT THE POWER PATTERNS OF BINDING INTO BLACK SKIN STRETCHED TAUT OVER HEAVING RIBS.
WHEN IT IS DONE, I TAKE HIM FAR AWAY, TO THE BARREN PLACE.
HERE THE SPIRIT WILL CONSUME HIM AND SO, CONSUME ITSELF.
I WALK AWAY. I DO NOT LOOK BACK.

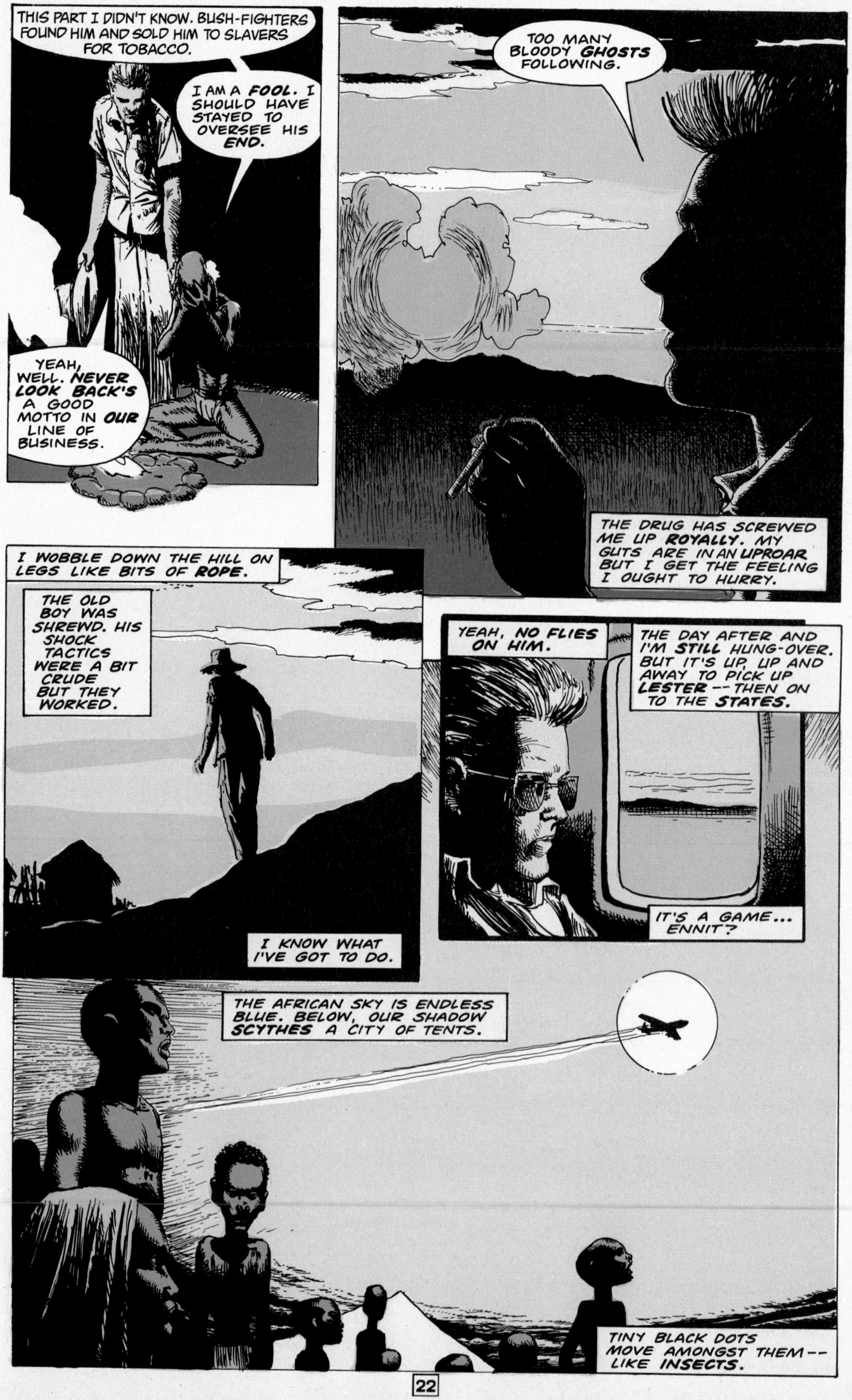
THIS PART I DIDN'T KNOW. BUSH-FIGHTERS FOUND HIM AND SOLD HIM TO SLAVERS FOR TOBACCO.
I AM A FOOL. I SHOULD HAVE STAYED TO OVERSEE HIS END.
YEAH, WELL. NEVER LOOK BACK'S A GOOD MOTTO IN OUR LINE OF BUSINESS.
TOO MANY BLOODY GHOSTS FOLLOWING.
THE DRUG HAS SCREWED ME UP ROYALLY. MY GUTS ARE IN AN UPROAR BUT I GET THE FEELING I OUGHT TO HURRY.
I WOBBLE DOWN THE HILL ON LEGS LIKE BITS OF ROPE.
THE OLD BOY WAS SHREWD. HIS SHOCK TACTICS WERE A BIT CRUDE BUT THEY WORKED.
I KNOW WHAT I'VE GOT TO DO.
YEAH, NO FLIES ON HIM.
THE DAY AFTER AND I'M STILL HUNG-OVER. BUT IT'S UP, UP AND AWAY TO PICK UP LESTER -- THEN ON TO THE STATES.
IT'S A GAME... ENNIT?
THE AFRICAN SKY IS ENDLESS BLUE. BELOW, OUR SHADOW SCYTHES A CITY OF TENTS.
TINY BLACK DOTS MOVE AMONGST THEM -- LIKE INSECTS.

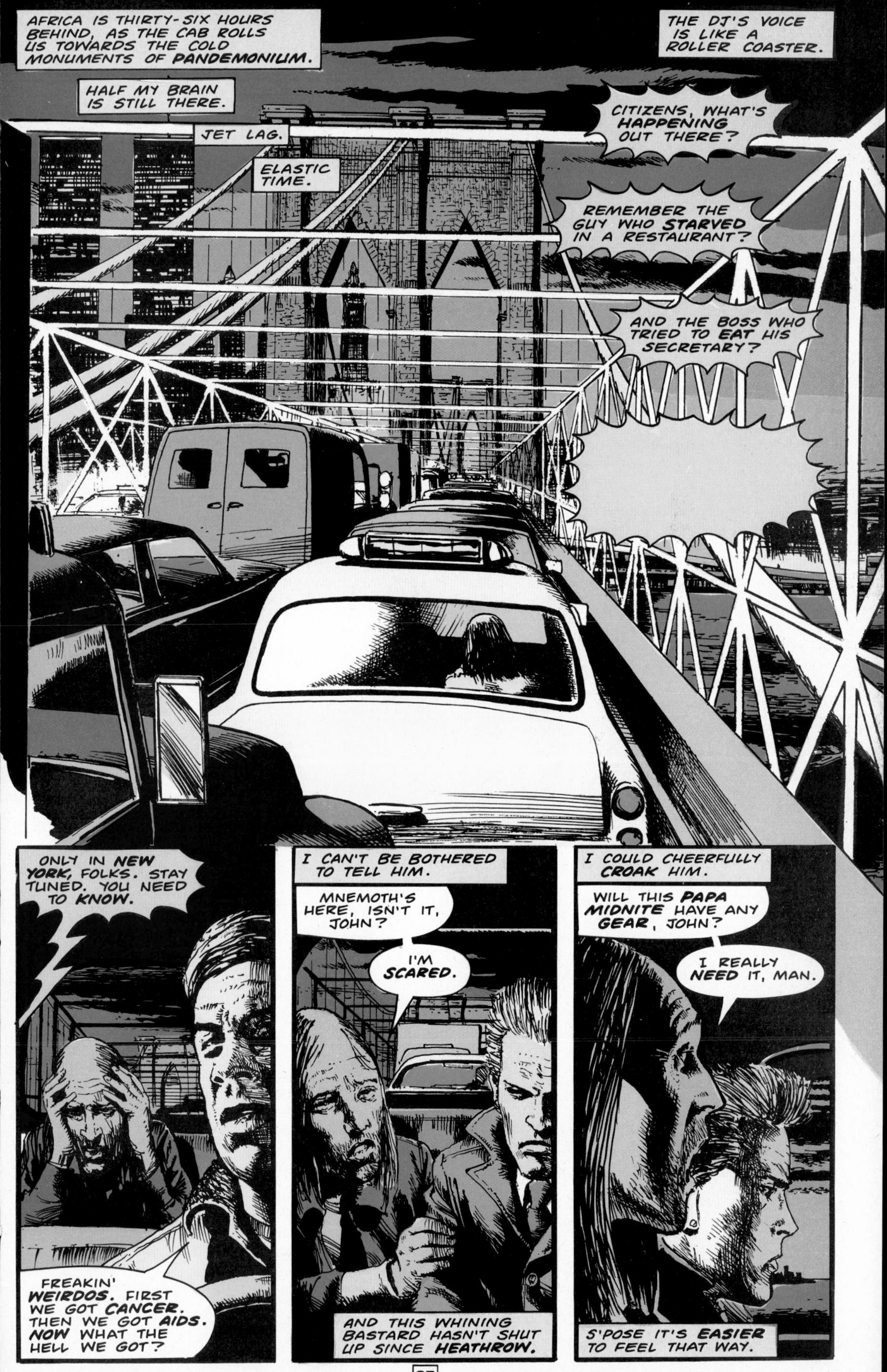

AFRICA IS THIRTY-SIX HOURS BEHIND, AS THE CAB ROLLS US TOWARDS THE COLD MONUMENTS OF PANDEMONIUM.
HALF MY BRAIN IS STILL THERE.
JET LAG.
ELASTIC TIME.
THE DJ'S VOICE IS LIKE A ROLLER COASTER.
CITIZENS, WHAT'S HAPPENING OUT THERE?
REMEMBER THE GUY WHO STARVED IN A RESTAURANT?
AND THE BOSS WHO TRIED TO EAT HIS SECRETARY?
ONLY IN NEW YORK, FOLKS. STAY TUNED. YOU NEED TO KNOW.
FREAKIN' WEIRDOS. FIRST WE GOT CANCER. THEN WE GOT AIDS. NOW WHAT THE HELL WE GOT?
I CAN'T BE BOTHERED TO TELL HIM.
MNEMOTH'S HERE, ISN'T IT, JOHN?
I'M SCARED.
AND THIS WHINING BASTARD HASN'T SHUT UP SINCE HEATHROW.
I COULD CHEERFULLY CROAK HIM.
WILL THIS PAPA MIDNITE HAVE ANY GEAR, JOHN?
I REALLY NEED IT, MAN.
S'POSE IT'S EASIER TO FEEL THAT WAY.

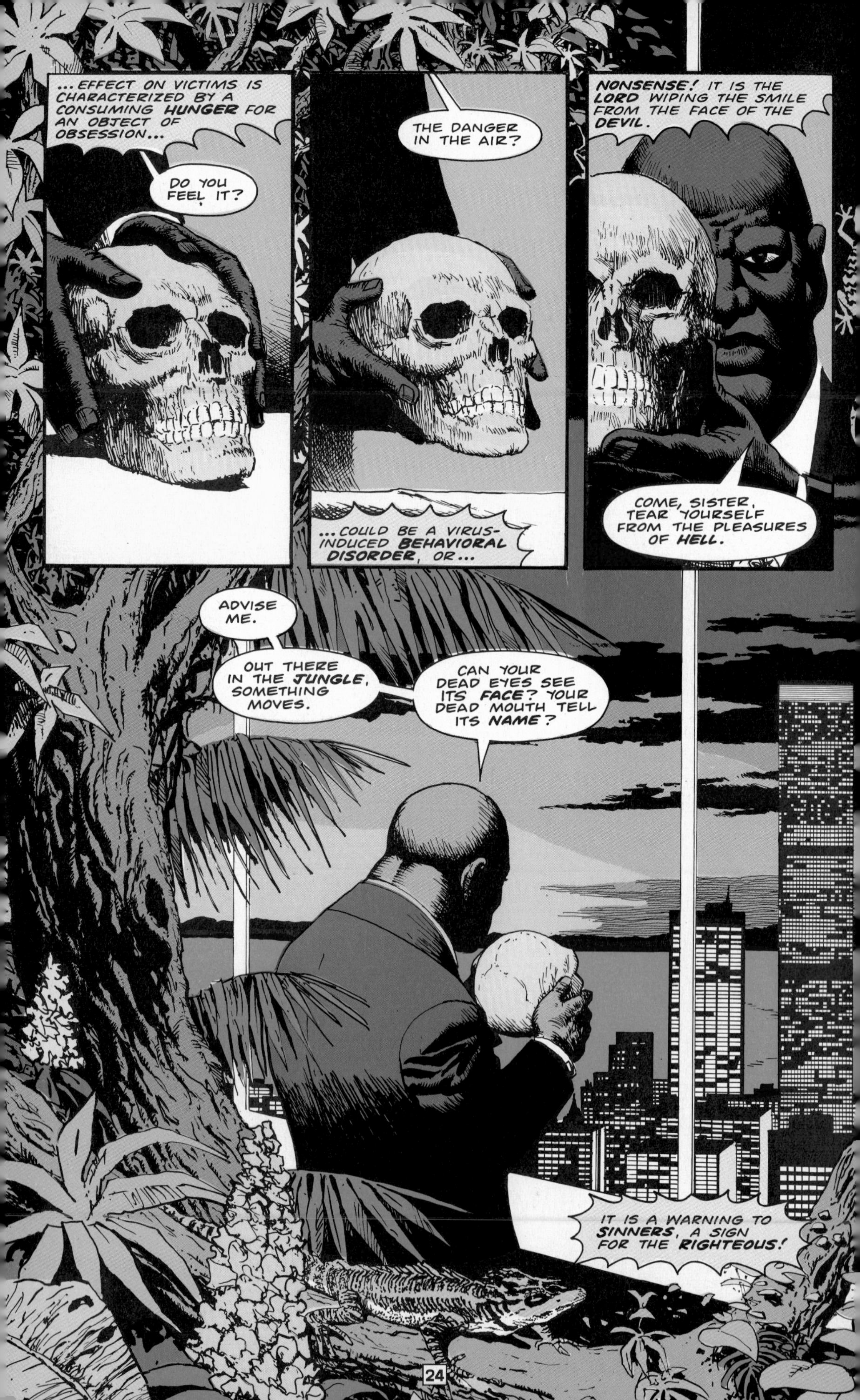
...EFFECT ON VICTIMS IS CHARACTERIZED BY A CONSUMING HUNGER FOR AN OBJECT OF OBSESSION...
DO YOU FEEL IT?
THE DANGER IN THE AIR?
...COULD BE A VIRUS-INDUCED BEHAVIORAL DISORDER, OR...
NONSENSE! IT IS THE LORD WIPING THE SMILE FROM THE FACE OF THE DEVIL.
COME, SISTER, TEAR YOURSELF FROM THE PLEASURES OF HELL.
ADVISE ME.
OUT THERE IN THE JUNGLE, SOMETHING MOVES.
CAN YOUR DEAD EYES SEE ITS FACE? YOUR DEAD MOUTH TELL ITS NAME?
IT IS A WARNING TO SINNERS, A SIGN FOR THE RIGHTEOUS!

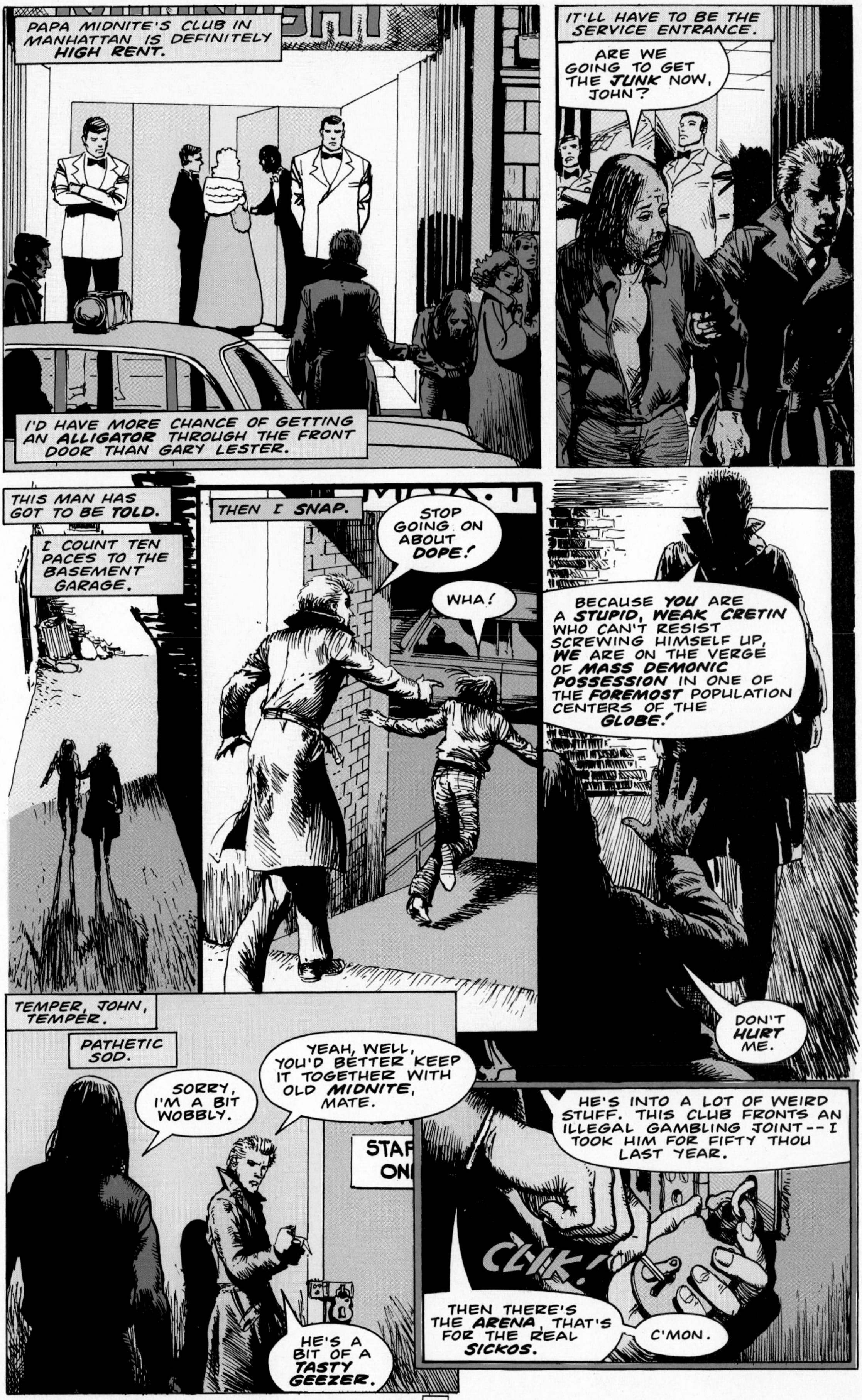
PAPA MIDNITE'S CLUB IN MANHATTAN IS DEFINITELY HIGH RENT.
I'D HAVE MORE CHANCE OF GETTING AN ALLIGATOR THROUGH THE FRONT DOOR THAN GARY LESTER.
IT'LL HAVE TO BE THE SERVICE ENTRANCE.
ARE WE GOING TO GET THE JUNK NOW, JOHN?
THIS MAN HAS GOT TO BE TOLD.
I COUNT TEN PACES TO THE BASEMENT GARAGE.
THEN I SNAP.
STOP GOING ON ABOUT DOPE!
WHA!
BECAUSE YOU ARE A STUPID, WEAK CRETIN WHO CAN'T RESIST SCREWING HIMSELF UP, WE ARE ON THE VERGE OF MASS DEMONIC POSSESSION IN ONE OF THE FOREMOST POPULATION CENTERS OF THE GLOBE!
DON'T HURT ME.
TEMPER, JOHN, TEMPER.
PATHETIC SOD.
SORRY, I'M A BIT WOBBLY.
YEAH, WELL, YOU'D BETTER KEEP IT TOGETHER WITH OLD MIDNITE, MATE.
HE'S A BIT OF A TASTY GEEZER.
HE'S INTO A LOT OF WEIRD STUFF. THIS CLUB FRONTS AN ILLEGAL GAMBLING JOINT -- I TOOK HIM FOR FIFTY THOU LAST YEAR.
CLIK!
THEN THERE'S THE ARENA, THAT'S FOR THE REAL SICKOS.
C'MON.

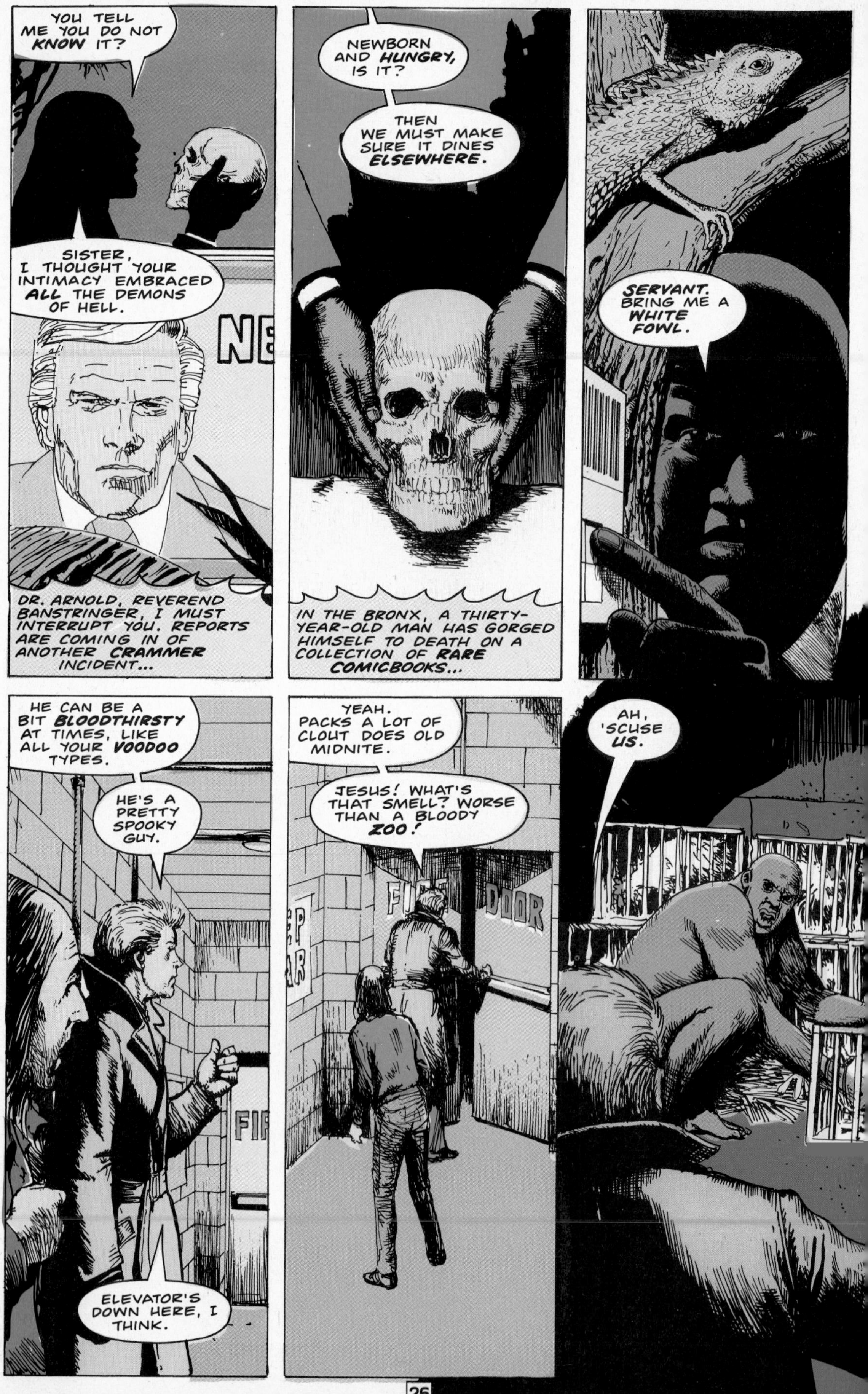
YOU TELL ME YOU DO NOT KNOW IT?
SISTER, I THOUGHT YOUR INTIMACY EMBRACED ALL THE DEMONS OF HELL.
DR. ARNOLD, REVEREND BANSTRINGER, I MUST INTERRUPT YOU. REPORTS ARE COMING IN OF ANOTHER CRAMMER INCIDENT...
NEWBORN AND HUNGRY, IS IT?
THEN WE MUST MAKE SURE IT DINES ELSEWHERE.
IN THE BRONX, A THIRTY-YEAR-OLD MAN HAS GORGED HIMSELF TO DEATH ON A COLLECTION OF RARE COMICBOOKS...
SERVANT. BRING ME A WHITE FOWL.
HE CAN BE A BIT BLOODTHIRSTY AT TIMES, LIKE ALL YOUR VOODOO TYPES.
HE'S A PRETTY SPOOKY GUY.
ELEVATOR'S DOWN HERE, I THINK.
YEAH. PACKS A LOT OF CLOUT DOES OLD MIDNITE.
JESUS! WHAT'S THAT SMELL? WORSE THAN A BLOODY ZOO!
AH, 'SCUSE US.

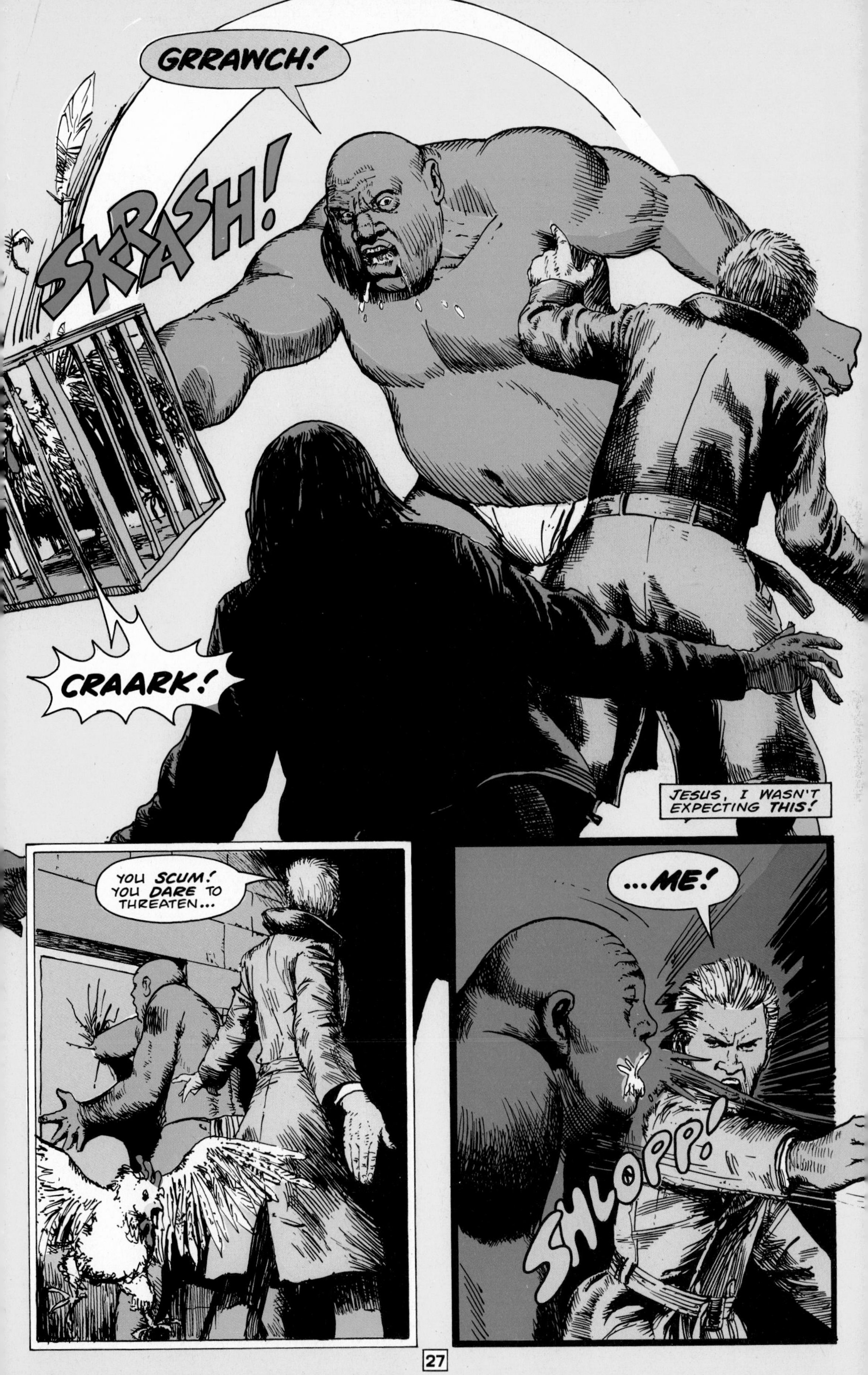
GRRAWCH!
SKRASH!
CRAARK!
JESUS, I WASN'T EXPECTING THIS!
YOU SCUM! YOU DARE TO THREATEN...
...ME!
SHLOPP!

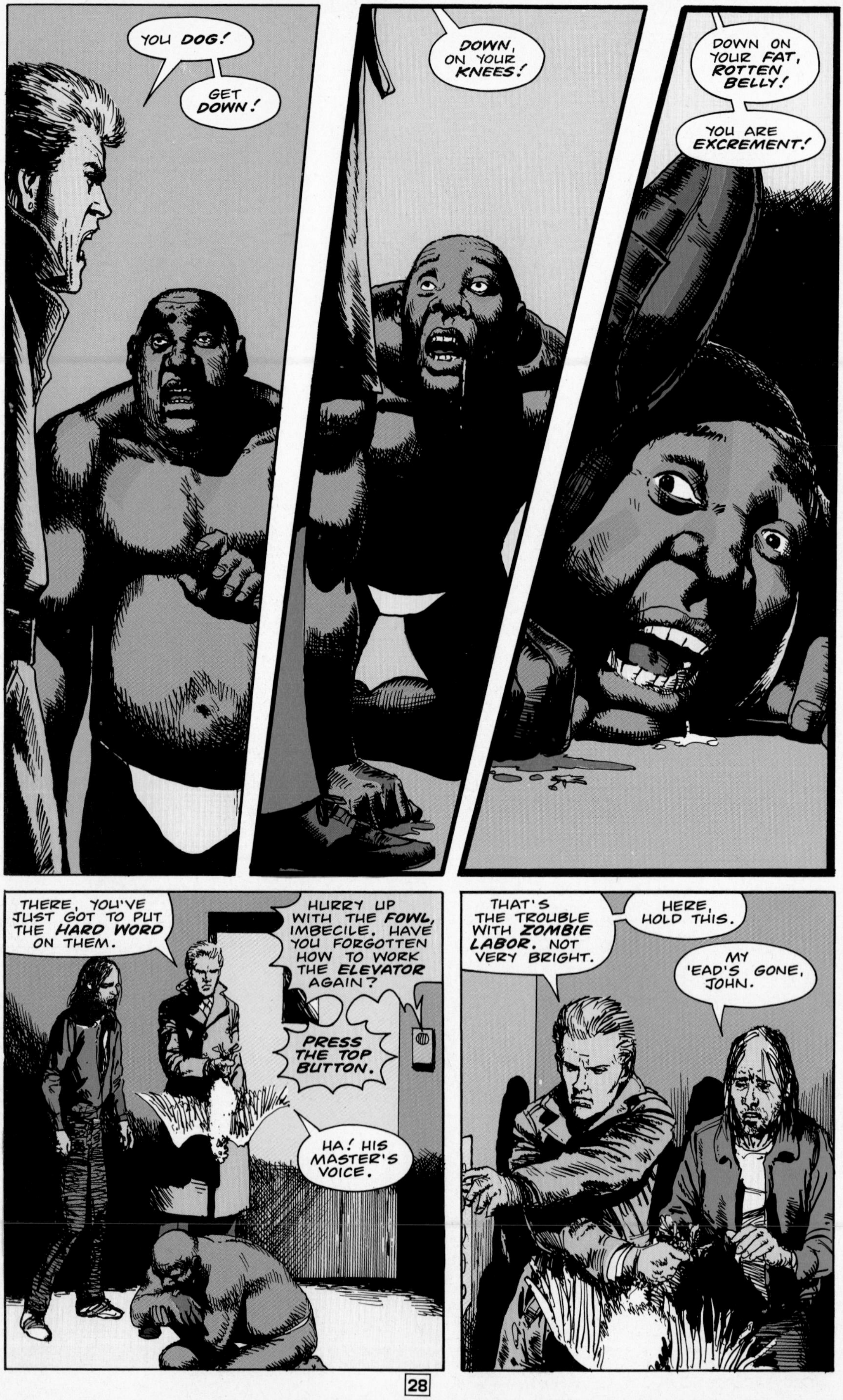
YOU DOG!
GET DOWN!
DOWN, ON YOUR KNEES!
DOWN ON YOUR FAT, ROTTEN BELLY!
YOU ARE EXCREMENT!
THERE, YOU'VE JUST GOT TO PUT THE HARD WORD ON THEM.
HURRY UP WITH THE FOWL, IMBECILE. HAVE YOU FORGOTTEN HOW TO WORK THE ELEVATOR AGAIN?
PRESS THE TOP BUTTON.
HA! HIS MASTER'S VOICE.
THAT'S THE TROUBLE WITH ZOMBIE LABOR. NOT VERY BRIGHT.
HERE, HOLD THIS.
MY 'EAD'S GONE, JOHN.

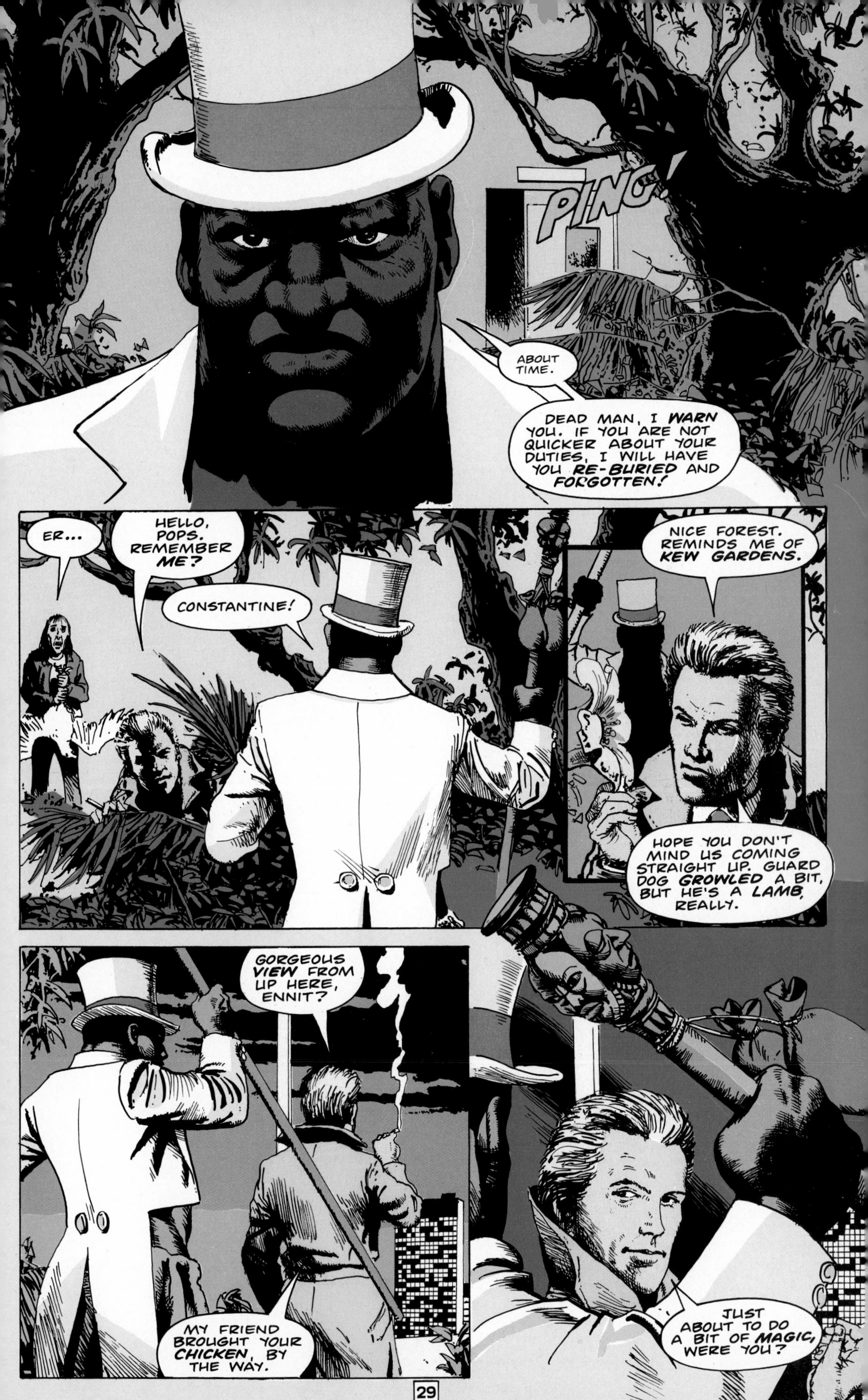
PING!
ABOUT TIME.
DEAD MAN, I WARN YOU. IF YOU ARE NOT QUICKER ABOUT YOUR DUTIES, I WILL HAVE YOU RE-BURIED AND FORGOTTEN!
ER...
HELLO, POPS. REMEMBER ME?
CONSTANTINE!
NICE FOREST. REMINDS ME OF KEW GARDENS.
HOPE YOU DON'T MIND US COMING STRAIGHT UP. GUARD DOG GROWLED A BIT, BUT HE'S A LAMB, REALLY.
GORGEOUS VIEW FROM UP HERE, ENNIT?
MY FRIEND BROUGHT YOUR CHICKEN, BY THE WAY.
JUST ABOUT TO DO A BIT OF MAGIC, WERE YOU?

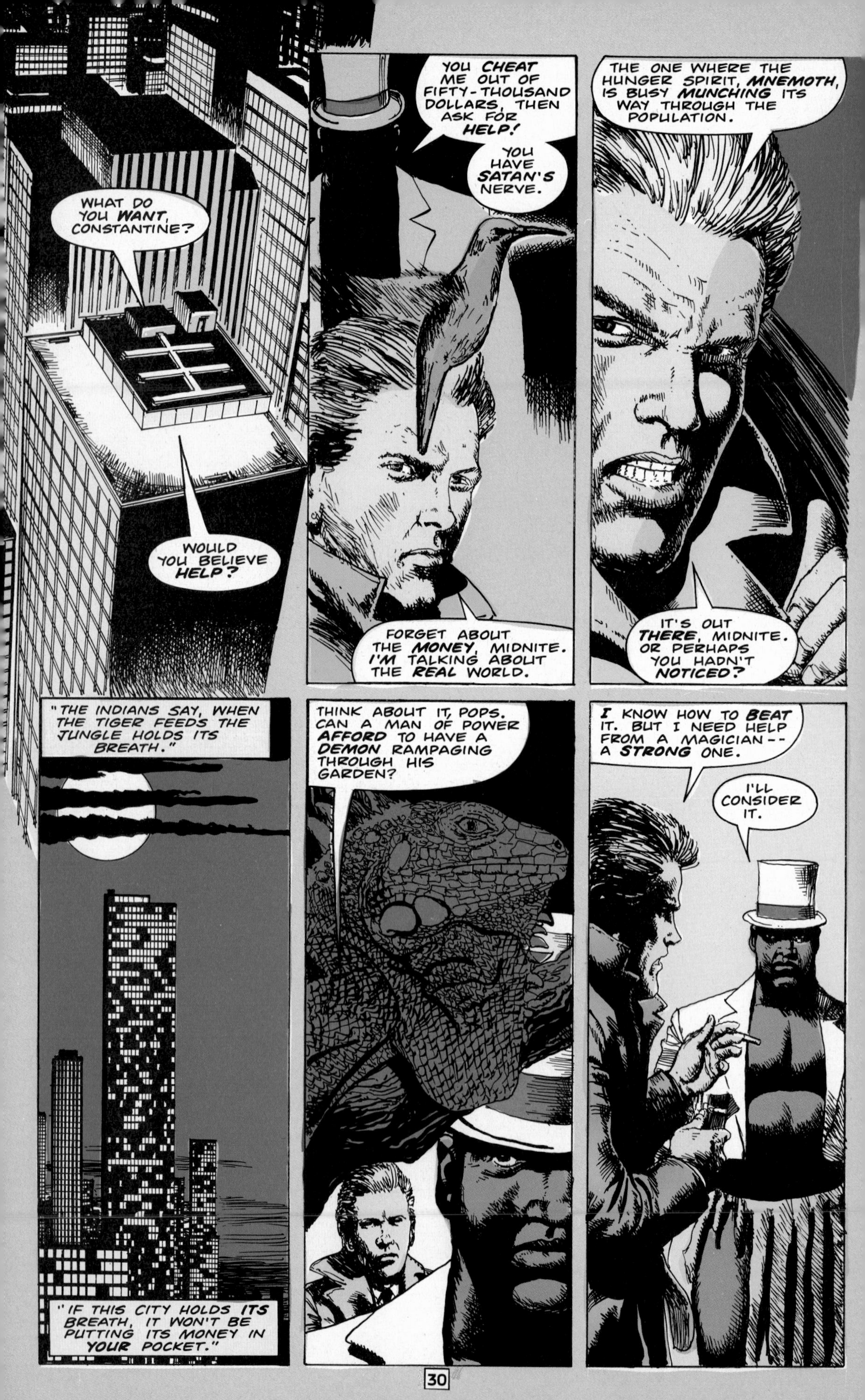
WHAT DO YOU WANT, CONSTANTINE?
WOULD YOU BELIEVE HELP?
YOU CHEAT ME OUT OF FIFTY-THOUSAND DOLLARS, THEN ASK FOR HELP!
YOU HAVE SATAN'S NERVE.
FORGET ABOUT THE MONEY, MIDNITE. I'M TALKING ABOUT THE REAL WORLD.
THE ONE WHERE THE HUNGER SPIRIT, MNEMOTH, IS BUSY MUNCHING ITS WAY THROUGH THE POPULATION.
IT'S OUT THERE, MIDNITE. OR PERHAPS YOU HADN'T NOTICED?
"THE INDIANS SAY, WHEN THE TIGER FEEDS THE JUNGLE HOLDS ITS BREATH."
"IF THIS CITY HOLDS ITS BREATH, IT WON'T BE PUTTING ITS MONEY IN YOUR POCKET."
THINK ABOUT IT, POPS. CAN A MAN OF POWER AFFORD TO HAVE A DEMON RAMPAGING THROUGH HIS GARDEN?
I KNOW HOW TO BEAT IT. BUT I NEED HELP FROM A MAGICIAN-- A STRONG ONE.
I'LL CONSIDER IT.

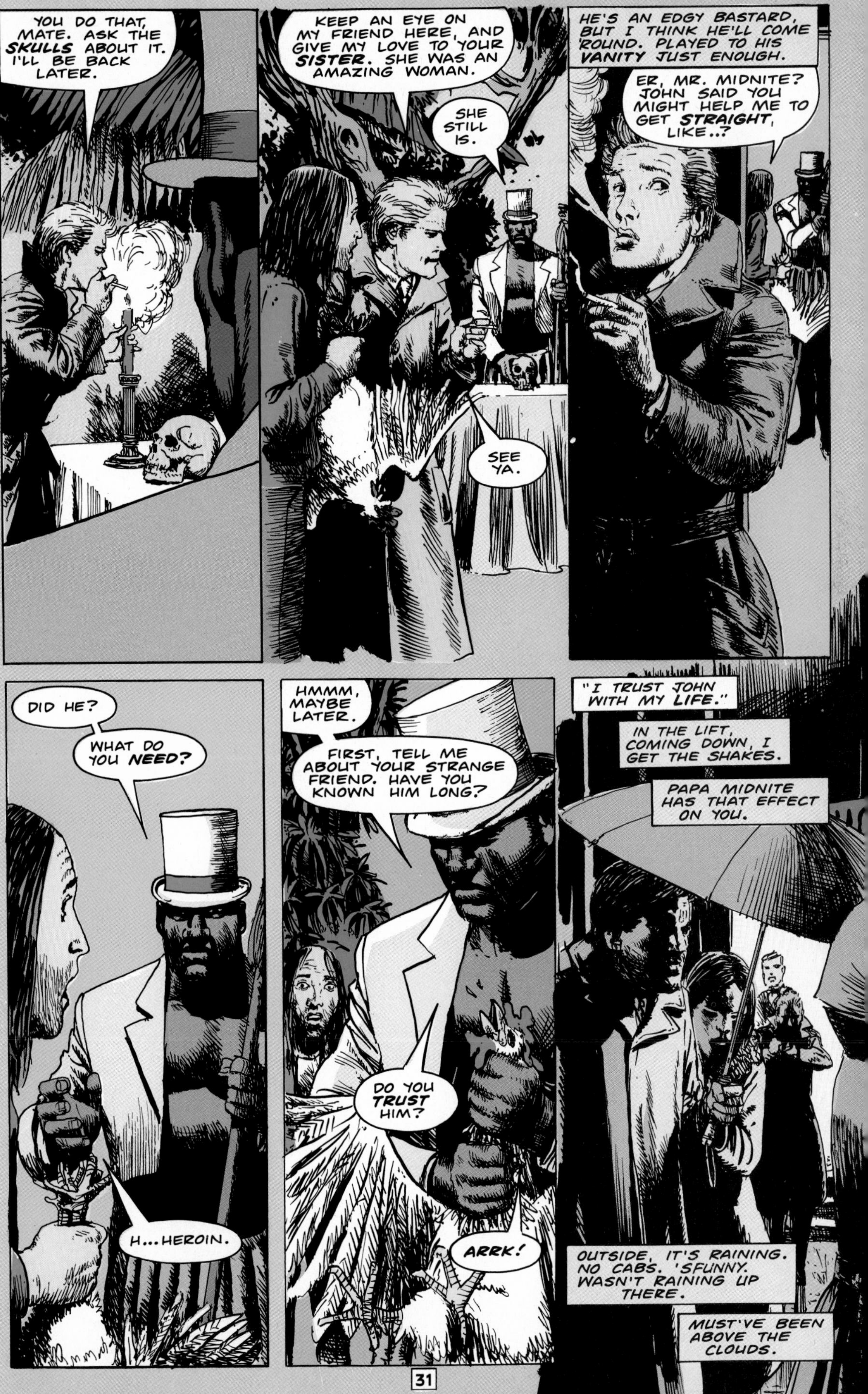
YOU DO THAT, MATE. ASK THE SKULLS ABOUT IT. I'LL BE BACK LATER.
KEEP AN EYE ON MY FRIEND HERE, AND GIVE MY LOVE TO YOUR SISTER. SHE WAS AN AMAZING WOMAN.
SHE STILL IS.
SEE YA.
HE'S AN EDGY BASTARD, BUT I THINK HE'LL COME 'ROUND. PLAYED TO HIS VANITY JUST ENOUGH.
ER, MR. MIDNITE? JOHN SAID YOU MIGHT HELP ME TO GET STRAIGHT, LIKE..?
DID HE?
WHAT DO YOU NEED?
H...HEROIN.
HMMM, MAYBE LATER.
FIRST, TELL ME ABOUT YOUR STRANGE FRIEND. HAVE YOU KNOWN HIM LONG?
DO YOU TRUST HIM?
ARRK!
"I TRUST JOHN WITH MY LIFE."
IN THE LIFT, COMING DOWN, I GET THE SHAKES.
PAPA MIDNITE HAS THAT EFFECT ON YOU.
OUTSIDE, IT'S RAINING. NO CABS. 'SFUNNY. WASN'T RAINING UP THERE.
MUST'VE BEEN ABOVE THE CLOUDS.

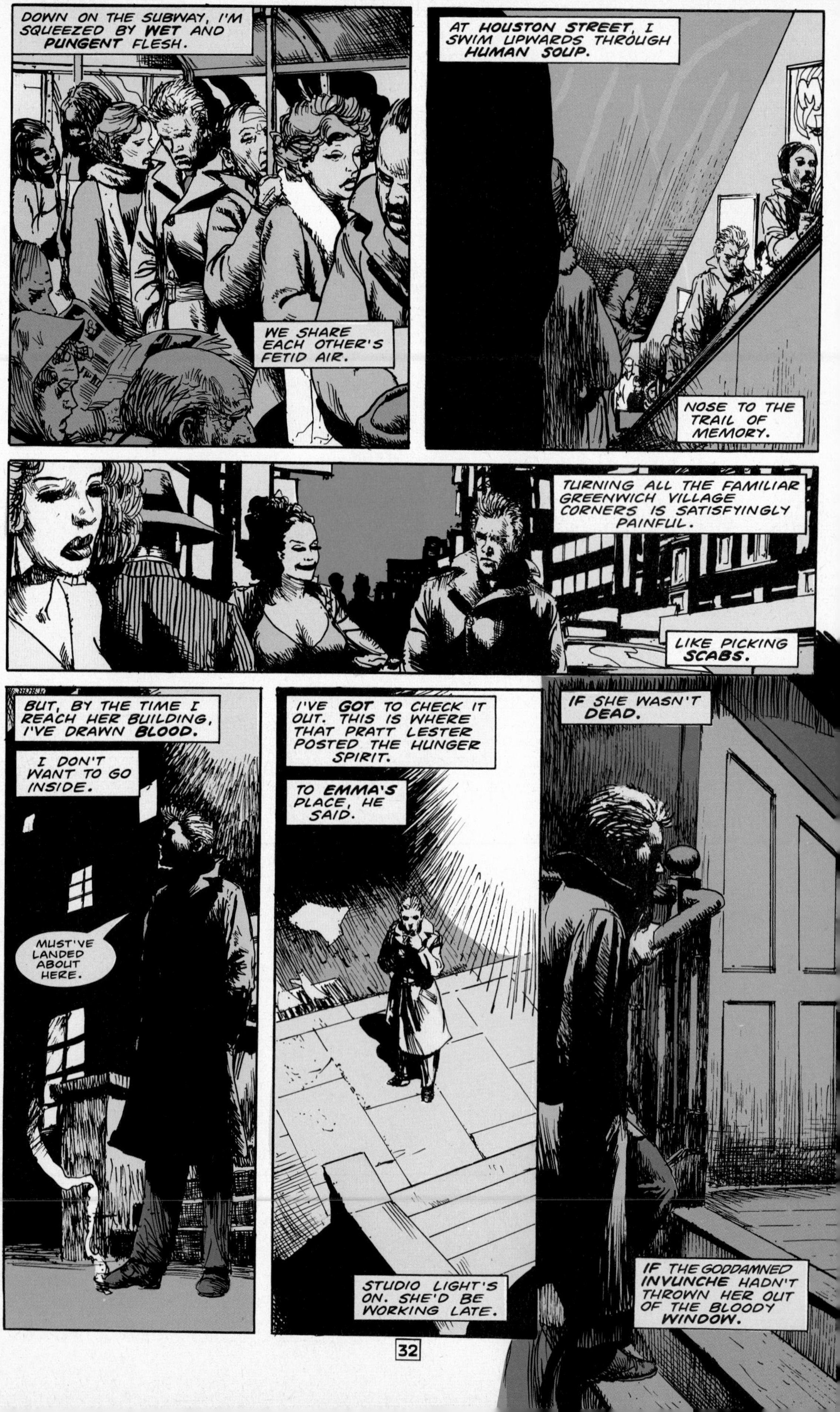

DOWN ON THE SUBWAY, I'M SQUEEZED BY WET AND PUNGENT FLESH.
WE SHARE EACH OTHER'S FETID AIR.
AT HOUSTON STREET, I SWIM UPWARDS THROUGH HUMAN SOUP.
NOSE TO THE TRAIL OF MEMORY.
TURNING ALL THE FAMILIAR GREENWICH VILLAGE CORNERS IS SATISFYINGLY PAINFUL.
LIKE PICKING SCABS.
BUT, BY THE TIME I REACH HER BUILDING, I'VE DRAWN BLOOD.
I DON'T WANT TO GO INSIDE.
MUST'VE LANDED ABOUT HERE.
I'VE GOT TO CHECK IT OUT. THIS IS WHERE THAT PRATT LESTER POSTED THE HUNGER SPIRIT.
TO EMMA'S PLACE, HE SAID.
STUDIO LIGHT'S ON. SHE'D BE WORKING LATE.
IF SHE WASN'T DEAD.
IF THE GODDAMNED INVUNCHE HADN'T THROWN HER OUT OF THE BLOODY WINDOW.

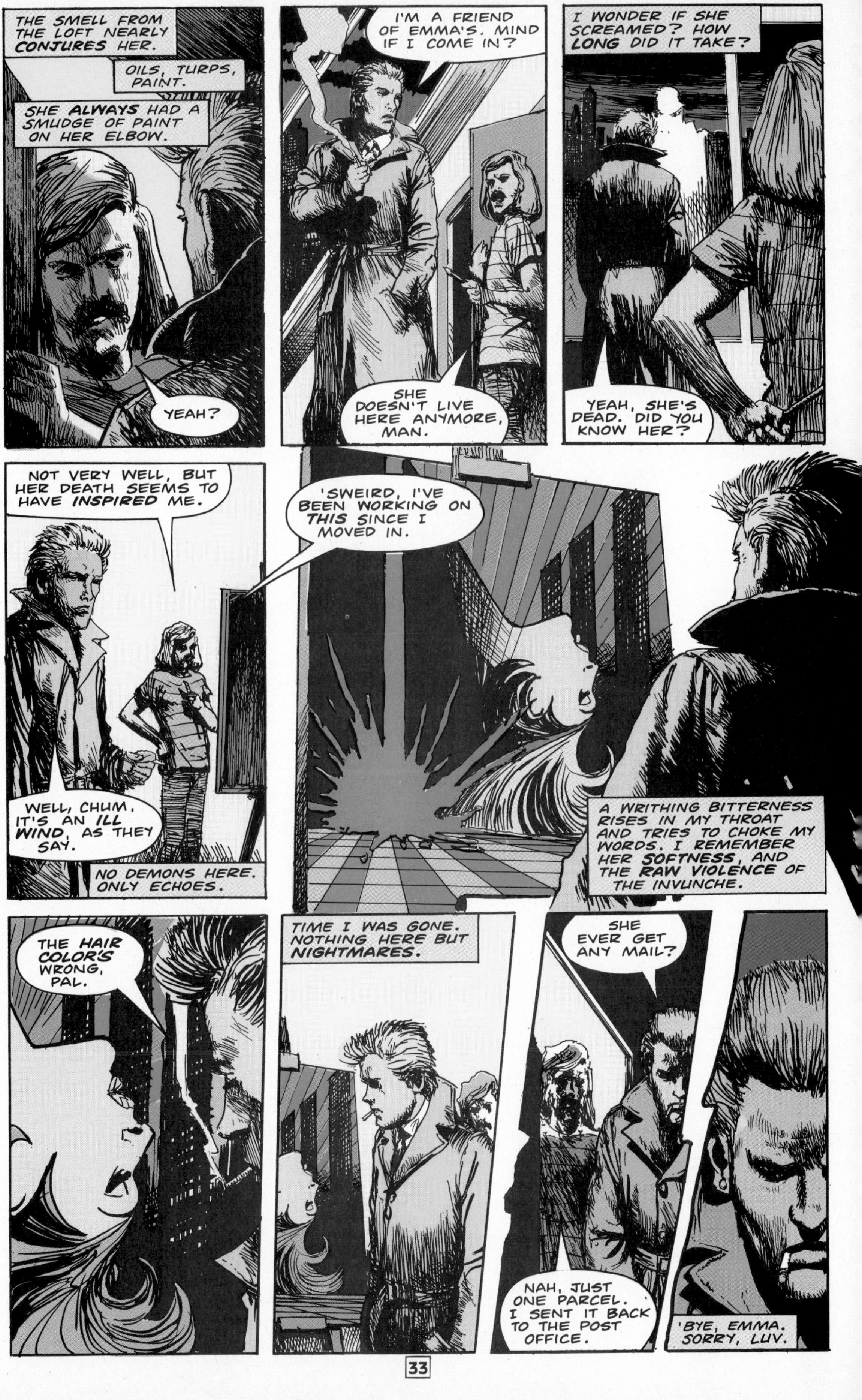
THE SMELL FROM THE LOFT NEARLY CONJURES HER.
OILS, TURPS, PAINT.
SHE ALWAYS HAD A SMUDGE OF PAINT ON HER ELBOW.
YEAH?
I'M A FRIEND OF EMMA'S. MIND IF I COME IN?
SHE DOESN'T LIVE HERE ANYMORE, MAN.
I WONDER IF SHE SCREAMED? HOW LONG DID IT TAKE?
YEAH, SHE'S DEAD. DID YOU KNOW HER?
NOT VERY WELL, BUT HER DEATH SEEMS TO HAVE INSPIRED ME.
WELL, CHUM, IT'S AN ILL WIND, AS THEY SAY.
NO DEMONS HERE. ONLY ECHOES.
'SWEIRD, I'VE BEEN WORKING ON THIS SINCE I MOVED IN.
A WRITHING BITTERNESS RISES IN MY THROAT AND TRIES TO CHOKE MY WORDS. I REMEMBER HER SOFTNESS, AND THE RAW VIOLENCE OF THE INVUNCHE.
THE HAIR COLOR'S WRONG, PAL.
TIME I WAS GONE. NOTHING HERE BUT NIGHTMARES.
SHE EVER GET ANY MAIL?
NAH, JUST ONE PARCEL. I SENT IT BACK TO THE POST OFFICE.
'BYE, EMMA. SORRY, LUV.

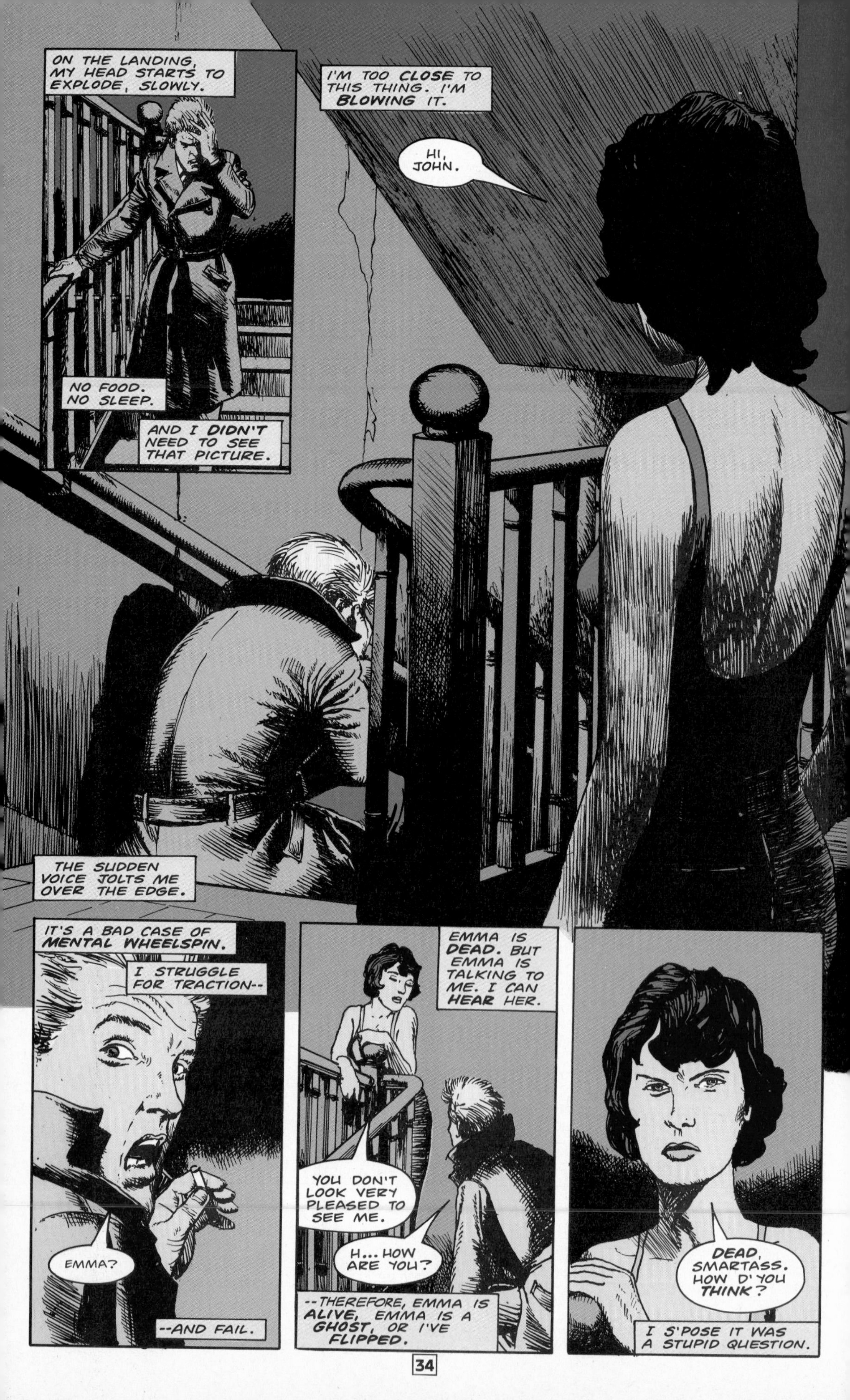

ON THE LANDING, MY HEAD STARTS TO EXPLODE, SLOWLY.
NO FOOD. NO SLEEP.
AND I DIDN'T NEED TO SEE THAT PICTURE.
I'M TOO CLOSE TO THIS THING. I'M BLOWING IT.
HI, JOHN.
THE SUDDEN VOICE JOLTS ME OVER THE EDGE.
IT'S A BAD CASE OF MENTAL WHEELSPIN.
I STRUGGLE FOR TRACTION--
EMMA?
--AND FAIL.
EMMA IS DEAD. BUT EMMA IS TALKING TO ME. I CAN HEAR HER.
YOU DON'T LOOK VERY PLEASED TO SEE ME.
H... HOW ARE YOU?
--THEREFORE, EMMA IS ALIVE, EMMA IS A GHOST, OR I'VE FLIPPED.
DEAD, SMARTASS. HOW D' YOU THINK?
I S'POSE IT WAS A STUPID QUESTION.

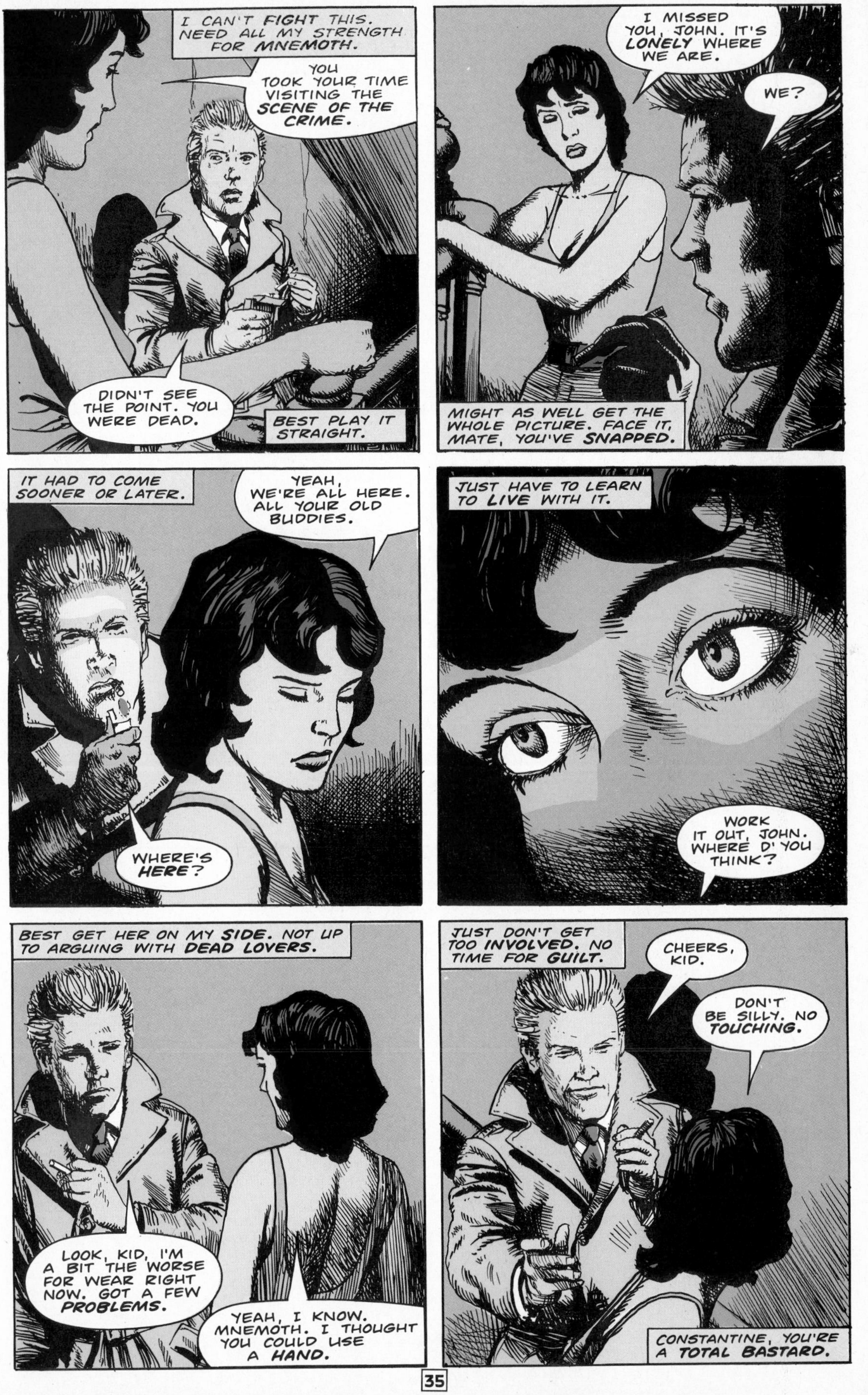

I CAN'T FIGHT THIS. NEED ALL MY STRENGTH FOR MNEMOTH.
YOU TOOK YOUR TIME VISITING THE SCENE OF THE CRIME.
DIDN'T SEE THE POINT. YOU WERE DEAD.
BEST PLAY IT STRAIGHT.
I MISSED YOU, JOHN. IT'S LONELY WHERE WE ARE.
WE?
MIGHT AS WELL GET THE WHOLE PICTURE. FACE IT, MATE, YOU'VE SNAPPED.
IT HAD TO COME SOONER OR LATER.
YEAH, WE'RE ALL HERE. ALL YOUR OLD BUDDIES.
WHERE'S HERE?
JUST HAVE TO LEARN TO LIVE WITH IT.
WORK IT OUT, JOHN. WHERE D' YOU THINK?
BEST GET HER ON MY SIDE. NOT UP TO ARGUING WITH DEAD LOVERS.
LOOK, KID, I'M A BIT THE WORSE FOR WEAR RIGHT NOW. GOT A FEW PROBLEMS.
YEAH, I KNOW. MNEMOTH. I THOUGHT YOU COULD USE A HAND.
JUST DON'T GET TOO INVOLVED. NO TIME FOR GUILT.
CHEERS, KID.
DON'T BE SILLY. NO TOUCHING.
CONSTANTINE, YOU'RE A TOTAL BASTARD.

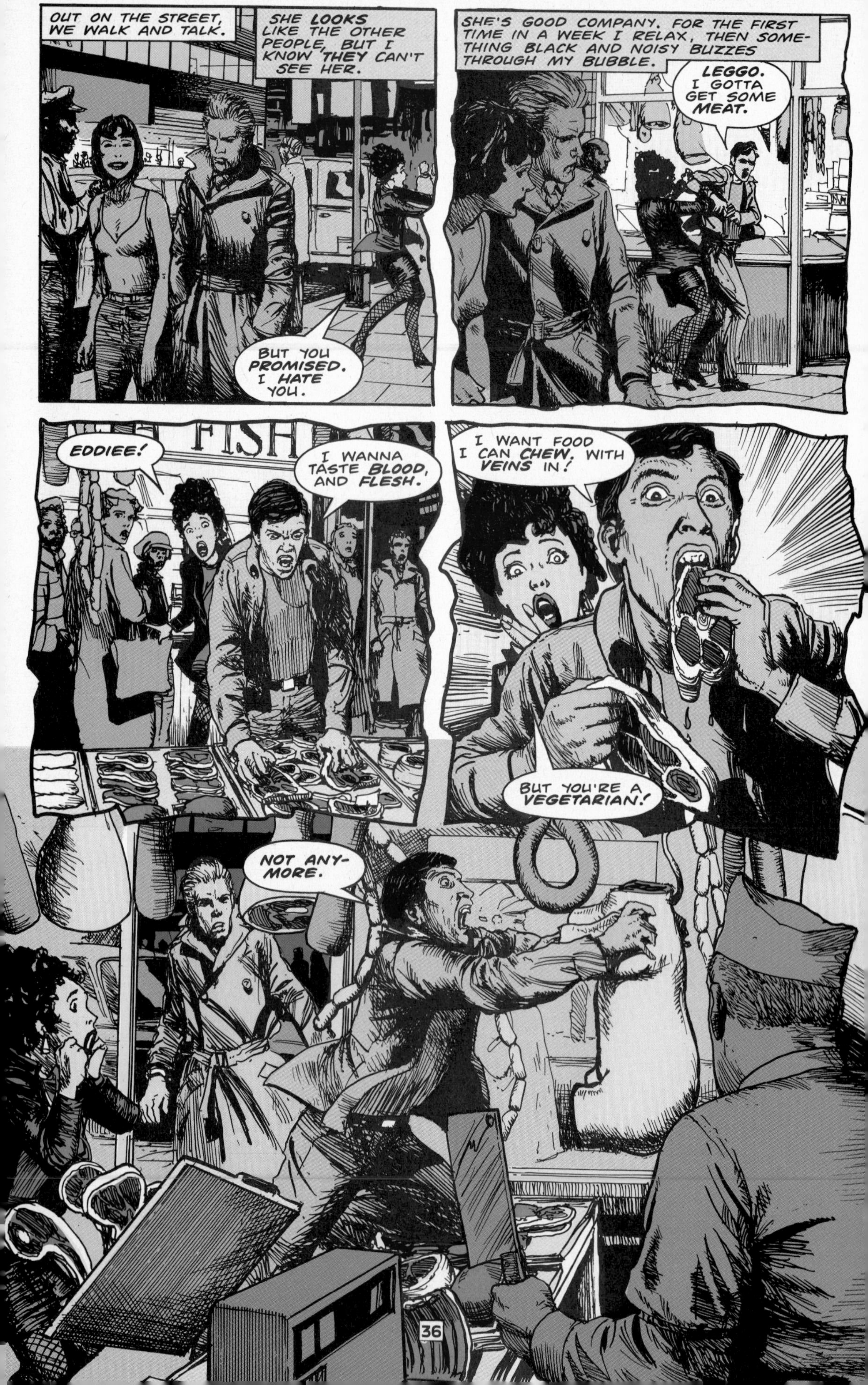
OUT ON THE STREET, WE WALK AND TALK.
SHE LOOKS LIKE THE OTHER PEOPLE, BUT I KNOW THEY CAN'T SEE HER.
BUT YOU PROMISED. I HATE YOU.
SHE'S GOOD COMPANY. FOR THE FIRST TIME IN A WEEK I RELAX, THEN SOMETHING BLACK AND NOISY BUZZES THROUGH MY BUBBLE.
LEGGO. I GOTTA GET SOME MEAT.
FISH
EDDIEE!
I WANNA TASTE BLOOD, AND FLESH.
I WANT FOOD I CAN CHEW. WITH VEINS IN!
BUT YOU'RE A VEGETARIAN!
NOT ANYMORE.

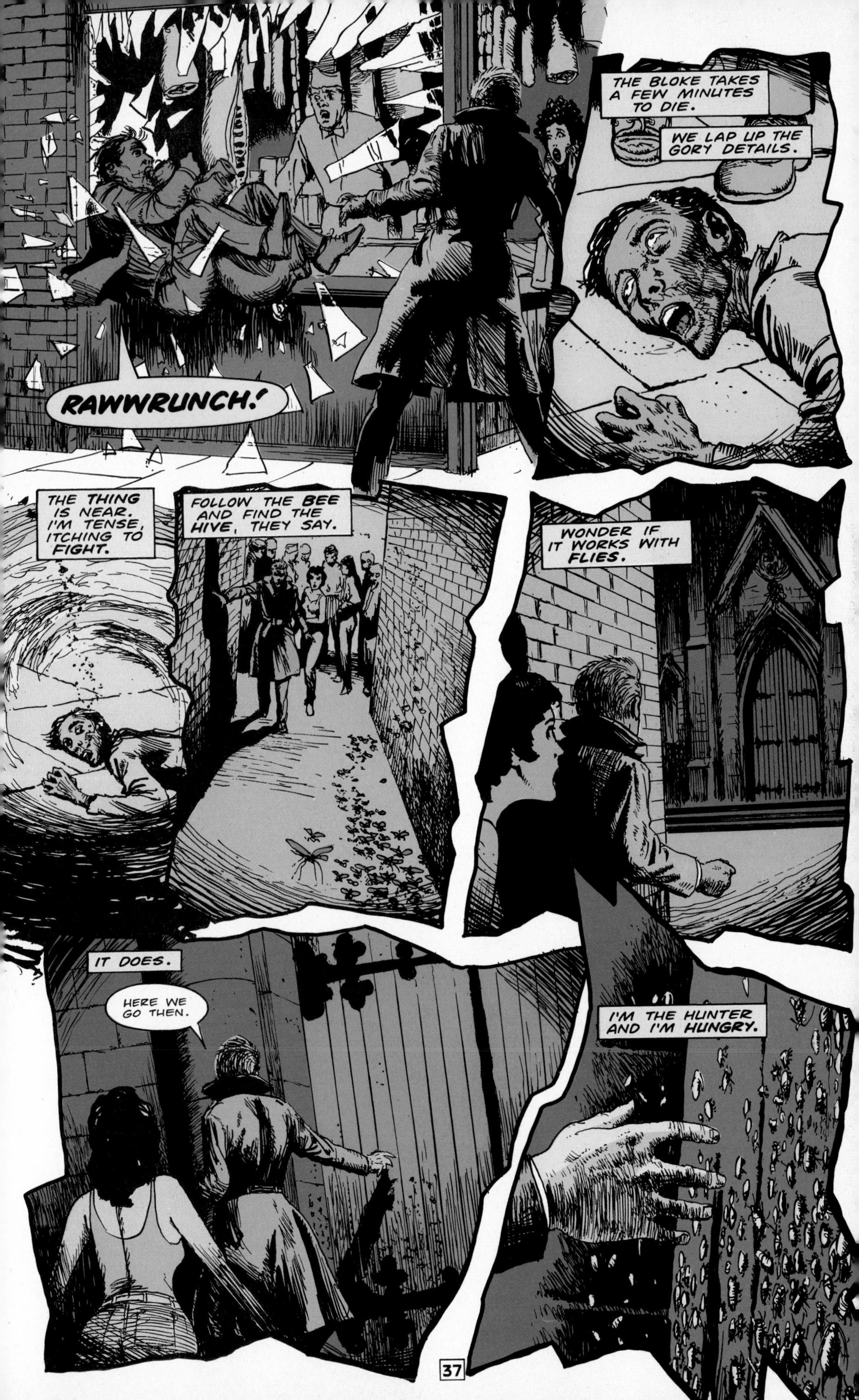

RAWWRUNCH!
THE BLOKE TAKES A FEW MINUTES TO DIE.
WE LAP UP THE GORY DETAILS.
THE THING IS NEAR. I'M TENSE, ITCHING TO FIGHT.
FOLLOW THE BEE AND FIND THE HIVE, THEY SAY.
WONDER IF IT WORKS WITH FLIES.
IT DOES.
HERE WE GO THEN.
I'M THE HUNTER AND I'M HUNGRY.

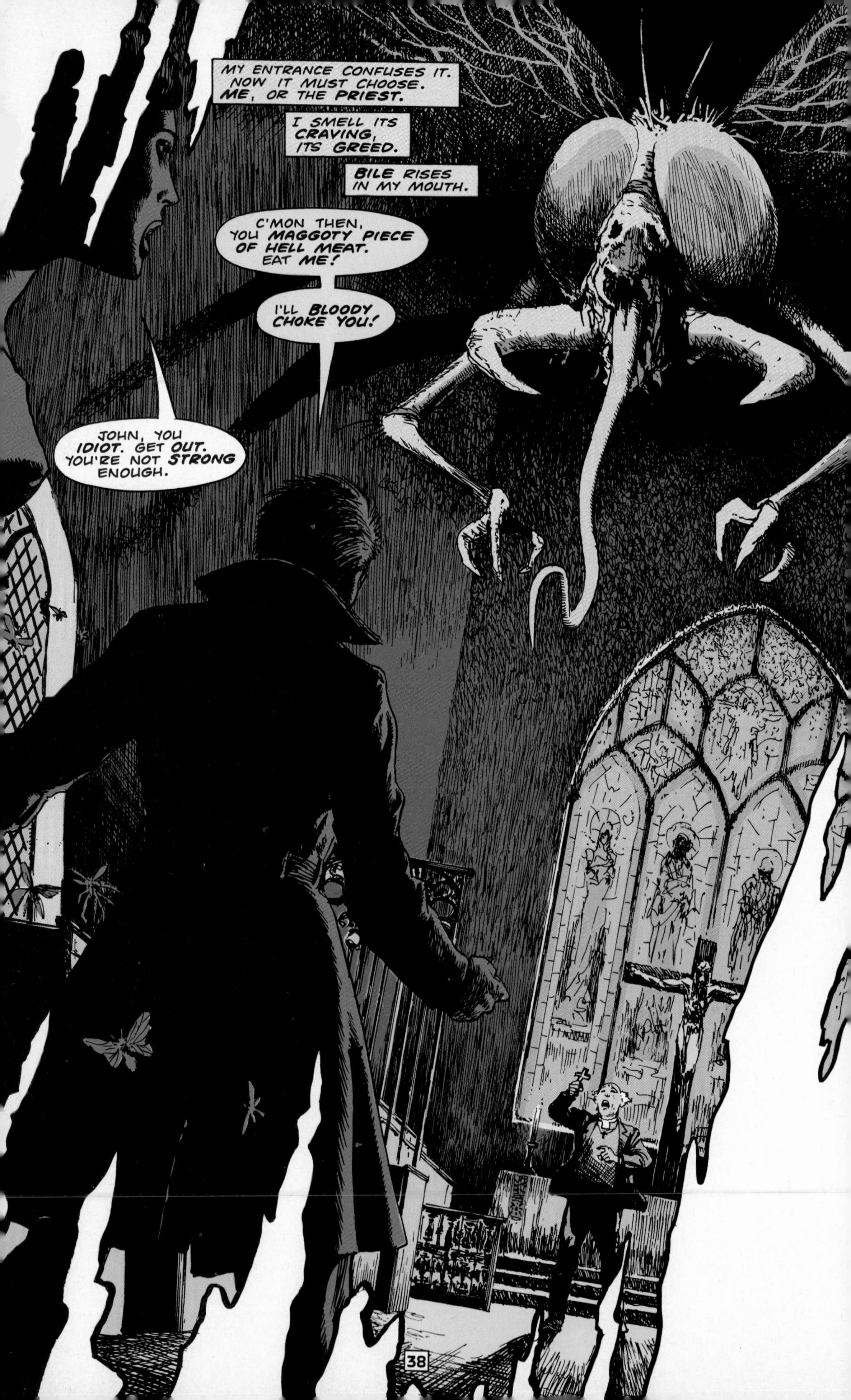
MY ENTRANCE CONFUSES IT. NOW IT MUST CHOOSE. ME, OR THE PRIEST.
I SMELL ITS CRAVING, ITS GREED.
BILE RISES IN MY MOUTH.
C'MON THEN, YOU MAGGOTY PIECE OF HELL MEAT. EAT ME!
I'LL BLOODY CHOKE YOU!
JOHN, YOU IDIOT. GET OUT. YOU'RE NOT STRONG ENOUGH.

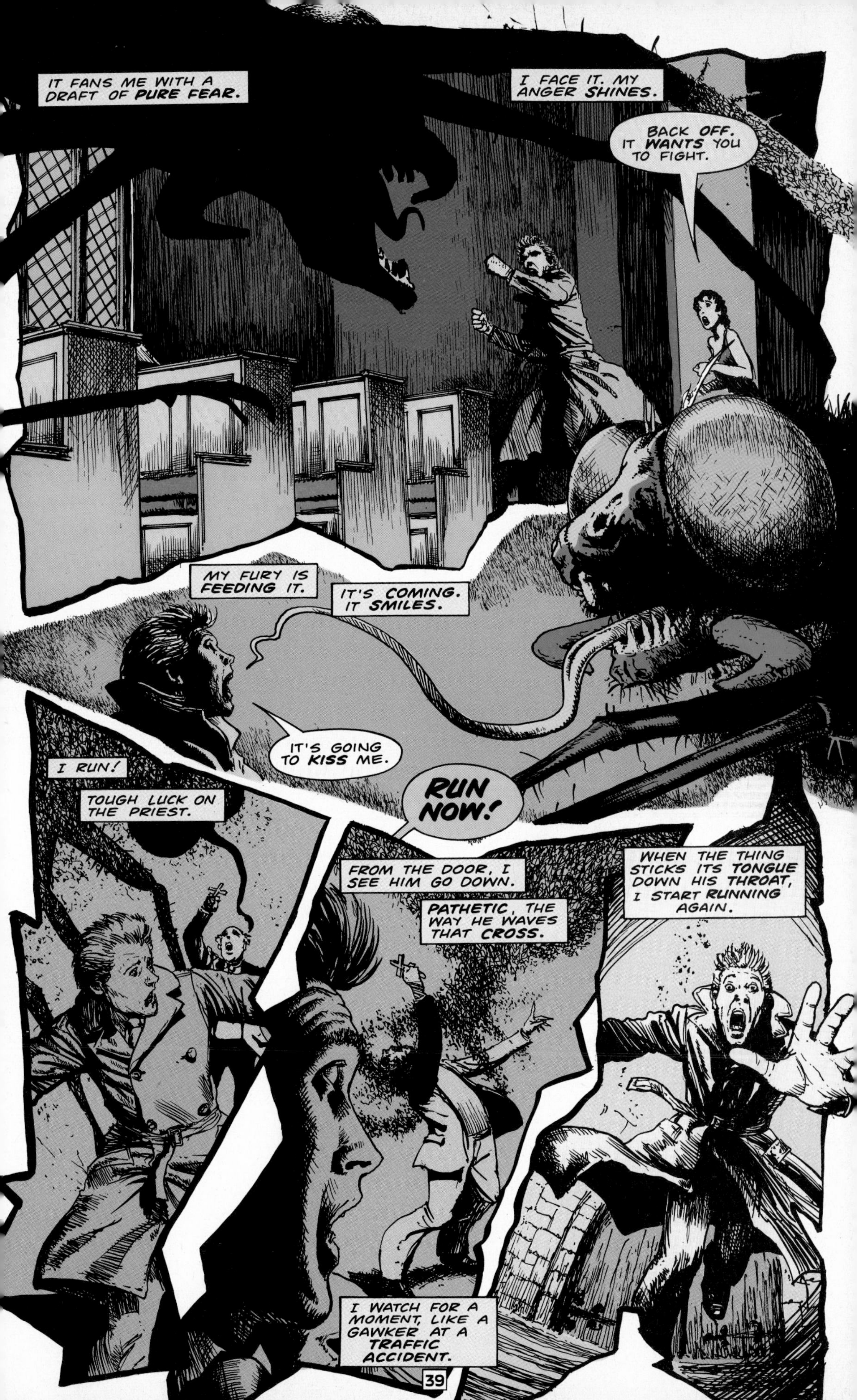

IT FANS ME WITH A DRAFT OF PURE FEAR.
I FACE IT. MY ANGER SHINES.
BACK OFF. IT WANTS YOU TO FIGHT.
MY FURY IS FEEDING IT.
IT'S COMING. IT SMILES.
IT'S GOING TO KISS ME.
RUN NOW!
I RUN!
TOUGH LUCK ON THE PRIEST.
FROM THE DOOR, I SEE HIM GO DOWN.
PATHETIC, THE WAY HE WAVES THAT CROSS.
I WATCH FOR A MOMENT, LIKE A GAWKER AT A TRAFFIC ACCIDENT.
WHEN THE THING STICKS ITS TONGUE DOWN HIS THROAT, I START RUNNING AGAIN.

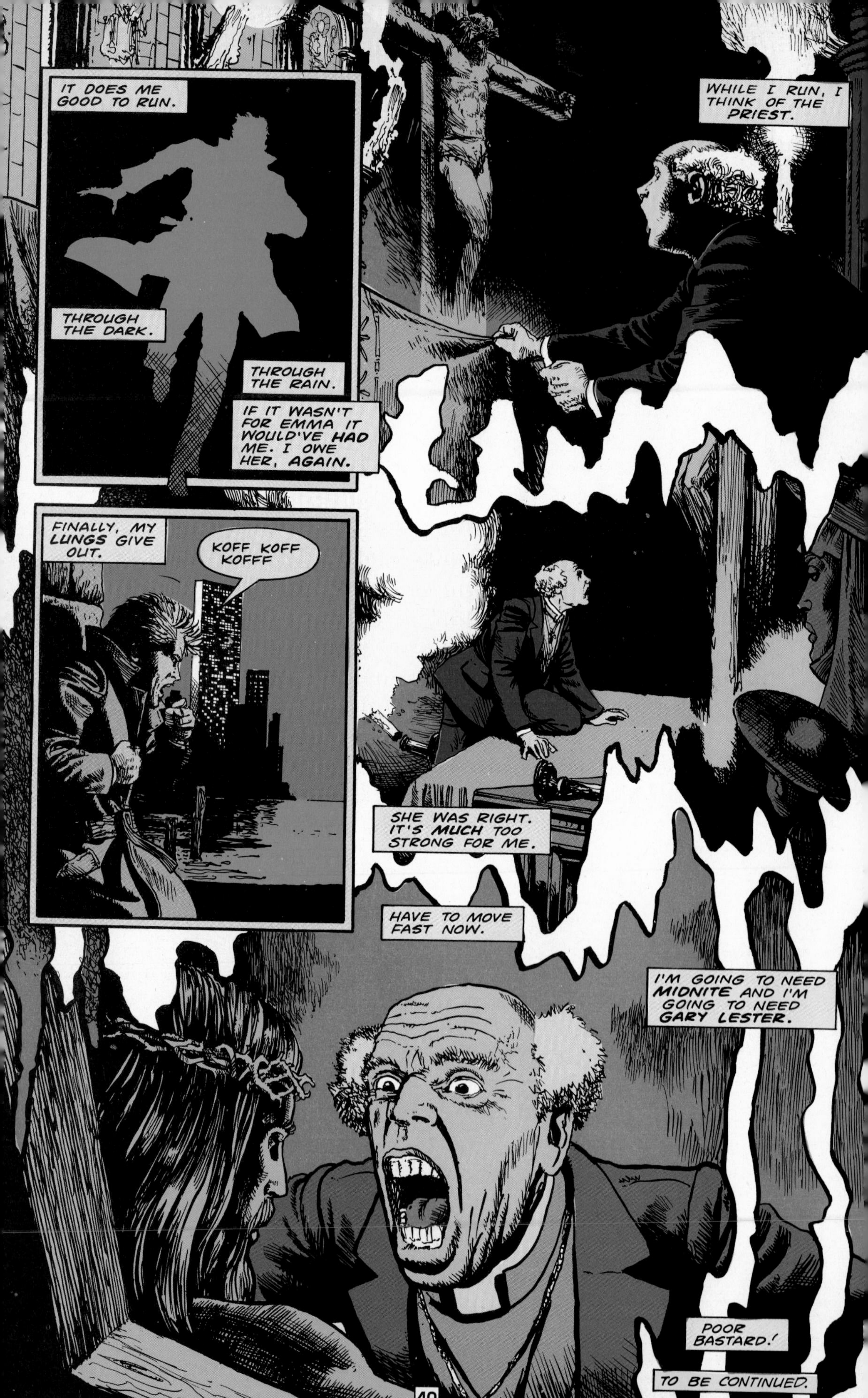
IT DOES ME GOOD TO RUN.
THROUGH THE DARK.
THROUGH THE RAIN.
IF IT WASN'T FOR EMMA IT WOULD'VE HAD ME. I OWE HER, AGAIN.
WHILE I RUN, I THINK OF THE PRIEST.
FINALLY, MY LUNGS GIVE OUT.
KOFF KOFF KOFFF
SHE WAS RIGHT. IT'S MUCH TOO STRONG FOR ME.
HAVE TO MOVE FAST NOW.
I'M GOING TO NEED MIDNITE AND I'M GOING TO NEED GARY LESTER.
POOR BASTARD!
TO BE CONTINUED.

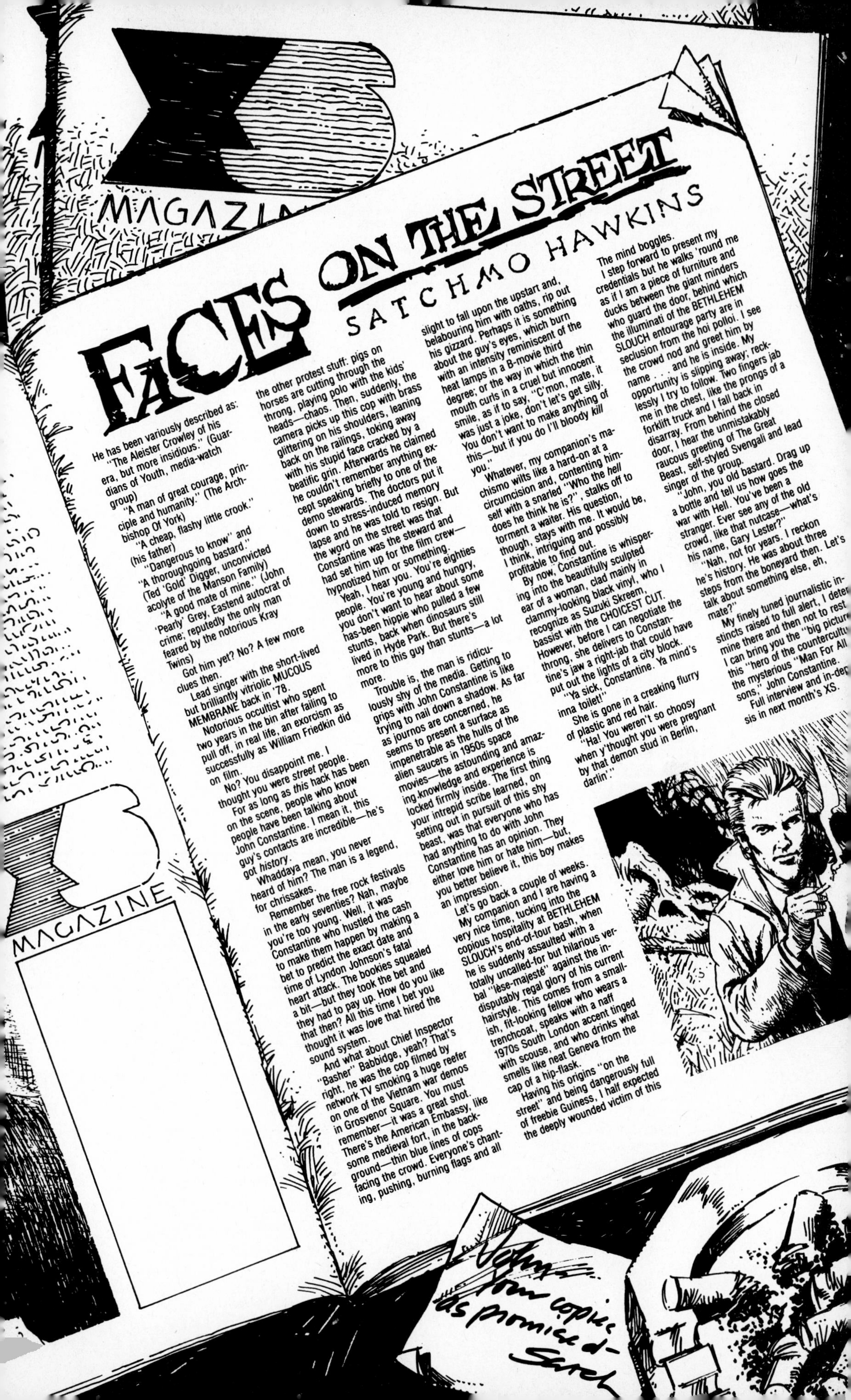
FACES ON THE STREET

SATCHMO HAWKINS

He has been variously described as: "The Aleister Crowley of his era, but more insidious." (Guardians of Youth, media-watch group)

"A man of great courage, principle and humanity." (The Archbishop Of York)

"A cheap, flashy little crook." (his father)

"Dangerous to know" and "A thoroughgoing bastard." (Ted 'Gold' Digger, unconvicted acolyte of the Manson Family)

"A good mate of mine." (John 'Pearly' Grey, Eastend autocrat of crime; reputedly the only man feared by the notorious Kray Twins)

Got him yet? No? A few more clues then.

Lead singer with the short-lived but brilliantly vitriolic MUCOUS MEMBRANE back in '78.

Notorious occultist who spent two years in the bin after failing to pull off, in real life, an exorcism as successfully as William Friedkin did on film.

No? You disappoint me. I thought you were *street* people.

For as long as *this* hack has been on the scene, people who know people have been talking about John Constantine. I mean it, this guy's contacts are incredible—he's got *history*.

Whaddaya mean, you never heard of him? The man is a legend, for chrissakes.

Remember the free rock festivals in the early seventies? Nah, maybe you're too young. Well, it was Constantine who hustled the cash to make them happen by making a bet to predict the exact date and time of Lyndon Johnson's fatal heart attack. The bookies squealed a bit—but they took the bet and they had to pay up. How do you like that then? All this time I bet you thought it was *love* that hired the sound system.

And what about Chief Inspector "Basher" Babbidge, yeah? That's right, he was the cop filmed by network TV smoking a huge reefer on one of the Vietnam war demos in Grosvenor Square. You must remember—it was a great shot. There's the American Embassy, like some medieval fort, in the background—thin blue lines of cops facing the crowd. Everyone's chanting, pushing, burning flags and all the other protest stuff: pigs on horses are cutting through the throng, playing polo with the kids' heads—chaos. Then, suddenly, the camera picks up this cop with brass glittering on his shoulders, leaning back on the railings, toking away with his stupid face cracked by a beatific grin. Afterwards he claimed he couldn't remember anything except speaking briefly to one of the demo stewards. The doctors put it down to stress-induced memory lapse and he was told to resign. But the word on the street was that Constantine was the steward and had set him up for the film crew—hypnotized him or something.

Yeah, I hear you. You're eighties people. You're young and hungry, you don't want to hear about some has-been hippie who pulled a few stunts, back when dinosaurs still lived in Hyde Park. But there's more to this guy than stunts—a lot more.

Trouble is, the man is ridiculously shy of the media. Getting to grips with John Constantine is like trying to nail down a shadow. As far as journos are concerned, he seems to present a surface as impenetrable as the hulls of the alien saucers in 1950s space movies—the astounding and amazing knowledge and experience is locked firmly inside. The first thing your intrepid scribe learned, on setting out in pursuit of this shy beast, was that everyone who has had anything to do with John Constantine has an opinion. They either love him or hate him—but, you better believe it, this boy makes an impression.

Let's go back a couple of weeks.

My companion and I are having a very nice time, tucking into the copious hospitality at BETHLEHEM SLOUCH's end-of-tour bash, when he is suddenly assaulted with a totally uncalled-for but hilarious verbal "lèse-majesté" against the indisputably regal glory of his current hairstyle. This comes from a smallish, fit-looking fellow who wears a naff trenchcoat, speaks with a 1970s South London accent tinged with scouse, and who drinks what smells like neat Geneva from the cap of a hip-flask.

Having his origins "on the street" and being dangerously full of freebie Guiness, I half expected the deeply wounded victim of this slight to fall upon the upstart and, belabouring him with oaths, rip out his gizzard. Perhaps it is something about the guy's eyes, which burn with an intensity reminiscent of the heat lamps in a B-movie third degree; or the way in which the thin mouth curls in a cruel but innocent smile, as if to say, "C'mon, mate, it was just a joke, don't let's get silly. You don't want to make anything of this—but if you do I'll bloody *kill* you."

Whatever, my companion's machismo wilts like a hard-on at a circumcision and, contenting himself with a snarled "Who the *hell* does he think he is?", stalks off to torment a waiter. His question, though, stays with me. It would be, I think, intriguing and possibly profitable to find out.

By now, Constantine is whispering into the beautifully sculpted ear of a woman, clad mainly in clammy-looking black vinyl, who I recognize as Suzuki Skreem, bassist with the CHOICEST CUT. However, before I can negotiate the throng, she delivers to Constantine's jaw a right-jab that could have put out the lights of a city block.

"Ya sick, Constantine. Ya mind's inna toilet!"

She is gone in a creaking flurry of plastic and red hair.

"Ha! You weren't so choosy when y'thought you were pregnant by that demon stud in Berlin, darlin'."

The mind boggles.

I step forward to present my credentials but he walks 'round me as if I am a piece of furniture and ducks between the giant minders who guard the door, behind which the illuminati of the BETHLEHEM SLOUCH entourage party are in seclusion from the hoi polloi. I see the crowd nod and greet him by name . . . and he is inside. My opportunity is slipping away; recklessly I try to follow. Two fingers jab me in the chest, like the prongs of a forklift truck and I fall back in disarray. From behind the closed door, I hear the unmistakably raucous greeting of The Great Beast, self-styled Svengali and lead singer of the group.

"John, you old bastard. Drag up a bottle and tell us how goes the war with Hell. You've been a stranger. Ever see any of the old crowd, like that nutcase—what's his name, Gary Lester?"

"Nah, not for years. I reckon he's history. He was about three steps from the boneyard then. Let's talk about something else, eh, mate?"

My finely tuned journalistic instincts raised to full alert, I deter-mine there and then not to rest [until] I can bring you the "big picture" [of] this "hero of the countercultu[re,]" the mysterious "Man For All [Sea]sons," John Constantine.

Full interview and in-dep[th analy]sis in next month's XS.

MAGAZINE
MAGAZINE
John
Your copies
as promised –
Satch

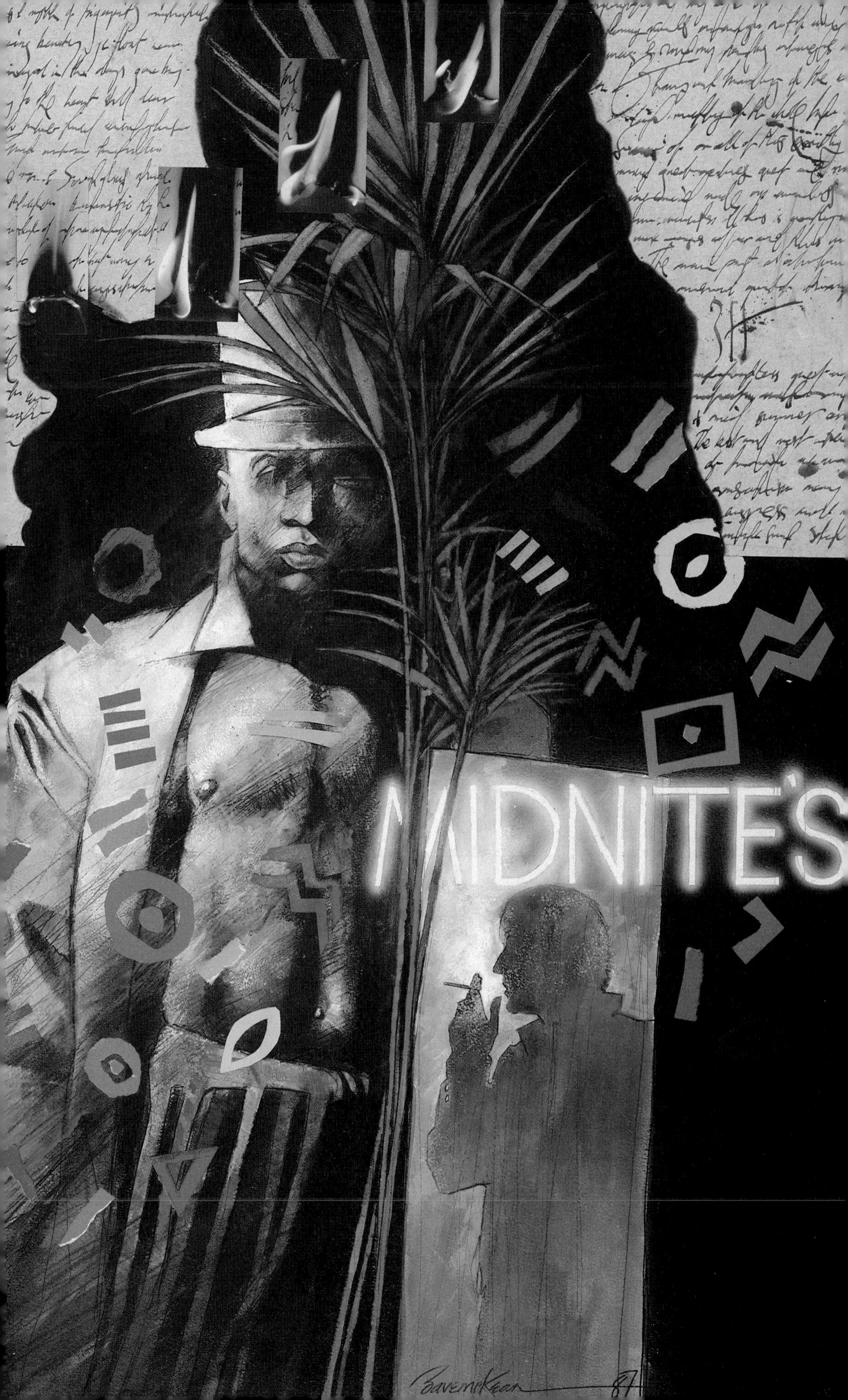
MIDNITE'S
DaveMcKean
87

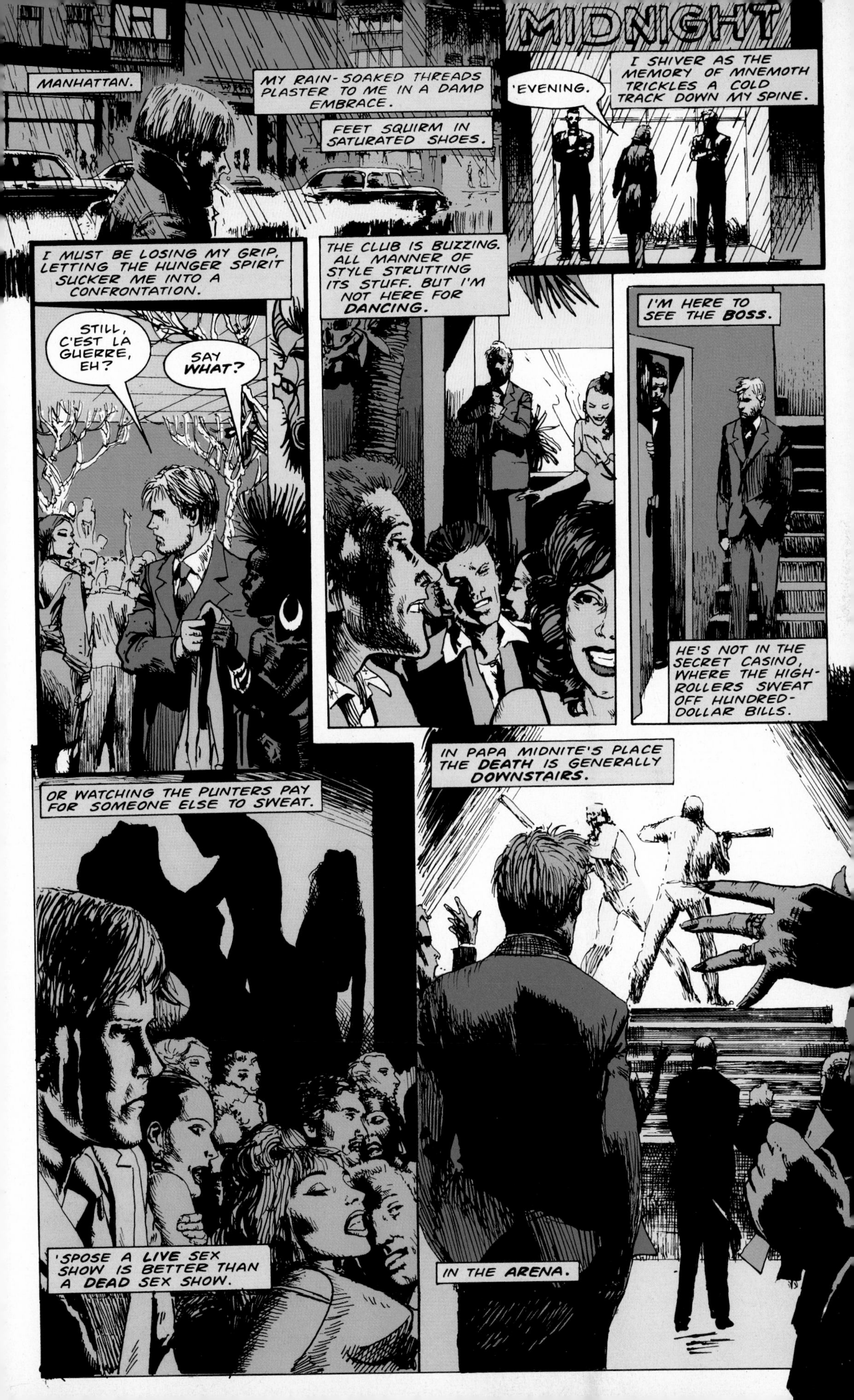
MIDNIGHT
MANHATTAN.
MY RAIN-SOAKED THREADS PLASTER TO ME IN A DAMP EMBRACE.
FEET SQUIRM IN SATURATED SHOES.
'EVENING.
I SHIVER AS THE MEMORY OF MNEMOTH TRICKLES A COLD TRACK DOWN MY SPINE.
I MUST BE LOSING MY GRIP, LETTING THE HUNGER SPIRIT SUCKER ME INTO A CONFRONTATION.
STILL, C'EST LA GUERRE, EH?
SAY WHAT?
THE CLUB IS BUZZING. ALL MANNER OF STYLE STRUTTING ITS STUFF. BUT I'M NOT HERE FOR DANCING.
I'M HERE TO SEE THE BOSS.
HE'S NOT IN THE SECRET CASINO, WHERE THE HIGH-ROLLERS SWEAT OFF HUNDRED-DOLLAR BILLS.
OR WATCHING THE PUNTERS PAY FOR SOMEONE ELSE TO SWEAT.
'SPOSE A LIVE SEX SHOW IS BETTER THAN A DEAD SEX SHOW.
IN PAPA MIDNITE'S PLACE THE DEATH IS GENERALLY DOWNSTAIRS.
IN THE ARENA.

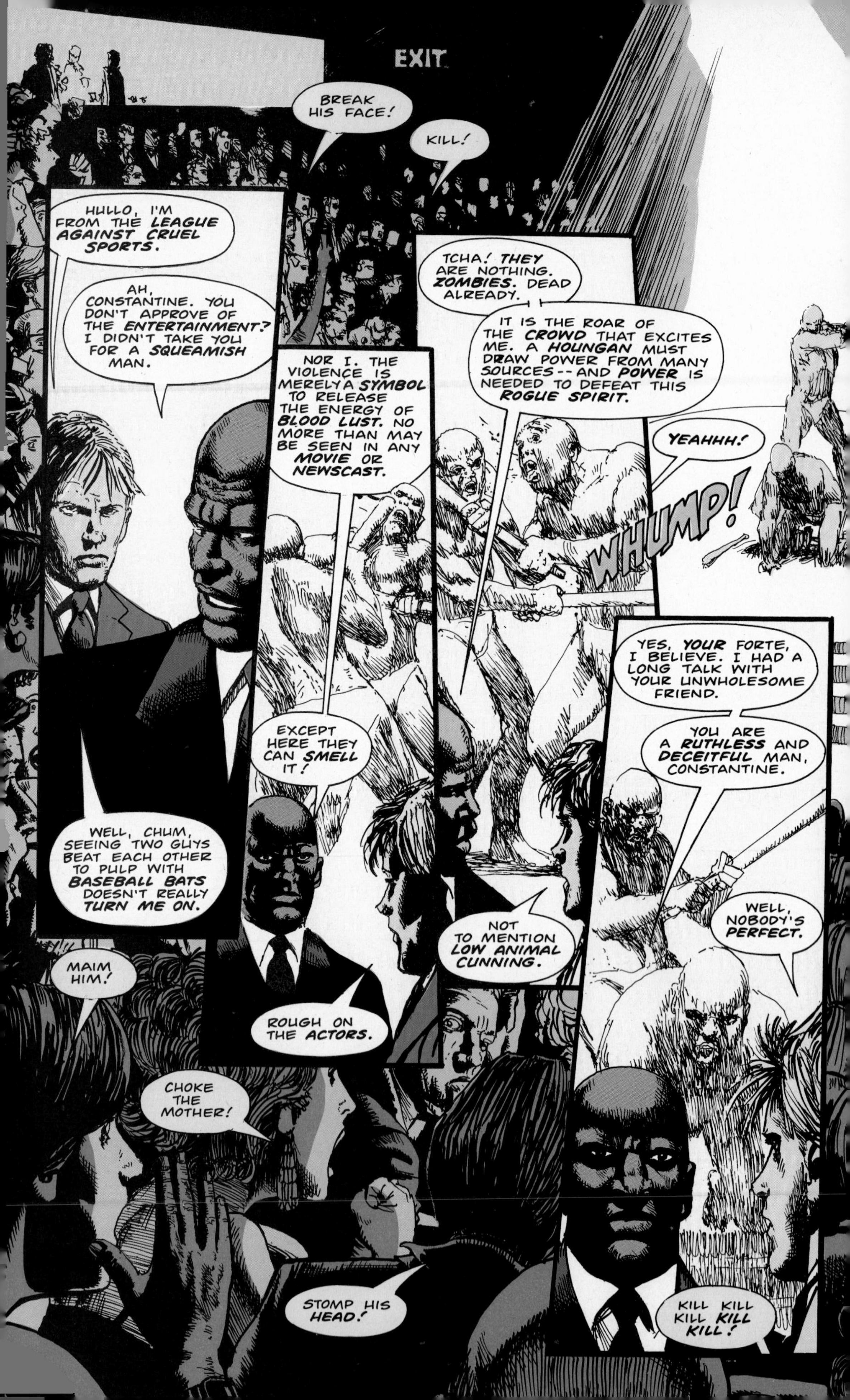
EXIT
BREAK HIS FACE!
KILL!
HULLO, I'M FROM THE LEAGUE AGAINST CRUEL SPORTS.
AH, CONSTANTINE. YOU DON'T APPROVE OF THE ENTERTAINMENT? I DIDN'T TAKE YOU FOR A SQUEAMISH MAN.
WELL, CHUM, SEEING TWO GUYS BEAT EACH OTHER TO PULP WITH BASEBALL BATS DOESN'T REALLY TURN ME ON.
NOR I. THE VIOLENCE IS MERELY A SYMBOL TO RELEASE THE ENERGY OF BLOOD LUST. NO MORE THAN MAY BE SEEN IN ANY MOVIE OR NEWSCAST.
EXCEPT HERE THEY CAN SMELL IT!
ROUGH ON THE ACTORS.
TCHA! THEY ARE NOTHING. ZOMBIES. DEAD ALREADY.
IT IS THE ROAR OF THE CROWD THAT EXCITES ME. A HOUNGAN MUST DRAW POWER FROM MANY SOURCES--AND POWER IS NEEDED TO DEFEAT THIS ROGUE SPIRIT.
NOT TO MENTION LOW ANIMAL CUNNING.
YEAHHH!
WHUMP!
YES, YOUR FORTE, I BELIEVE. I HAD A LONG TALK WITH YOUR UNWHOLESOME FRIEND.
YOU ARE A RUTHLESS AND DECEITFUL MAN, CONSTANTINE.
WELL, NOBODY'S PERFECT.
MAIM HIM!
CHOKE THE MOTHER!
STOMP HIS HEAD!
KILL KILL KILL KILL KILL!

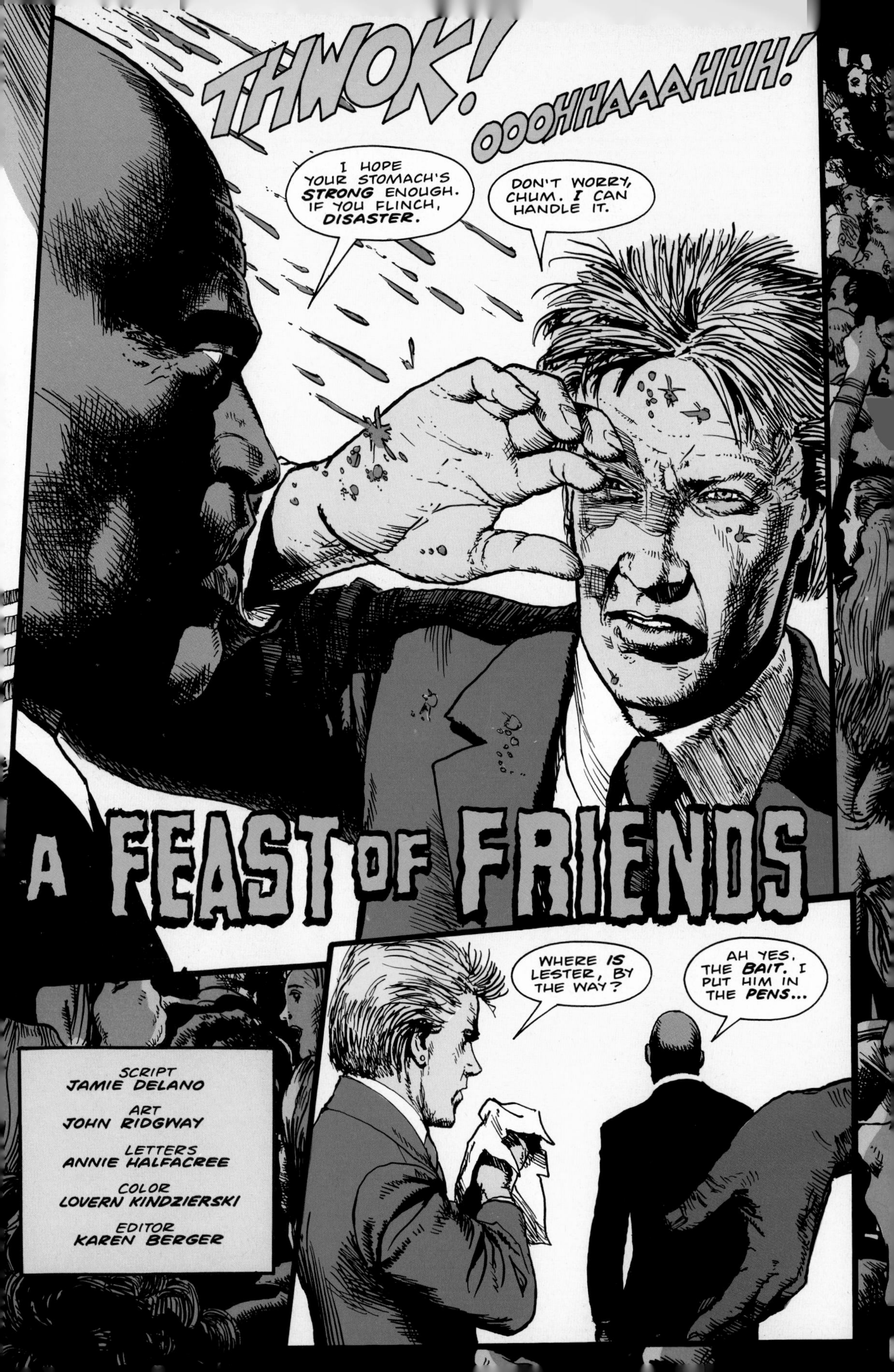
THWOK!
OOOHHAAAHHH!
I HOPE YOUR STOMACH'S STRONG ENOUGH. IF YOU FLINCH, DISASTER.
DON'T WORRY, CHUM. I CAN HANDLE IT.
A FEAST OF FRIENDS
SCRIPT JAMIE DELANO
ART JOHN RIDGWAY
LETTERS ANNIE HALFACREE
COLOR LOVERN KINDZIERSKI
EDITOR KAREN BERGER
WHERE IS LESTER, BY THE WAY?
AH YES. THE BAIT. I PUT HIM IN THE PENS...

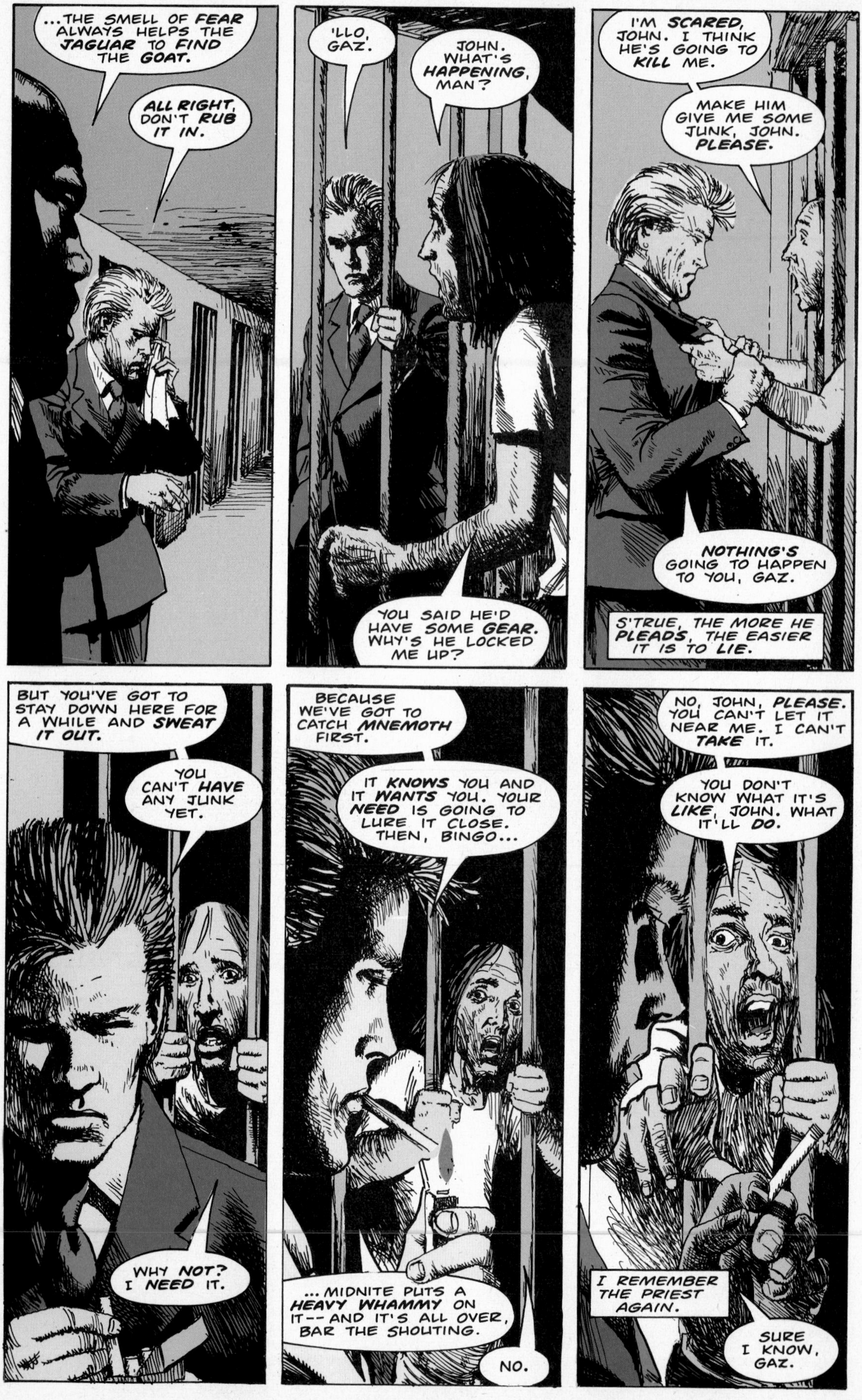
...THE SMELL OF FEAR ALWAYS HELPS THE JAGUAR TO FIND THE GOAT.
ALL RIGHT, DON'T RUB IT IN.
'LLO, GAZ.
JOHN. WHAT'S HAPPENING, MAN?
YOU SAID HE'D HAVE SOME GEAR. WHY'S HE LOCKED ME UP?
I'M SCARED, JOHN. I THINK HE'S GOING TO KILL ME.
MAKE HIM GIVE ME SOME JUNK, JOHN. PLEASE.
NOTHING'S GOING TO HAPPEN TO YOU, GAZ.
S'TRUE, THE MORE HE PLEADS, THE EASIER IT IS TO LIE.
BUT YOU'VE GOT TO STAY DOWN HERE FOR A WHILE AND SWEAT IT OUT.
YOU CAN'T HAVE ANY JUNK YET.
WHY NOT? I NEED IT.
BECAUSE WE'VE GOT TO CATCH MNEMOTH FIRST.
IT KNOWS YOU AND IT WANTS YOU. YOUR NEED IS GOING TO LURE IT CLOSE. THEN, BINGO...
...MIDNITE PUTS A HEAVY WHAMMY ON IT-- AND IT'S ALL OVER, BAR THE SHOUTING.
NO.
NO, JOHN, PLEASE. YOU CAN'T LET IT NEAR ME. I CAN'T TAKE IT.
YOU DON'T KNOW WHAT IT'S LIKE, JOHN. WHAT IT'LL DO.
I REMEMBER THE PRIEST AGAIN.
SURE I KNOW, GAZ.

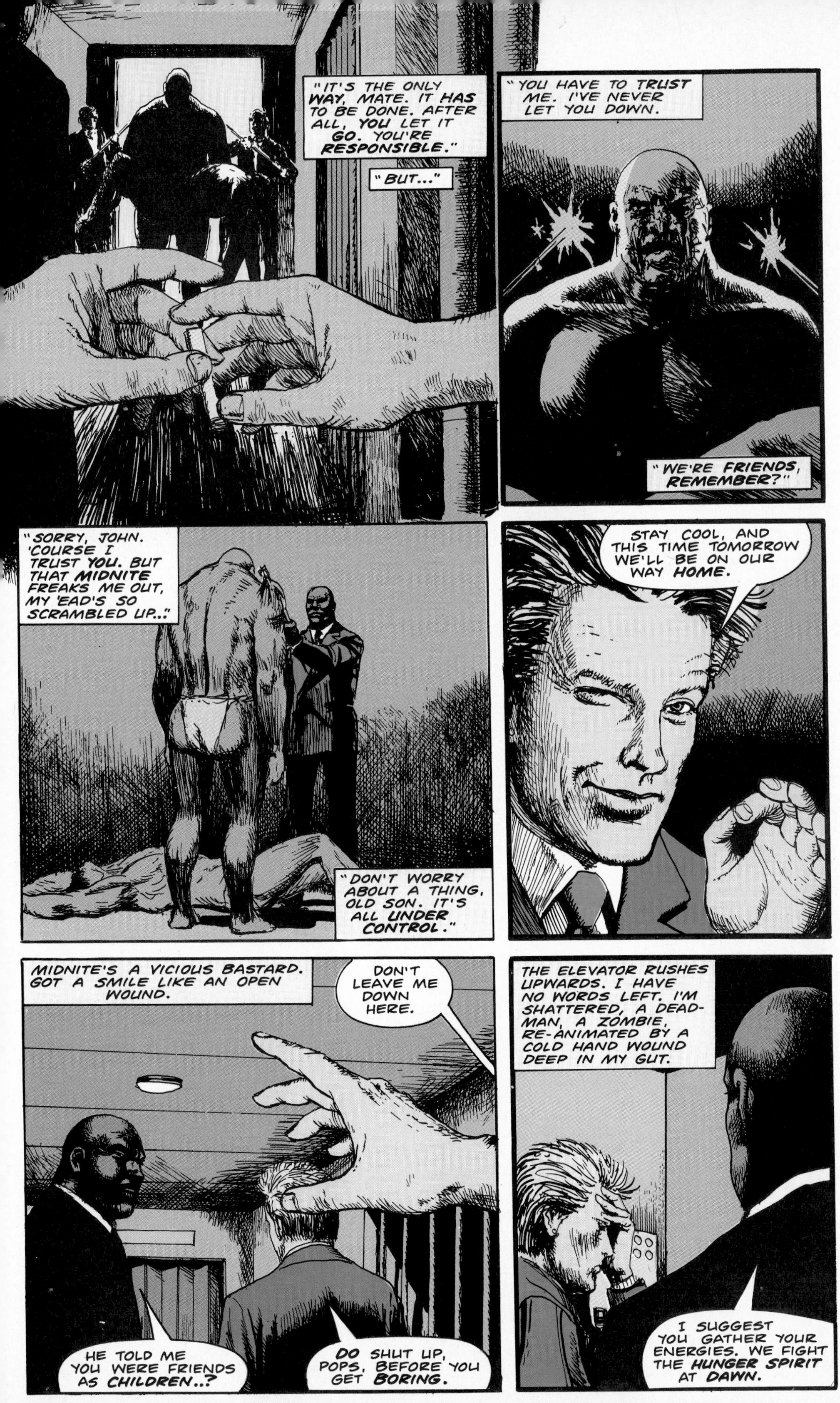
"IT'S THE ONLY WAY, MATE. IT HAS TO BE DONE. AFTER ALL, YOU LET IT GO. YOU'RE RESPONSIBLE."
"BUT..."
"YOU HAVE TO TRUST ME. I'VE NEVER LET YOU DOWN.
"WE'RE FRIENDS, REMEMBER?"
"SORRY, JOHN. 'COURSE I TRUST YOU. BUT THAT MIDNITE FREAKS ME OUT, MY 'EAD'S SO SCRAMBLED UP..."
"DON'T WORRY ABOUT A THING, OLD SON. IT'S ALL UNDER CONTROL."
STAY COOL, AND THIS TIME TOMORROW WE'LL BE ON OUR WAY HOME.
MIDNITE'S A VICIOUS BASTARD. GOT A SMILE LIKE AN OPEN WOUND.
DON'T LEAVE ME DOWN HERE.
HE TOLD ME YOU WERE FRIENDS AS CHILDREN..?
DO SHUT UP, POPS, BEFORE YOU GET BORING.
THE ELEVATOR RUSHES UPWARDS. I HAVE NO WORDS LEFT. I'M SHATTERED, A DEAD-MAN, A ZOMBIE, RE-ANIMATED BY A COLD HAND WOUND DEEP IN MY GUT.
I SUGGEST YOU GATHER YOUR ENERGIES. WE FIGHT THE HUNGER SPIRIT AT DAWN.

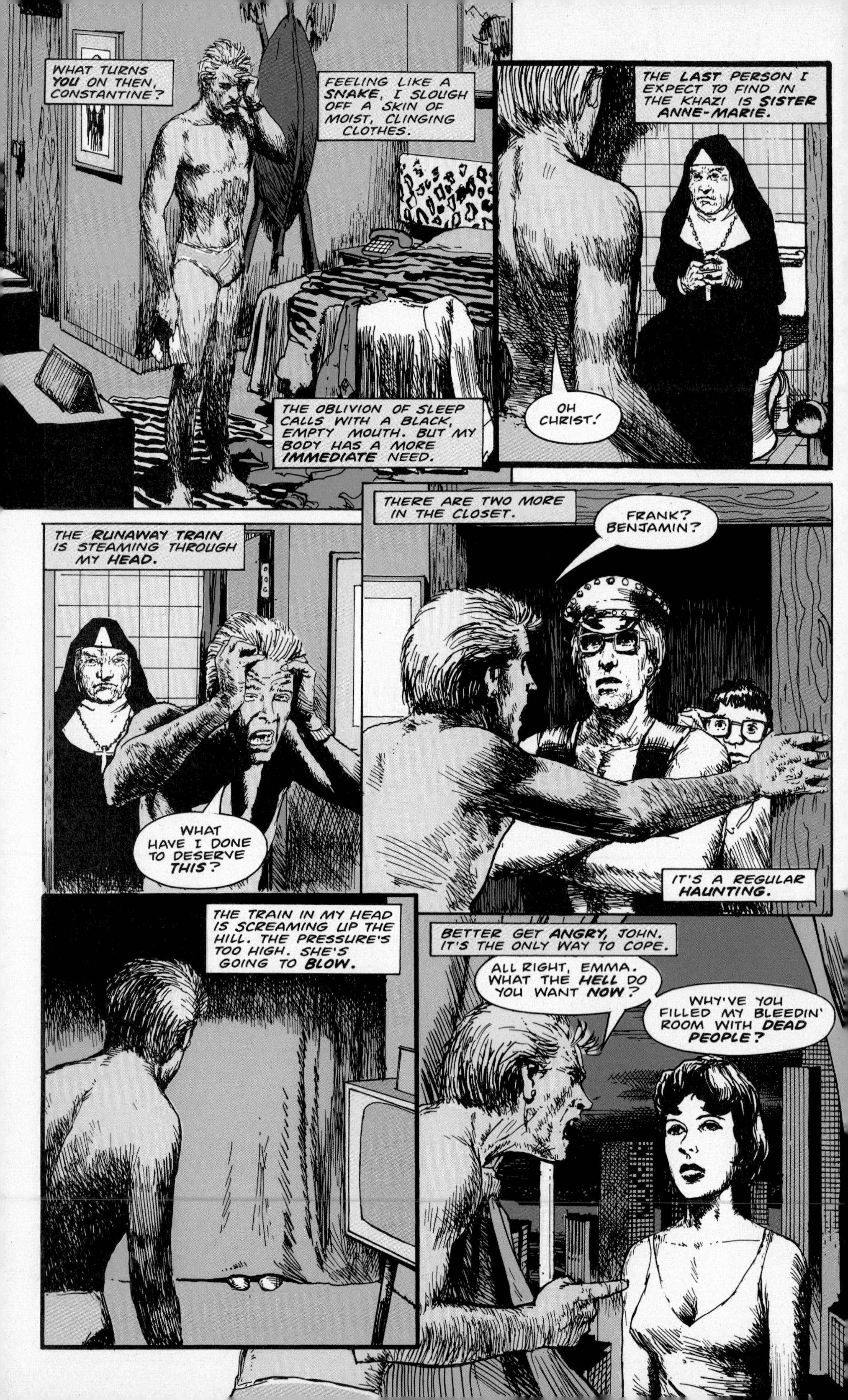
WHAT TURNS YOU ON THEN, CONSTANTINE?
FEELING LIKE A SNAKE, I SLOUGH OFF A SKIN OF MOIST, CLINGING CLOTHES.
THE OBLIVION OF SLEEP CALLS WITH A BLACK, EMPTY MOUTH. BUT MY BODY HAS A MORE IMMEDIATE NEED.
THE LAST PERSON I EXPECT TO FIND IN THE KHAZI IS SISTER ANNE-MARIE.
OH CHRIST!
THE RUNAWAY TRAIN IS STEAMING THROUGH MY HEAD.
WHAT HAVE I DONE TO DESERVE THIS?
THERE ARE TWO MORE IN THE CLOSET.
FRANK? BENJAMIN?
IT'S A REGULAR HAUNTING.
THE TRAIN IN MY HEAD IS SCREAMING UP THE HILL. THE PRESSURE'S TOO HIGH. SHE'S GOING TO BLOW.
BETTER GET ANGRY, JOHN. IT'S THE ONLY WAY TO COPE.
ALL RIGHT, EMMA. WHAT THE HELL DO YOU WANT NOW?
WHY'VE YOU FILLED MY BLEEDIN' ROOM WITH DEAD PEOPLE?

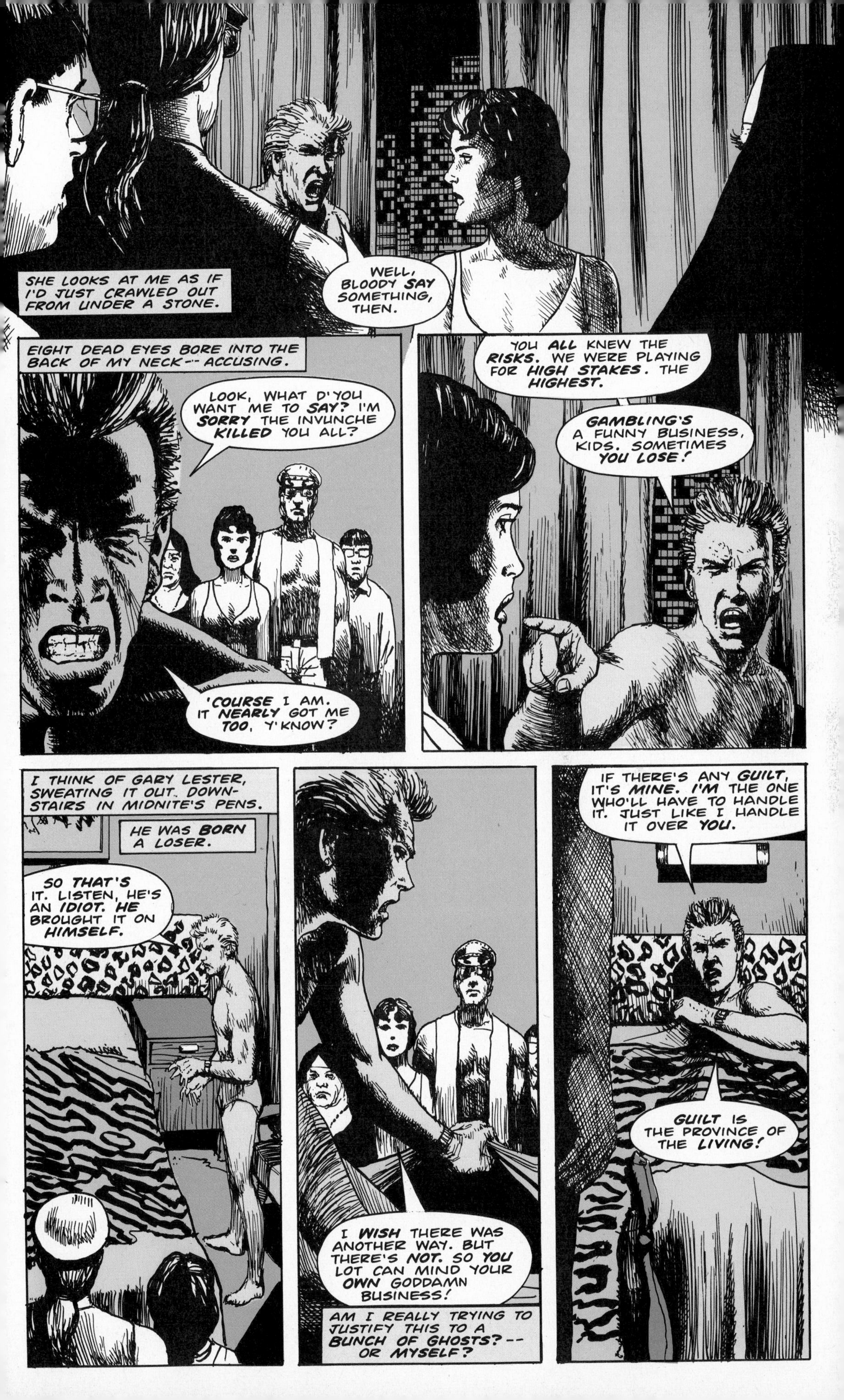
SHE LOOKS AT ME AS IF I'D JUST CRAWLED OUT FROM UNDER A STONE.
WELL, BLOODY SAY SOMETHING, THEN.
EIGHT DEAD EYES BORE INTO THE BACK OF MY NECK--- ACCUSING.
LOOK, WHAT D'YOU WANT ME TO SAY? I'M SORRY THE INVUNCHE KILLED YOU ALL?
'COURSE I AM. IT NEARLY GOT ME TOO, Y'KNOW?
YOU ALL KNEW THE RISKS. WE WERE PLAYING FOR HIGH STAKES. THE HIGHEST.
GAMBLING'S A FUNNY BUSINESS, KIDS. SOMETIMES YOU LOSE!
I THINK OF GARY LESTER, SWEATING IT OUT. DOWN-STAIRS IN MIDNITE'S PENS.
HE WAS BORN A LOSER.
SO THAT'S IT. LISTEN, HE'S AN IDIOT. HE BROUGHT IT ON HIMSELF.
I WISH THERE WAS ANOTHER WAY. BUT THERE'S NOT. SO YOU LOT CAN MIND YOUR OWN GODDAMN BUSINESS!
AM I REALLY TRYING TO JUSTIFY THIS TO A BUNCH OF GHOSTS?-- OR MYSELF?
IF THERE'S ANY GUILT, IT'S MINE. I'M THE ONE WHO'LL HAVE TO HANDLE IT. JUST LIKE I HANDLE IT OVER YOU.
GUILT IS THE PROVINCE OF THE LIVING!

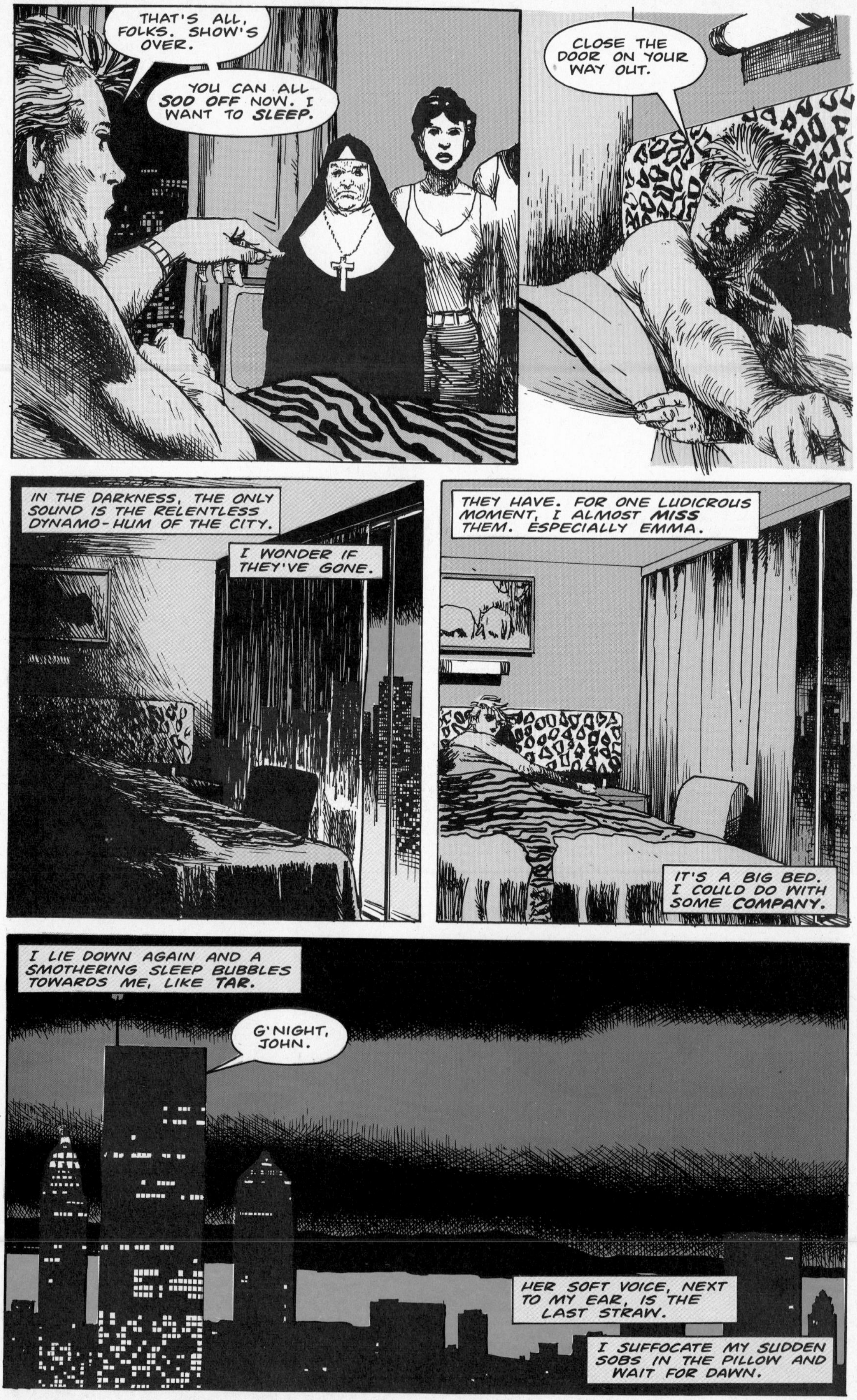
THAT'S ALL, FOLKS. SHOW'S OVER.
YOU CAN ALL SOD OFF NOW. I WANT TO SLEEP.
CLOSE THE DOOR ON YOUR WAY OUT.
IN THE DARKNESS, THE ONLY SOUND IS THE RELENTLESS DYNAMO-HUM OF THE CITY.
I WONDER IF THEY'VE GONE.
THEY HAVE. FOR ONE LUDICROUS MOMENT, I ALMOST MISS THEM. ESPECIALLY EMMA.
IT'S A BIG BED. I COULD DO WITH SOME COMPANY.
I LIE DOWN AGAIN AND A SMOTHERING SLEEP BUBBLES TOWARDS ME, LIKE TAR.
G'NIGHT, JOHN.
HER SOFT VOICE, NEXT TO MY EAR, IS THE LAST STRAW.
I SUFFOCATE MY SUDDEN SOBS IN THE PILLOW AND WAIT FOR DAWN.

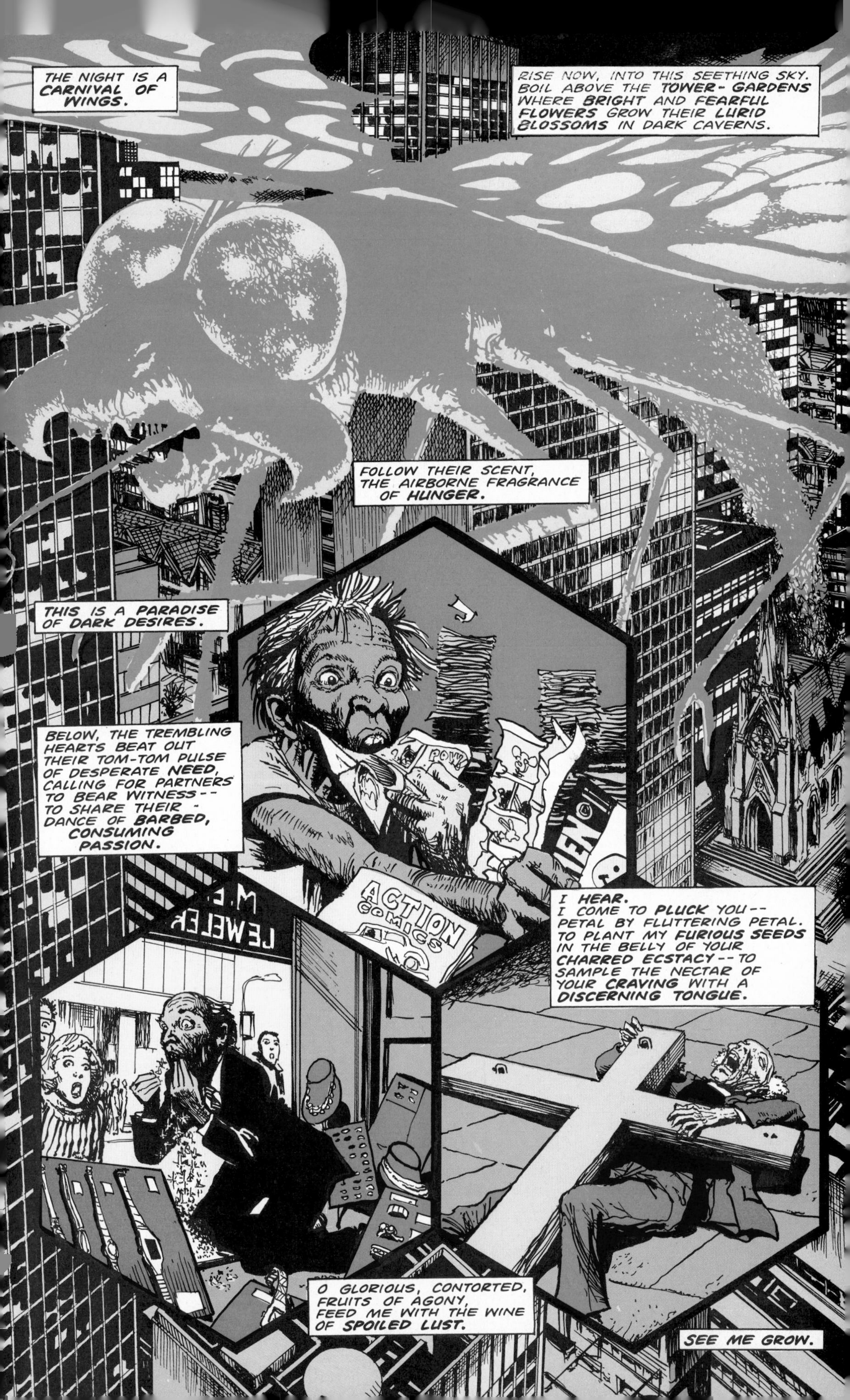
THE NIGHT IS A CARNIVAL OF WINGS.
RISE NOW, INTO THIS SEETHING SKY. BOIL ABOVE THE TOWER-GARDENS WHERE BRIGHT AND FEARFUL FLOWERS GROW THEIR LURID BLOSSOMS IN DARK CAVERNS.
FOLLOW THEIR SCENT, THE AIRBORNE FRAGRANCE OF HUNGER.
THIS IS A PARADISE OF DARK DESIRES.
BELOW, THE TREMBLING HEARTS BEAT OUT THEIR TOM-TOM PULSE OF DESPERATE NEED, CALLING FOR PARTNERS TO BEAR WITNESS-- TO SHARE THEIR DANCE OF BARBED, CONSUMING PASSION.
POW
ACTION COMICS
JEWELER
I HEAR. I COME TO PLUCK YOU-- PETAL BY FLUTTERING PETAL. TO PLANT MY FURIOUS SEEDS IN THE BELLY OF YOUR CHARRED ECSTACY--TO SAMPLE THE NECTAR OF YOUR CRAVING WITH A DISCERNING TONGUE.
O GLORIOUS, CONTORTED, FRUITS OF AGONY, FEED ME WITH THE WINE OF SPOILED LUST.
SEE ME GROW.

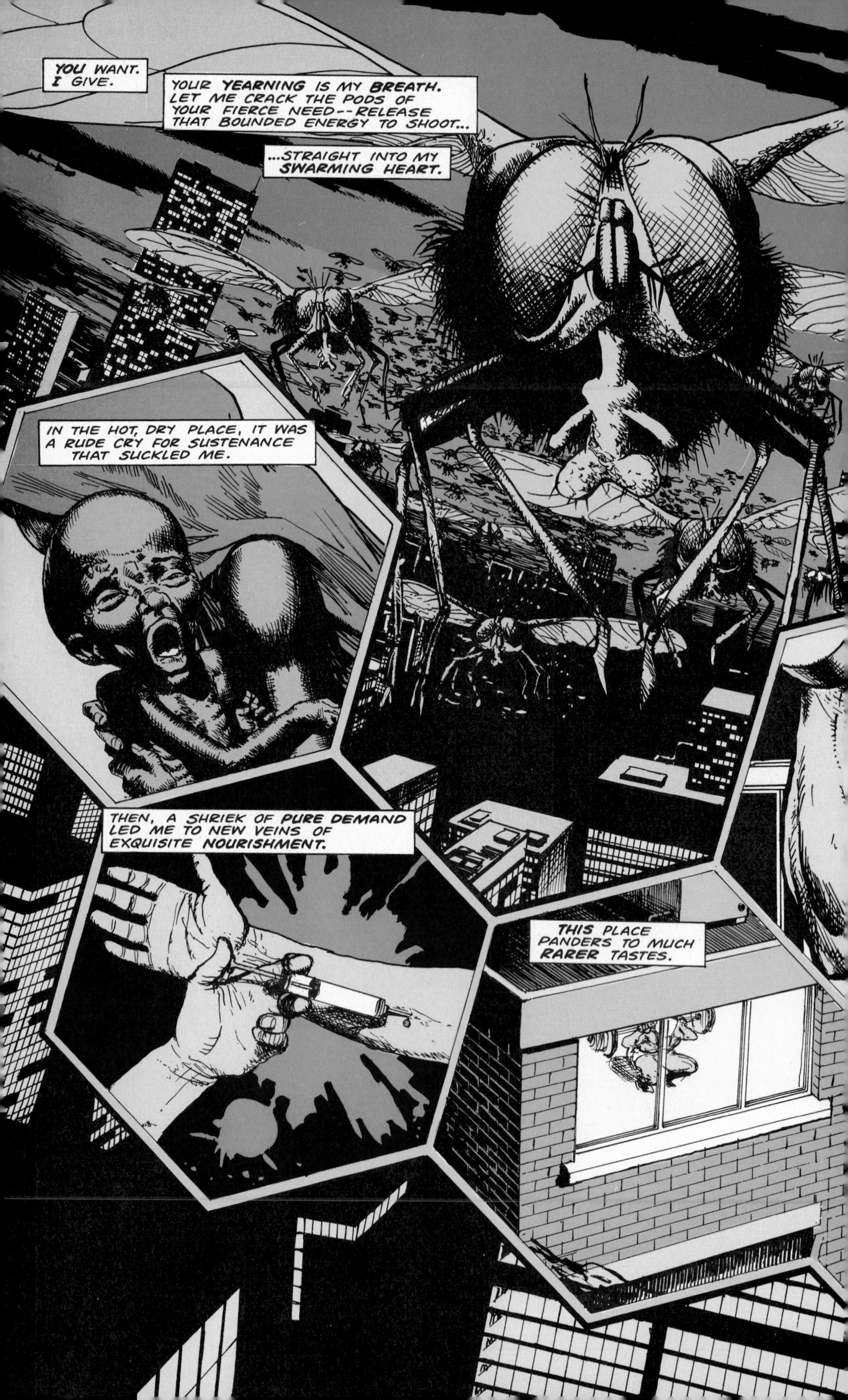
YOU WANT. I GIVE.
YOUR YEARNING IS MY BREATH. LET ME CRACK THE PODS OF YOUR FIERCE NEED--RELEASE THAT BOUNDED ENERGY TO SHOOT...
...STRAIGHT INTO MY SWARMING HEART.
IN THE HOT, DRY PLACE, IT WAS A RUDE CRY FOR SUSTENANCE THAT SUCKLED ME.
THEN, A SHRIEK OF PURE DEMAND LED ME TO NEW VEINS OF EXQUISITE NOURISHMENT.
THIS PLACE PANDERS TO MUCH RARER TASTES.

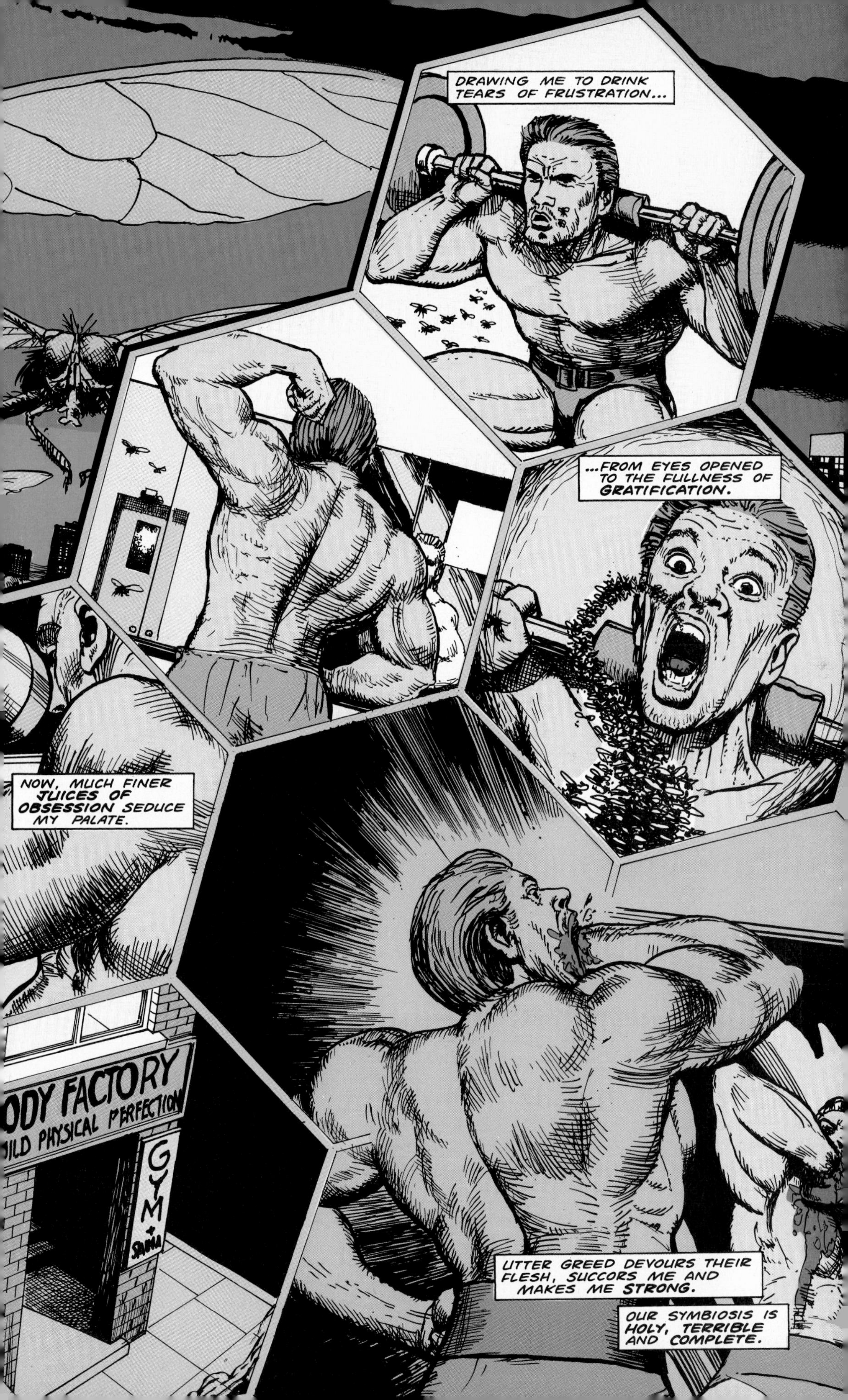
DRAWING ME TO DRINK TEARS OF FRUSTRATION...
...FROM EYES OPENED TO THE FULLNESS OF GRATIFICATION.
NOW, MUCH FINER JUICES OF OBSESSION SEDUCE MY PALATE.
ODY FACTORY
UILD PHYSICAL PERFECTION
GYM + SAUNA
UTTER GREED DEVOURS THEIR FLESH, SUCCORS ME AND MAKES ME STRONG.
OUR SYMBIOSIS IS HOLY, TERRIBLE AND COMPLETE.

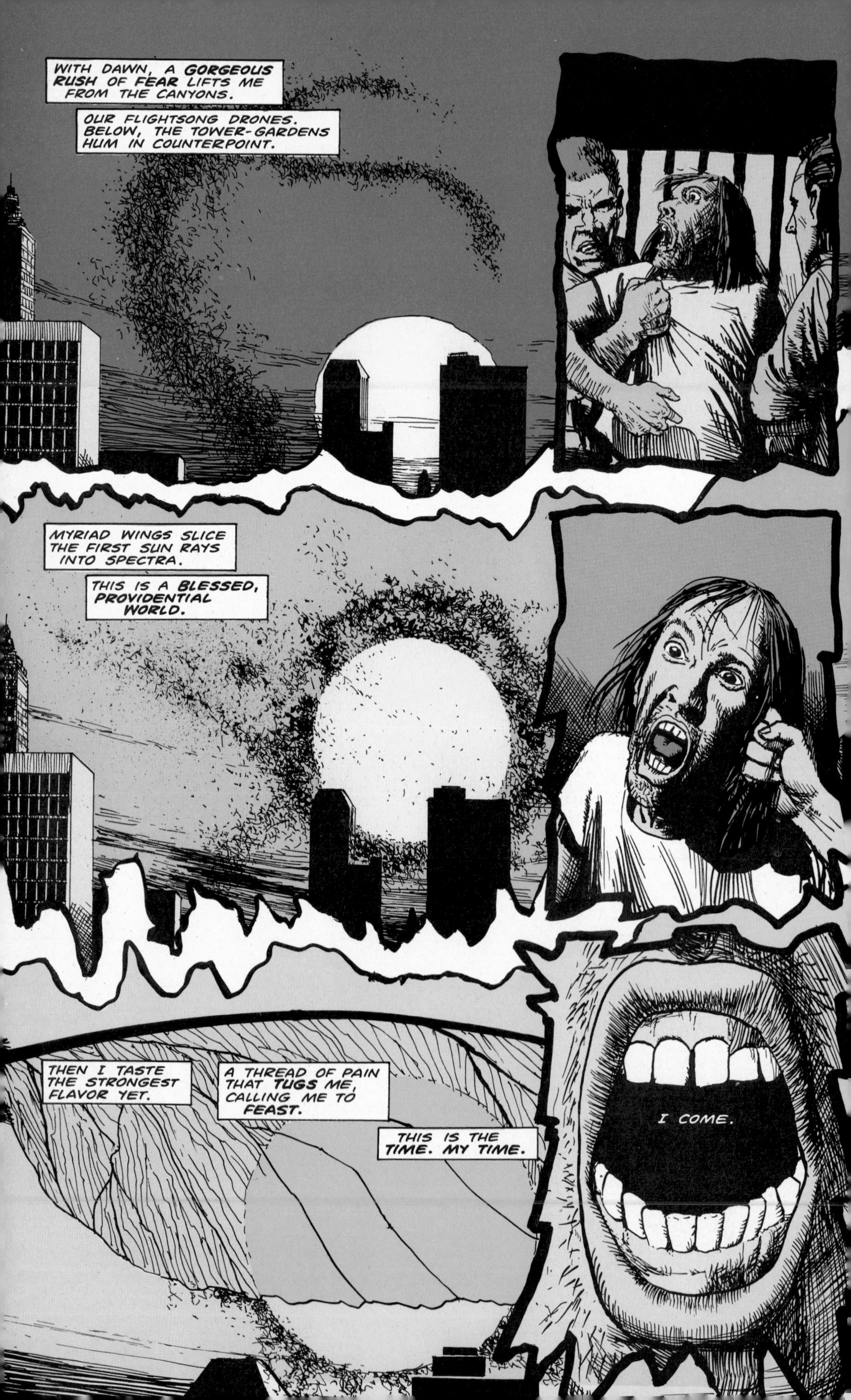
WITH DAWN, A GORGEOUS RUSH OF FEAR LIFTS ME FROM THE CANYONS.
OUR FLIGHTSONG DRONES. BELOW, THE TOWER-GARDENS HUM IN COUNTERPOINT.
MYRIAD WINGS SLICE THE FIRST SUN RAYS INTO SPECTRA.
THIS IS A BLESSED, PROVIDENTIAL WORLD.
THEN I TASTE THE STRONGEST FLAVOR YET.
A THREAD OF PAIN THAT TUGS ME, CALLING ME TO FEAST.
THIS IS THE TIME. MY TIME.
I COME.

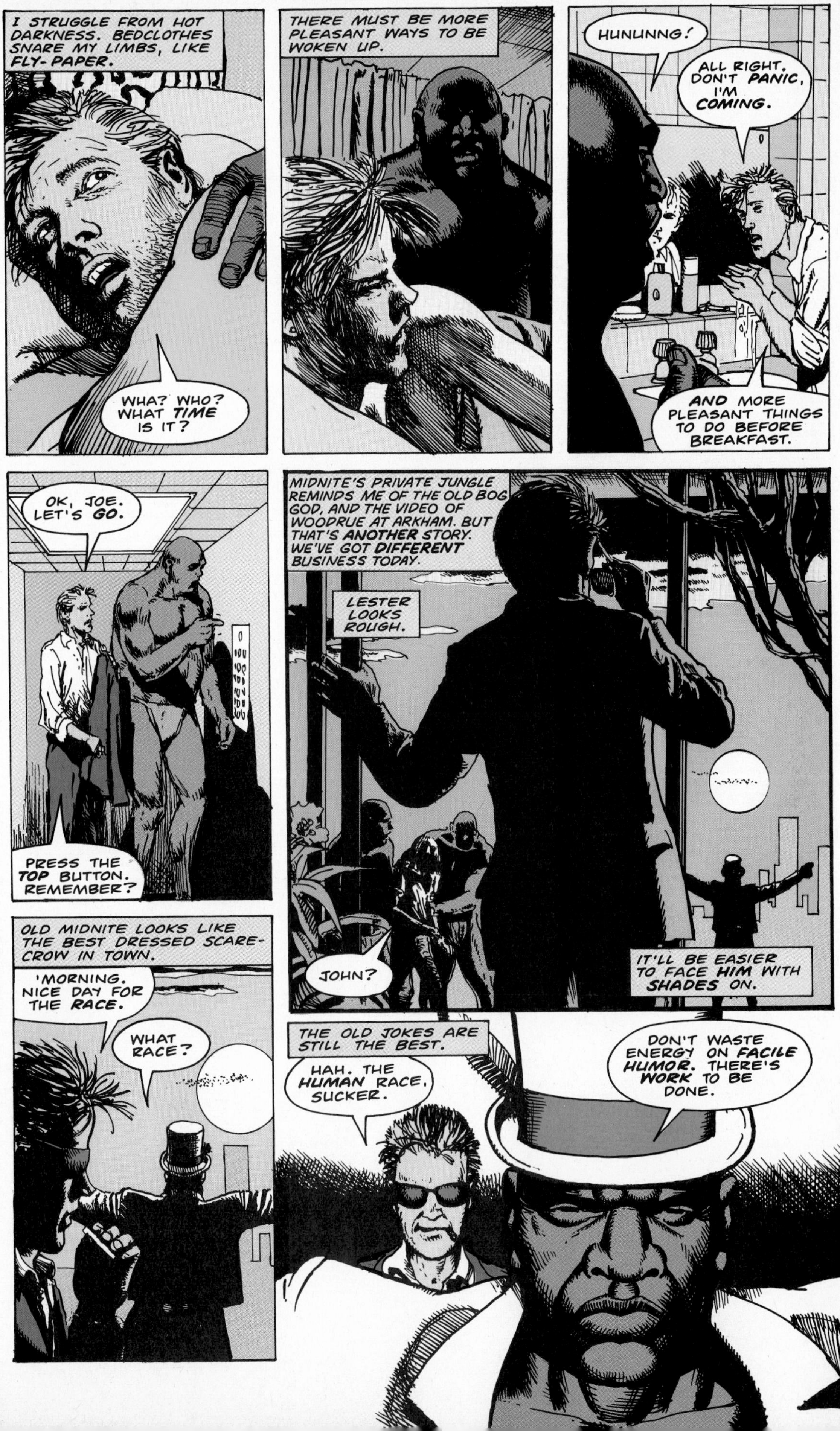

I STRUGGLE FROM HOT DARKNESS. BEDCLOTHES SNARE MY LIMBS, LIKE FLY-PAPER.
WHAT? WHO? WHAT TIME IS IT?
THERE MUST BE MORE PLEASANT WAYS TO BE WOKEN UP.
HUNUNNG!
ALL RIGHT. DON'T PANIC, I'M COMING.
AND MORE PLEASANT THINGS TO DO BEFORE BREAKFAST.
OK, JOE. LET'S GO.
PRESS THE TOP BUTTON. REMEMBER?
MIDNITE'S PRIVATE JUNGLE REMINDS ME OF THE OLD BOG GOD, AND THE VIDEO OF WOODRUE AT ARKHAM. BUT THAT'S ANOTHER STORY. WE'VE GOT DIFFERENT BUSINESS TODAY.
LESTER LOOKS ROUGH.
JOHN?
IT'LL BE EASIER TO FACE HIM WITH SHADES ON.
OLD MIDNITE LOOKS LIKE THE BEST DRESSED SCARE-CROW IN TOWN.
'MORNING. NICE DAY FOR THE RACE.
WHAT RACE?
THE OLD JOKES ARE STILL THE BEST.
HAH. THE HUMAN RACE, SUCKER.
DON'T WASTE ENERGY ON FACILE HUMOR. THERE'S WORK TO BE DONE.

JUST TRYING TO KEEP OUR *SPIRITS* UP.

BEST CHECK THE *EQUIPMENT.* TATTOOING NEEDLES, INK, STRAIT-JACKET, HYPO AND THE CHAIR. LET'S HAVE A LOOK AT THE *CHAIR.*

BLOODY HELL! WHERE'D YOU GET *THIS?*

PRIVATE AUCTION. IT CAME FROM *SING SING.*

OVER THREE-HUNDRED LIVES HAVE SIZZLED TO EXTINCTION ON THAT SEAT.

IT'S A BIT *OVER* THE TOP.

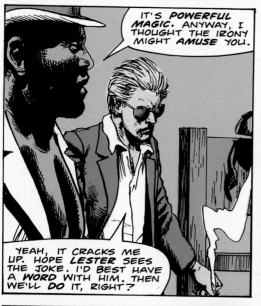

IT'S *POWERFUL MAGIC.* ANYWAY, I THOUGHT THE IRONY MIGHT *AMUSE* YOU.

YEAH, IT CRACKS ME UP. HOPE *LESTER* SEES THE JOKE. I'D BEST HAVE A *WORD* WITH HIM. THEN WE'LL *DO* IT, RIGHT?

I FEEL LIKE A *PRIEST,* BESTOWING A *NICOTINE ABSOLUTION.*

'MORNING, GAZ. HOW'RE Y'DOING?

IT'S NO GOOD, JOHN. I CAN'T GO THROUGH WITH IT. I'M OUT OF MY *DEPTH.*

OUT OF HIS DEPTH, HE SAYS-- AS HE GOES DOWN FOR THE *THIRD* TIME.

DON'T BE DAFT, PAL. IT'LL BE A *DODDLE.*

THE MAN'S AN *OPTIMIST.*

I *MEAN* IT. YOU'LL HAVE TO CALL IT OFF.

NO CAN DO, OLD SON. JUST IMAGINE YOU'RE AT THE *DENTIST*-- AND I'M YOUR *MUM.*

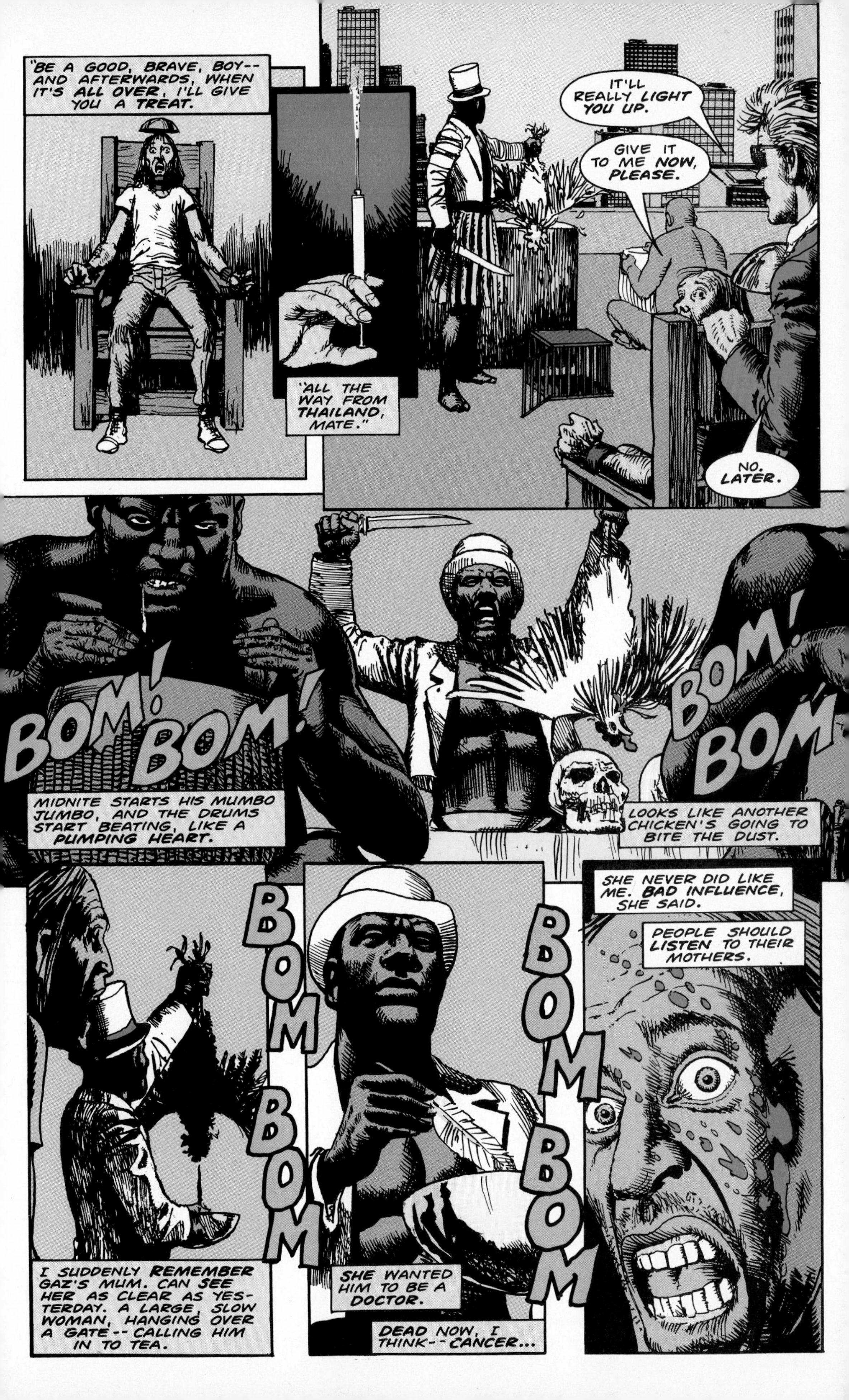
"BE A GOOD, BRAVE, BOY-- AND AFTERWARDS, WHEN IT'S ALL OVER, I'LL GIVE YOU A TREAT.
"ALL THE WAY FROM THAILAND, MATE."
IT'LL REALLY LIGHT YOU UP.
GIVE IT TO ME NOW, PLEASE.
NO. LATER.
BOM! BOM!
MIDNITE STARTS HIS MUMBO JUMBO, AND THE DRUMS START BEATING, LIKE A PUMPING HEART.
BOM! BOM!
LOOKS LIKE ANOTHER CHICKEN'S GOING TO BITE THE DUST.
I SUDDENLY REMEMBER GAZ'S MUM. CAN SEE HER AS CLEAR AS YESTERDAY. A LARGE, SLOW WOMAN, HANGING OVER A GATE-- CALLING HIM IN TO TEA.
BOM BOM BOM BOM
SHE WANTED HIM TO BE A DOCTOR.
DEAD NOW, I THINK--CANCER...
BOM BOM BOM BOM
SHE NEVER DID LIKE ME. BAD INFLUENCE, SHE SAID.
PEOPLE SHOULD LISTEN TO THEIR MOTHERS.

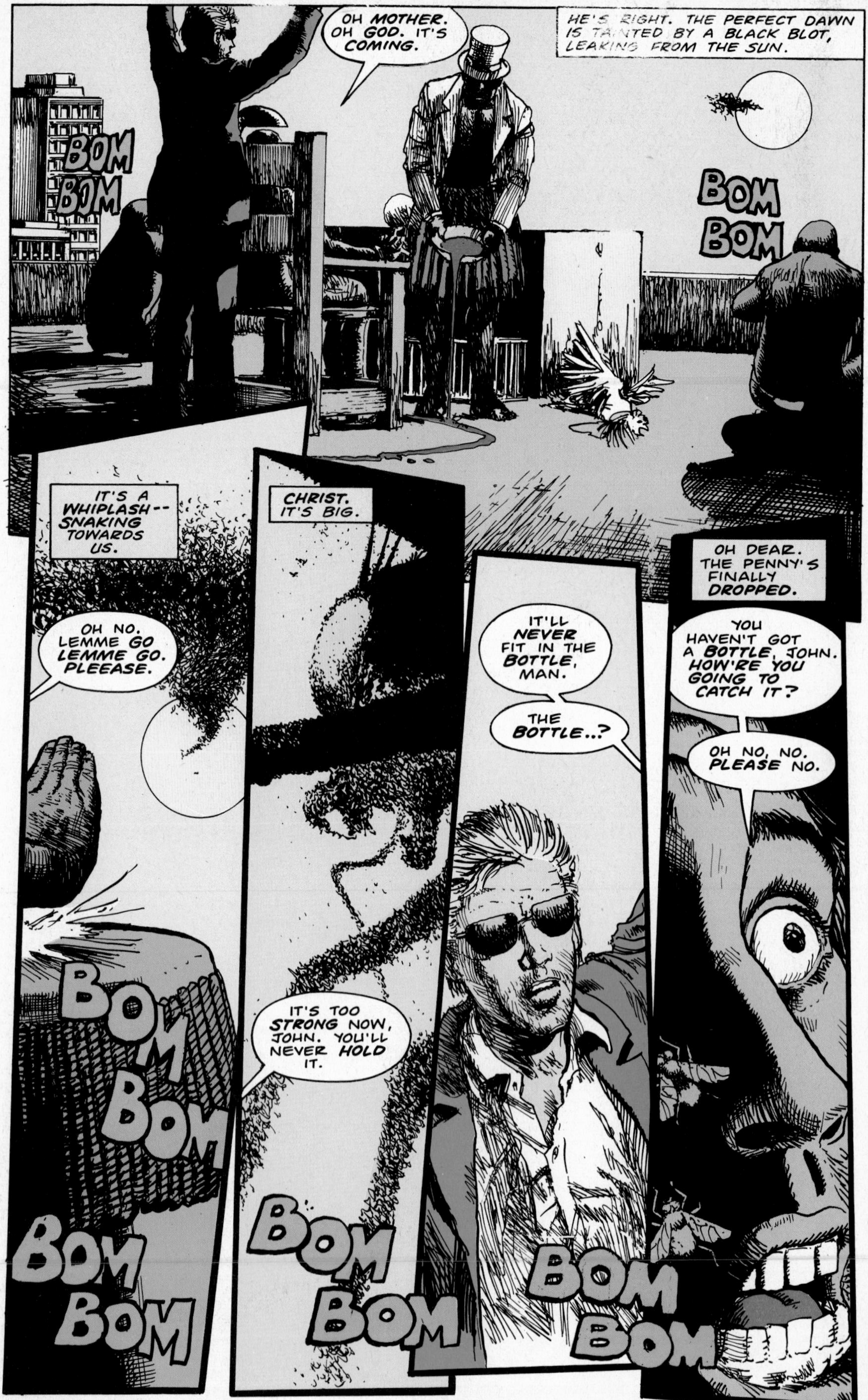
OH MOTHER. OH GOD. IT'S COMING.
HE'S RIGHT. THE PERFECT DAWN IS TAINTED BY A BLACK BLOT, LEAKING FROM THE SUN.
BOM BOM
BOM BOM
IT'S A WHIPLASH-- SNAKING TOWARDS US.
OH NO. LEMME GO LEMME GO. PLEEASE.
BOM BOM
BOM BOM
CHRIST. IT'S BIG.
IT'S TOO STRONG NOW, JOHN. YOU'LL NEVER HOLD IT.
BOM BOM
IT'LL NEVER FIT IN THE BOTTLE, MAN.
THE BOTTLE..?
BOM BOM
OH DEAR. THE PENNY'S FINALLY DROPPED.
YOU HAVEN'T GOT A BOTTLE, JOHN. HOW'RE YOU GOING TO CATCH IT?
OH NO, NO. PLEASE NO.

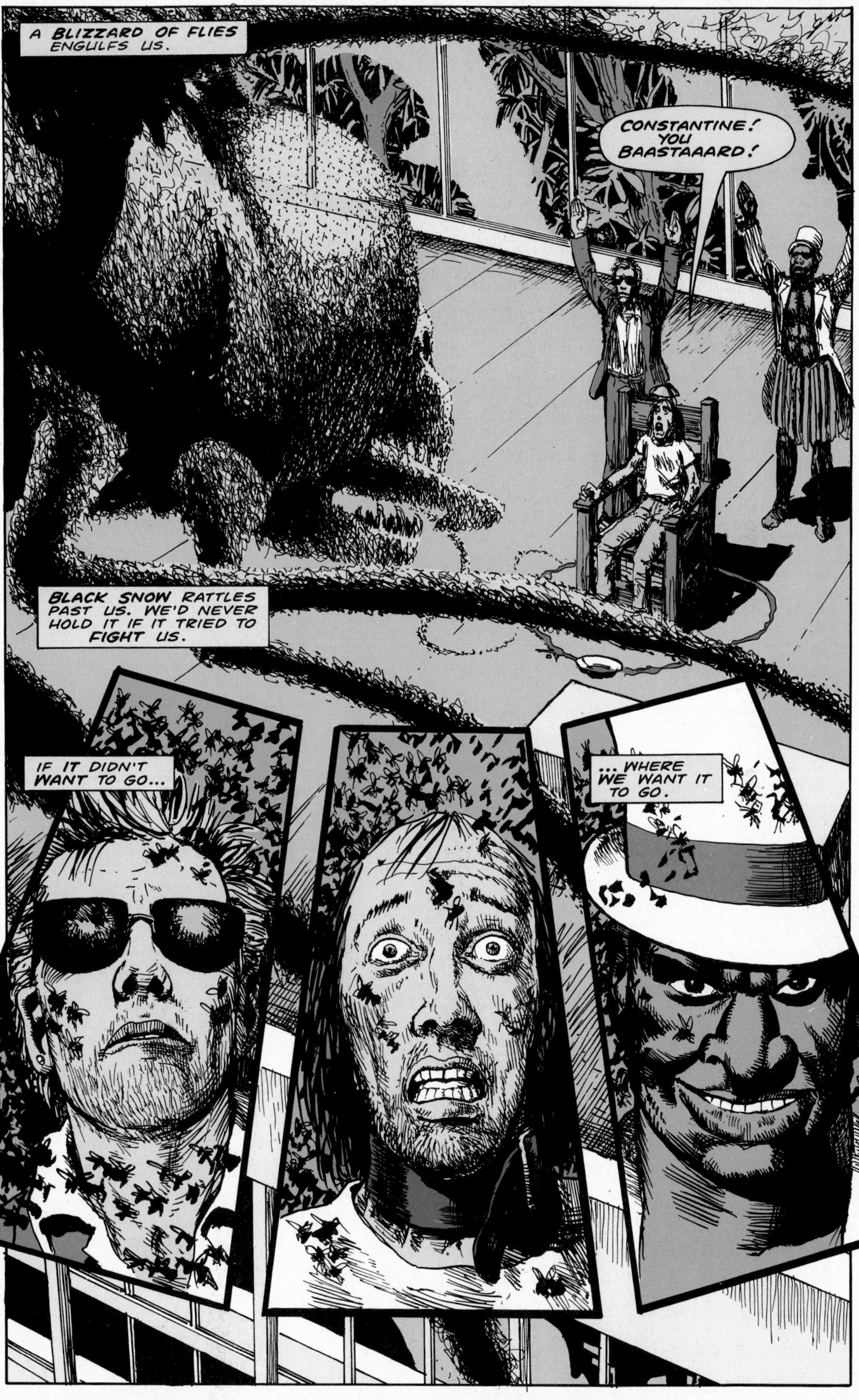
A BLIZZARD OF FLIES ENGULFS US.
CONSTANTINE! YOU BAASTAAARD!
BLACK SNOW RATTLES PAST US. WE'D NEVER HOLD IT IF IT TRIED TO FIGHT US.
IF IT DIDN'T WANT TO GO...
...WHERE WE WANT IT TO GO.

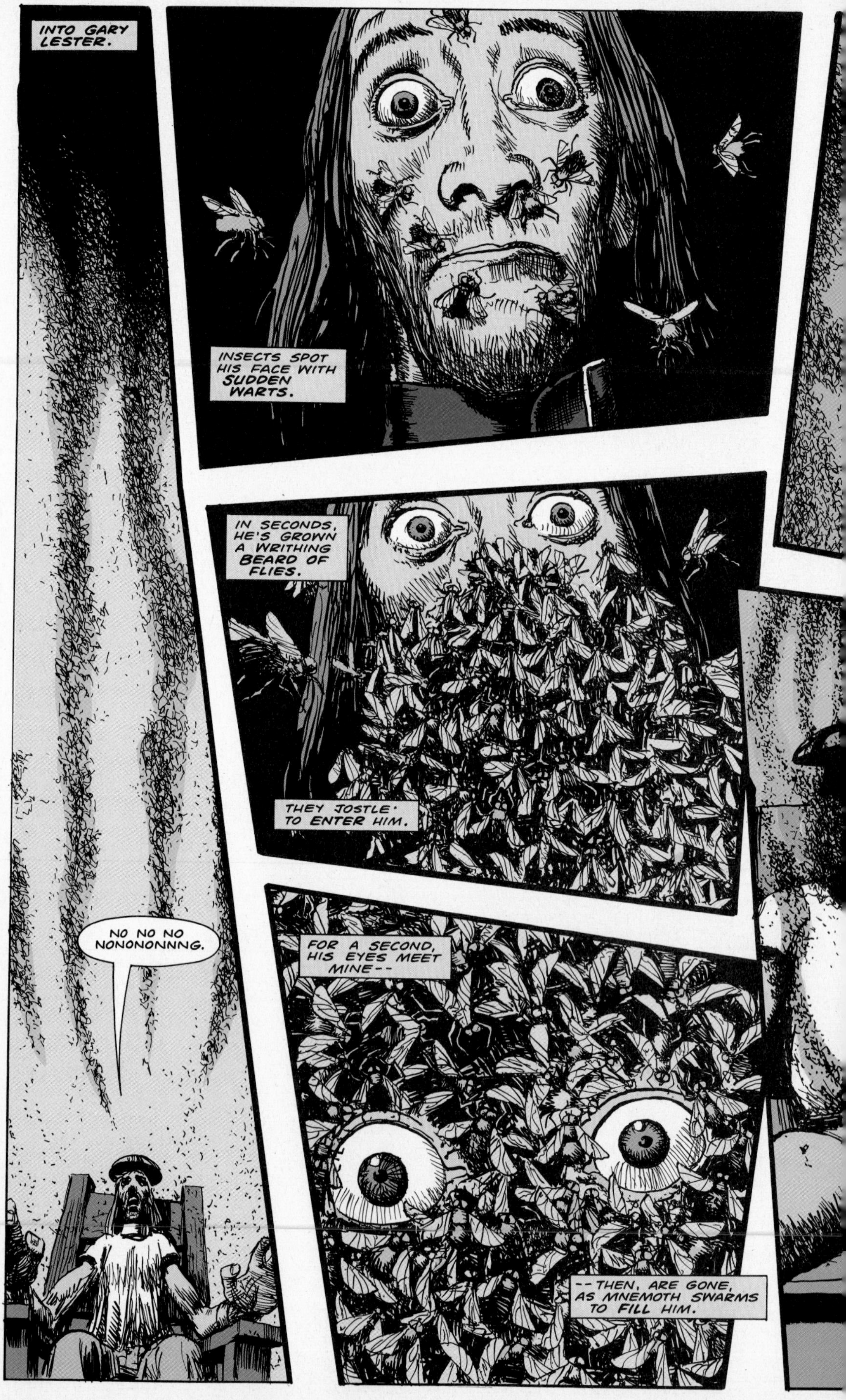
INTO GARY LESTER.
INSECTS SPOT HIS FACE WITH SUDDEN WARTS.
IN SECONDS, HE'S GROWN A WRITHING BEARD OF FLIES.
THEY JOSTLE TO ENTER HIM.
NO NO NO NONONONNNG.
FOR A SECOND, HIS EYES MEET MINE--
--THEN, ARE GONE, AS MNEMOTH SWARMS TO FILL HIM.

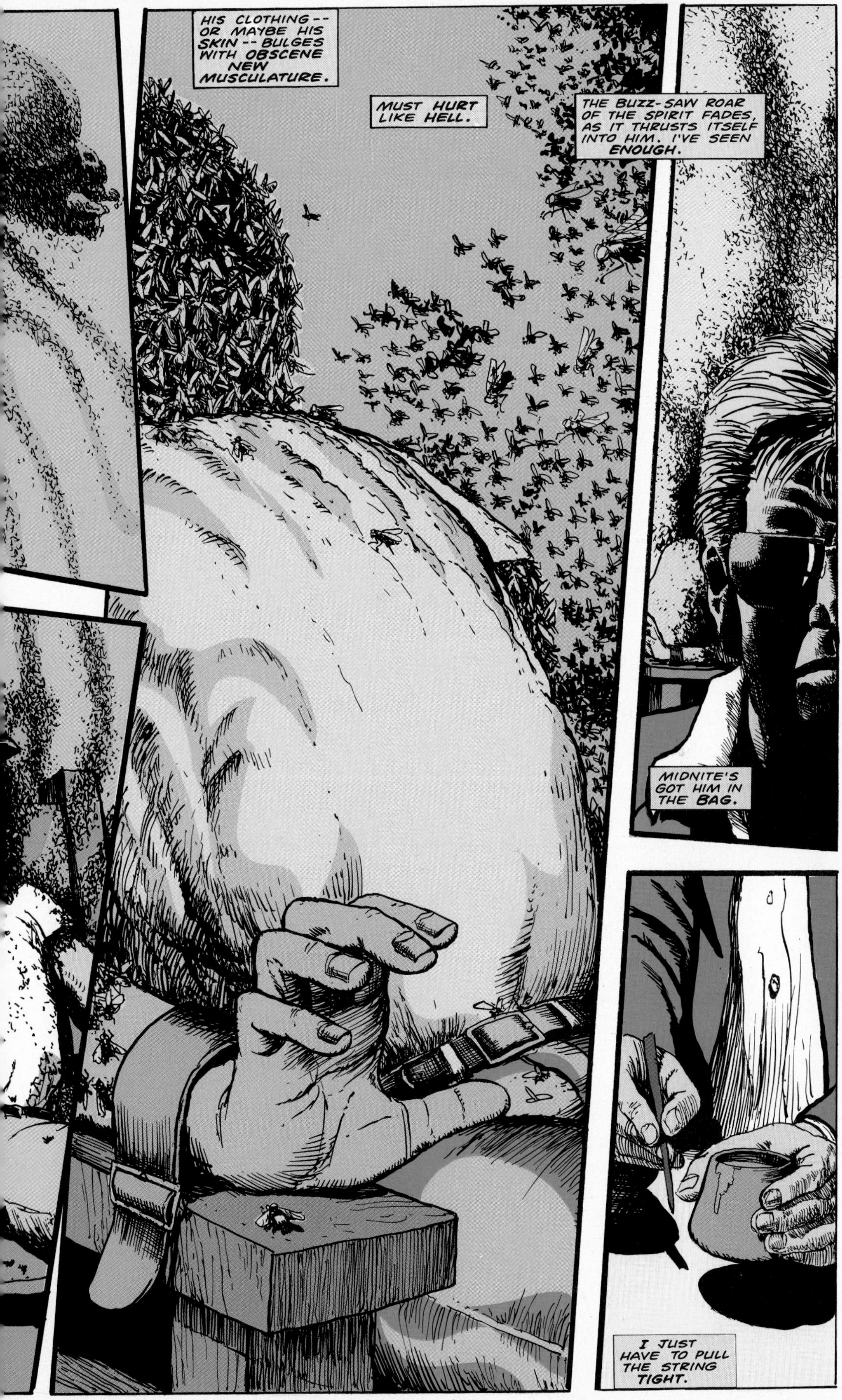
HIS CLOTHING -- OR MAYBE HIS SKIN -- BULGES WITH OBSCENE NEW MUSCULATURE.
MUST HURT LIKE HELL.
THE BUZZ-SAW ROAR OF THE SPIRIT FADES, AS IT THRUSTS ITSELF INTO HIM. I'VE SEEN ENOUGH.
MIDNITE'S GOT HIM IN THE BAG.
I JUST HAVE TO PULL THE STRING TIGHT.

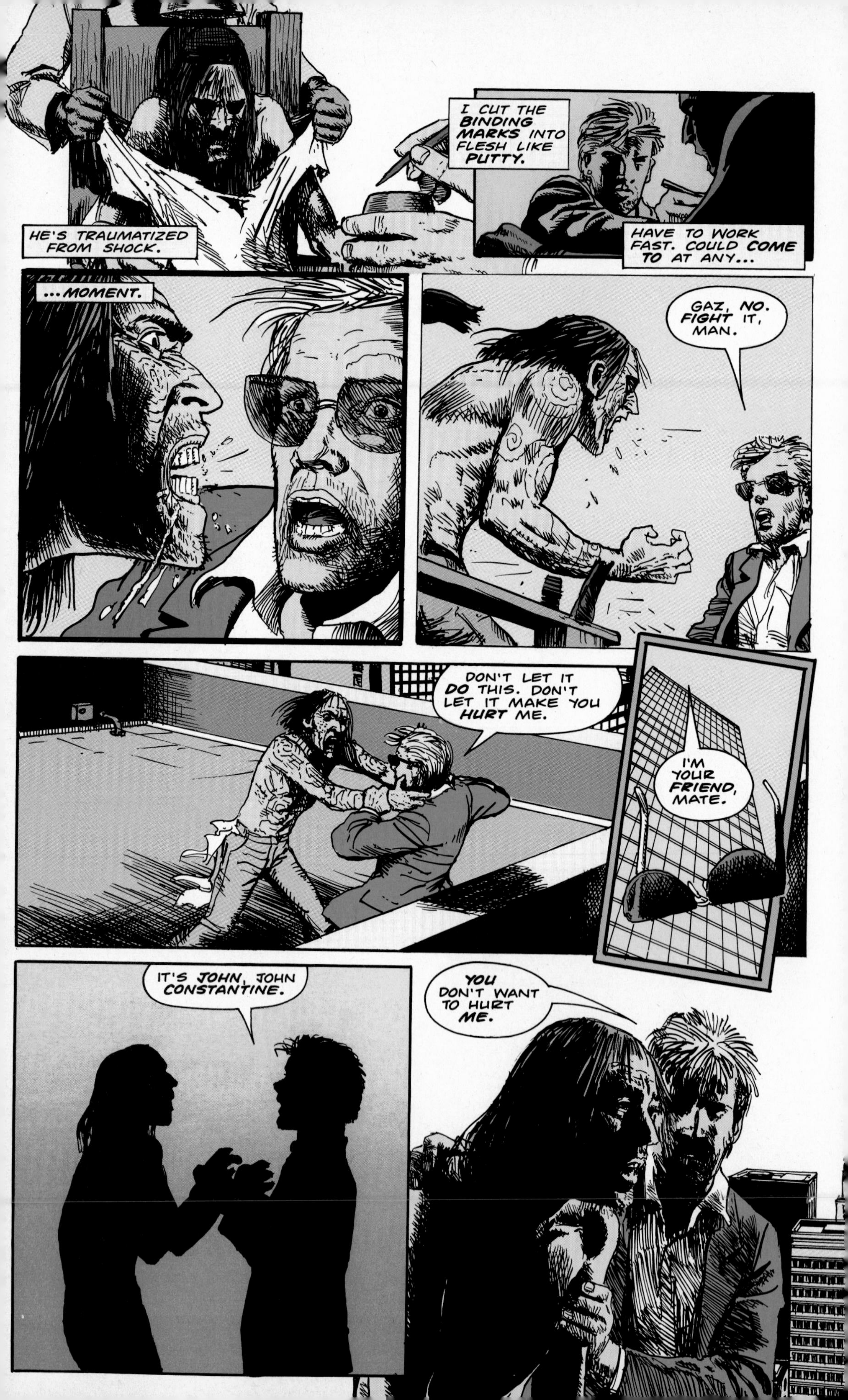
I CUT THE BINDING MARKS INTO FLESH LIKE PUTTY.
HE'S TRAUMATIZED FROM SHOCK.
HAVE TO WORK FAST. COULD COME TO AT ANY...
...MOMENT.
GAZ, NO. FIGHT IT, MAN.
DON'T LET IT DO THIS. DON'T LET IT MAKE YOU HURT ME.
I'M YOUR FRIEND, MATE.
IT'S JOHN, JOHN CONSTANTINE.
YOU DON'T WANT TO HURT ME.

JUST SLIP THIS ON. IT'LL KEEP YOU SAFE AND WARM.

WHAT'VE YOU DONE TO ME, JOHN?

I FEEL HIM START TO TENSE AGAIN.

KILL ME, JOHN. DON'T LET IT HAVE ME.

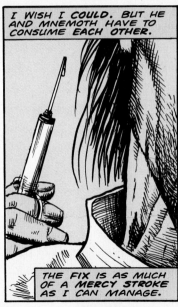

I WISH I COULD. BUT HE AND MNEMOTH HAVE TO CONSUME EACH OTHER.

THE FIX IS AS MUCH OF A MERCY STROKE AS I CAN MANAGE.

WHY HAS THIS HAPPENED TO ME?

HE WOULDN'T UNDERSTAND -- HOW SOME PEOPLE ARE DOOMED FROM THE WORD GO. HOW THEY DEVOUR THEMSELVES -- SEARCHING FOR ANNIHILATION.

HIS FOREHEAD IS COLD TO MY LIPS, LIKE A DEAD MAN'S.

TAKE HIM DOWN. I'LL FOLLOW.

MIDNITE, I WANT WHISKY AND CIGARETTES. LOTS OF THEM!

OOAARGCHHH.'

IT'S EATING ME.

YU-U YEURGH!

ON AVERAGE, IT TAKES FOUR MINUTES TO SMOKE A CIGARETTE.

HRAGH GUGU

A BOTTLE OF WHISKY LASTS TWO HOURS.

REEARGH!

BUT HOW BLOODY LONG CAN A MAN KEEP SCREAMING?

FOR AS LONG AS IT HURTS, MATE, I SUPPOSE.

PLEEEASE.

I NEED MORE ANESTHETIC.

BY THE END OF THE BOTTLE, THE SCREAMING HAS FINALLY STOPPED.

AND I THINK I'M SLIGHTLY PISSED.

I'M GLAD ABOUT THAT.

'CAUSE THE GHOSTS ARE HAVING A PARTY. AND I DON'T SEEM TO BE WELCOME.

ONE GLANCE IS ALL I GET. THEN EVERYTHING CATCHES FIRE AROUND THE EDGES.

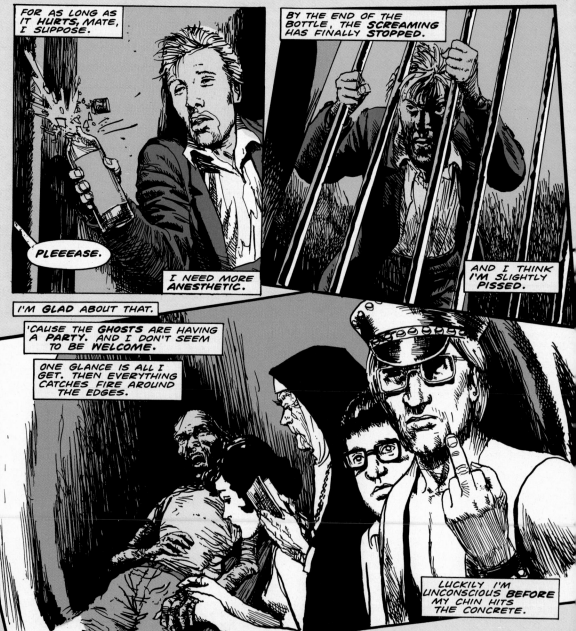

LUCKILY I'M UNCONSCIOUS BEFORE MY CHIN HITS THE CONCRETE.

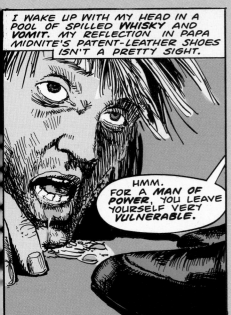

I WAKE UP WITH MY HEAD IN A POOL OF SPILLED *WHISKY* AND *VOMIT*. MY REFLECTION IN PAPA MIDNITE'S PATENT-LEATHER SHOES ISN'T A PRETTY SIGHT.

HMM. FOR A *MAN OF POWER*, YOU LEAVE YOURSELF VERY *VULNERABLE*.

AT LEAST THE *GHOSTS* HAVE GONE.

WELL, Y'KNOW WHAT THEY SAY -- *WORK HARD, PLAY HARD.* MAN'S GOT TO RELAX *SOMETIMES.*

ANYWAY, FUNERALS ARE *EASIER* IF THERE'S A *WAKE.*

LESTER'S BODY IS COMPLETELY *DESSICATED --* MUMMIFIED.

GRIEF, CONSTANTINE, IS A *LUXURY.*

EYES TOO DRY TO CLOSE.

JUST LIKE A *PHARAOH.*

A *MAGICIAN* MUST SEPARATE HIMSELF FROM HIS *HUMANITY.*

SORRY, MATE. NO *PYRAMID* FOR YOU.

Y'KNOW SOMETHING, MIDNITE? YOU GET *RIGHT* UP MY *BLOODY NOSE!*

BRICK IT UP.

I'LL SEE YA!

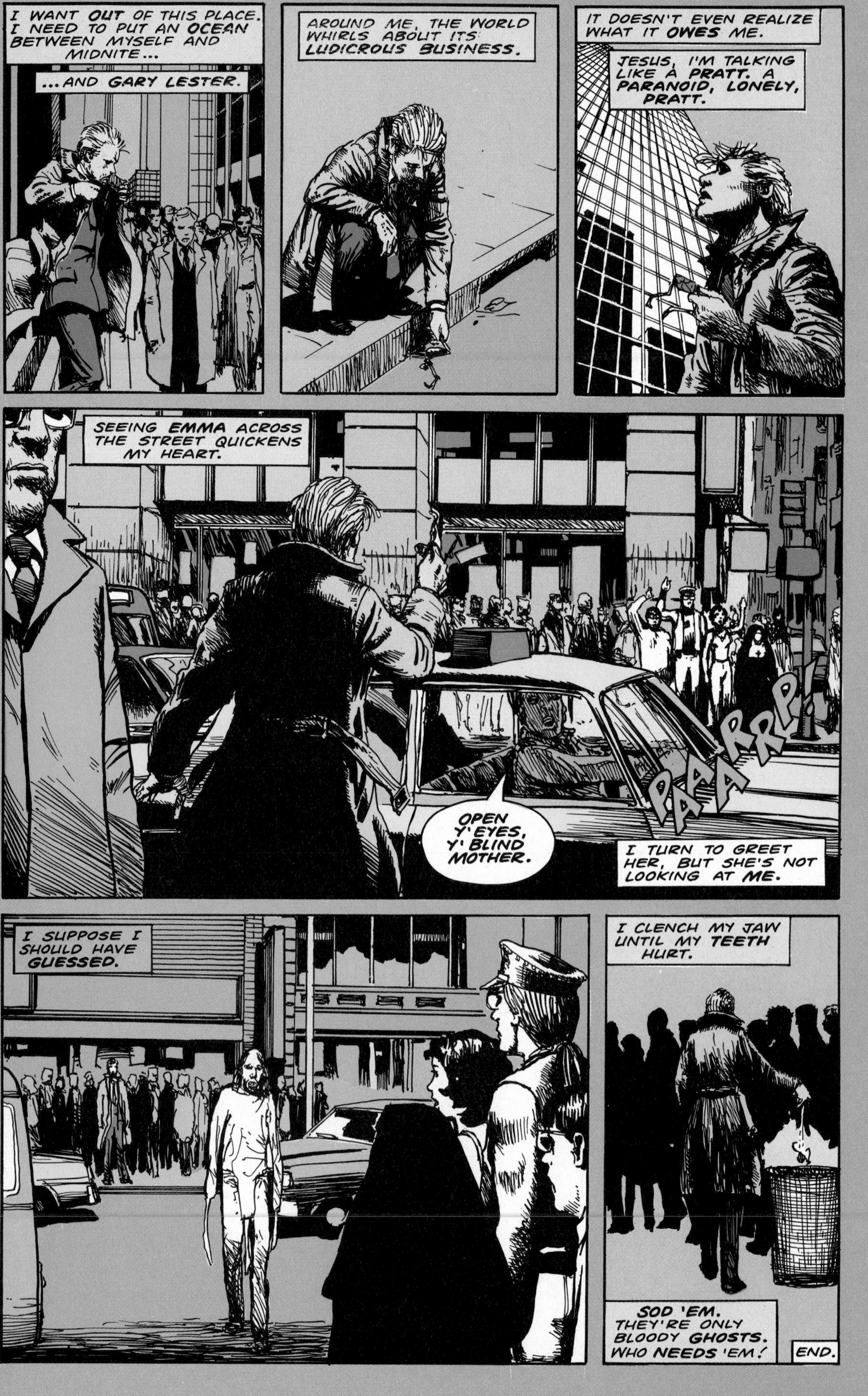
I WANT OUT OF THIS PLACE. I NEED TO PUT AN OCEAN BETWEEN MYSELF AND MIDNITE...
...AND GARY LESTER.
AROUND ME, THE WORLD WHIRLS ABOUT ITS LUDICROUS BUSINESS.
IT DOESN'T EVEN REALIZE WHAT IT OWES ME.
JESUS, I'M TALKING LIKE A PRATT. A PARANOID, LONELY, PRATT.
SEEING EMMA ACROSS THE STREET QUICKENS MY HEART.
OPEN Y'EYES, Y' BLIND MOTHER.
PAAARRP!
I TURN TO GREET HER, BUT SHE'S NOT LOOKING AT ME.
I SUPPOSE I SHOULD HAVE GUESSED.
I CLENCH MY JAW UNTIL MY TEETH HURT.
SOD 'EM. THEY'RE ONLY BLOODY GHOSTS. WHO NEEDS 'EM!
END.

FACES ON THE STREET

SATCHMO HAWKINS

FACE TO FACE with JOHN CONSTANTINE

Those of you with short-term memories unimpaired by habitual consumption of exotic cheroots or addiction to cable TV, may recall my promise to secure a fearless interview/exposé on the life and times of one JOHN CONSTANTINE.

How fascinating, I thought, and relevant to our lives to sift through the enigmatic variations of this secretive man's experience. Teams of dedicated researchers, more diligent than the FBI, were employed. Surreptitious deals were made—closely-guarded phone-numbers coaxed or extorted from unwilling trustees. At last, contact was achieved, and a meet, on neutral territory, arranged.

Thus is was that a hot and gritty summer evening found me forsaking my customary happy-hour cocktails to cross the river, South, into 'Injun country'. My mood was buoyant. I could already see the cover-spread. 'Satchmo Hawkins—John Constantine exclusive.'

So, faithful side-kicks, stick some Tom Waits on the stereo, unfetter your imaginations, and follow me into the heart of darkness. Believe me, I could use the company!

★ ★ ★

Not far from Clapham Junction, after much meandering up and down dark, narrow streets and blind alleys, the cabby ceases his torrent of invective—mainly illustrative of some of the finer aspects of inter-species sex—and brings his chariot to a squealing halt outside a public house of less than salubrious demeanour called THE BUTCHER'S HOOK. Great, you think, tremendous atmosphere: working-class street cred...perfect. You pay the cabby (over the odds, but what the hell, nobody's going to query the expenses for a John Constantine interview)!

The interior of the dingy bar is reminiscent, in atmosphere and colour, to the lungs of a forty-a-day man. The walls practically drip nicotine. You regret wearing white!

No sign of Constantine yet—just a couple of solitary geriatrics silently watching their half-pints of mild ale evaporating. Poor old sods, you think. Must be hard to keep yourself in beer and fags when you've living on a pension.

You order a pint of lager from a barman who is doubtless an ex-wrestler—his head looks like an engine block perched on a neck of old, bald, tyres. He overcharges you by at least a pound. He knows you won't argue. He's right!

Arriving before Constantine gives you a chance to check that the new Jap recorder is working and run through your interview strategy.

Start off with a bit of harmless chatter about music—the rise and fall of punk, etcetera—while you loosen him up with a few drinks. Then perhaps you'll hit him with the 'Super-hero connection'—should get a good quote out of the rumours about him and ZATANNA. That might lead us into the occult stuff, the Newcastle exorcism, the haunted cabinet-minister and such-like stories. You'll have to go steady on Newcastle, though. He might be a bit touchy about that one...

Three hours and eight pints of strong lager later, it dawns on you that Constantine isn't going to show. The bar is now jam-packed full of serious drinkers. The conversation at the table next to you—between some very heavy looking types—although largely inaudible, has been providing intriguing snippets which seem to concern the proposed route for a 'Securicor' armoured car and possible methods of detaining and opening said vehicle.

You decide to have one more drink to give Constantine a final chance for a late appearance. You struggle through the press toward the bar, which appears to be at least three-deep in copulating hippopotami—an illusion brought about by alcohol and air practically opaque with cheap cigarette smoke. The hippos are, in reality, thirsty building workers—dangerous but not so exotic. As you have no desire to end your life by coming between an uncontrollable beer-belly and its tenth pint of Friday-night Guinness, you hang a swift left and veer into the toilet.

It's like stepping into Hell. The toilet gully is choked with sodden fag-ends, the floor awash with a malodorous lake that laps around the welts of your sky-blue, Italian leather shoes. Before you think to hike up your Chinos, the turn-ups have darkened ominously. Necessity overcomes distaste. You steady yourself with one hand pressed against the clammy wall, idly wondering what diseases are transmittable cutaneously. A line of graffiti snarls bitterly at eye-level—DROP THE BLOODY BOMB, NOW! PUT US ALL OUT OF OUR MISERY. The sentiment seems eminently agreeable.

The interview of the decade has turned into a total debacle.

As you turn to paddle gingerly out of the festering swamp, the door opens and two of the armoured car freaks from the next table walk in. They have faces like matching tombstones. With downcast eyes, you move to pass them. A hand the size of a small car leaps toward your face. There is a sharp crunch somewhere deep inside your head—suddenly you are sitting on your backside in two inches of stagnant micturition.

A heavy brogue shoe plants itself firmly in your ribs. You feel the new tape-recorder disintegrate. The pain makes you feel sick. You are sick!

One of the tombstones looms towards you and a hand rips the fragmented electronics from your inside pocket.

"See—told yer 'e was wired. Who d'yer reckon 'e is, then? The Old Bill?" "Nah, even the Bill wouldn't 'ave a nancy boy like 'im on the force. 'E's just some soddin' reporter!"

One of the giant hands crushes your windpipe and lifts you, dripping, from the floor. With graveyard breath, the tombstone speaks into your face. "Lissen, you effin' nosy bastard. We're the Dodkins Bruvvers, see. An' if yer come snoopin' arahnd dahn 'ere again, we're goin' ter nail yer effin' 'ands ter the floor. Geddit?"

They drag you, leaving a stinking, wet slug-trail, through the bar and propel you, sprawling—inexpressibly grateful for their mercy—into the gutter. A minicab pulls up. The driver winds down his window and speaks.

"You a party name of Satchmo 'Awkins?"

You nod dumbly.

"John Constantine sent me. Says 'e's sorry but somethin's come up. 'E's gone to New York.

"I'm s'posed to take you 'ome—but you ain't getting in my car in a state like that! You smell like a dead dog, mate!"

You watch as he speeds off up the street. You feel sick again. It's a two-hour walk to get home.

★ ★ ★

And that, gentle reader, is the story of the interview that never was. So, if sometime we're ligging around the same bar, introduce yourself. We'll talk about the weather, the Gross National Product or the plot of Dynasty—but don't mention John Constantine to me. I never want to hear that bastard's name again!

The BUTCHER'S HOOK

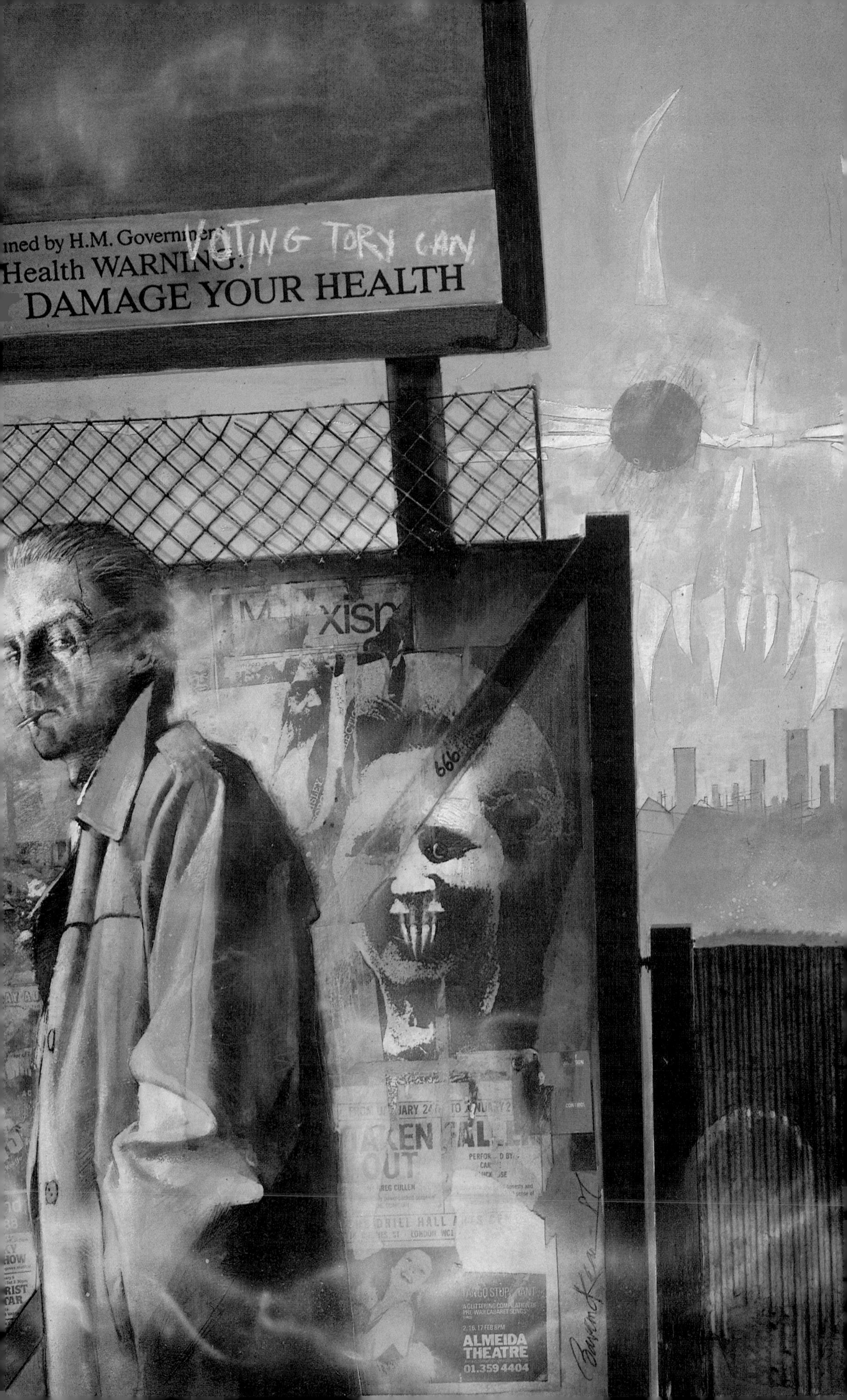
Health WARNING:
VOTING TORY CAN
DAMAGE YOUR HEALTH
xisn
666
OUT
PERFOR D BY
GREG CULLEN
DRILL HALL
LONDON WC1
CONTROL
A GLITTERING COMPILATION OF PRE-WAR CABARET SONGS
2.16.17 FEB 8PM
ALMEIDA THEATRE
01.359 4404

A FEAR OF FAILURE SPURS HIM LONG INTO THE SUMMER EVENING.

IT'S TOO MUCH TO TAKE ON BOARD.

A WEEK AGO HE WAS FIRMLY IN THE SPREAD. LIFE WAS PURE GOLD. NOW, THE CITY HAS SHUT ITS DOORS ON HIM.

HE'S GETTING SHAFTED-- BUT WHY?

FIRST, HE'D TAKEN A TUMBLE ON SOME HIGH-RISK FUTURES. HE COULD HAVE STOOD THAT -- BUT SARAH'S GUCCI TAB HAD COME IN, AND THE COKE BILL.

THEN SOME PEASANTS HAD POURED PAINT-STRIPPER ON THE JAGUAR. OVER-EXTENDED, HE'D MISSED SOME CREDIT CARD PAYMENTS AND THE BASTARDS HAD SLASHED HIS RATING.

EVENTS ARE OVERTAKING HIM.

OF COURSE SARAH HAD LEFT AS SOON AS THE CASH FLOW DRIED UP.

NOW, UNBELIEVABLY, HE IS OVERDUE ON THE COMMISSION FOR THE YOUNG TURKS AT MAMMON INVESTMENTS.

IF HE CAN KEEP AHEAD OF THEM FOR A FEW MORE DAYS, HE MIGHT JUST STAY IN THE RACE.

BUT ROGER RANDALL, IS RUNNING OUT OF TIME.

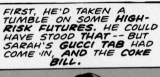

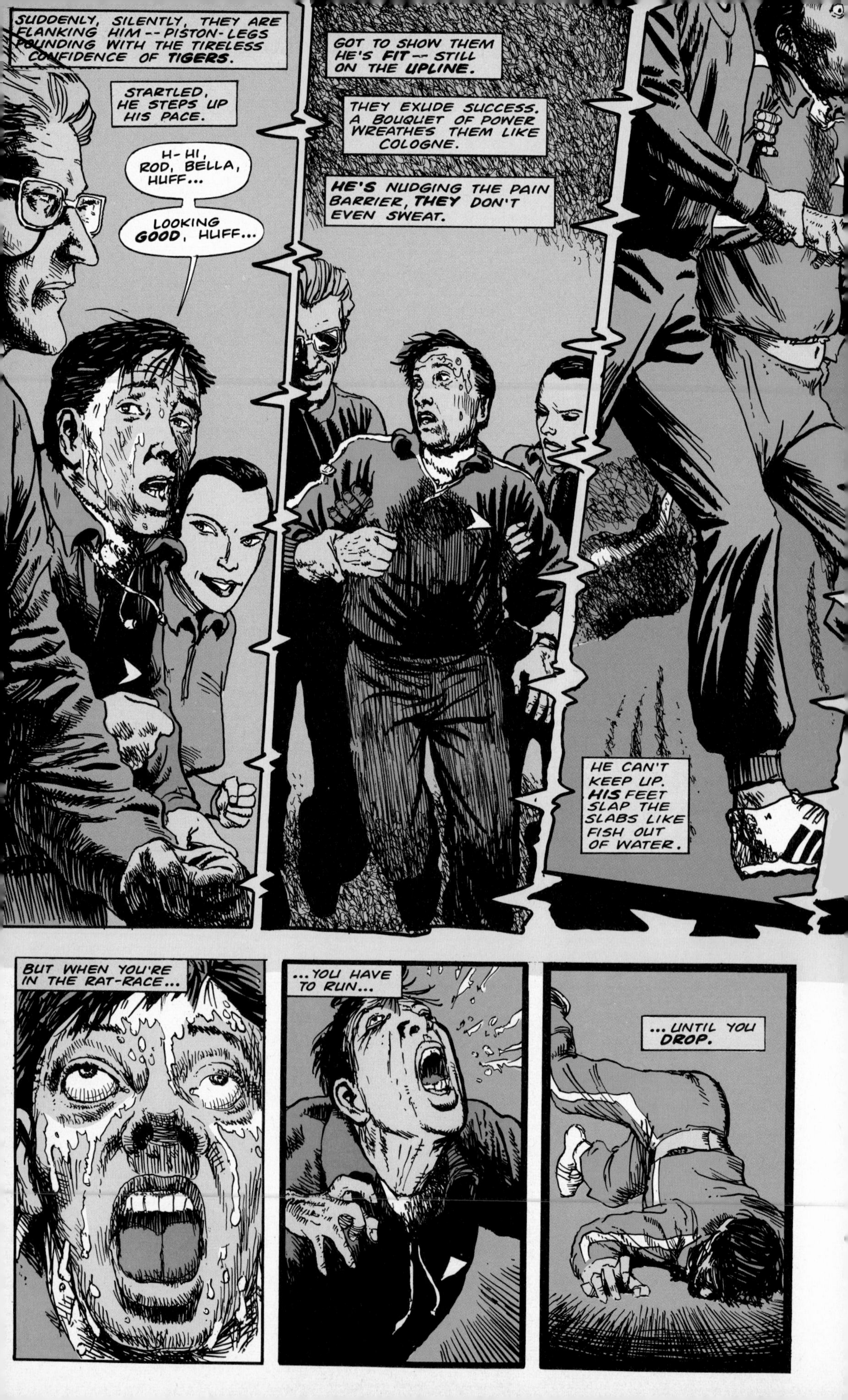
SUDDENLY, SILENTLY, THEY ARE FLANKING HIM -- PISTON-LEGS POUNDING WITH THE TIRELESS CONFIDENCE OF TIGERS.
STARTLED, HE STEPS UP HIS PACE.
H-HI, ROD, BELLA, HUFF...
LOOKING GOOD, HUFF...
GOT TO SHOW THEM HE'S FIT -- STILL ON THE UPLINE.
THEY EXUDE SUCCESS. A BOUQUET OF POWER WREATHES THEM LIKE COLOGNE.
HE'S NUDGING THE PAIN BARRIER, THEY DON'T EVEN SWEAT.
HE CAN'T KEEP UP. HIS FEET SLAP THE SLABS LIKE FISH OUT OF WATER.
BUT WHEN YOU'RE IN THE RAT-RACE...
...YOU HAVE TO RUN...
...UNTIL YOU DROP.

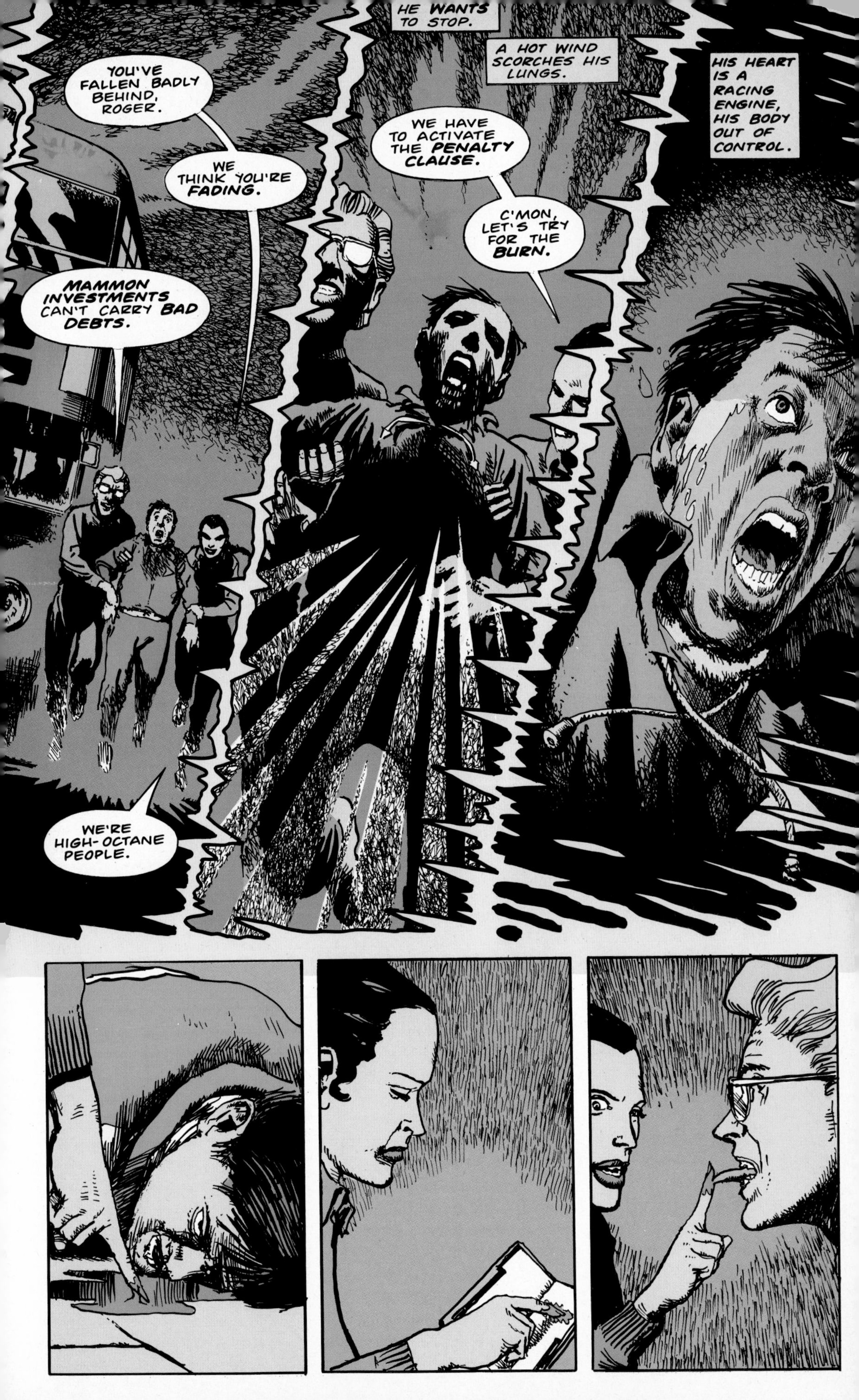
HE WANTS TO STOP.
YOU'VE FALLEN BADLY BEHIND, ROGER.
WE THINK YOU'RE FADING.
MAMMON INVESTMENTS CAN'T CARRY BAD DEBTS.
WE'RE HIGH-OCTANE PEOPLE.
A HOT WIND SCORCHES HIS LUNGS.
WE HAVE TO ACTIVATE THE PENALTY CLAUSE.
C'MON, LET'S TRY FOR THE BURN.
HIS HEART IS A RACING ENGINE, HIS BODY OUT OF CONTROL.

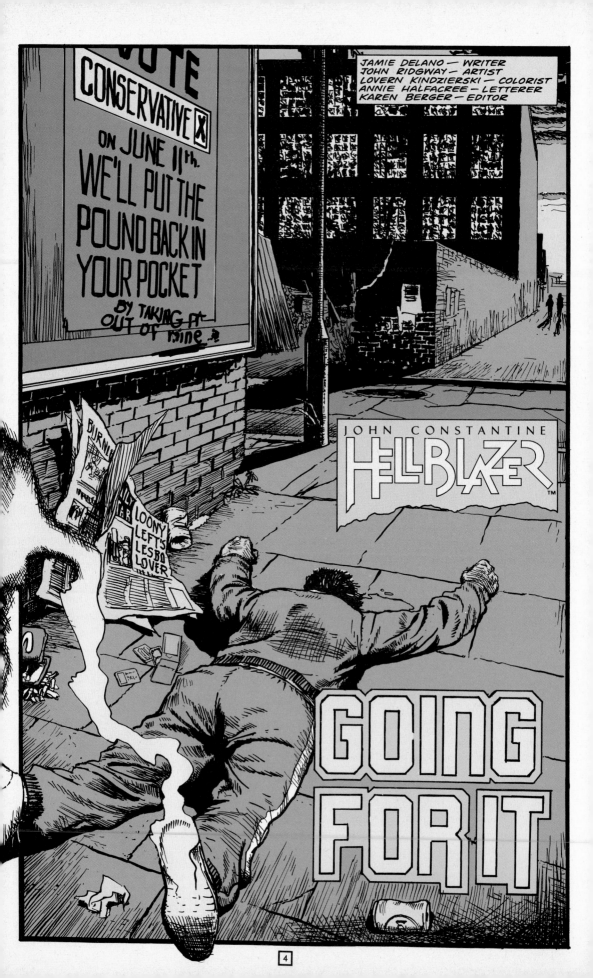

JAMIE DELANO — WRITER
JOHN RIDGWAY — ARTIST
LOVERN KINDZIERSKI — COLORIST
ANNIE HALFACREE — LETTERER
KAREN BERGER — EDITOR

VOTE
CONSERVATIVE X
ON JUNE 11th.
WE'LL PUT THE
POUND BACK IN
YOUR POCKET
BY TAKING IT
OUT OF MINE

BURN...

LOONY
LEFT'S
LESBO
LOVER

JOHN CONSTANTINE
HELLBLAZER™

GOING
FOR IT

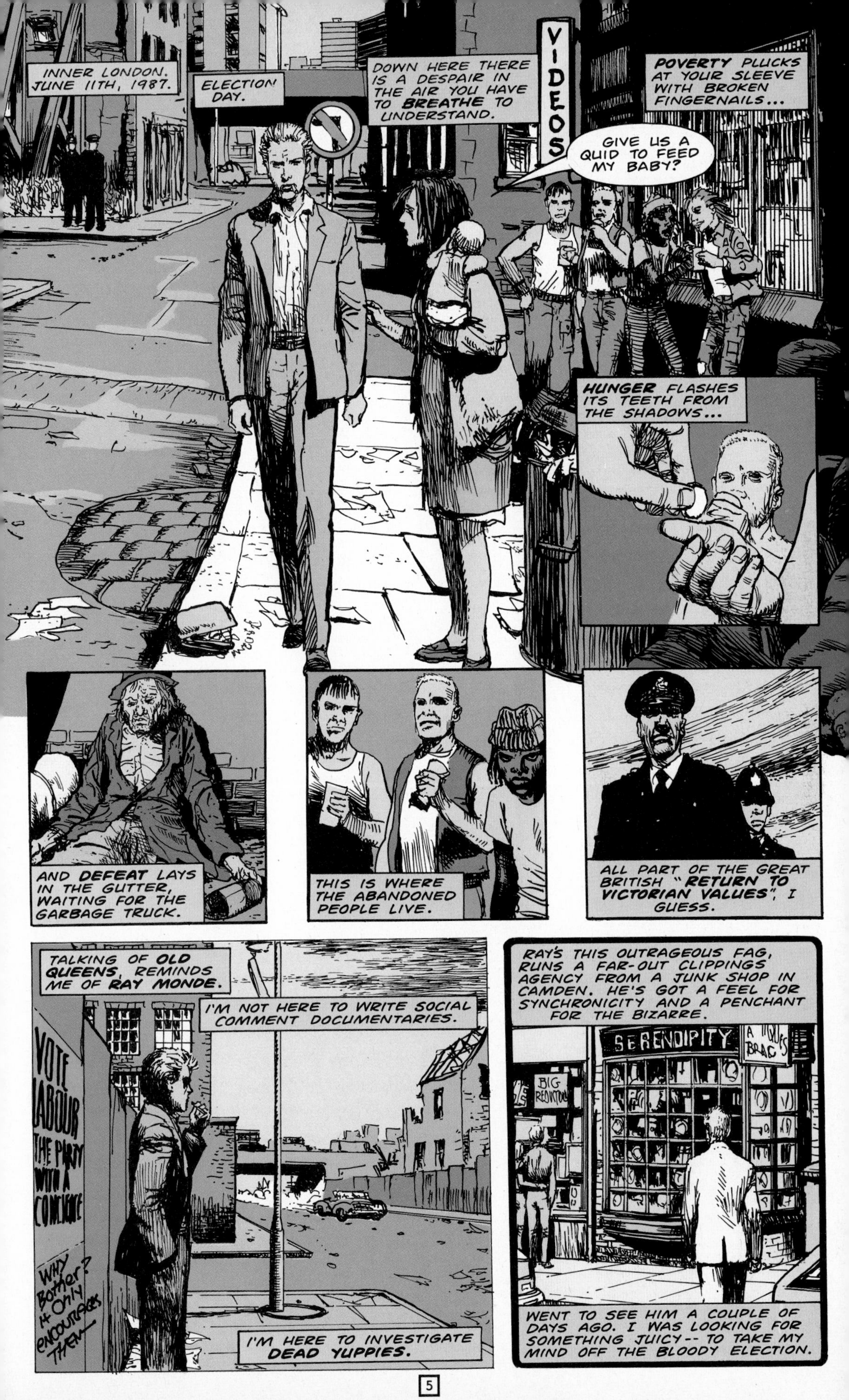
INNER LONDON. JUNE 11TH, 1987.
ELECTION DAY.
DOWN HERE THERE IS A DESPAIR IN THE AIR YOU HAVE TO BREATHE TO UNDERSTAND.
VIDEOS
POVERTY PLUCKS AT YOUR SLEEVE WITH BROKEN FINGERNAILS...
GIVE US A QUID TO FEED MY BABY?
HUNGER FLASHES ITS TEETH FROM THE SHADOWS...
AND DEFEAT LAYS IN THE GUTTER, WAITING FOR THE GARBAGE TRUCK.
THIS IS WHERE THE ABANDONED PEOPLE LIVE.
ALL PART OF THE GREAT BRITISH "RETURN TO VICTORIAN VALUES", I GUESS.
TALKING OF OLD QUEENS, REMINDS ME OF RAY MONDE.
I'M NOT HERE TO WRITE SOCIAL COMMENT DOCUMENTARIES.
VOTE LABOUR THE PARTY WITH A CONSCIENCE
WHY Bother? It Only encourages THEM
I'M HERE TO INVESTIGATE DEAD YUPPIES.
RAY'S THIS OUTRAGEOUS FAG, RUNS A FAR-OUT CLIPPINGS AGENCY FROM A JUNK SHOP IN CAMDEN. HE'S GOT A FEEL FOR SYNCHRONICITY AND A PENCHANT FOR THE BIZARRE.
SERENDIPITY
BIG REDUCTIONS
WENT TO SEE HIM A COUPLE OF DAYS AGO. I WAS LOOKING FOR SOMETHING JUICY-- TO TAKE MY MIND OFF THE BLOODY ELECTION.

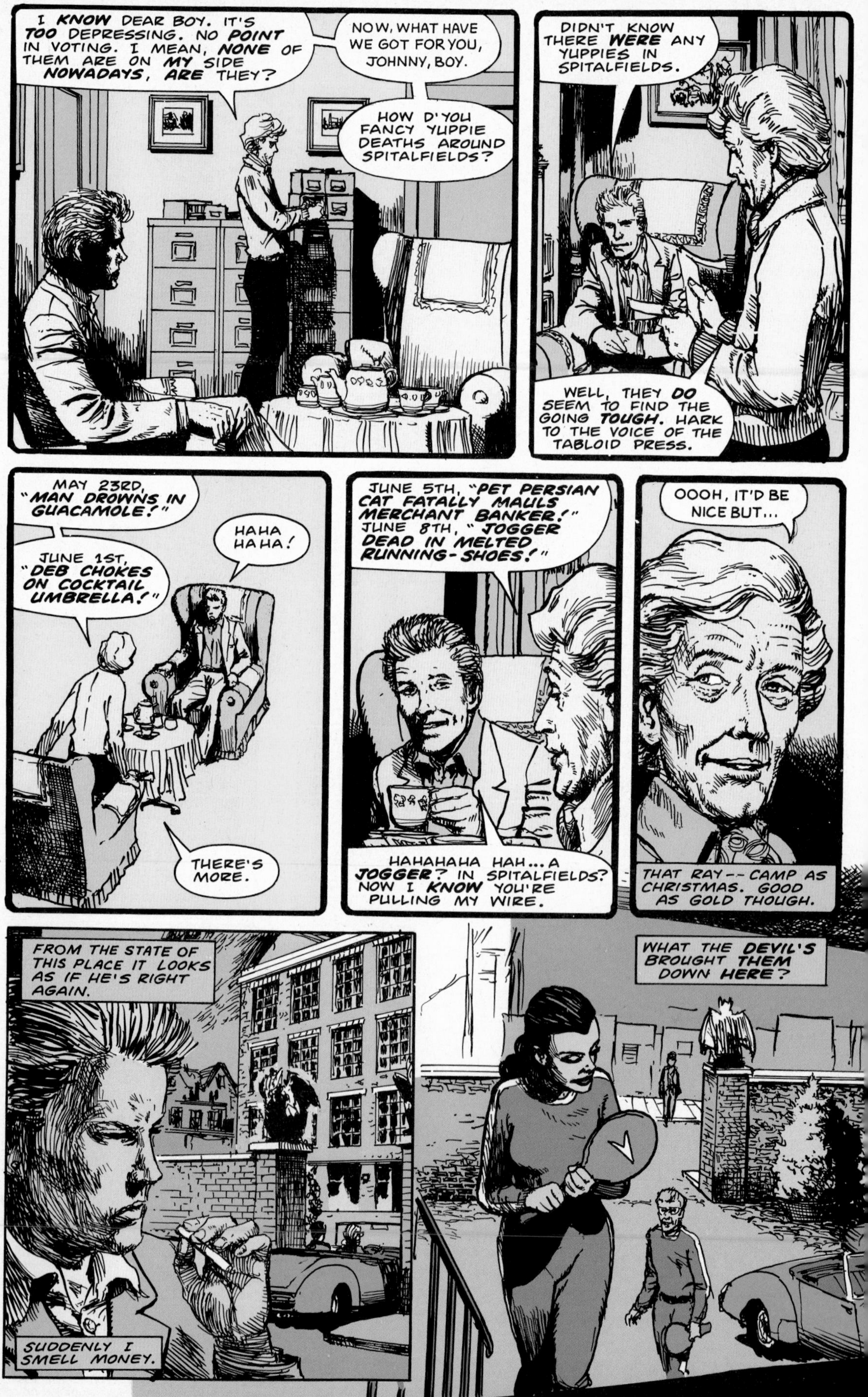
I KNOW DEAR BOY. IT'S TOO DEPRESSING. NO POINT IN VOTING. I MEAN, NONE OF THEM ARE ON MY SIDE NOWADAYS, ARE THEY?
NOW, WHAT HAVE WE GOT FOR YOU, JOHNNY, BOY.
HOW D'YOU FANCY YUPPIE DEATHS AROUND SPITALFIELDS?
DIDN'T KNOW THERE WERE ANY YUPPIES IN SPITALFIELDS.
WELL, THEY DO SEEM TO FIND THE GOING TOUGH. HARK TO THE VOICE OF THE TABLOID PRESS.
MAY 23RD, "MAN DROWNS IN GUACAMOLE!"
HAHA HAHA!
JUNE 1ST, "DEB CHOKES ON COCKTAIL UMBRELLA!"
THERE'S MORE.
JUNE 5TH, "PET PERSIAN CAT FATALLY MAULS MERCHANT BANKER!" JUNE 8TH, "JOGGER DEAD IN MELTED RUNNING-SHOES!"
HAHAHAHA HAH... A JOGGER? IN SPITALFIELDS? NOW I KNOW YOU'RE PULLING MY WIRE.
OOOH, IT'D BE NICE BUT...
THAT RAY-- CAMP AS CHRISTMAS. GOOD AS GOLD THOUGH.
FROM THE STATE OF THIS PLACE IT LOOKS AS IF HE'S RIGHT AGAIN.
SUDDENLY I SMELL MONEY.
WHAT THE DEVIL'S BROUGHT THEM DOWN HERE?

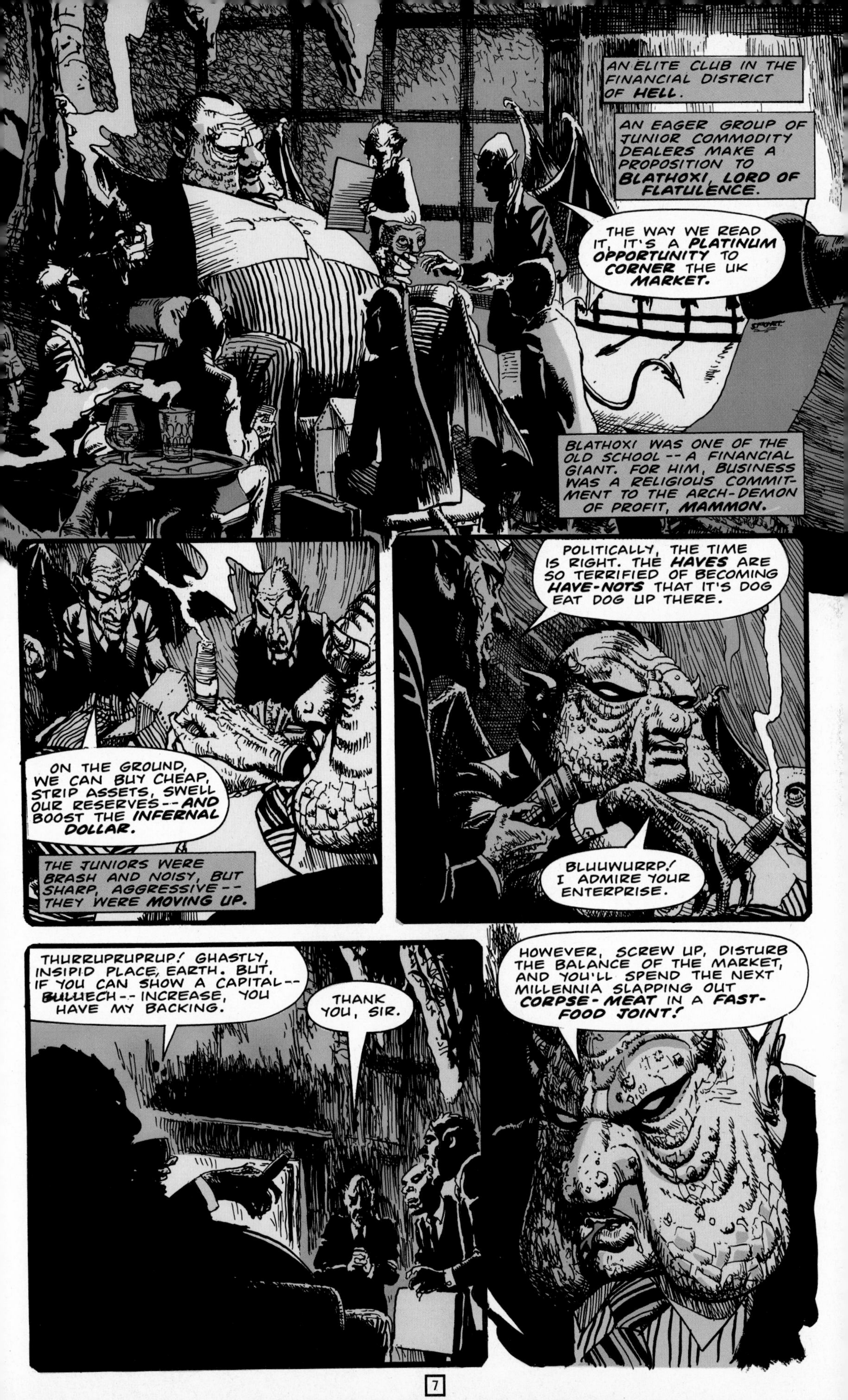

AN ELITE CLUB IN THE FINANCIAL DISTRICT OF HELL.
AN EAGER GROUP OF JUNIOR COMMODITY DEALERS MAKE A PROPOSITION TO BLATHOXI, LORD OF FLATULENCE.
THE WAY WE READ IT, IT'S A PLATINUM OPPORTUNITY TO CORNER THE UK MARKET.
BLATHOXI WAS ONE OF THE OLD SCHOOL -- A FINANCIAL GIANT. FOR HIM, BUSINESS WAS A RELIGIOUS COMMITMENT TO THE ARCH-DEMON OF PROFIT, MAMMON.
ON THE GROUND, WE CAN BUY CHEAP, STRIP ASSETS, SWELL OUR RESERVES--AND BOOST THE INFERNAL DOLLAR.
THE JUNIORS WERE BRASH AND NOISY, BUT SHARP, AGGRESSIVE -- THEY WERE MOVING UP.
POLITICALLY, THE TIME IS RIGHT. THE HAVES ARE SO TERRIFIED OF BECOMING HAVE-NOTS THAT IT'S DOG EAT DOG UP THERE.
BLUUWURRP! I ADMIRE YOUR ENTERPRISE.
THURRUPRUPRUP! GHASTLY, INSIPID PLACE, EARTH. BUT, IF YOU CAN SHOW A CAPITAL-- BULLIECH-- INCREASE, YOU HAVE MY BACKING.
THANK YOU, SIR.
HOWEVER, SCREW UP, DISTURB THE BALANCE OF THE MARKET, AND YOU'LL SPEND THE NEXT MILLENNIA SLAPPING OUT CORPSE-MEAT IN A FAST-FOOD JOINT!

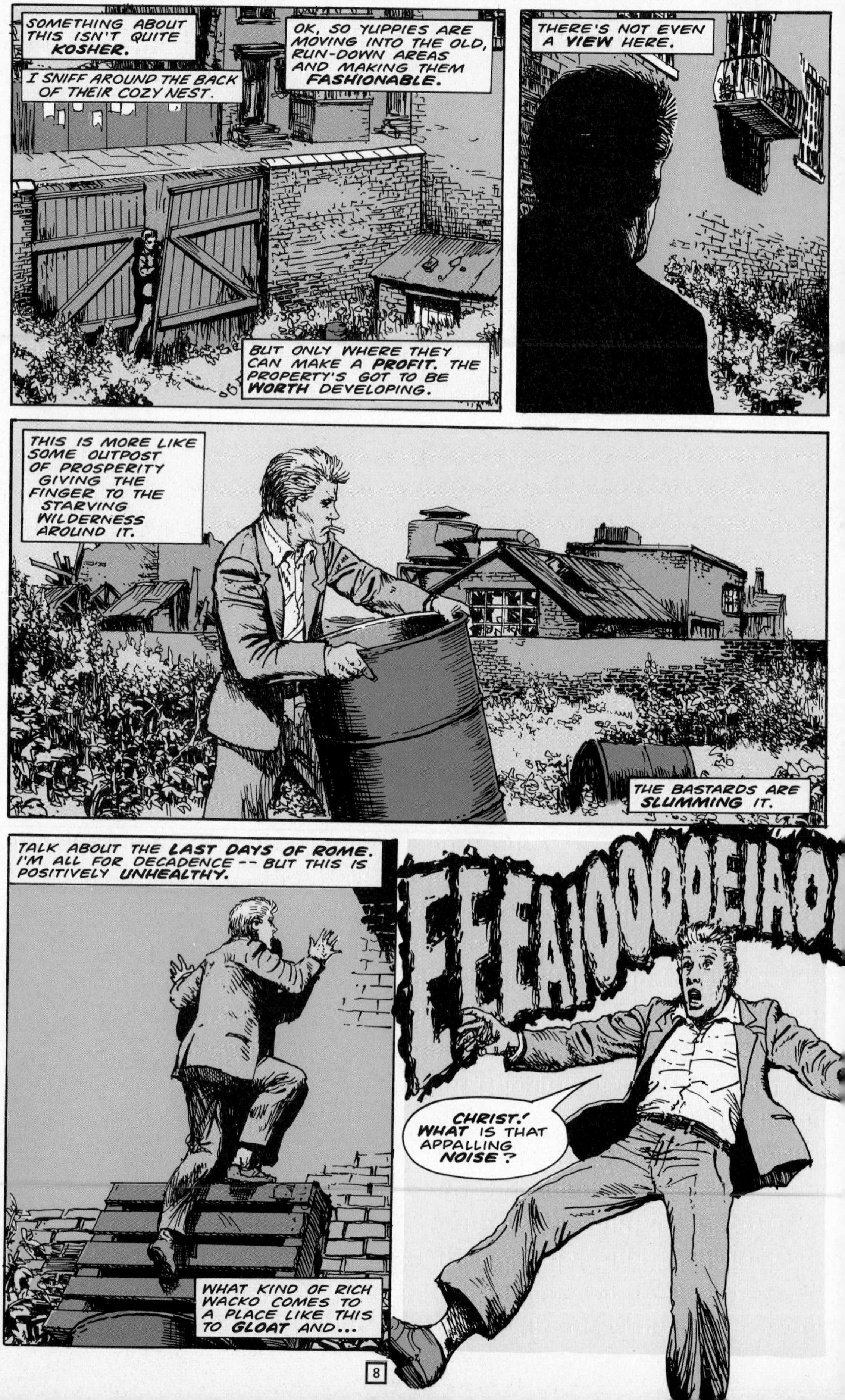
SOMETHING ABOUT THIS ISN'T QUITE KOSHER.
I SNIFF AROUND THE BACK OF THEIR COZY NEST.
OK, SO YUPPIES ARE MOVING INTO THE OLD, RUN-DOWN AREAS AND MAKING THEM FASHIONABLE.
BUT ONLY WHERE THEY CAN MAKE A PROFIT. THE PROPERTY'S GOT TO BE WORTH DEVELOPING.
THERE'S NOT EVEN A VIEW HERE.
THIS IS MORE LIKE SOME OUTPOST OF PROSPERITY GIVING THE FINGER TO THE STARVING WILDERNESS AROUND IT.
THE BASTARDS ARE SLUMMING IT.
TALK ABOUT THE LAST DAYS OF ROME. I'M ALL FOR DECADENCE -- BUT THIS IS POSITIVELY UNHEALTHY.
WHAT KIND OF RICH WACKO COMES TO A PLACE LIKE THIS TO GLOAT AND...
EEEAIOOOOEIAO
CHRIST! WHAT IS THAT APPALLING NOISE?

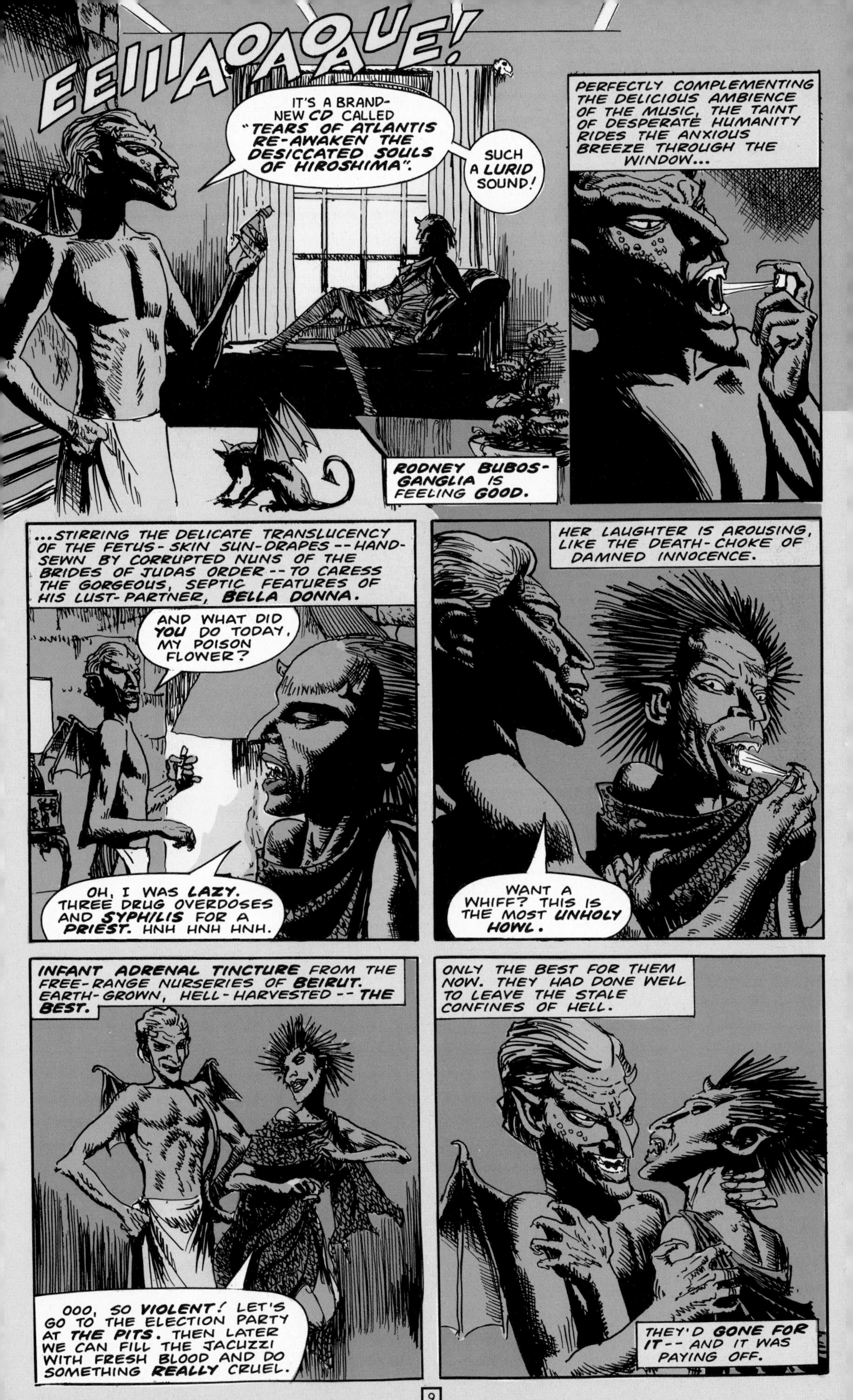

EEIIIAOAOAUE!
IT'S A BRAND-NEW CD CALLED "TEARS OF ATLANTIS RE-AWAKEN THE DESICCATED SOULS OF HIROSHIMA".
SUCH A LURID SOUND!
RODNEY BUBOSGANGLIA IS FEELING GOOD.
PERFECTLY COMPLEMENTING THE DELICIOUS AMBIENCE OF THE MUSIC, THE TAINT OF DESPERATE HUMANITY RIDES THE ANXIOUS BREEZE THROUGH THE WINDOW...
...STIRRING THE DELICATE TRANSLUCENCY OF THE FETUS-SKIN SUN-DRAPES -- HAND-SEWN BY CORRUPTED NUNS OF THE BRIDES OF JUDAS ORDER -- TO CARESS THE GORGEOUS, SEPTIC FEATURES OF HIS LUST-PARTNER, BELLA DONNA.
AND WHAT DID YOU DO TODAY, MY POISON FLOWER?
OH, I WAS LAZY. THREE DRUG OVERDOSES AND SYPHILIS FOR A PRIEST. HNH HNH HNH.
HER LAUGHTER IS AROUSING, LIKE THE DEATH-CHOKE OF DAMNED INNOCENCE.
WANT A WHIFF? THIS IS THE MOST UNHOLY HOWL.
INFANT ADRENAL TINCTURE FROM THE FREE-RANGE NURSERIES OF BEIRUT. EARTH-GROWN, HELL-HARVESTED -- THE BEST.
OOO, SO VIOLENT! LET'S GO TO THE ELECTION PARTY AT THE PITS. THEN LATER WE CAN FILL THE JACUZZI WITH FRESH BLOOD AND DO SOMETHING REALLY CRUEL.
ONLY THE BEST FOR THEM NOW. THEY HAD DONE WELL TO LEAVE THE STALE CONFINES OF HELL.
THEY'D GONE FOR IT -- AND IT WAS PAYING OFF.

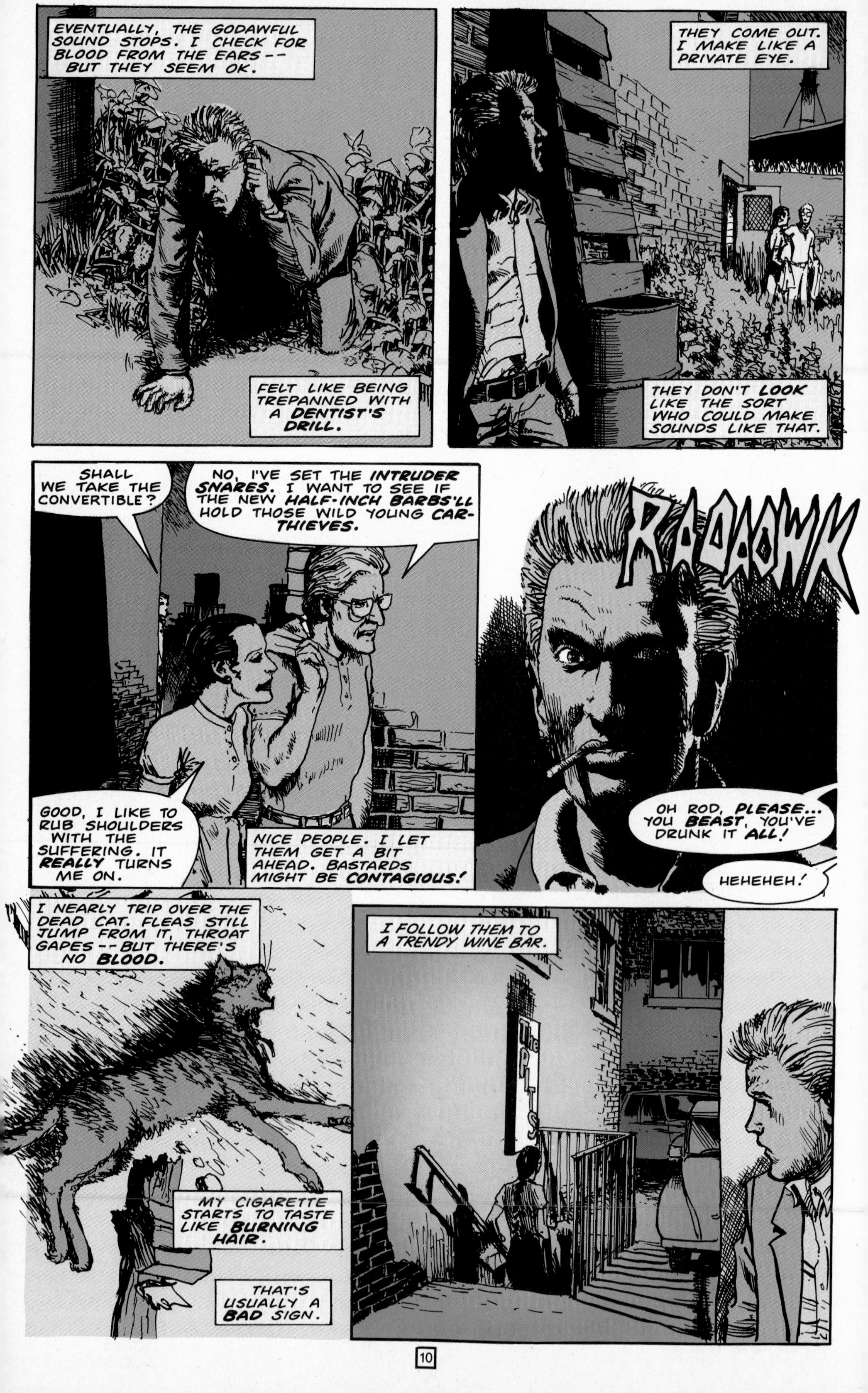

EVENTUALLY, THE GODAWFUL SOUND STOPS. I CHECK FOR BLOOD FROM THE EARS -- BUT THEY SEEM OK.
FELT LIKE BEING TREPANNED WITH A DENTIST'S DRILL.
THEY COME OUT. I MAKE LIKE A PRIVATE EYE.
THEY DON'T LOOK LIKE THE SORT WHO COULD MAKE SOUNDS LIKE THAT.
SHALL WE TAKE THE CONVERTIBLE?
NO, I'VE SET THE INTRUDER SNARES. I WANT TO SEE IF THE NEW HALF-INCH BARBS'LL HOLD THOSE WILD YOUNG CAR-THIEVES.
GOOD, I LIKE TO RUB SHOULDERS WITH THE SUFFERING. IT REALLY TURNS ME ON.
NICE PEOPLE. I LET THEM GET A BIT AHEAD. BASTARDS MIGHT BE CONTAGIOUS!
RAOAOWK
OH ROD, PLEASE... YOU BEAST, YOU'VE DRUNK IT ALL!
HEHEHEH!
I NEARLY TRIP OVER THE DEAD CAT. FLEAS STILL JUMP FROM IT, THROAT GAPES -- BUT THERE'S NO BLOOD.
MY CIGARETTE STARTS TO TASTE LIKE BURNING HAIR.
THAT'S USUALLY A BAD SIGN.
I FOLLOW THEM TO A TRENDY WINE BAR.

IF YOU WANT TO KNOW ABOUT PEOPLE, WATCH THEM AT *PLAY*-- WHEN THEIR *GUARD'S* DOWN.

I'LL JUST SLIP IN, MINGLE WITH THE CROWD AND GET THE STORY ON THESE CREEPS.

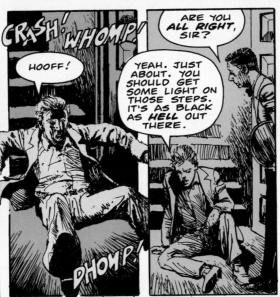

CRASH! WHOMP!

HOOFF!

ARE YOU ALL RIGHT, SIR?

YEAH. JUST ABOUT. YOU SHOULD GET SOME LIGHT ON THOSE STEPS. IT'S AS BLACK AS *HELL* OUT THERE.

DHOMP!

MOST OF OUR PATRONS *PREFER* IT THAT WAY.

NOBODY PAYS ME MUCH ATTENTION. THAT'S FINE BY ME. I DON'T WANT TO MAKE FRIENDS WITH *THIS* CLASS OF *SPOON-FED PONDLIFE.*

I TRY TO MAKE SENSE OF THEIR VACUOUS BRAYING.

HE'D *ALREADY* PAID AN *ARM* AND A *LEG!*

THAT'S WHAT I LIKE ABOUT BUSINESS. IT'S SO MUCH *FUN.*

SO I GAZUMPED HIM THROUGH THE ROOF. UNFORTUNATELY, IT *BROKE* HIM. HAW HAW.

A FEW SECONDS CONVINCES ME THAT I'M GOING TO NEED A DRINK. AS I LOOK FOR THE WAITER, MY EYES TUNE IN TO THE WEIRD LIGHTING...

...AND I REALIZE THAT THE LAMPSHADE HAS A *TATTOO.*

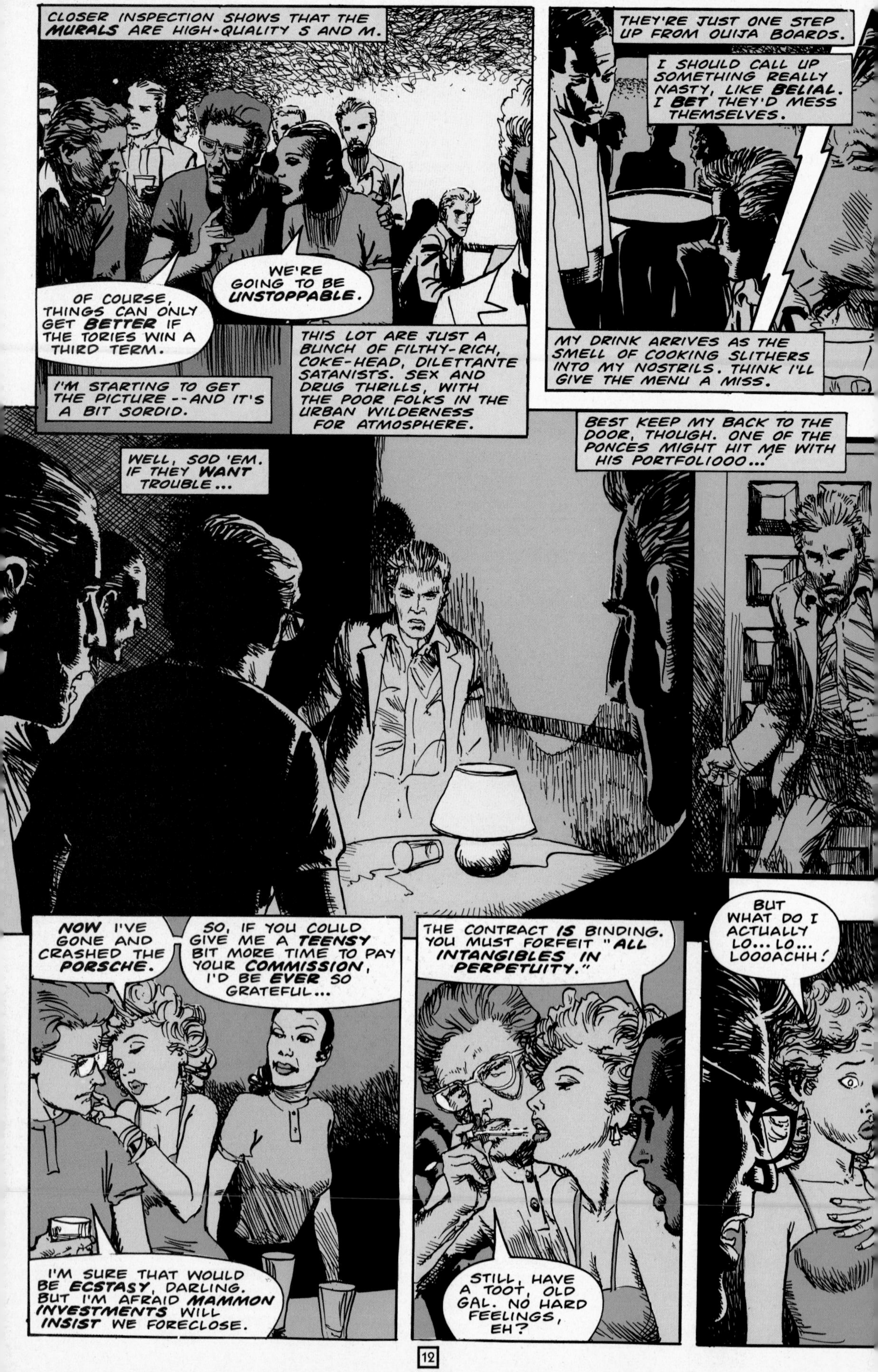

CLOSER INSPECTION SHOWS THAT THE MURALS ARE HIGH-QUALITY S AND M.
WE'RE GOING TO BE UNSTOPPABLE.
OF COURSE, THINGS CAN ONLY GET BETTER IF THE TORIES WIN A THIRD TERM.
I'M STARTING TO GET THE PICTURE--AND IT'S A BIT SORDID.
THIS LOT ARE JUST A BUNCH OF FILTHY-RICH, COKE-HEAD, DILETTANTE SATANISTS. SEX AND DRUG THRILLS, WITH THE POOR FOLKS IN THE URBAN WILDERNESS FOR ATMOSPHERE.
THEY'RE JUST ONE STEP UP FROM OUIJA BOARDS.
I SHOULD CALL UP SOMETHING REALLY NASTY, LIKE BELIAL. I BET THEY'D MESS THEMSELVES.
MY DRINK ARRIVES AS THE SMELL OF COOKING SLITHERS INTO MY NOSTRILS. THINK I'LL GIVE THE MENU A MISS.
WELL, SOD 'EM. IF THEY WANT TROUBLE...
BEST KEEP MY BACK TO THE DOOR, THOUGH. ONE OF THE PONCES MIGHT HIT ME WITH HIS PORTFOLIOOO...'
NOW I'VE GONE AND CRASHED THE PORSCHE.
SO, IF YOU COULD GIVE ME A TEENSY BIT MORE TIME TO PAY YOUR COMMISSION, I'D BE EVER SO GRATEFUL...
I'M SURE THAT WOULD BE ECSTASY, DARLING. BUT I'M AFRAID MAMMON INVESTMENTS WILL INSIST WE FORECLOSE.
THE CONTRACT IS BINDING. YOU MUST FORFEIT "ALL INTANGIBLES IN PERPETUITY."
STILL, HAVE A TOOT, OLD GAL. NO HARD FEELINGS, EH?
BUT WHAT DO I ACTUALLY LO... LO... LOOOACHH!

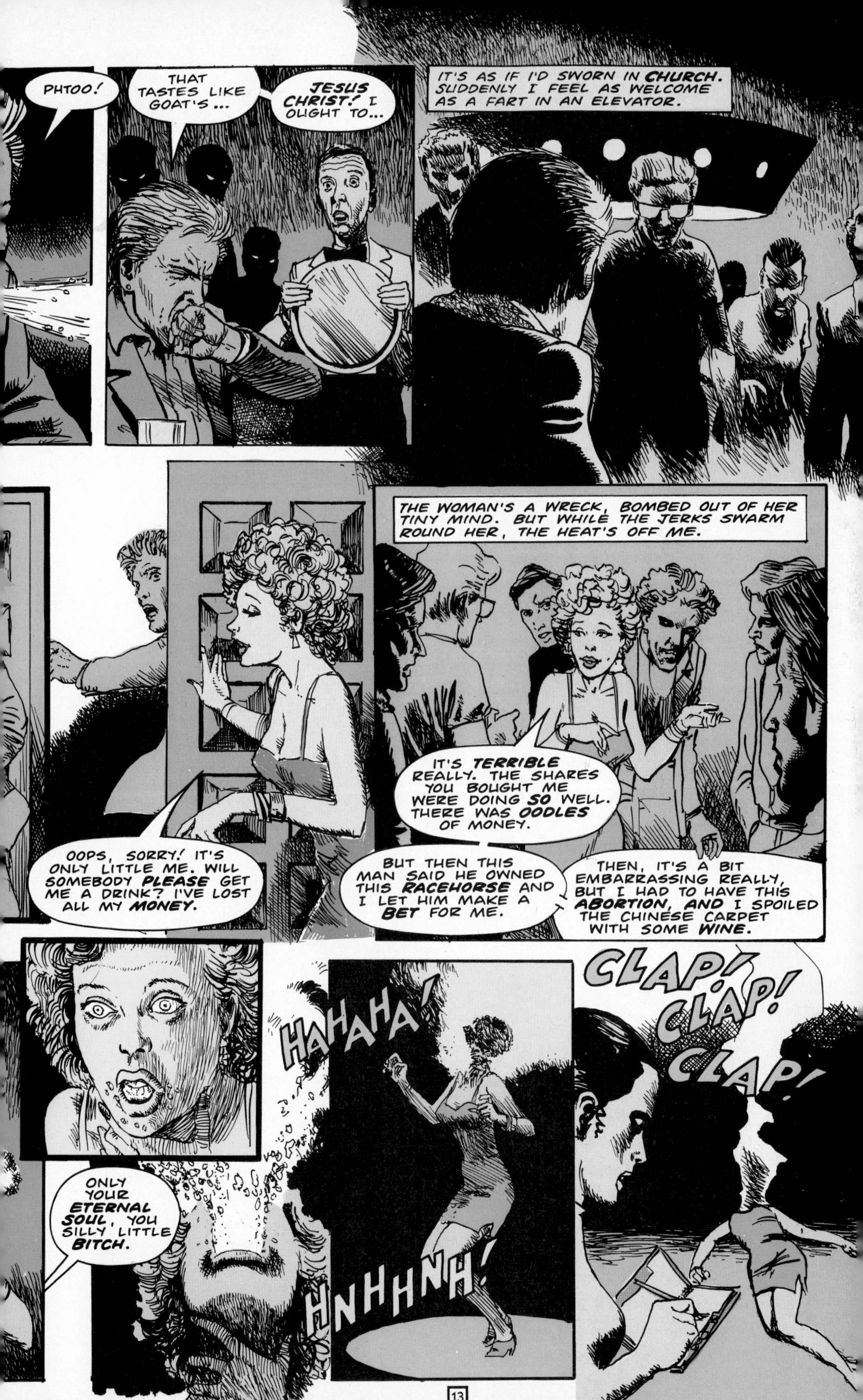
PHTOO!
THAT TASTES LIKE GOAT'S...
JESUS CHRIST! I OUGHT TO...
IT'S AS IF I'D SWORN IN CHURCH. SUDDENLY I FEEL AS WELCOME AS A FART IN AN ELEVATOR.
OOPS, SORRY! IT'S ONLY LITTLE ME. WILL SOMEBODY PLEASE GET ME A DRINK? I'VE LOST ALL MY MONEY.
THE WOMAN'S A WRECK, BOMBED OUT OF HER TINY MIND. BUT WHILE THE JERKS SWARM ROUND HER, THE HEAT'S OFF ME.
IT'S TERRIBLE REALLY. THE SHARES YOU BOUGHT ME WERE DOING SO WELL. THERE WAS OODLES OF MONEY.
BUT THEN THIS MAN SAID HE OWNED THIS RACEHORSE AND I LET HIM MAKE A BET FOR ME.
THEN, IT'S A BIT EMBARRASSING REALLY, BUT I HAD TO HAVE THIS ABORTION, AND I SPOILED THE CHINESE CARPET WITH SOME WINE.
ONLY YOUR ETERNAL SOUL, YOU SILLY LITTLE BITCH.
HAHAHA!
HNHHHNH!
CLAP! CLAP! CLAP!

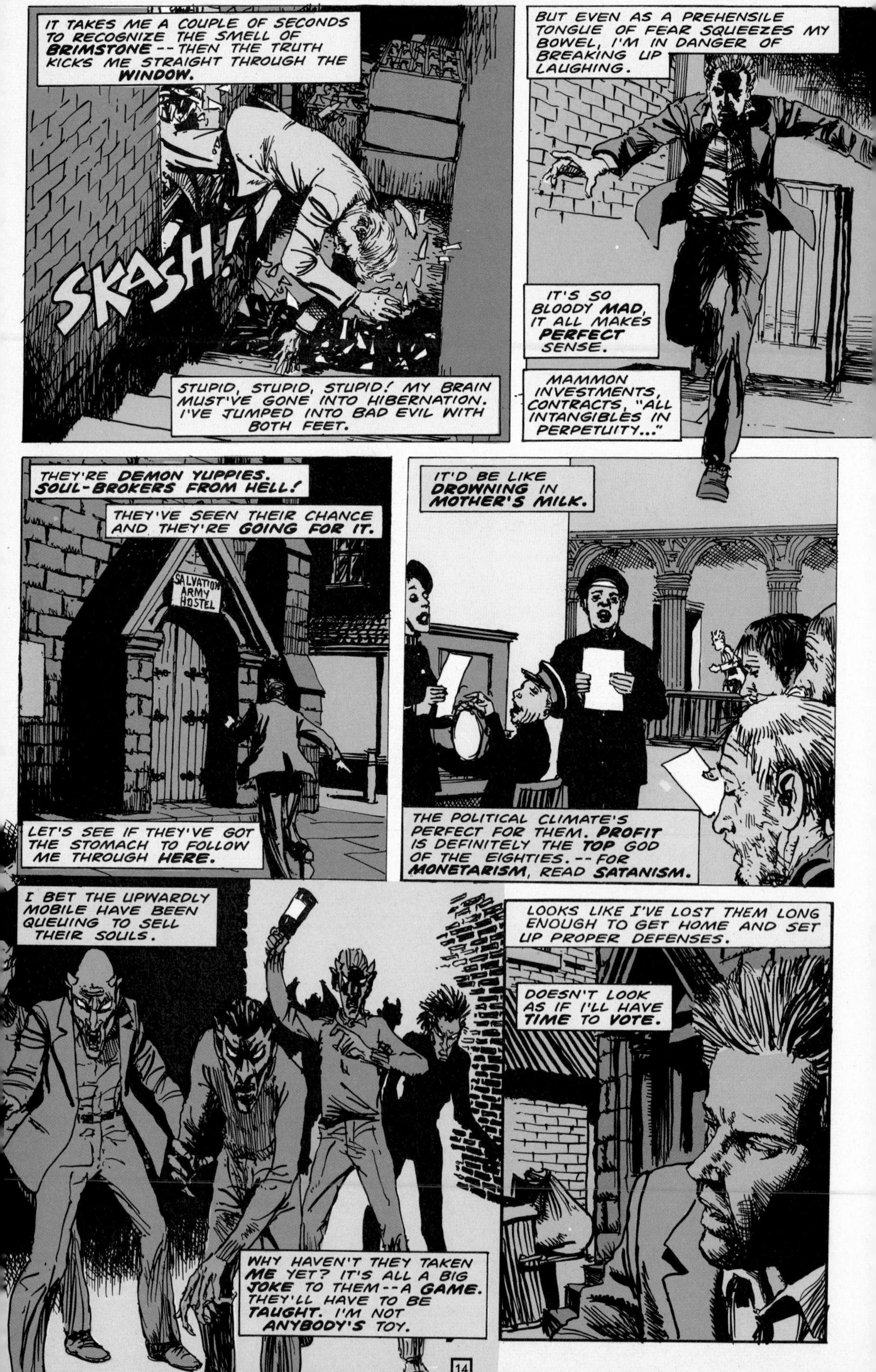
IT TAKES ME A COUPLE OF SECONDS TO RECOGNIZE THE SMELL OF BRIMSTONE--THEN THE TRUTH KICKS ME STRAIGHT THROUGH THE WINDOW.
SKASH!
STUPID, STUPID, STUPID! MY BRAIN MUST'VE GONE INTO HIBERNATION. I'VE JUMPED INTO BAD EVIL WITH BOTH FEET.
BUT EVEN AS A PREHENSILE TONGUE OF FEAR SQUEEZES MY BOWEL, I'M IN DANGER OF BREAKING UP LAUGHING.
IT'S SO BLOODY MAD, IT ALL MAKES PERFECT SENSE.
MAMMON INVESTMENTS, CONTRACTS, "ALL INTANGIBLES IN PERPETUITY..."
THEY'RE DEMON YUPPIES. SOUL-BROKERS FROM HELL!
THEY'VE SEEN THEIR CHANCE AND THEY'RE GOING FOR IT.
SALVATION ARMY HOSTEL
LET'S SEE IF THEY'VE GOT THE STOMACH TO FOLLOW ME THROUGH HERE.
IT'D BE LIKE DROWNING IN MOTHER'S MILK.
THE POLITICAL CLIMATE'S PERFECT FOR THEM. PROFIT IS DEFINITELY THE TOP GOD OF THE EIGHTIES.--FOR MONETARISM, READ SATANISM.
I BET THE UPWARDLY MOBILE HAVE BEEN QUEUING TO SELL THEIR SOULS.
WHY HAVEN'T THEY TAKEN ME YET? IT'S ALL A BIG JOKE TO THEM--A GAME. THEY'LL HAVE TO BE TAUGHT. I'M NOT ANYBODY'S TOY.
LOOKS LIKE I'VE LOST THEM LONG ENOUGH TO GET HOME AND SET UP PROPER DEFENSES.
DOESN'T LOOK AS IF I'LL HAVE TIME TO VOTE.

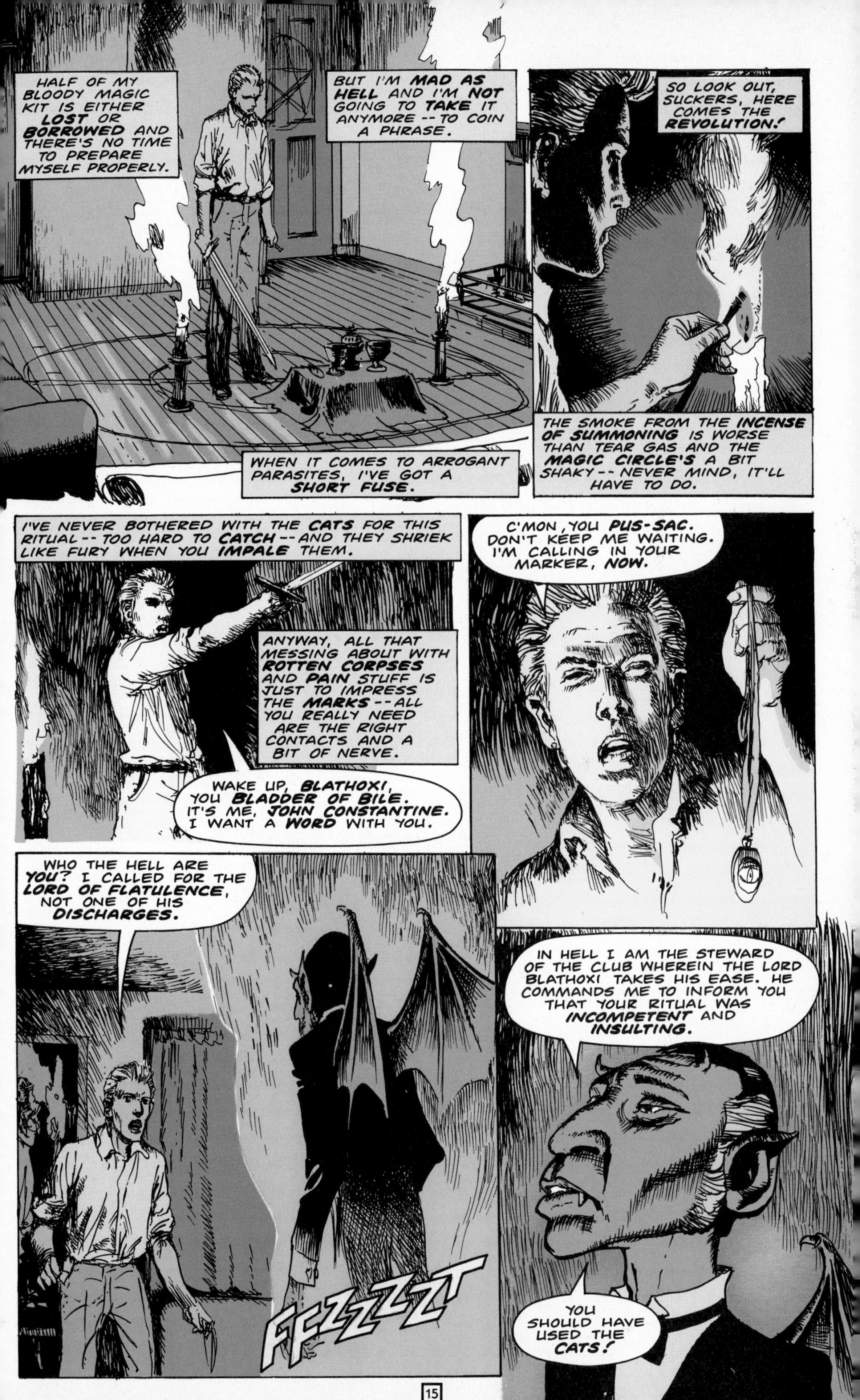
HALF OF MY BLOODY MAGIC KIT IS EITHER LOST OR BORROWED AND THERE'S NO TIME TO PREPARE MYSELF PROPERLY.
BUT I'M MAD AS HELL AND I'M NOT GOING TO TAKE IT ANYMORE -- TO COIN A PHRASE.
WHEN IT COMES TO ARROGANT PARASITES, I'VE GOT A SHORT FUSE.
SO LOOK OUT, SUCKERS, HERE COMES THE REVOLUTION!
THE SMOKE FROM THE INCENSE OF SUMMONING IS WORSE THAN TEAR GAS AND THE MAGIC CIRCLE'S A BIT SHAKY -- NEVER MIND, IT'LL HAVE TO DO.
I'VE NEVER BOTHERED WITH THE CATS FOR THIS RITUAL -- TOO HARD TO CATCH -- AND THEY SHRIEK LIKE FURY WHEN YOU IMPALE THEM.
ANYWAY, ALL THAT MESSING ABOUT WITH ROTTEN CORPSES AND PAIN STUFF IS JUST TO IMPRESS THE MARKS -- ALL YOU REALLY NEED ARE THE RIGHT CONTACTS AND A BIT OF NERVE.
WAKE UP, BLATHOXI, YOU BLADDER OF BILE. IT'S ME, JOHN CONSTANTINE. I WANT A WORD WITH YOU.
C'MON, YOU PUS-SAC. DON'T KEEP ME WAITING. I'M CALLING IN YOUR MARKER, NOW.
WHO THE HELL ARE YOU? I CALLED FOR THE LORD OF FLATULENCE, NOT ONE OF HIS DISCHARGES.
FFZZZZT
IN HELL I AM THE STEWARD OF THE CLUB WHEREIN THE LORD BLATHOXI TAKES HIS EASE. HE COMMANDS ME TO INFORM YOU THAT YOUR RITUAL WAS INCOMPETENT AND INSULTING.
YOU SHOULD HAVE USED THE CATS!

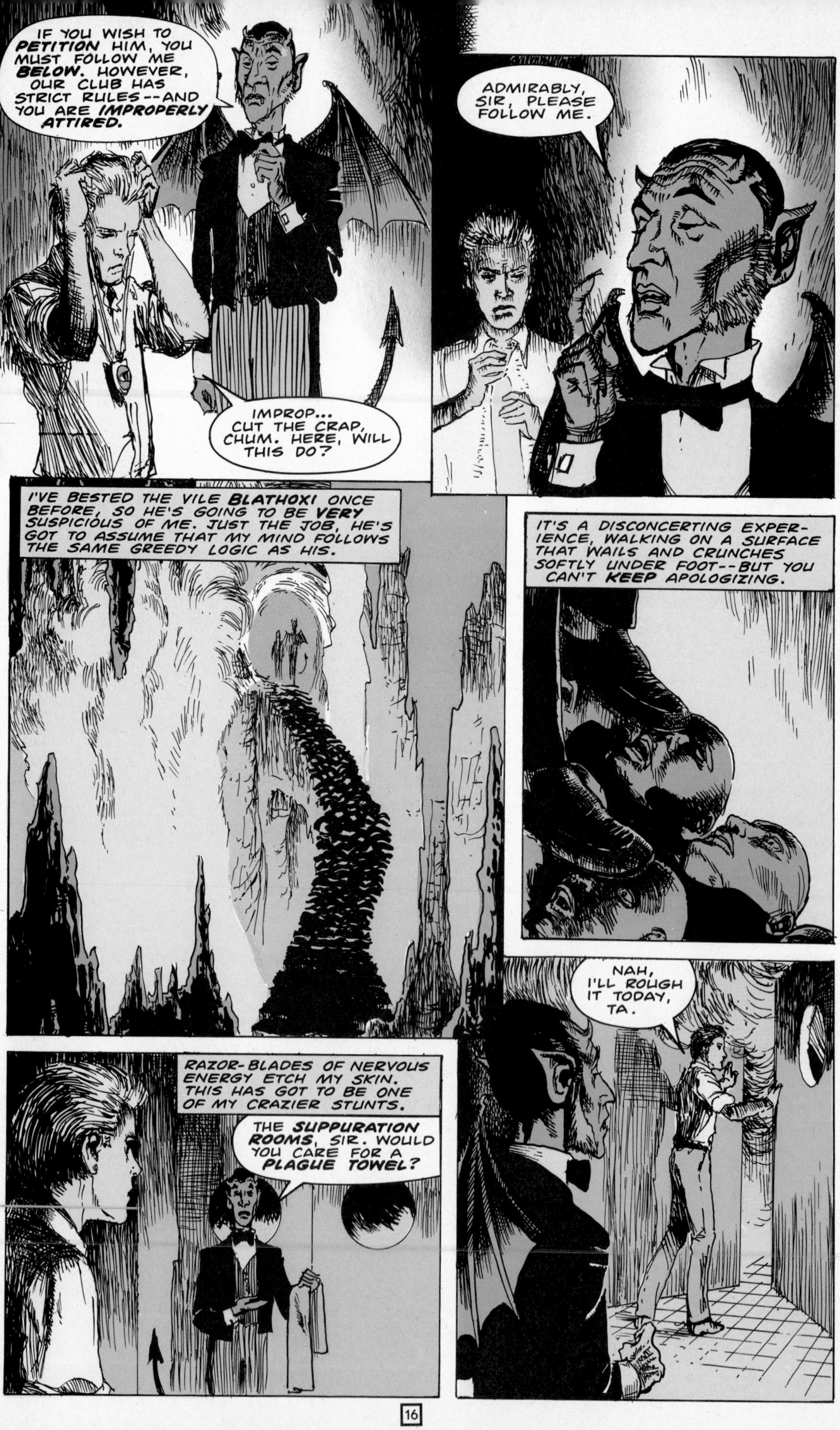

IF YOU WISH TO PETITION HIM, YOU MUST FOLLOW ME BELOW. HOWEVER, OUR CLUB HAS STRICT RULES--AND YOU ARE IMPROPERLY ATTIRED.
IMPROP... CUT THE CRAP, CHUM. HERE, WILL THIS DO?
ADMIRABLY, SIR, PLEASE FOLLOW ME.
I'VE BESTED THE VILE BLATHOXI ONCE BEFORE, SO HE'S GOING TO BE VERY SUSPICIOUS OF ME. JUST THE JOB, HE'S GOT TO ASSUME THAT MY MIND FOLLOWS THE SAME GREEDY LOGIC AS HIS.
IT'S A DISCONCERTING EXPERIENCE, WALKING ON A SURFACE THAT WAILS AND CRUNCHES SOFTLY UNDER FOOT--BUT YOU CAN'T KEEP APOLOGIZING.
RAZOR-BLADES OF NERVOUS ENERGY ETCH MY SKIN. THIS HAS GOT TO BE ONE OF MY CRAZIER STUNTS.
THE SUPPURATION ROOMS, SIR. WOULD YOU CARE FOR A PLAGUE TOWEL?
NAH, I'LL ROUGH IT TODAY, TA.

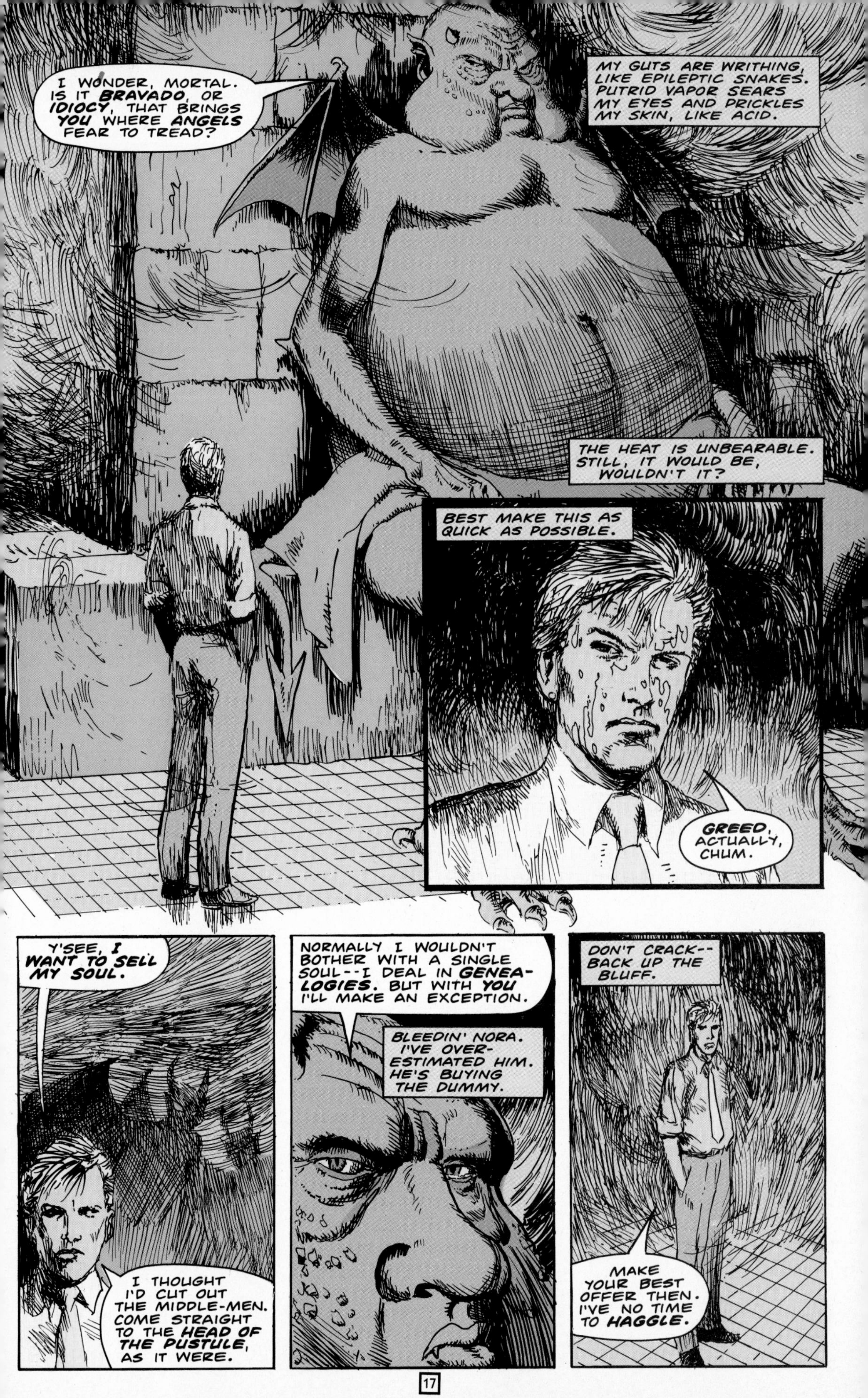
I WONDER, MORTAL. IS IT BRAVADO, OR IDIOCY, THAT BRINGS YOU WHERE ANGELS FEAR TO TREAD?
MY GUTS ARE WRITHING, LIKE EPILEPTIC SNAKES. PUTRID VAPOR SEARS MY EYES AND PRICKLES MY SKIN, LIKE ACID.
THE HEAT IS UNBEARABLE. STILL, IT WOULD BE, WOULDN'T IT?
BEST MAKE THIS AS QUICK AS POSSIBLE.
GREED, ACTUALLY, CHUM.
Y'SEE, I WANT TO SELL MY SOUL.
I THOUGHT I'D CUT OUT THE MIDDLE-MEN. COME STRAIGHT TO THE HEAD OF THE PUSTULE, AS IT WERE.
NORMALLY I WOULDN'T BOTHER WITH A SINGLE SOUL--I DEAL IN GENEALOGIES. BUT WITH YOU I'LL MAKE AN EXCEPTION.
BLEEDIN' NORA. I'VE OVER-ESTIMATED HIM. HE'S BUYING THE DUMMY.
DON'T CRACK--BACK UP THE BLUFF.
MAKE YOUR BEST OFFER THEN. I'VE NO TIME TO HAGGLE.

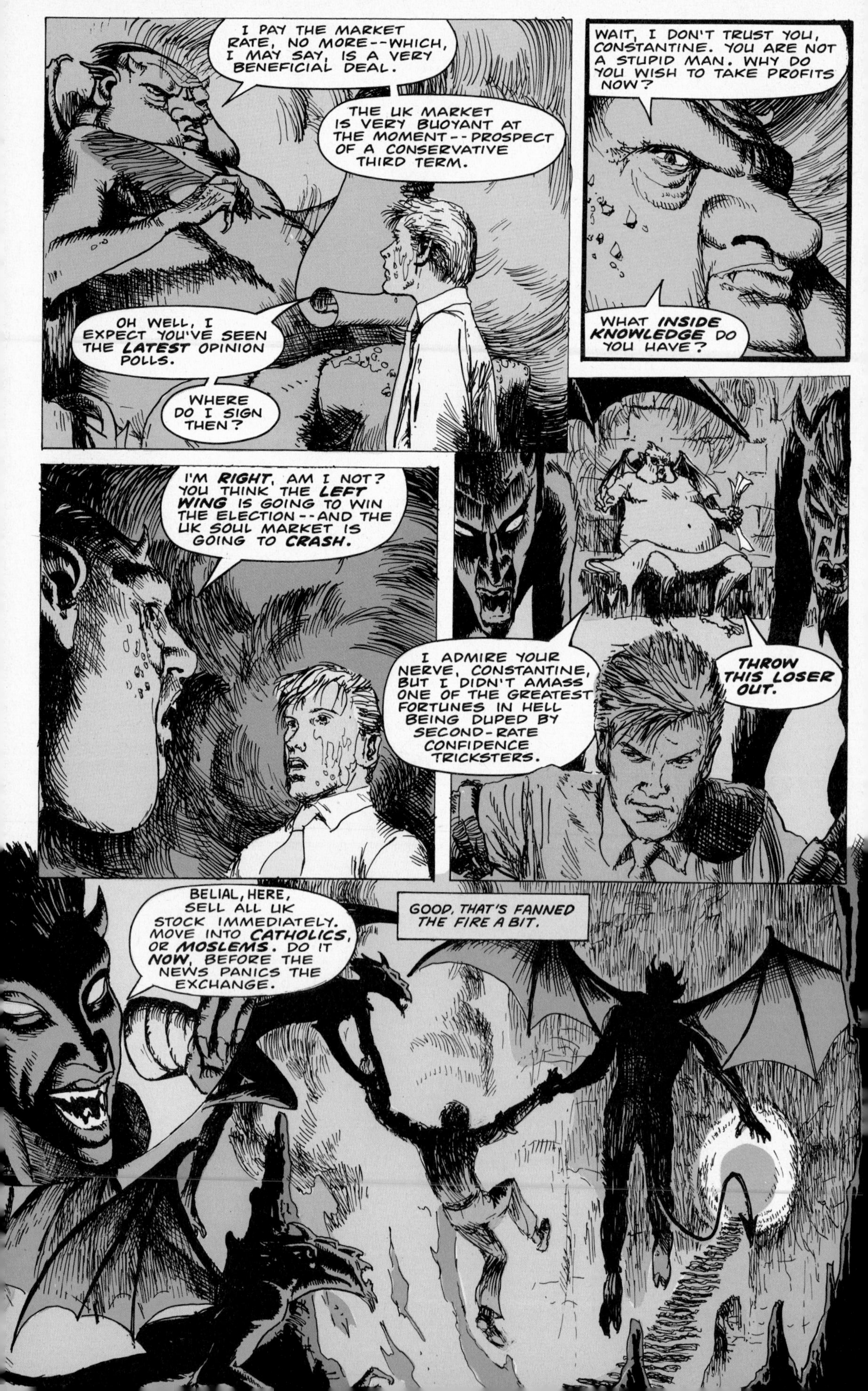
I PAY THE MARKET RATE, NO MORE--WHICH, I MAY SAY, IS A VERY BENEFICIAL DEAL.
THE UK MARKET IS VERY BUOYANT AT THE MOMENT--PROSPECT OF A CONSERVATIVE THIRD TERM.
OH WELL, I EXPECT YOU'VE SEEN THE LATEST OPINION POLLS.
WHERE DO I SIGN THEN?
WAIT, I DON'T TRUST YOU, CONSTANTINE. YOU ARE NOT A STUPID MAN. WHY DO YOU WISH TO TAKE PROFITS NOW?
WHAT INSIDE KNOWLEDGE DO YOU HAVE?
I'M RIGHT, AM I NOT? YOU THINK THE LEFT WING IS GOING TO WIN THE ELECTION--AND THE UK SOUL MARKET IS GOING TO CRASH.
I ADMIRE YOUR NERVE, CONSTANTINE, BUT I DIDN'T AMASS ONE OF THE GREATEST FORTUNES IN HELL BEING DUPED BY SECOND-RATE CONFIDENCE TRICKSTERS.
THROW THIS LOSER OUT.
BELIAL, HERE, SELL ALL UK STOCK IMMEDIATELY. MOVE INTO CATHOLICS, OR MOSLEMS. DO IT NOW, BEFORE THE NEWS PANICS THE EXCHANGE.
GOOD, THAT'S FANNED THE FIRE A BIT.

SEEMS LIKE THE PARTY'S COME TO MY PLACE.

STILL, THERE'S MORE THAN *ONE* ROAD LEADS TO *HELL*, AS THEY SAY.

GUESS I SHOULD'VE TAKEN MORE CARE OVER THE MAGIC CIRCLE.

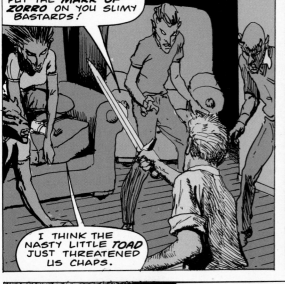

KEEP BACK--OR I'LL PUT THE *MARK OF ZORRO* ON YOU SLIMY BASTARDS!

I THINK THE NASTY LITTLE *TOAD* JUST THREATENED US CHAPS.

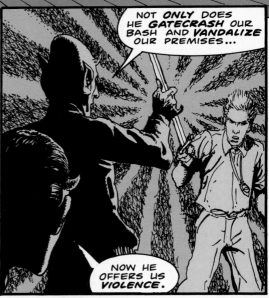

NOT *ONLY* DOES HE *GATECRASH* OUR BASH AND *VANDALIZE* OUR PREMISES...

NOW HE OFFERS US *VIOLENCE*.

I THINK WE'RE GOING TO HAVE TO *SKIN* HIM AND TAN HIS *HIDE*.

GOOD, I NEED SOME NEW SEAT-COVERS FOR THE BMW.

I S'POSE IT WAS A BIT OF A FUTILE GESTURE.

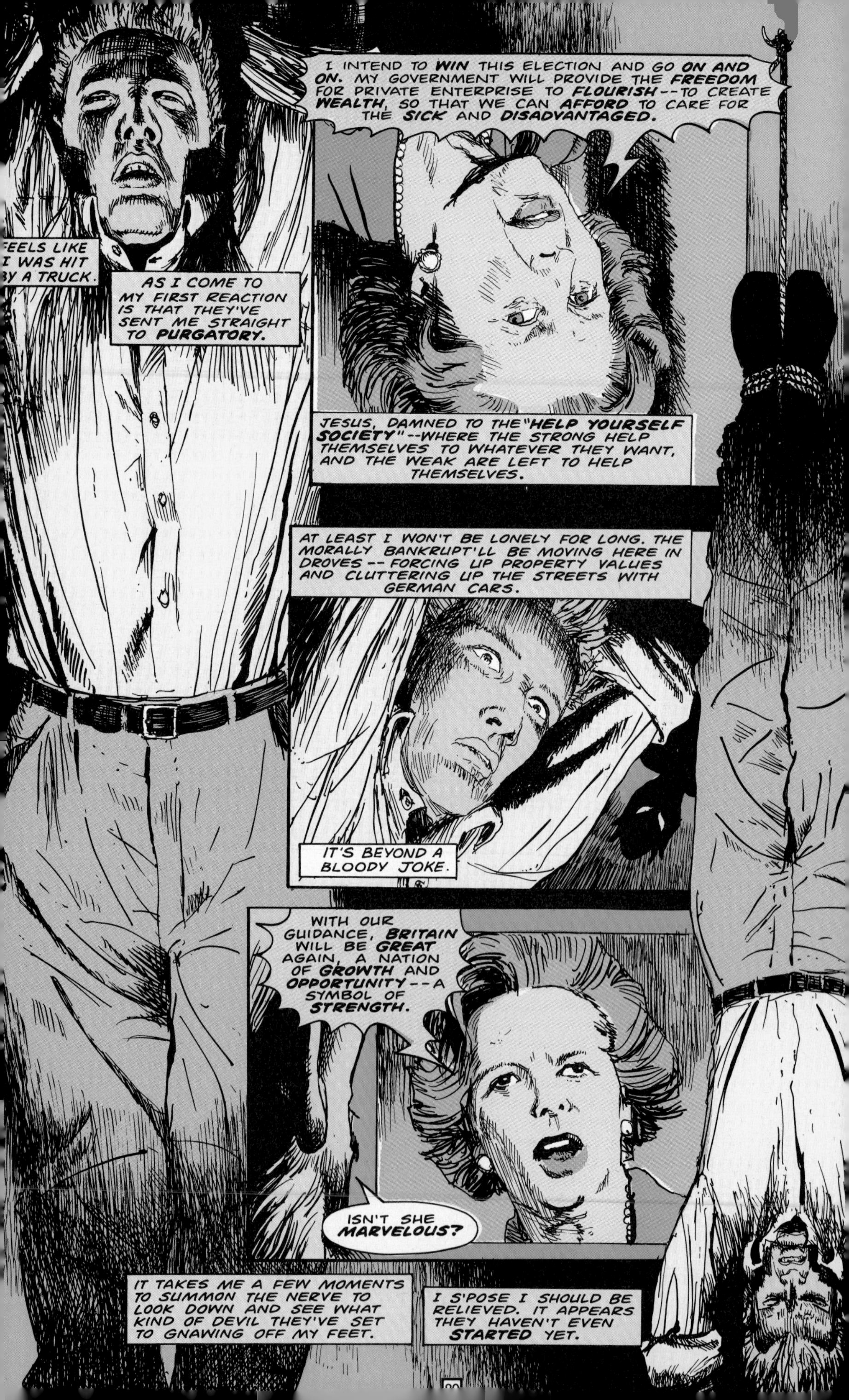

FEELS LIKE I WAS HIT BY A TRUCK.
AS I COME TO MY FIRST REACTION IS THAT THEY'VE SENT ME STRAIGHT TO **PURGATORY.**
I INTEND TO **WIN** THIS ELECTION AND GO **ON AND ON.** MY GOVERNMENT WILL PROVIDE THE **FREEDOM** FOR PRIVATE ENTERPRISE TO **FLOURISH**--TO CREATE **WEALTH**, SO THAT WE CAN **AFFORD** TO CARE FOR THE **SICK** AND **DISADVANTAGED.**
JESUS, DAMNED TO THE "**HELP YOURSELF SOCIETY**"--WHERE THE STRONG HELP THEMSELVES TO WHATEVER THEY WANT, AND THE WEAK ARE LEFT TO HELP THEMSELVES.
AT LEAST I WON'T BE LONELY FOR LONG. THE MORALLY BANKRUPT'LL BE MOVING HERE IN DROVES -- FORCING UP PROPERTY VALUES AND CLUTTERING UP THE STREETS WITH GERMAN CARS.
IT'S BEYOND A BLOODY JOKE.
WITH OUR GUIDANCE, **BRITAIN** WILL BE **GREAT** AGAIN, A NATION OF **GROWTH** AND **OPPORTUNITY**--A SYMBOL OF **STRENGTH.**
ISN'T SHE **MARVELOUS?**
IT TAKES ME A FEW MOMENTS TO SUMMON THE NERVE TO LOOK DOWN AND SEE WHAT KIND OF DEVIL THEY'VE SET TO GNAWING OFF MY FEET.
I S'POSE I SHOULD BE RELIEVED. IT APPEARS THEY HAVEN'T EVEN **STARTED** YET.

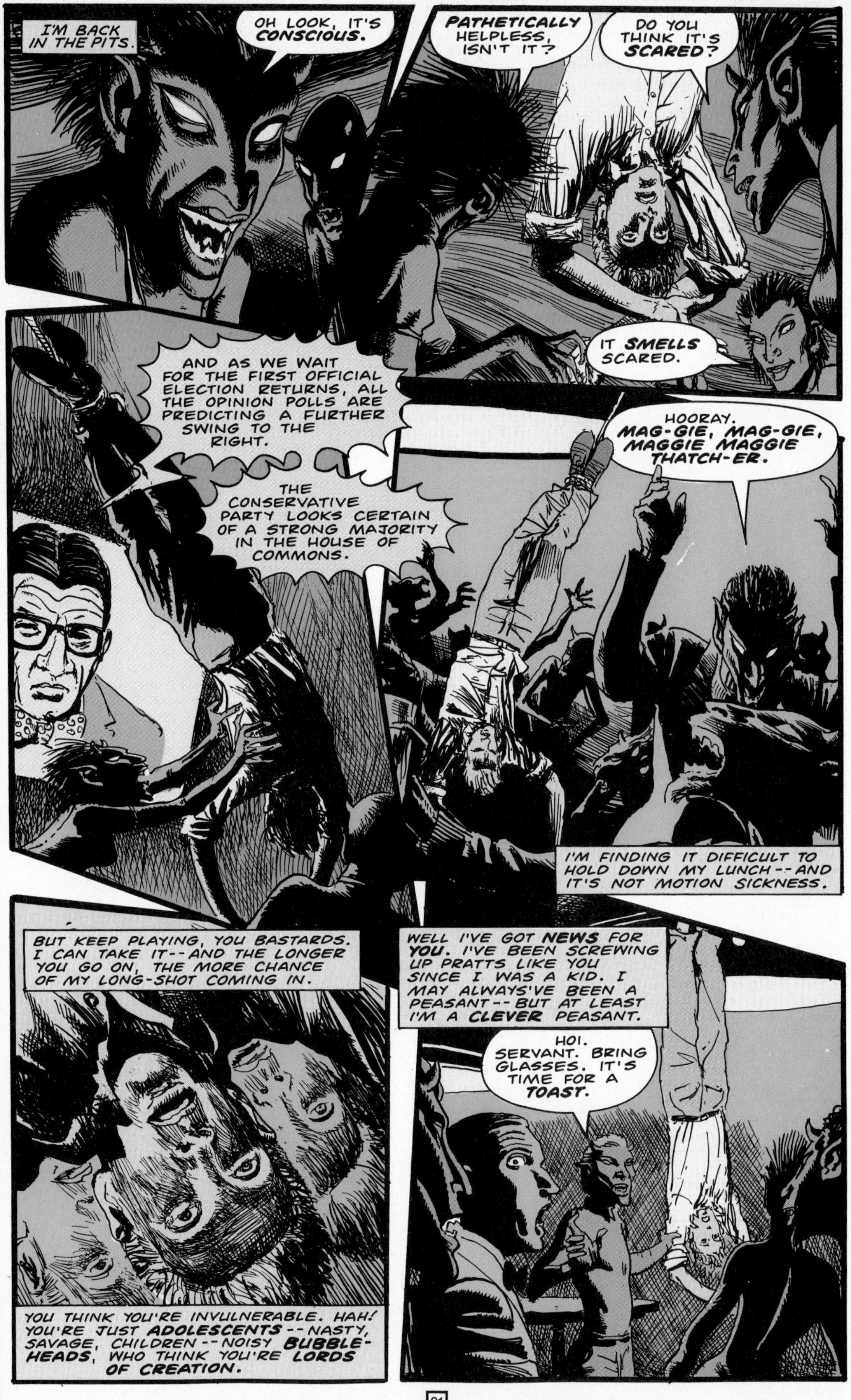
I'M BACK IN THE PITS.
OH LOOK, IT'S CONSCIOUS.
PATHETICALLY HELPLESS, ISN'T IT?
DO YOU THINK IT'S SCARED?
IT SMELLS SCARED.
AND AS WE WAIT FOR THE FIRST OFFICIAL ELECTION RETURNS, ALL THE OPINION POLLS ARE PREDICTING A FURTHER SWING TO THE RIGHT.
THE CONSERVATIVE PARTY LOOKS CERTAIN OF A STRONG MAJORITY IN THE HOUSE OF COMMONS.
HOORAY. MAG-GIE, MAG-GIE, MAGGIE MAGGIE THATCH-ER.
I'M FINDING IT DIFFICULT TO HOLD DOWN MY LUNCH--AND IT'S NOT MOTION SICKNESS.
BUT KEEP PLAYING, YOU BASTARDS. I CAN TAKE IT--AND THE LONGER YOU GO ON, THE MORE CHANCE OF MY LONG-SHOT COMING IN.
YOU THINK YOU'RE INVULNERABLE. HAH! YOU'RE JUST ADOLESCENTS--NASTY, SAVAGE, CHILDREN--NOISY BUBBLE-HEADS, WHO THINK YOU'RE LORDS OF CREATION.
WELL I'VE GOT NEWS FOR YOU. I'VE BEEN SCREWING UP PRATTS LIKE YOU SINCE I WAS A KID. I MAY ALWAYS'VE BEEN A PEASANT--BUT AT LEAST I'M A CLEVER PEASANT.
HOI. SERVANT. BRING GLASSES. IT'S TIME FOR A TOAST.

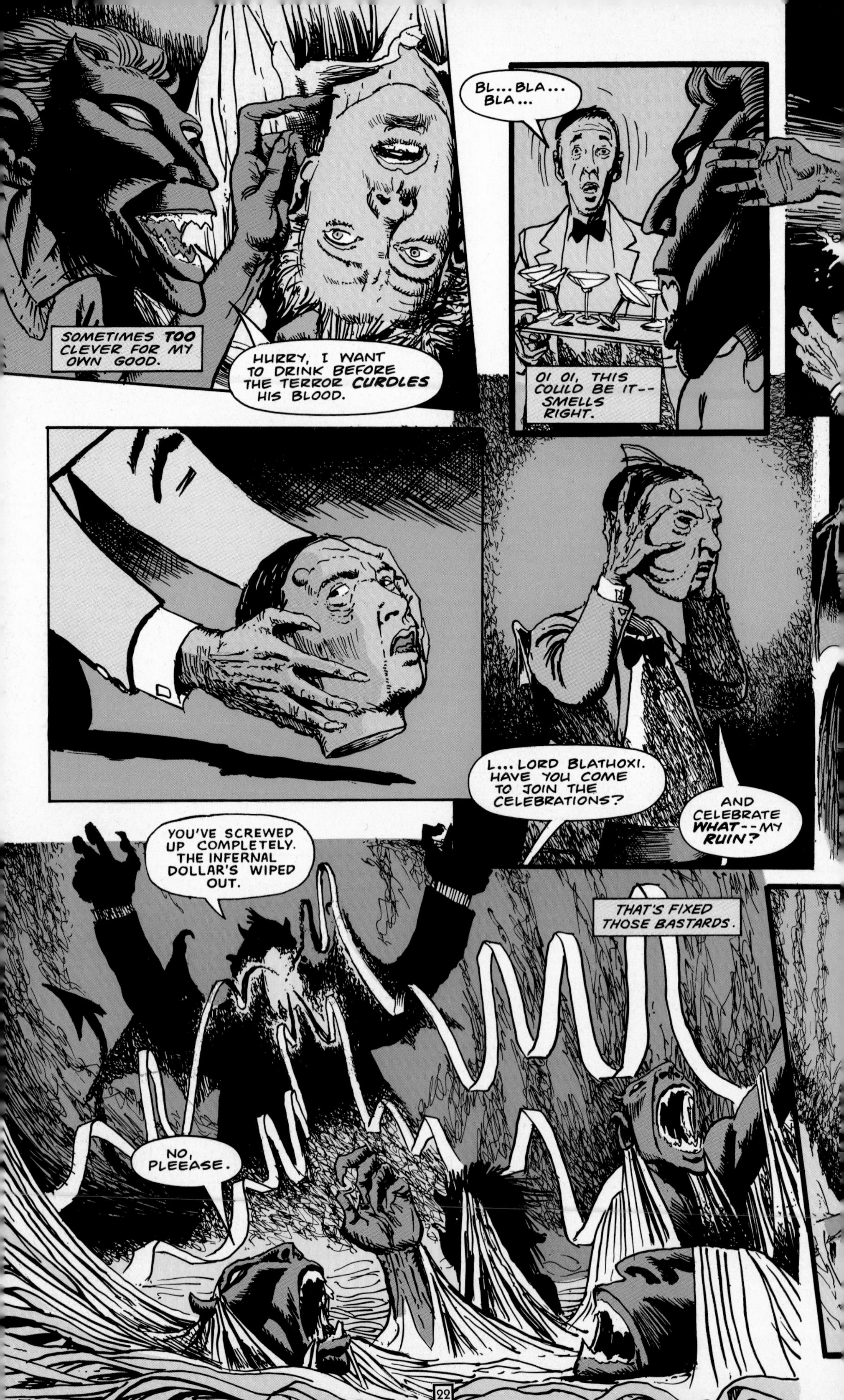
SOMETIMES TOO CLEVER FOR MY OWN GOOD.
HURRY, I WANT TO DRINK BEFORE THE TERROR CURDLES HIS BLOOD.
BL... BLA... BLA...
OI OI, THIS COULD BE IT-- SMELLS RIGHT.
L... LORD BLATHOXI. HAVE YOU COME TO JOIN THE CELEBRATIONS?
AND CELEBRATE WHAT--MY RUIN?
YOU'VE SCREWED UP COMPLETELY. THE INFERNAL DOLLAR'S WIPED OUT.
THAT'S FIXED THOSE BASTARDS.
NO, PLEEASE.

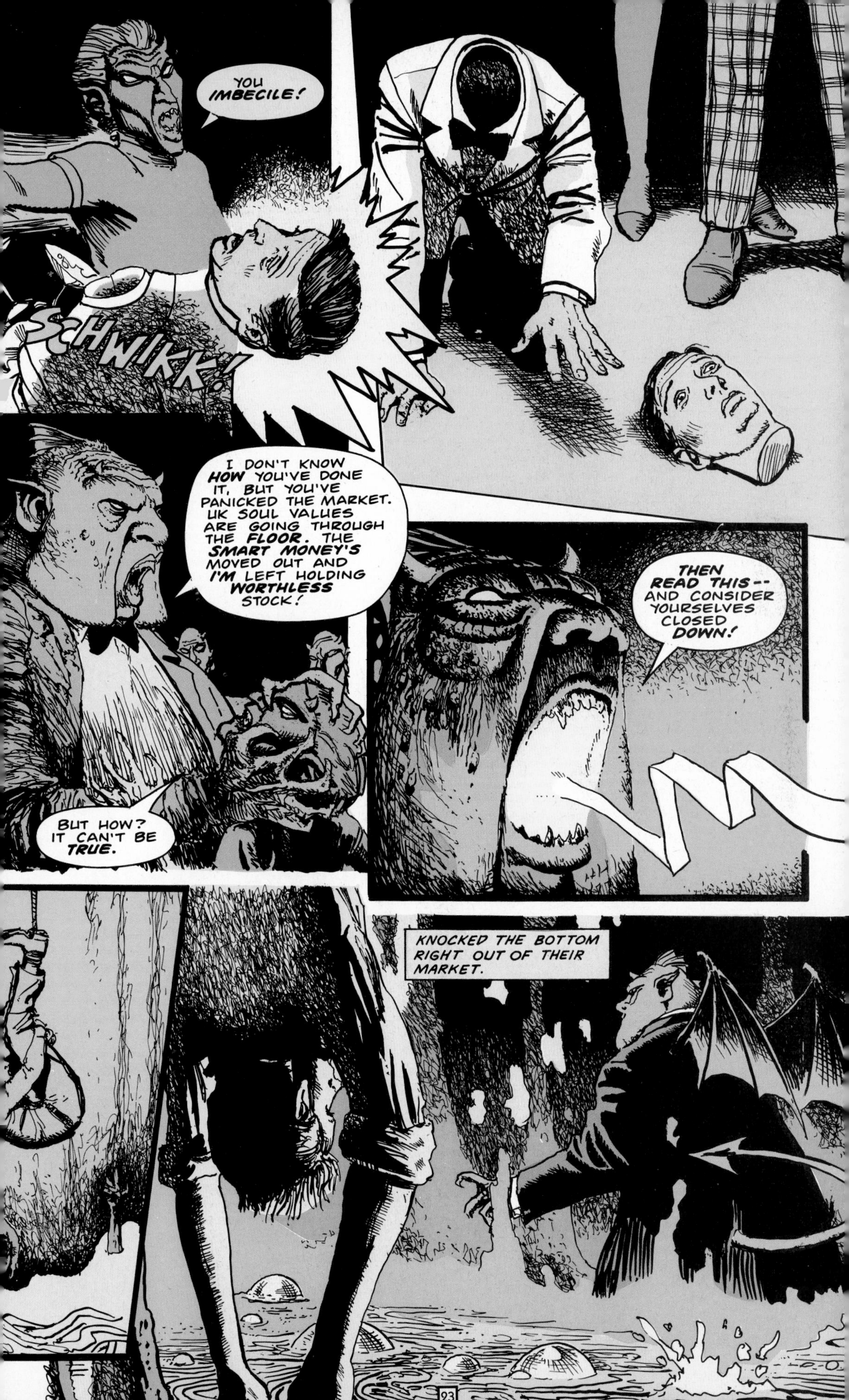
YOU IMBECILE!
SCHWIKK!
I DON'T KNOW HOW YOU'VE DONE IT, BUT YOU'VE PANICKED THE MARKET. UK SOUL VALUES ARE GOING THROUGH THE FLOOR. THE SMART MONEY'S MOVED OUT AND I'M LEFT HOLDING WORTHLESS STOCK!
BUT HOW? IT CAN'T BE TRUE.
THEN READ THIS-- AND CONSIDER YOURSELVES CLOSED DOWN!
KNOCKED THE BOTTOM RIGHT OUT OF THEIR MARKET.

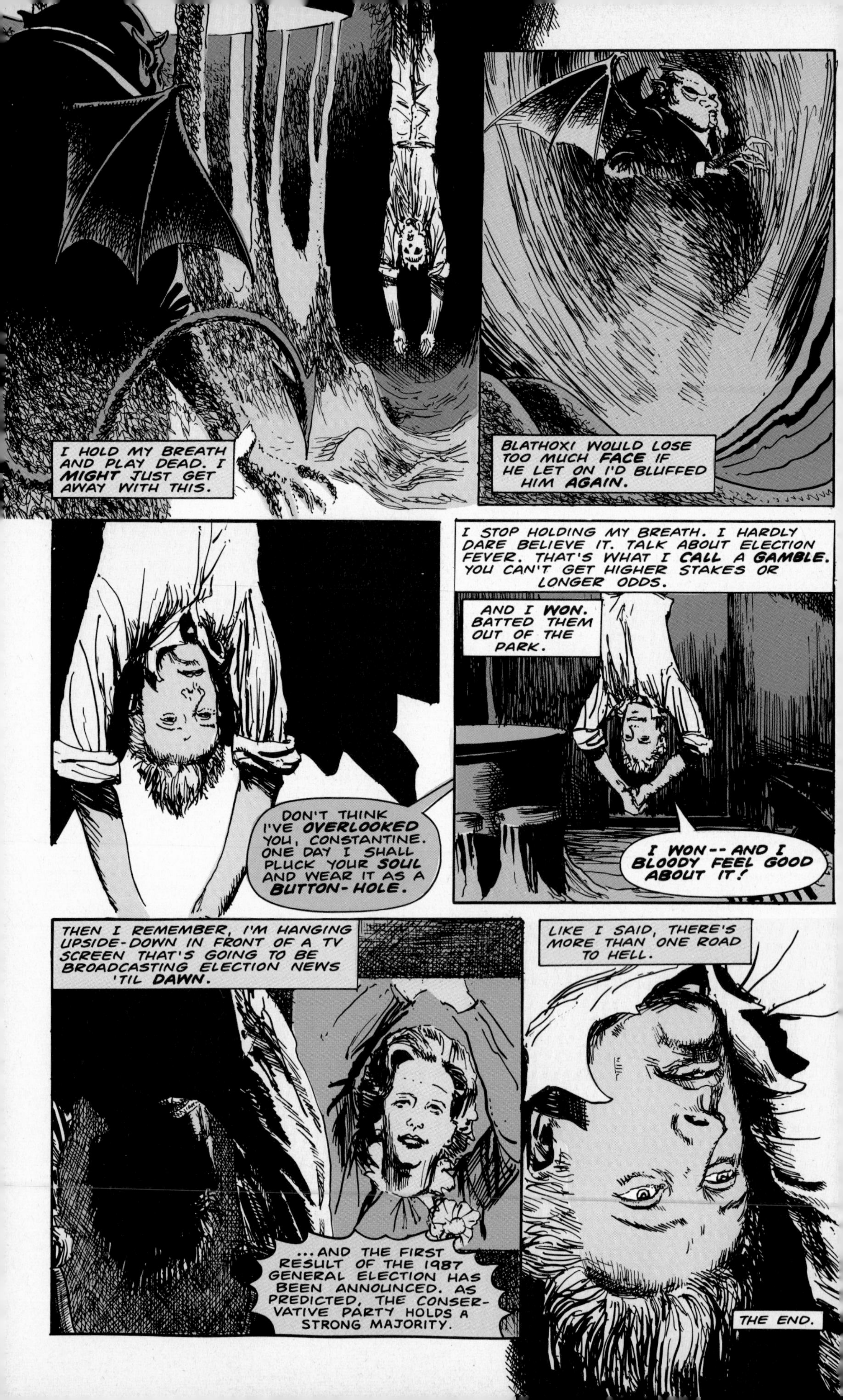

I HOLD MY BREATH AND PLAY DEAD. I MIGHT JUST GET AWAY WITH THIS.
BLATHOXI WOULD LOSE TOO MUCH FACE IF HE LET ON I'D BLUFFED HIM AGAIN.
DON'T THINK I'VE OVERLOOKED YOU, CONSTANTINE. ONE DAY I SHALL PLUCK YOUR SOUL AND WEAR IT AS A BUTTON-HOLE.
I STOP HOLDING MY BREATH. I HARDLY DARE BELIEVE IT. TALK ABOUT ELECTION FEVER. THAT'S WHAT I CALL A GAMBLE. YOU CAN'T GET HIGHER STAKES OR LONGER ODDS.
AND I WON. BATTED THEM OUT OF THE PARK.
I WON--AND I BLOODY FEEL GOOD ABOUT IT!
THEN I REMEMBER, I'M HANGING UPSIDE-DOWN IN FRONT OF A TV SCREEN THAT'S GOING TO BE BROADCASTING ELECTION NEWS 'TIL DAWN.
...AND THE FIRST RESULT OF THE 1987 GENERAL ELECTION HAS BEEN ANNOUNCED. AS PREDICTED, THE CONSER-VATIVE PARTY HOLDS A STRONG MAJORITY.
LIKE I SAID, THERE'S MORE THAN ONE ROAD TO HELL.
THE END.

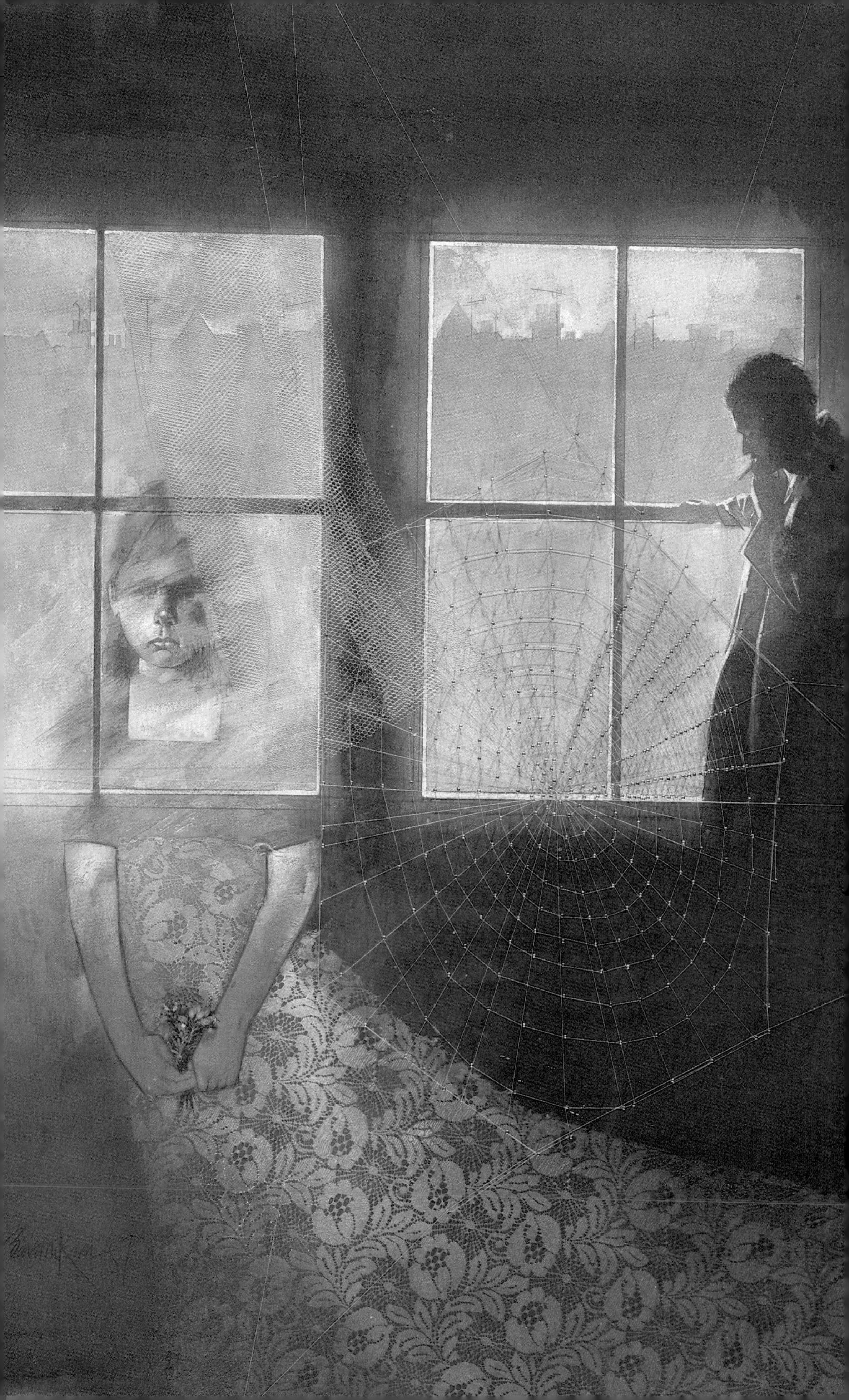

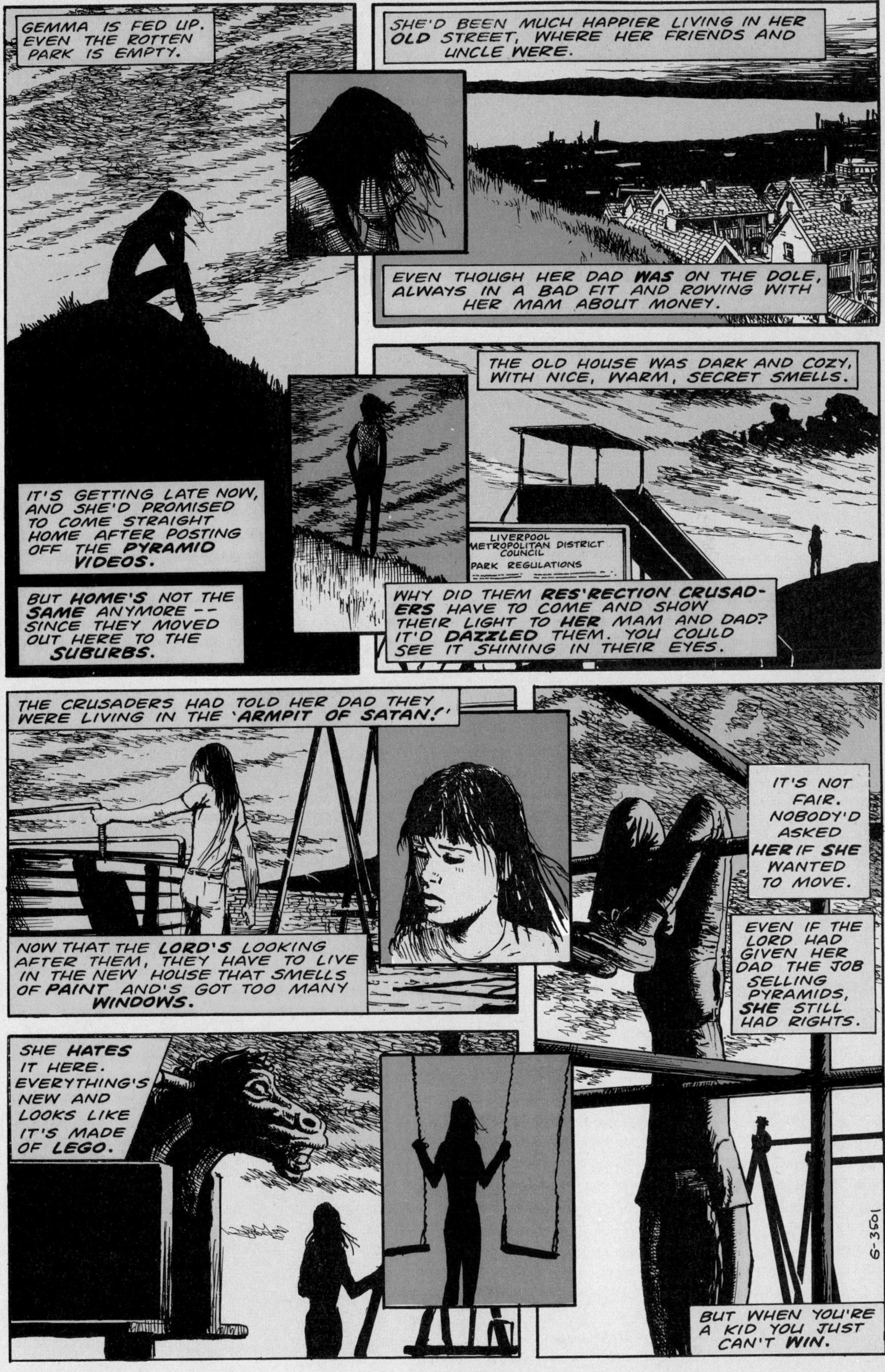
GEMMA IS FED UP. EVEN THE ROTTEN PARK IS EMPTY.
IT'S GETTING LATE NOW, AND SHE'D PROMISED TO COME STRAIGHT HOME AFTER POSTING OFF THE PYRAMID VIDEOS.
BUT HOME'S NOT THE SAME ANYMORE -- SINCE THEY MOVED OUT HERE TO THE SUBURBS.
SHE'D BEEN MUCH HAPPIER LIVING IN HER OLD STREET, WHERE HER FRIENDS AND UNCLE WERE.
EVEN THOUGH HER DAD WAS ON THE DOLE, ALWAYS IN A BAD FIT AND ROWING WITH HER MAM ABOUT MONEY.
THE OLD HOUSE WAS DARK AND COZY, WITH NICE, WARM, SECRET SMELLS.
LIVERPOOL METROPOLITAN DISTRICT COUNCIL
PARK REGULATIONS
WHY DID THEM RES'RECTION CRUSADERS HAVE TO COME AND SHOW THEIR LIGHT TO HER MAM AND DAD? IT'D DAZZLED THEM. YOU COULD SEE IT SHINING IN THEIR EYES.
THE CRUSADERS HAD TOLD HER DAD THEY WERE LIVING IN THE 'ARMPIT OF SATAN!'
NOW THAT THE LORD'S LOOKING AFTER THEM, THEY HAVE TO LIVE IN THE NEW HOUSE THAT SMELLS OF PAINT AND'S GOT TOO MANY WINDOWS.
IT'S NOT FAIR. NOBODY'D ASKED HER IF SHE WANTED TO MOVE.
EVEN IF THE LORD HAD GIVEN HER DAD THE JOB SELLING PYRAMIDS, SHE STILL HAD RIGHTS.
SHE HATES IT HERE. EVERYTHING'S NEW AND LOOKS LIKE IT'S MADE OF LEGO.
BUT WHEN YOU'RE A KID YOU JUST CAN'T WIN.
6-3501

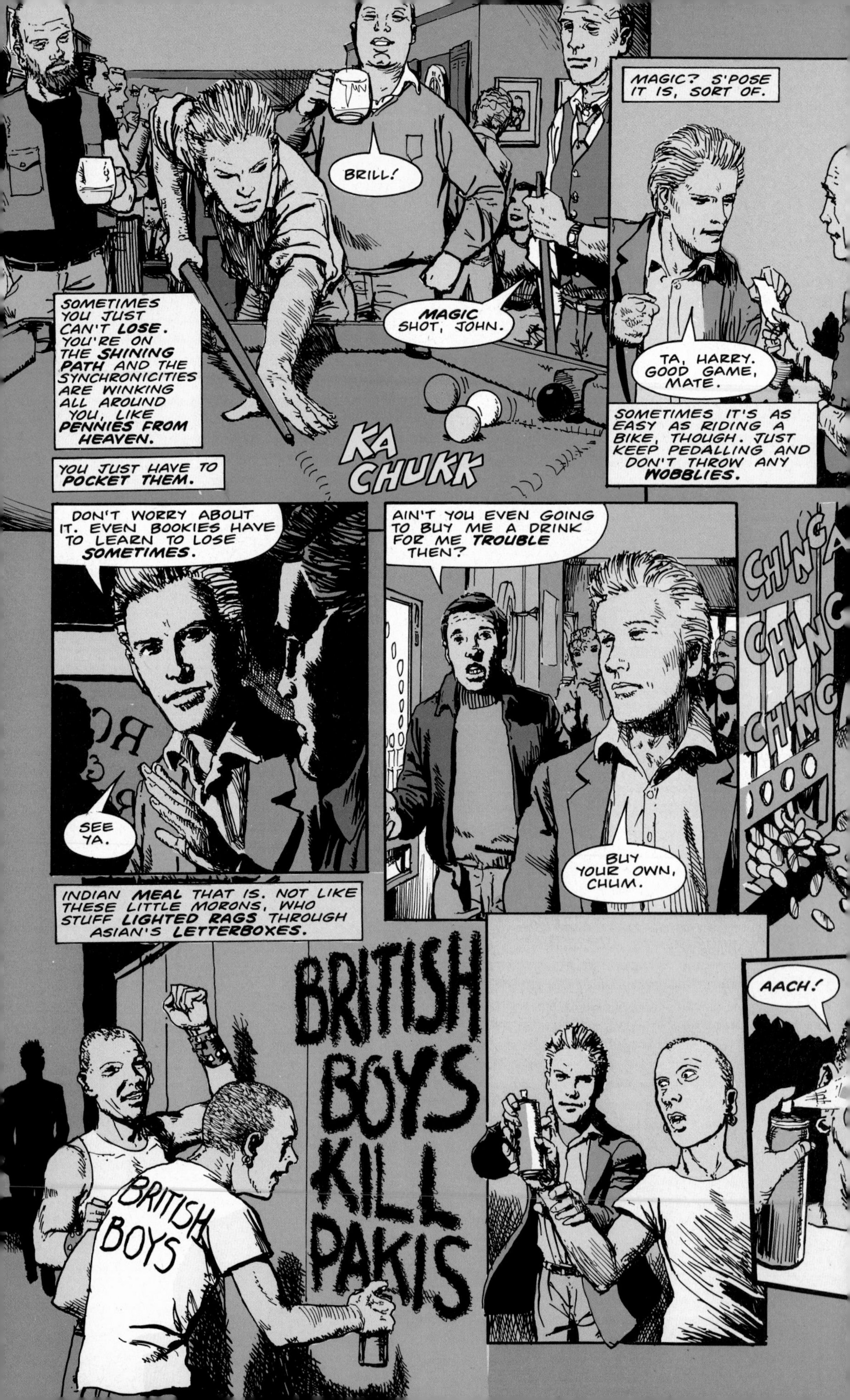
BRILL!
SOMETIMES YOU JUST CAN'T LOSE. YOU'RE ON THE SHINING PATH AND THE SYNCHRONICITIES ARE WINKING ALL AROUND YOU, LIKE PENNIES FROM HEAVEN.
YOU JUST HAVE TO POCKET THEM.
MAGIC SHOT, JOHN.
KA CHUKK
MAGIC? S'POSE IT IS, SORT OF.
TA, HARRY. GOOD GAME, MATE.
SOMETIMES IT'S AS EASY AS RIDING A BIKE, THOUGH. JUST KEEP PEDALLING AND DON'T THROW ANY WOBBLIES.
DON'T WORRY ABOUT IT. EVEN BOOKIES HAVE TO LEARN TO LOSE SOMETIMES.
SEE YA.
AIN'T YOU EVEN GOING TO BUY ME A DRINK FOR ME TROUBLE THEN?
BUY YOUR OWN, CHUM.
CHINGA CHING CHING
INDIAN MEAL THAT IS. NOT LIKE THESE LITTLE MORONS, WHO STUFF LIGHTED RAGS THROUGH ASIAN'S LETTERBOXES.
BRITISH BOYS KILL PAKIS
BRITISH BOYS
AACH!

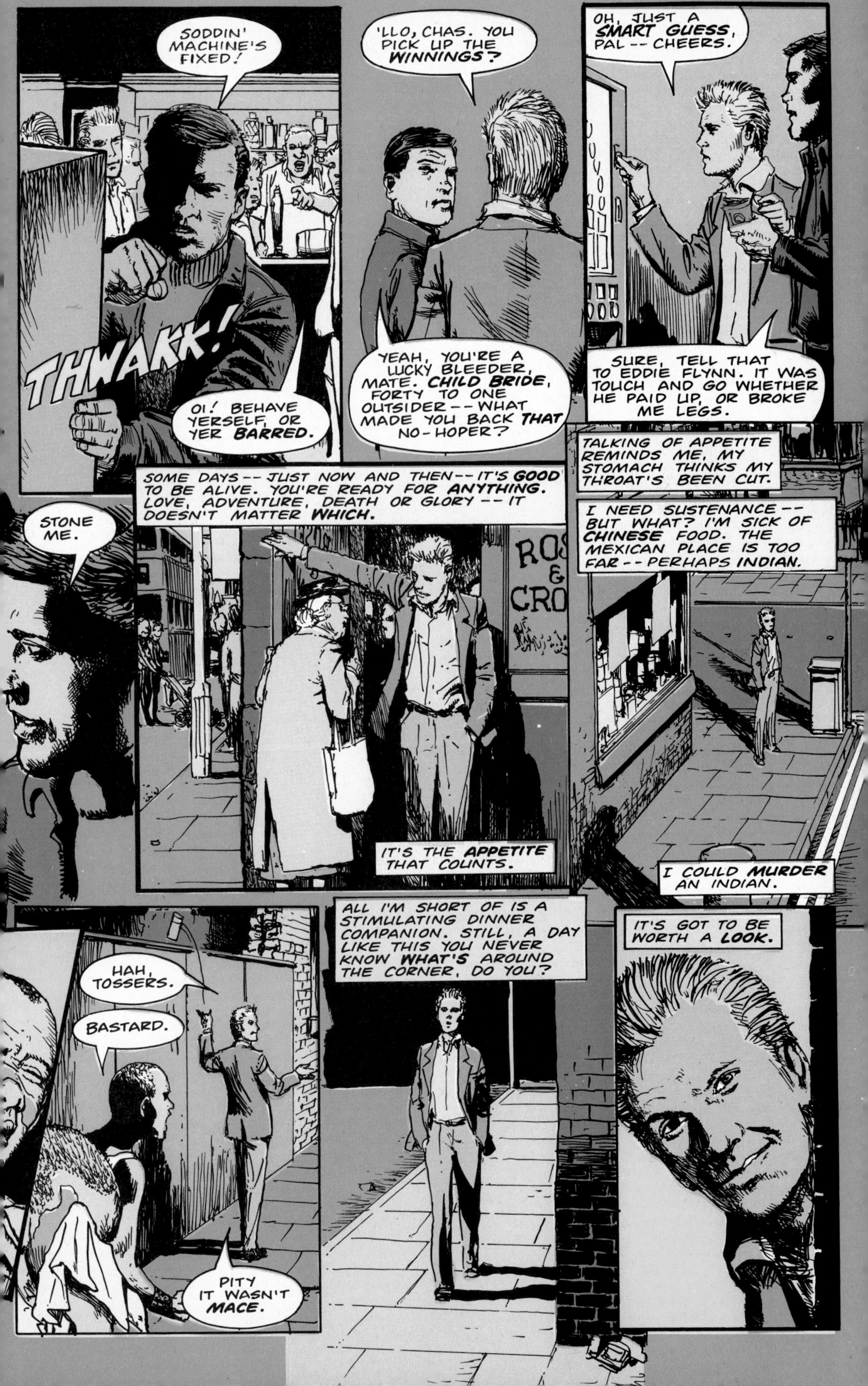
SODDIN' MACHINE'S FIXED!
THWAKK!
OI! BEHAVE YERSELF, OR YER BARRED.
'LLO, CHAS. YOU PICK UP THE WINNINGS?
YEAH, YOU'RE A LUCKY BLEEDER, MATE. CHILD BRIDE, FORTY TO ONE OUTSIDER -- WHAT MADE YOU BACK THAT NO-HOPER?
OH, JUST A SMART GUESS, PAL -- CHEERS.
SURE, TELL THAT TO EDDIE FLYNN. IT WAS TOUCH AND GO WHETHER HE PAID UP, OR BROKE ME LEGS.
STONE ME.
SOME DAYS -- JUST NOW AND THEN -- IT'S GOOD TO BE ALIVE. YOU'RE READY FOR ANYTHING. LOVE, ADVENTURE, DEATH OR GLORY -- IT DOESN'T MATTER WHICH.
IT'S THE APPETITE THAT COUNTS.
TALKING OF APPETITE REMINDS ME, MY STOMACH THINKS MY THROAT'S BEEN CUT.
I NEED SUSTENANCE -- BUT WHAT? I'M SICK OF CHINESE FOOD. THE MEXICAN PLACE IS TOO FAR -- PERHAPS INDIAN.
I COULD MURDER AN INDIAN.
HAH, TOSSERS.
BASTARD.
PITY IT WASN'T MACE.
ALL I'M SHORT OF IS A STIMULATING DINNER COMPANION. STILL, A DAY LIKE THIS YOU NEVER KNOW WHAT'S AROUND THE CORNER, DO YOU?
IT'S GOT TO BE WORTH A LOOK.

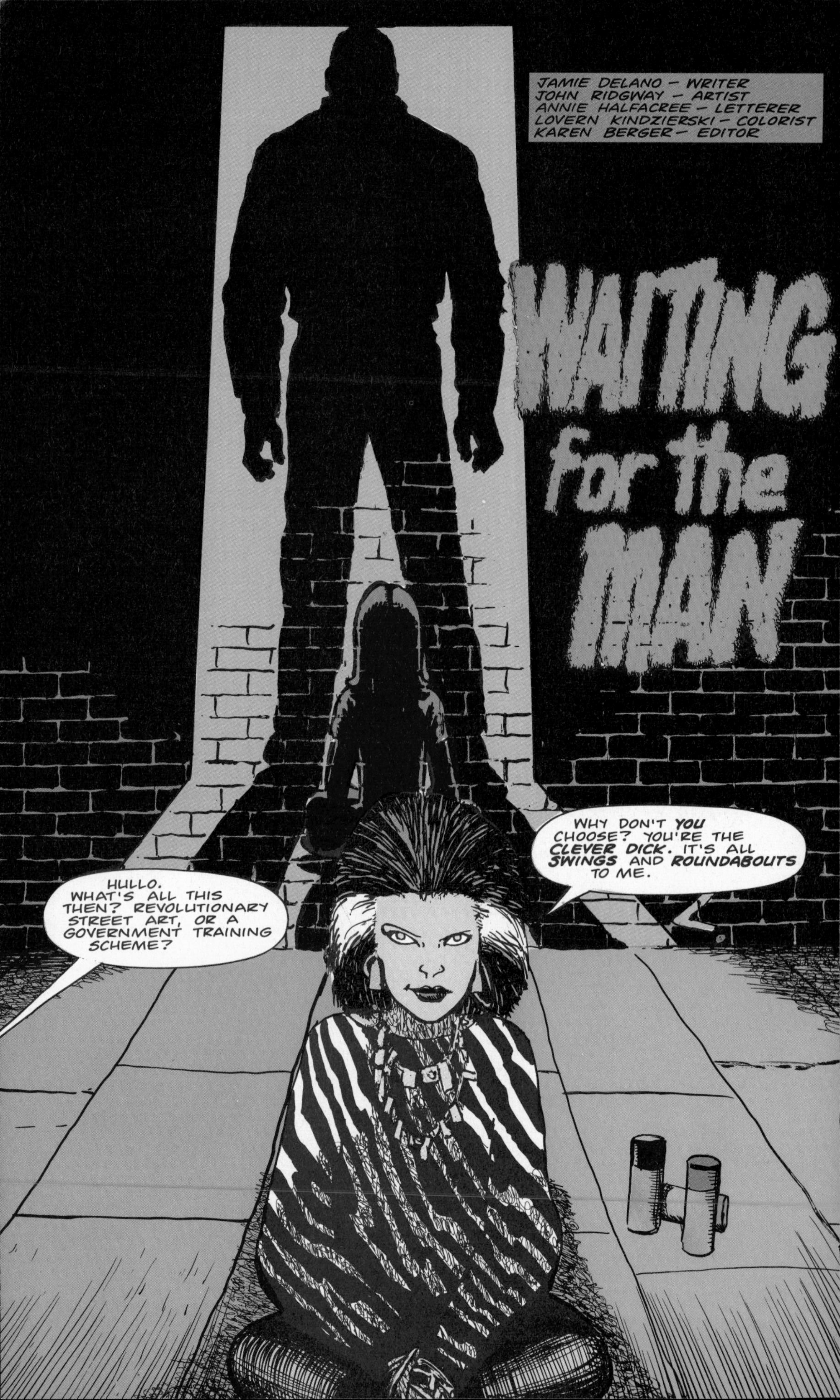
JAMIE DELANO - WRITER
JOHN RIDGWAY - ARTIST
ANNIE HALFACREE - LETTERER
LOVERN KINDZIERSKI - COLORIST
KAREN BERGER - EDITOR
WAITING for the MAN
HULLO. WHAT'S ALL THIS THEN? REVOLUTIONARY STREET ART, OR A GOVERNMENT TRAINING SCHEME?
WHY DON'T YOU CHOOSE? YOU'RE THE CLEVER DICK. IT'S ALL SWINGS AND ROUNDABOUTS TO ME.

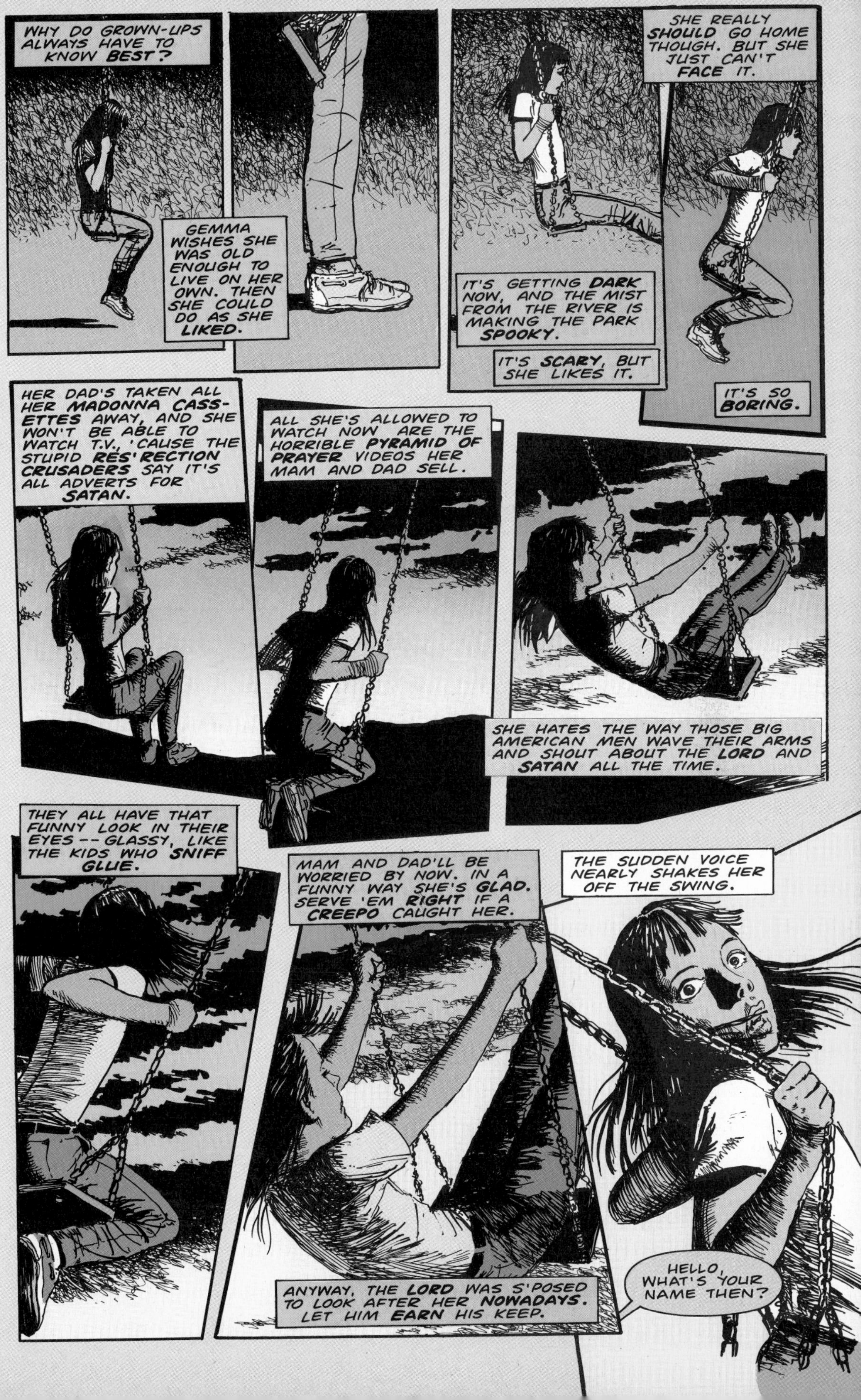
WHY DO GROWN-UPS ALWAYS HAVE TO KNOW BEST?
GEMMA WISHES SHE WAS OLD ENOUGH TO LIVE ON HER OWN. THEN SHE COULD DO AS SHE LIKED.
SHE REALLY SHOULD GO HOME THOUGH. BUT SHE JUST CAN'T FACE IT.
IT'S GETTING DARK NOW, AND THE MIST FROM THE RIVER IS MAKING THE PARK SPOOKY.
IT'S SCARY, BUT SHE LIKES IT.
IT'S SO BORING.
HER DAD'S TAKEN ALL HER MADONNA CASS-ETTES AWAY, AND SHE WON'T BE ABLE TO WATCH T.V., 'CAUSE THE STUPID RES'RECTION CRUSADERS SAY IT'S ALL ADVERTS FOR SATAN.
ALL SHE'S ALLOWED TO WATCH NOW ARE THE HORRIBLE PYRAMID OF PRAYER VIDEOS HER MAM AND DAD SELL.
SHE HATES THE WAY THOSE BIG AMERICAN MEN WAVE THEIR ARMS AND SHOUT ABOUT THE LORD AND SATAN ALL THE TIME.
THEY ALL HAVE THAT FUNNY LOOK IN THEIR EYES--GLASSY, LIKE THE KIDS WHO SNIFF GLUE.
MAM AND DAD'LL BE WORRIED BY NOW. IN A FUNNY WAY SHE'S GLAD. SERVE 'EM RIGHT IF A CREEPO CAUGHT HER.
ANYWAY, THE LORD WAS S'POSED TO LOOK AFTER HER NOWADAYS. LET HIM EARN HIS KEEP.
THE SUDDEN VOICE NEARLY SHAKES HER OFF THE SWING.
HELLO, WHAT'S YOUR NAME THEN?

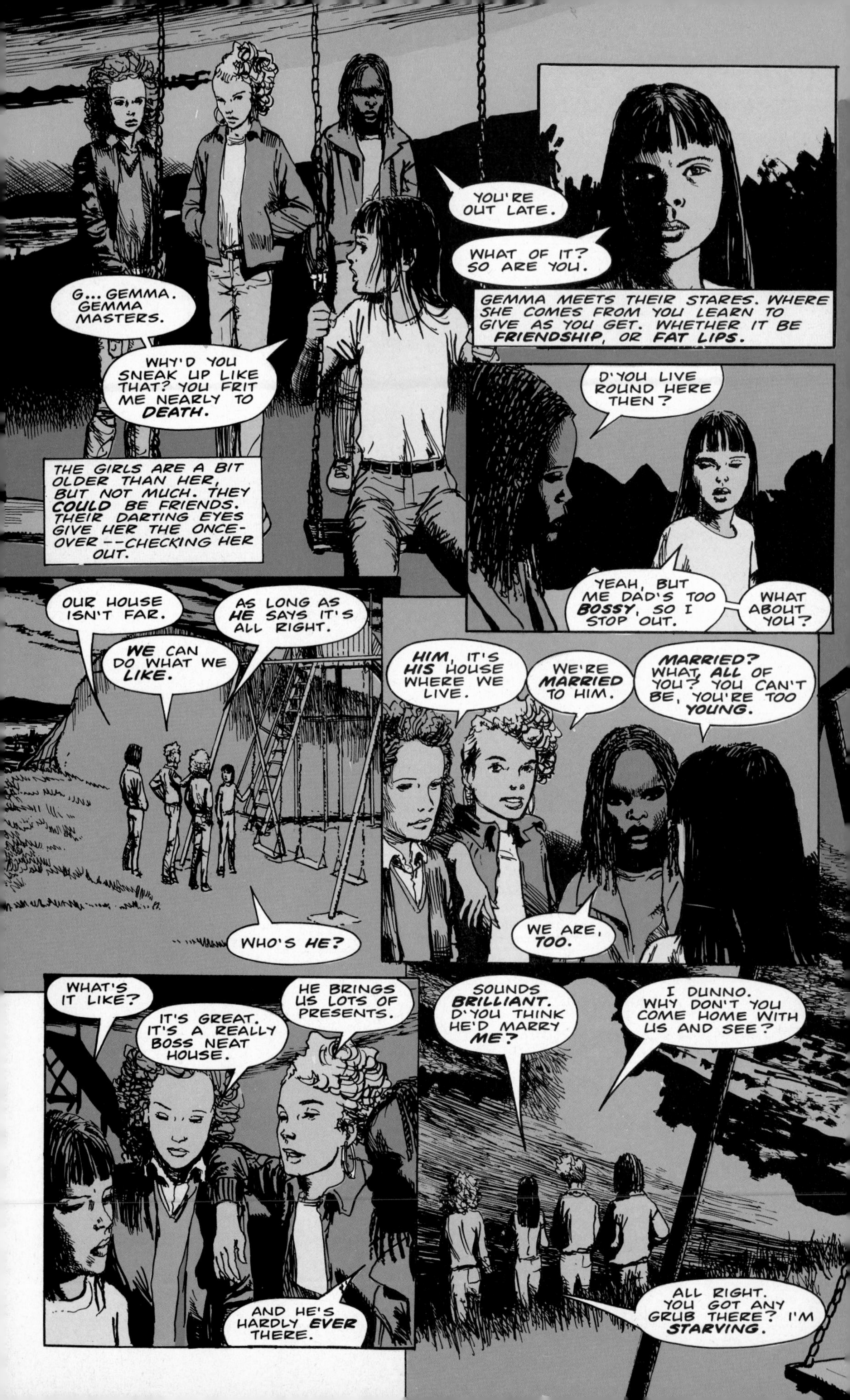
YOU'RE OUT LATE.
WHAT OF IT? SO ARE YOU.
GEMMA MEETS THEIR STARES. WHERE SHE COMES FROM YOU LEARN TO GIVE AS YOU GET. WHETHER IT BE FRIENDSHIP, OR FAT LIPS.
G... GEMMA. GEMMA MASTERS.
WHY'D YOU SNEAK UP LIKE THAT? YOU FRIT ME NEARLY TO DEATH.
THE GIRLS ARE A BIT OLDER THAN HER, BUT NOT MUCH. THEY COULD BE FRIENDS. THEIR DARTING EYES GIVE HER THE ONCE-OVER--CHECKING HER OUT.
D'YOU LIVE ROUND HERE THEN?
YEAH, BUT ME DAD'S TOO BOSSY, SO I STOP OUT.
WHAT ABOUT YOU?
OUR HOUSE ISN'T FAR.
WE CAN DO WHAT WE LIKE.
AS LONG AS HE SAYS IT'S ALL RIGHT.
WHO'S HE?
HIM, IT'S HIS HOUSE WHERE WE LIVE.
WE'RE MARRIED TO HIM.
MARRIED? WHAT, ALL OF YOU? YOU CAN'T BE, YOU'RE TOO YOUNG.
WE ARE, TOO.
WHAT'S IT LIKE?
IT'S GREAT. IT'S A REALLY BOSS NEAT HOUSE.
HE BRINGS US LOTS OF PRESENTS.
AND HE'S HARDLY EVER THERE.
SOUNDS BRILLIANT. D'YOU THINK HE'D MARRY ME?
I DUNNO. WHY DON'T YOU COME HOME WITH US AND SEE?
ALL RIGHT. YOU GOT ANY GRUB THERE? I'M STARVING.

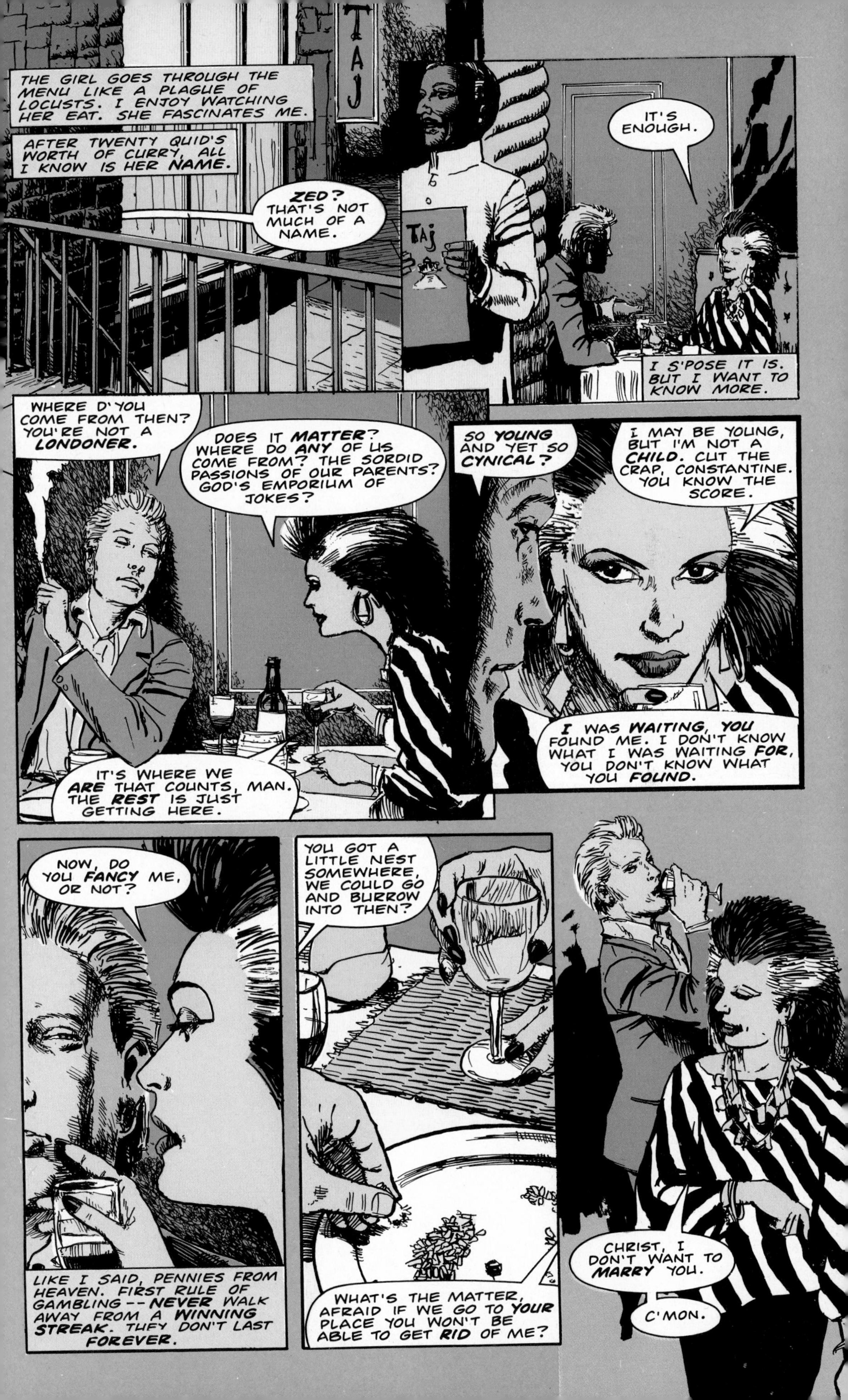

THE GIRL GOES THROUGH THE MENU LIKE A PLAGUE OF LOCUSTS. I ENJOY WATCHING HER EAT. SHE FASCINATES ME.
AFTER TWENTY QUID'S WORTH OF CURRY, ALL I KNOW IS HER NAME.
ZED? THAT'S NOT MUCH OF A NAME.
TAJ
IT'S ENOUGH.
I S'POSE IT IS. BUT I WANT TO KNOW MORE.
WHERE D'YOU COME FROM THEN? YOU'RE NOT A LONDONER.
DOES IT MATTER? WHERE DO ANY OF US COME FROM? THE SORDID PASSIONS OF OUR PARENTS? GOD'S EMPORIUM OF JOKES?
IT'S WHERE WE ARE THAT COUNTS, MAN. THE REST IS JUST GETTING HERE.
SO YOUNG AND YET SO CYNICAL?
I MAY BE YOUNG, BUT I'M NOT A CHILD. CUT THE CRAP, CONSTANTINE. YOU KNOW THE SCORE.
I WAS WAITING, YOU FOUND ME. I DON'T KNOW WHAT I WAS WAITING FOR, YOU DON'T KNOW WHAT YOU FOUND.
NOW, DO YOU FANCY ME, OR NOT?
LIKE I SAID, PENNIES FROM HEAVEN. FIRST RULE OF GAMBLING--NEVER WALK AWAY FROM A WINNING STREAK. THEY DON'T LAST FOREVER.
YOU GOT A LITTLE NEST SOMEWHERE, WE COULD GO AND BURROW INTO THEN?
WHAT'S THE MATTER, AFRAID IF WE GO TO YOUR PLACE YOU WON'T BE ABLE TO GET RID OF ME?
CHRIST, I DON'T WANT TO MARRY YOU.
C'MON.

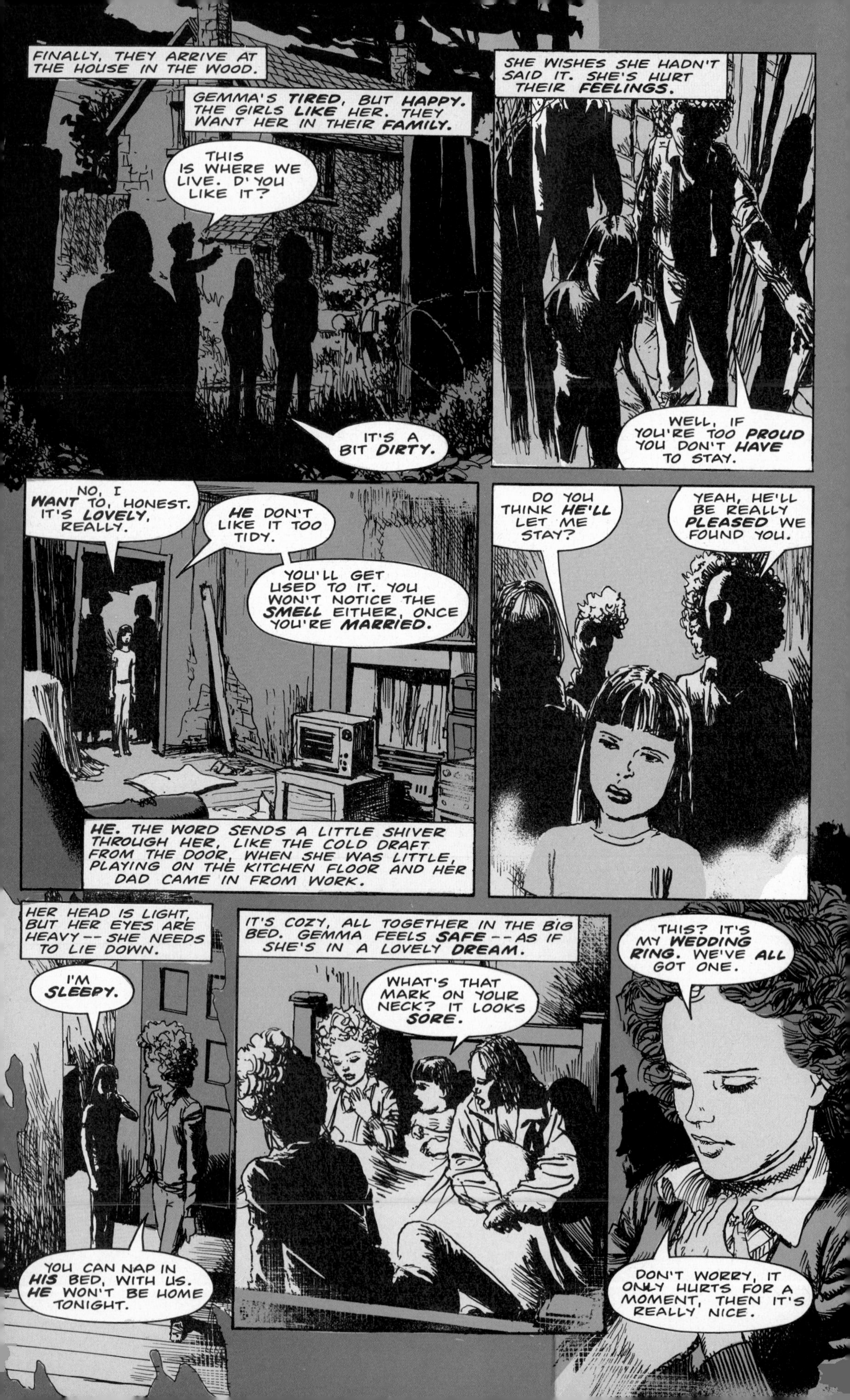
FINALLY, THEY ARRIVE AT THE HOUSE IN THE WOOD.
GEMMA'S TIRED, BUT HAPPY. THE GIRLS LIKE HER. THEY WANT HER IN THEIR FAMILY.
THIS IS WHERE WE LIVE. D'YOU LIKE IT?
IT'S A BIT DIRTY.
SHE WISHES SHE HADN'T SAID IT. SHE'S HURT THEIR FEELINGS.
WELL, IF YOU'RE TOO PROUD YOU DON'T HAVE TO STAY.
NO, I WANT TO, HONEST. IT'S LOVELY, REALLY.
HE DON'T LIKE IT TOO TIDY.
YOU'LL GET USED TO IT. YOU WON'T NOTICE THE SMELL EITHER, ONCE YOU'RE MARRIED.
HE. THE WORD SENDS A LITTLE SHIVER THROUGH HER, LIKE THE COLD DRAFT FROM THE DOOR, WHEN SHE WAS LITTLE, PLAYING ON THE KITCHEN FLOOR AND HER DAD CAME IN FROM WORK.
DO YOU THINK HE'LL LET ME STAY?
YEAH, HE'LL BE REALLY PLEASED WE FOUND YOU.
HER HEAD IS LIGHT, BUT HER EYES ARE HEAVY -- SHE NEEDS TO LIE DOWN.
I'M SLEEPY.
YOU CAN NAP IN HIS BED, WITH US. HE WON'T BE HOME TONIGHT.
IT'S COZY, ALL TOGETHER IN THE BIG BED. GEMMA FEELS SAFE -- AS IF SHE'S IN A LOVELY DREAM.
WHAT'S THAT MARK ON YOUR NECK? IT LOOKS SORE.
THIS? IT'S MY WEDDING RING. WE'VE ALL GOT ONE.
DON'T WORRY, IT ONLY HURTS FOR A MOMENT, THEN IT'S REALLY NICE.

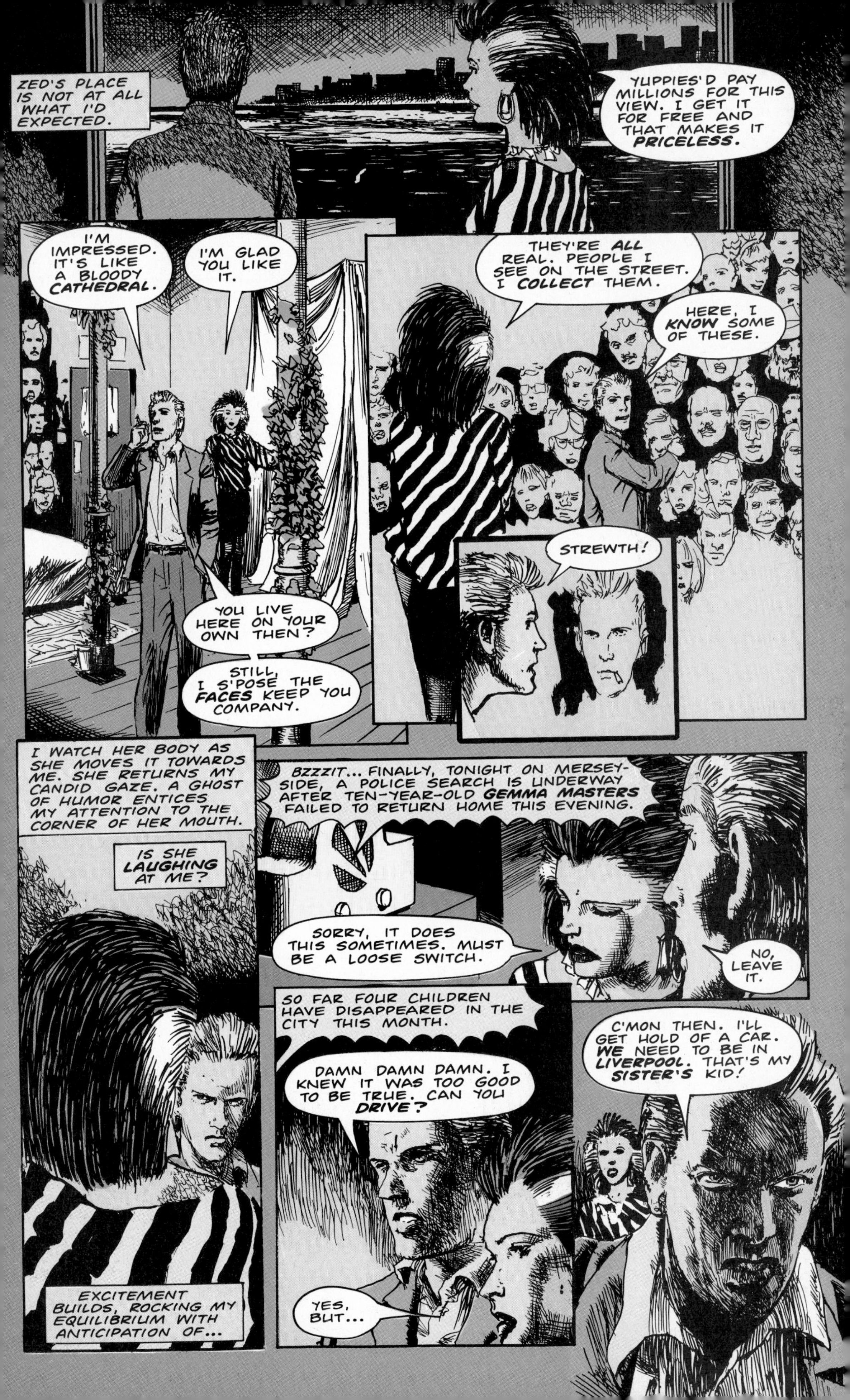
ZED'S PLACE IS NOT AT ALL WHAT I'D EXPECTED.
YUPPIES'D PAY MILLIONS FOR THIS VIEW. I GET IT FOR FREE AND THAT MAKES IT PRICELESS.
I'M IMPRESSED. IT'S LIKE A BLOODY CATHEDRAL.
I'M GLAD YOU LIKE IT.
YOU LIVE HERE ON YOUR OWN THEN?
STILL, I S'POSE THE FACES KEEP YOU COMPANY.
THEY'RE ALL REAL. PEOPLE I SEE ON THE STREET. I COLLECT THEM.
HERE, I KNOW SOME OF THESE.
STREWTH!
I WATCH HER BODY AS SHE MOVES IT TOWARDS ME. SHE RETURNS MY CANDID GAZE. A GHOST OF HUMOR ENTICES MY ATTENTION TO THE CORNER OF HER MOUTH.
IS SHE LAUGHING AT ME?
EXCITEMENT BUILDS, ROCKING MY EQUILIBRIUM WITH ANTICIPATION OF...
BZZZIT... FINALLY, TONIGHT ON MERSEY-SIDE, A POLICE SEARCH IS UNDERWAY AFTER TEN-YEAR-OLD GEMMA MASTERS FAILED TO RETURN HOME THIS EVENING.
SORRY, IT DOES THIS SOMETIMES. MUST BE A LOOSE SWITCH.
NO, LEAVE IT.
SO FAR FOUR CHILDREN HAVE DISAPPEARED IN THE CITY THIS MONTH.
DAMN DAMN DAMN. I KNEW IT WAS TOO GOOD TO BE TRUE. CAN YOU DRIVE?
YES, BUT...
C'MON THEN. I'LL GET HOLD OF A CAR. WE NEED TO BE IN LIVERPOOL. THAT'S MY SISTER'S KID!

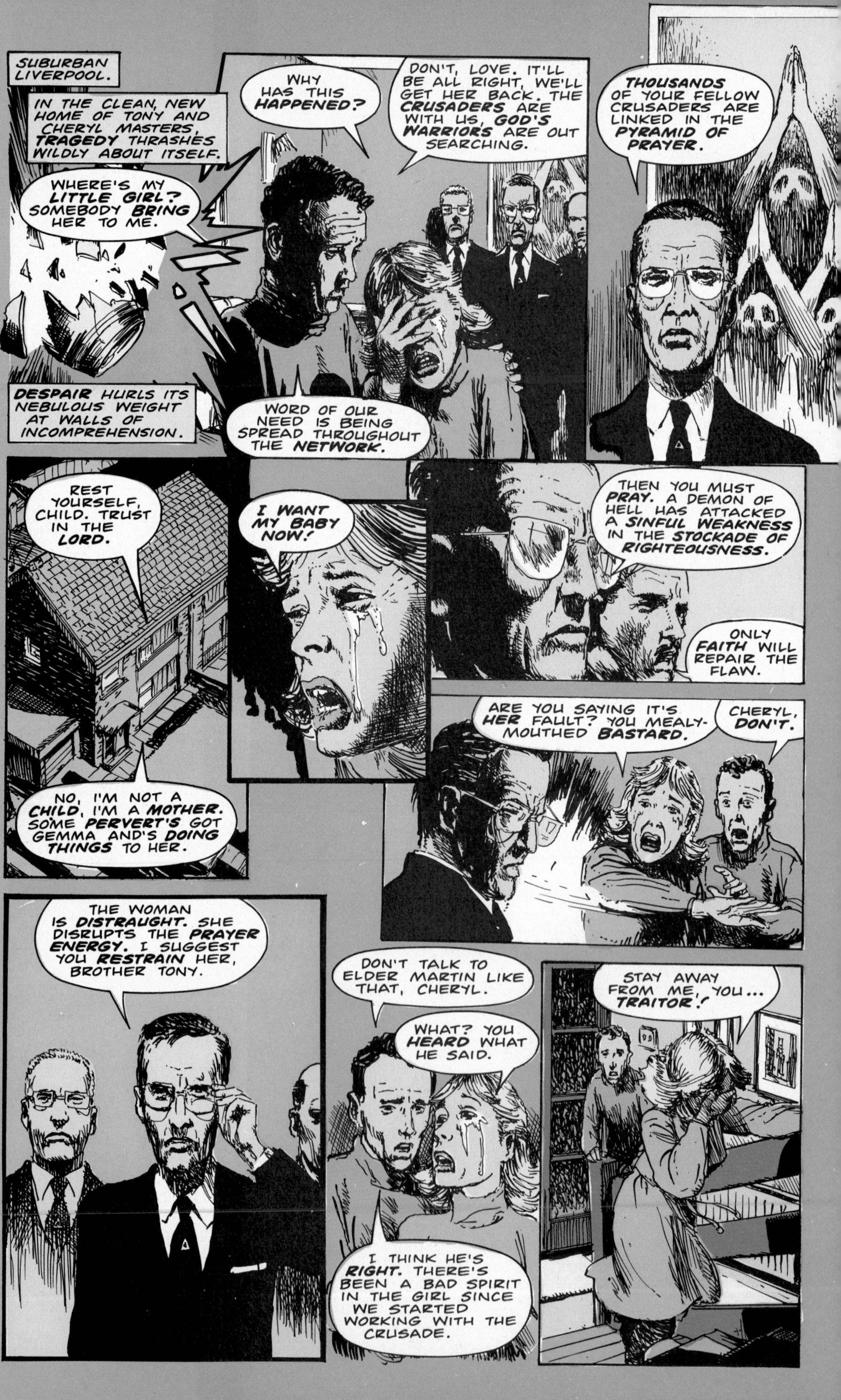

SUBURBAN LIVERPOOL.
IN THE CLEAN, NEW HOME OF TONY AND CHERYL MASTERS, TRAGEDY THRASHES WILDLY ABOUT ITSELF.
WHERE'S MY LITTLE GIRL? SOMEBODY BRING HER TO ME.
WHY HAS THIS HAPPENED?
DON'T, LOVE. IT'LL BE ALL RIGHT, WE'LL GET HER BACK. THE CRUSADERS ARE WITH US, GOD'S WARRIORS ARE OUT SEARCHING.
DESPAIR HURLS ITS NEBULOUS WEIGHT AT WALLS OF INCOMPREHENSION.
WORD OF OUR NEED IS BEING SPREAD THROUGHOUT THE NETWORK.
THOUSANDS OF YOUR FELLOW CRUSADERS ARE LINKED IN THE PYRAMID OF PRAYER.
REST YOURSELF, CHILD. TRUST IN THE LORD.
NO, I'M NOT A CHILD, I'M A MOTHER. SOME PERVERT'S GOT GEMMA AND'S DOING THINGS TO HER.
I WANT MY BABY NOW!
THEN YOU MUST PRAY. A DEMON OF HELL HAS ATTACKED A SINFUL WEAKNESS IN THE STOCKADE OF RIGHTEOUSNESS.
ONLY FAITH WILL REPAIR THE FLAW.
ARE YOU SAYING IT'S HER FAULT? YOU MEALY-MOUTHED BASTARD.
CHERYL, DON'T.
THE WOMAN IS DISTRAUGHT. SHE DISRUPTS THE PRAYER ENERGY. I SUGGEST YOU RESTRAIN HER, BROTHER TONY.
DON'T TALK TO ELDER MARTIN LIKE THAT, CHERYL.
WHAT? YOU HEARD WHAT HE SAID.
I THINK HE'S RIGHT. THERE'S BEEN A BAD SPIRIT IN THE GIRL SINCE WE STARTED WORKING WITH THE CRUSADE.
STAY AWAY FROM ME, YOU... TRAITOR!

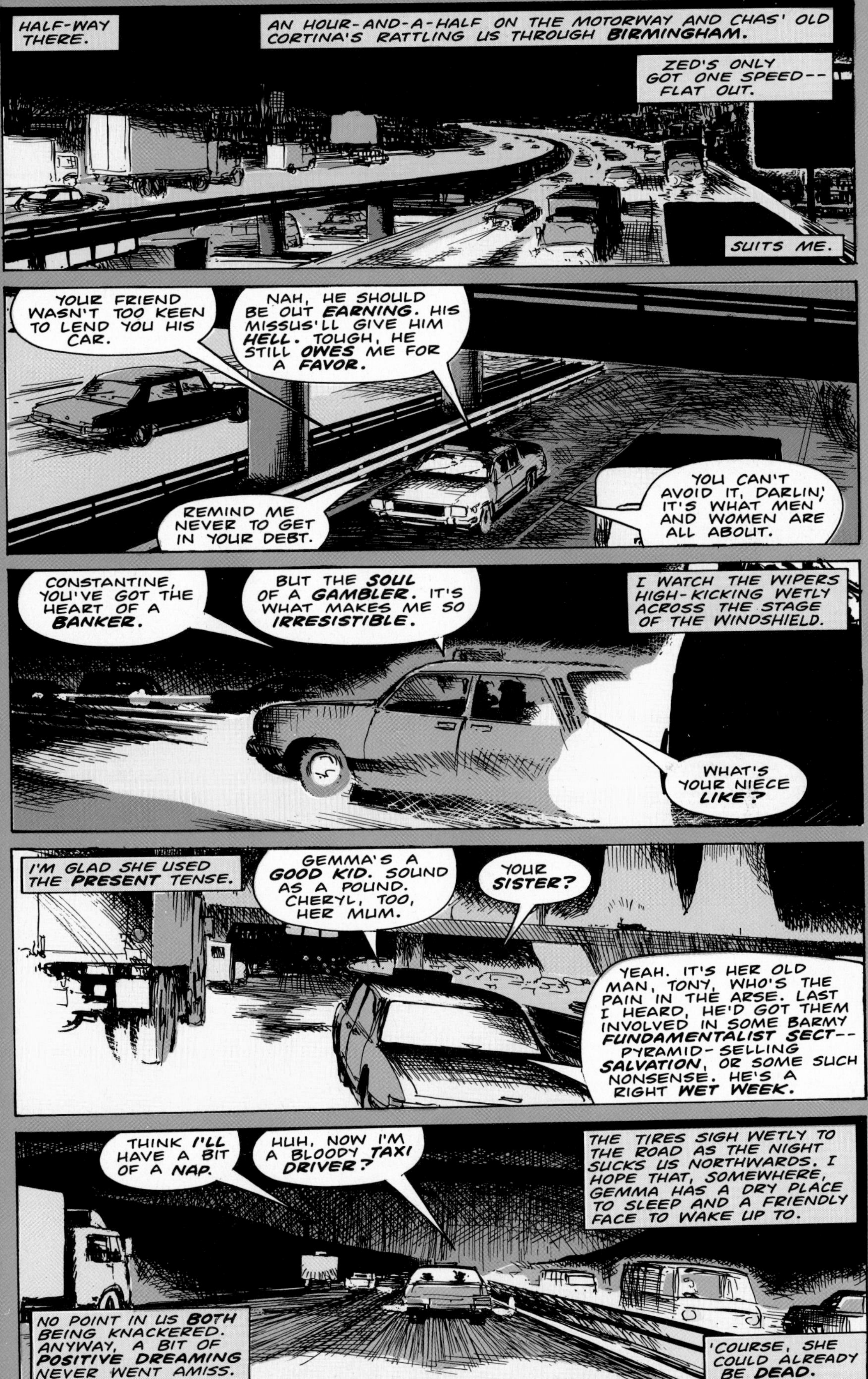
HALF-WAY THERE.
AN HOUR-AND-A-HALF ON THE MOTORWAY AND CHAS' OLD CORTINA'S RATTLING US THROUGH BIRMINGHAM.
ZED'S ONLY GOT ONE SPEED-- FLAT OUT.
SUITS ME.
YOUR FRIEND WASN'T TOO KEEN TO LEND YOU HIS CAR.
NAH, HE SHOULD BE OUT EARNING. HIS MISSUS'LL GIVE HIM HELL. TOUGH, HE STILL OWES ME FOR A FAVOR.
REMIND ME NEVER TO GET IN YOUR DEBT.
YOU CAN'T AVOID IT, DARLIN', IT'S WHAT MEN AND WOMEN ARE ALL ABOUT.
CONSTANTINE, YOU'VE GOT THE HEART OF A BANKER.
BUT THE SOUL OF A GAMBLER. IT'S WHAT MAKES ME SO IRRESISTIBLE.
I WATCH THE WIPERS HIGH-KICKING WETLY ACROSS THE STAGE OF THE WINDSHIELD.
WHAT'S YOUR NIECE LIKE?
I'M GLAD SHE USED THE PRESENT TENSE.
GEMMA'S A GOOD KID. SOUND AS A POUND. CHERYL, TOO, HER MUM.
YOUR SISTER?
YEAH. IT'S HER OLD MAN, TONY, WHO'S THE PAIN IN THE ARSE. LAST I HEARD, HE'D GOT THEM INVOLVED IN SOME BARMY FUNDAMENTALIST SECT-- PYRAMID-SELLING SALVATION, OR SOME SUCH NONSENSE. HE'S A RIGHT WET WEEK.
THINK I'LL HAVE A BIT OF A NAP.
HUH, NOW I'M A BLOODY TAXI DRIVER?
THE TIRES SIGH WETLY TO THE ROAD AS THE NIGHT SUCKS US NORTHWARDS. I HOPE THAT, SOMEWHERE, GEMMA HAS A DRY PLACE TO SLEEP AND A FRIENDLY FACE TO WAKE UP TO.
NO POINT IN US BOTH BEING KNACKERED. ANYWAY, A BIT OF POSITIVE DREAMING NEVER WENT AMISS.
'COURSE, SHE COULD ALREADY BE DEAD.

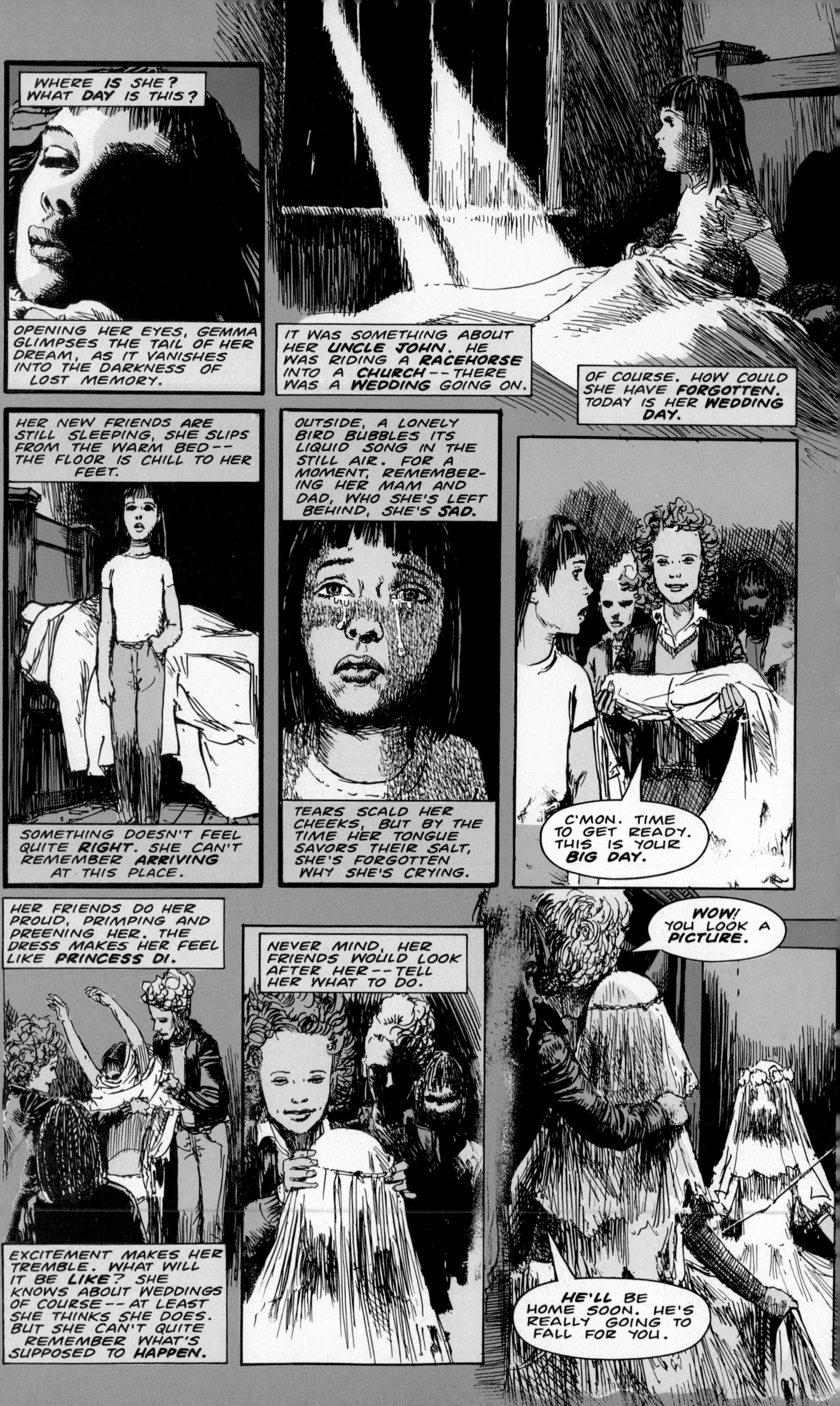
WHERE IS SHE? WHAT DAY IS THIS?
OPENING HER EYES, GEMMA GLIMPSES THE TAIL OF HER DREAM, AS IT VANISHES INTO THE DARKNESS OF LOST MEMORY.
IT WAS SOMETHING ABOUT HER UNCLE JOHN. HE WAS RIDING A RACEHORSE INTO A CHURCH--THERE WAS A WEDDING GOING ON.
OF COURSE. HOW COULD SHE HAVE FORGOTTEN. TODAY IS HER WEDDING DAY.
HER NEW FRIENDS ARE STILL SLEEPING, SHE SLIPS FROM THE WARM BED-- THE FLOOR IS CHILL TO HER FEET.
SOMETHING DOESN'T FEEL QUITE RIGHT. SHE CAN'T REMEMBER ARRIVING AT THIS PLACE.
OUTSIDE, A LONELY BIRD BUBBLES ITS LIQUID SONG IN THE STILL AIR. FOR A MOMENT, REMEMBERING HER MAM AND DAD, WHO SHE'S LEFT BEHIND, SHE'S SAD.
TEARS SCALD HER CHEEKS, BUT BY THE TIME HER TONGUE SAVORS THEIR SALT, SHE'S FORGOTTEN WHY SHE'S CRYING.
C'MON. TIME TO GET READY. THIS IS YOUR BIG DAY.
HER FRIENDS DO HER PROUD, PRIMPING AND PREENING HER. THE DRESS MAKES HER FEEL LIKE PRINCESS DI.
EXCITEMENT MAKES HER TREMBLE. WHAT WILL IT BE LIKE? SHE KNOWS ABOUT WEDDINGS OF COURSE-- AT LEAST SHE THINKS SHE DOES. BUT SHE CAN'T QUITE REMEMBER WHAT'S SUPPOSED TO HAPPEN.
NEVER MIND, HER FRIENDS WOULD LOOK AFTER HER--TELL HER WHAT TO DO.
WOW! YOU LOOK A PICTURE.
HE'LL BE HOME SOON. HE'S REALLY GOING TO FALL FOR YOU.

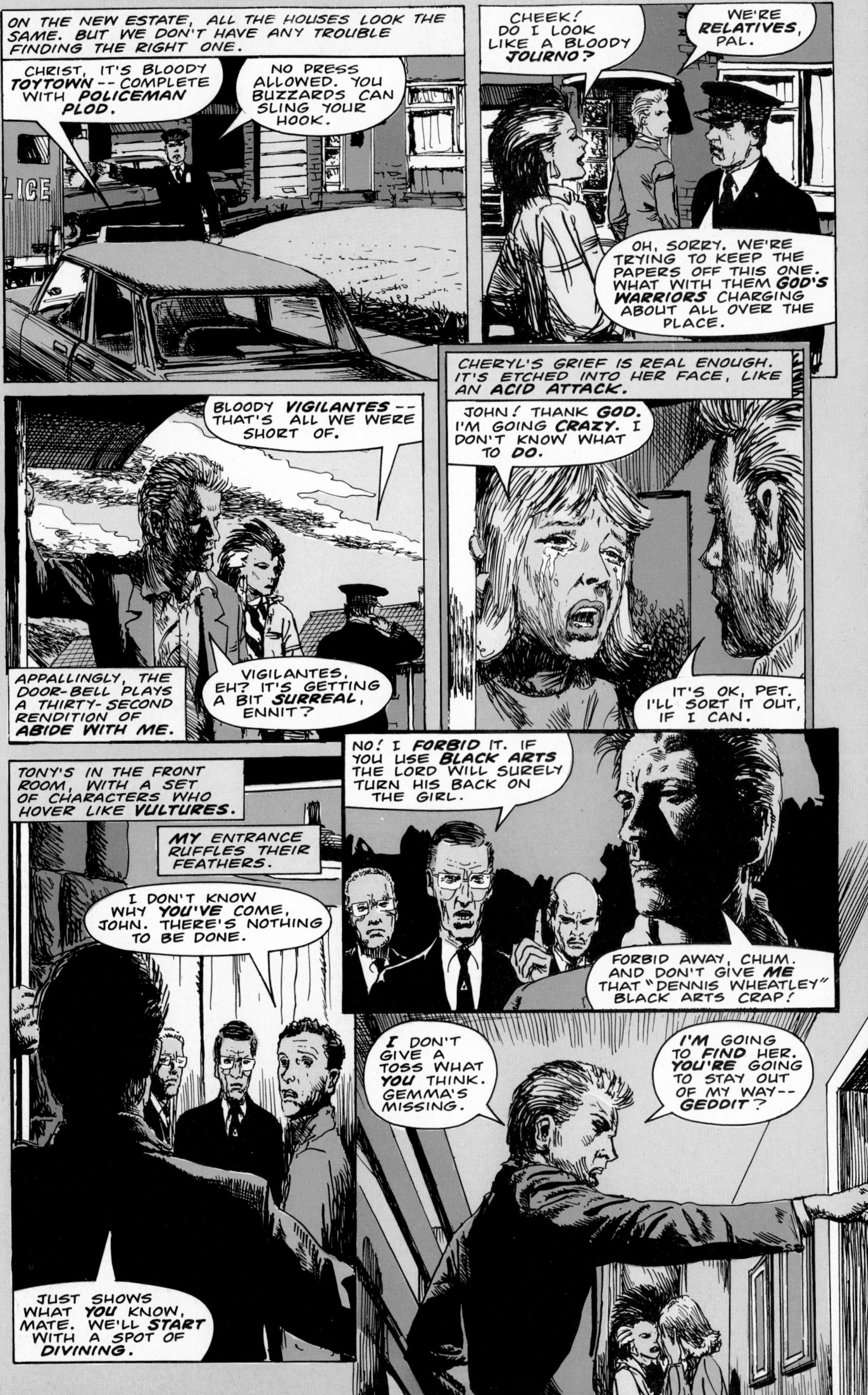
ON THE NEW ESTATE, ALL THE HOUSES LOOK THE SAME. BUT WE DON'T HAVE ANY TROUBLE FINDING THE RIGHT ONE.
CHRIST, IT'S BLOODY TOYTOWN -- COMPLETE WITH POLICEMAN PLOD.
NO PRESS ALLOWED. YOU BUZZARDS CAN SLING YOUR HOOK.
LICE
CHEEK! DO I LOOK LIKE A BLOODY JOURNO?
WE'RE RELATIVES, PAL.
OH, SORRY. WE'RE TRYING TO KEEP THE PAPERS OFF THIS ONE. WHAT WITH THEM GOD'S WARRIORS CHARGING ABOUT ALL OVER THE PLACE.
BLOODY VIGILANTES -- THAT'S ALL WE WERE SHORT OF.
APPALLINGLY, THE DOOR-BELL PLAYS A THIRTY-SECOND RENDITION OF ABIDE WITH ME.
VIGILANTES, EH? IT'S GETTING A BIT SURREAL, ENNIT?
CHERYL'S GRIEF IS REAL ENOUGH. IT'S ETCHED INTO HER FACE, LIKE AN ACID ATTACK.
JOHN! THANK GOD. I'M GOING CRAZY. I DON'T KNOW WHAT TO DO.
IT'S OK, PET. I'LL SORT IT OUT, IF I CAN.
TONY'S IN THE FRONT ROOM, WITH A SET OF CHARACTERS WHO HOVER LIKE VULTURES.
MY ENTRANCE RUFFLES THEIR FEATHERS.
I DON'T KNOW WHY YOU'VE COME, JOHN. THERE'S NOTHING TO BE DONE.
JUST SHOWS WHAT YOU KNOW, MATE. WE'LL START WITH A SPOT OF DIVINING.
NO! I FORBID IT. IF YOU USE BLACK ARTS THE LORD WILL SURELY TURN HIS BACK ON THE GIRL.
FORBID AWAY, CHUM. AND DON'T GIVE ME THAT "DENNIS WHEATLEY" BLACK ARTS CRAP!
I DON'T GIVE A TOSS WHAT YOU THINK. GEMMA'S MISSING.
I'M GOING TO FIND HER. YOU'RE GOING TO STAY OUT OF MY WAY-- GEDDIT?

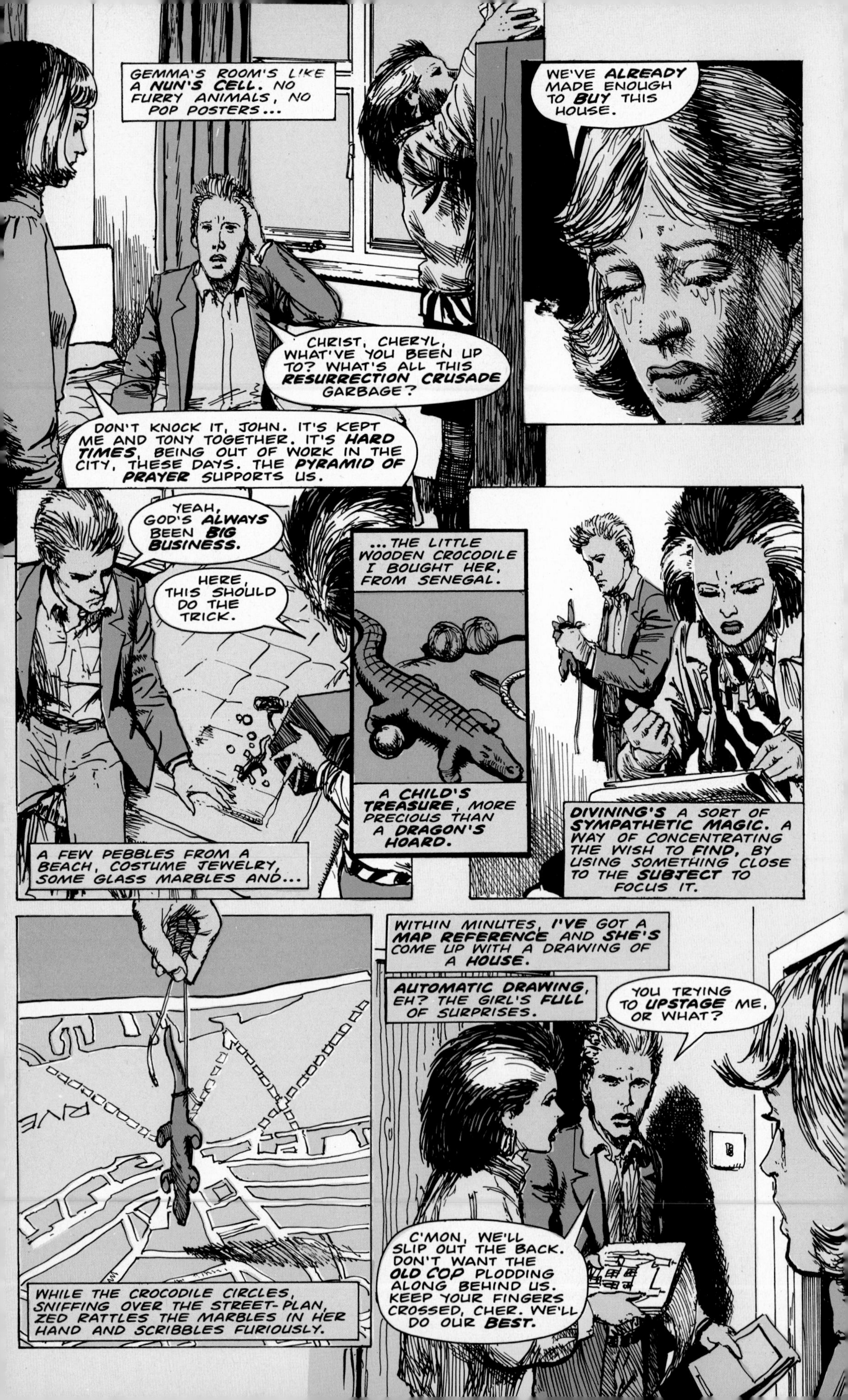

GEMMA'S ROOM'S LIKE A NUN'S CELL. NO FURRY ANIMALS, NO POP POSTERS...
WE'VE ALREADY MADE ENOUGH TO BUY THIS HOUSE.
CHRIST, CHERYL, WHAT'VE YOU BEEN UP TO? WHAT'S ALL THIS RESURRECTION CRUSADE GARBAGE?
DON'T KNOCK IT, JOHN. IT'S KEPT ME AND TONY TOGETHER. IT'S HARD TIMES, BEING OUT OF WORK IN THE CITY, THESE DAYS. THE PYRAMID OF PRAYER SUPPORTS US.
YEAH, GOD'S ALWAYS BEEN BIG BUSINESS.
HERE, THIS SHOULD DO THE TRICK.
A FEW PEBBLES FROM A BEACH, COSTUME JEWELRY, SOME GLASS MARBLES AND...
...THE LITTLE WOODEN CROCODILE I BOUGHT HER, FROM SENEGAL.
A CHILD'S TREASURE, MORE PRECIOUS THAN A DRAGON'S HOARD.
DIVINING'S A SORT OF SYMPATHETIC MAGIC. A WAY OF CONCENTRATING THE WISH TO FIND, BY USING SOMETHING CLOSE TO THE SUBJECT TO FOCUS IT.
WHILE THE CROCODILE CIRCLES, SNIFFING OVER THE STREET-PLAN, ZED RATTLES THE MARBLES IN HER HAND AND SCRIBBLES FURIOUSLY.
WITHIN MINUTES, I'VE GOT A MAP REFERENCE AND SHE'S COME UP WITH A DRAWING OF A HOUSE.
AUTOMATIC DRAWING, EH? THE GIRL'S FULL OF SURPRISES.
YOU TRYING TO UPSTAGE ME, OR WHAT?
C'MON, WE'LL SLIP OUT THE BACK. DON'T WANT THE OLD COP PLODDING ALONG BEHIND US. KEEP YOUR FINGERS CROSSED, CHER. WE'LL DO OUR BEST.

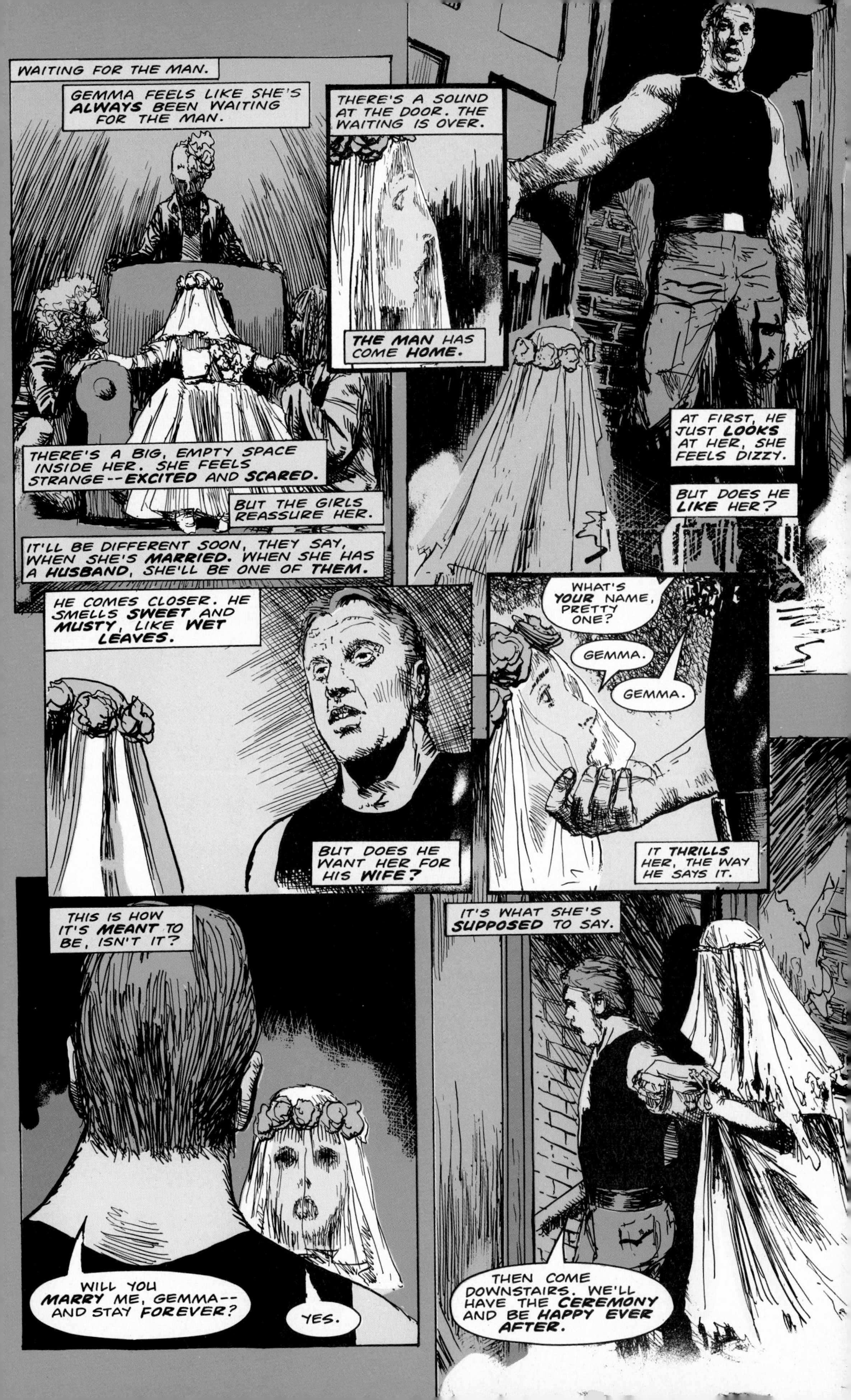
WAITING FOR THE MAN.
GEMMA FEELS LIKE SHE'S ALWAYS BEEN WAITING FOR THE MAN.
THERE'S A BIG, EMPTY SPACE INSIDE HER. SHE FEELS STRANGE--EXCITED AND SCARED.
BUT THE GIRLS REASSURE HER.
IT'LL BE DIFFERENT SOON, THEY SAY, WHEN SHE'S MARRIED. WHEN SHE HAS A HUSBAND, SHE'LL BE ONE OF THEM.
THERE'S A SOUND AT THE DOOR. THE WAITING IS OVER.
THE MAN HAS COME HOME.
AT FIRST, HE JUST LOOKS AT HER, SHE FEELS DIZZY.
BUT DOES HE LIKE HER?
HE COMES CLOSER. HE SMELLS SWEET AND MUSTY, LIKE WET LEAVES.
BUT DOES HE WANT HER FOR HIS WIFE?
WHAT'S YOUR NAME, PRETTY ONE?
GEMMA.
GEMMA.
IT THRILLS HER, THE WAY HE SAYS IT.
THIS IS HOW IT'S MEANT TO BE, ISN'T IT?
WILL YOU MARRY ME, GEMMA--AND STAY FOREVER?
YES.
IT'S WHAT SHE'S SUPPOSED TO SAY.
THEN COME DOWNSTAIRS. WE'LL HAVE THE CEREMONY AND BE HAPPY EVER AFTER.

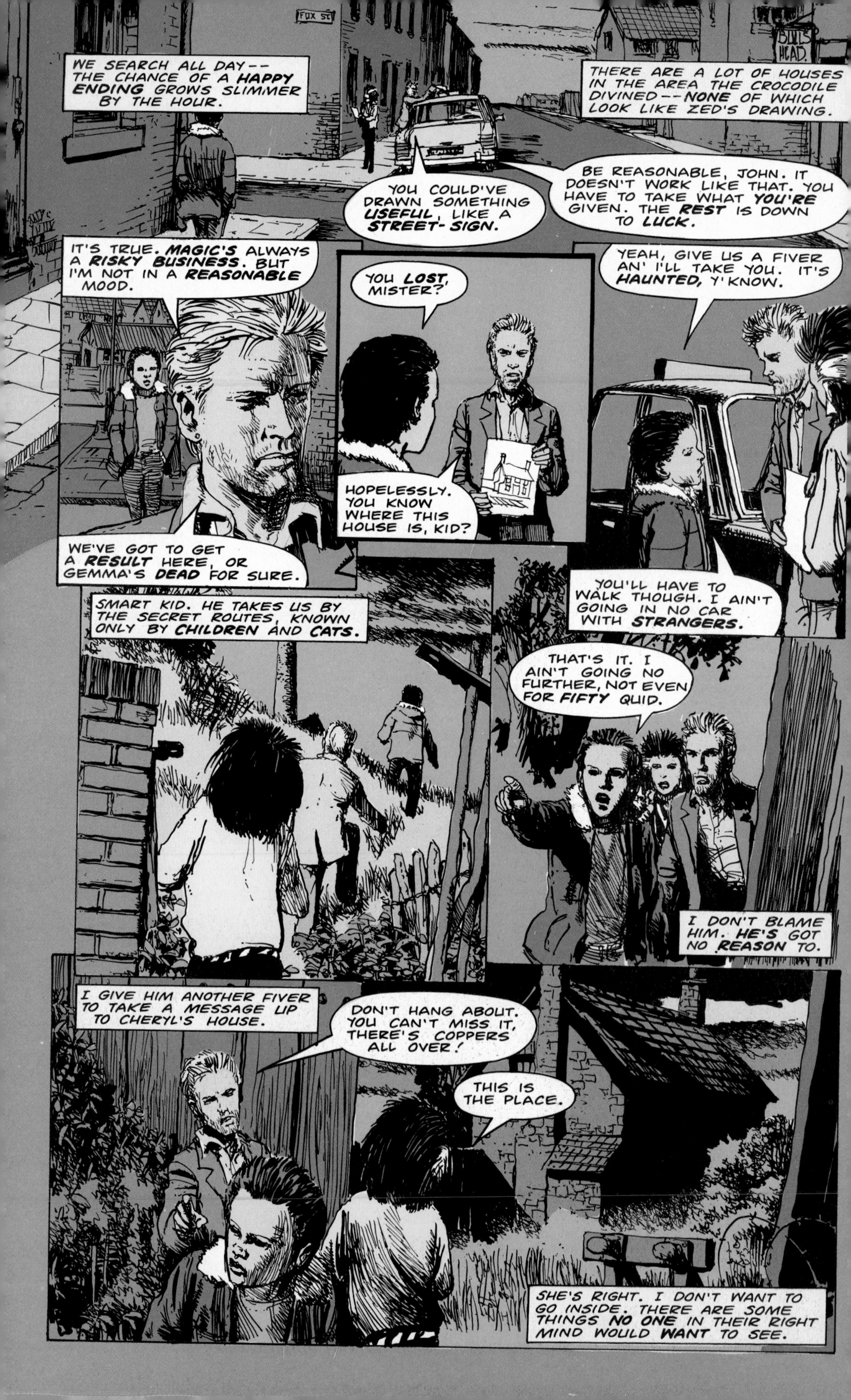
FOX ST
BULLS HEAD
WE SEARCH ALL DAY-- THE CHANCE OF A HAPPY ENDING GROWS SLIMMER BY THE HOUR.
THERE ARE A LOT OF HOUSES IN THE AREA THE CROCODILE DIVINED--NONE OF WHICH LOOK LIKE ZED'S DRAWING.
YOU COULD'VE DRAWN SOMETHING USEFUL, LIKE A STREET-SIGN.
BE REASONABLE, JOHN. IT DOESN'T WORK LIKE THAT. YOU HAVE TO TAKE WHAT YOU'RE GIVEN. THE REST IS DOWN TO LUCK.
IT'S TRUE. MAGIC'S ALWAYS A RISKY BUSINESS. BUT I'M NOT IN A REASONABLE MOOD.
WE'VE GOT TO GET A RESULT HERE, OR GEMMA'S DEAD FOR SURE.
YOU LOST, MISTER?
HOPELESSLY. YOU KNOW WHERE THIS HOUSE IS, KID?
YEAH, GIVE US A FIVER AN' I'LL TAKE YOU. IT'S HAUNTED, Y'KNOW.
YOU'LL HAVE TO WALK THOUGH. I AIN'T GOING IN NO CAR WITH STRANGERS.
SMART KID. HE TAKES US BY THE SECRET ROUTES, KNOWN ONLY BY CHILDREN AND CATS.
THAT'S IT. I AIN'T GOING NO FURTHER, NOT EVEN FOR FIFTY QUID.
I DON'T BLAME HIM. HE'S GOT NO REASON TO.
I GIVE HIM ANOTHER FIVER TO TAKE A MESSAGE UP TO CHERYL'S HOUSE.
DON'T HANG ABOUT. YOU CAN'T MISS IT, THERE'S COPPERS ALL OVER!
THIS IS THE PLACE.
SHE'S RIGHT. I DON'T WANT TO GO INSIDE. THERE ARE SOME THINGS NO ONE IN THEIR RIGHT MIND WOULD WANT TO SEE.

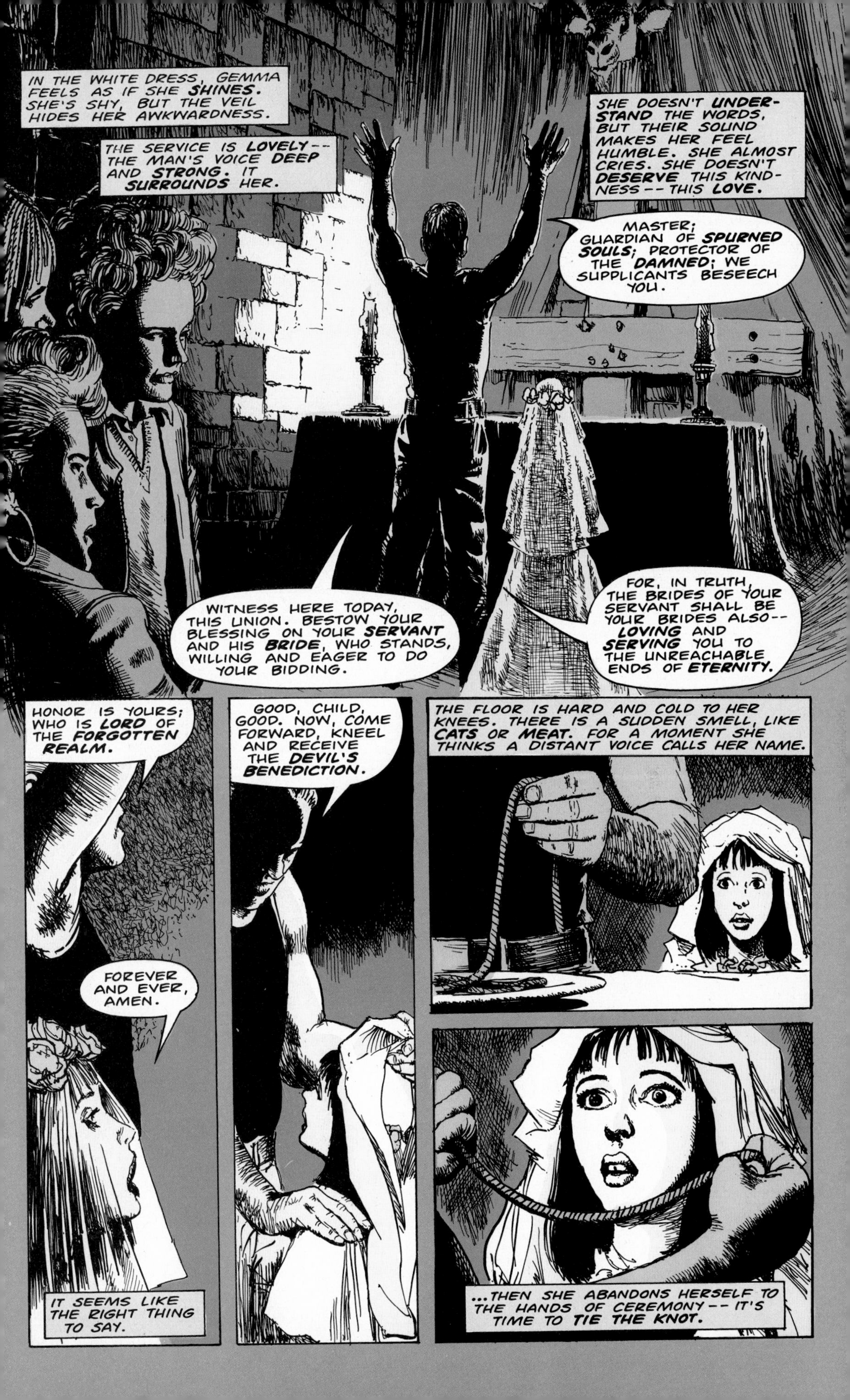

IN THE WHITE DRESS, GEMMA FEELS AS IF SHE SHINES. SHE'S SHY, BUT THE VEIL HIDES HER AWKWARDNESS.
THE SERVICE IS LOVELY-- THE MAN'S VOICE DEEP AND STRONG. IT SURROUNDS HER.
SHE DOESN'T UNDERSTAND THE WORDS, BUT THEIR SOUND MAKES HER FEEL HUMBLE. SHE ALMOST CRIES. SHE DOESN'T DESERVE THIS KINDNESS -- THIS LOVE.
MASTER; GUARDIAN OF SPURNED SOULS; PROTECTOR OF THE DAMNED; WE SUPPLICANTS BESEECH YOU.
WITNESS HERE TODAY, THIS UNION. BESTOW YOUR BLESSING ON YOUR SERVANT AND HIS BRIDE, WHO STANDS, WILLING AND EAGER TO DO YOUR BIDDING.
FOR, IN TRUTH, THE BRIDES OF YOUR SERVANT SHALL BE YOUR BRIDES ALSO-- LOVING AND SERVING YOU TO THE UNREACHABLE ENDS OF ETERNITY.
HONOR IS YOURS; WHO IS LORD OF THE FORGOTTEN REALM.
FOREVER AND EVER, AMEN.
IT SEEMS LIKE THE RIGHT THING TO SAY.
GOOD, CHILD, GOOD. NOW, COME FORWARD, KNEEL AND RECEIVE THE DEVIL'S BENEDICTION.
THE FLOOR IS HARD AND COLD TO HER KNEES. THERE IS A SUDDEN SMELL, LIKE CATS OR MEAT. FOR A MOMENT SHE THINKS A DISTANT VOICE CALLS HER NAME.
...THEN SHE ABANDONS HERSELF TO THE HANDS OF CEREMONY-- IT'S TIME TO TIE THE KNOT.

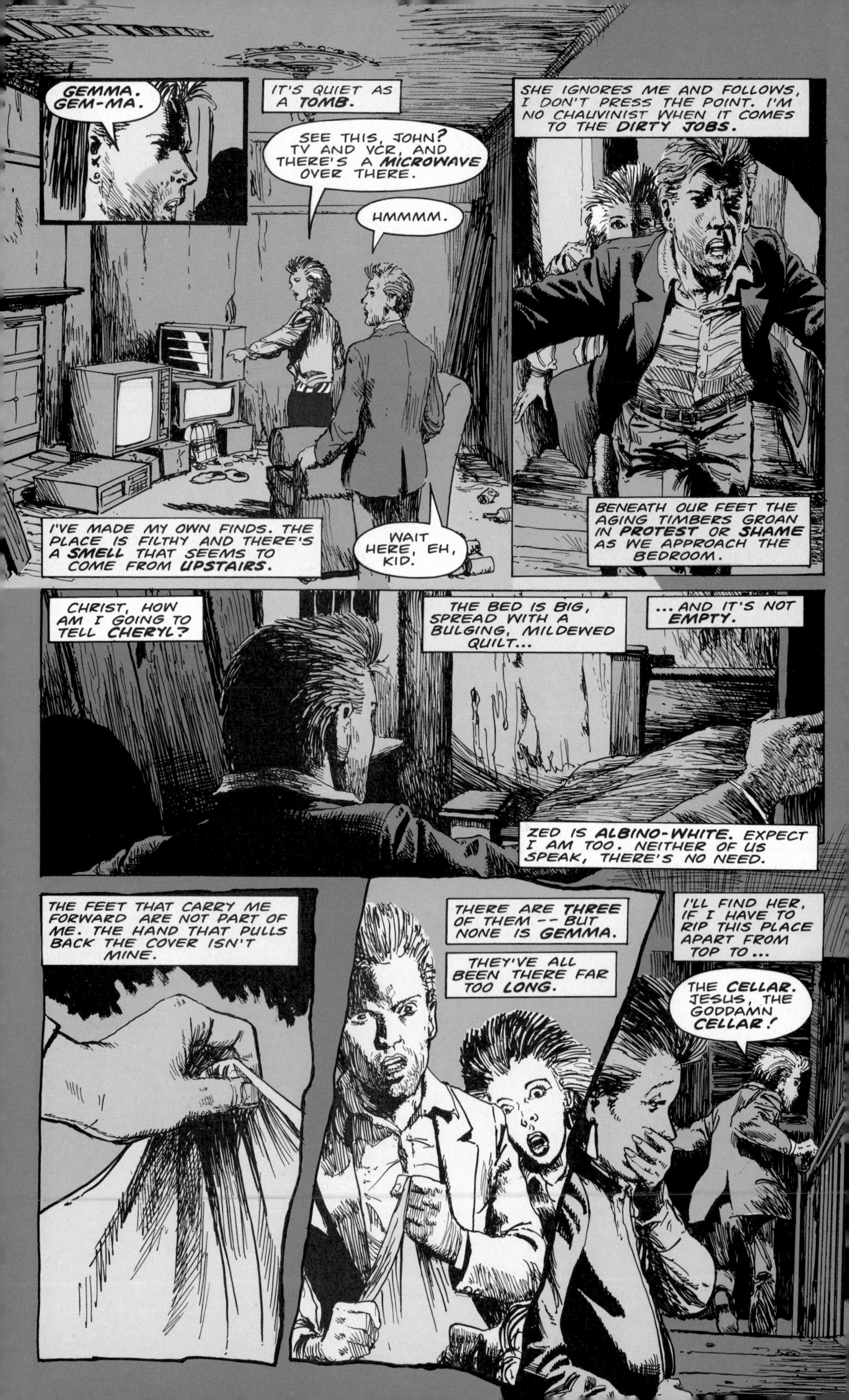
GEMMA. GEM-MA.
IT'S QUIET AS A TOMB.
SEE THIS, JOHN? TV AND VCR, AND THERE'S A MICROWAVE OVER THERE.
HMMMM.
I'VE MADE MY OWN FINDS. THE PLACE IS FILTHY AND THERE'S A SMELL THAT SEEMS TO COME FROM UPSTAIRS.
WAIT HERE, EH, KID.
SHE IGNORES ME AND FOLLOWS, I DON'T PRESS THE POINT. I'M NO CHAUVINIST WHEN IT COMES TO THE DIRTY JOBS.
BENEATH OUR FEET THE AGING TIMBERS GROAN IN PROTEST OR SHAME AS WE APPROACH THE BEDROOM.
CHRIST, HOW AM I GOING TO TELL CHERYL?
THE BED IS BIG, SPREAD WITH A BULGING, MILDEWED QUILT...
...AND IT'S NOT EMPTY.
ZED IS ALBINO-WHITE. EXPECT I AM TOO. NEITHER OF US SPEAK, THERE'S NO NEED.
THE FEET THAT CARRY ME FORWARD ARE NOT PART OF ME. THE HAND THAT PULLS BACK THE COVER ISN'T MINE.
THERE ARE THREE OF THEM -- BUT NONE IS GEMMA.
THEY'VE ALL BEEN THERE FAR TOO LONG.
I'LL FIND HER, IF I HAVE TO RIP THIS PLACE APART FROM TOP TO...
THE CELLAR. JESUS, THE GODDAMN CELLAR!

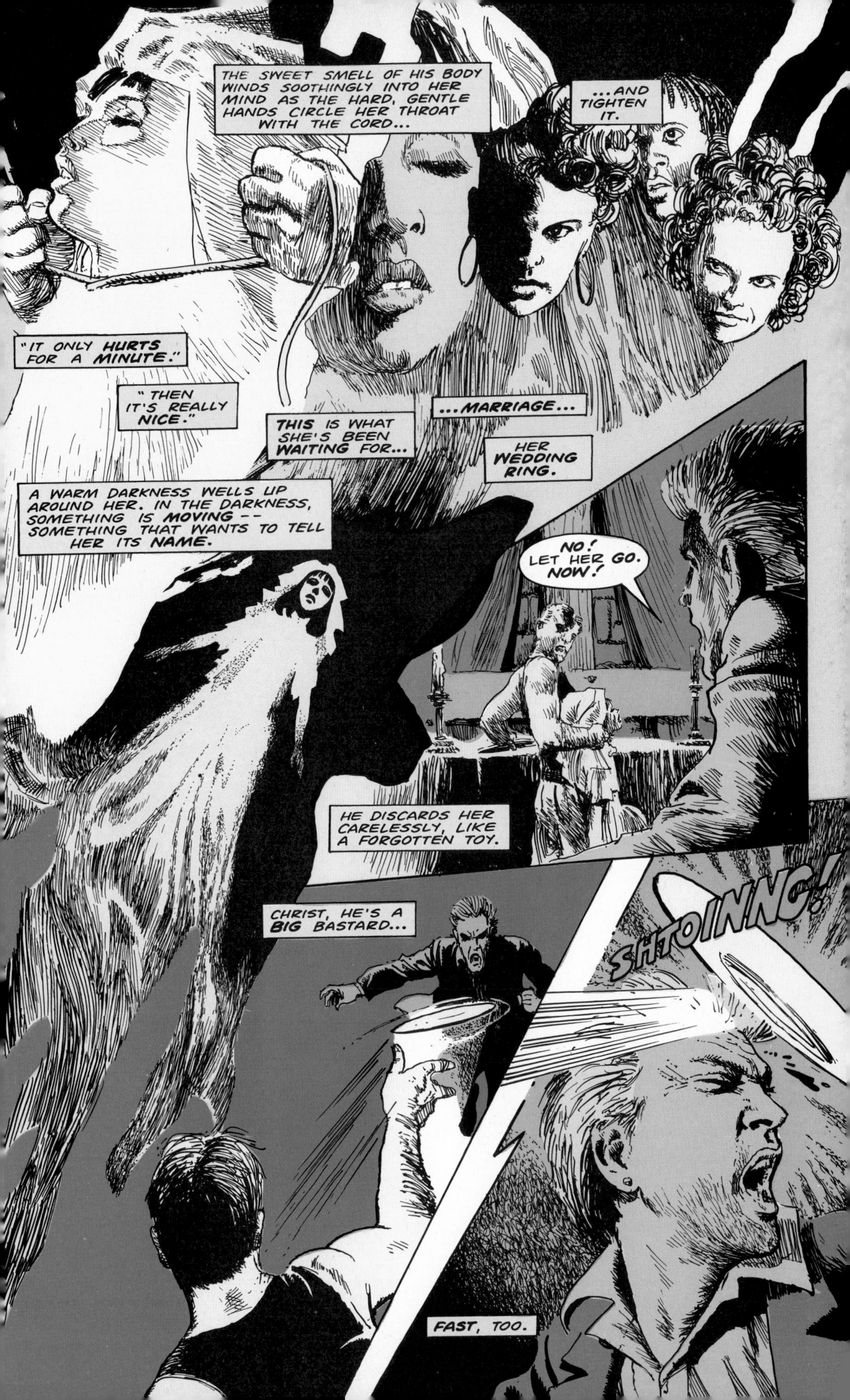
THE SWEET SMELL OF HIS BODY WINDS SOOTHINGLY INTO HER MIND AS THE HARD, GENTLE HANDS CIRCLE HER THROAT WITH THE CORD...
...AND TIGHTEN IT.
"IT ONLY HURTS FOR A MINUTE."
"THEN IT'S REALLY NICE."
THIS IS WHAT SHE'S BEEN WAITING FOR...
...MARRIAGE...
HER WEDDING RING.
A WARM DARKNESS WELLS UP AROUND HER. IN THE DARKNESS, SOMETHING IS MOVING -- SOMETHING THAT WANTS TO TELL HER ITS NAME.
NO! LET HER GO. NOW!
HE DISCARDS HER CARELESSLY, LIKE A FORGOTTEN TOY.
CHRIST, HE'S A BIG BASTARD...
SHTOINNG!
FAST, TOO.

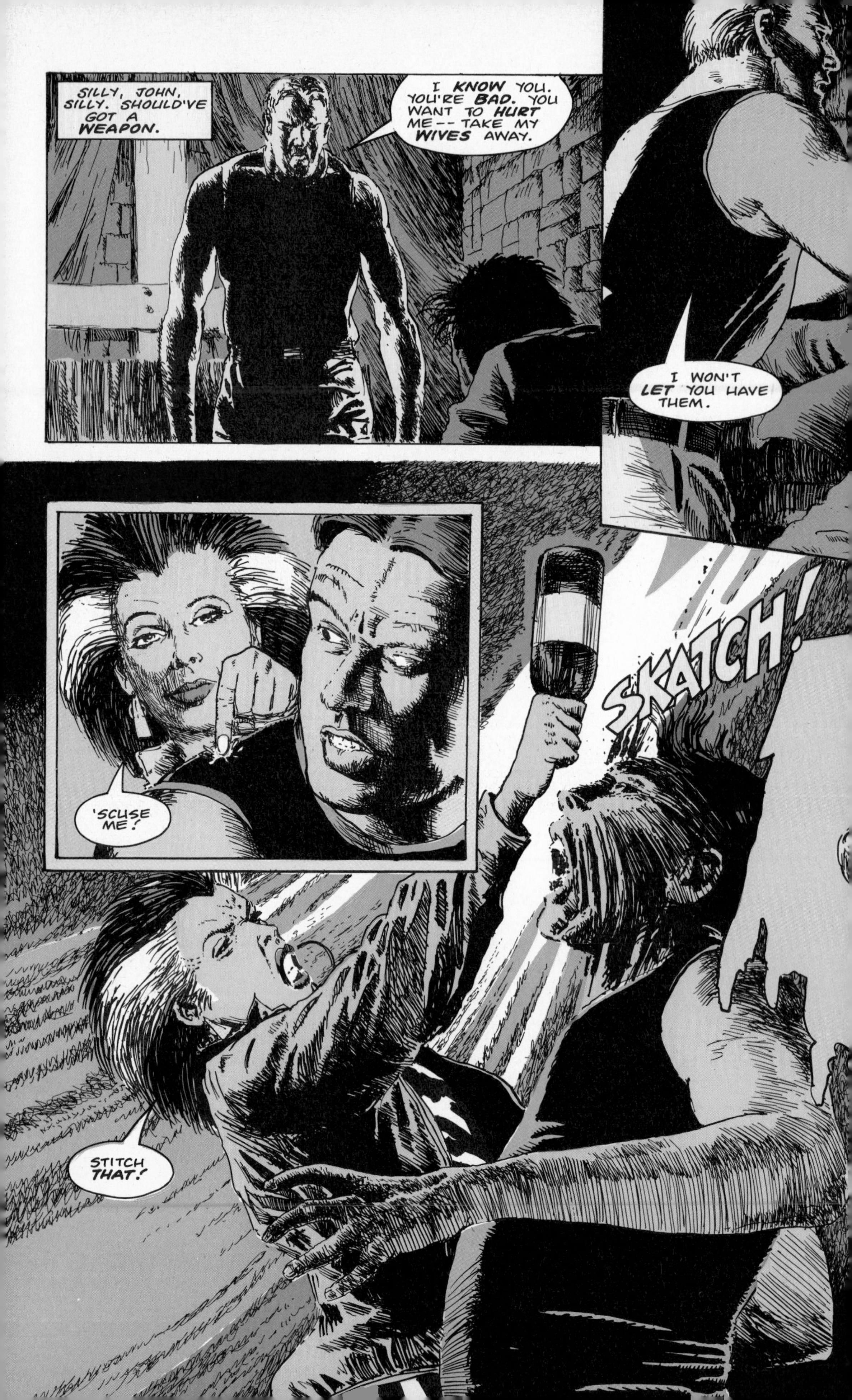
SILLY, JOHN, SILLY. SHOULD'VE GOT A WEAPON.
I KNOW YOU. YOU'RE BAD. YOU WANT TO HURT ME-- TAKE MY WIVES AWAY.
I WON'T LET YOU HAVE THEM.
'SCUSE ME!
SKATCH!
STITCH THAT!

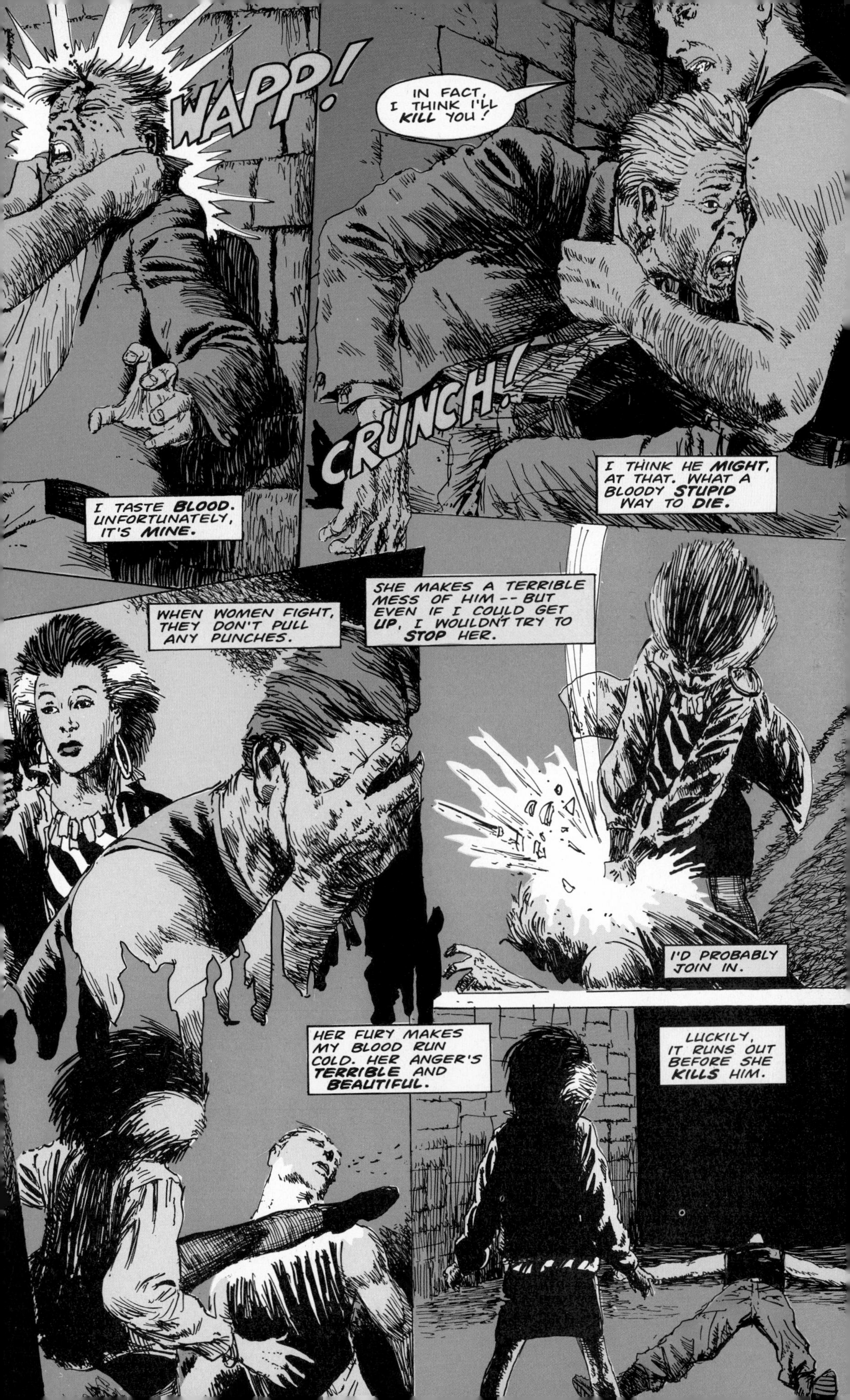
WAPP!
IN FACT, I THINK I'LL KILL YOU!
CRUNCH!
I TASTE BLOOD. UNFORTUNATELY, IT'S MINE.
I THINK HE MIGHT, AT THAT. WHAT A BLOODY STUPID WAY TO DIE.
WHEN WOMEN FIGHT, THEY DON'T PULL ANY PUNCHES.
SHE MAKES A TERRIBLE MESS OF HIM -- BUT EVEN IF I COULD GET UP, I WOULDN'T TRY TO STOP HER.
I'D PROBABLY JOIN IN.
HER FURY MAKES MY BLOOD RUN COLD. HER ANGER'S TERRIBLE AND BEAUTIFUL.
LUCKILY, IT RUNS OUT BEFORE SHE KILLS HIM.

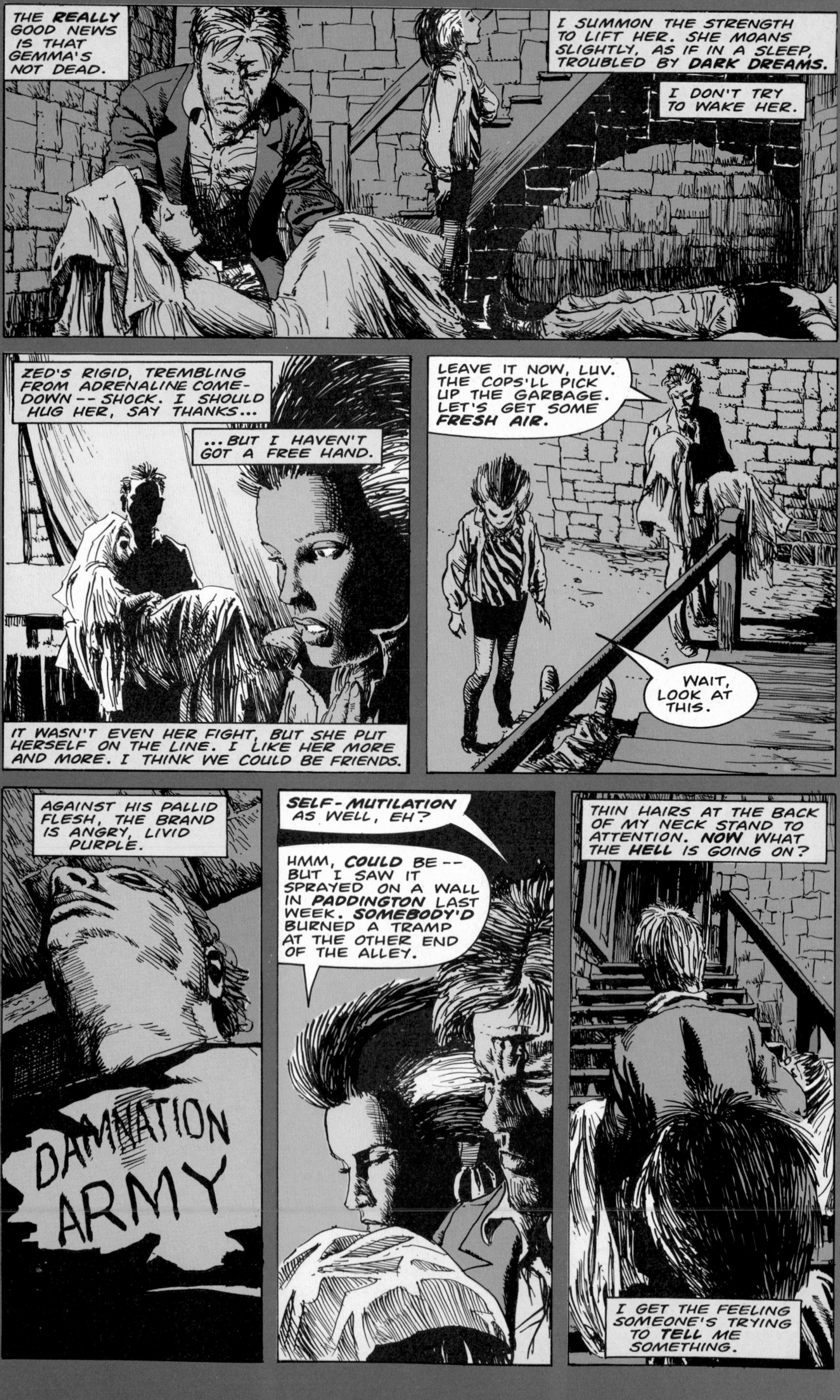
THE REALLY GOOD NEWS IS THAT GEMMA'S NOT DEAD.
I SUMMON THE STRENGTH TO LIFT HER. SHE MOANS SLIGHTLY, AS IF IN A SLEEP, TROUBLED BY DARK DREAMS.
I DON'T TRY TO WAKE HER.
ZED'S RIGID, TREMBLING FROM ADRENALINE COME-DOWN -- SHOCK. I SHOULD HUG HER, SAY THANKS...
...BUT I HAVEN'T GOT A FREE HAND.
IT WASN'T EVEN HER FIGHT, BUT SHE PUT HERSELF ON THE LINE. I LIKE HER MORE AND MORE. I THINK WE COULD BE FRIENDS.
LEAVE IT NOW, LUV. THE COPS'LL PICK UP THE GARBAGE. LET'S GET SOME FRESH AIR.
WAIT, LOOK AT THIS.
AGAINST HIS PALLID FLESH, THE BRAND IS ANGRY, LIVID PURPLE.
DAMNATION ARMY
SELF-MUTILATION AS WELL, EH?
HMM, COULD BE -- BUT I SAW IT SPRAYED ON A WALL IN PADDINGTON LAST WEEK. SOMEBODY'D BURNED A TRAMP AT THE OTHER END OF THE ALLEY.
THIN HAIRS AT THE BACK OF MY NECK STAND TO ATTENTION. NOW WHAT THE HELL IS GOING ON?
I GET THE FEELING SOMEONE'S TRYING TO TELL ME SOMETHING.

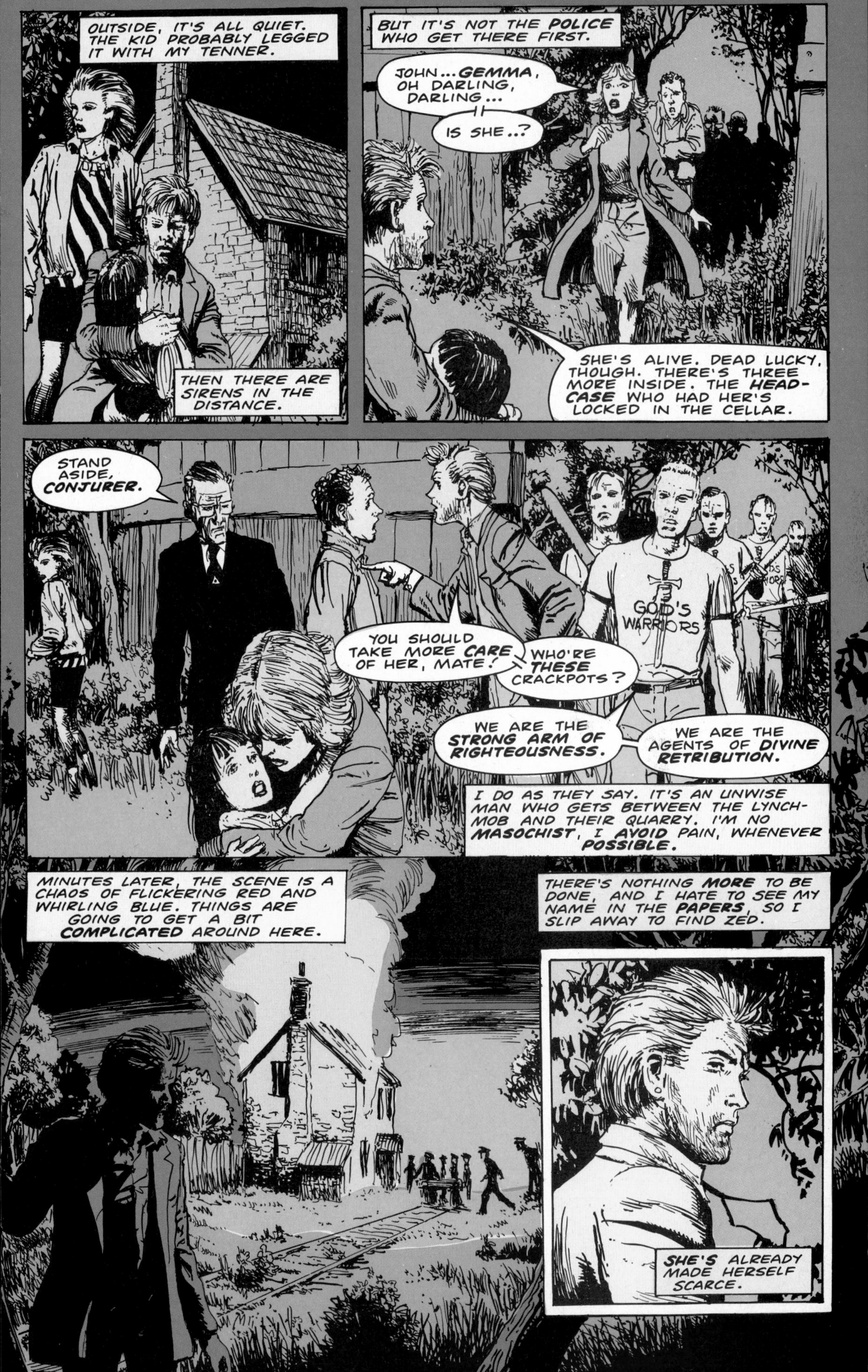
OUTSIDE, IT'S ALL QUIET. THE KID PROBABLY LEGGED IT WITH MY TENNER.
THEN THERE ARE SIRENS IN THE DISTANCE.
BUT IT'S NOT THE POLICE WHO GET THERE FIRST.
JOHN... GEMMA, OH DARLING, DARLING...
IS SHE..?
SHE'S ALIVE. DEAD LUCKY, THOUGH. THERE'S THREE MORE INSIDE. THE HEAD-CASE WHO HAD HER'S LOCKED IN THE CELLAR.
STAND ASIDE, CONJURER.
YOU SHOULD TAKE MORE CARE OF HER, MATE!
WHO'RE THESE CRACKPOTS?
GOD'S WARRIORS
WE ARE THE STRONG ARM OF RIGHTEOUSNESS.
WE ARE THE AGENTS OF DIVINE RETRIBUTION.
I DO AS THEY SAY. IT'S AN UNWISE MAN WHO GETS BETWEEN THE LYNCH-MOB AND THEIR QUARRY. I'M NO MASOCHIST, I AVOID PAIN, WHENEVER POSSIBLE.
MINUTES LATER, THE SCENE IS A CHAOS OF FLICKERING RED AND WHIRLING BLUE. THINGS ARE GOING TO GET A BIT COMPLICATED AROUND HERE.
THERE'S NOTHING MORE TO BE DONE, AND I HATE TO SEE MY NAME IN THE PAPERS, SO I SLIP AWAY TO FIND ZED.
SHE'S ALREADY MADE HERSELF SCARCE.

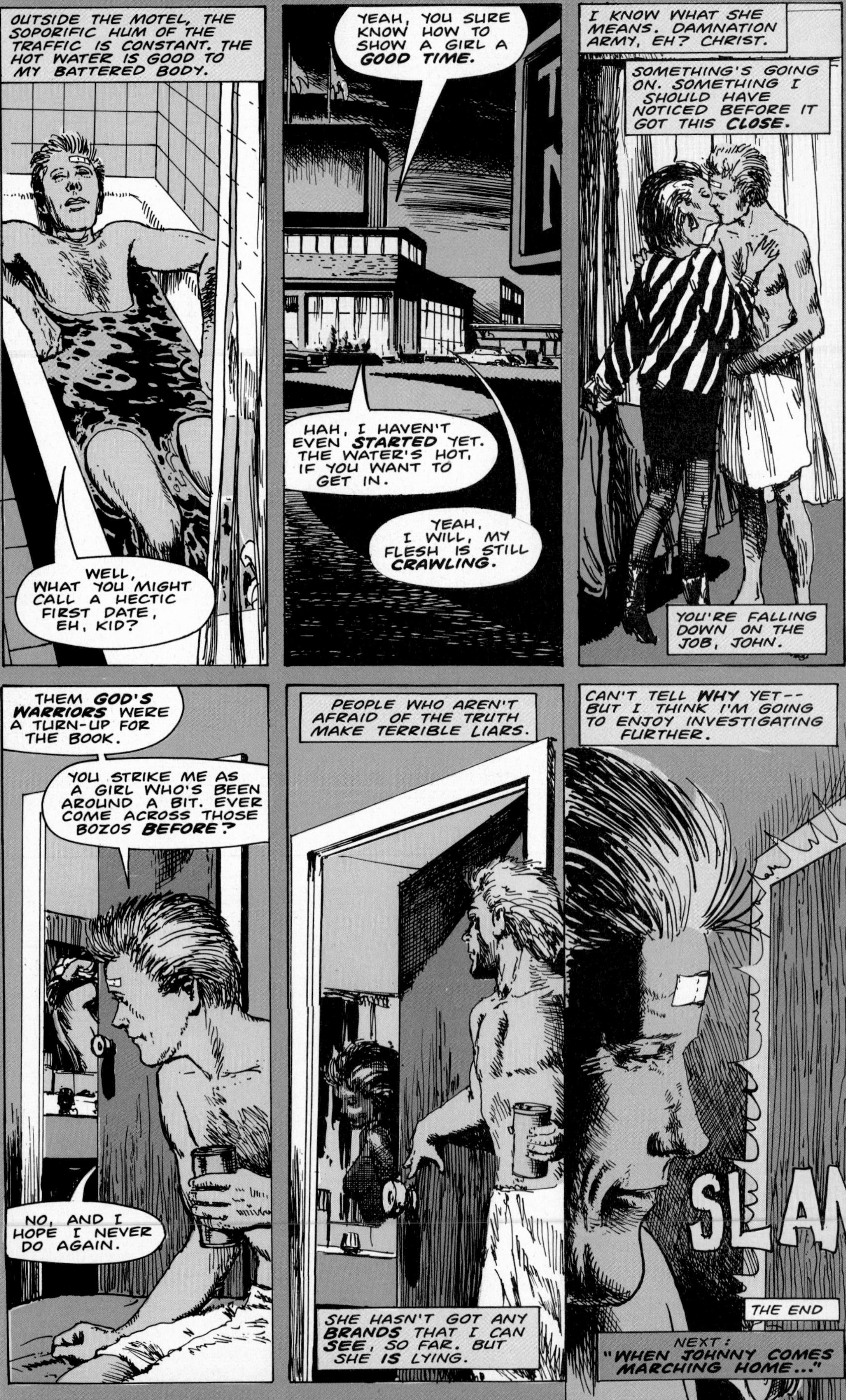
OUTSIDE THE MOTEL, THE SOPORIFIC HUM OF THE TRAFFIC IS CONSTANT. THE HOT WATER IS GOOD TO MY BATTERED BODY.
WELL, WHAT YOU MIGHT CALL A HECTIC FIRST DATE, EH, KID?
YEAH, YOU SURE KNOW HOW TO SHOW A GIRL A GOOD TIME.
HAH, I HAVEN'T EVEN STARTED YET. THE WATER'S HOT, IF YOU WANT TO GET IN.
YEAH, I WILL, MY FLESH IS STILL CRAWLING.
I KNOW WHAT SHE MEANS. DAMNATION ARMY, EH? CHRIST.
SOMETHING'S GOING ON. SOMETHING I SHOULD HAVE NOTICED BEFORE IT GOT THIS CLOSE.
YOU'RE FALLING DOWN ON THE JOB, JOHN.
THEM GOD'S WARRIORS WERE A TURN-UP FOR THE BOOK.
YOU STRIKE ME AS A GIRL WHO'S BEEN AROUND A BIT. EVER COME ACROSS THOSE BOZOS BEFORE?
NO, AND I HOPE I NEVER DO AGAIN.
PEOPLE WHO AREN'T AFRAID OF THE TRUTH MAKE TERRIBLE LIARS.
SHE HASN'T GOT ANY BRANDS THAT I CAN SEE, SO FAR. BUT SHE IS LYING.
CAN'T TELL WHY YET-- BUT I THINK I'M GOING TO ENJOY INVESTIGATING FURTHER.
SLAM
THE END
NEXT: "WHEN JOHNNY COMES MARCHING HOME..."

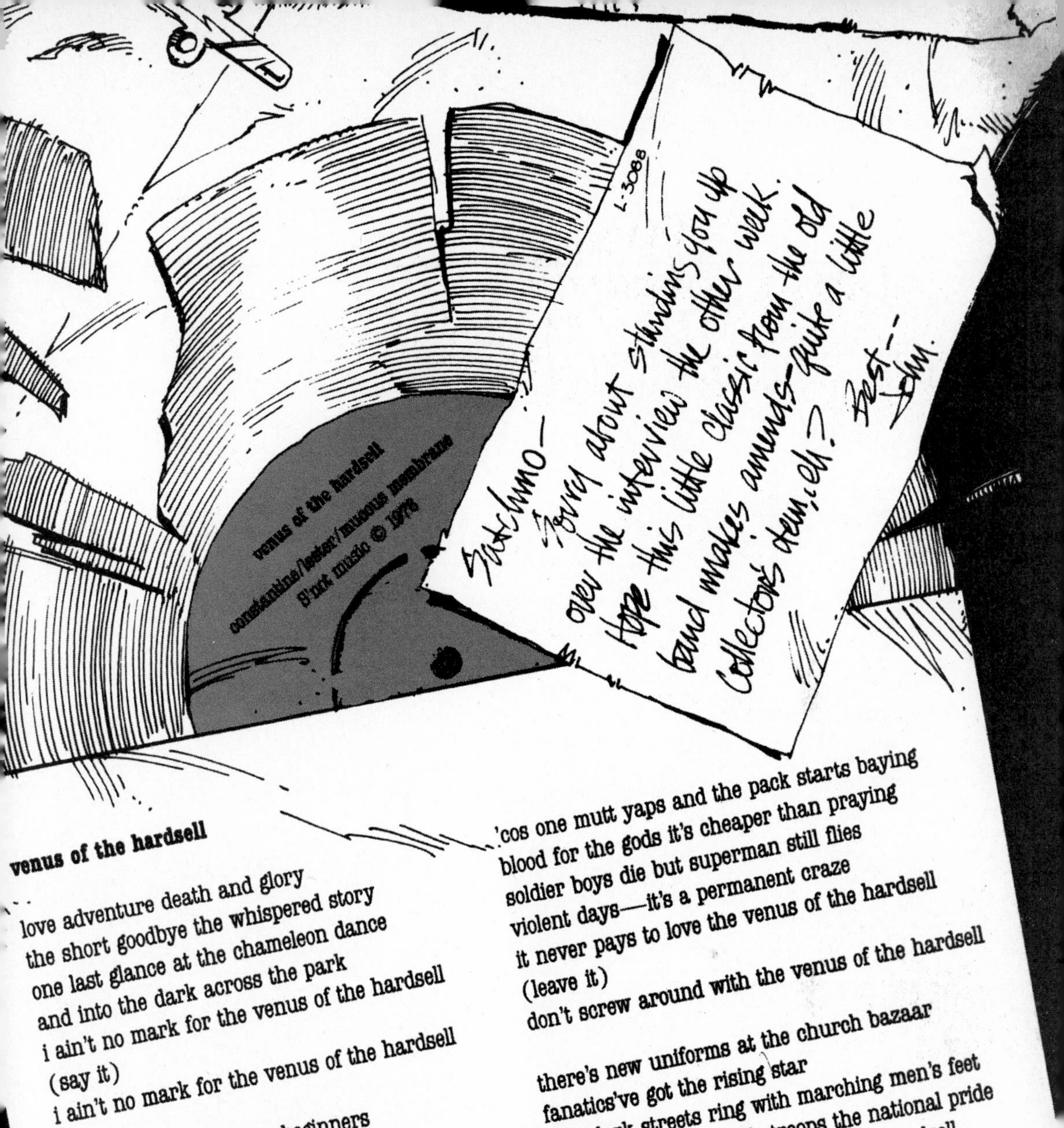
venus of the hardsell
constantine/lester/mucous membrane
S'not music © 1978
L-3088
Satchmo—
Sorry about standing you up
over the interview the other week.
Hope this little classic from the old
band makes amends—quite a little
collector's item, eh? Best—
John.

venus of the hardsell

love adventure death and glory
the short goodbye the whispered story
one last glance at the chameleon dance
and into the dark across the park
i ain't no mark for the venus of the hardsell
(say it)
i ain't no mark for the venus of the hardsell

saints and sinners raw beginners
lipstick traces and tv dinners
cigarsmoke bars and expensive new cars
the acapulco dive and the media jive
they all survive for the venus of the hardsell
(know it)
they all survive for the venus of the hardsell

empty graves and shallow heads
shallow smiles and empty beds
betta get a room without a view
sail out of sight of land
momma won't like it but you should/
travel with a rough-neck crew
listen out for all that's said
just worry when the hounds ain't fed
(gotta)
worry when the hounds ain't fed

'cos one mutt yaps and the pack starts baying
blood for the gods it's cheaper than praying
soldier boys die but superman still flies
violent days—it's a permanent craze
it never pays to love the venus of the hardsell
(leave it)
don't screw around with the venus of the hardsell

there's new uniforms at the church bazaar
fanatics've got the rising star
thin dark streets ring with marching men's feet
past the billboard bride troops the national pride
it's all supplied by the venus of the hardsell
(f**k it)
it's all supplied by the venus of the hardsell.

constantine/lester/mucous membrane
S'not music © 1978

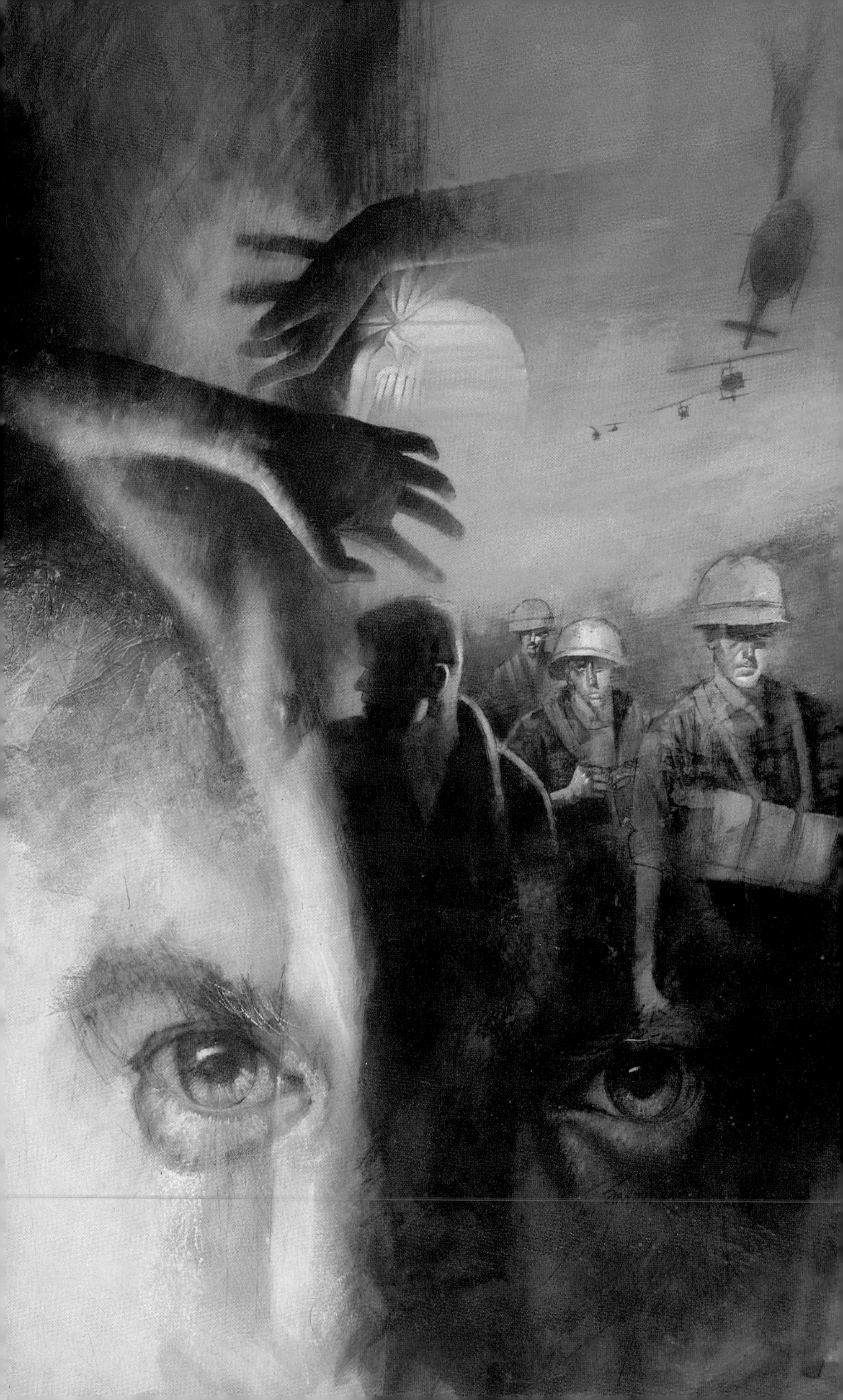

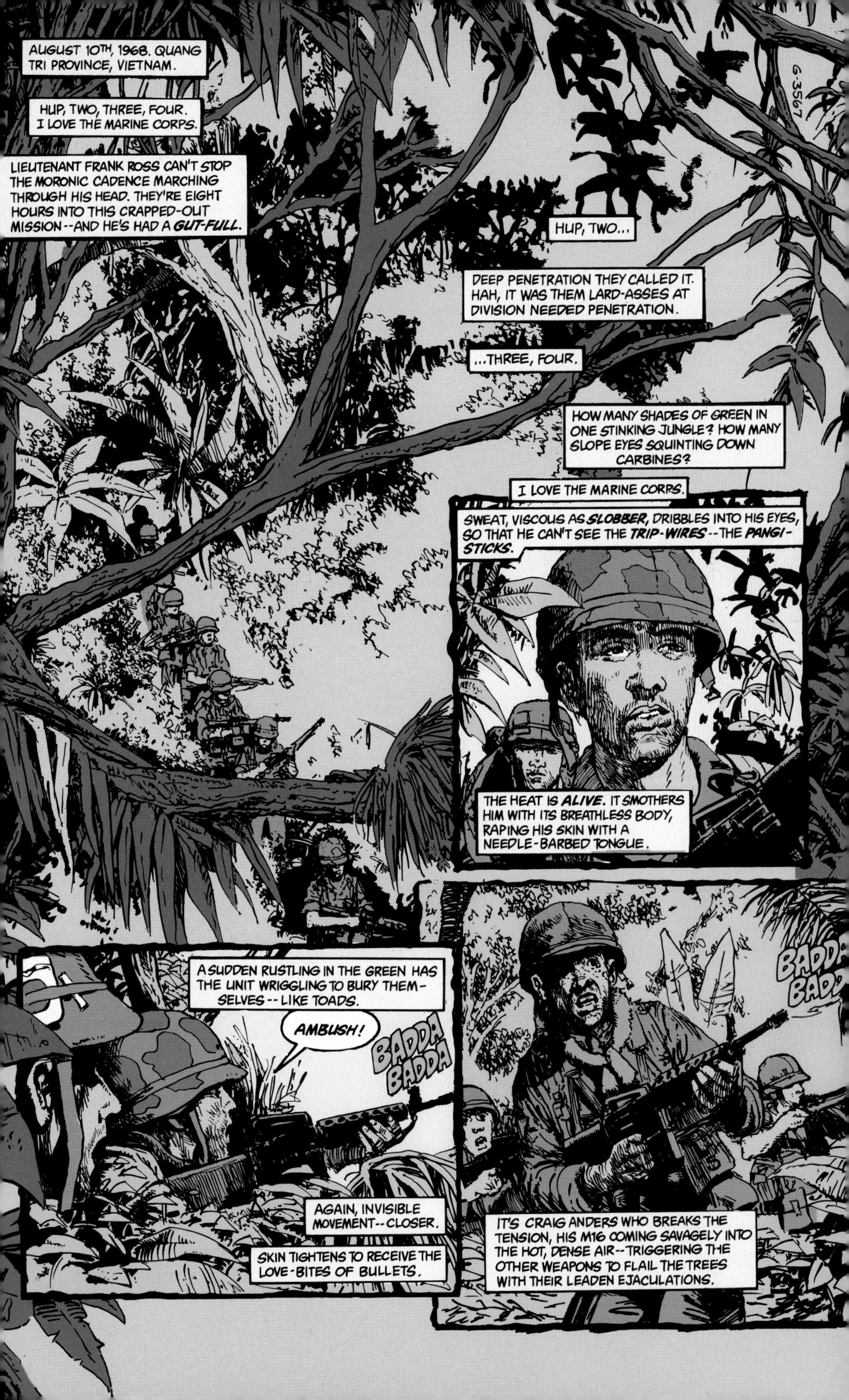

G-3567
AUGUST 10TH, 1968. QUANG TRI PROVINCE, VIETNAM.
HUP, TWO, THREE, FOUR. I LOVE THE MARINE CORPS.
LIEUTENANT FRANK ROSS CAN'T STOP THE MORONIC CADENCE MARCHING THROUGH HIS HEAD. THEY'RE EIGHT HOURS INTO THIS CRAPPED-OUT MISSION--AND HE'S HAD A GUT-FULL.
HUP, TWO...
DEEP PENETRATION THEY CALLED IT. HAH, IT WAS THEM LARD-ASSES AT DIVISION NEEDED PENETRATION.
...THREE, FOUR.
HOW MANY SHADES OF GREEN IN ONE STINKING JUNGLE? HOW MANY SLOPE EYES SQUINTING DOWN CARBINES?
I LOVE THE MARINE CORPS.
SWEAT, VISCOUS AS SLOBBER, DRIBBLES INTO HIS EYES, SO THAT HE CAN'T SEE THE TRIP-WIRES--THE PANGI-STICKS.
THE HEAT IS ALIVE. IT SMOTHERS HIM WITH ITS BREATHLESS BODY, RAPING HIS SKIN WITH A NEEDLE-BARBED TONGUE.
A SUDDEN RUSTLING IN THE GREEN HAS THE UNIT WRIGGLING TO BURY THEMSELVES--LIKE TOADS.
AMBUSH!
BADDA BADDA
AGAIN, INVISIBLE MOVEMENT--CLOSER.
SKIN TIGHTENS TO RECEIVE THE LOVE-BITES OF BULLETS.
IT'S CRAIG ANDERS WHO BREAKS THE TENSION, HIS M16 COMING SAVAGELY INTO THE HOT, DENSE AIR--TRIGGERING THE OTHER WEAPONS TO FLAIL THE TREES WITH THEIR LEADEN EJACULATIONS.

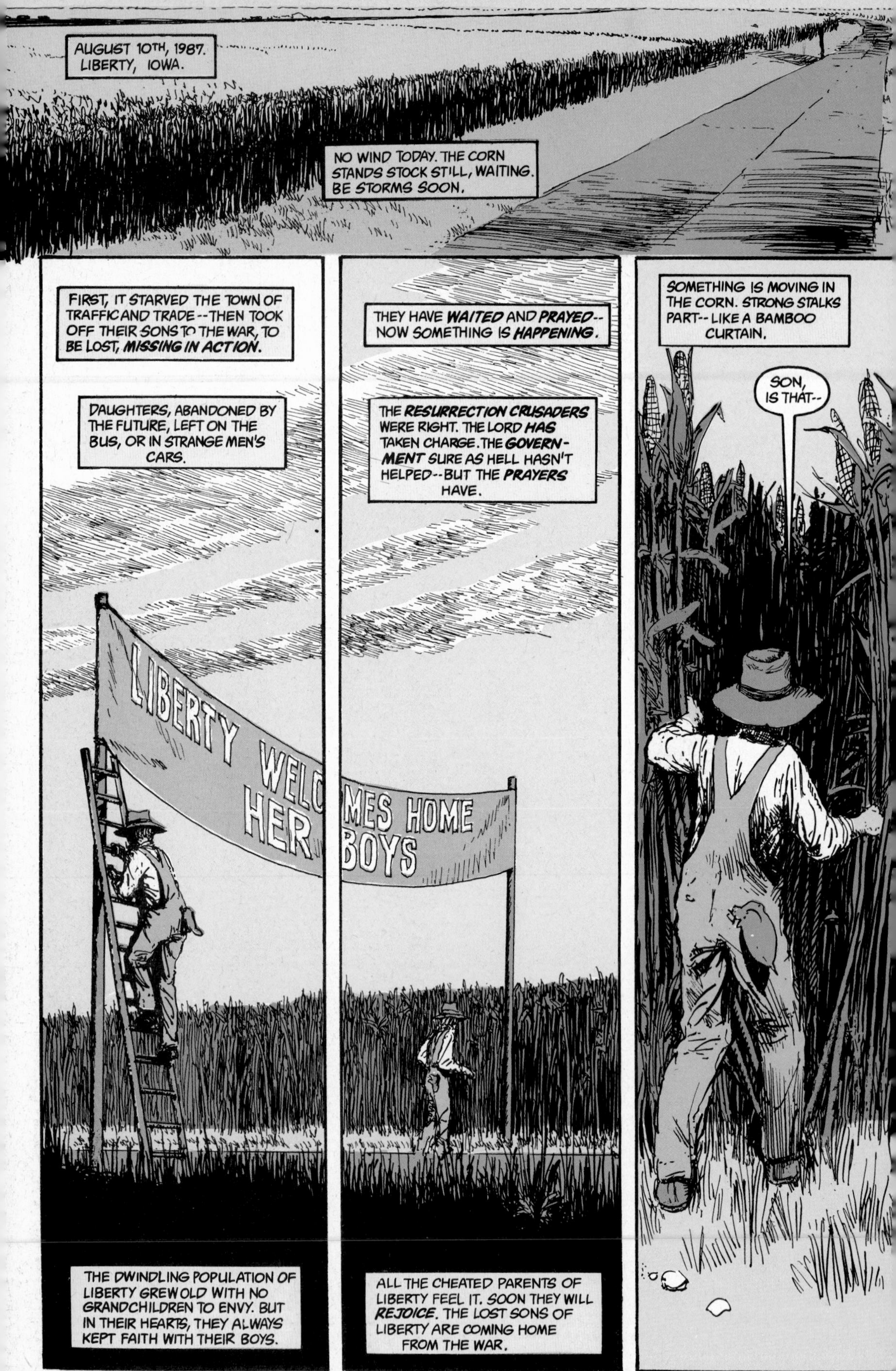

AUGUST 10TH, 1987. LIBERTY, IOWA.
NO WIND TODAY. THE CORN STANDS STOCK STILL, WAITING. BE STORMS SOON.
FIRST, IT STARVED THE TOWN OF TRAFFIC AND TRADE--THEN TOOK OFF THEIR SONS TO THE WAR, TO BE LOST, MISSING IN ACTION.
DAUGHTERS, ABANDONED BY THE FUTURE, LEFT ON THE BUS, OR IN STRANGE MEN'S CARS.
LIBERTY WELCOMES HOME HER BOYS
THE DWINDLING POPULATION OF LIBERTY GREW OLD WITH NO GRANDCHILDREN TO ENVY. BUT IN THEIR HEARTS, THEY ALWAYS KEPT FAITH WITH THEIR BOYS.
THEY HAVE WAITED AND PRAYED--NOW SOMETHING IS HAPPENING.
THE RESURRECTION CRUSADERS WERE RIGHT. THE LORD HAS TAKEN CHARGE. THE GOVERNMENT SURE AS HELL HASN'T HELPED--BUT THE PRAYERS HAVE.
ALL THE CHEATED PARENTS OF LIBERTY FEEL IT. SOON THEY WILL REJOICE. THE LOST SONS OF LIBERTY ARE COMING HOME FROM THE WAR.
SOMETHING IS MOVING IN THE CORN. STRONG STALKS PART--LIKE A BAMBOO CURTAIN.
SON, IS THAT--

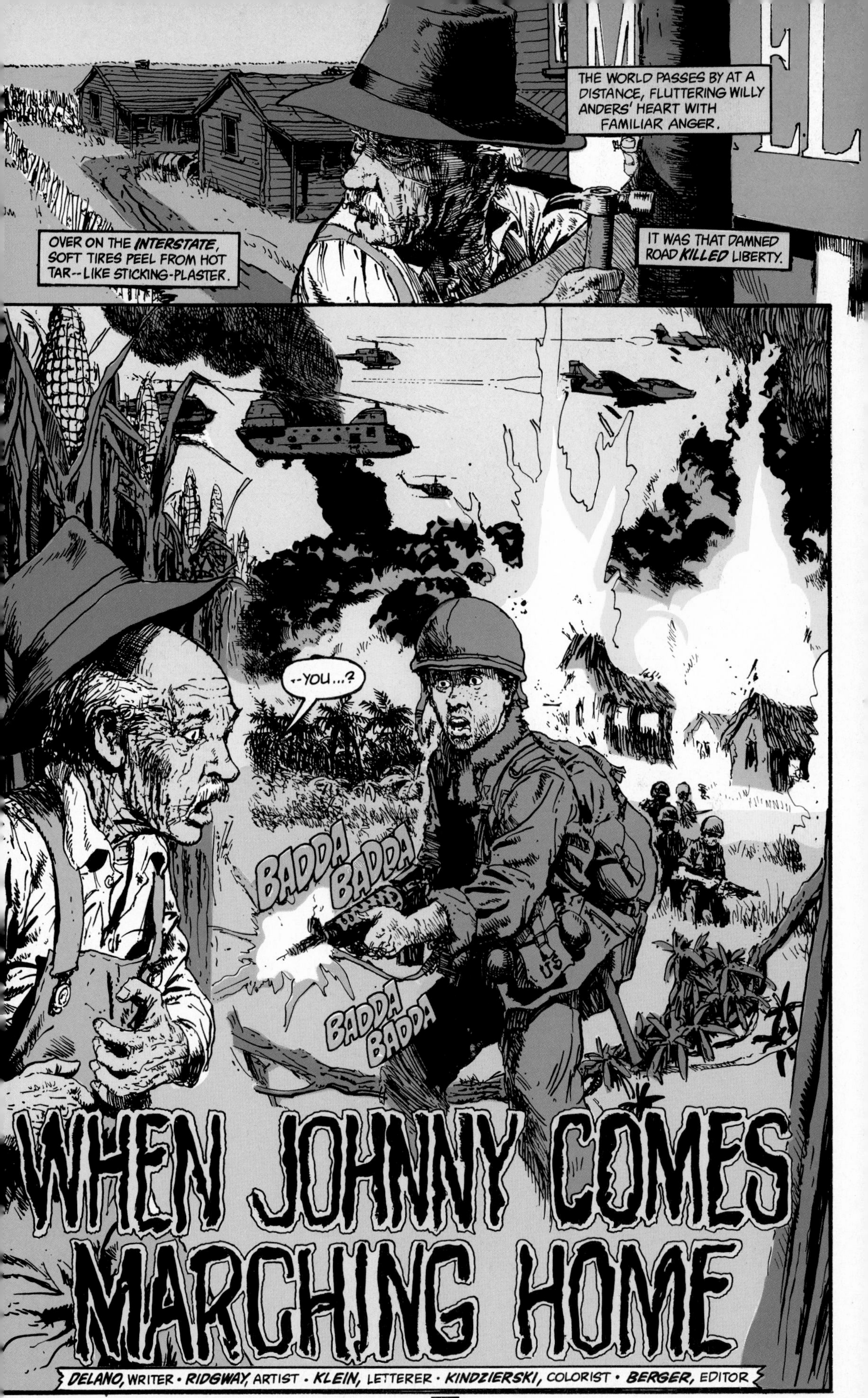
THE WORLD PASSES BY AT A DISTANCE, FLUTTERING WILLY ANDERS' HEART WITH FAMILIAR ANGER.
OVER ON THE INTERSTATE, SOFT TIRES PEEL FROM HOT TAR--LIKE STICKING-PLASTER.
IT WAS THAT DAMNED ROAD KILLED LIBERTY.
--YOU...?
BADDA BADDA
BADDA BADDA
WHEN JOHNNY COMES MARCHING HOME
DELANO, WRITER · RIDGWAY, ARTIST · KLEIN, LETTERER · KINDZIERSKI, COLORIST · BERGER, EDITOR

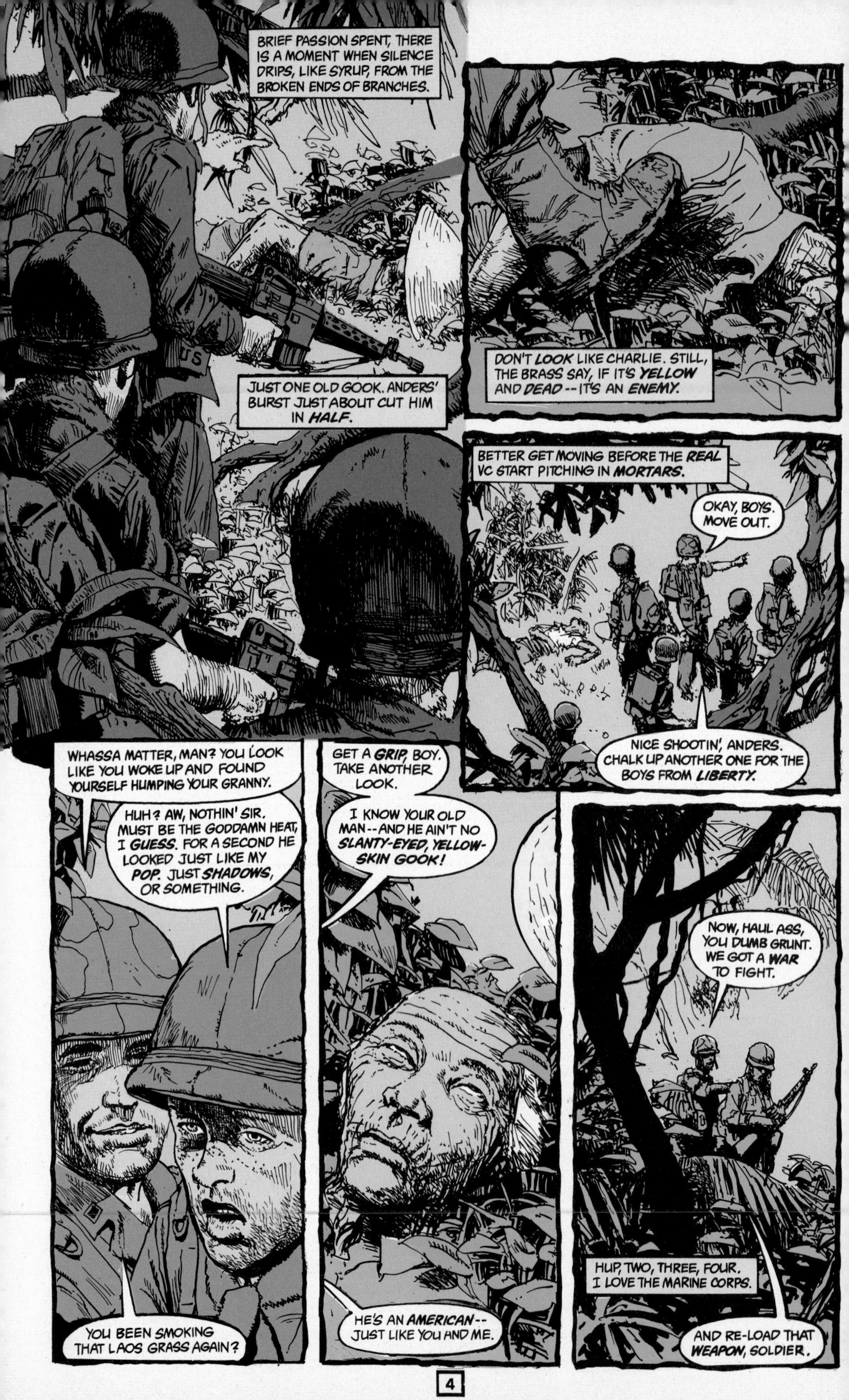

BRIEF PASSION SPENT, THERE IS A MOMENT WHEN SILENCE DRIPS, LIKE SYRUP, FROM THE BROKEN ENDS OF BRANCHES.
US
JUST ONE OLD GOOK. ANDERS' BURST JUST ABOUT CUT HIM IN HALF.
DON'T LOOK LIKE CHARLIE. STILL, THE BRASS SAY, IF IT'S YELLOW AND DEAD -- IT'S AN ENEMY.
BETTER GET MOVING BEFORE THE REAL VC START PITCHING IN MORTARS.
OKAY, BOYS. MOVE OUT.
NICE SHOOTIN', ANDERS. CHALK UP ANOTHER ONE FOR THE BOYS FROM LIBERTY.
WHASSA MATTER, MAN? YOU LOOK LIKE YOU WOKE UP AND FOUND YOURSELF HUMPING YOUR GRANNY.
HUH? AW, NOTHIN' SIR. MUST BE THE GODDAMN HEAT, I GUESS. FOR A SECOND HE LOOKED JUST LIKE MY POP. JUST SHADOWS, OR SOMETHING.
YOU BEEN SMOKING THAT LAOS GRASS AGAIN?
GET A GRIP, BOY. TAKE ANOTHER LOOK.
I KNOW YOUR OLD MAN--AND HE AIN'T NO SLANTY-EYED, YELLOW-SKIN GOOK!
HE'S AN AMERICAN-- JUST LIKE YOU AND ME.
NOW, HAUL ASS, YOU DUMB GRUNT. WE GOT A WAR TO FIGHT.
HUP, TWO, THREE, FOUR. I LOVE THE MARINE CORPS.
AND RE-LOAD THAT WEAPON, SOLDIER.

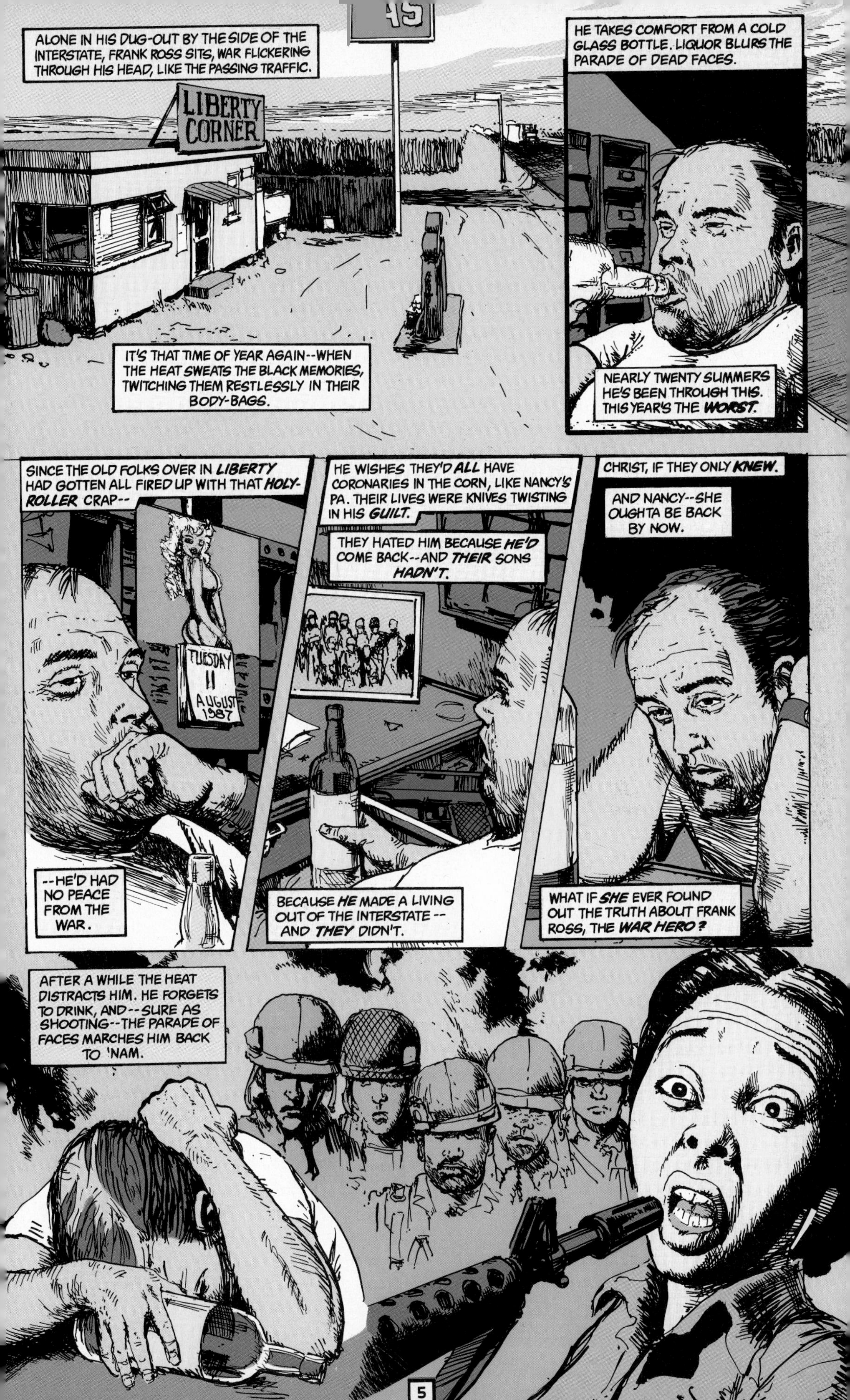

AS
ALONE IN HIS DUG-OUT BY THE SIDE OF THE INTERSTATE, FRANK ROSS SITS, WAR FLICKERING THROUGH HIS HEAD, LIKE THE PASSING TRAFFIC.
LIBERTY CORNER
IT'S THAT TIME OF YEAR AGAIN--WHEN THE HEAT SWEATS THE BLACK MEMORIES, TWITCHING THEM RESTLESSLY IN THEIR BODY-BAGS.
HE TAKES COMFORT FROM A COLD GLASS BOTTLE. LIQUOR BLURS THE PARADE OF DEAD FACES.
NEARLY TWENTY SUMMERS HE'S BEEN THROUGH THIS. THIS YEAR'S THE ***WORST.***
SINCE THE OLD FOLKS OVER IN ***LIBERTY*** HAD GOTTEN ALL FIRED UP WITH THAT ***HOLY-ROLLER*** CRAP--
TUESDAY 11 AUGUST 1987
--HE'D HAD NO PEACE FROM THE WAR.
HE WISHES THEY'D ***ALL*** HAVE CORONARIES IN THE CORN, LIKE NANCY'S PA. THEIR LIVES WERE KNIVES TWISTING IN HIS ***GUILT.***
THEY HATED HIM BECAUSE ***HE'D*** COME BACK--AND ***THEIR*** SONS ***HADN'T.***
BECAUSE ***HE*** MADE A LIVING OUT OF THE INTERSTATE --AND ***THEY*** DIDN'T.
CHRIST, IF THEY ONLY ***KNEW.***
AND NANCY--SHE OUGHTA BE BACK BY NOW.
WHAT IF ***SHE*** EVER FOUND OUT THE TRUTH ABOUT FRANK ROSS, THE ***WAR HERO?***
AFTER A WHILE THE HEAT DISTRACTS HIM. HE FORGETS TO DRINK, AND--SURE AS SHOOTING--THE PARADE OF FACES MARCHES HIM BACK TO 'NAM.

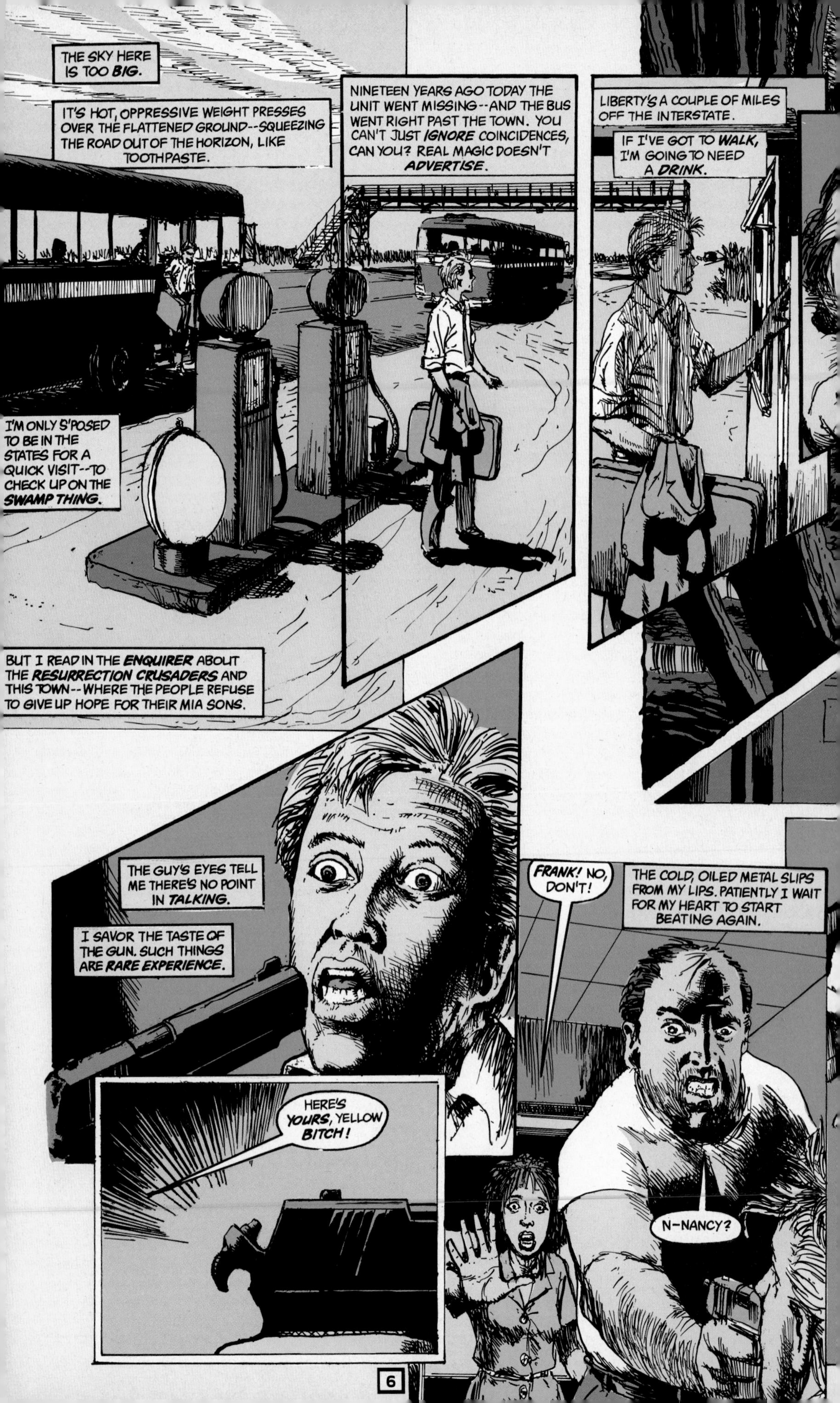

THE SKY HERE IS TOO BIG.
IT'S HOT, OPPRESSIVE WEIGHT PRESSES OVER THE FLATTENED GROUND--SQUEEZING THE ROAD OUT OF THE HORIZON, LIKE TOOTHPASTE.
I'M ONLY S'POSED TO BE IN THE STATES FOR A QUICK VISIT--TO CHECK UP ON THE SWAMP THING.
BUT I READ IN THE ENQUIRER ABOUT THE RESURRECTION CRUSADERS AND THIS TOWN--WHERE THE PEOPLE REFUSE TO GIVE UP HOPE FOR THEIR MIA SONS.
NINETEEN YEARS AGO TODAY THE UNIT WENT MISSING--AND THE BUS WENT RIGHT PAST THE TOWN. YOU CAN'T JUST IGNORE COINCIDENCES, CAN YOU? REAL MAGIC DOESN'T ADVERTISE.
LIBERTY'S A COUPLE OF MILES OFF THE INTERSTATE.
IF I'VE GOT TO WALK, I'M GOING TO NEED A DRINK.
THE GUY'S EYES TELL ME THERE'S NO POINT IN TALKING.
I SAVOR THE TASTE OF THE GUN. SUCH THINGS ARE RARE EXPERIENCE.
HERE'S YOURS, YELLOW BITCH!
FRANK! NO, DON'T!
THE COLD, OILED METAL SLIPS FROM MY LIPS. PATIENTLY I WAIT FOR MY HEART TO START BEATING AGAIN.
N-NANCY?

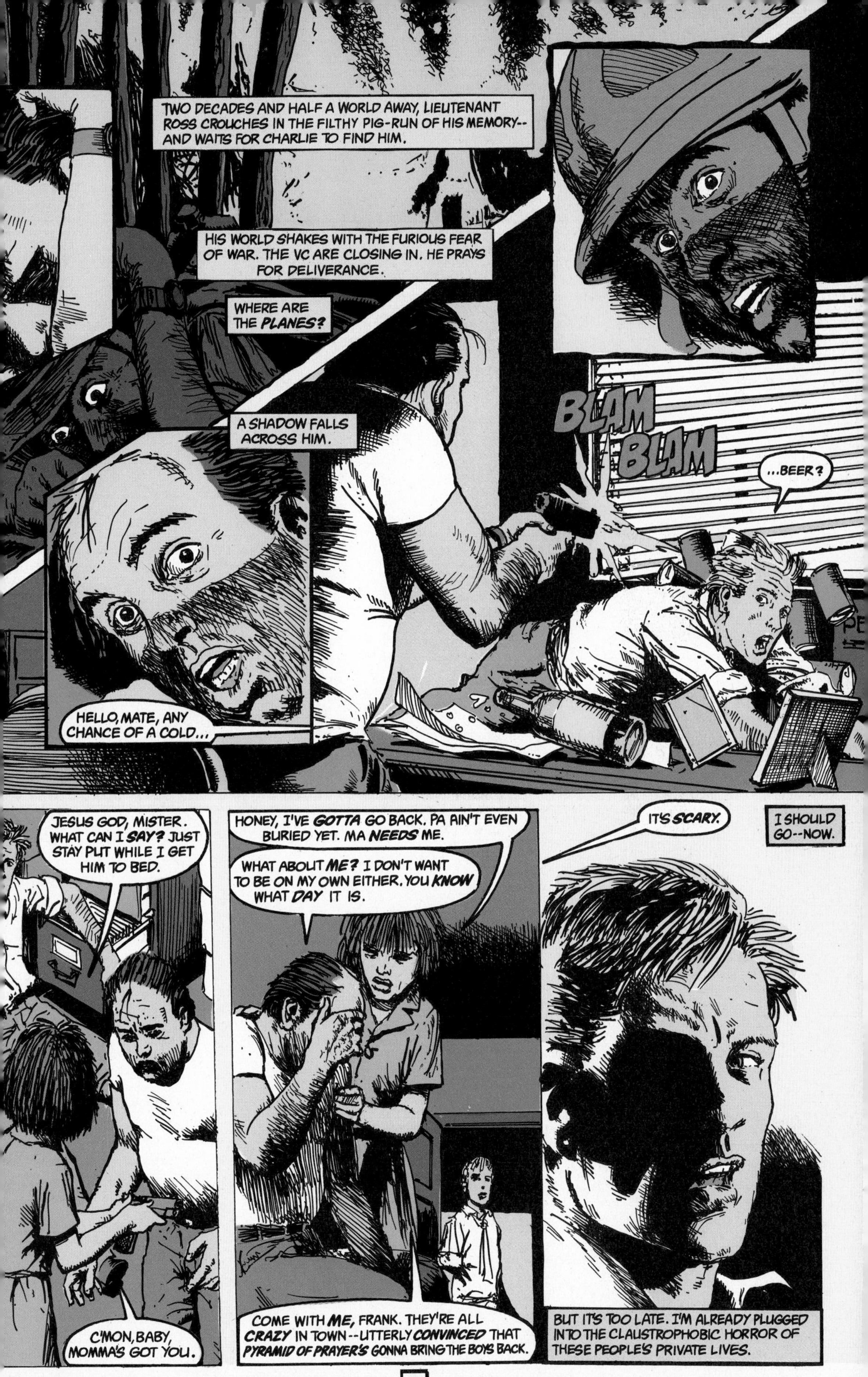
TWO DECADES AND HALF A WORLD AWAY, LIEUTENANT ROSS CROUCHES IN THE FILTHY PIG-RUN OF HIS MEMORY-- AND WAITS FOR CHARLIE TO FIND HIM.
HIS WORLD SHAKES WITH THE FURIOUS FEAR OF WAR. THE VC ARE CLOSING IN. HE PRAYS FOR DELIVERANCE.
WHERE ARE THE PLANES?
A SHADOW FALLS ACROSS HIM.
HELLO, MATE, ANY CHANCE OF A COLD...
BLAM
BLAM
...BEER?
JESUS GOD, MISTER. WHAT CAN I SAY? JUST STAY PUT WHILE I GET HIM TO BED.
C'MON, BABY, MOMMA'S GOT YOU.
HONEY, I'VE GOTTA GO BACK. PA AIN'T EVEN BURIED YET. MA NEEDS ME.
WHAT ABOUT ME? I DON'T WANT TO BE ON MY OWN EITHER. YOU KNOW WHAT DAY IT IS.
COME WITH ME, FRANK. THEY'RE ALL CRAZY IN TOWN--UTTERLY CONVINCED THAT PYRAMID OF PRAYER'S GONNA BRING THE BOYS BACK.
IT'S SCARY.
I SHOULD GO--NOW.
BUT IT'S TOO LATE. I'M ALREADY PLUGGED INTO THE CLAUSTROPHOBIC HORROR OF THESE PEOPLE'S PRIVATE LIVES.

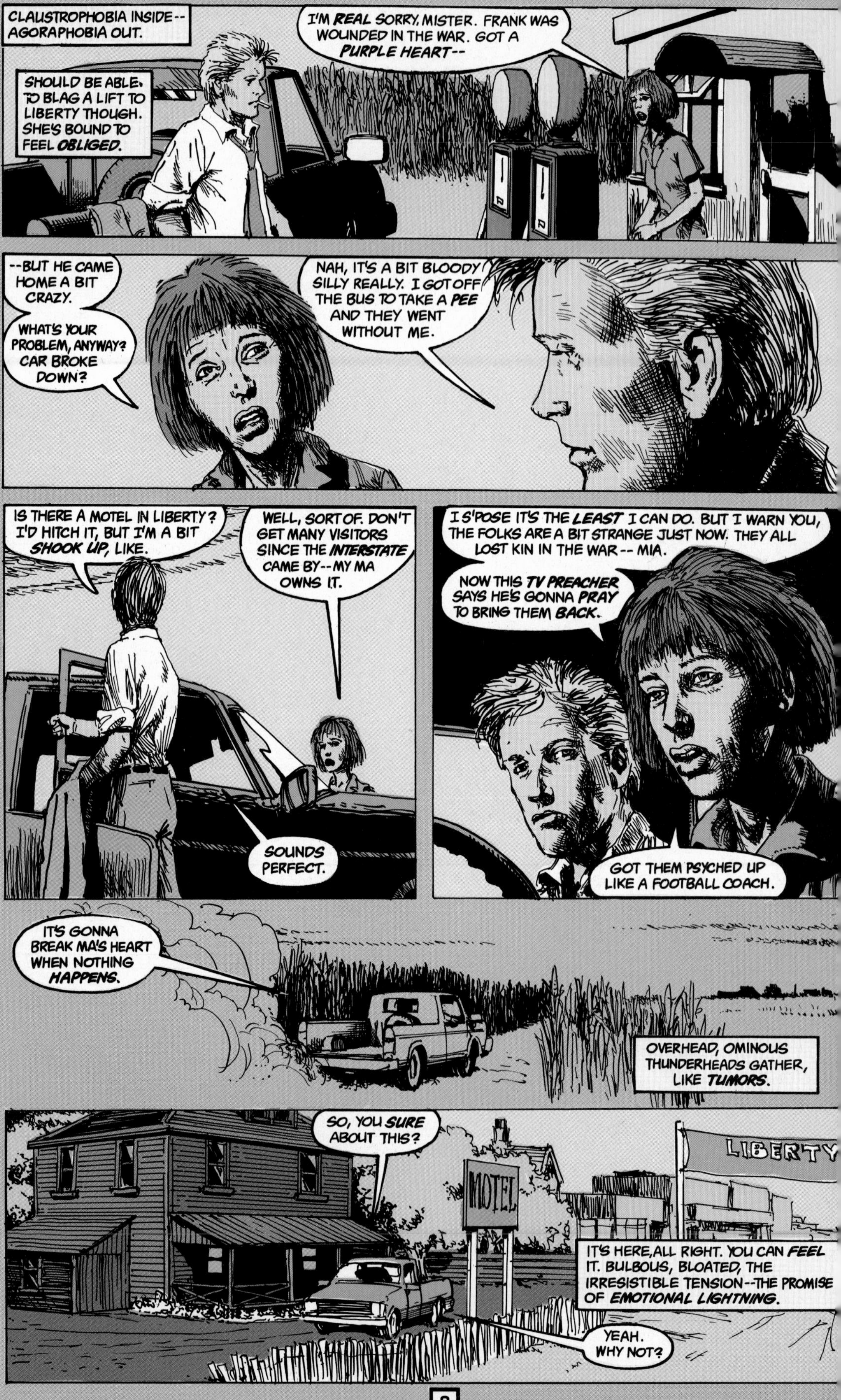
CLAUSTROPHOBIA INSIDE-- AGORAPHOBIA OUT.
SHOULD BE ABLE TO BLAG A LIFT TO LIBERTY THOUGH. SHE'S BOUND TO FEEL OBLIGED.
I'M REAL SORRY, MISTER. FRANK WAS WOUNDED IN THE WAR. GOT A PURPLE HEART--
--BUT HE CAME HOME A BIT CRAZY.
WHAT'S YOUR PROBLEM, ANYWAY? CAR BROKE DOWN?
NAH, IT'S A BIT BLOODY SILLY REALLY. I GOT OFF THE BUS TO TAKE A PEE AND THEY WENT WITHOUT ME.
IS THERE A MOTEL IN LIBERTY? I'D HITCH IT, BUT I'M A BIT SHOOK UP, LIKE.
WELL, SORT OF. DON'T GET MANY VISITORS SINCE THE INTERSTATE CAME BY--MY MA OWNS IT.
SOUNDS PERFECT.
I S'POSE IT'S THE LEAST I CAN DO. BUT I WARN YOU, THE FOLKS ARE A BIT STRANGE JUST NOW. THEY ALL LOST KIN IN THE WAR -- MIA.
NOW THIS TV PREACHER SAYS HE'S GONNA PRAY TO BRING THEM BACK.
GOT THEM PSYCHED UP LIKE A FOOTBALL COACH.
IT'S GONNA BREAK MA'S HEART WHEN NOTHING HAPPENS.
OVERHEAD, OMINOUS THUNDERHEADS GATHER, LIKE TUMORS.
SO, YOU SURE ABOUT THIS?
MOTEL
LIBERTY
IT'S HERE, ALL RIGHT. YOU CAN FEEL IT. BULBOUS, BLOATED, THE IRRESISTIBLE TENSION--THE PROMISE OF EMOTIONAL LIGHTNING.
YEAH. WHY NOT?

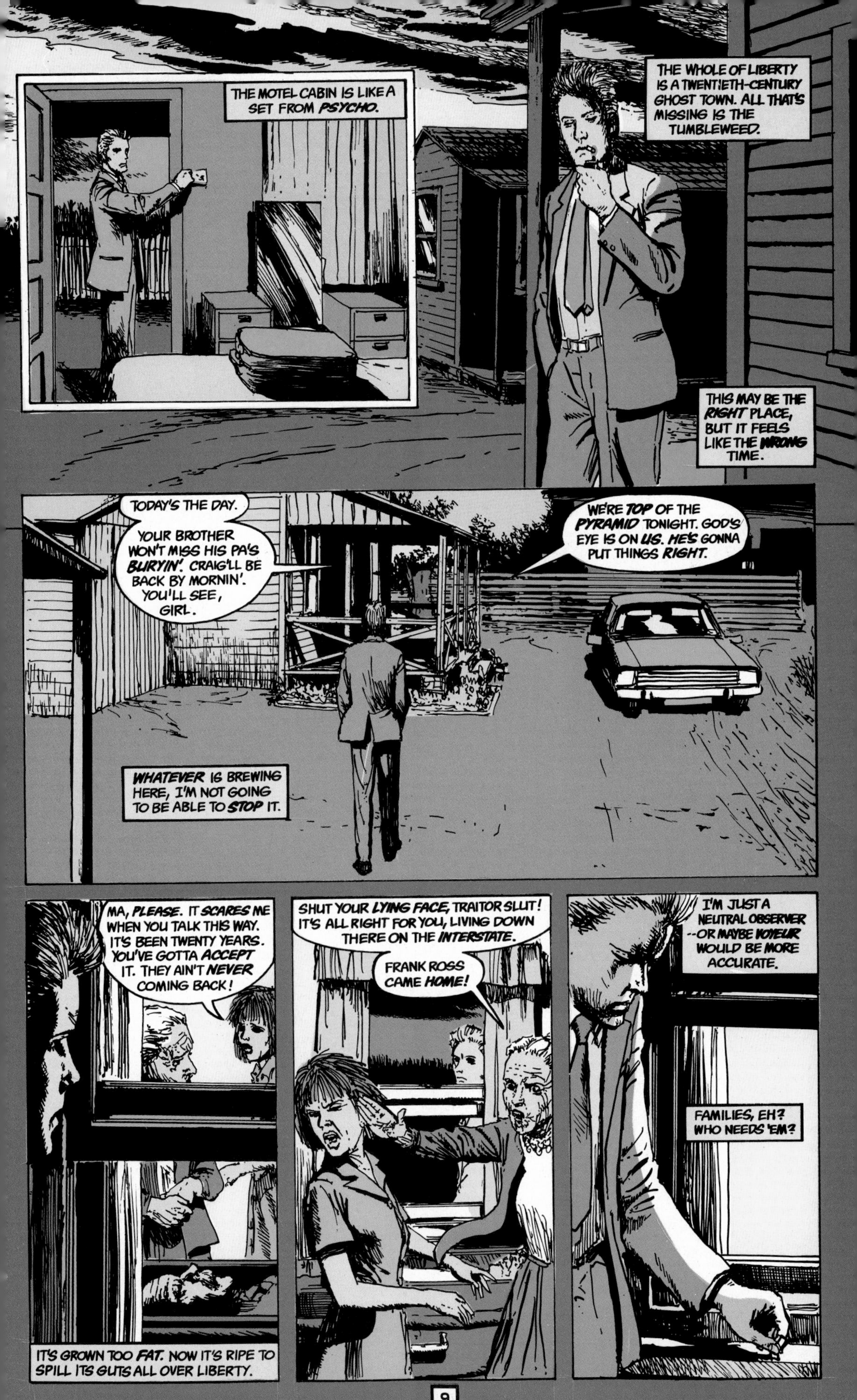
THE MOTEL CABIN IS LIKE A SET FROM PSYCHO.
THE WHOLE OF LIBERTY IS A TWENTIETH-CENTURY GHOST TOWN. ALL THAT'S MISSING IS THE TUMBLEWEED.
THIS MAY BE THE RIGHT PLACE, BUT IT FEELS LIKE THE WRONG TIME.
TODAY'S THE DAY.
YOUR BROTHER WON'T MISS HIS PA'S BURYIN'. CRAIG'LL BE BACK BY MORNIN'. YOU'LL SEE, GIRL.
WE'RE TOP OF THE PYRAMID TONIGHT. GOD'S EYE IS ON US. HE'S GONNA PUT THINGS RIGHT.
WHATEVER IS BREWING HERE, I'M NOT GOING TO BE ABLE TO STOP IT.
MA, PLEASE. IT SCARES ME WHEN YOU TALK THIS WAY. IT'S BEEN TWENTY YEARS. YOU'VE GOTTA ACCEPT IT. THEY AIN'T NEVER COMING BACK!
IT'S GROWN TOO FAT. NOW IT'S RIPE TO SPILL ITS GUTS ALL OVER LIBERTY.
SHUT YOUR LYING FACE, TRAITOR SLUT! IT'S ALL RIGHT FOR YOU, LIVING DOWN THERE ON THE INTERSTATE.
FRANK ROSS CAME HOME!
I'M JUST A NEUTRAL OBSERVER --OR MAYBE VOYEUR WOULD BE MORE ACCURATE.
FAMILIES, EH? WHO NEEDS 'EM?

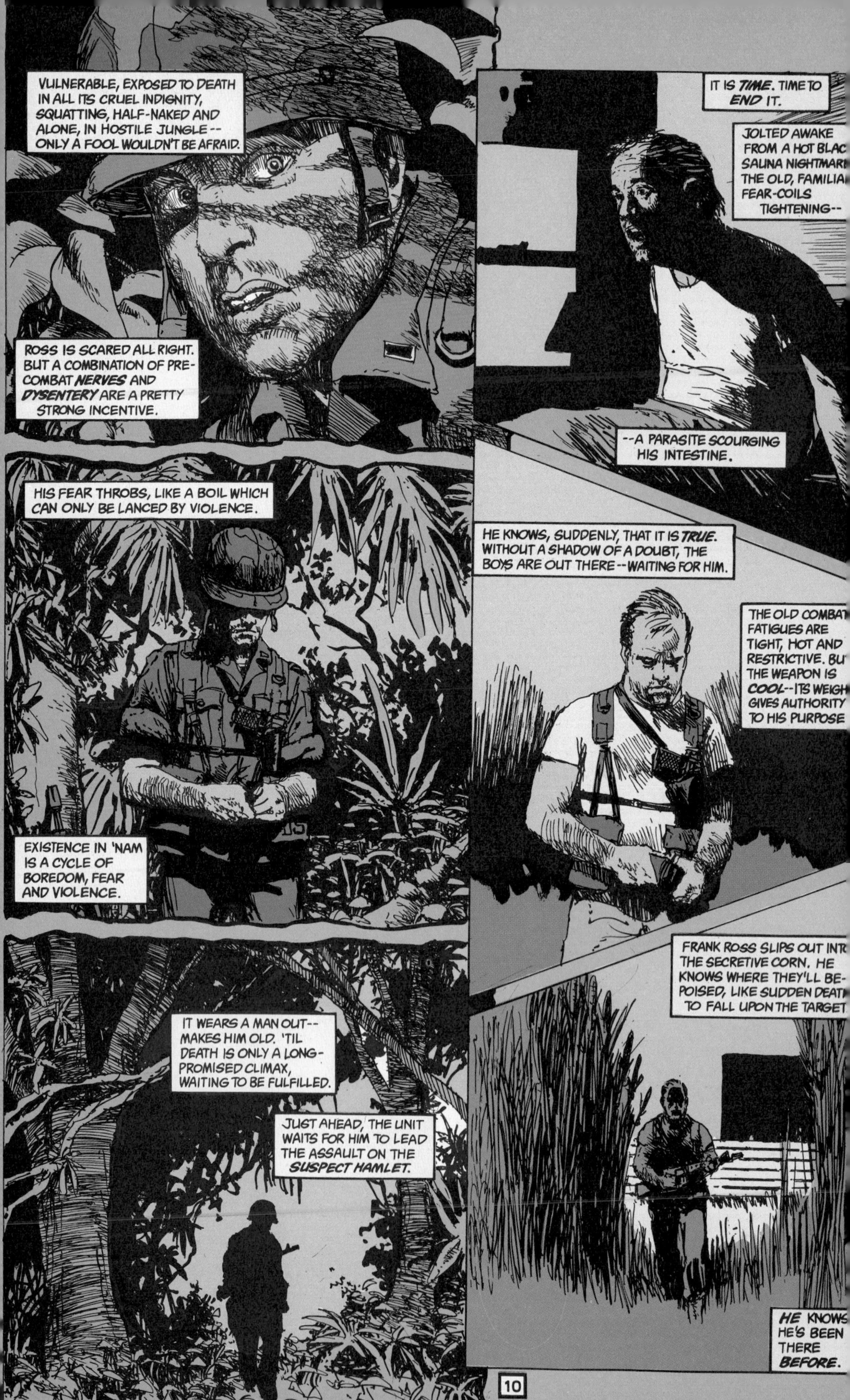

VULNERABLE, EXPOSED TO DEATH IN ALL ITS CRUEL INDIGNITY, SQUATTING, HALF-NAKED AND ALONE, IN HOSTILE JUNGLE -- ONLY A FOOL WOULDN'T BE AFRAID.
ROSS IS SCARED ALL RIGHT. BUT A COMBINATION OF PRE-COMBAT NERVES AND DYSENTERY ARE A PRETTY STRONG INCENTIVE.
IT IS TIME. TIME TO END IT.
JOLTED AWAKE FROM A HOT BLAC SAUNA NIGHTMAR THE OLD, FAMILIA FEAR-COILS TIGHTENING--
--A PARASITE SCOURGING HIS INTESTINE.
HIS FEAR THROBS, LIKE A BOIL WHICH CAN ONLY BE LANCED BY VIOLENCE.
EXISTENCE IN 'NAM IS A CYCLE OF BOREDOM, FEAR AND VIOLENCE.
HE KNOWS, SUDDENLY, THAT IT IS TRUE. WITHOUT A SHADOW OF A DOUBT, THE BOYS ARE OUT THERE--WAITING FOR HIM.
THE OLD COMBA FATIGUES ARE TIGHT, HOT AND RESTRICTIVE. BU THE WEAPON IS COOL--ITS WEIGH GIVES AUTHORITY TO HIS PURPOSE
IT WEARS A MAN OUT-- MAKES HIM OLD. 'TIL DEATH IS ONLY A LONG-PROMISED CLIMAX, WAITING TO BE FULFILLED.
JUST AHEAD, THE UNIT WAITS FOR HIM TO LEAD THE ASSAULT ON THE SUSPECT HAMLET.
FRANK ROSS SLIPS OUT INT THE SECRETIVE CORN. HE KNOWS WHERE THEY'LL BE-POISED, LIKE SUDDEN DEAT TO FALL UPON THE TARGET
HE KNOWS HE'S BEEN THERE BEFORE.

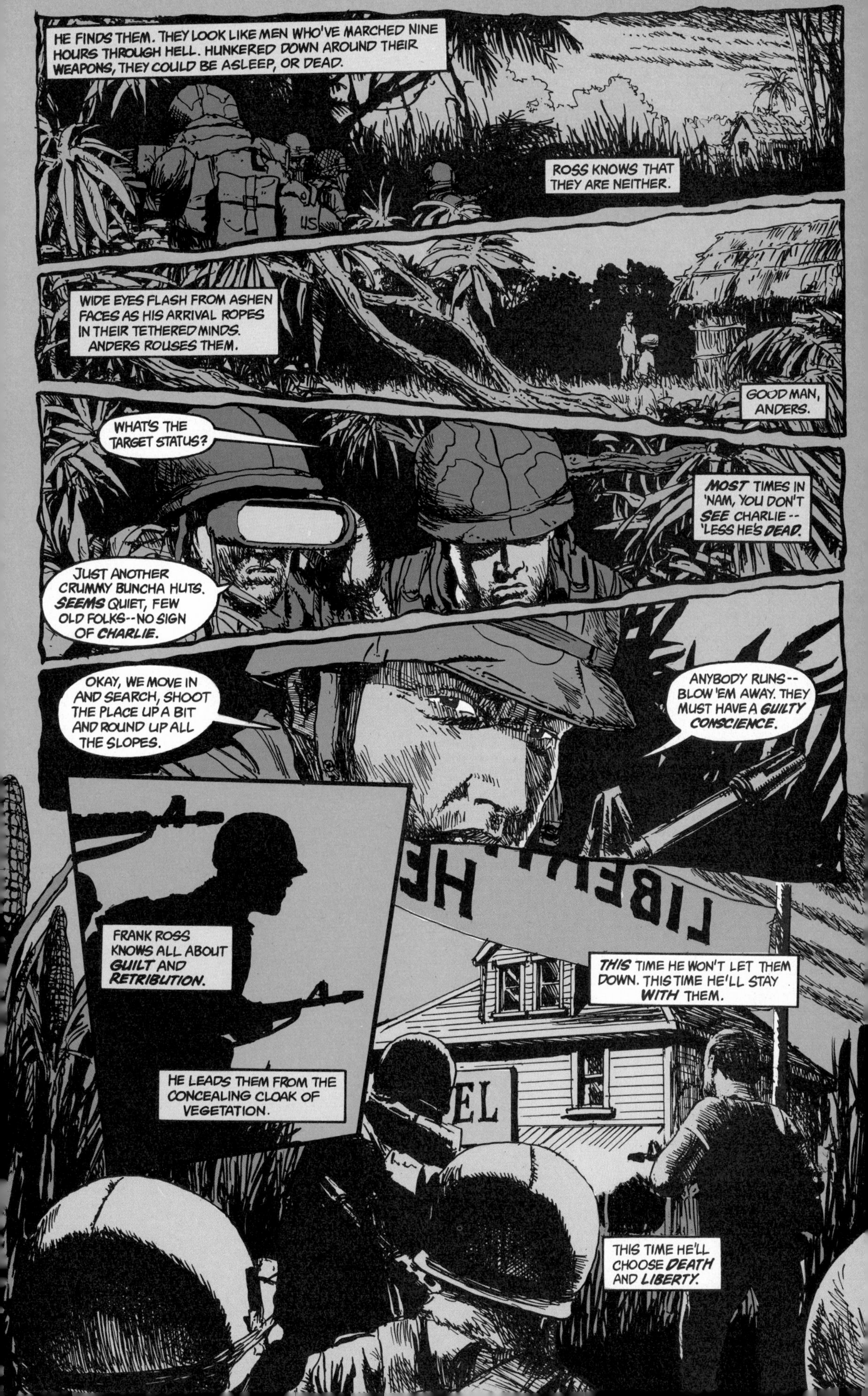
HE FINDS THEM. THEY LOOK LIKE MEN WHO'VE MARCHED NINE HOURS THROUGH HELL. HUNKERED DOWN AROUND THEIR WEAPONS, THEY COULD BE ASLEEP, OR DEAD.
ROSS KNOWS THAT THEY ARE NEITHER.
US
WIDE EYES FLASH FROM ASHEN FACES AS HIS ARRIVAL ROPES IN THEIR TETHERED MINDS. ANDERS ROUSES THEM.
GOOD MAN, ANDERS.
WHAT'S THE TARGET STATUS?
MOST TIMES IN 'NAM, YOU DON'T SEE CHARLIE -- 'LESS HE'S DEAD.
JUST ANOTHER CRUMMY BUNCHA HUTS. SEEMS QUIET, FEW OLD FOLKS--NO SIGN OF CHARLIE.
OKAY, WE MOVE IN AND SEARCH, SHOOT THE PLACE UP A BIT AND ROUND UP ALL THE SLOPES.
ANYBODY RUNS-- BLOW 'EM AWAY. THEY MUST HAVE A GUILTY CONSCIENCE.
FRANK ROSS KNOWS ALL ABOUT GUILT AND RETRIBUTION.
THIS TIME HE WON'T LET THEM DOWN. THIS TIME HE'LL STAY WITH THEM.
HE LEADS THEM FROM THE CONCEALING CLOAK OF VEGETATION.
EL
THIS TIME HE'LL CHOOSE DEATH AND LIBERTY.

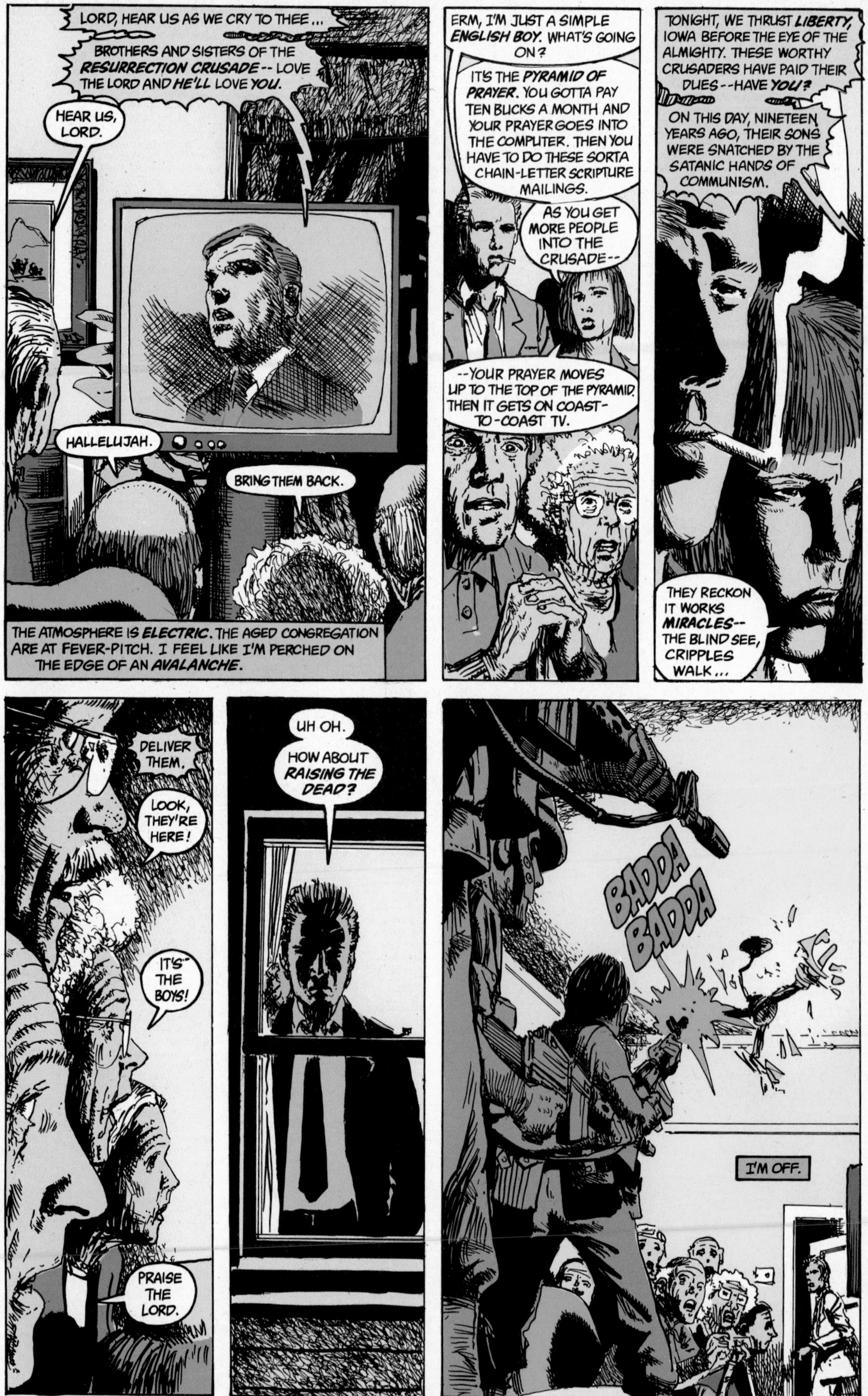
LORD, HEAR US AS WE CRY TO THEE...
BROTHERS AND SISTERS OF THE RESURRECTION CRUSADE -- LOVE THE LORD AND HE'LL LOVE YOU.
HEAR US, LORD.
HALLELUJAH.
BRING THEM BACK.
THE ATMOSPHERE IS ELECTRIC. THE AGED CONGREGATION ARE AT FEVER-PITCH. I FEEL LIKE I'M PERCHED ON THE EDGE OF AN AVALANCHE.
ERM, I'M JUST A SIMPLE ENGLISH BOY. WHAT'S GOING ON?
IT'S THE PYRAMID OF PRAYER. YOU GOTTA PAY TEN BUCKS A MONTH AND YOUR PRAYER GOES INTO THE COMPUTER. THEN YOU HAVE TO DO THESE SORTA CHAIN-LETTER SCRIPTURE MAILINGS.
AS YOU GET MORE PEOPLE INTO THE CRUSADE--
--YOUR PRAYER MOVES UP TO THE TOP OF THE PYRAMID. THEN IT GETS ON COAST-TO-COAST TV.
TONIGHT, WE THRUST LIBERTY, IOWA BEFORE THE EYE OF THE ALMIGHTY. THESE WORTHY CRUSADERS HAVE PAID THEIR DUES--HAVE YOU?
ON THIS DAY, NINETEEN YEARS AGO, THEIR SONS WERE SNATCHED BY THE SATANIC HANDS OF COMMUNISM.
THEY RECKON IT WORKS MIRACLES-- THE BLIND SEE, CRIPPLES WALK...
DELIVER THEM.
LOOK, THEY'RE HERE!
IT'S THE BOYS!
PRAISE THE LORD.
UH OH.
HOW ABOUT RAISING THE DEAD?
BADDA BADDA
I'M OFF.

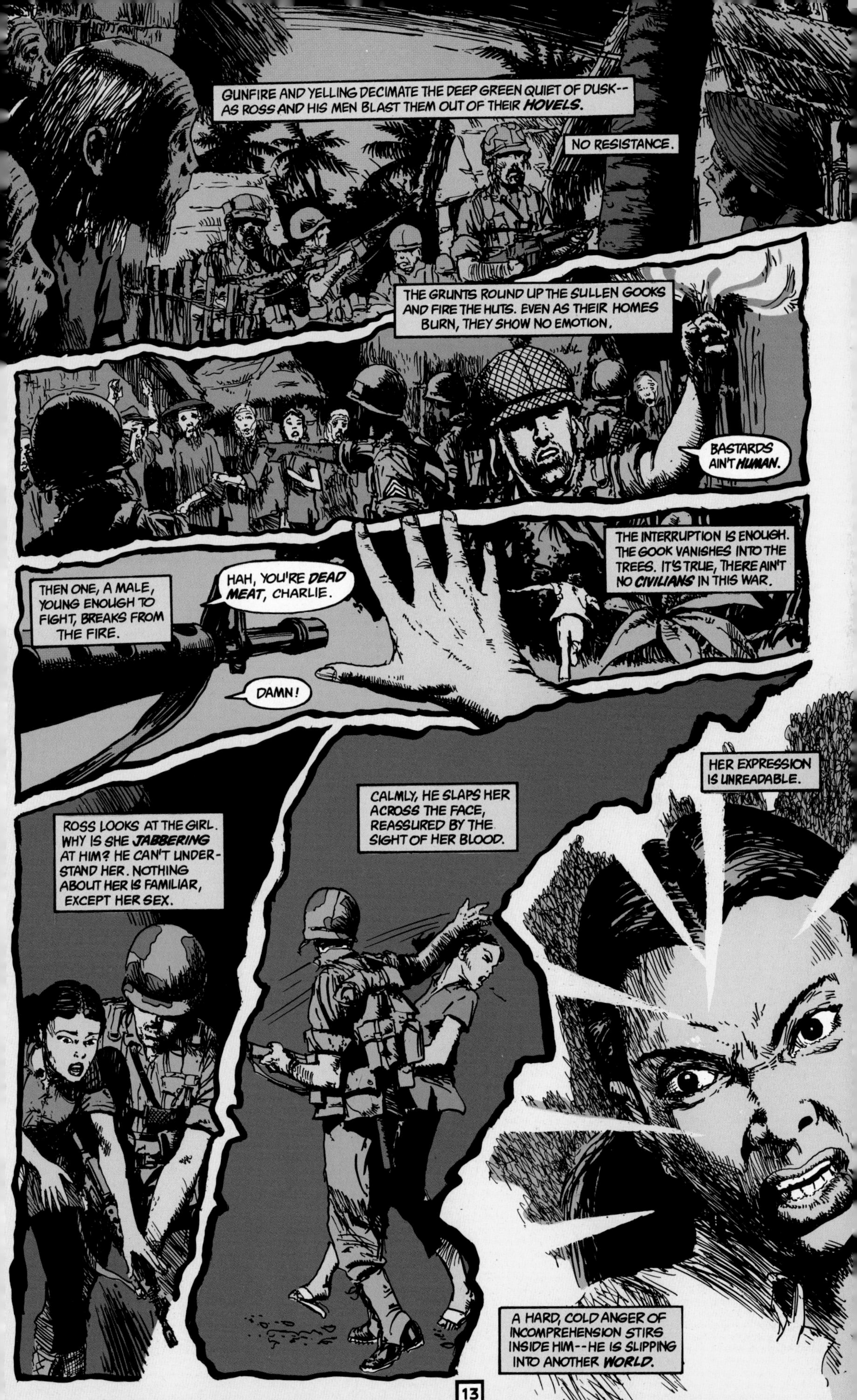

GUNFIRE AND YELLING DECIMATE THE DEEP GREEN QUIET OF DUSK-- AS ROSS AND HIS MEN BLAST THEM OUT OF THEIR HOVELS.
NO RESISTANCE.
THE GRUNTS ROUND UP THE SULLEN GOOKS AND FIRE THE HUTS. EVEN AS THEIR HOMES BURN, THEY SHOW NO EMOTION.
BASTARDS AIN'T HUMAN.
THEN ONE, A MALE, YOUNG ENOUGH TO FIGHT, BREAKS FROM THE FIRE.
HAH, YOU'RE DEAD MEAT, CHARLIE.
DAMN!
THE INTERRUPTION IS ENOUGH. THE GOOK VANISHES INTO THE TREES. IT'S TRUE, THERE AIN'T NO CIVILIANS IN THIS WAR.
ROSS LOOKS AT THE GIRL. WHY IS SHE JABBERING AT HIM? HE CAN'T UNDERSTAND HER. NOTHING ABOUT HER IS FAMILIAR, EXCEPT HER SEX.
CALMLY, HE SLAPS HER ACROSS THE FACE, REASSURED BY THE SIGHT OF HER BLOOD.
HER EXPRESSION IS UNREADABLE.
A HARD, COLD ANGER OF INCOMPREHENSION STIRS INSIDE HIM--HE IS SLIPPING INTO ANOTHER WORLD.

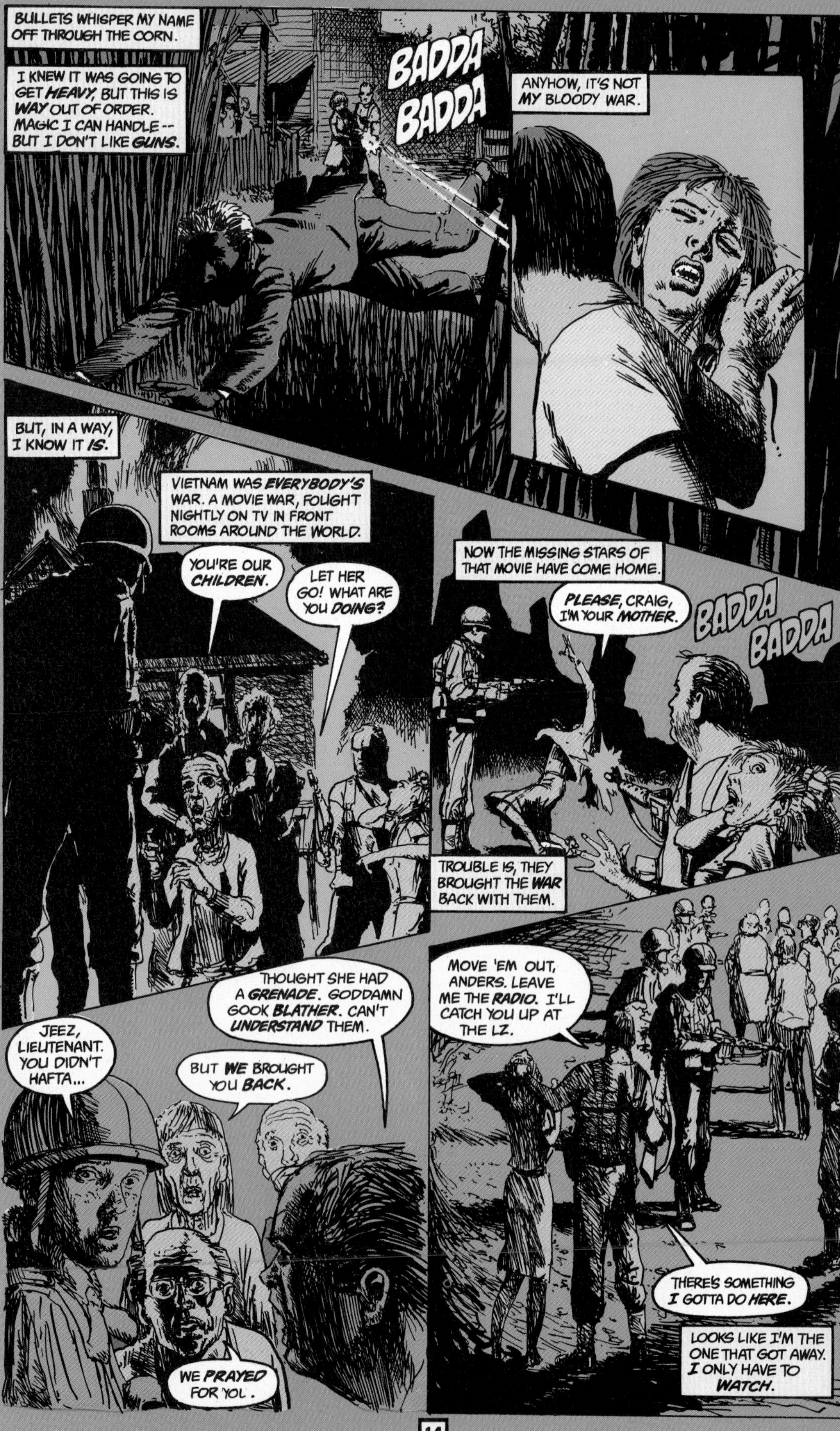

BULLETS WHISPER MY NAME OFF THROUGH THE CORN.
I KNEW IT WAS GOING TO GET HEAVY, BUT THIS IS WAY OUT OF ORDER. MAGIC I CAN HANDLE -- BUT I DON'T LIKE GUNS.
BADDA BADDA
ANYHOW, IT'S NOT MY BLOODY WAR.
BUT, IN A WAY, I KNOW IT IS.
VIETNAM WAS EVERYBODY'S WAR. A MOVIE WAR, FOUGHT NIGHTLY ON TV IN FRONT ROOMS AROUND THE WORLD.
YOU'RE OUR CHILDREN.
LET HER GO! WHAT ARE YOU DOING?
NOW THE MISSING STARS OF THAT MOVIE HAVE COME HOME.
PLEASE, CRAIG, I'M YOUR MOTHER.
BADDA BADDA
TROUBLE IS, THEY BROUGHT THE WAR BACK WITH THEM.
THOUGHT SHE HAD A GRENADE. GODDAMN GOOK BLATHER. CAN'T UNDERSTAND THEM.
JEEZ, LIEUTENANT. YOU DIDN'T HAFTA...
BUT WE BROUGHT YOU BACK.
WE PRAYED FOR YOU.
MOVE 'EM OUT, ANDERS. LEAVE ME THE RADIO. I'LL CATCH YOU UP AT THE LZ.
THERE'S SOMETHING I GOTTA DO HERE.
LOOKS LIKE I'M THE ONE THAT GOT AWAY. I ONLY HAVE TO WATCH.

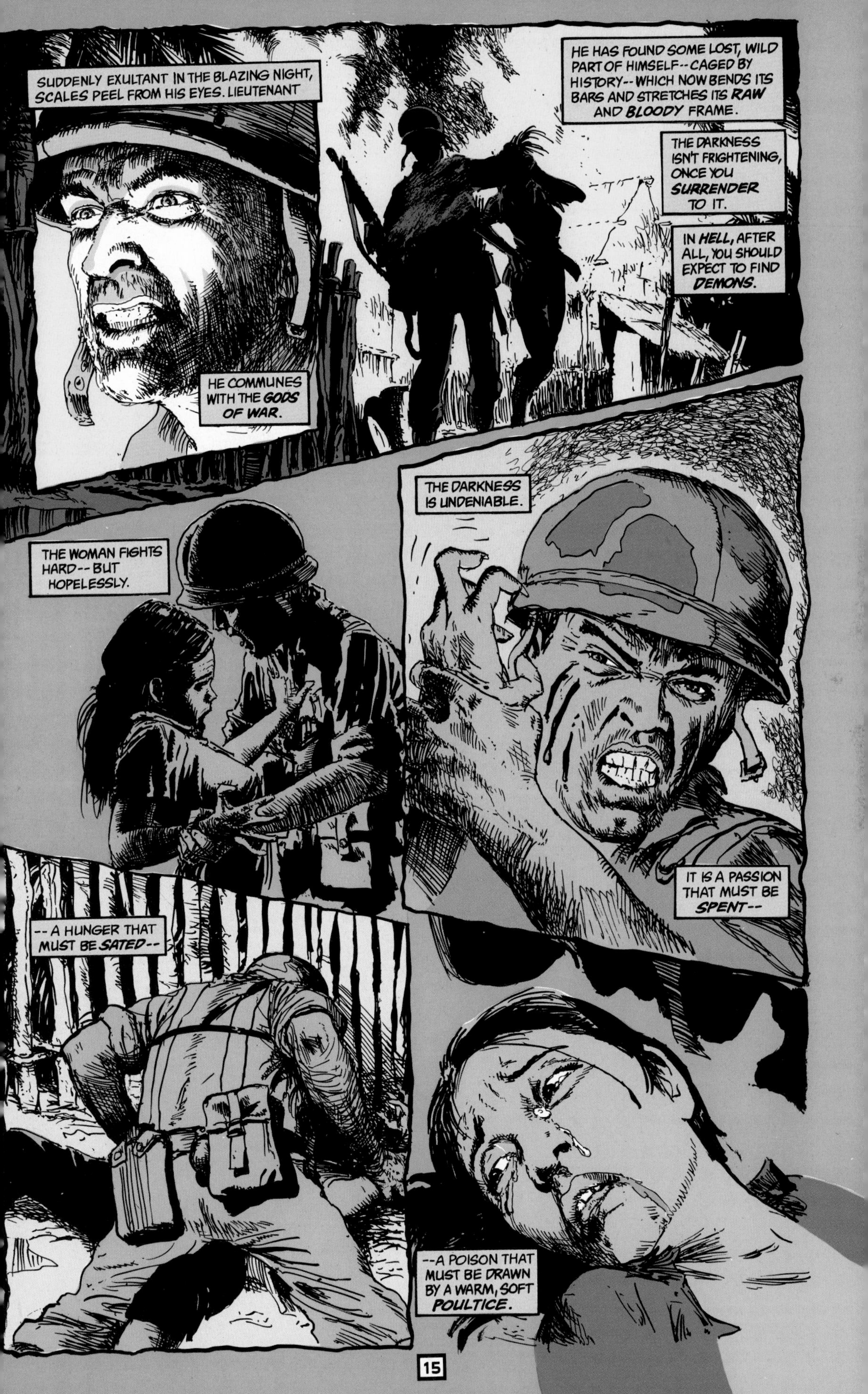
SUDDENLY EXULTANT IN THE BLAZING NIGHT, SCALES PEEL FROM HIS EYES. LIEUTENANT
HE COMMUNES WITH THE GODS OF WAR.
HE HAS FOUND SOME LOST, WILD PART OF HIMSELF--CAGED BY HISTORY--WHICH NOW BENDS ITS BARS AND STRETCHES ITS RAW AND BLOODY FRAME.
THE DARKNESS ISN'T FRIGHTENING, ONCE YOU SURRENDER TO IT.
IN HELL, AFTER ALL, YOU SHOULD EXPECT TO FIND DEMONS.
THE WOMAN FIGHTS HARD--BUT HOPELESSLY.
THE DARKNESS IS UNDENIABLE.
IT IS A PASSION THAT MUST BE SPENT--
--A HUNGER THAT MUST BE SATED--
--A POISON THAT MUST BE DRAWN BY A WARM, SOFT POULTICE.

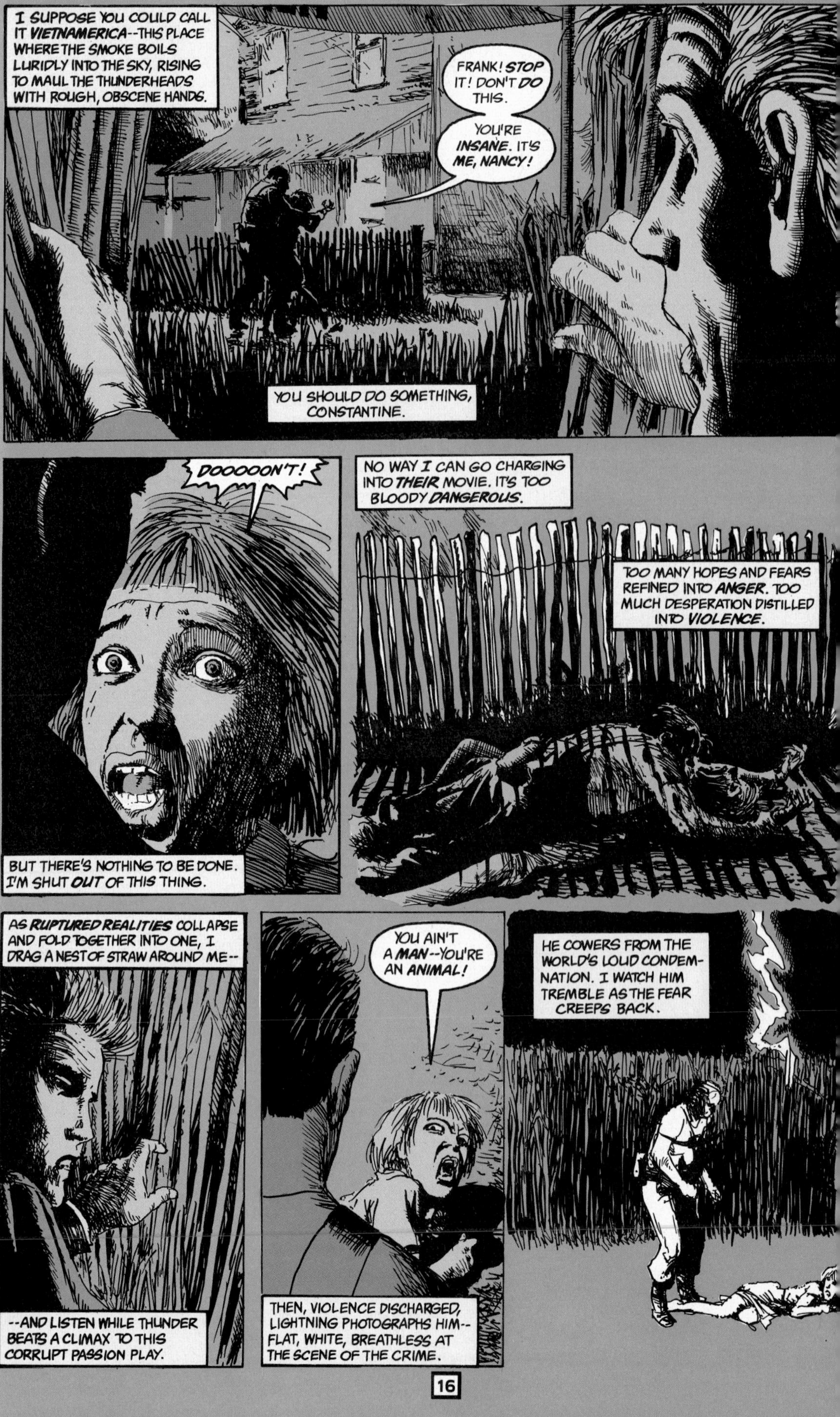
I SUPPOSE YOU COULD CALL IT VIETNAMERICA--THIS PLACE WHERE THE SMOKE BOILS LURIDLY INTO THE SKY, RISING TO MAUL THE THUNDERHEADS WITH ROUGH, OBSCENE HANDS.
FRANK! STOP IT! DON'T DO THIS.
YOU'RE INSANE. IT'S ME, NANCY!
YOU SHOULD DO SOMETHING, CONSTANTINE.
DOOOOOON'T!
BUT THERE'S NOTHING TO BE DONE. I'M SHUT OUT OF THIS THING.
NO WAY I CAN GO CHARGING INTO THEIR MOVIE. IT'S TOO BLOODY DANGEROUS.
TOO MANY HOPES AND FEARS REFINED INTO ANGER. TOO MUCH DESPERATION DISTILLED INTO VIOLENCE.
AS RUPTURED REALITIES COLLAPSE AND FOLD TOGETHER INTO ONE, I DRAG A NEST OF STRAW AROUND ME--
--AND LISTEN WHILE THUNDER BEATS A CLIMAX TO THIS CORRUPT PASSION PLAY.
YOU AIN'T A MAN--YOU'RE AN ANIMAL!
THEN, VIOLENCE DISCHARGED, LIGHTNING PHOTOGRAPHS HIM--FLAT, WHITE, BREATHLESS AT THE SCENE OF THE CRIME.
HE COWERS FROM THE WORLD'S LOUD CONDEMNATION. I WATCH HIM TREMBLE AS THE FEAR CREEPS BACK.

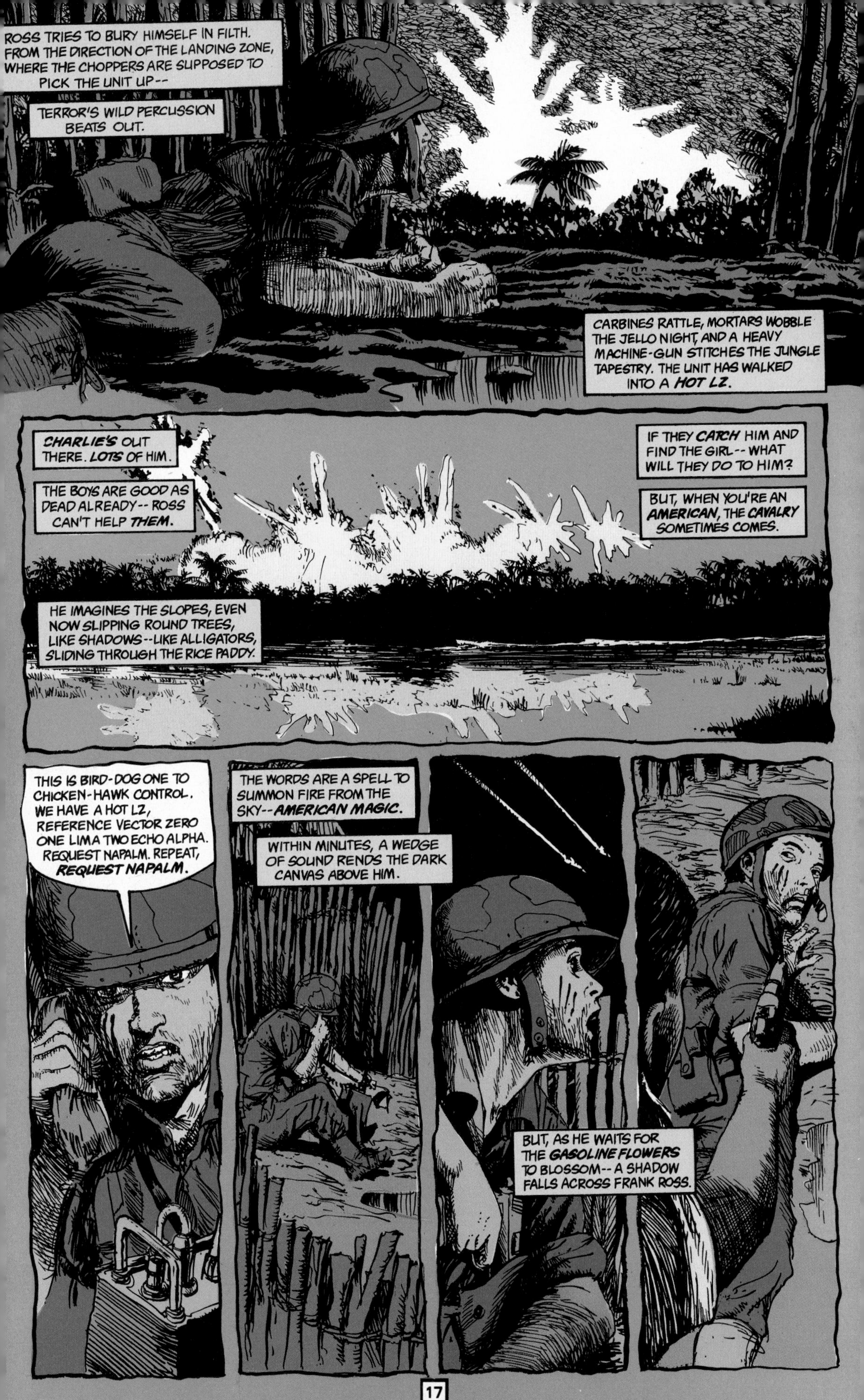
ROSS TRIES TO BURY HIMSELF IN FILTH. FROM THE DIRECTION OF THE LANDING ZONE, WHERE THE CHOPPERS ARE SUPPOSED TO PICK THE UNIT UP--
TERROR'S WILD PERCUSSION BEATS OUT.
CARBINES RATTLE, MORTARS WOBBLE THE JELLO NIGHT, AND A HEAVY MACHINE-GUN STITCHES THE JUNGLE TAPESTRY. THE UNIT HAS WALKED INTO A **HOT LZ**.
CHARLIE'S OUT THERE. **LOTS** OF HIM.
THE BOYS ARE GOOD AS DEAD ALREADY-- ROSS CAN'T HELP **THEM**.
IF THEY **CATCH** HIM AND FIND THE GIRL-- WHAT WILL THEY DO TO HIM?
BUT, WHEN YOU'RE AN **AMERICAN**, THE **CAVALRY** SOMETIMES COMES.
HE IMAGINES THE SLOPES, EVEN NOW SLIPPING ROUND TREES, LIKE SHADOWS--LIKE ALLIGATORS, SLIDING THROUGH THE RICE PADDY.
THIS IS BIRD-DOG ONE TO CHICKEN-HAWK CONTROL. WE HAVE A HOT LZ, REFERENCE VECTOR ZERO ONE LIMA TWO ECHO ALPHA. REQUEST NAPALM. REPEAT, **REQUEST NAPALM**.
THE WORDS ARE A SPELL TO SUMMON FIRE FROM THE SKY--**AMERICAN MAGIC**.
WITHIN MINUTES, A WEDGE OF SOUND RENDS THE DARK CANVAS ABOVE HIM.
BUT, AS HE WAITS FOR THE **GASOLINE FLOWERS** TO BLOSSOM-- A SHADOW FALLS ACROSS FRANK ROSS.

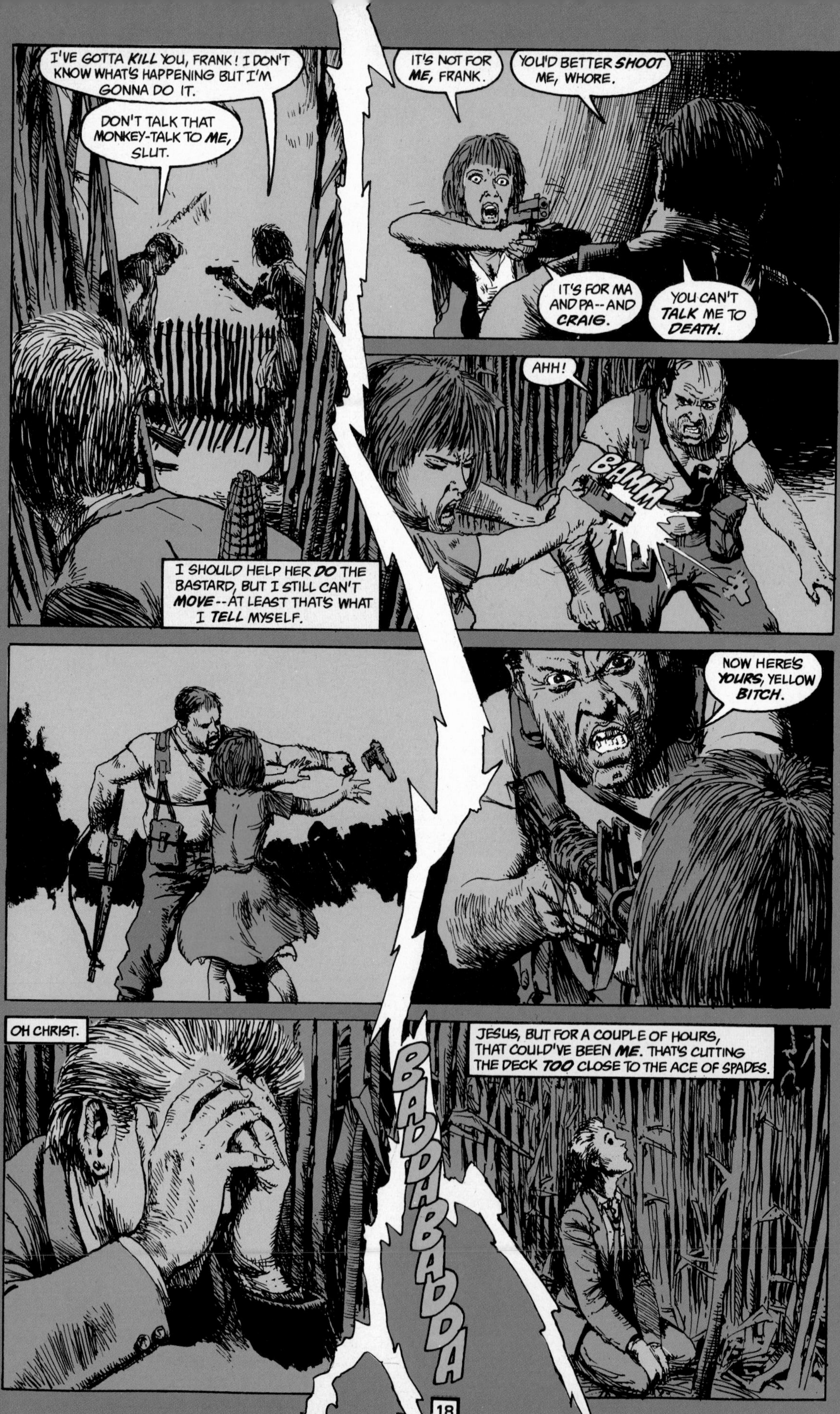

I'VE GOTTA KILL YOU, FRANK! I DON'T KNOW WHAT'S HAPPENING BUT I'M GONNA DO IT.
DON'T TALK THAT MONKEY-TALK TO ME, SLUT.
IT'S NOT FOR ME, FRANK.
YOU'D BETTER SHOOT ME, WHORE.
IT'S FOR MA AND PA--AND CRAIG.
YOU CAN'T TALK ME TO DEATH.
AHH!
BAMM
I SHOULD HELP HER DO THE BASTARD, BUT I STILL CAN'T MOVE--AT LEAST THAT'S WHAT I TELL MYSELF.
NOW HERE'S YOURS, YELLOW BITCH.
OH CHRIST.
BADDADADADADA
JESUS, BUT FOR A COUPLE OF HOURS, THAT COULD'VE BEEN ME. THAT'S CUTTING THE DECK TOO CLOSE TO THE ACE OF SPADES.

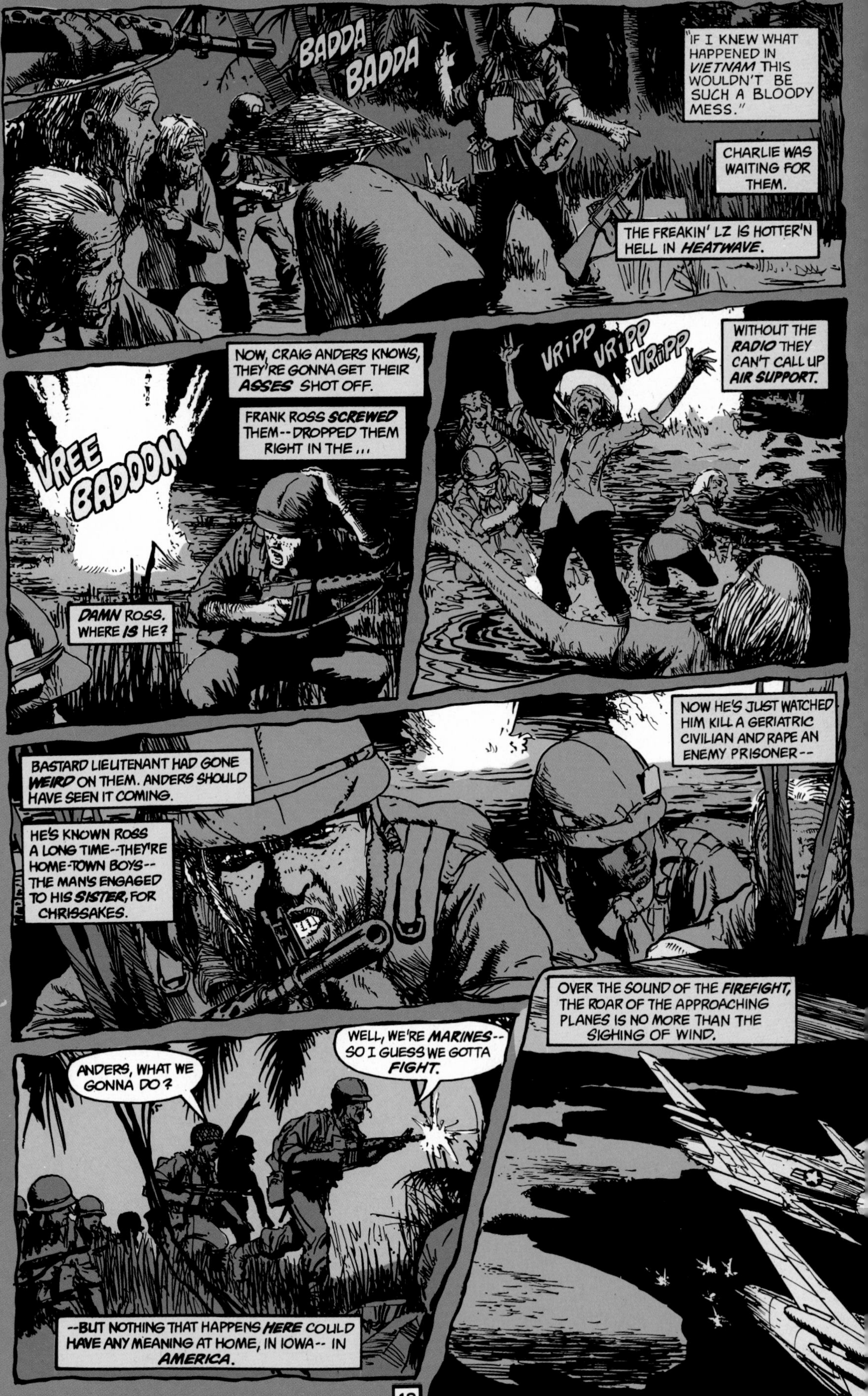
BADDA BADDA
"IF I KNEW WHAT HAPPENED IN VIETNAM THIS WOULDN'T BE SUCH A BLOODY MESS."
CHARLIE WAS WAITING FOR THEM.
THE FREAKIN' LZ IS HOTTER'N HELL IN HEATWAVE.
NOW, CRAIG ANDERS KNOWS, THEY'RE GONNA GET THEIR ASSES SHOT OFF.
FRANK ROSS SCREWED THEM--DROPPED THEM RIGHT IN THE...
VREE BADOOM
DAMN ROSS. WHERE IS HE?
VRIPP VRIPP VRIPP
WITHOUT THE RADIO THEY CAN'T CALL UP AIR SUPPORT.
NOW HE'S JUST WATCHED HIM KILL A GERIATRIC CIVILIAN AND RAPE AN ENEMY PRISONER--
BASTARD LIEUTENANT HAD GONE WEIRD ON THEM. ANDERS SHOULD HAVE SEEN IT COMING.
HE'S KNOWN ROSS A LONG TIME--THEY'RE HOME-TOWN BOYS--THE MAN'S ENGAGED TO HIS SISTER, FOR CHRISSAKES.
OVER THE SOUND OF THE FIREFIGHT, THE ROAR OF THE APPROACHING PLANES IS NO MORE THAN THE SIGHING OF WIND.
ANDERS, WHAT WE GONNA DO?
WELL, WE'RE MARINES--SO I GUESS WE GOTTA FIGHT.
--BUT NOTHING THAT HAPPENS HERE COULD HAVE ANY MEANING AT HOME, IN IOWA-- IN AMERICA.

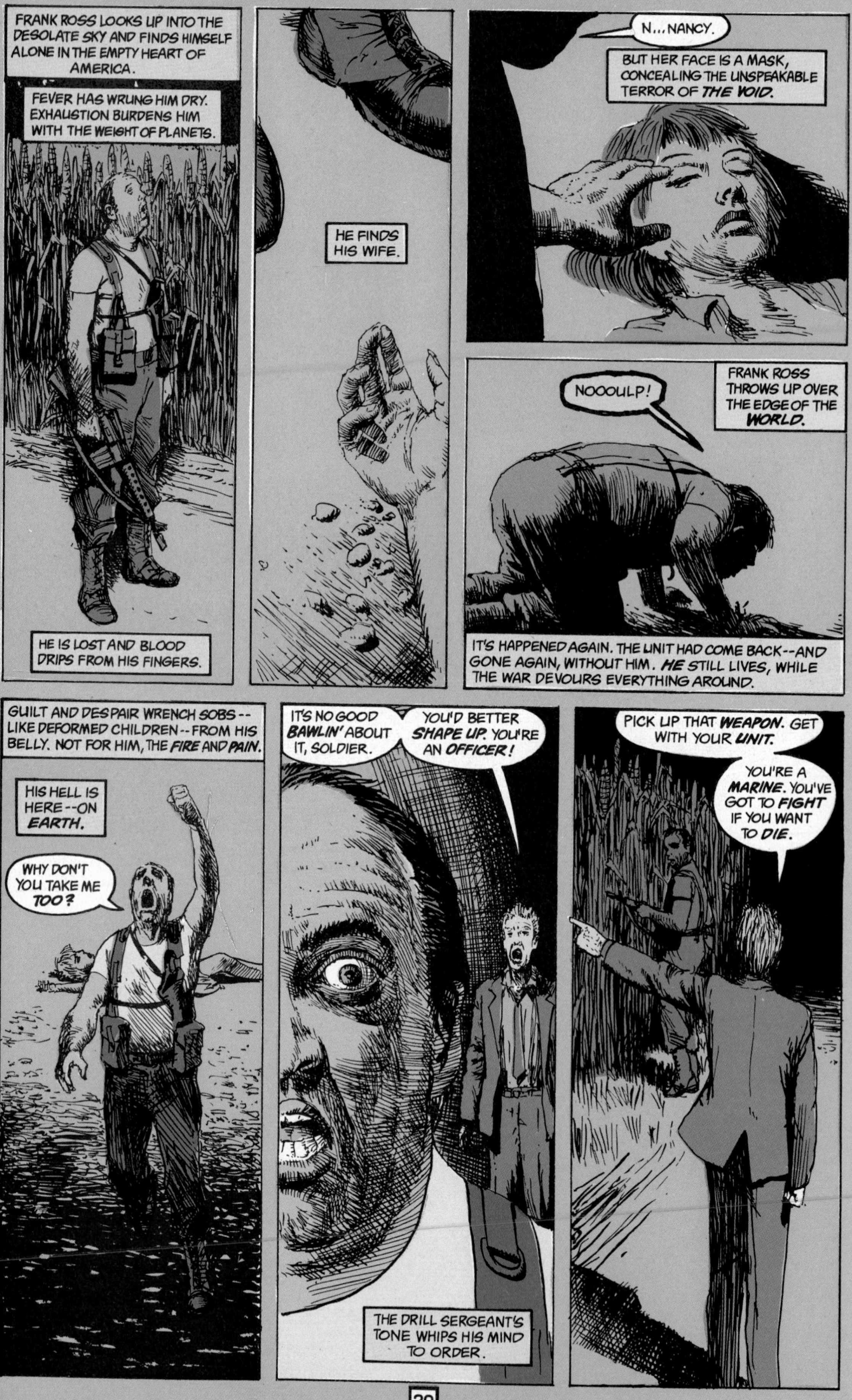
FRANK ROSS LOOKS UP INTO THE DESOLATE SKY AND FINDS HIMSELF ALONE IN THE EMPTY HEART OF AMERICA.
FEVER HAS WRUNG HIM DRY. EXHAUSTION BURDENS HIM WITH THE WEIGHT OF PLANETS.
HE IS LOST AND BLOOD DRIPS FROM HIS FINGERS.
HE FINDS HIS WIFE.
N...NANCY.
BUT HER FACE IS A MASK, CONCEALING THE UNSPEAKABLE TERROR OF THE VOID.
NOOOULP!
FRANK ROSS THROWS UP OVER THE EDGE OF THE WORLD.
IT'S HAPPENED AGAIN. THE UNIT HAD COME BACK--AND GONE AGAIN, WITHOUT HIM. HE STILL LIVES, WHILE THE WAR DEVOURS EVERYTHING AROUND.
GUILT AND DESPAIR WRENCH SOBS--LIKE DEFORMED CHILDREN--FROM HIS BELLY. NOT FOR HIM, THE FIRE AND PAIN.
HIS HELL IS HERE--ON EARTH.
WHY DON'T YOU TAKE ME TOO?
IT'S NO GOOD BAWLIN' ABOUT IT, SOLDIER.
YOU'D BETTER SHAPE UP. YOU'RE AN OFFICER!
THE DRILL SERGEANT'S TONE WHIPS HIS MIND TO ORDER.
PICK UP THAT WEAPON. GET WITH YOUR UNIT.
YOU'RE A MARINE. YOU'VE GOT TO FIGHT IF YOU WANT TO DIE.

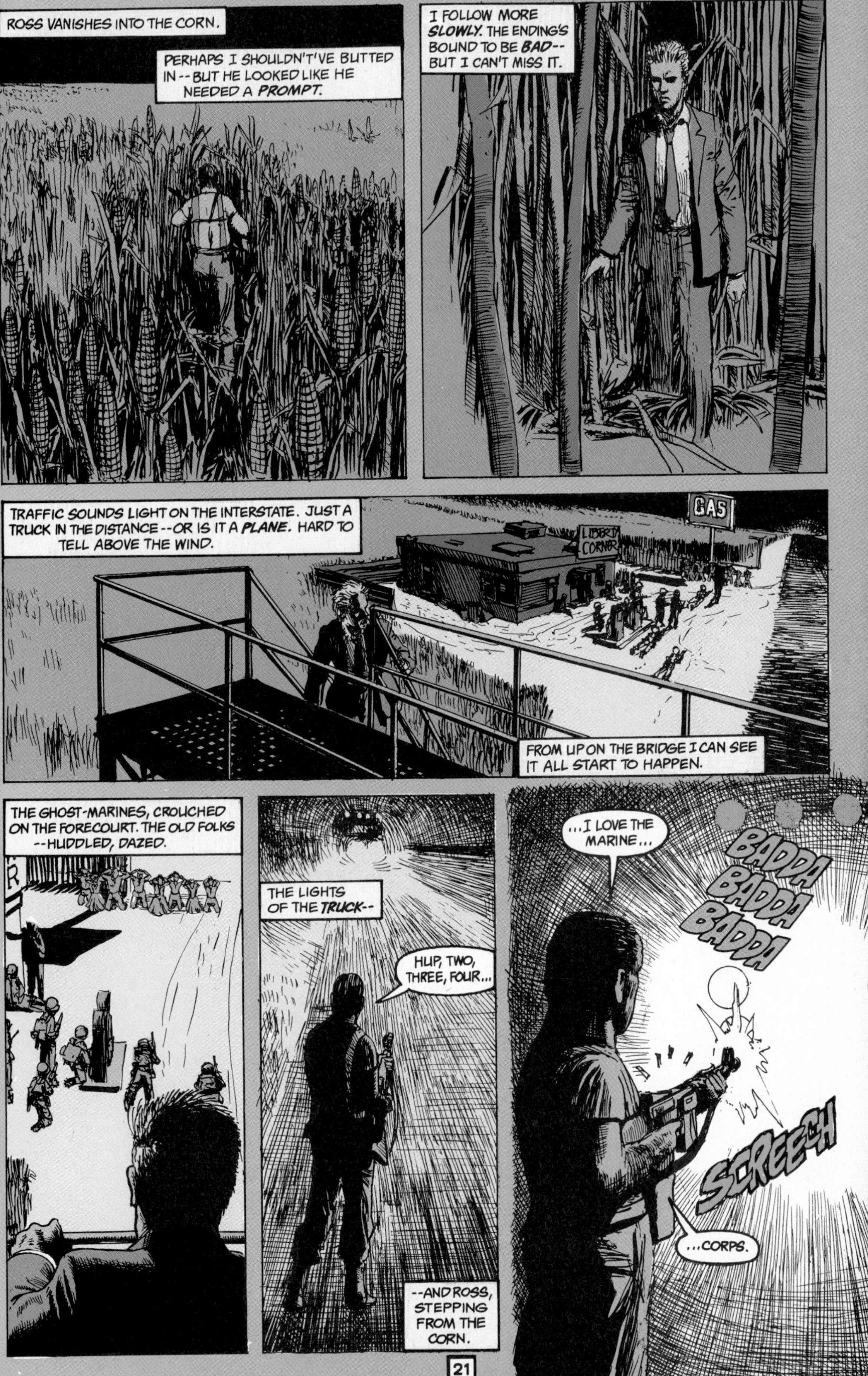
ROSS VANISHES INTO THE CORN.
PERHAPS I SHOULDN'T'VE BUTTED IN--BUT HE LOOKED LIKE HE NEEDED A PROMPT.
I FOLLOW MORE SLOWLY. THE ENDING'S BOUND TO BE BAD--BUT I CAN'T MISS IT.
TRAFFIC SOUNDS LIGHT ON THE INTERSTATE. JUST A TRUCK IN THE DISTANCE--OR IS IT A PLANE. HARD TO TELL ABOVE THE WIND.
GAS
CORNER
FROM UP ON THE BRIDGE I CAN SEE IT ALL START TO HAPPEN.
THE GHOST-MARINES, CROUCHED ON THE FORECOURT. THE OLD FOLKS--HUDDLED, DAZED.
THE LIGHTS OF THE TRUCK--
HUP, TWO, THREE, FOUR...
--AND ROSS, STEPPING FROM THE CORN.
...I LOVE THE MARINE...
BADDA BADDA BADDA
SCREECH
...CORPS.

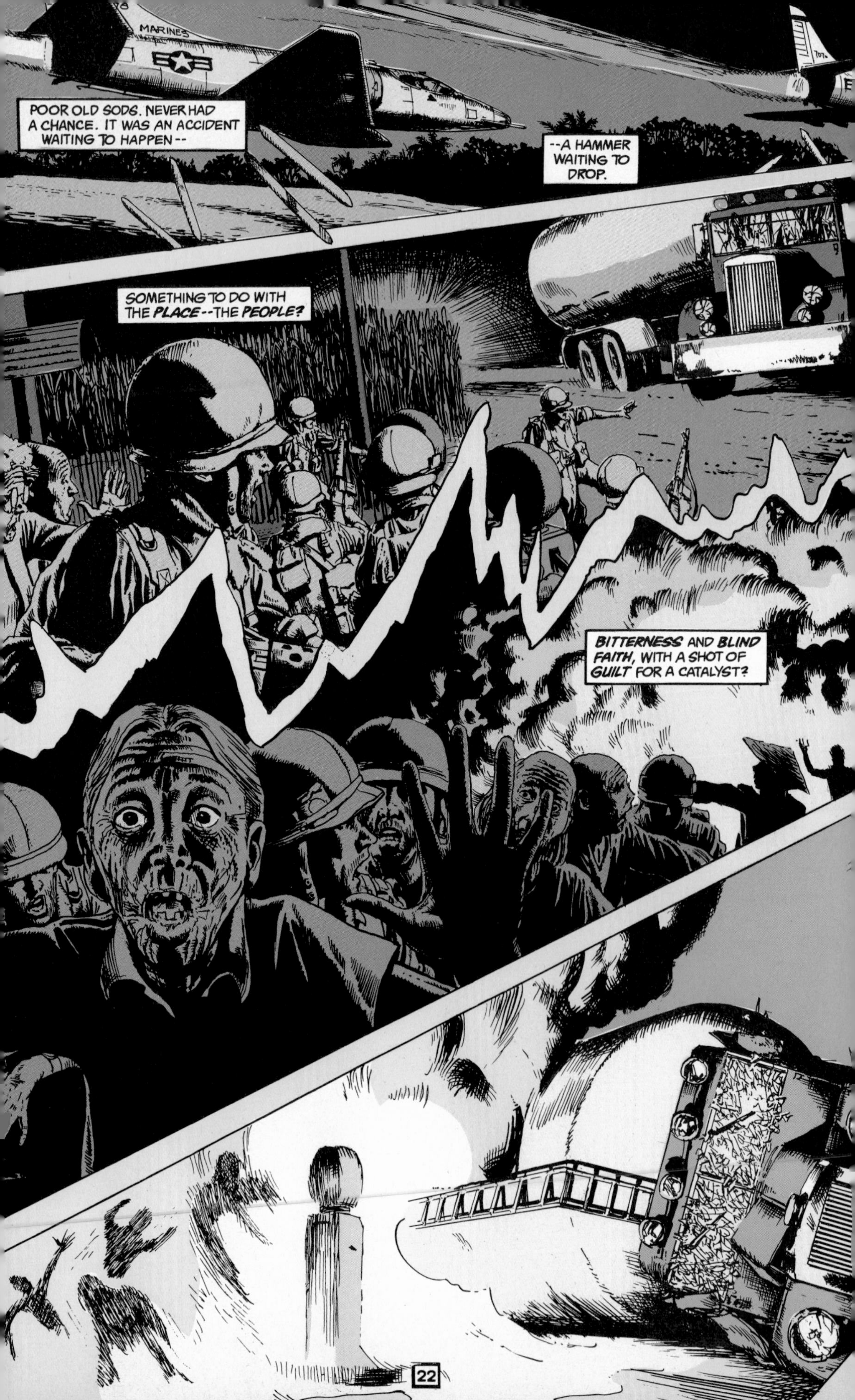
MARINES
POOR OLD SODS. NEVER HAD A CHANCE. IT WAS AN ACCIDENT WAITING TO HAPPEN--
--A HAMMER WAITING TO DROP.
SOMETHING TO DO WITH THE *PLACE*--THE *PEOPLE*?
BITTERNESS AND *BLIND FAITH*, WITH A SHOT OF *GUILT* FOR A CATALYST?

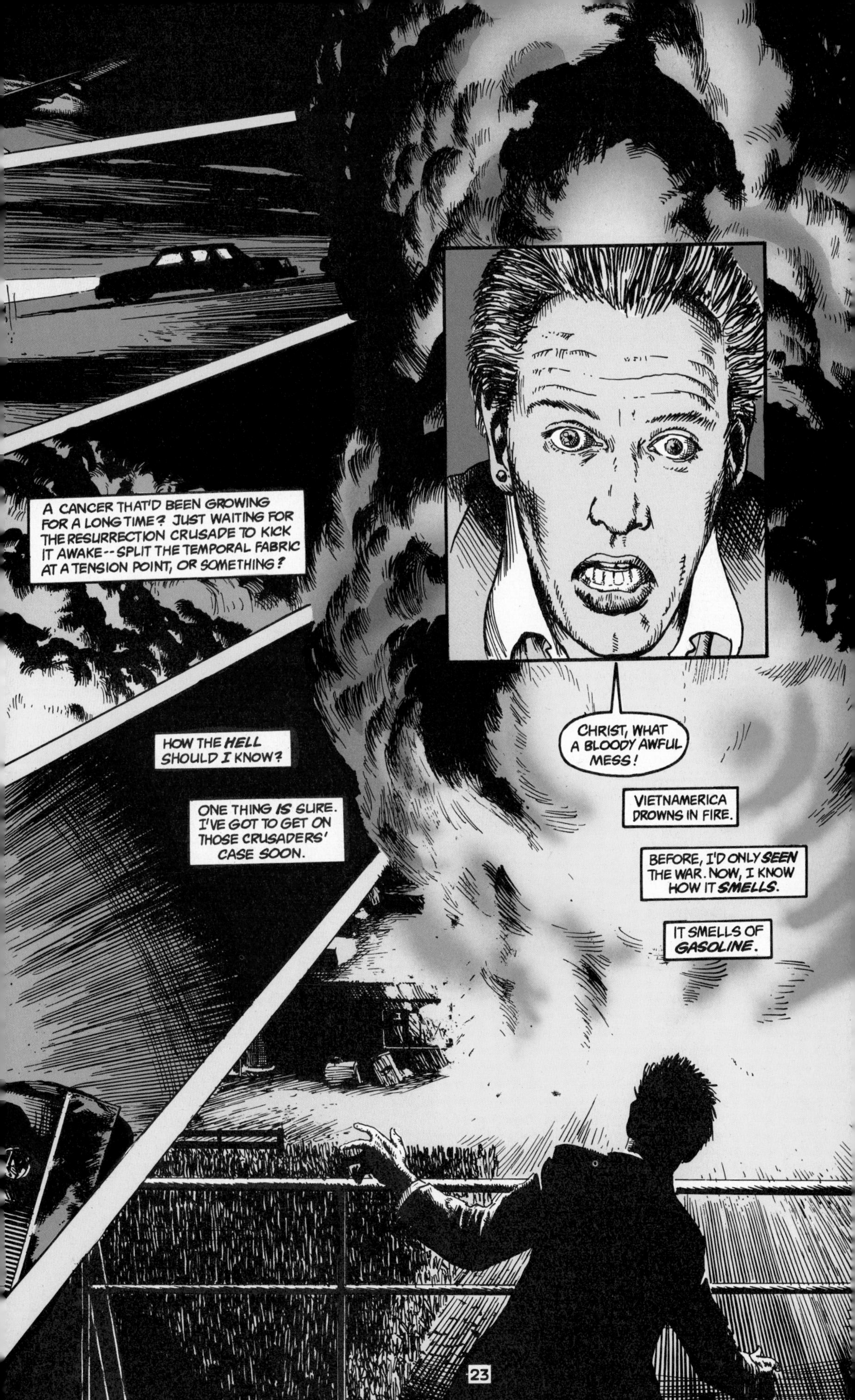
A CANCER THAT'D BEEN GROWING FOR A LONG TIME? JUST WAITING FOR THE RESURRECTION CRUSADE TO KICK IT AWAKE--SPLIT THE TEMPORAL FABRIC AT A TENSION POINT, OR SOMETHING?
HOW THE HELL SHOULD I KNOW?
ONE THING IS SURE. I'VE GOT TO GET ON THOSE CRUSADERS' CASE SOON.
CHRIST, WHAT A BLOODY AWFUL MESS!
VIETNAMERICA DROWNS IN FIRE.
BEFORE, I'D ONLY SEEN THE WAR. NOW, I KNOW HOW IT SMELLS.
IT SMELLS OF GASOLINE.

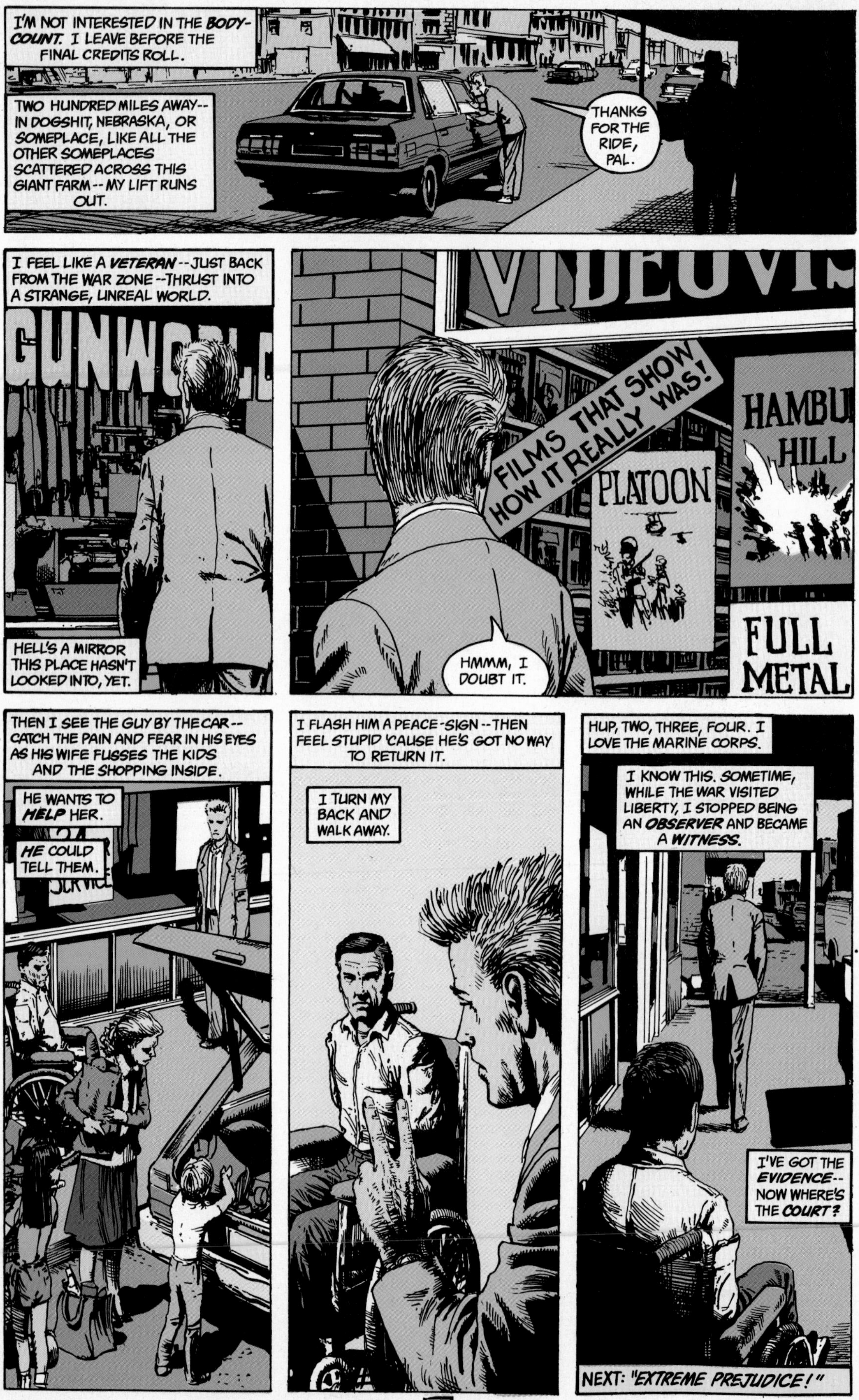

I'M NOT INTERESTED IN THE BODY-COUNT. I LEAVE BEFORE THE FINAL CREDITS ROLL.
TWO HUNDRED MILES AWAY-- IN DOGSHIT, NEBRASKA, OR SOMEPLACE, LIKE ALL THE OTHER SOMEPLACES SCATTERED ACROSS THIS GIANT FARM -- MY LIFT RUNS OUT.
THANKS FOR THE RIDE, PAL.
I FEEL LIKE A VETERAN -- JUST BACK FROM THE WAR ZONE --THRUST INTO A STRANGE, UNREAL WORLD.
HELL'S A MIRROR THIS PLACE HASN'T LOOKED INTO, YET.
FILMS THAT SHOW HOW IT REALLY WAS!
PLATOON
HILL
FULL METAL
HMMM, I DOUBT IT.
THEN I SEE THE GUY BY THE CAR -- CATCH THE PAIN AND FEAR IN HIS EYES AS HIS WIFE FUSSES THE KIDS AND THE SHOPPING INSIDE.
HE WANTS TO HELP HER.
HE COULD TELL THEM.
I FLASH HIM A PEACE-SIGN --THEN FEEL STUPID 'CAUSE HE'S GOT NO WAY TO RETURN IT.
I TURN MY BACK AND WALK AWAY.
HUP, TWO, THREE, FOUR. I LOVE THE MARINE CORPS.
I KNOW THIS. SOMETIME, WHILE THE WAR VISITED LIBERTY, I STOPPED BEING AN OBSERVER AND BECAME A WITNESS.
I'VE GOT THE EVIDENCE-- NOW WHERE'S THE COURT?
NEXT: "EXTREME PREJUDICE!"

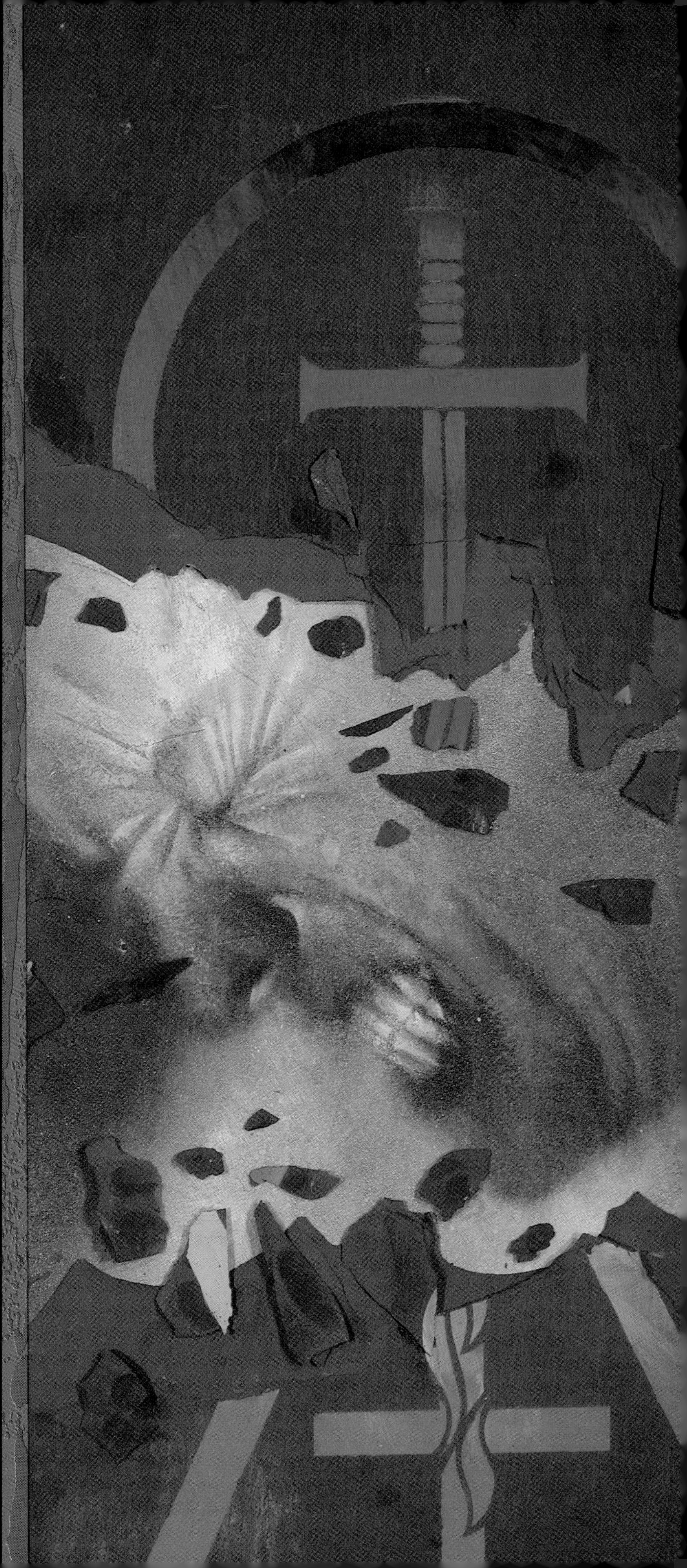

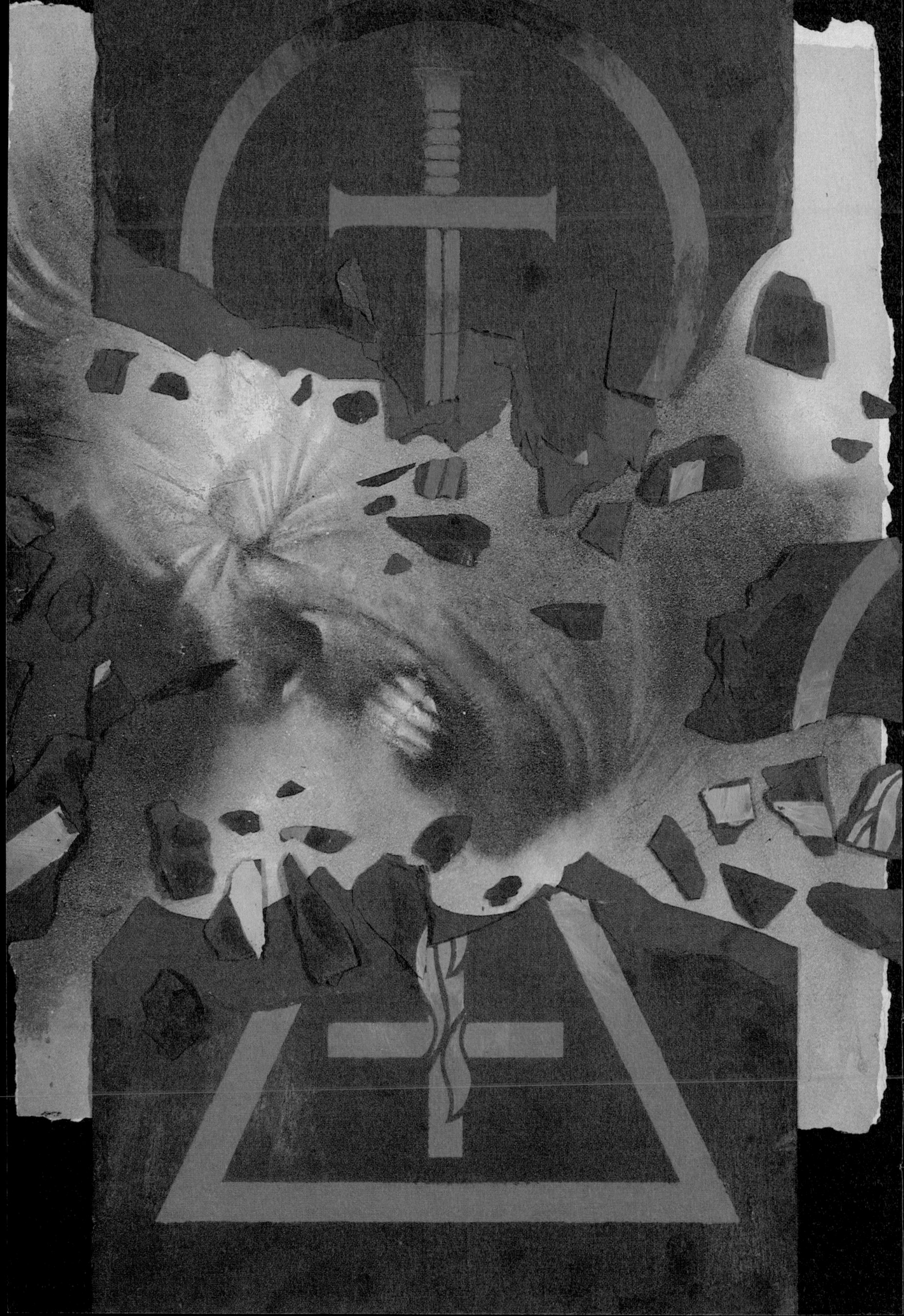

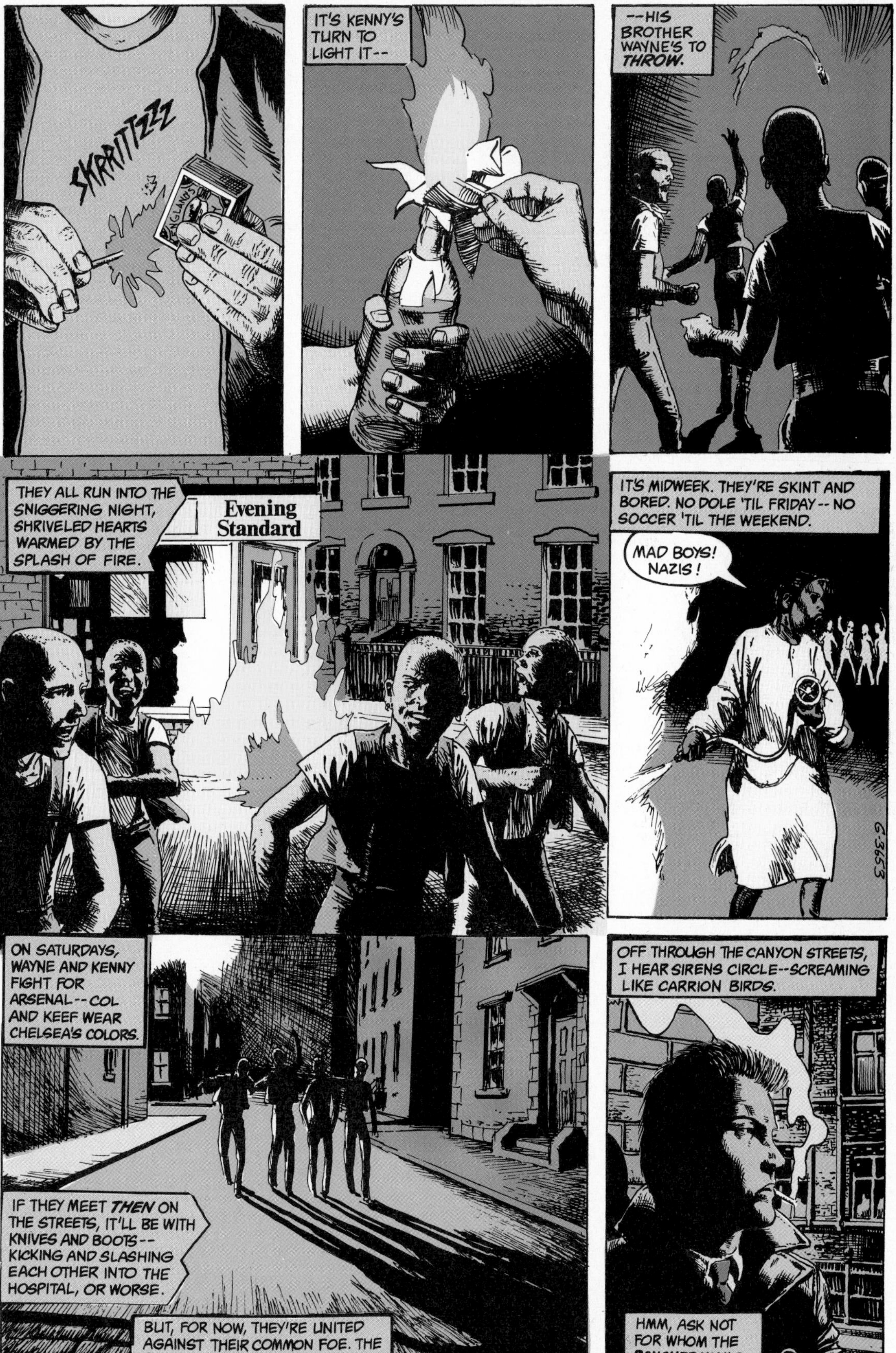
SKRRITTZZZ
IT'S KENNY'S TURN TO LIGHT IT--
--HIS BROTHER WAYNE'S TO THROW.
THEY ALL RUN INTO THE SNIGGERING NIGHT, SHRIVELED HEARTS WARMED BY THE SPLASH OF FIRE.
Evening Standard
IT'S MIDWEEK. THEY'RE SKINT AND BORED. NO DOLE 'TIL FRIDAY -- NO SOCCER 'TIL THE WEEKEND.
MAD BOYS! NAZIS!
G-3653
ON SATURDAYS, WAYNE AND KENNY FIGHT FOR ARSENAL--COL AND KEEF WEAR CHELSEA'S COLORS.
IF THEY MEET THEN ON THE STREETS, IT'LL BE WITH KNIVES AND BOOTS-- KICKING AND SLASHING EACH OTHER INTO THE HOSPITAL, OR WORSE.
BUT, FOR NOW, THEY'RE UNITED AGAINST THEIR COMMON FOE. THE BRITISH BOYS ARE ON PATROL.
OFF THROUGH THE CANYON STREETS, I HEAR SIRENS CIRCLE--SCREAMING LIKE CARRION BIRDS.
HMM, ASK NOT FOR WHOM THE BANSHEE WAILS...

IT WAILS FOR THEE.

HAH! MADE THAT BASTARD SHOUT, EH?

STILL, THEY *LIKE* IT *HOT*, DON'T THEY?

BRITISH BOYS *HATE PAKIS*--AND *WOGS*--AND *YIDS*--AND *LEFTIES.*

AND *QUEERS*--

QUEERS SHOULD BE *EXTERMINATED.*

OI OI, WHAT'RE THE *HITLER YOUTH* UP TO NOW?

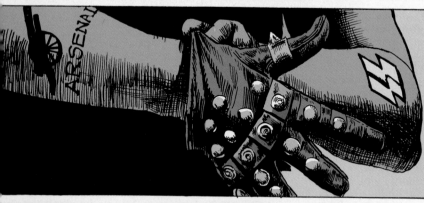

WITH HIS MATES BESIDE HIM, KENNY FEELS *HARD* AND *SHARP.* HE PULLS ON HIS *FIGHTING GLOVE* AND BECOMES *IRONFIST THE AVENGER.*

IT'S SHAPING INTO A *GOOD* NIGHT.

MOST GAYS'D HAVE MORE SENSE THAN TO COME "COTTAGING" IN *THIS* MANOR.

POOR BASTARD'S GOING TO GET A *RIGHT* KICKING.

GENTS

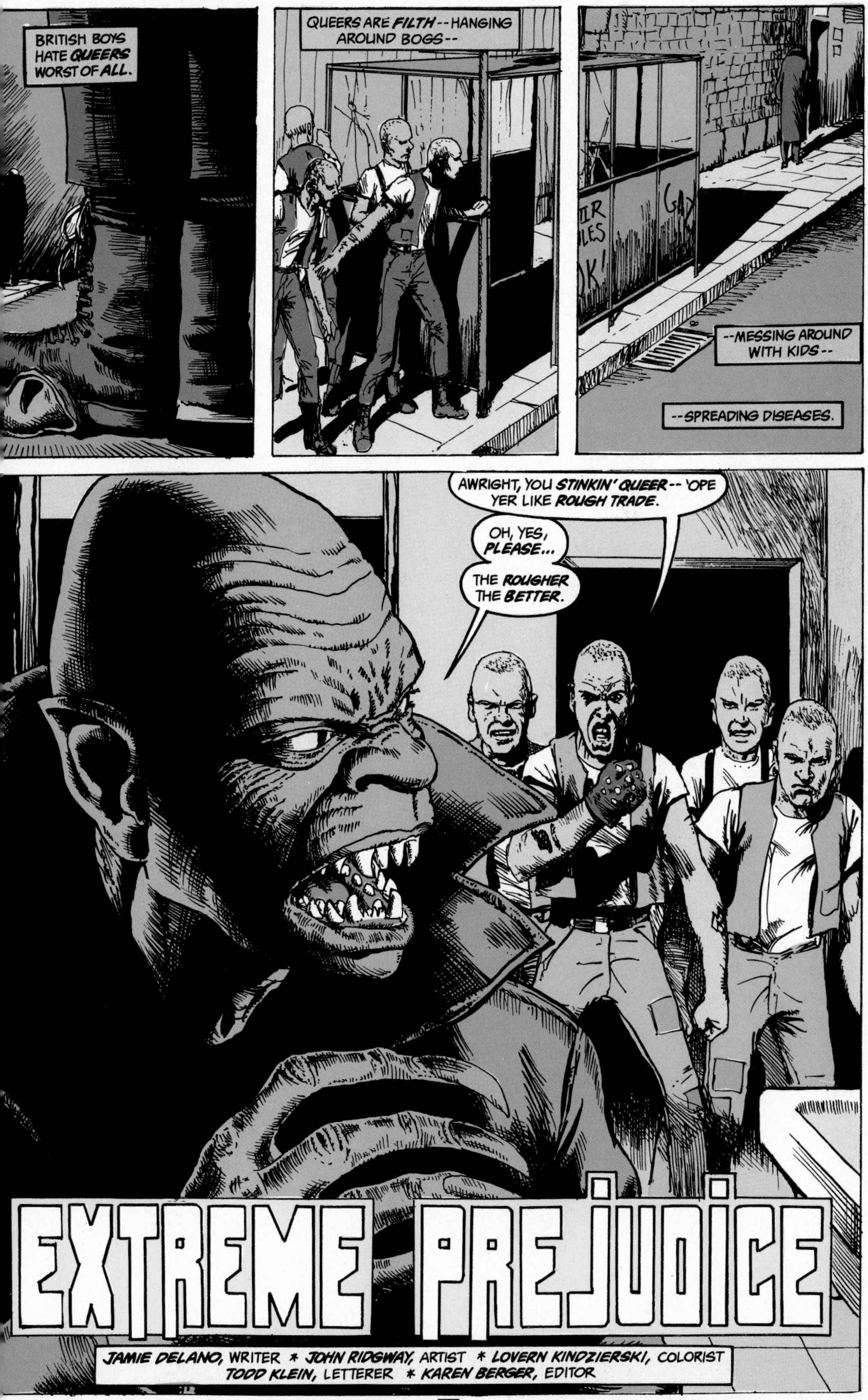

BRITISH BOYS HATE QUEERS WORST OF ALL.
QUEERS ARE FILTH--HANGING AROUND BOGS--
--MESSING AROUND WITH KIDS--
--SPREADING DISEASES.
AWRIGHT, YOU STINKIN' QUEER--'OPE YER LIKE ROUGH TRADE.
OH, YES, PLEASE...
THE ROUGHER THE BETTER.
EXTREME PREJUDICE
JAMIE DELANO, WRITER * JOHN RIDGWAY, ARTIST * LOVERN KINDZIERSKI, COLORIST
TODD KLEIN, LETTERER * KAREN BERGER, EDITOR

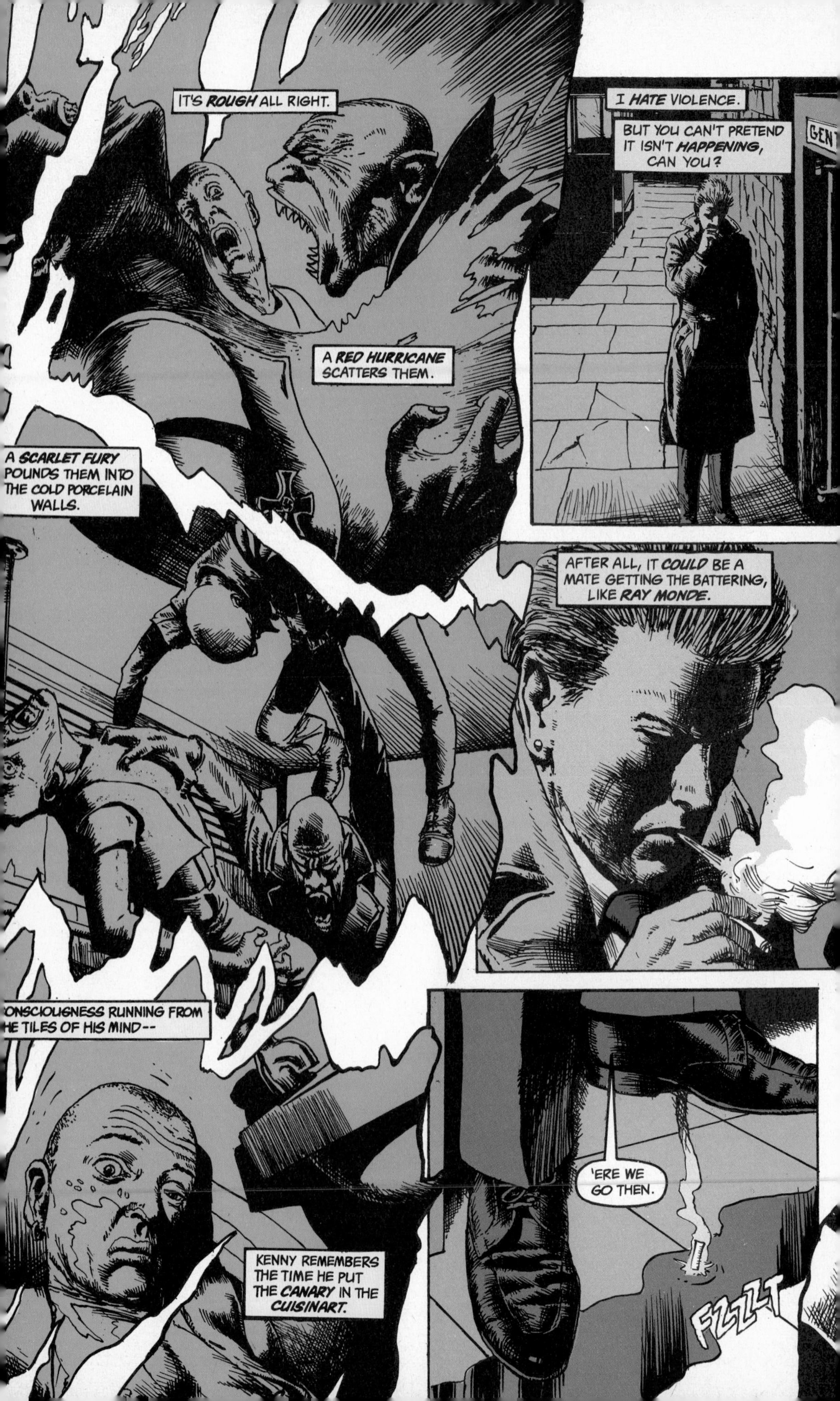
IT'S ROUGH ALL RIGHT.
I HATE VIOLENCE.
BUT YOU CAN'T PRETEND IT ISN'T HAPPENING, CAN YOU?
GENT
A RED HURRICANE SCATTERS THEM.
A SCARLET FURY POUNDS THEM INTO THE COLD PORCELAIN WALLS.
AFTER ALL, IT COULD BE A MATE GETTING THE BATTERING, LIKE RAY MONDE.
ONSCIOUSNESS RUNNING FROM HE TILES OF HIS MIND--
'ERE WE GO THEN.
KENNY REMEMBERS THE TIME HE PUT THE CANARY IN THE CUISINART.
FZZZT

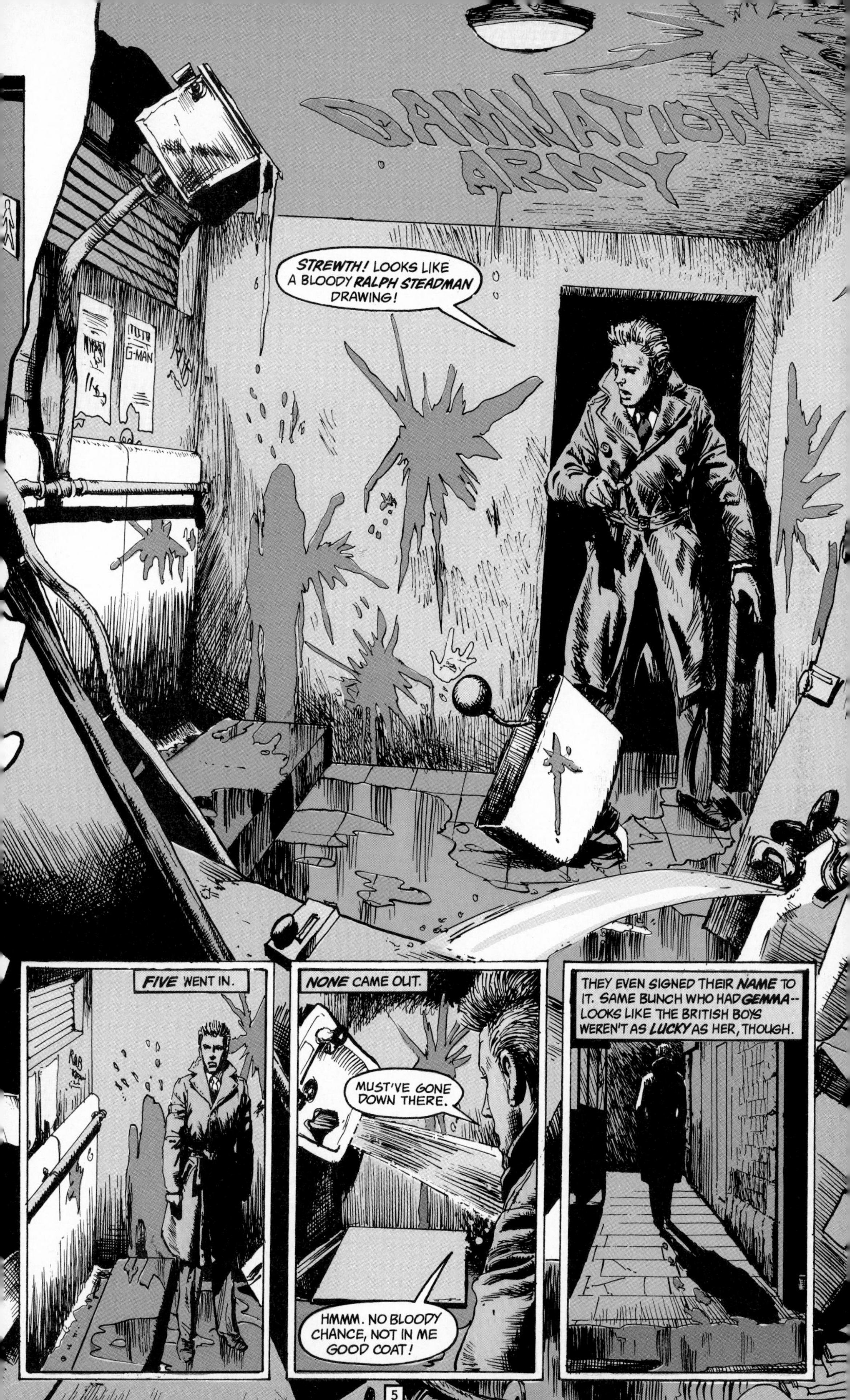
DAMNATION ARMY
STREWTH! LOOKS LIKE A BLOODY RALPH STEADMAN DRAWING!
G-MAN
FIVE WENT IN.
NONE CAME OUT.
MUST'VE GONE DOWN THERE.
HMMM. NO BLOODY CHANCE, NOT IN ME GOOD COAT!
THEY EVEN SIGNED THEIR NAME TO IT. SAME BUNCH WHO HAD GEMMA-- LOOKS LIKE THE BRITISH BOYS WEREN'T AS LUCKY AS HER, THOUGH.

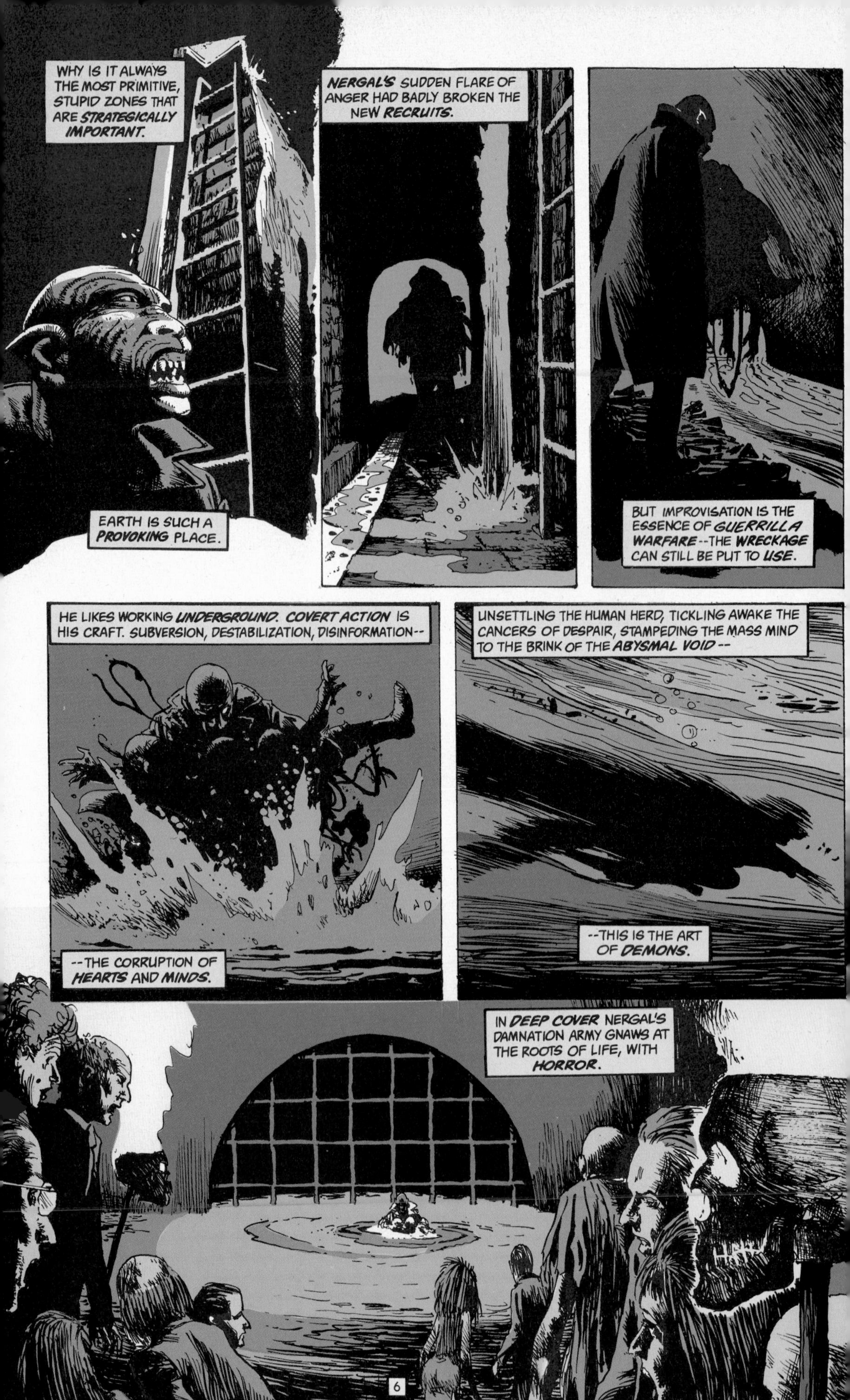
WHY IS IT ALWAYS THE MOST PRIMITIVE, STUPID ZONES THAT ARE STRATEGICALLY IMPORTANT.
EARTH IS SUCH A PROVOKING PLACE.
NERGAL'S SUDDEN FLARE OF ANGER HAD BADLY BROKEN THE NEW RECRUITS.
BUT IMPROVISATION IS THE ESSENCE OF GUERRILLA WARFARE--THE WRECKAGE CAN STILL BE PUT TO USE.
HE LIKES WORKING UNDERGROUND. COVERT ACTION IS HIS CRAFT. SUBVERSION, DESTABILIZATION, DISINFORMATION--
--THE CORRUPTION OF HEARTS AND MINDS.
UNSETTLING THE HUMAN HERD, TICKLING AWAKE THE CANCERS OF DESPAIR, STAMPEDING THE MASS MIND TO THE BRINK OF THE ABYSMAL VOID--
--THIS IS THE ART OF DEMONS.
IN DEEP COVER NERGAL'S DAMNATION ARMY GNAWS AT THE ROOTS OF LIFE, WITH HORROR.

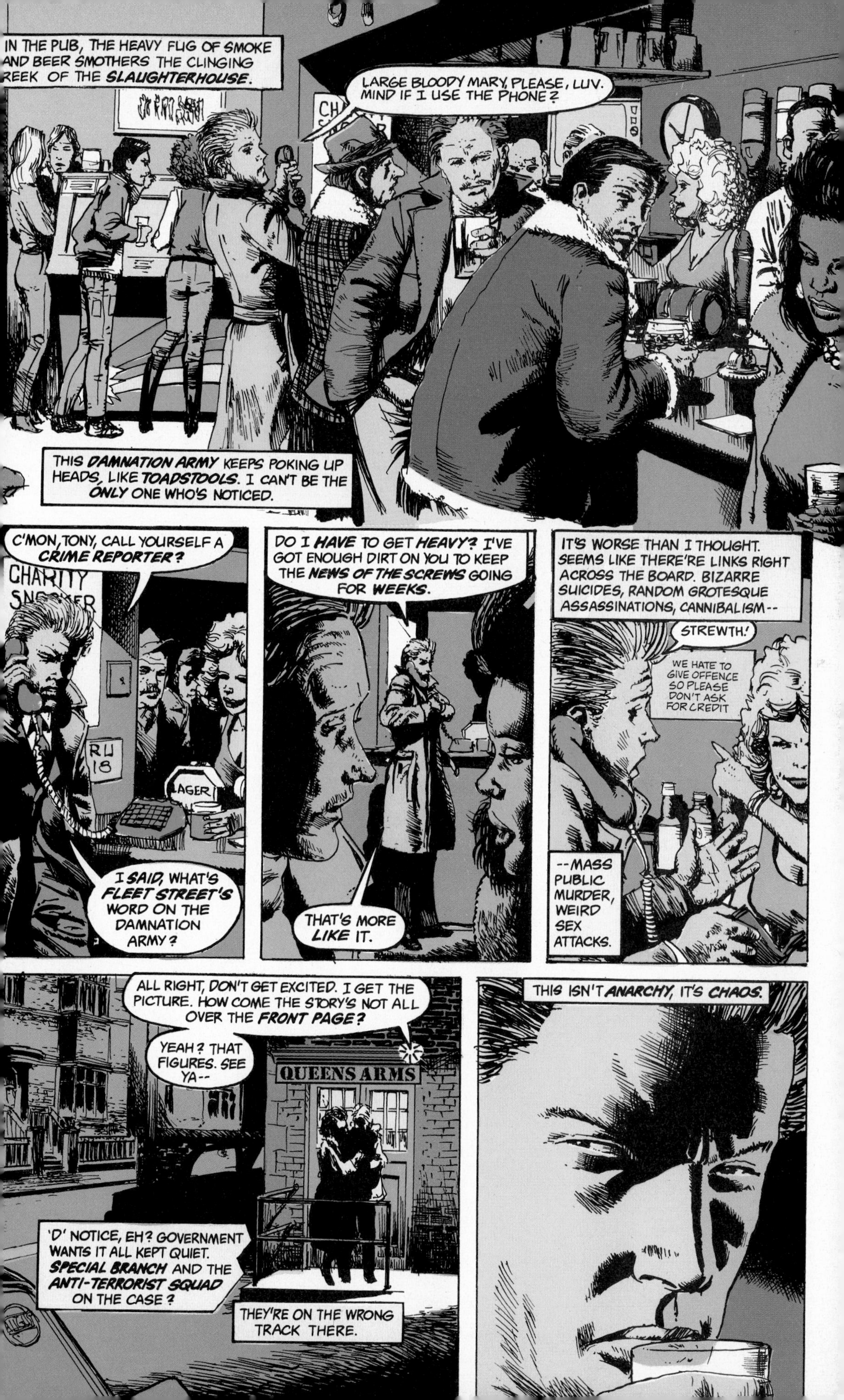
IN THE PUB, THE HEAVY FUG OF SMOKE AND BEER SMOTHERS THE CLINGING REEK OF THE SLAUGHTERHOUSE.
LARGE BLOODY MARY, PLEASE, LUV. MIND IF I USE THE PHONE?
THIS DAMNATION ARMY KEEPS POKING UP HEADS, LIKE TOADSTOOLS. I CAN'T BE THE ONLY ONE WHO'S NOTICED.
C'MON, TONY, CALL YOURSELF A CRIME REPORTER?
CHARITY SNOOKER
LAGER
I SAID, WHAT'S FLEET STREET'S WORD ON THE DAMNATION ARMY?
DO I HAVE TO GET HEAVY? I'VE GOT ENOUGH DIRT ON YOU TO KEEP THE NEWS OF THE SCREWS GOING FOR WEEKS.
THAT'S MORE LIKE IT.
IT'S WORSE THAN I THOUGHT. SEEMS LIKE THERE'RE LINKS RIGHT ACROSS THE BOARD. BIZARRE SUICIDES, RANDOM GROTESQUE ASSASSINATIONS, CANNIBALISM--
STREWTH!
WE HATE TO GIVE OFFENCE SO PLEASE DON'T ASK FOR CREDIT
--MASS PUBLIC MURDER, WEIRD SEX ATTACKS.
ALL RIGHT, DON'T GET EXCITED. I GET THE PICTURE. HOW COME THE STORY'S NOT ALL OVER THE FRONT PAGE?
YEAH? THAT FIGURES. SEE YA--
QUEENS ARMS
'D' NOTICE, EH? GOVERNMENT WANTS IT ALL KEPT QUIET. SPECIAL BRANCH AND THE ANTI-TERRORIST SQUAD ON THE CASE?
THEY'RE ON THE WRONG TRACK THERE.
THIS ISN'T ANARCHY, IT'S CHAOS.

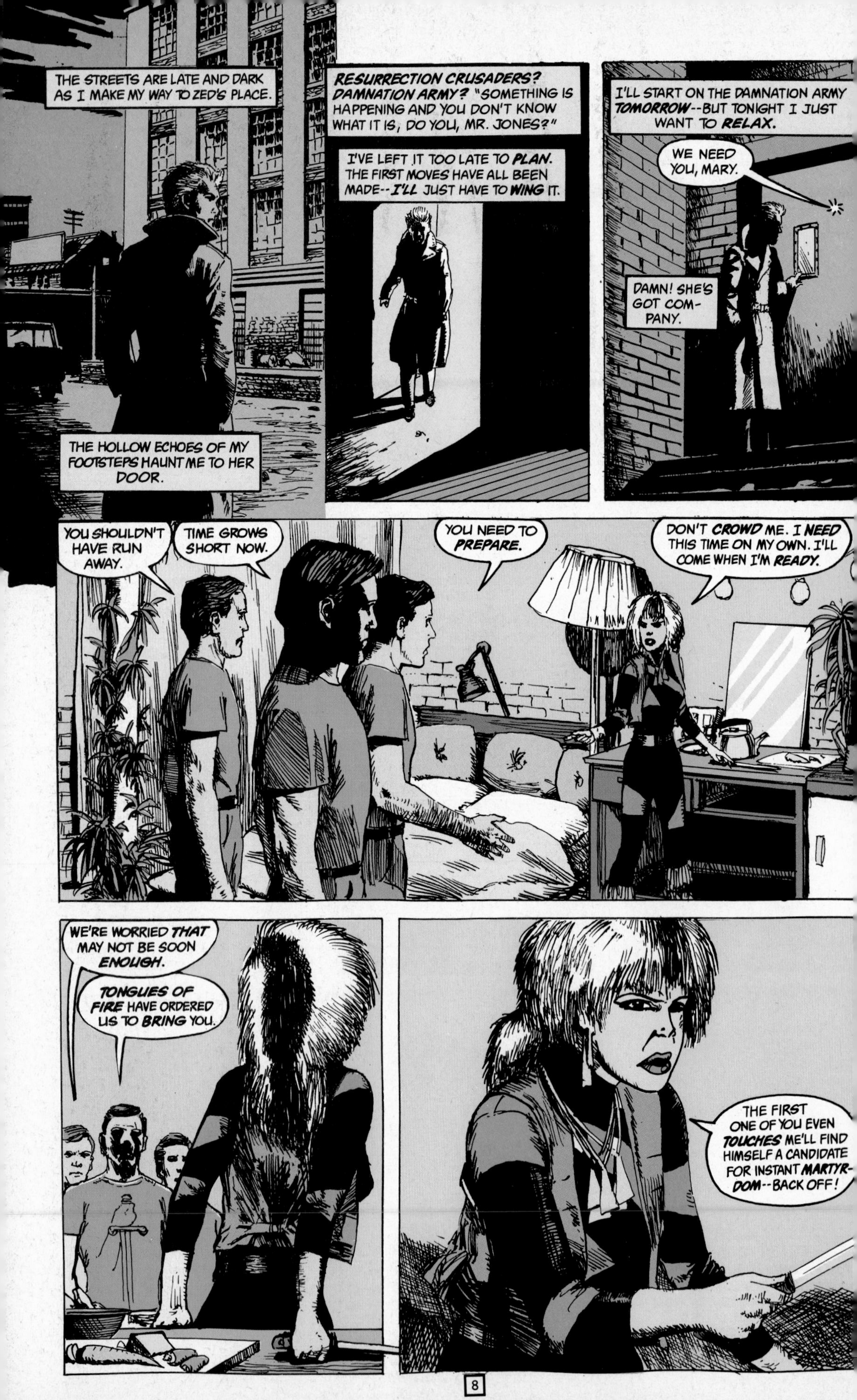
THE STREETS ARE LATE AND DARK AS I MAKE MY WAY TO ZED'S PLACE.
THE HOLLOW ECHOES OF MY FOOTSTEPS HAUNT ME TO HER DOOR.
RESURRECTION CRUSADERS? DAMNATION ARMY? "SOMETHING IS HAPPENING AND YOU DON'T KNOW WHAT IT IS, DO YOU, MR. JONES?"
I'VE LEFT IT TOO LATE TO PLAN. THE FIRST MOVES HAVE ALL BEEN MADE--I'LL JUST HAVE TO WING IT.
I'LL START ON THE DAMNATION ARMY TOMORROW--BUT TONIGHT I JUST WANT TO RELAX.
WE NEED YOU, MARY.
DAMN! SHE'S GOT COM-PANY.
YOU SHOULDN'T HAVE RUN AWAY.
TIME GROWS SHORT NOW.
YOU NEED TO PREPARE.
DON'T CROWD ME. I NEED THIS TIME ON MY OWN. I'LL COME WHEN I'M READY.
WE'RE WORRIED THAT MAY NOT BE SOON ENOUGH.
TONGUES OF FIRE HAVE ORDERED US TO BRING YOU.
THE FIRST ONE OF YOU EVEN TOUCHES ME'LL FIND HIMSELF A CANDIDATE FOR INSTANT MARTYR-DOM--BACK OFF!

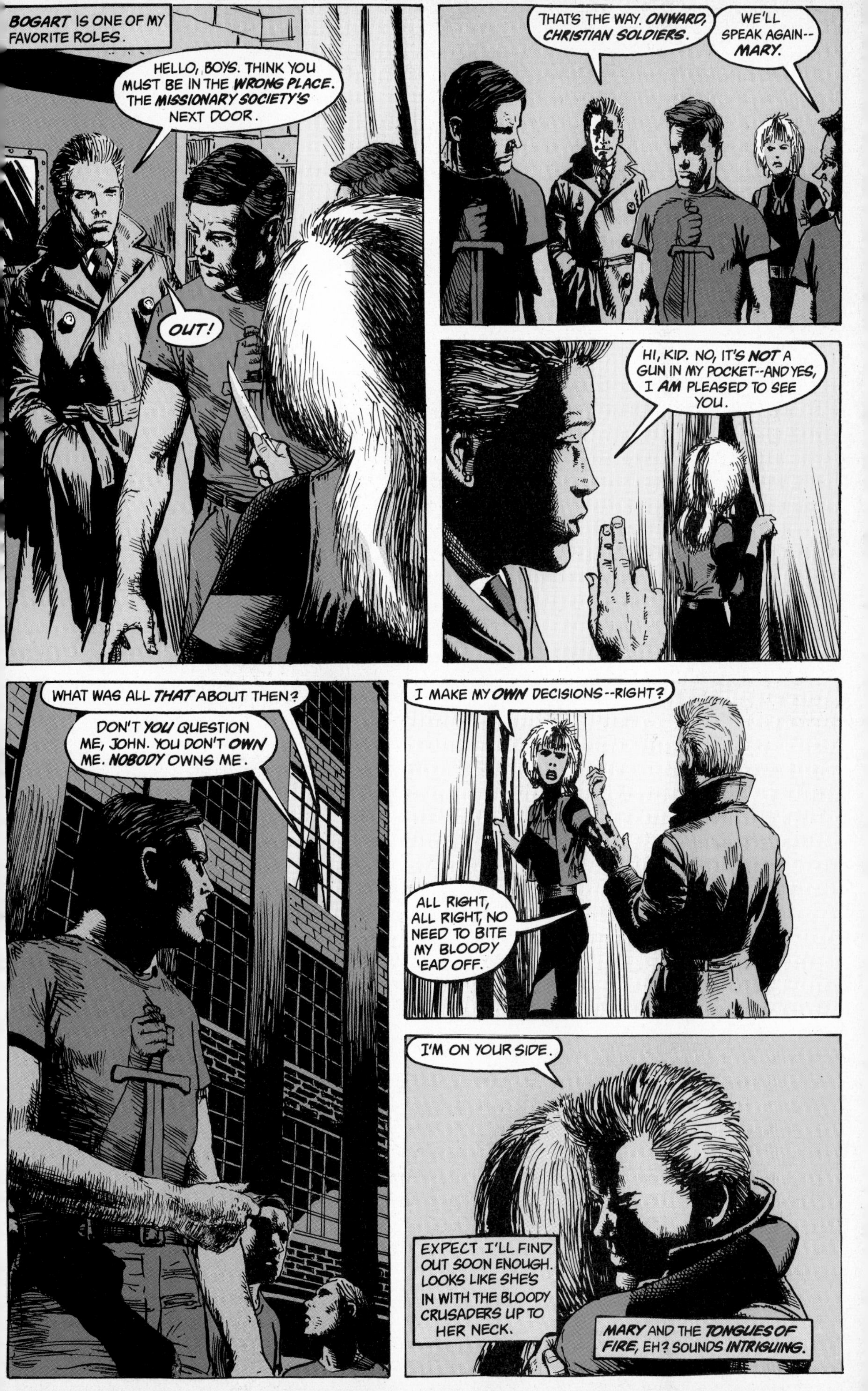
BOGART IS ONE OF MY FAVORITE ROLES.
HELLO, BOYS. THINK YOU MUST BE IN THE WRONG PLACE. THE MISSIONARY SOCIETY'S NEXT DOOR.
OUT!
THAT'S THE WAY. ONWARD, CHRISTIAN SOLDIERS.
WE'LL SPEAK AGAIN-- MARY.
HI, KID. NO, IT'S NOT A GUN IN MY POCKET--AND YES, I AM PLEASED TO SEE YOU.
WHAT WAS ALL THAT ABOUT THEN?
DON'T YOU QUESTION ME, JOHN. YOU DON'T OWN ME. NOBODY OWNS ME.
I MAKE MY OWN DECISIONS--RIGHT?
ALL RIGHT, ALL RIGHT, NO NEED TO BITE MY BLOODY 'EAD OFF.
I'M ON YOUR SIDE.
EXPECT I'LL FIND OUT SOON ENOUGH. LOOKS LIKE SHE'S IN WITH THE BLOODY CRUSADERS UP TO HER NECK.
MARY AND THE TONGUES OF FIRE, EH? SOUNDS INTRIGUING.

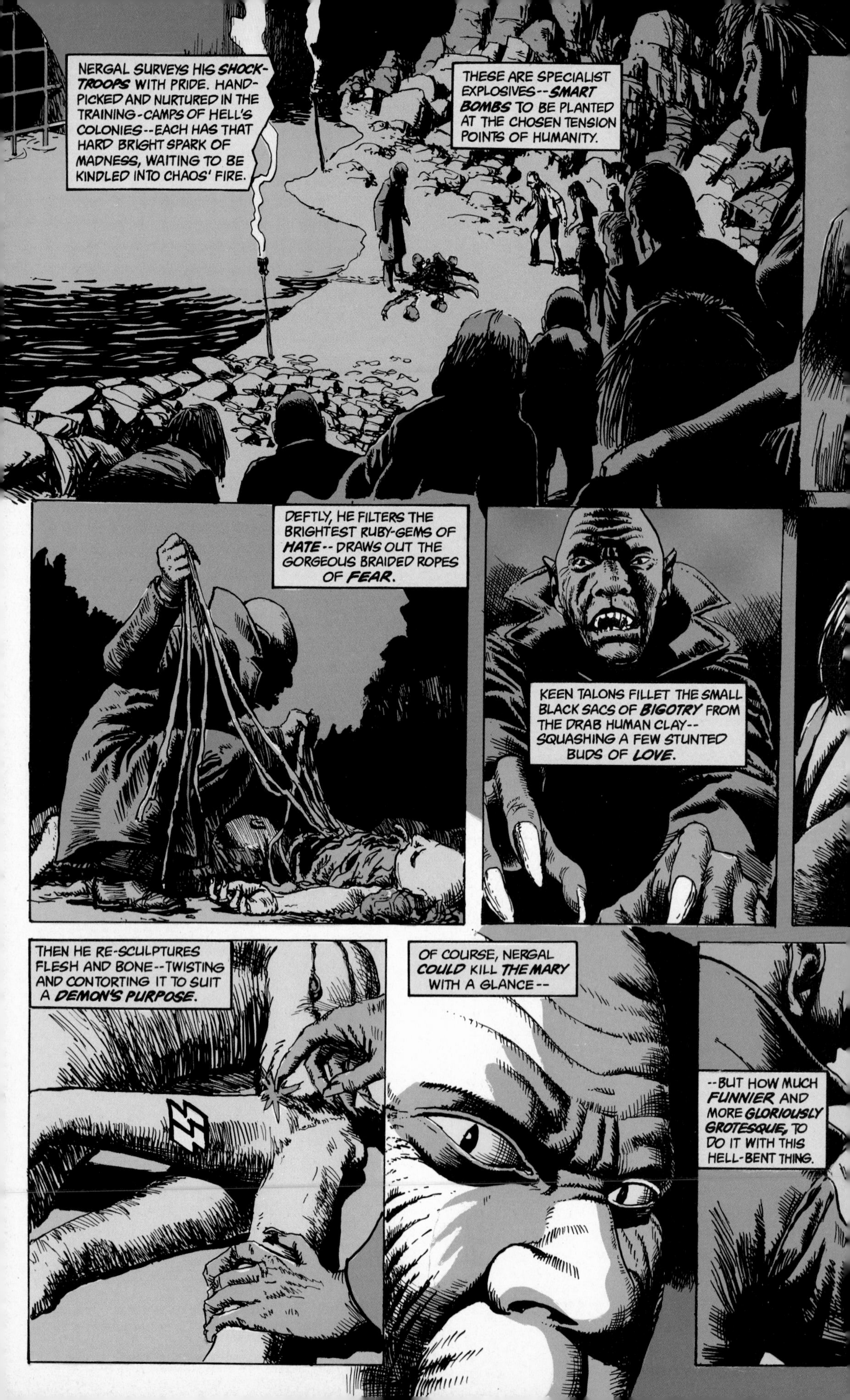
NERGAL SURVEYS HIS SHOCK-TROOPS WITH PRIDE. HAND-PICKED AND NURTURED IN THE TRAINING-CAMPS OF HELL'S COLONIES--EACH HAS THAT HARD BRIGHT SPARK OF MADNESS, WAITING TO BE KINDLED INTO CHAOS' FIRE.
THESE ARE SPECIALIST EXPLOSIVES--SMART BOMBS TO BE PLANTED AT THE CHOSEN TENSION POINTS OF HUMANITY.
DEFTLY, HE FILTERS THE BRIGHTEST RUBY-GEMS OF HATE--DRAWS OUT THE GORGEOUS BRAIDED ROPES OF FEAR.
KEEN TALONS FILLET THE SMALL BLACK SACS OF BIGOTRY FROM THE DRAB HUMAN CLAY--SQUASHING A FEW STUNTED BUDS OF LOVE.
THEN HE RE-SCULPTURES FLESH AND BONE--TWISTING AND CONTORTING IT TO SUIT A DEMON'S PURPOSE.
OF COURSE, NERGAL COULD KILL THE MARY WITH A GLANCE--
--BUT HOW MUCH FUNNIER AND MORE GLORIOUSLY GROTESQUE, TO DO IT WITH THIS HELL-BENT THING.

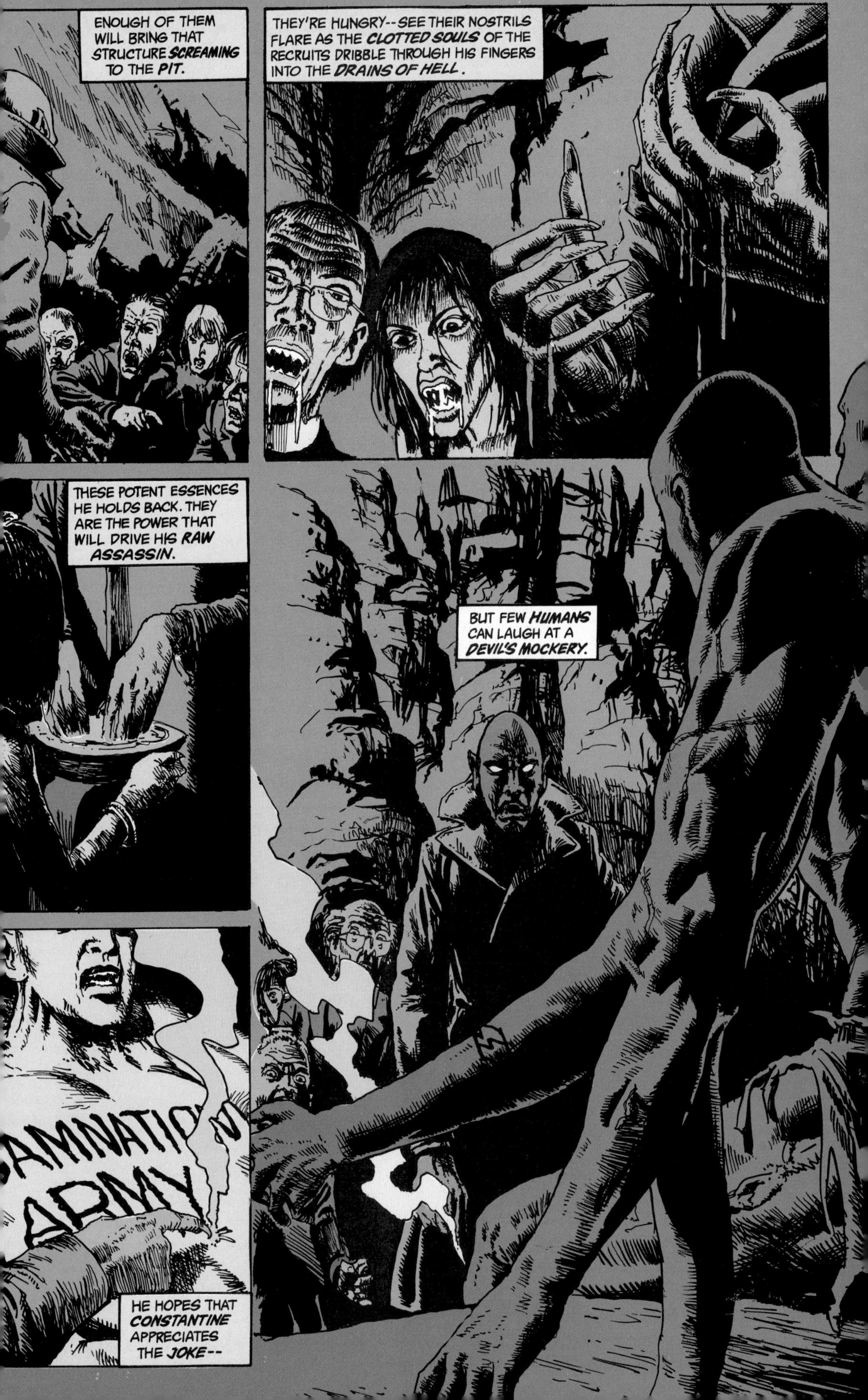

ENOUGH OF THEM WILL BRING THAT STRUCTURE SCREAMING TO THE PIT.
THEY'RE HUNGRY--SEE THEIR NOSTRILS FLARE AS THE CLOTTED SOULS OF THE RECRUITS DRIBBLE THROUGH HIS FINGERS INTO THE DRAINS OF HELL.
THESE POTENT ESSENCES HE HOLDS BACK. THEY ARE THE POWER THAT WILL DRIVE HIS RAW ASSASSIN.
BUT FEW HUMANS CAN LAUGH AT A DEVIL'S MOCKERY.
AMNATIO
ARMY
HE HOPES THAT CONSTANTINE APPRECIATES THE JOKE--

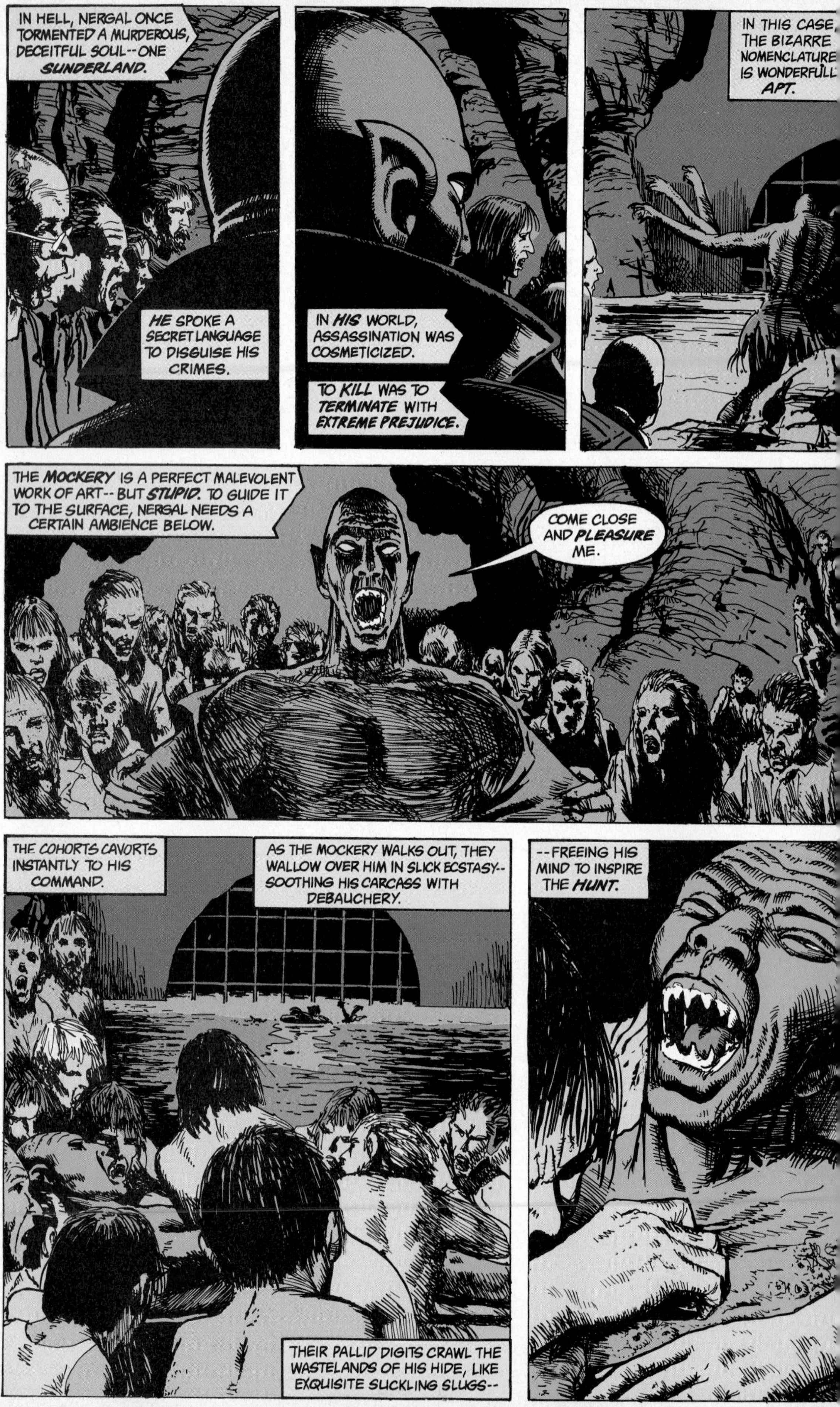
IN HELL, NERGAL ONCE TORMENTED A MURDEROUS, DECEITFUL SOUL--ONE SUNDERLAND.
HE SPOKE A SECRET LANGUAGE TO DISGUISE HIS CRIMES.
IN HIS WORLD, ASSASSINATION WAS COSMETICIZED.
TO KILL WAS TO TERMINATE WITH EXTREME PREJUDICE.
IN THIS CASE, THE BIZARRE NOMENCLATURE IS WONDERFULLY APT.
THE MOCKERY IS A PERFECT MALEVOLENT WORK OF ART-- BUT STUPID. TO GUIDE IT TO THE SURFACE, NERGAL NEEDS A CERTAIN AMBIENCE BELOW.
COME CLOSE AND PLEASURE ME.
THE COHORTS CAVORTS INSTANTLY TO HIS COMMAND.
AS THE MOCKERY WALKS OUT, THEY WALLOW OVER HIM IN SLICK ECSTASY-- SOOTHING HIS CARCASS WITH DEBAUCHERY.
THEIR PALLID DIGITS CRAWL THE WASTELANDS OF HIS HIDE, LIKE EXQUISITE SUCKLING SLUGS--
--FREEING HIS MIND TO INSPIRE THE HUNT.

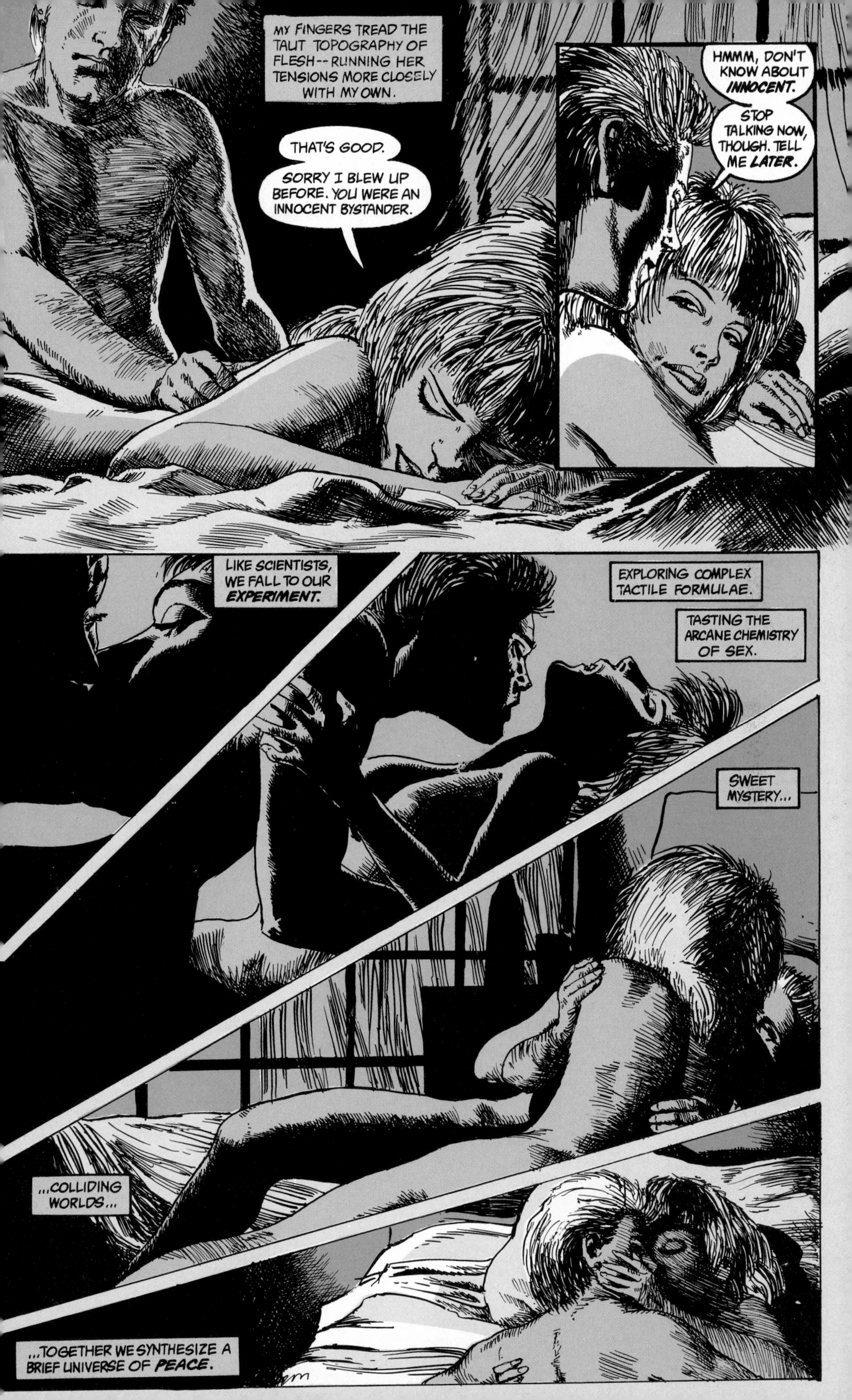
MY FINGERS TREAD THE TAUT TOPOGRAPHY OF FLESH--RUNNING HER TENSIONS MORE CLOSELY WITH MY OWN.
THAT'S GOOD.
SORRY I BLEW UP BEFORE. YOU WERE AN INNOCENT BYSTANDER.
HMMM, DON'T KNOW ABOUT INNOCENT.
STOP TALKING NOW, THOUGH. TELL ME LATER.
LIKE SCIENTISTS, WE FALL TO OUR EXPERIMENT.
EXPLORING COMPLEX TACTILE FORMULAE.
TASTING THE ARCANE CHEMISTRY OF SEX.
SWEET MYSTERY...
...COLLIDING WORLDS...
...TOGETHER WE SYNTHESIZE A BRIEF UNIVERSE OF PEACE.

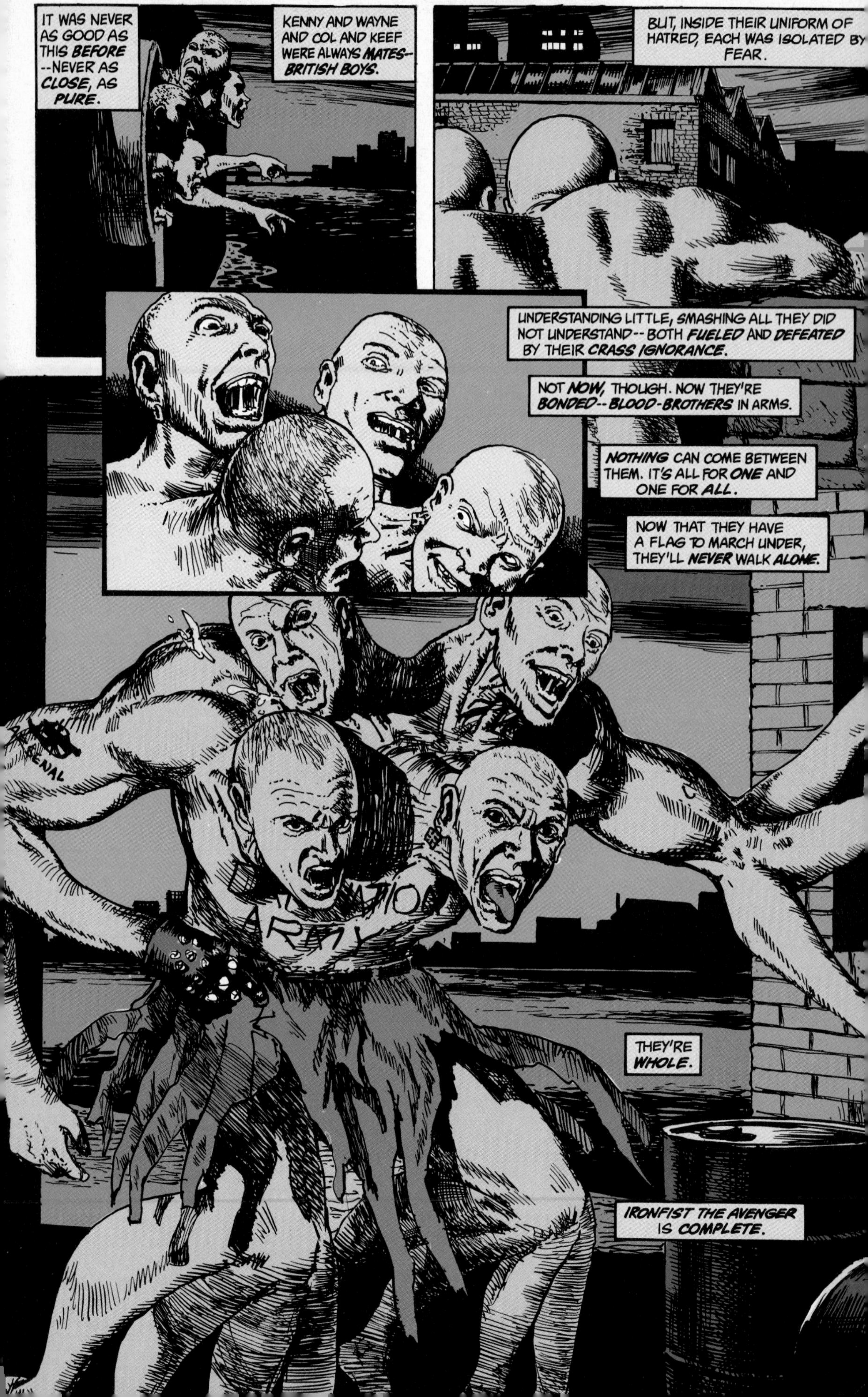
IT WAS NEVER AS GOOD AS THIS BEFORE --NEVER AS CLOSE, AS PURE.
KENNY AND WAYNE AND COL AND KEEF WERE ALWAYS MATES-- BRITISH BOYS.
BUT, INSIDE THEIR UNIFORM OF HATRED, EACH WAS ISOLATED BY FEAR.
UNDERSTANDING LITTLE, SMASHING ALL THEY DID NOT UNDERSTAND-- BOTH FUELED AND DEFEATED BY THEIR CRASS IGNORANCE.
NOT NOW, THOUGH. NOW THEY'RE BONDED-- BLOOD-BROTHERS IN ARMS.
NOTHING CAN COME BETWEEN THEM. IT'S ALL FOR ONE AND ONE FOR ALL.
NOW THAT THEY HAVE A FLAG TO MARCH UNDER, THEY'LL NEVER WALK ALONE.
THEY'RE WHOLE.
IRONFIST THE AVENGER IS COMPLETE.

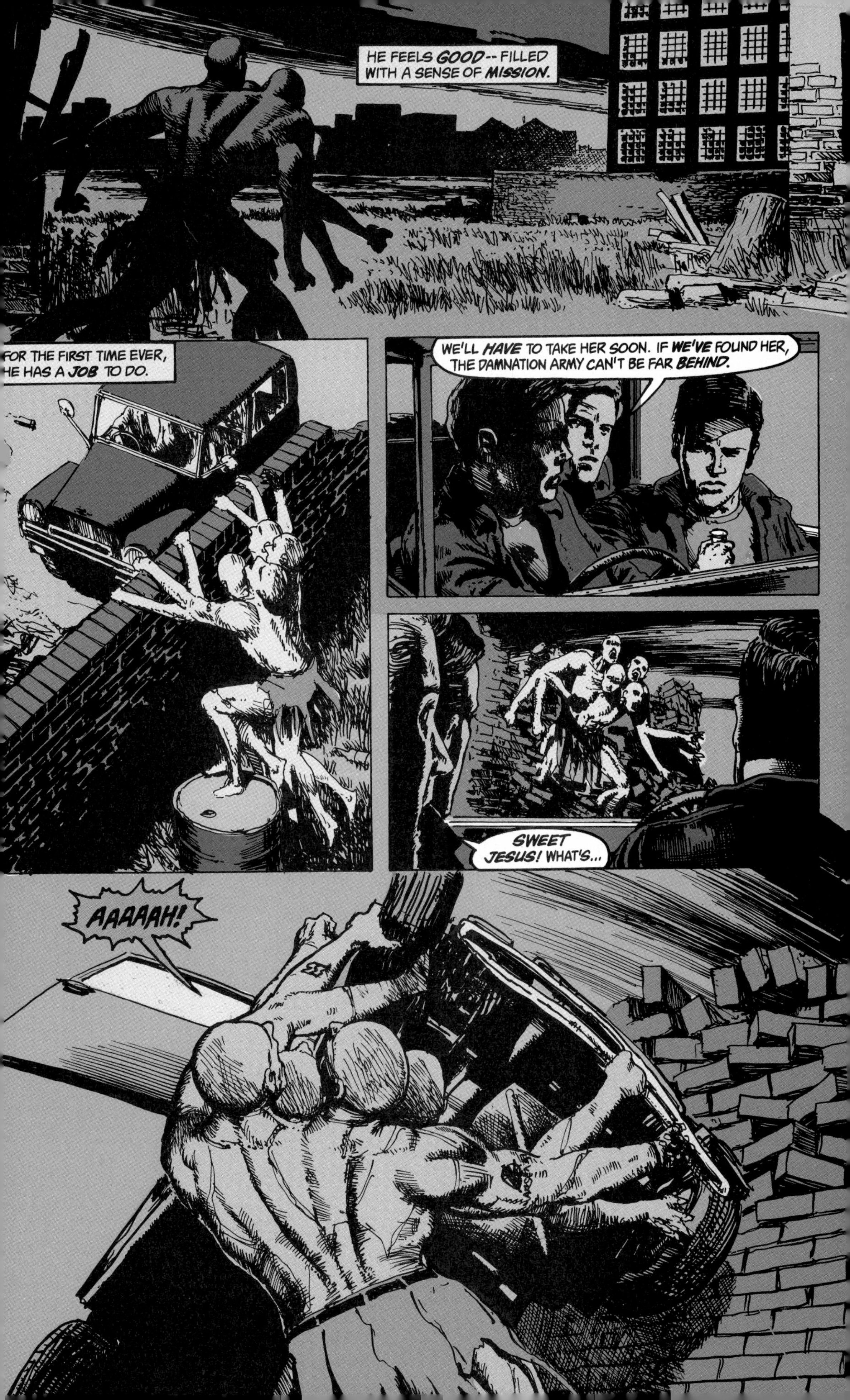

HE FEELS GOOD -- FILLED WITH A SENSE OF MISSION.
FOR THE FIRST TIME EVER, HE HAS A JOB TO DO.
WE'LL HAVE TO TAKE HER SOON. IF WE'VE FOUND HER, THE DAMNATION ARMY CAN'T BE FAR BEHIND.
SWEET JESUS! WHAT'S...
AAAAAH!

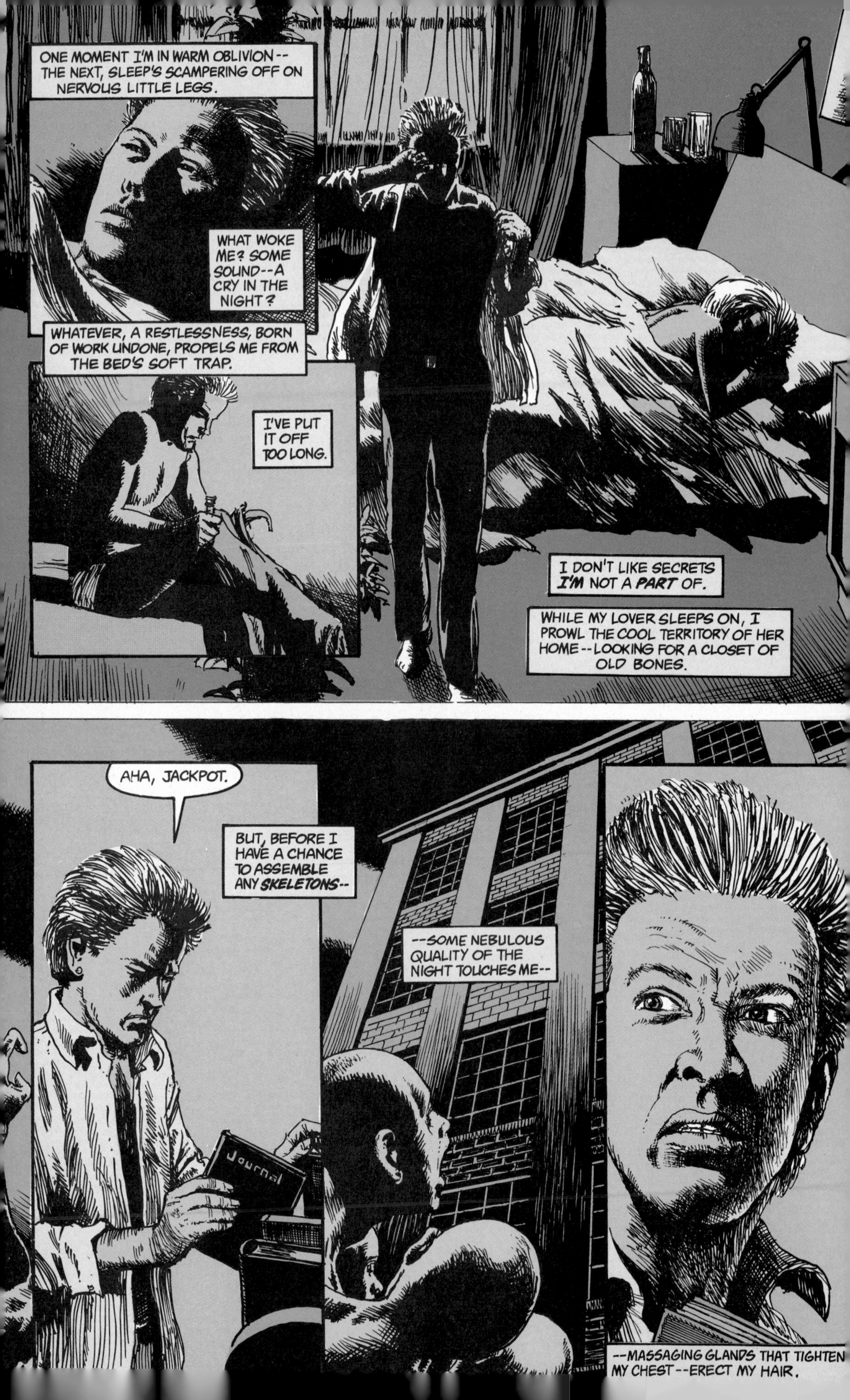
ONE MOMENT I'M IN WARM OBLIVION -- THE NEXT, SLEEP'S SCAMPERING OFF ON NERVOUS LITTLE LEGS.
WHAT WOKE ME? SOME SOUND--A CRY IN THE NIGHT?
WHATEVER, A RESTLESSNESS, BORN OF WORK UNDONE, PROPELS ME FROM THE BED'S SOFT TRAP.
I'VE PUT IT OFF TOO LONG.
I DON'T LIKE SECRETS I'M NOT A PART OF.
WHILE MY LOVER SLEEPS ON, I PROWL THE COOL TERRITORY OF HER HOME--LOOKING FOR A CLOSET OF OLD BONES.
AHA, JACKPOT.
BUT, BEFORE I HAVE A CHANCE TO ASSEMBLE ANY SKELETONS--
Journal
--SOME NEBULOUS QUALITY OF THE NIGHT TOUCHES ME--
--MASSAGING GLANDS THAT TIGHTEN MY CHEST--ERECT MY HAIR.

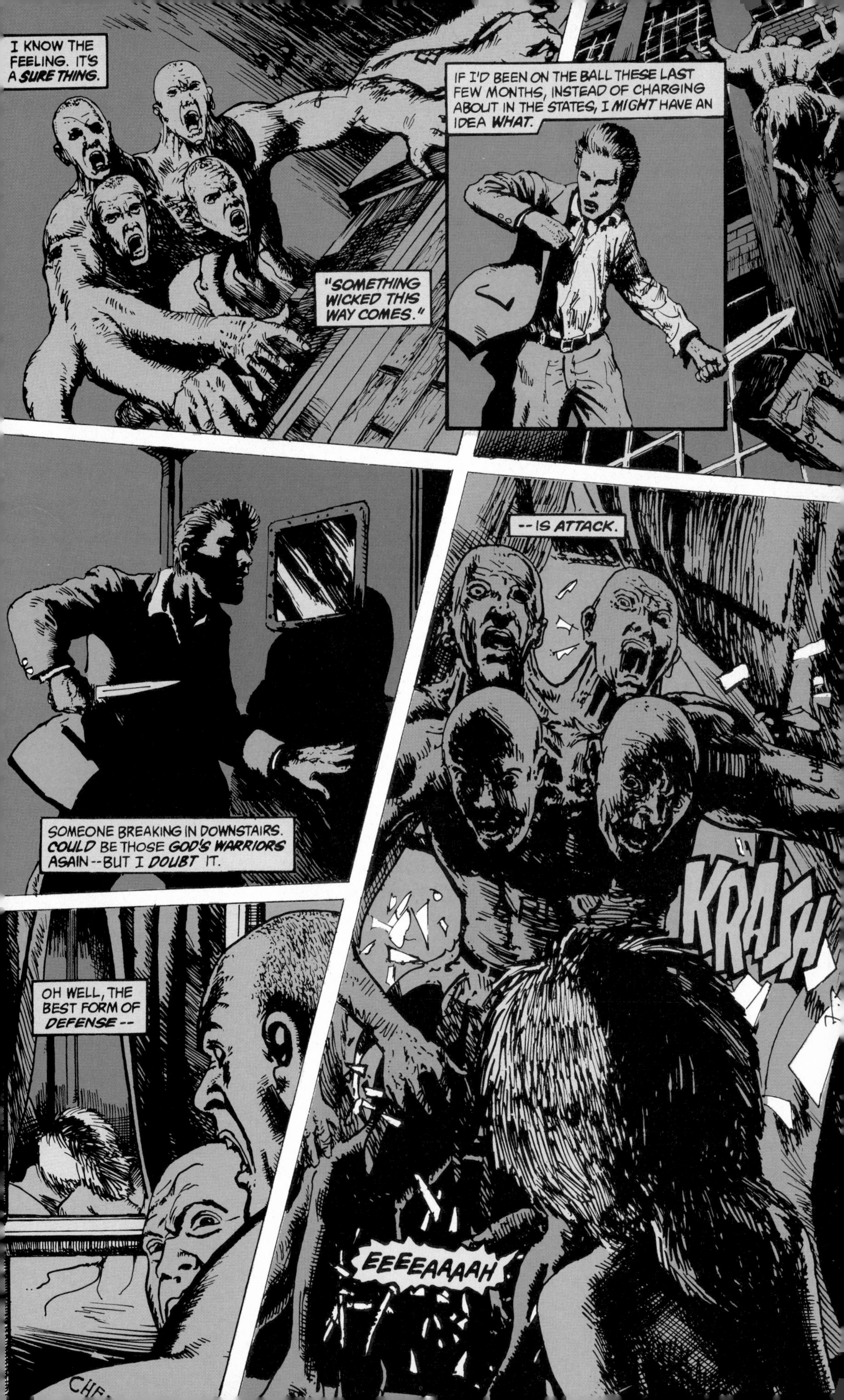
I KNOW THE FEELING. IT'S A SURE THING.
"SOMETHING WICKED THIS WAY COMES."
IF I'D BEEN ON THE BALL THESE LAST FEW MONTHS, INSTEAD OF CHARGING ABOUT IN THE STATES, I MIGHT HAVE AN IDEA WHAT.
SOMEONE BREAKING IN DOWNSTAIRS. COULD BE THOSE GOD'S WARRIORS AGAIN--BUT I DOUBT IT.
OH WELL, THE BEST FORM OF DEFENSE--
--IS ATTACK.
KRASH
EEEEAAAAH

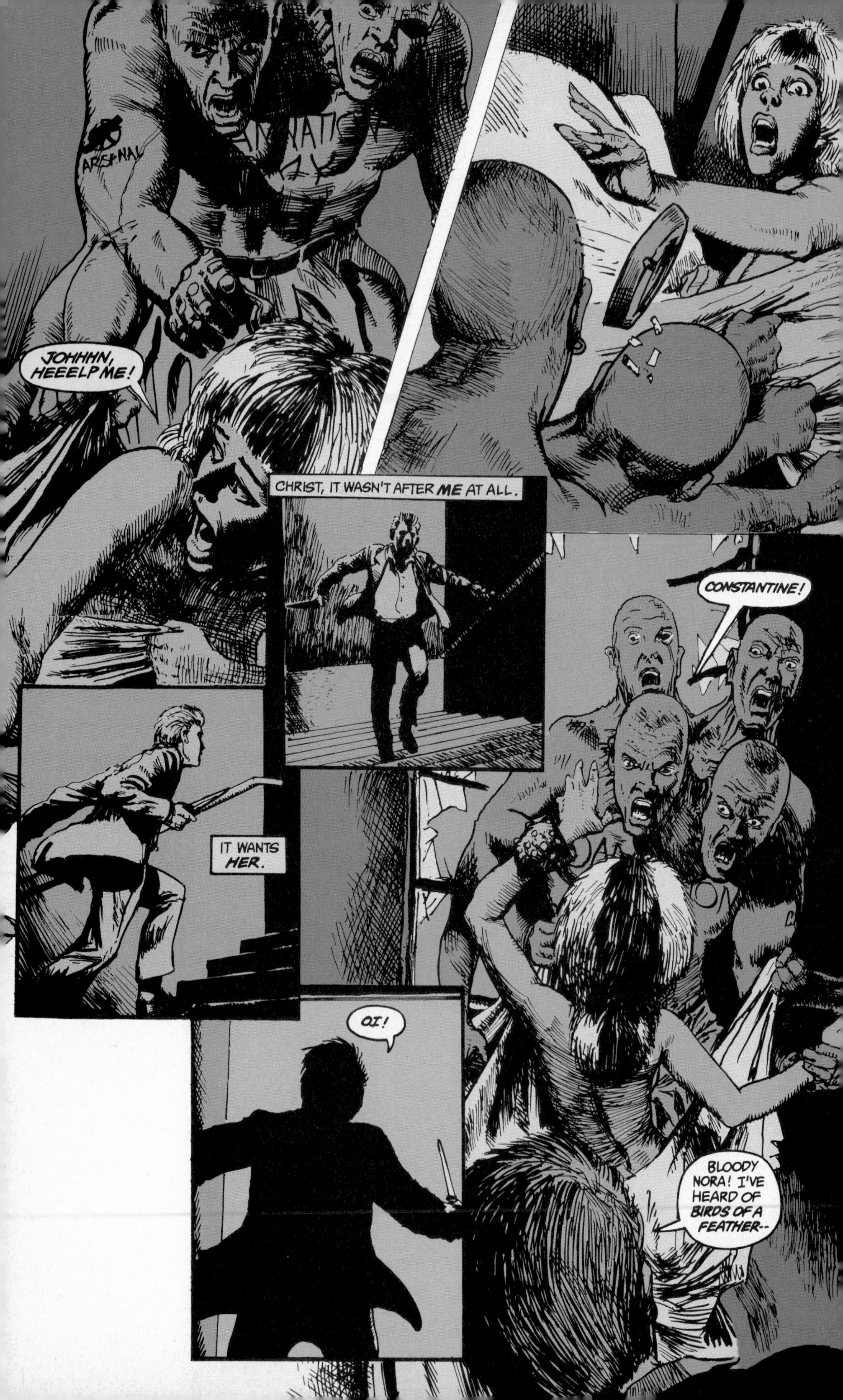

JOHHHN, HEEELP ME!
CHRIST, IT WASN'T AFTER ME AT ALL.
IT WANTS HER.
CONSTANTINE!
OI!
BLOODY NORA! I'VE HEARD OF BIRDS OF A FEATHER--

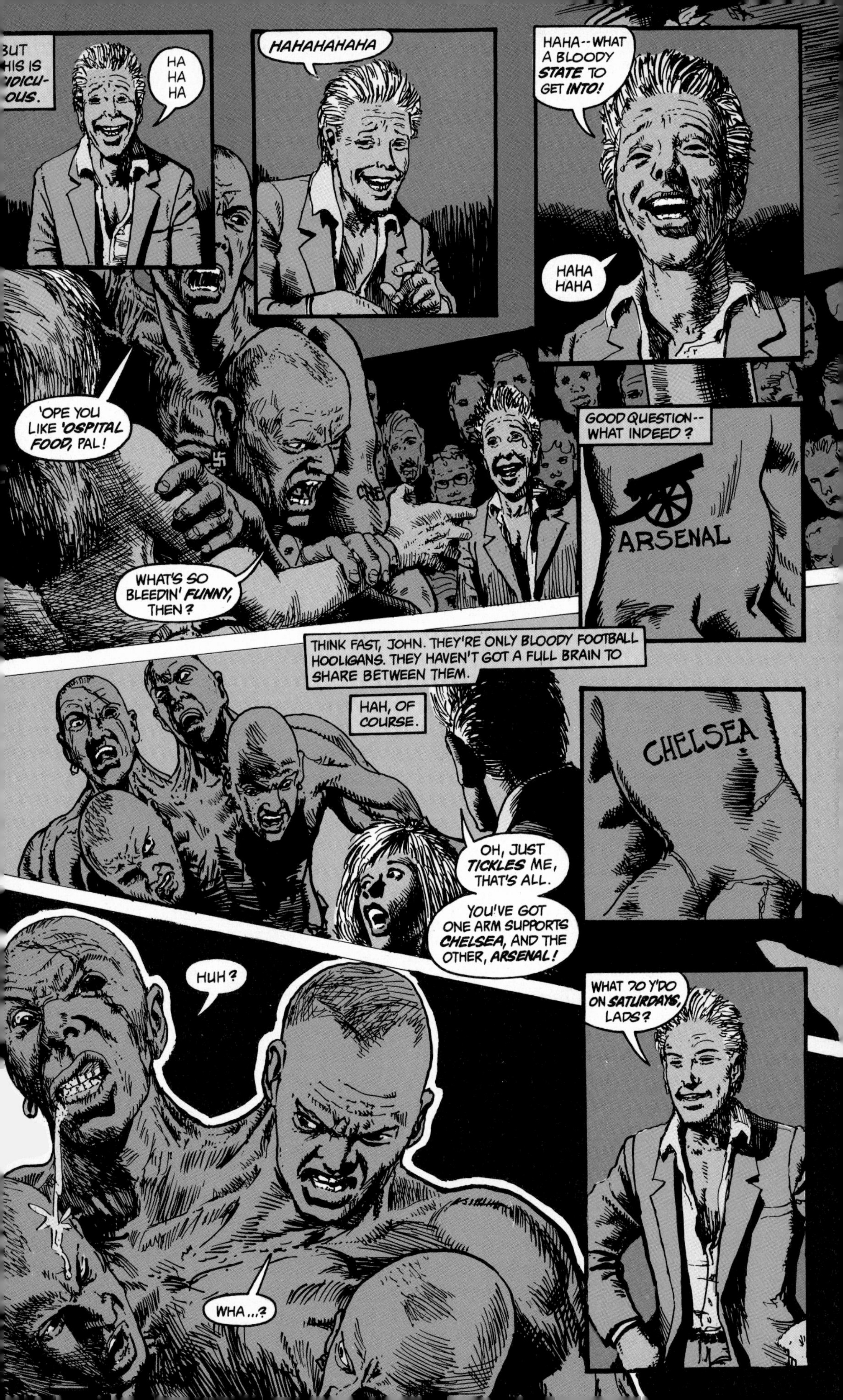
BUT THIS IS RIDICULOUS.
HA HA HA
HAHAHAHAHA
HAHA--WHAT A BLOODY STATE TO GET INTO!
HAHA HAHA
'OPE YOU LIKE 'OSPITAL FOOD, PAL!
GOOD QUESTION--WHAT INDEED?
ARSENAL
WHAT'S SO BLEEDIN' FUNNY, THEN?
THINK FAST, JOHN. THEY'RE ONLY BLOODY FOOTBALL HOOLIGANS. THEY HAVEN'T GOT A FULL BRAIN TO SHARE BETWEEN THEM.
HAH, OF COURSE.
CHELSEA
OH, JUST TICKLES ME, THAT'S ALL.
YOU'VE GOT ONE ARM SUPPORTS CHELSEA, AND THE OTHER, ARSENAL!
HUH?
WHAT DO Y'DO ON SATURDAYS, LADS?
WHA...?

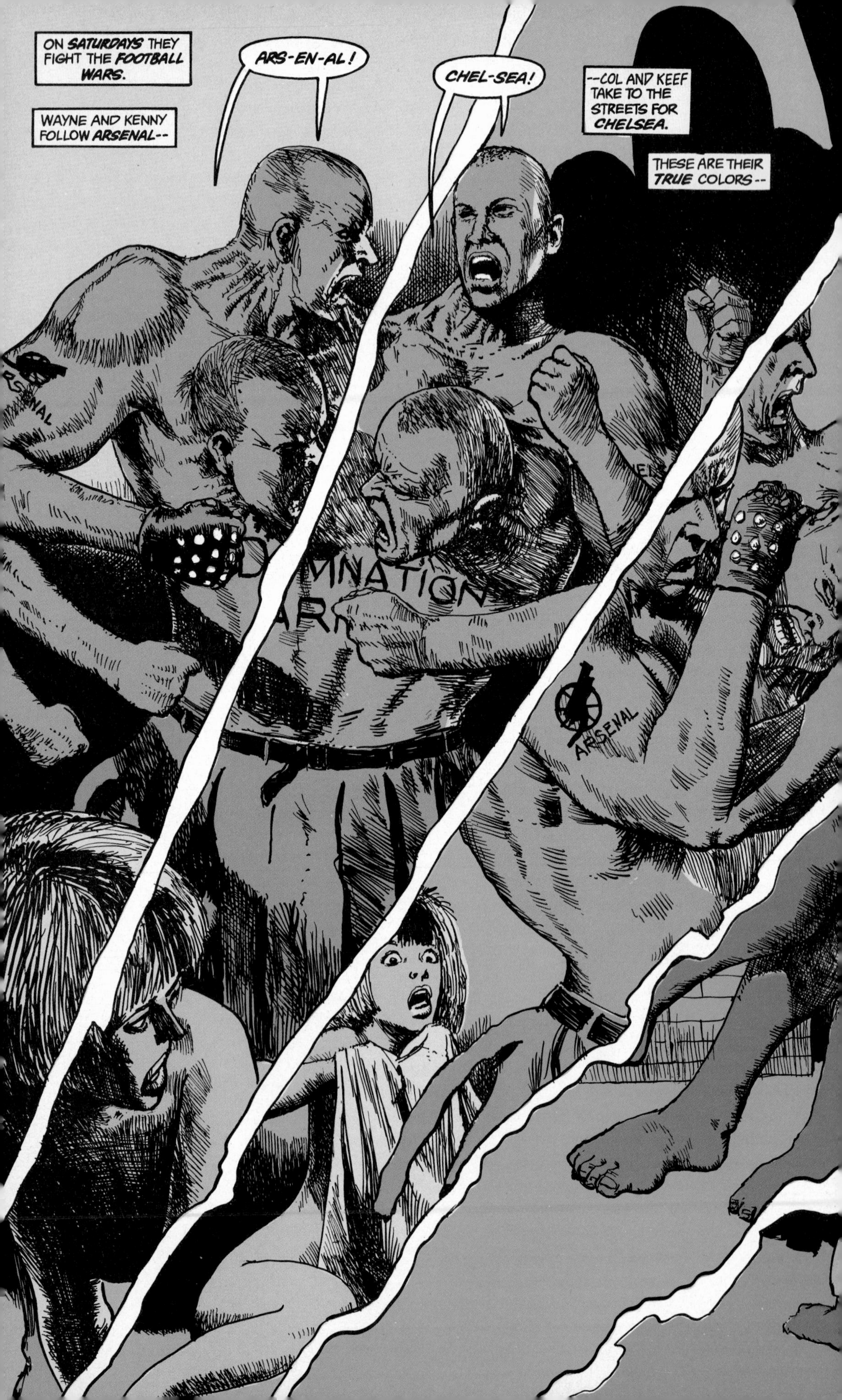

ON SATURDAYS THEY FIGHT THE FOOTBALL WARS.
WAYNE AND KENNY FOLLOW ARSENAL--
ARS-EN-AL!
CHEL-SEA!
--COL AND KEEF TAKE TO THE STREETS FOR CHELSEA.
THESE ARE THEIR TRUE COLORS--
ARSENAL
ARSENAL

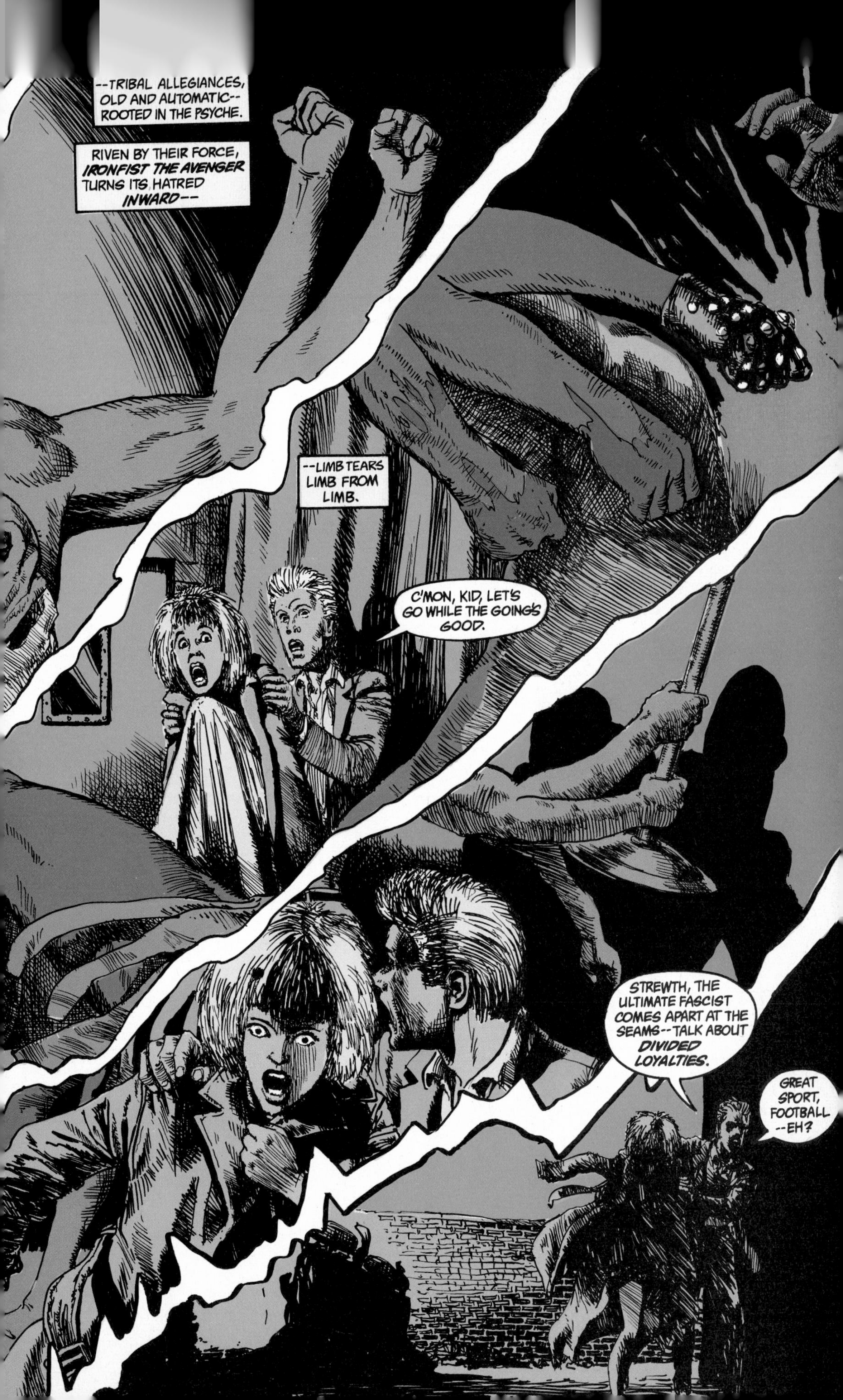
--TRIBAL ALLEGIANCES, OLD AND AUTOMATIC-- ROOTED IN THE PSYCHE.
RIVEN BY THEIR FORCE, IRONFIST THE AVENGER TURNS ITS HATRED INWARD--
--LIMB TEARS LIMB FROM LIMB.
C'MON, KID, LET'S GO WHILE THE GOING'S GOOD.
STREWTH, THE ULTIMATE FASCIST COMES APART AT THE SEAMS--TALK ABOUT DIVIDED LOYALTIES.
GREAT SPORT, FOOTBALL --EH?

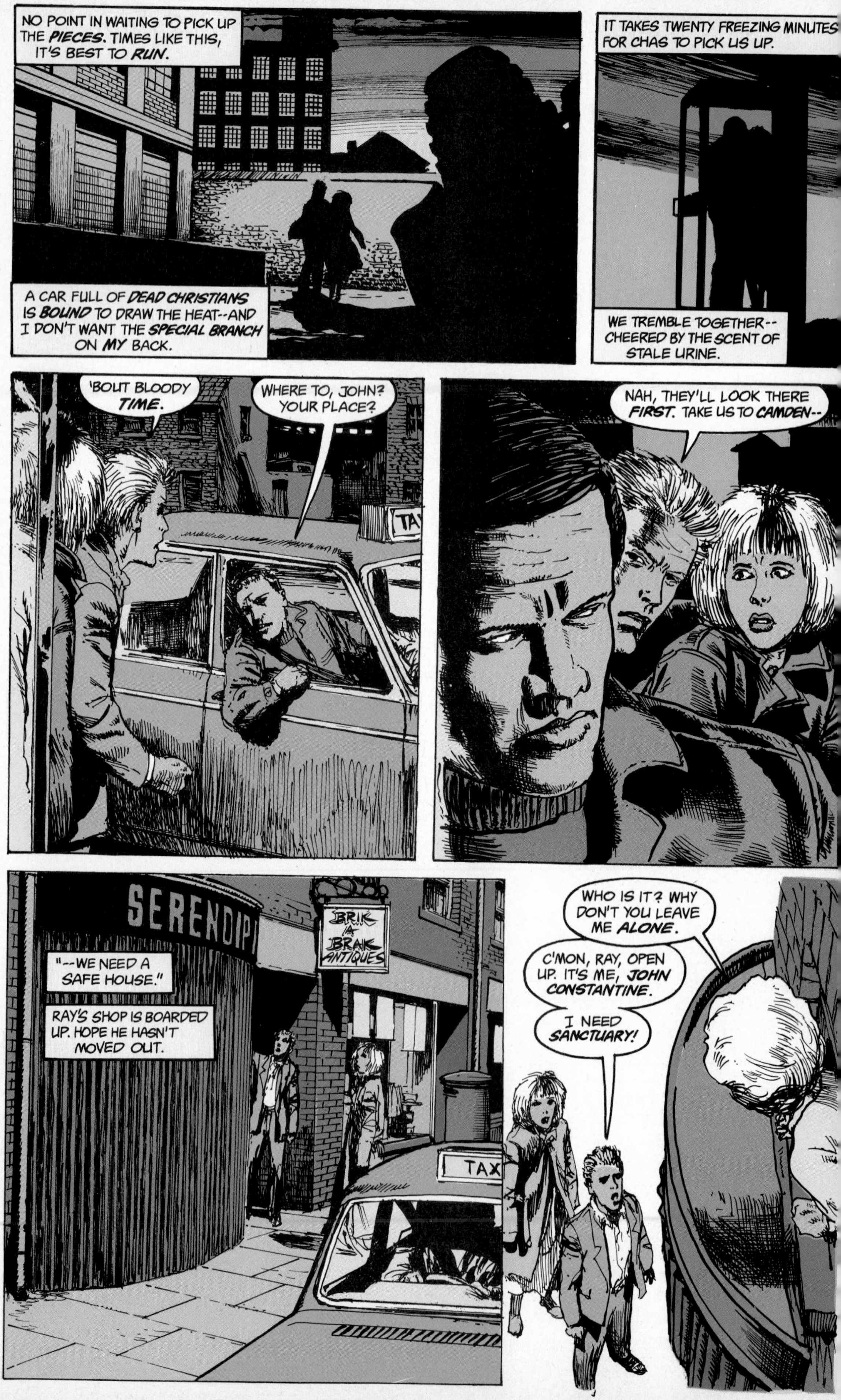

NO POINT IN WAITING TO PICK UP THE PIECES. TIMES LIKE THIS, IT'S BEST TO RUN.
A CAR FULL OF DEAD CHRISTIANS IS BOUND TO DRAW THE HEAT--AND I DON'T WANT THE SPECIAL BRANCH ON MY BACK.
IT TAKES TWENTY FREEZING MINUTES FOR CHAS TO PICK US UP.
WE TREMBLE TOGETHER--CHEERED BY THE SCENT OF STALE URINE.
'BOUT BLOODY TIME.
WHERE TO, JOHN? YOUR PLACE?
NAH, THEY'LL LOOK THERE FIRST. TAKE US TO CAMDEN--
SERENDIP
BRIK A BRAK ANTIQUES
"--WE NEED A SAFE HOUSE."
RAY'S SHOP IS BOARDED UP. HOPE HE HASN'T MOVED OUT.
TAX
WHO IS IT? WHY DON'T YOU LEAVE ME ALONE.
C'MON, RAY, OPEN UP. IT'S ME, JOHN CONSTANTINE.
I NEED SANCTUARY!

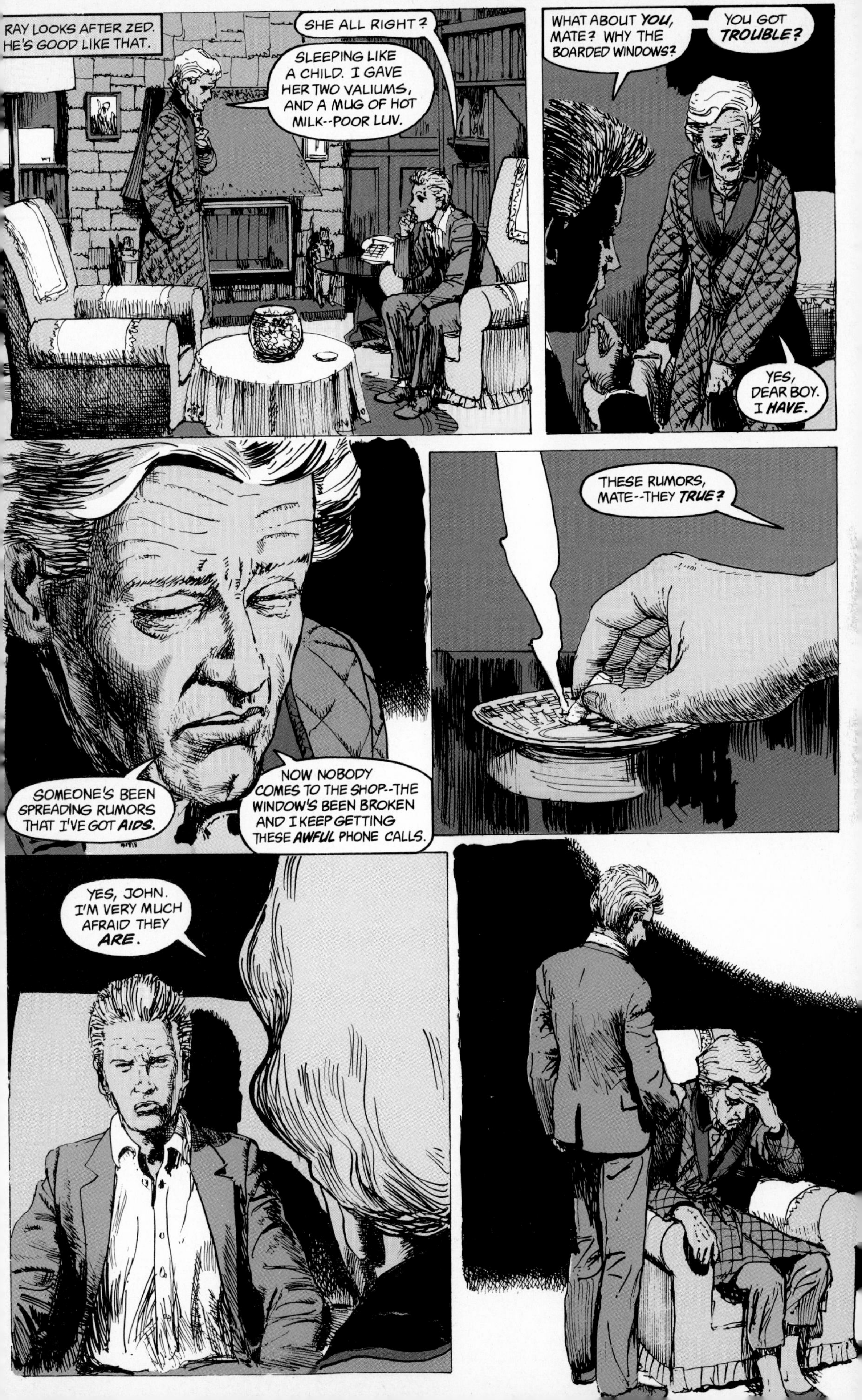
RAY LOOKS AFTER ZED. HE'S GOOD LIKE THAT.
SHE ALL RIGHT?
SLEEPING LIKE A CHILD. I GAVE HER TWO VALIUMS, AND A MUG OF HOT MILK--POOR LUV.
WHAT ABOUT YOU, MATE? WHY THE BOARDED WINDOWS?
YOU GOT TROUBLE?
YES, DEAR BOY. I HAVE.
SOMEONE'S BEEN SPREADING RUMORS THAT I'VE GOT AIDS.
NOW NOBODY COMES TO THE SHOP--THE WINDOW'S BEEN BROKEN AND I KEEP GETTING THESE AWFUL PHONE CALLS.
THESE RUMORS, MATE--THEY TRUE?
YES, JOHN. I'M VERY MUCH AFRAID THEY ARE.

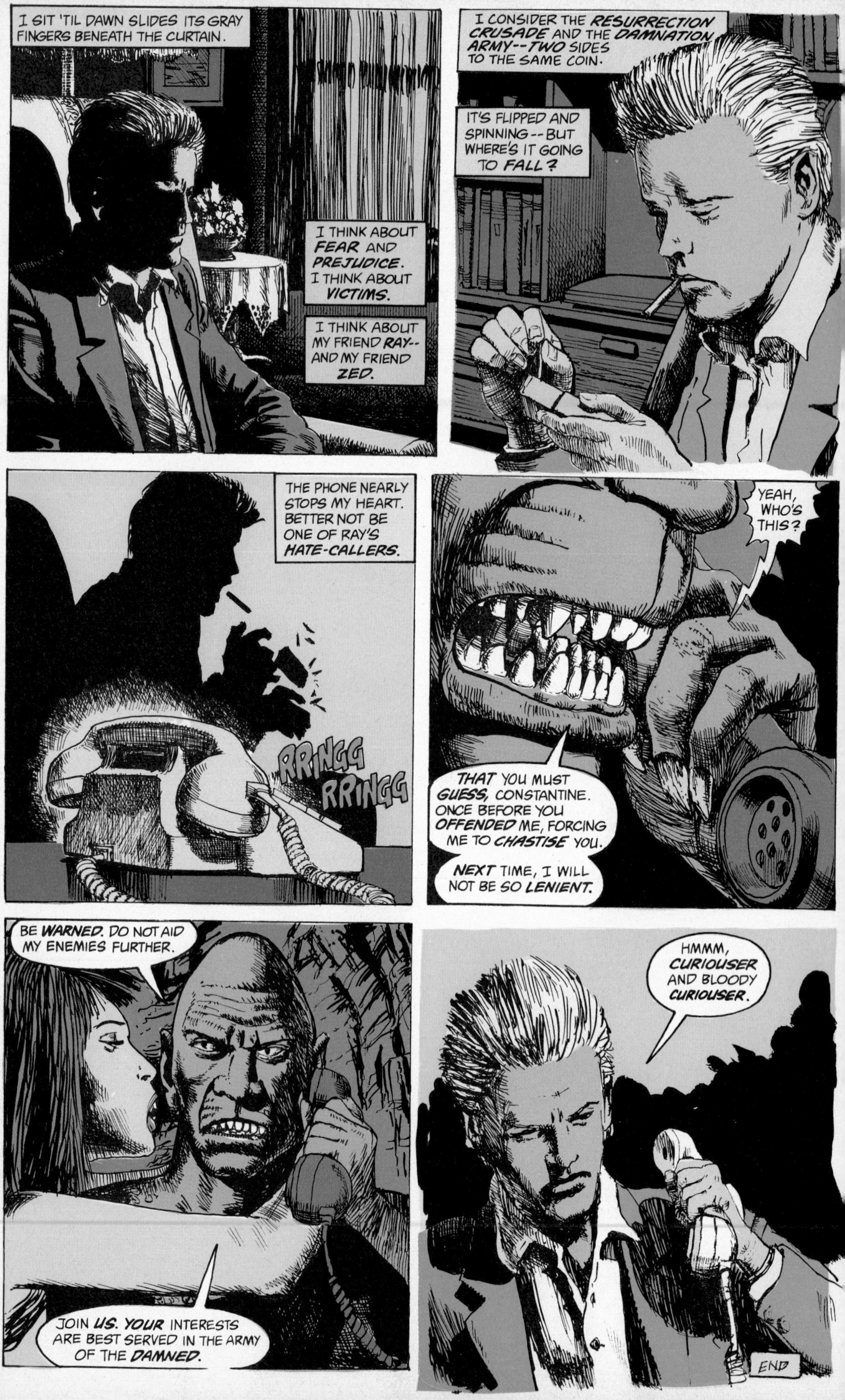
I SIT 'TIL DAWN SLIDES ITS GRAY FINGERS BENEATH THE CURTAIN.
I THINK ABOUT FEAR AND PREJUDICE. I THINK ABOUT VICTIMS.
I THINK ABOUT MY FRIEND RAY-- AND MY FRIEND ZED.
I CONSIDER THE RESURRECTION CRUSADE AND THE DAMNATION ARMY--TWO SIDES TO THE SAME COIN.
IT'S FLIPPED AND SPINNING -- BUT WHERE'S IT GOING TO FALL?
THE PHONE NEARLY STOPS MY HEART. BETTER NOT BE ONE OF RAY'S HATE-CALLERS.
RRINGG
RRINGG
YEAH, WHO'S THIS?
THAT YOU MUST GUESS, CONSTANTINE. ONCE BEFORE YOU OFFENDED ME, FORCING ME TO CHASTISE YOU.
NEXT TIME, I WILL NOT BE SO LENIENT.
BE WARNED. DO NOT AID MY ENEMIES FURTHER.
JOIN US. YOUR INTERESTS ARE BEST SERVED IN THE ARMY OF THE DAMNED.
HMMM, CURIOUSER AND BLOODY CURIOUSER.
END

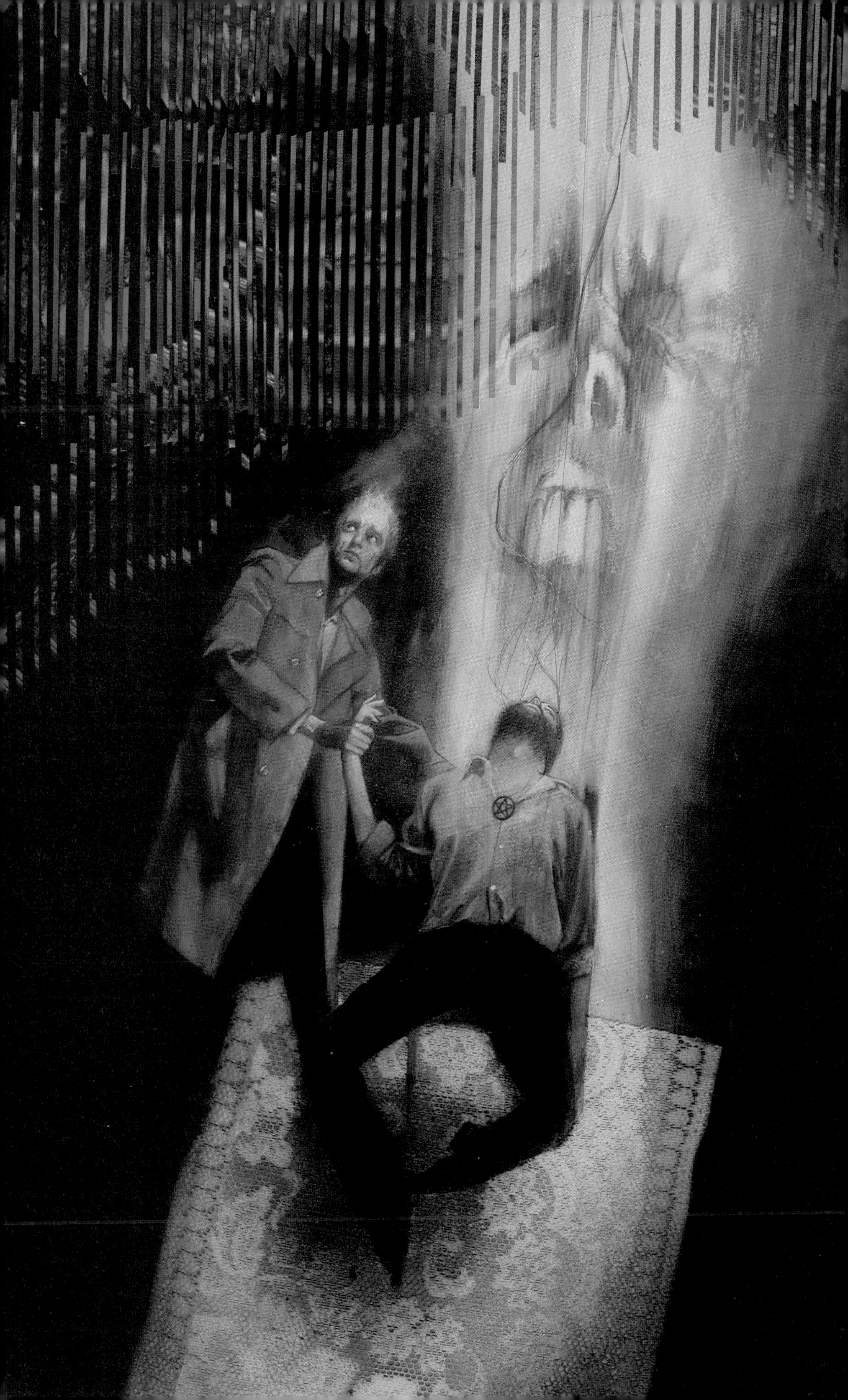

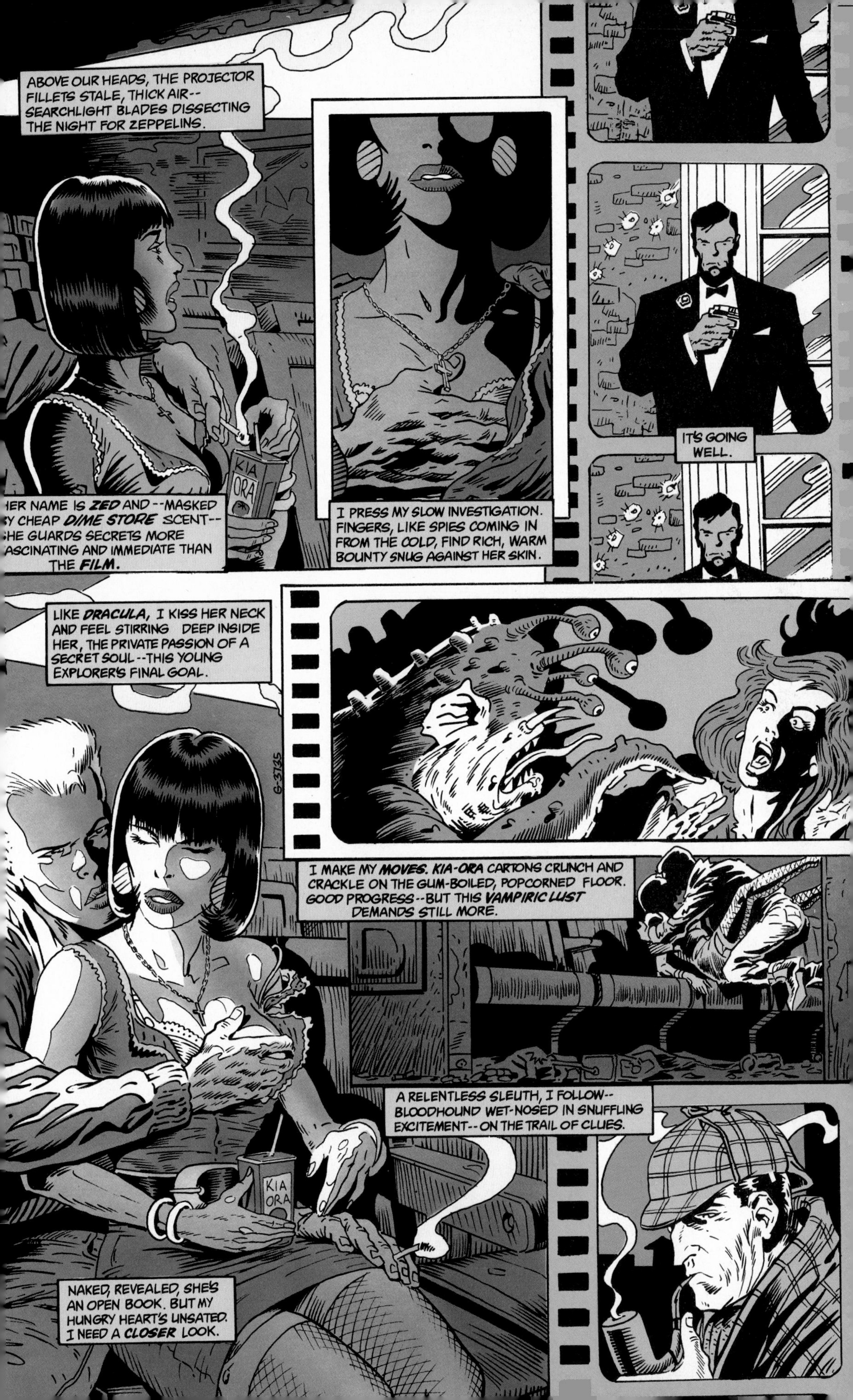
ABOVE OUR HEADS, THE PROJECTOR FILLETS STALE, THICK AIR-- SEARCHLIGHT BLADES DISSECTING THE NIGHT FOR ZEPPELINS.
KIA ORA
HER NAME IS ZED AND --MASKED Y CHEAP DIME STORE SCENT-- HE GUARDS SECRETS MORE ASCINATING AND IMMEDIATE THAN THE FILM.
I PRESS MY SLOW INVESTIGATION. FINGERS, LIKE SPIES COMING IN FROM THE COLD, FIND RICH, WARM BOUNTY SNUG AGAINST HER SKIN.
IT'S GOING WELL.
LIKE DRACULA, I KISS HER NECK AND FEEL STIRRING DEEP INSIDE HER, THE PRIVATE PASSION OF A SECRET SOUL --THIS YOUNG EXPLORER'S FINAL GOAL.
I MAKE MY MOVES. KIA-ORA CARTONS CRUNCH AND CRACKLE ON THE GUM-BOILED, POPCORNED FLOOR. GOOD PROGRESS--BUT THIS VAMPIRIC LUST DEMANDS STILL MORE.
A RELENTLESS SLEUTH, I FOLLOW-- BLOODHOUND WET-NOSED IN SNUFFLING EXCITEMENT--ON THE TRAIL OF CLUES.
KIA ORA
NAKED, REVEALED, SHE'S AN OPEN BOOK. BUT MY HUNGRY HEART'S UNSATED. I NEED A CLOSER LOOK.

I'M UNSTOPPABLE. I HAVE NO CHOICE, I MUST INQUIRE WITHIN. STRUGGLING, LIKE SOME VILE PARASITE, TO GET BENEATH HER SKIN.

GENTLY--SO DELICATELY--I SEARCH HER. SHE SQUIRMS AS MY QUESTING HANDS PUSH AND CLEAVE THROUGH SOFT FABRIC--

--SLICK PLANES OF TISSUE--

OILED WITH THE CLAMMY SWEAT OF ADOLESCENT ARDOR, I REACH OUT FOR THE HEART OF THE MATTER.

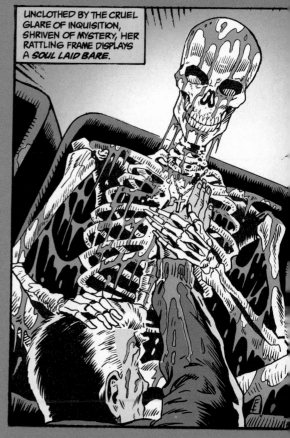

UNCLOTHED BY THE CRUEL GLARE OF INQUISITION, SHRIVEN OF MYSTERY, HER RATTLING FRAME DISPLAYS A *SOUL LAID BARE.*

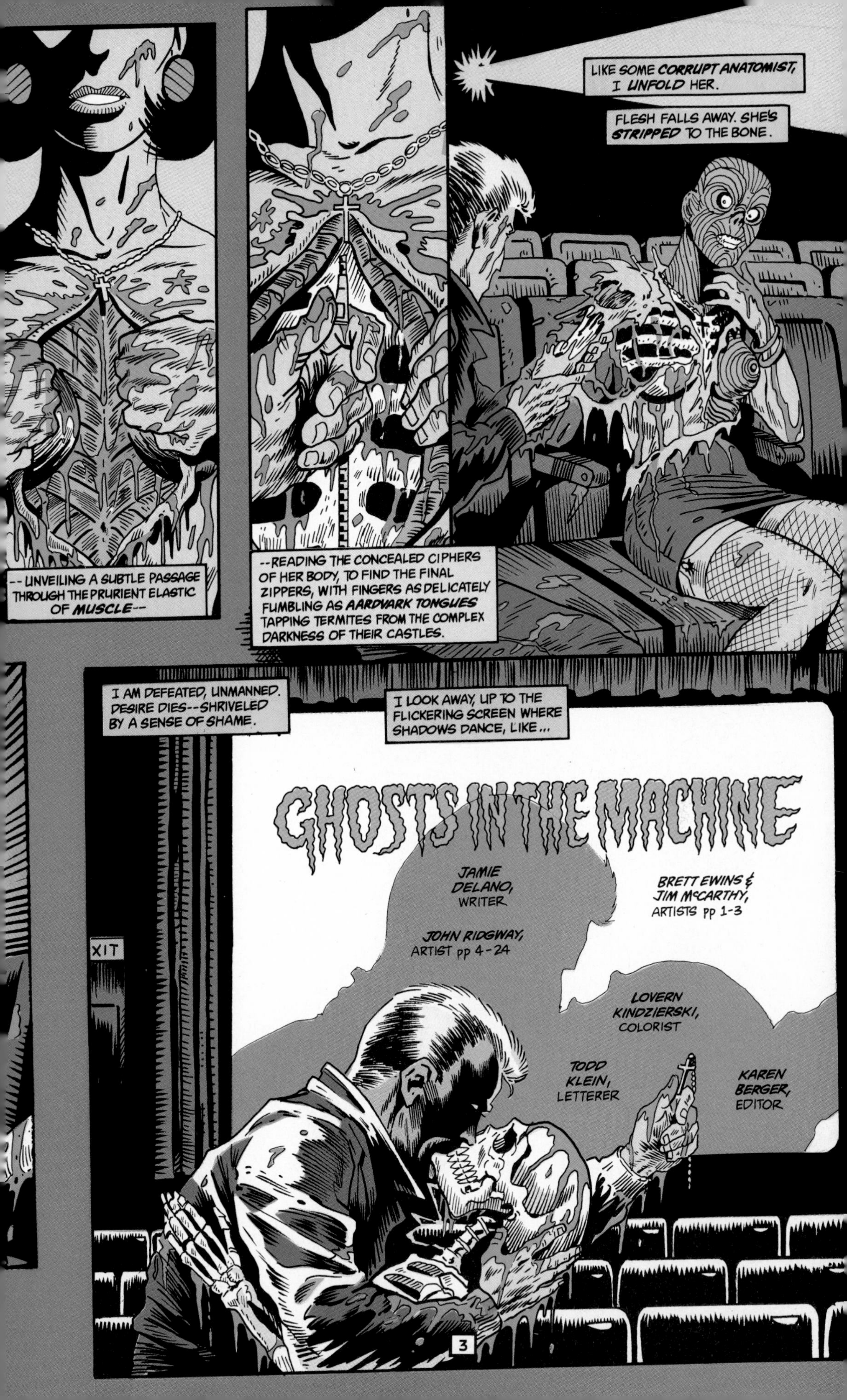
LIKE SOME CORRUPT ANATOMIST, I UNFOLD HER.
FLESH FALLS AWAY. SHE'S STRIPPED TO THE BONE.
--UNVEILING A SUBTLE PASSAGE THROUGH THE PRURIENT ELASTIC OF MUSCLE--
--READING THE CONCEALED CIPHERS OF HER BODY, TO FIND THE FINAL ZIPPERS, WITH FINGERS AS DELICATELY FUMBLING AS AARDVARK TONGUES TAPPING TERMITES FROM THE COMPLEX DARKNESS OF THEIR CASTLES.
I AM DEFEATED, UNMANNED. DESIRE DIES--SHRIVELED BY A SENSE OF SHAME.
I LOOK AWAY, UP TO THE FLICKERING SCREEN WHERE SHADOWS DANCE, LIKE...
GHOSTS IN THE MACHINE
JAMIE DELANO, WRITER
BRETT EWINS & JIM McCARTHY, ARTISTS pp 1-3
JOHN RIDGWAY, ARTIST pp 4-24
LOVERN KINDZIERSKI, COLORIST
TODD KLEIN, LETTERER
KAREN BERGER, EDITOR
XIT
3

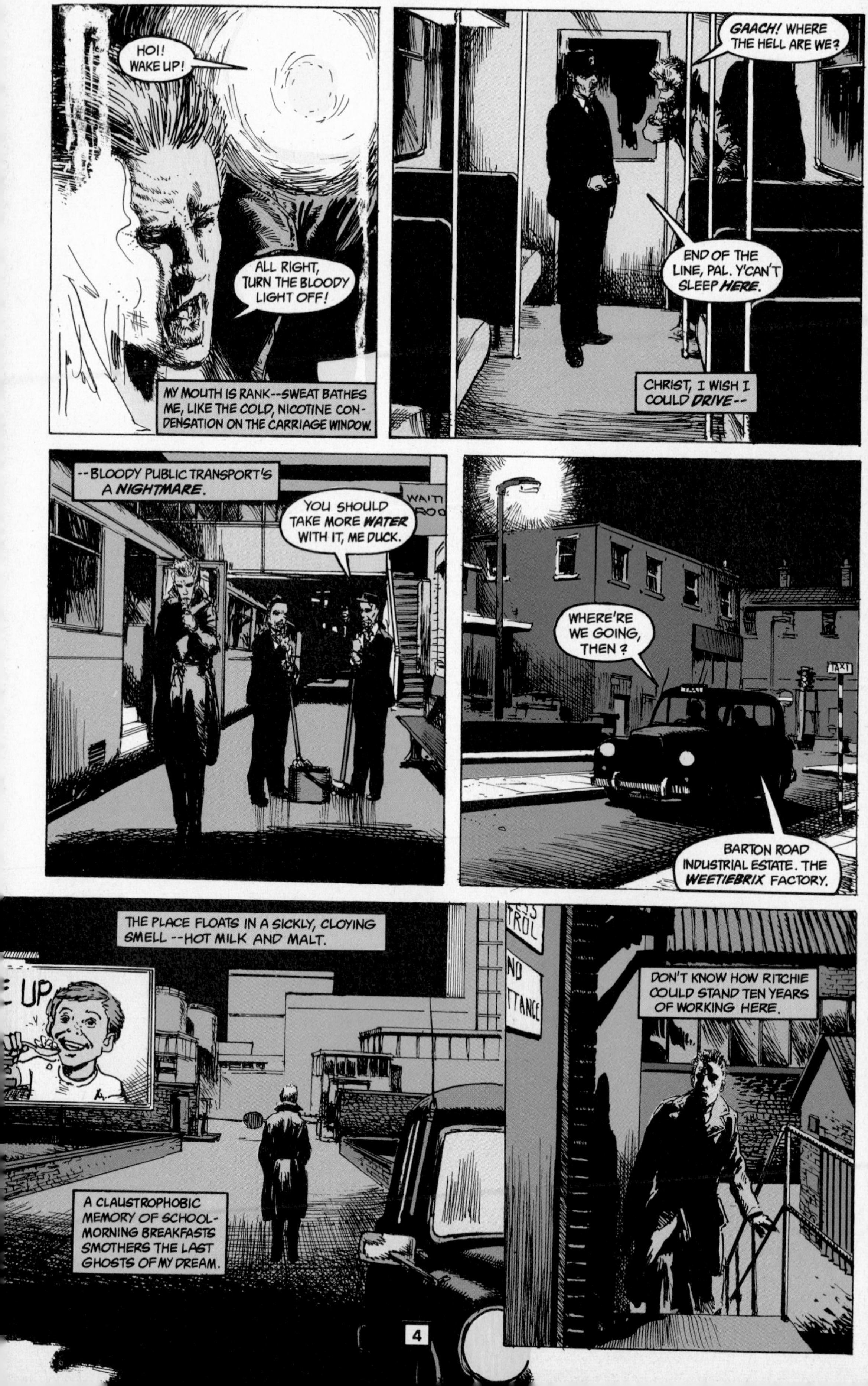
HOI! WAKE UP!
ALL RIGHT, TURN THE BLOODY LIGHT OFF!
MY MOUTH IS RANK--SWEAT BATHES ME, LIKE THE COLD, NICOTINE CON-DENSATION ON THE CARRIAGE WINDOW.
GAACH! WHERE THE HELL ARE WE?
END OF THE LINE, PAL. Y'CAN'T SLEEP HERE.
CHRIST, I WISH I COULD DRIVE--
--BLOODY PUBLIC TRANSPORT'S A NIGHTMARE.
YOU SHOULD TAKE MORE WATER WITH IT, ME DUCK.
WHERE'RE WE GOING, THEN?
TAXI
BARTON ROAD INDUSTRIAL ESTATE. THE WEETIEBRIX FACTORY.
THE PLACE FLOATS IN A SICKLY, CLOYING SMELL--HOT MILK AND MALT.
A CLAUSTROPHOBIC MEMORY OF SCHOOL-MORNING BREAKFASTS SMOTHERS THE LAST GHOSTS OF MY DREAM.
DON'T KNOW HOW RITCHIE COULD STAND TEN YEARS OF WORKING HERE.

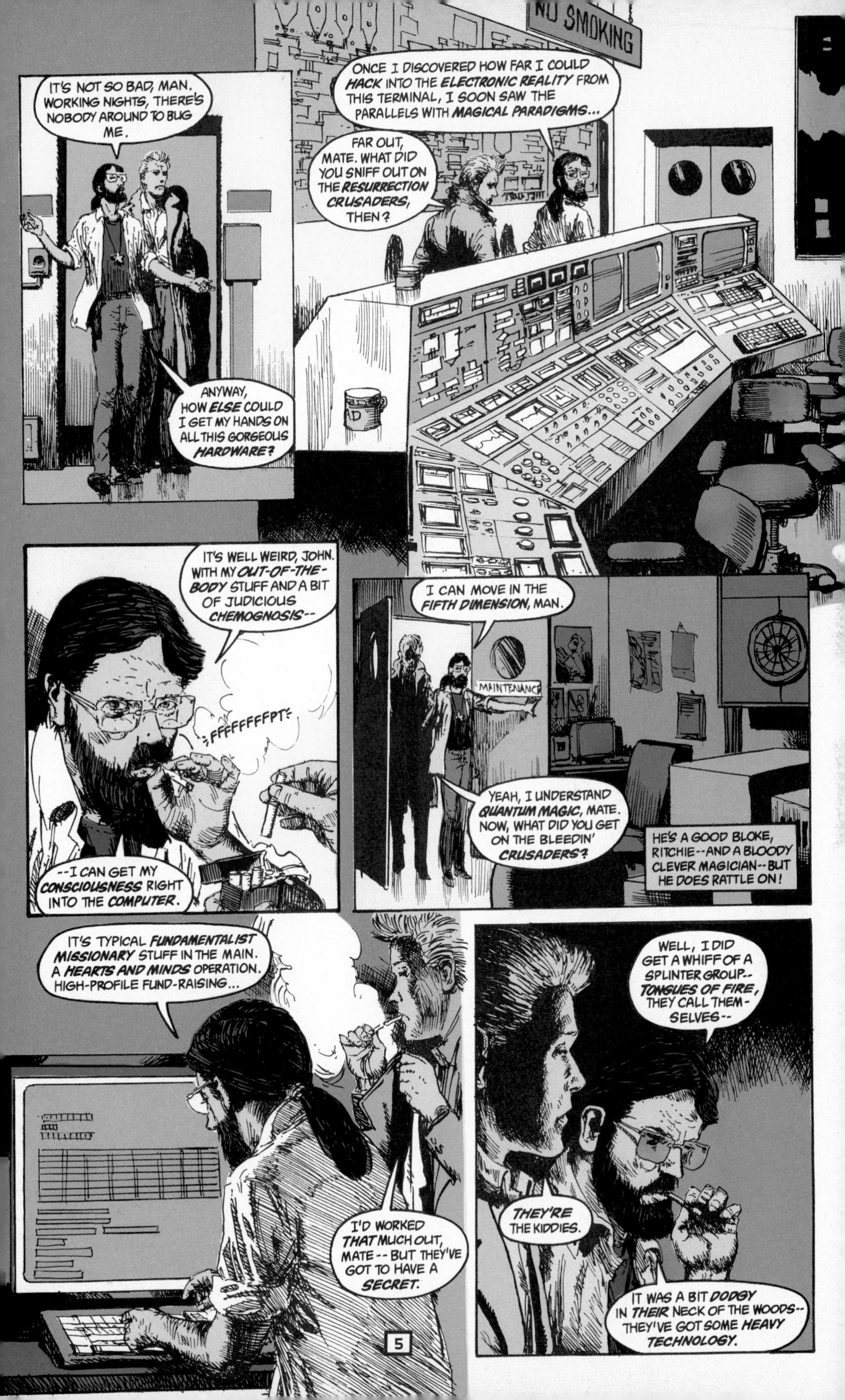
NO SMOKING
IT'S NOT SO BAD, MAN. WORKING NIGHTS, THERE'S NOBODY AROUND TO BUG ME.
ONCE I DISCOVERED HOW FAR I COULD HACK INTO THE ELECTRONIC REALITY FROM THIS TERMINAL, I SOON SAW THE PARALLELS WITH MAGICAL PARADIGMS...
FAR OUT, MATE. WHAT DID YOU SNIFF OUT ON THE RESURRECTION CRUSADERS, THEN?
ANYWAY, HOW ELSE COULD I GET MY HANDS ON ALL THIS GORGEOUS HARDWARE?
IT'S WELL WEIRD, JOHN. WITH MY OUT-OF-THE-BODY STUFF AND A BIT OF JUDICIOUS CHEMOGNOSIS--
FFFFFFFFPT
--I CAN GET MY CONSCIOUSNESS RIGHT INTO THE COMPUTER.
I CAN MOVE IN THE FIFTH DIMENSION, MAN.
MAINTENANCE
YEAH, I UNDERSTAND QUANTUM MAGIC, MATE. NOW, WHAT DID YOU GET ON THE BLEEDIN' CRUSADERS?
HE'S A GOOD BLOKE, RITCHIE--AND A BLOODY CLEVER MAGICIAN--BUT HE DOES RATTLE ON!
IT'S TYPICAL FUNDAMENTALIST MISSIONARY STUFF IN THE MAIN. A HEARTS AND MINDS OPERATION. HIGH-PROFILE FUND-RAISING...
I'D WORKED THAT MUCH OUT, MATE -- BUT THEY'VE GOT TO HAVE A SECRET.
WELL, I DID GET A WHIFF OF A SPLINTER GROUP-- TONGUES OF FIRE, THEY CALL THEM-SELVES--
THEY'RE THE KIDDIES.
IT WAS A BIT DODGY IN THEIR NECK OF THE WOODS-- THEY'VE GOT SOME HEAVY TECHNOLOGY.

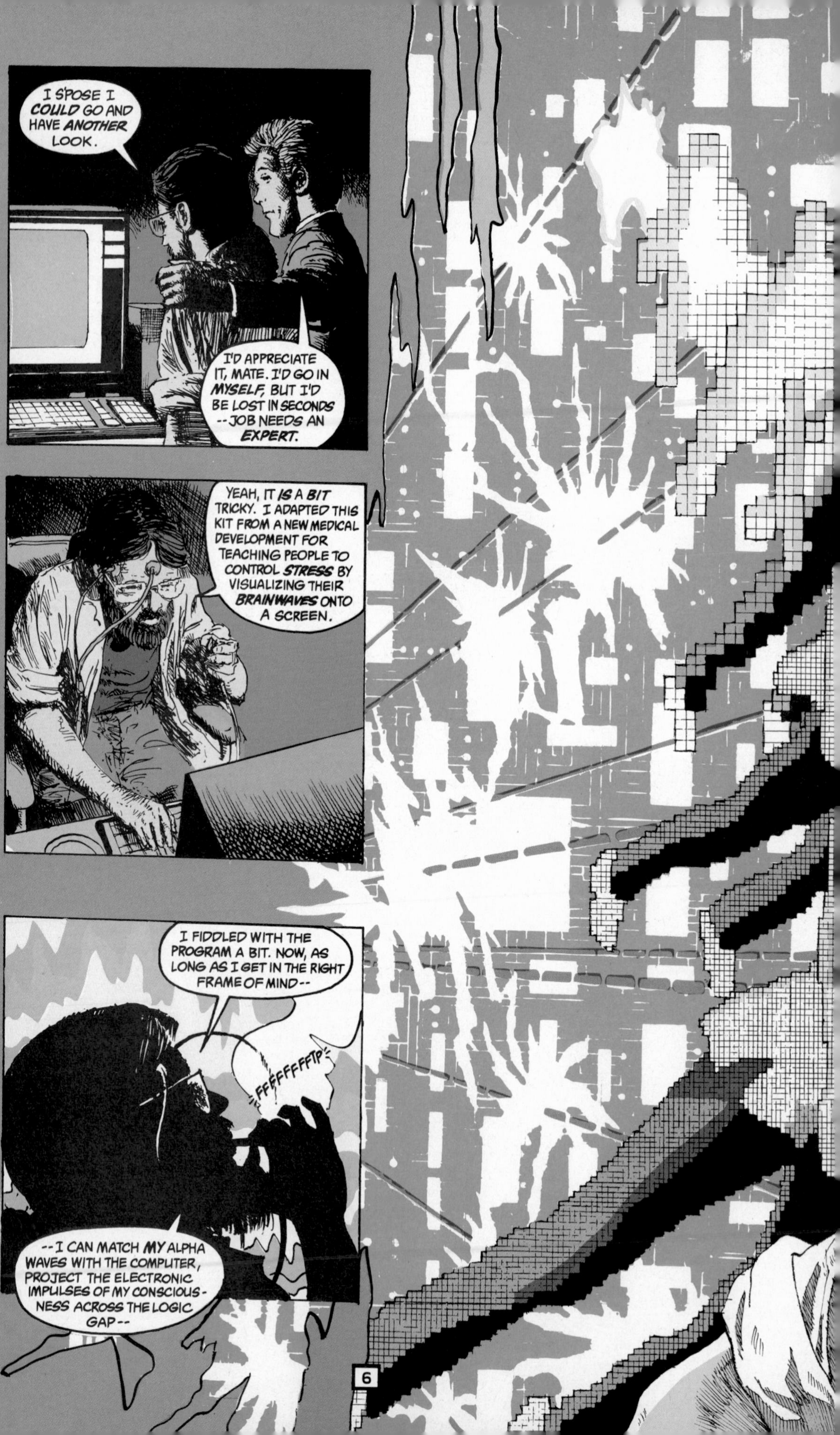
I S'POSE I COULD GO AND HAVE ANOTHER LOOK.
I'D APPRECIATE IT, MATE. I'D GO IN MYSELF, BUT I'D BE LOST IN SECONDS --JOB NEEDS AN EXPERT.
YEAH, IT IS A BIT TRICKY. I ADAPTED THIS KIT FROM A NEW MEDICAL DEVELOPMENT FOR TEACHING PEOPLE TO CONTROL STRESS BY VISUALIZING THEIR BRAINWAVES ONTO A SCREEN.
I FIDDLED WITH THE PROGRAM A BIT. NOW, AS LONG AS I GET IN THE RIGHT FRAME OF MIND--
FFFFFFFFTP
--I CAN MATCH MY ALPHA WAVES WITH THE COMPUTER, PROJECT THE ELECTRONIC IMPULSES OF MY CONSCIOUSNESS ACROSS THE LOGIC GAP--

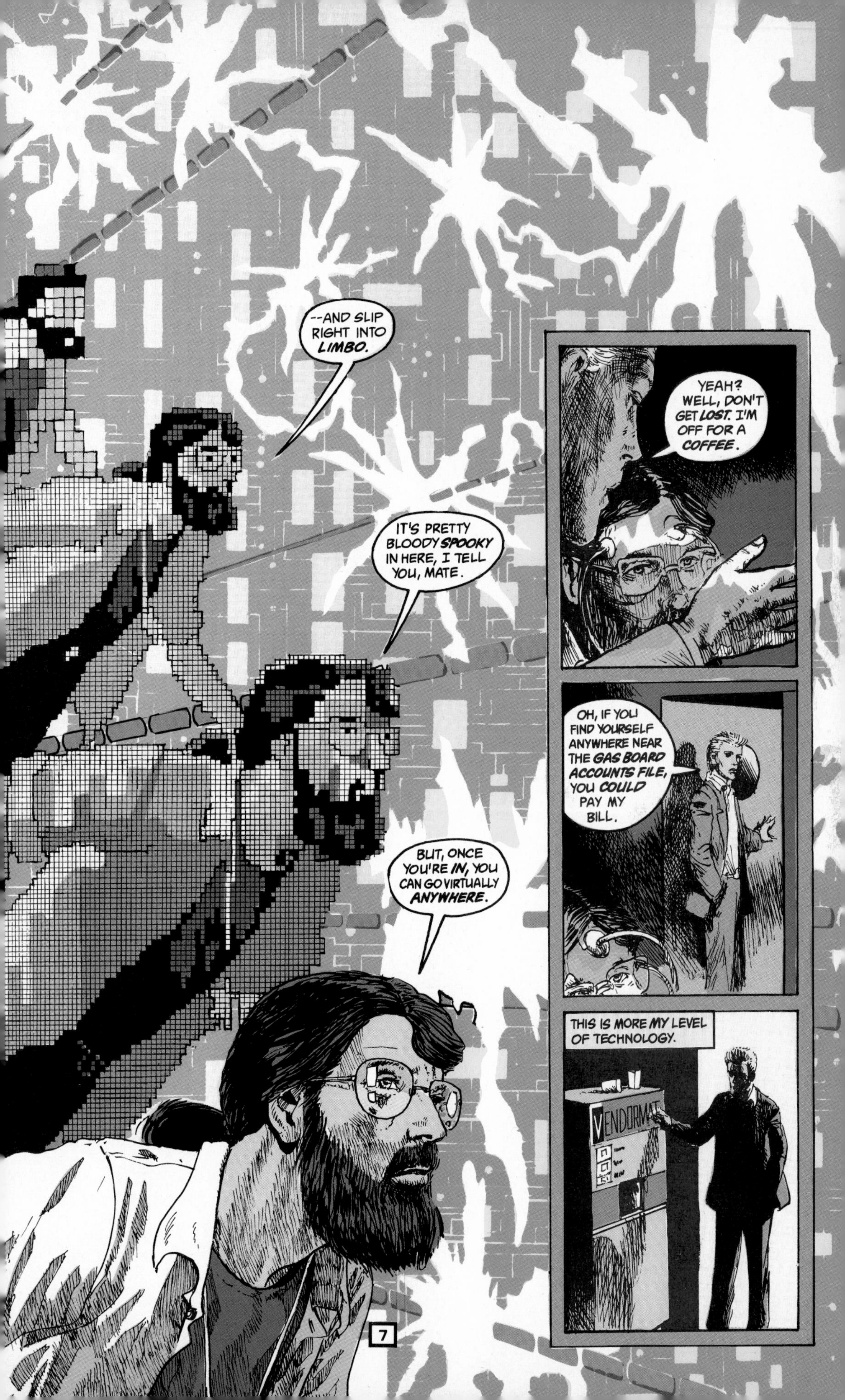
--AND SLIP RIGHT INTO LIMBO.
IT'S PRETTY BLOODY SPOOKY IN HERE, I TELL YOU, MATE.
BUT, ONCE YOU'RE IN, YOU CAN GO VIRTUALLY ANYWHERE.
YEAH? WELL, DON'T GET LOST. I'M OFF FOR A COFFEE.
OH, IF YOU FIND YOURSELF ANYWHERE NEAR THE GAS BOARD ACCOUNTS FILE, YOU COULD PAY MY BILL.
THIS IS MORE MY LEVEL OF TECHNOLOGY.
VENDORMAT

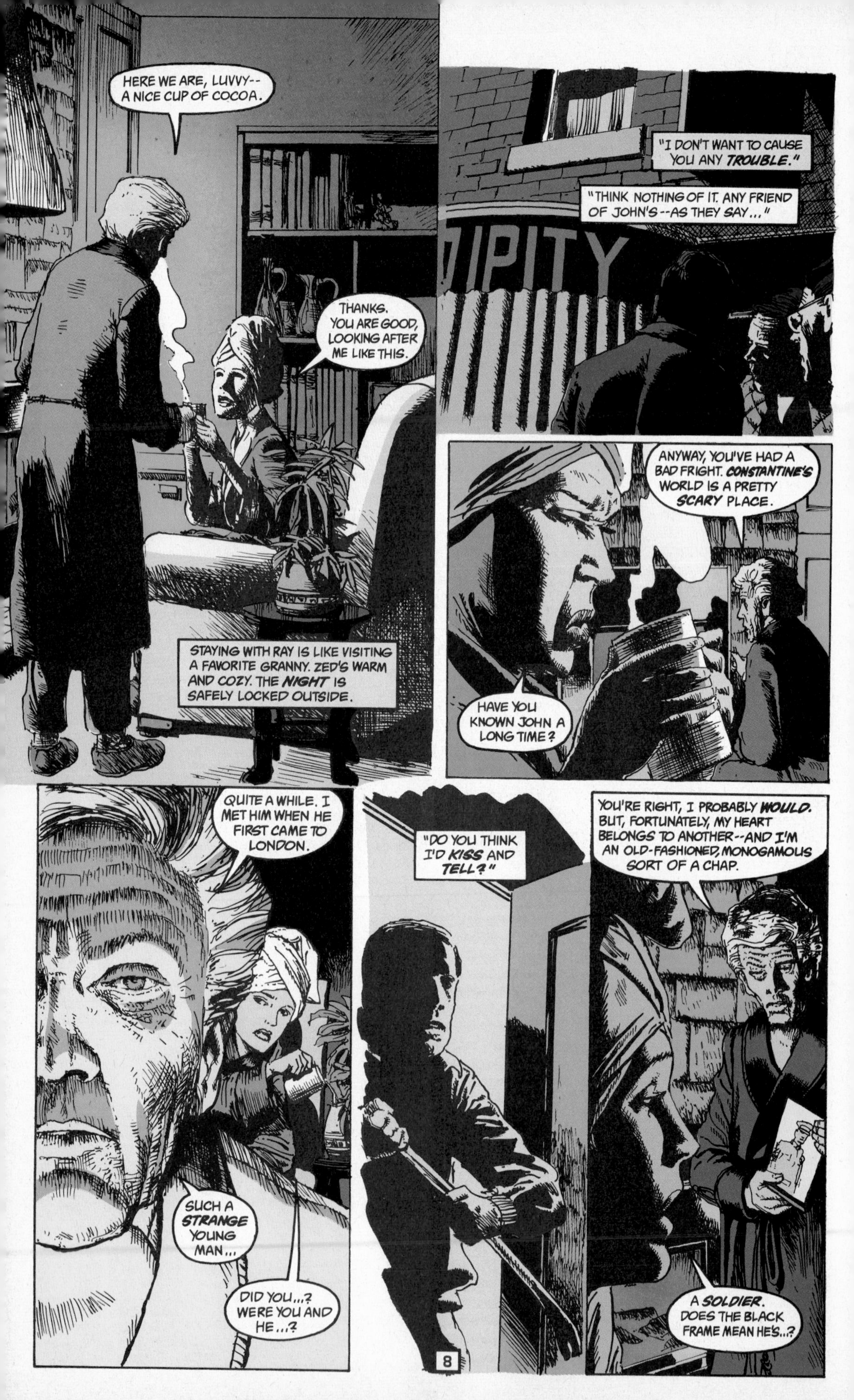
HERE WE ARE, LUVVY--
A NICE CUP OF COCOA.
THANKS. YOU ARE GOOD, LOOKING AFTER ME LIKE THIS.
STAYING WITH RAY IS LIKE VISITING A FAVORITE GRANNY. ZED'S WARM AND COZY. THE NIGHT IS SAFELY LOCKED OUTSIDE.
"I DON'T WANT TO CAUSE YOU ANY TROUBLE."
"THINK NOTHING OF IT. ANY FRIEND OF JOHN'S--AS THEY SAY..."
DIPITY
ANYWAY, YOU'VE HAD A BAD FRIGHT. CONSTANTINE'S WORLD IS A PRETTY SCARY PLACE.
HAVE YOU KNOWN JOHN A LONG TIME?
QUITE A WHILE. I MET HIM WHEN HE FIRST CAME TO LONDON.
SUCH A STRANGE YOUNG MAN...
DID YOU...? WERE YOU AND HE...?
"DO YOU THINK I'D KISS AND TELL?"
YOU'RE RIGHT, I PROBABLY WOULD. BUT, FORTUNATELY, MY HEART BELONGS TO ANOTHER--AND I'M AN OLD-FASHIONED, MONOGAMOUS SORT OF A CHAP.
A SOLDIER. DOES THE BLACK FRAME MEAN HE'S...?

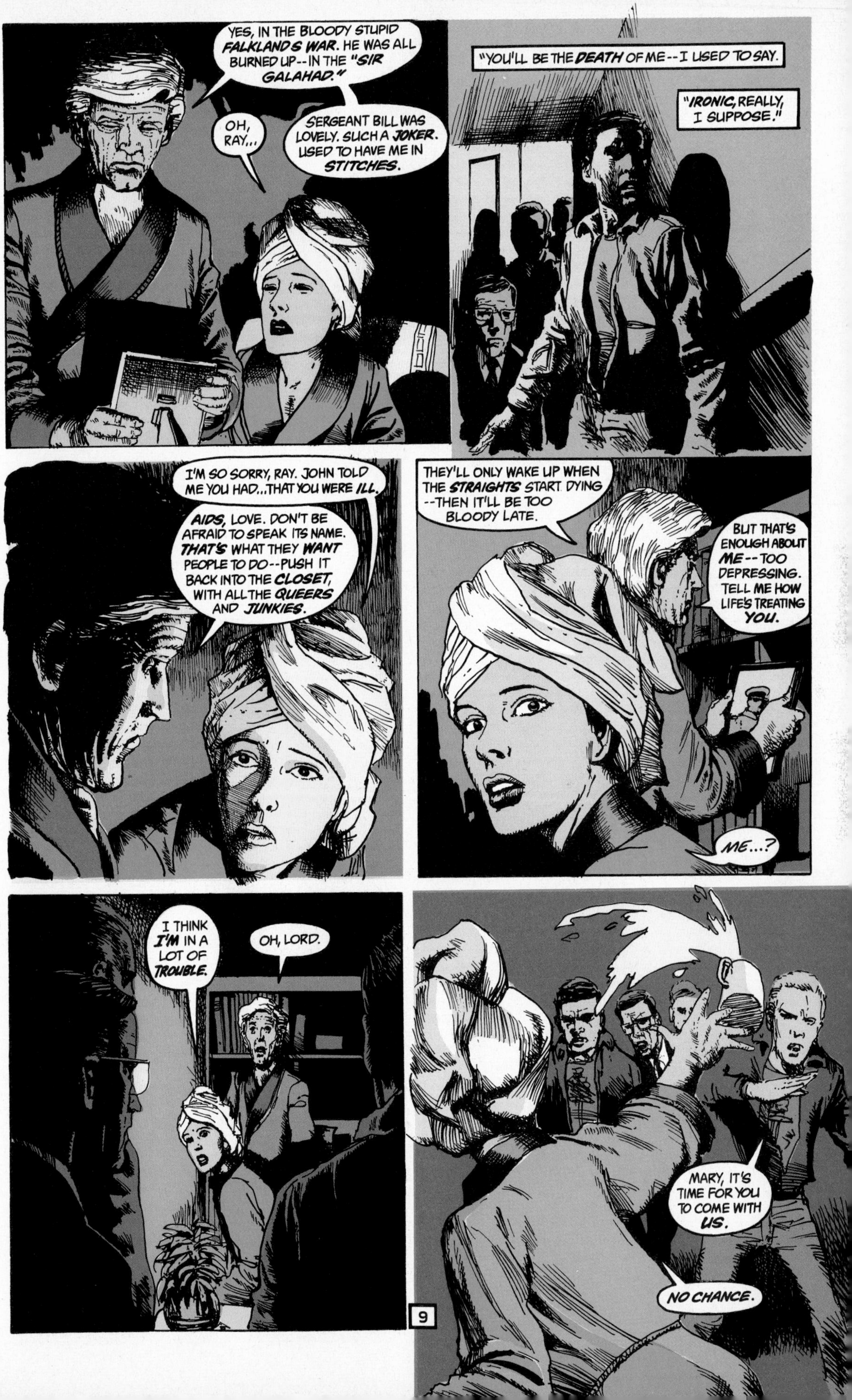
YES, IN THE BLOODY STUPID FALKLANDS WAR. HE WAS ALL BURNED UP--IN THE "SIR GALAHAD."
OH, RAY...
SERGEANT BILL WAS LOVELY. SUCH A JOKER. USED TO HAVE ME IN STITCHES.
"YOU'LL BE THE DEATH OF ME--I USED TO SAY.
"IRONIC, REALLY, I SUPPOSE."
I'M SO SORRY, RAY. JOHN TOLD ME YOU HAD...THAT YOU WERE ILL.
AIDS, LOVE. DON'T BE AFRAID TO SPEAK ITS NAME. THAT'S WHAT THEY WANT PEOPLE TO DO--PUSH IT BACK INTO THE CLOSET, WITH ALL THE QUEERS AND JUNKIES.
THEY'LL ONLY WAKE UP WHEN THE STRAIGHTS START DYING --THEN IT'LL BE TOO BLOODY LATE.
BUT THAT'S ENOUGH ABOUT ME--TOO DEPRESSING. TELL ME HOW LIFE'S TREATING YOU.
ME...?
I THINK I'M IN A LOT OF TROUBLE.
OH, LORD.
MARY, IT'S TIME FOR YOU TO COME WITH US.
NO CHANCE.

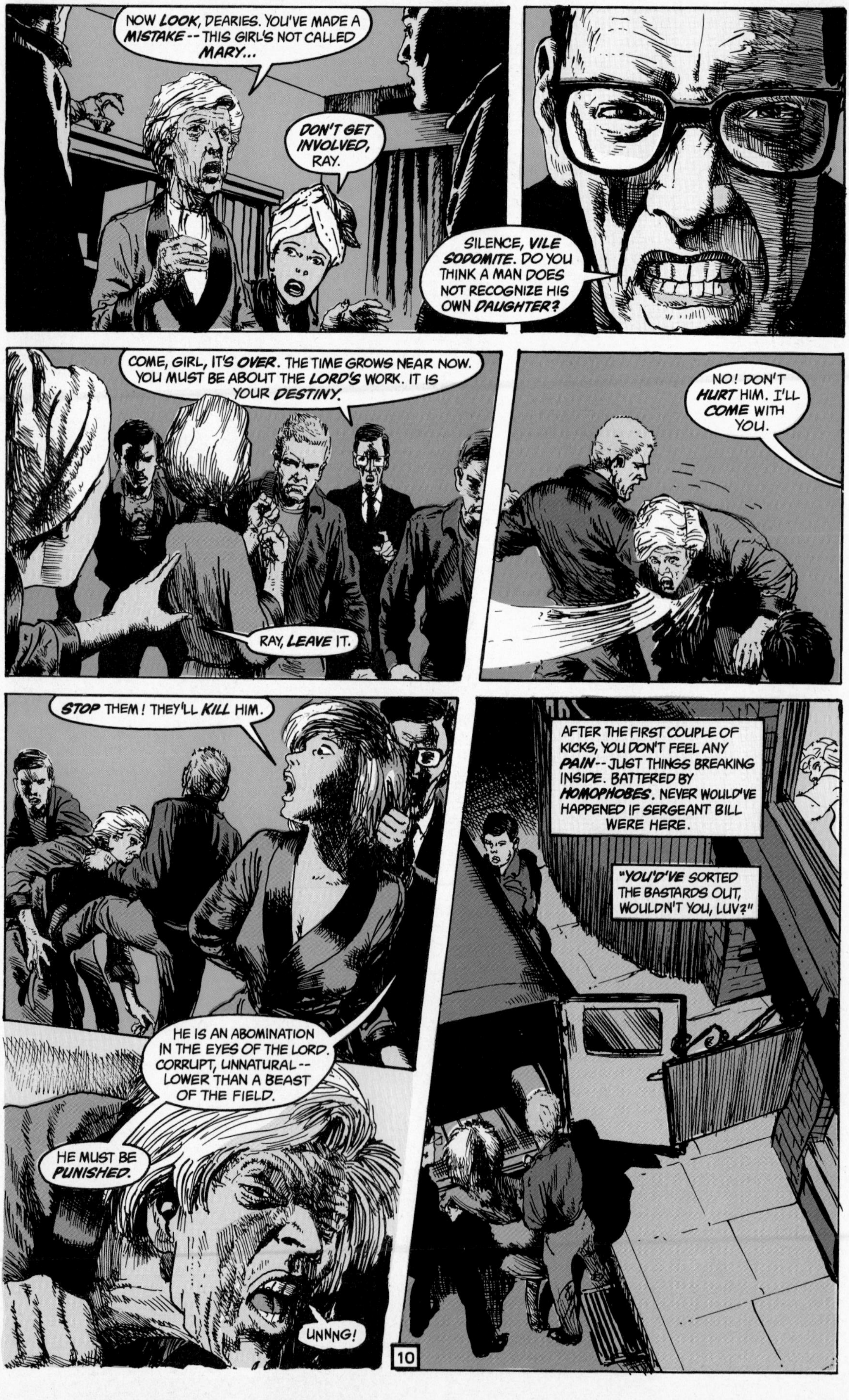
NOW LOOK, DEARIES. YOU'VE MADE A MISTAKE -- THIS GIRL'S NOT CALLED MARY...
DON'T GET INVOLVED, RAY.
SILENCE, VILE SODOMITE. DO YOU THINK A MAN DOES NOT RECOGNIZE HIS OWN DAUGHTER?
COME, GIRL, IT'S OVER. THE TIME GROWS NEAR NOW. YOU MUST BE ABOUT THE LORD'S WORK. IT IS YOUR DESTINY.
RAY, LEAVE IT.
NO! DON'T HURT HIM. I'LL COME WITH YOU.
STOP THEM! THEY'LL KILL HIM.
HE IS AN ABOMINATION IN THE EYES OF THE LORD. CORRUPT, UNNATURAL -- LOWER THAN A BEAST OF THE FIELD.
HE MUST BE PUNISHED.
UNNNG!
AFTER THE FIRST COUPLE OF KICKS, YOU DON'T FEEL ANY PAIN -- JUST THINGS BREAKING INSIDE. BATTERED BY HOMOPHOBES. NEVER WOULD'VE HAPPENED IF SERGEANT BILL WERE HERE.
"YOU'D'VE SORTED THE BASTARDS OUT, WOULDN'T YOU, LUV?"

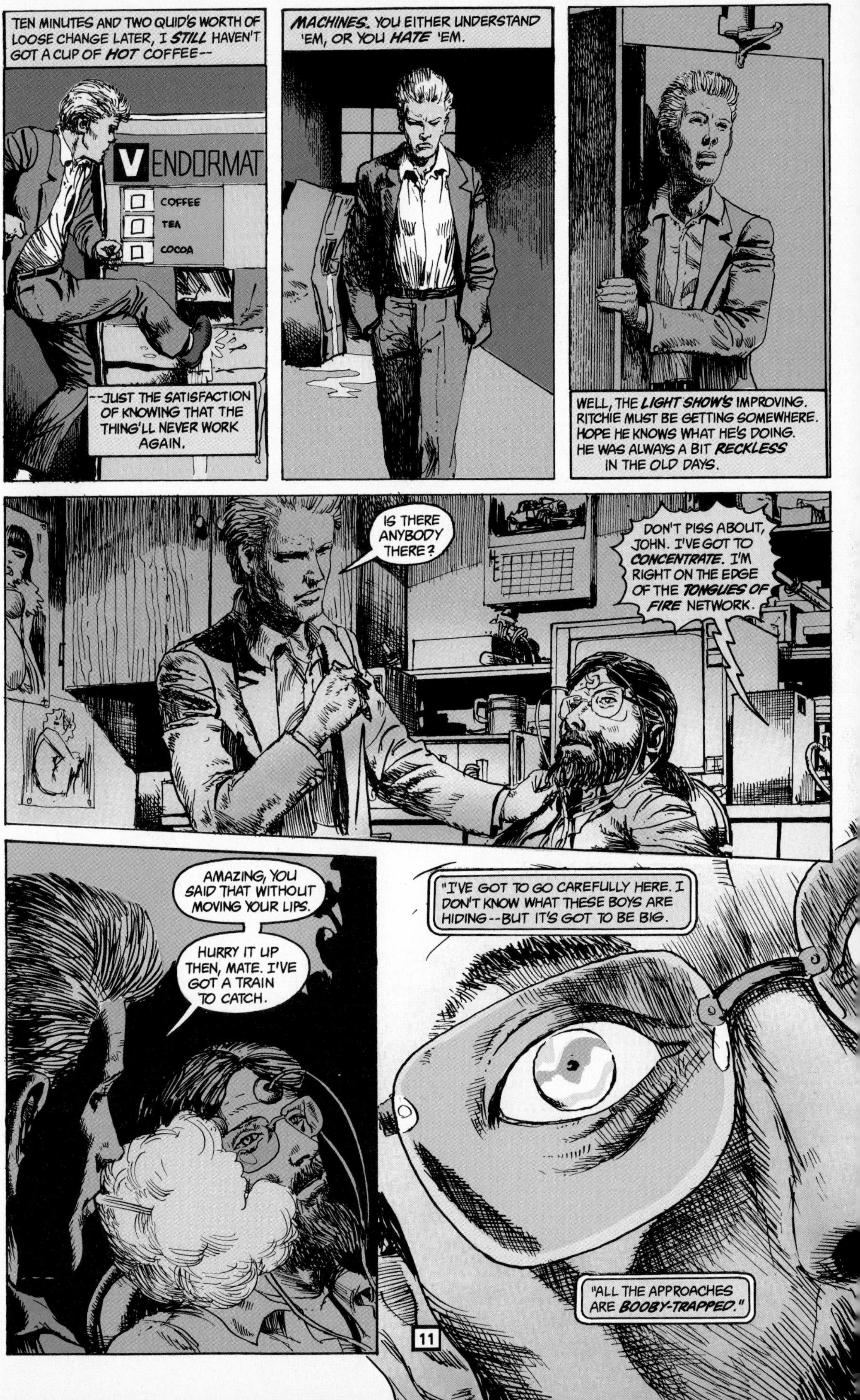

TEN MINUTES AND TWO QUID'S WORTH OF LOOSE CHANGE LATER, I STILL HAVEN'T GOT A CUP OF HOT COFFEE--
VENDORMAT
COFFEE
TEA
COCOA
--JUST THE SATISFACTION OF KNOWING THAT THE THING'LL NEVER WORK AGAIN.
MACHINES. YOU EITHER UNDERSTAND 'EM, OR YOU HATE 'EM.
WELL, THE LIGHT SHOW'S IMPROVING. RITCHIE MUST BE GETTING SOMEWHERE. HOPE HE KNOWS WHAT HE'S DOING. HE WAS ALWAYS A BIT RECKLESS IN THE OLD DAYS.
IS THERE ANYBODY THERE?
DON'T PISS ABOUT, JOHN. I'VE GOT TO CONCENTRATE. I'M RIGHT ON THE EDGE OF THE TONGUES OF FIRE NETWORK.
AMAZING, YOU SAID THAT WITHOUT MOVING YOUR LIPS.
HURRY IT UP THEN, MATE. I'VE GOT A TRAIN TO CATCH.
"I'VE GOT TO GO CAREFULLY HERE. I DON'T KNOW WHAT THESE BOYS ARE HIDING--BUT IT'S GOT TO BE BIG.
"ALL THE APPROACHES ARE BOOBY-TRAPPED."

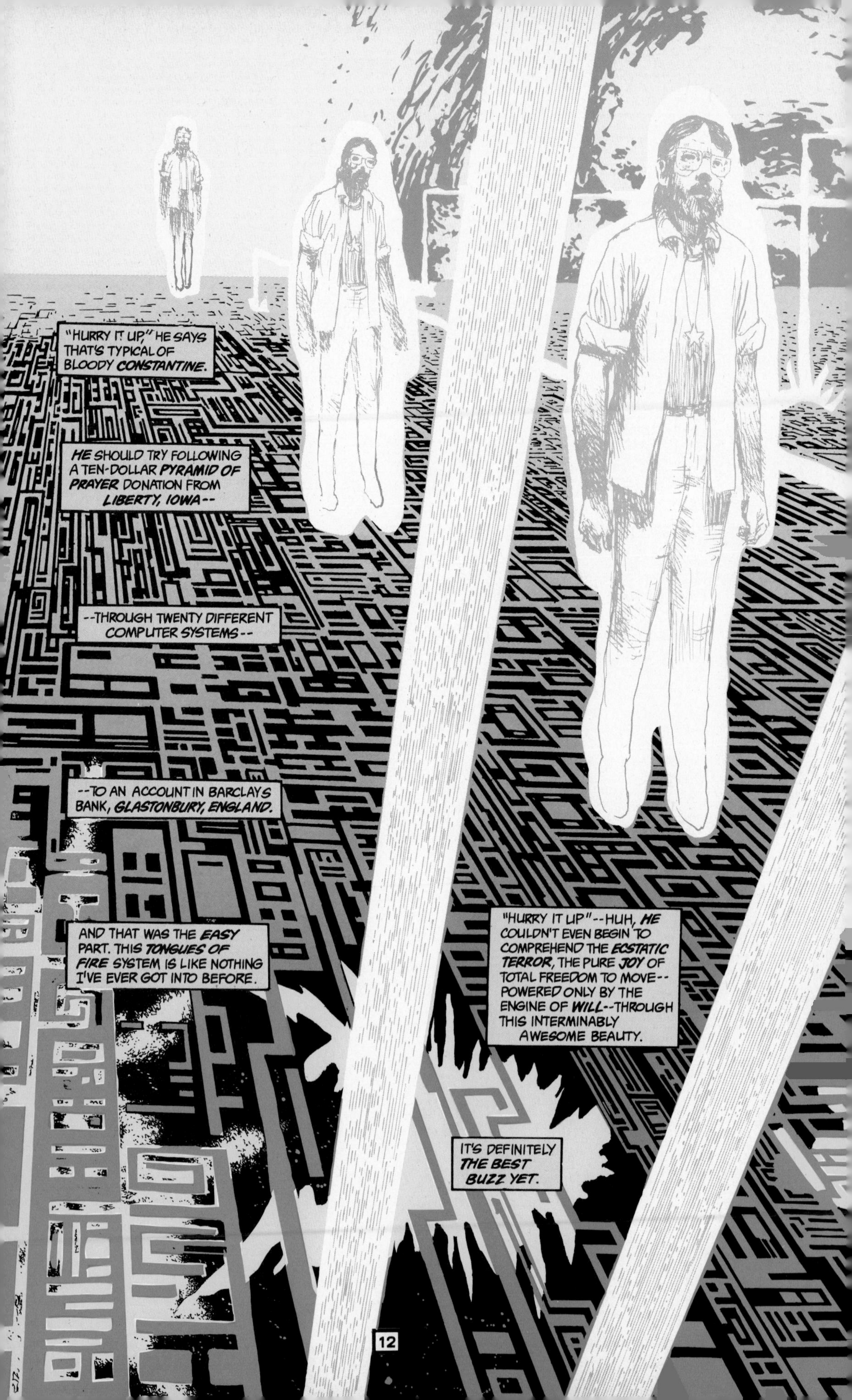
"HURRY IT UP," HE SAYS THAT'S TYPICAL OF BLOODY CONSTANTINE.
HE SHOULD TRY FOLLOWING A TEN-DOLLAR PYRAMID OF PRAYER DONATION FROM LIBERTY, IOWA--
--THROUGH TWENTY DIFFERENT COMPUTER SYSTEMS--
--TO AN ACCOUNT IN BARCLAYS BANK, GLASTONBURY, ENGLAND.
AND THAT WAS THE EASY PART. THIS TONGUES OF FIRE SYSTEM IS LIKE NOTHING I'VE EVER GOT INTO BEFORE.
"HURRY IT UP"--HUH, HE COULDN'T EVEN BEGIN TO COMPREHEND THE ECSTATIC TERROR, THE PURE JOY OF TOTAL FREEDOM TO MOVE--POWERED ONLY BY THE ENGINE OF WILL--THROUGH THIS INTERMINABLY AWESOME BEAUTY.
IT'S DEFINITELY THE BEST BUZZ YET.

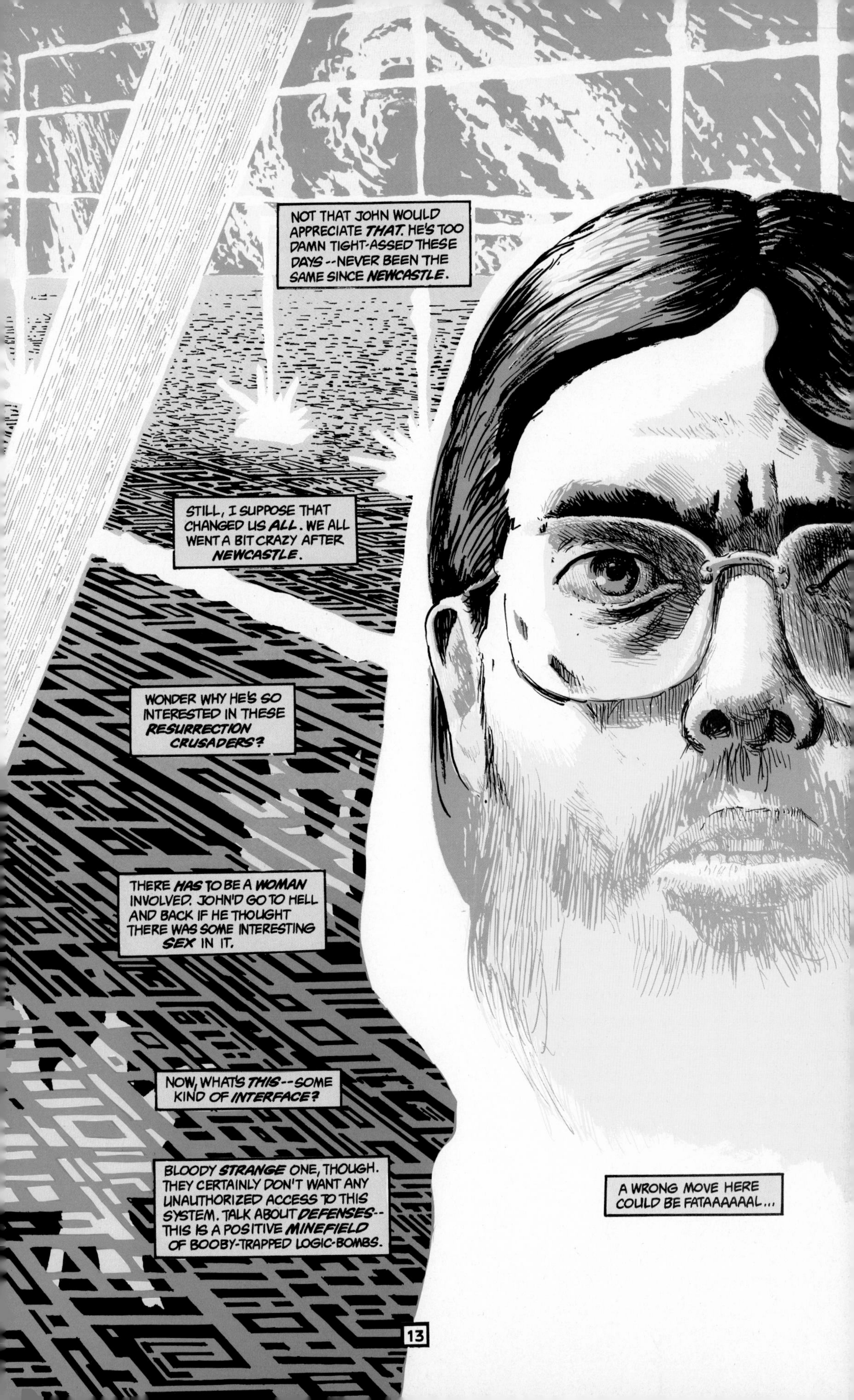
NOT THAT JOHN WOULD APPRECIATE THAT. HE'S TOO DAMN TIGHT-ASSED THESE DAYS--NEVER BEEN THE SAME SINCE NEWCASTLE.
STILL, I SUPPOSE THAT CHANGED US ALL. WE ALL WENT A BIT CRAZY AFTER NEWCASTLE.
WONDER WHY HE'S SO INTERESTED IN THESE RESURRECTION CRUSADERS?
THERE HAS TO BE A WOMAN INVOLVED. JOHN'D GO TO HELL AND BACK IF HE THOUGHT THERE WAS SOME INTERESTING SEX IN IT.
NOW, WHAT'S THIS--SOME KIND OF INTERFACE?
BLOODY STRANGE ONE, THOUGH. THEY CERTAINLY DON'T WANT ANY UNAUTHORIZED ACCESS TO THIS SYSTEM. TALK ABOUT DEFENSES--THIS IS A POSITIVE MINEFIELD OF BOOBY-TRAPPED LOGIC-BOMBS.
A WRONG MOVE HERE COULD BE FATAAAAAAL...

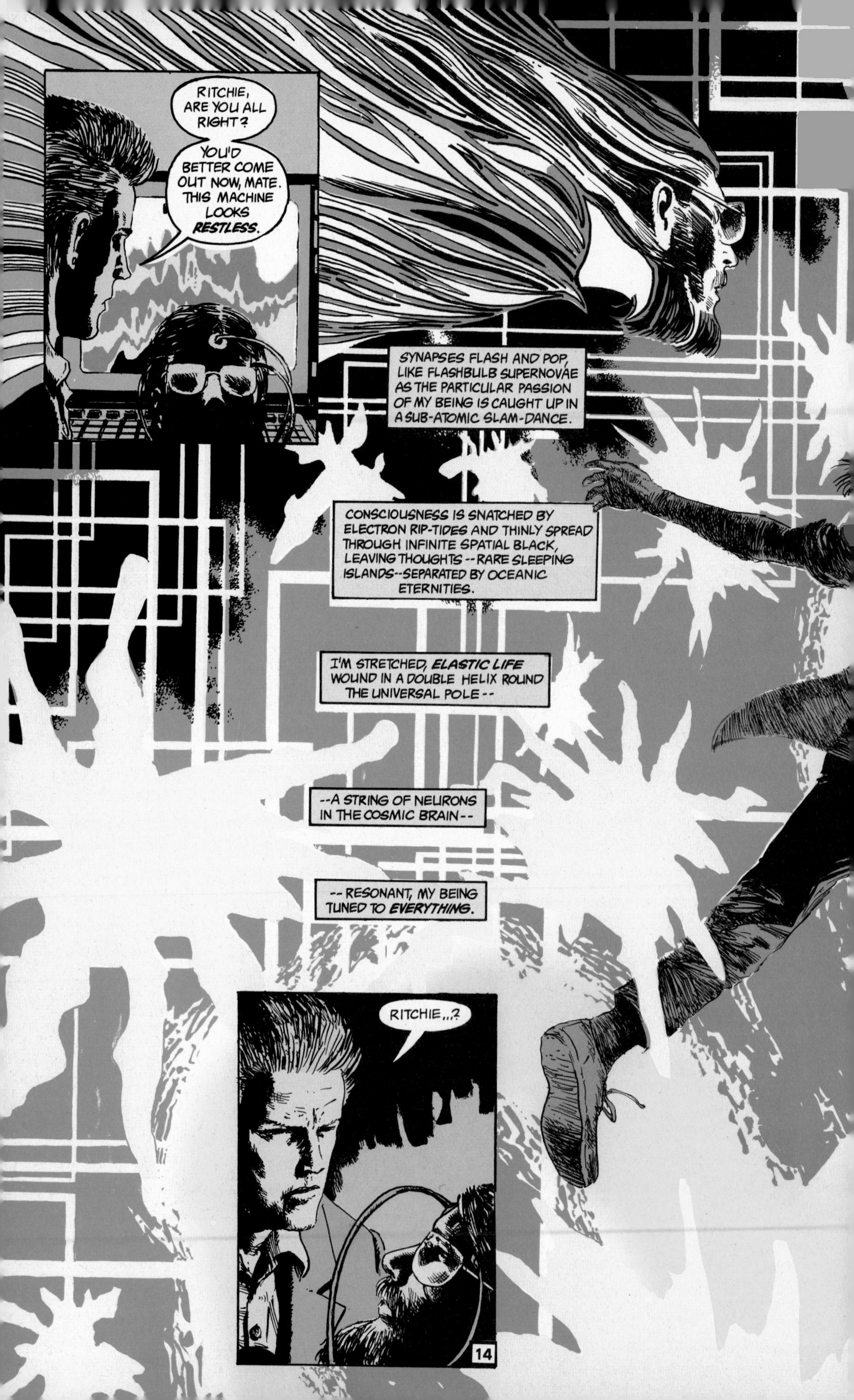

RITCHIE, ARE YOU ALL RIGHT?
YOU'D BETTER COME OUT NOW, MATE. THIS MACHINE LOOKS *RESTLESS*.
SYNAPSES FLASH AND POP, LIKE FLASHBULB SUPERNOVAE AS THE PARTICULAR PASSION OF MY BEING IS CAUGHT UP IN A SUB-ATOMIC SLAM-DANCE.
CONSCIOUSNESS IS SNATCHED BY ELECTRON RIP-TIDES AND THINLY SPREAD THROUGH INFINITE SPATIAL BLACK, LEAVING THOUGHTS -- RARE SLEEPING ISLANDS--SEPARATED BY OCEANIC ETERNITIES.
I'M STRETCHED, *ELASTIC LIFE* WOUND IN A DOUBLE HELIX ROUND THE UNIVERSAL POLE --
--A STRING OF NEURONS IN THE COSMIC BRAIN--
-- RESONANT, MY BEING TUNED TO *EVERYTHING*.
RITCHIE...?
14

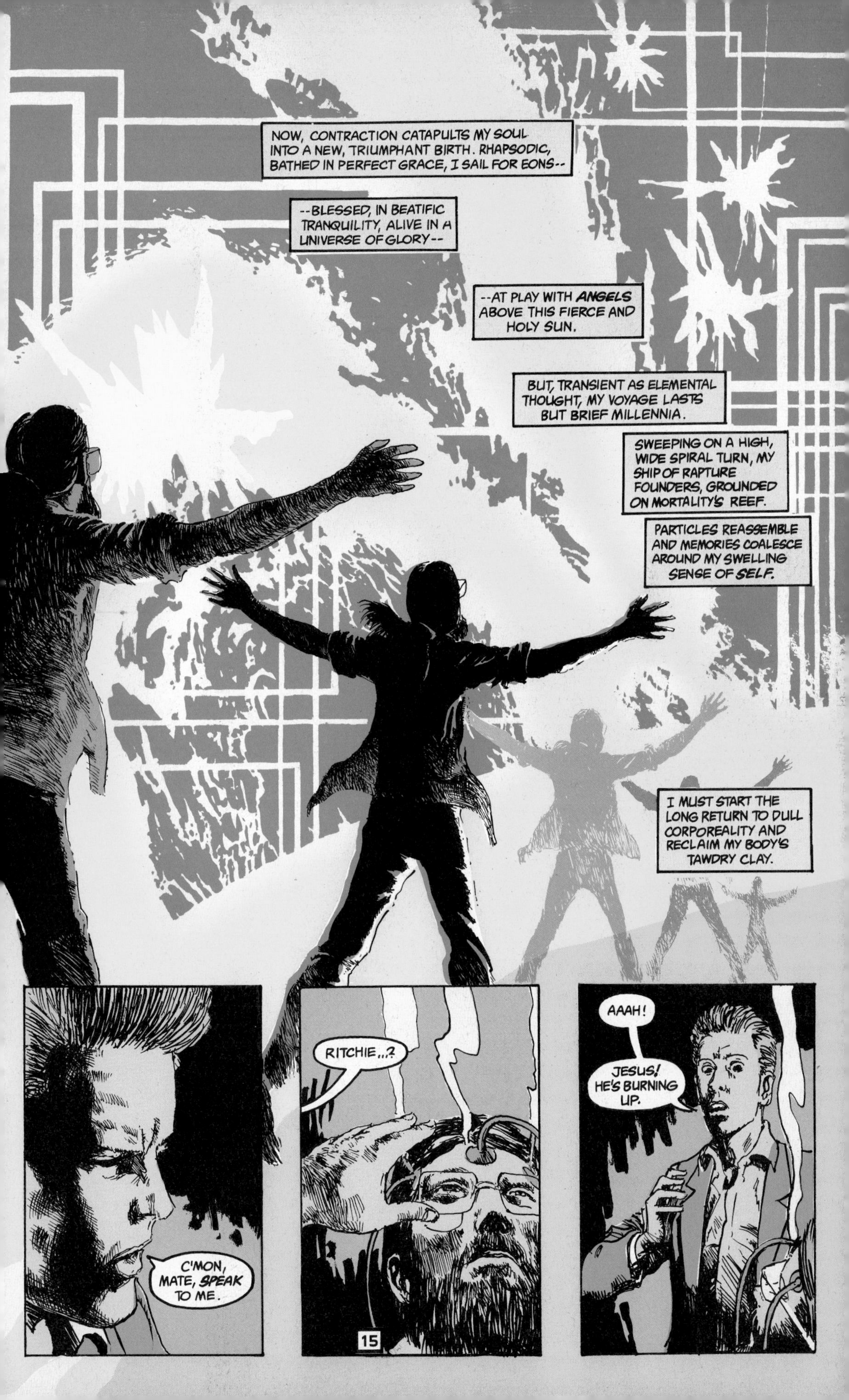
NOW, CONTRACTION CATAPULTS MY SOUL INTO A NEW, TRIUMPHANT BIRTH. RHAPSODIC, BATHED IN PERFECT GRACE, I SAIL FOR EONS--
--BLESSED, IN BEATIFIC TRANQUILITY, ALIVE IN A UNIVERSE OF GLORY--
--AT PLAY WITH *ANGELS* ABOVE THIS FIERCE AND HOLY SUN.
BUT, TRANSIENT AS ELEMENTAL THOUGHT, MY VOYAGE LASTS BUT BRIEF MILLENNIA.
SWEEPING ON A HIGH, WIDE SPIRAL TURN, MY SHIP OF RAPTURE FOUNDERS, GROUNDED ON MORTALITY'S REEF.
PARTICLES REASSEMBLE AND MEMORIES COALESCE AROUND MY SWELLING SENSE OF *SELF*.
I MUST START THE LONG RETURN TO DULL CORPOREALITY AND RECLAIM MY BODY'S TAWDRY CLAY.
C'MON, MATE, *SPEAK* TO ME.
RITCHIE...?
AAAH!
JESUS! HE'S BURNING UP.

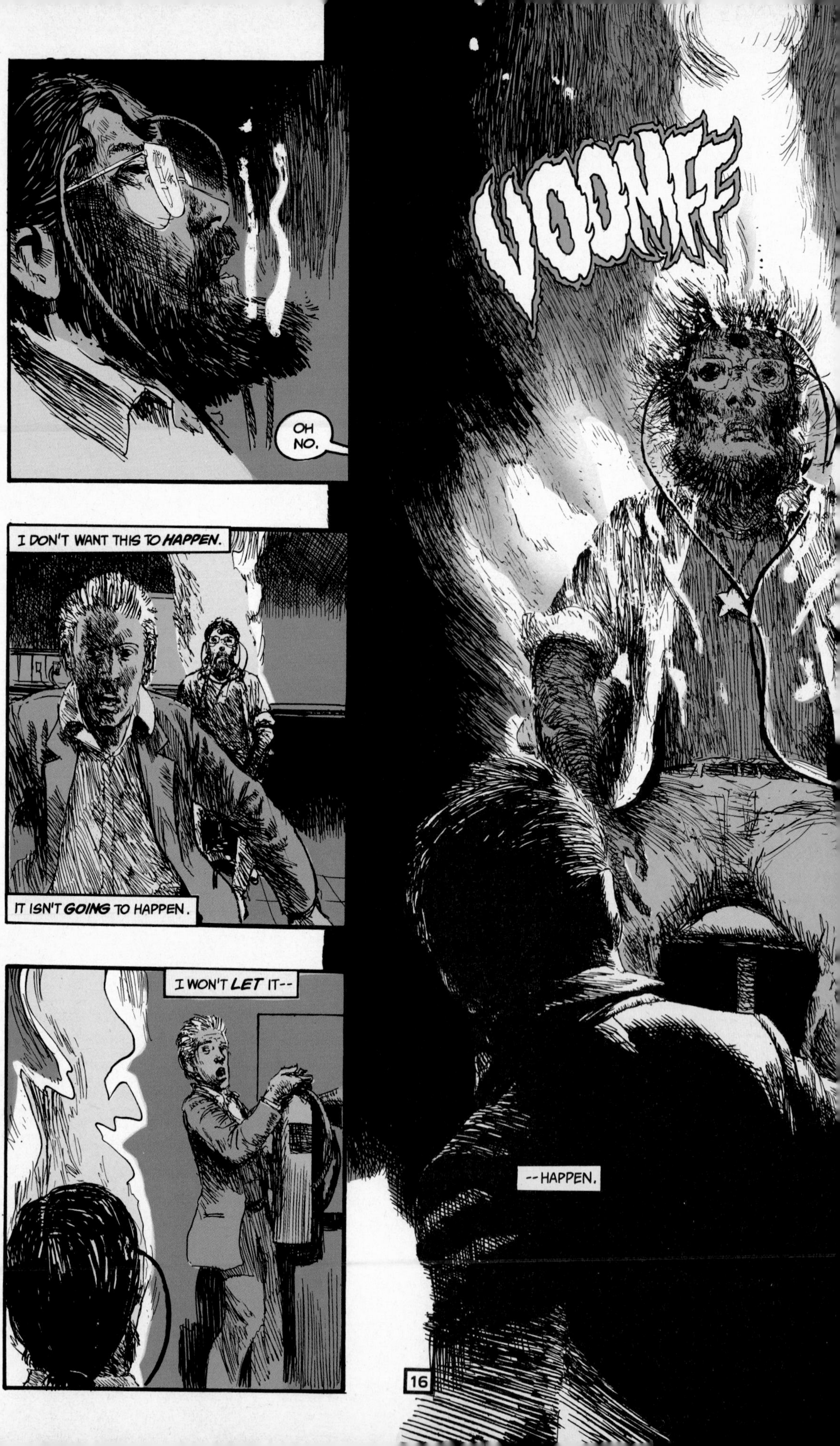
OH NO.
I DON'T WANT THIS TO HAPPEN.
IT ISN'T GOING TO HAPPEN.
I WON'T LET IT--
VOOMFF
--HAPPEN.

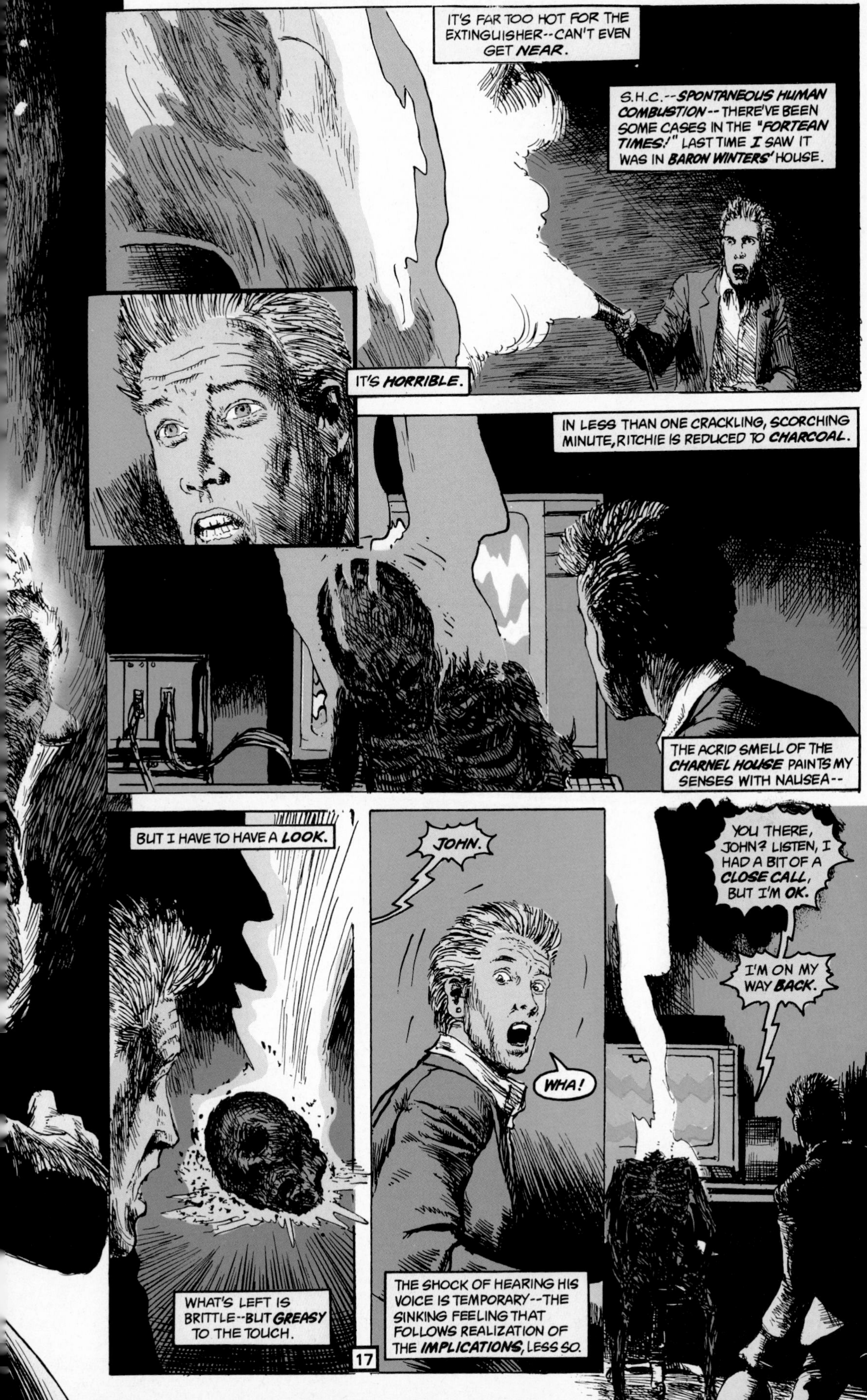

IT'S FAR TOO HOT FOR THE EXTINGUISHER--CAN'T EVEN GET NEAR.
S.H.C.--SPONTANEOUS HUMAN COMBUSTION--THERE'VE BEEN SOME CASES IN THE "FORTEAN TIMES!" LAST TIME I SAW IT WAS IN BARON WINTERS' HOUSE.
IT'S HORRIBLE.
IN LESS THAN ONE CRACKLING, SCORCHING MINUTE, RITCHIE IS REDUCED TO CHARCOAL.
THE ACRID SMELL OF THE CHARNEL HOUSE PAINTS MY SENSES WITH NAUSEA--
BUT I HAVE TO HAVE A LOOK.
WHAT'S LEFT IS BRITTLE--BUT GREASY TO THE TOUCH.
JOHN.
WHA!
THE SHOCK OF HEARING HIS VOICE IS TEMPORARY--THE SINKING FEELING THAT FOLLOWS REALIZATION OF THE IMPLICATIONS, LESS SO.
YOU THERE, JOHN? LISTEN, I HAD A BIT OF A CLOSE CALL, BUT I'M OK.
I'M ON MY WAY BACK.

LOOK, MATE, I DON'T KNOW HOW TO TELL YOU THIS...

YOU WON'T *BELIEVE* WHERE I'VE BEEN...

RITCHIE, I...

COLUMBUS ONLY DISCOVERED A *NEW WORLD*. RITCHIE SIMPSON FOUND A WHOLE NEW *UNIVERSE*.

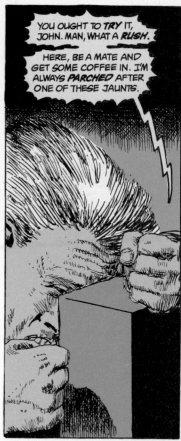

YOU OUGHT TO *TRY* IT, JOHN. MAN, WHAT A *RUSH*.

HERE, BE A MATE AND GET *SOME* COFFEE IN. I'M ALWAYS *PARCHED* AFTER ONE OF THESE JAUNTS.

GODDAMN IT ALL TO HELL. WHY...?

WHY IS IT THAT, LATELY, EVERYTHING I TOUCH--

--TURNS TO *SHIT* IN MY HANDS.

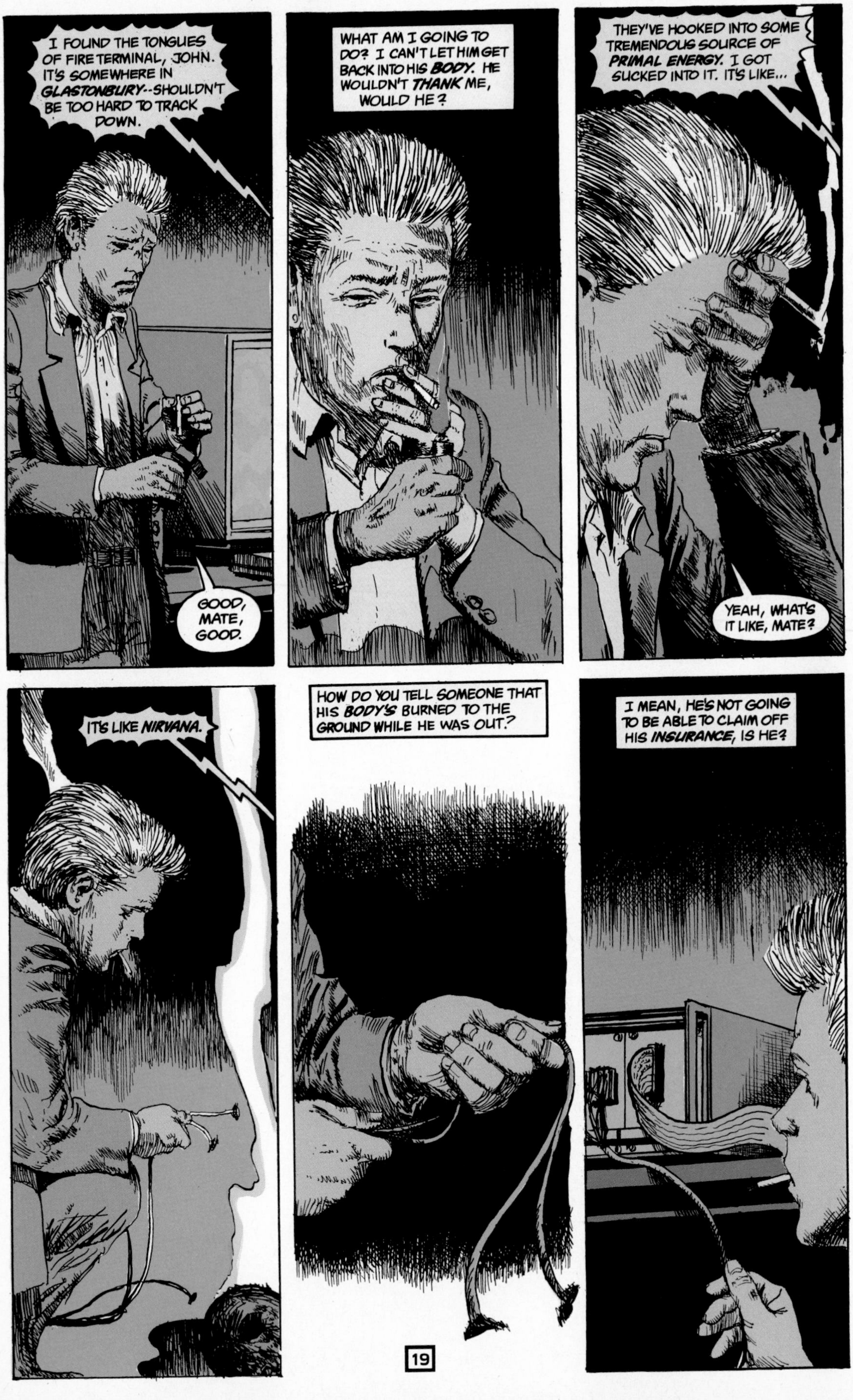
I FOUND THE TONGUES OF FIRE TERMINAL, JOHN. IT'S SOMEWHERE IN GLASTONBURY--SHOULDN'T BE TOO HARD TO TRACK DOWN.
GOOD, MATE, GOOD.
WHAT AM I GOING TO DO? I CAN'T LET HIM GET BACK INTO HIS BODY. HE WOULDN'T THANK ME, WOULD HE?
THEY'VE HOOKED INTO SOME TREMENDOUS SOURCE OF PRIMAL ENERGY. I GOT SUCKED INTO IT. IT'S LIKE...
YEAH, WHAT'S IT LIKE, MATE?
IT'S LIKE NIRVANA.
HOW DO YOU TELL SOMEONE THAT HIS BODY'S BURNED TO THE GROUND WHILE HE WAS OUT?
I MEAN, HE'S NOT GOING TO BE ABLE TO CLAIM OFF HIS INSURANCE, IS HE?

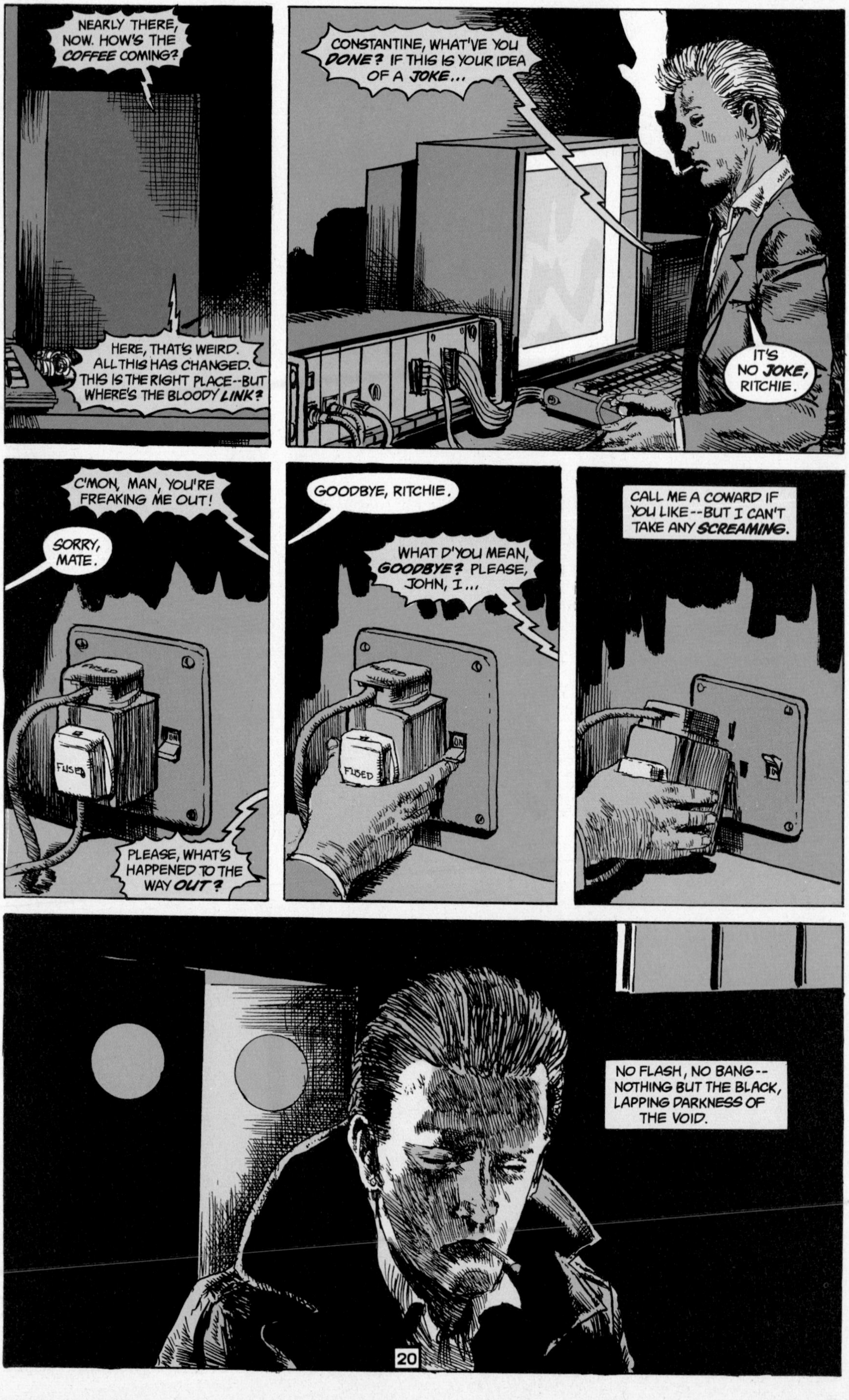
NEARLY THERE, NOW. HOW'S THE COFFEE COMING?
HERE, THAT'S WEIRD. ALL THIS HAS CHANGED. THIS IS THE RIGHT PLACE--BUT WHERE'S THE BLOODY LINK?
CONSTANTINE, WHAT'VE YOU DONE? IF THIS IS YOUR IDEA OF A JOKE...
IT'S NO JOKE, RITCHIE.
C'MON, MAN, YOU'RE FREAKING ME OUT!
SORRY, MATE.
PLEASE, WHAT'S HAPPENED TO THE WAY OUT?
GOODBYE, RITCHIE.
WHAT D'YOU MEAN, GOODBYE? PLEASE, JOHN, I...
CALL ME A COWARD IF YOU LIKE--BUT I CAN'T TAKE ANY SCREAMING.
NO FLASH, NO BANG--NOTHING BUT THE BLACK, LAPPING DARKNESS OF THE VOID.

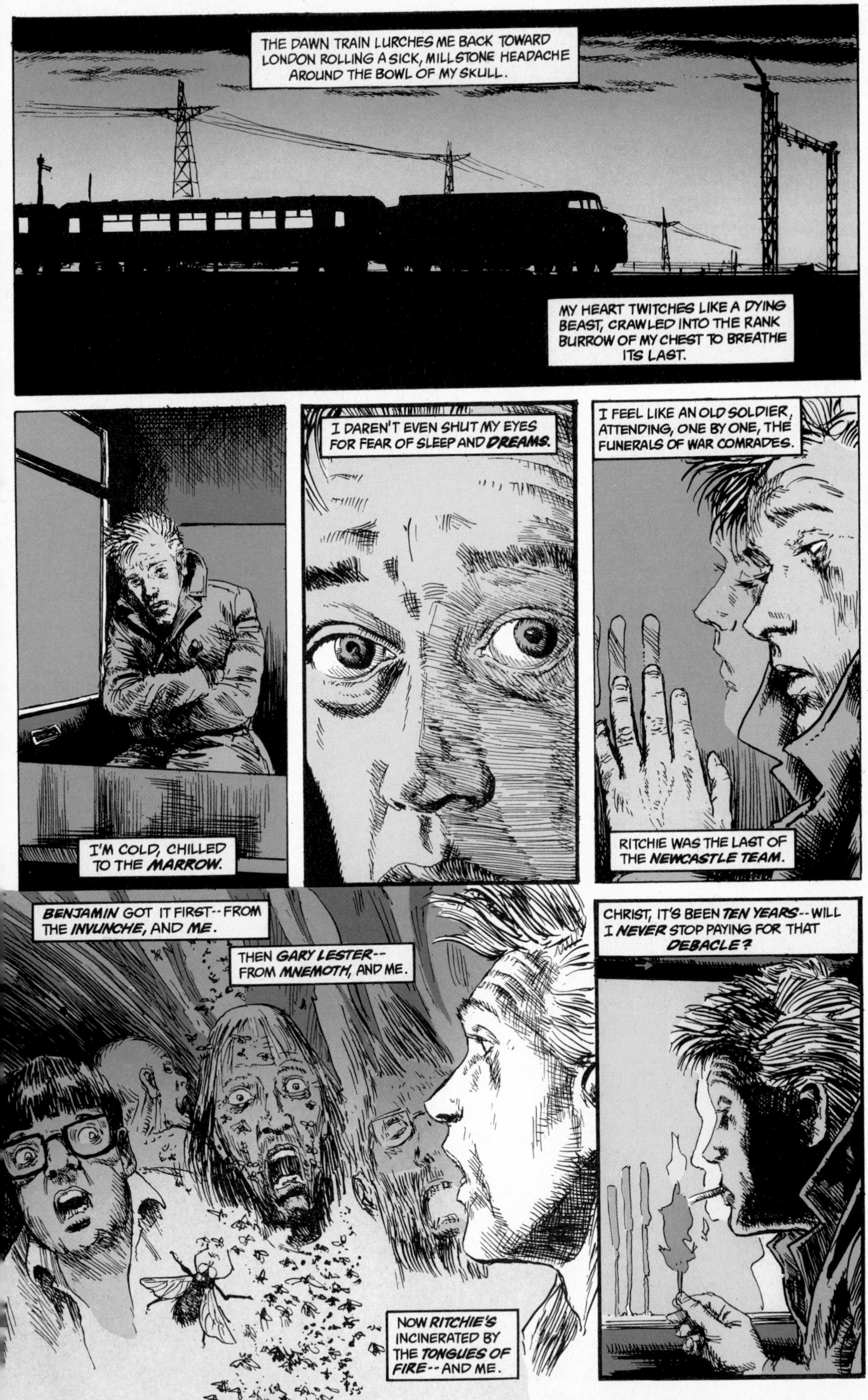

THE DAWN TRAIN LURCHES ME BACK TOWARD LONDON ROLLING A SICK, MILLSTONE HEADACHE AROUND THE BOWL OF MY SKULL.
MY HEART TWITCHES LIKE A DYING BEAST, CRAWLED INTO THE RANK BURROW OF MY CHEST TO BREATHE ITS LAST.
I'M COLD, CHILLED TO THE MARROW.
I DAREN'T EVEN SHUT MY EYES FOR FEAR OF SLEEP AND DREAMS.
I FEEL LIKE AN OLD SOLDIER, ATTENDING, ONE BY ONE, THE FUNERALS OF WAR COMRADES.
RITCHIE WAS THE LAST OF THE NEWCASTLE TEAM.
BENJAMIN GOT IT FIRST--FROM THE INVUNCHE, AND ME.
THEN GARY LESTER--FROM MNEMOTH, AND ME.
NOW RITCHIE'S INCINERATED BY THE TONGUES OF FIRE--AND ME.
CHRIST, IT'S BEEN TEN YEARS--WILL I NEVER STOP PAYING FOR THAT DEBACLE?

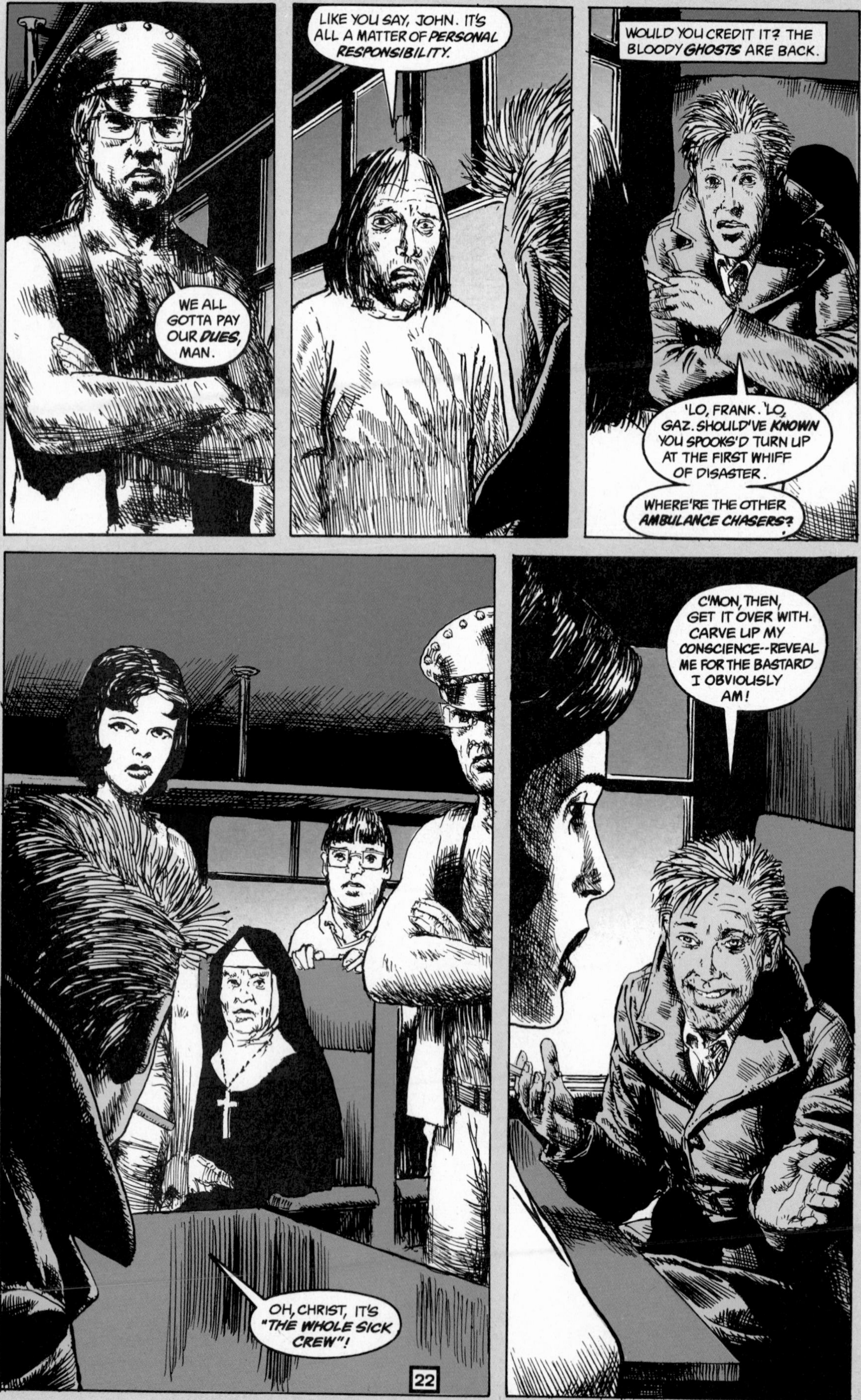
WE ALL GOTTA PAY OUR DUES, MAN.
LIKE YOU SAY, JOHN. IT'S ALL A MATTER OF PERSONAL RESPONSIBILITY.
WOULD YOU CREDIT IT? THE BLOODY GHOSTS ARE BACK.
'LO, FRANK. 'LO, GAZ. SHOULD'VE KNOWN YOU SPOOKS'D TURN UP AT THE FIRST WHIFF OF DISASTER.
WHERE'RE THE OTHER AMBULANCE CHASERS?
OH, CHRIST, IT'S "THE WHOLE SICK CREW"!
C'MON, THEN, GET IT OVER WITH. CARVE UP MY CONSCIENCE--REVEAL ME FOR THE BASTARD I OBVIOUSLY AM!

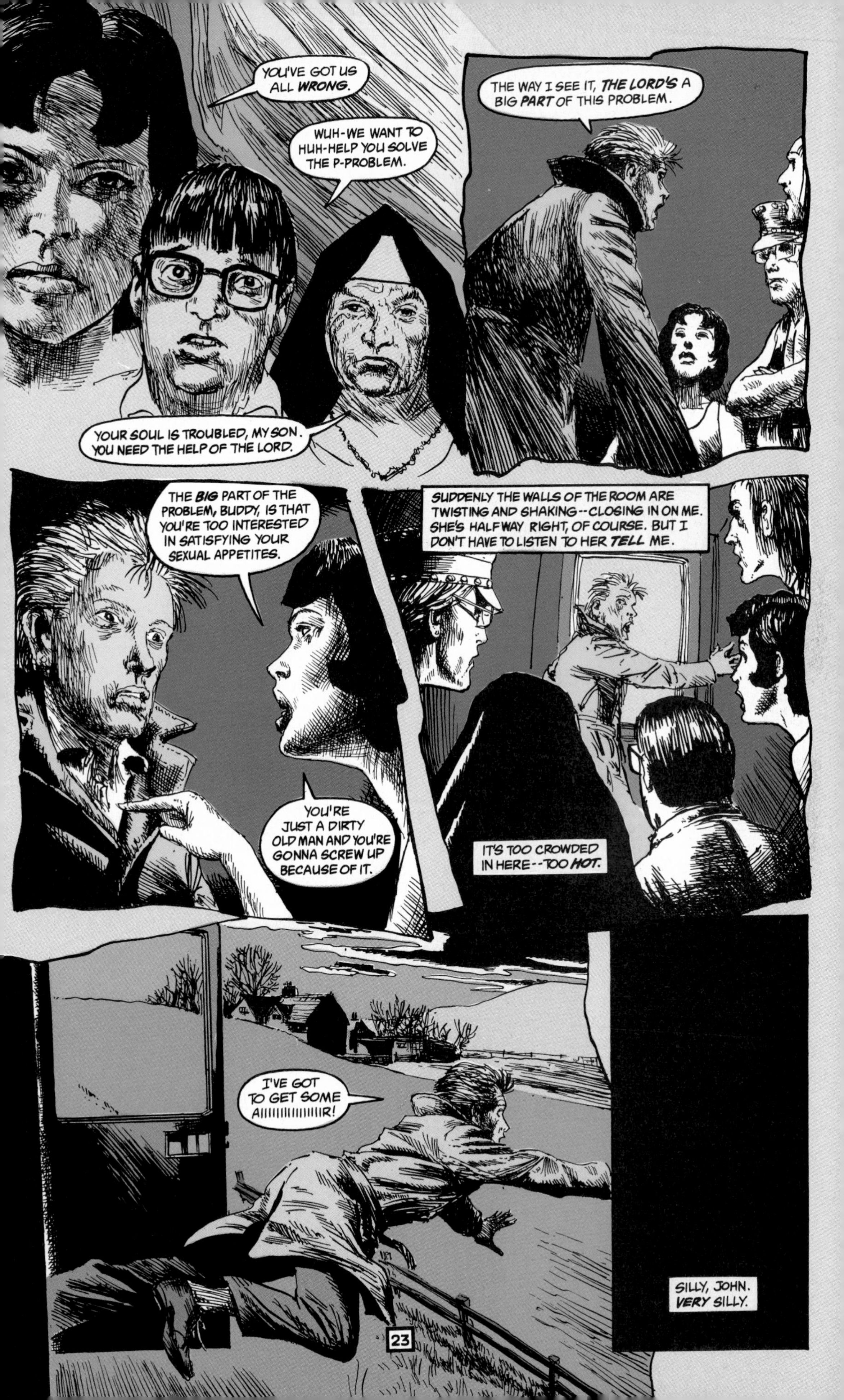
YOU'VE GOT US ALL WRONG.
WUH-WE WANT TO HUH-HELP YOU SOLVE THE P-PROBLEM.
YOUR SOUL IS TROUBLED, MY SON. YOU NEED THE HELP OF THE LORD.
THE WAY I SEE IT, THE LORD'S A BIG PART OF THIS PROBLEM.
THE BIG PART OF THE PROBLEM, BUDDY, IS THAT YOU'RE TOO INTERESTED IN SATISFYING YOUR SEXUAL APPETITES.
YOU'RE JUST A DIRTY OLD MAN AND YOU'RE GONNA SCREW UP BECAUSE OF IT.
SUDDENLY THE WALLS OF THE ROOM ARE TWISTING AND SHAKING--CLOSING IN ON ME. SHE'S HALFWAY RIGHT, OF COURSE. BUT I DON'T HAVE TO LISTEN TO HER TELL ME.
IT'S TOO CROWDED IN HERE--TOO HOT.
I'VE GOT TO GET SOME AIIIIIIIIIIIIIR!
SILLY, JOHN. VERY SILLY.

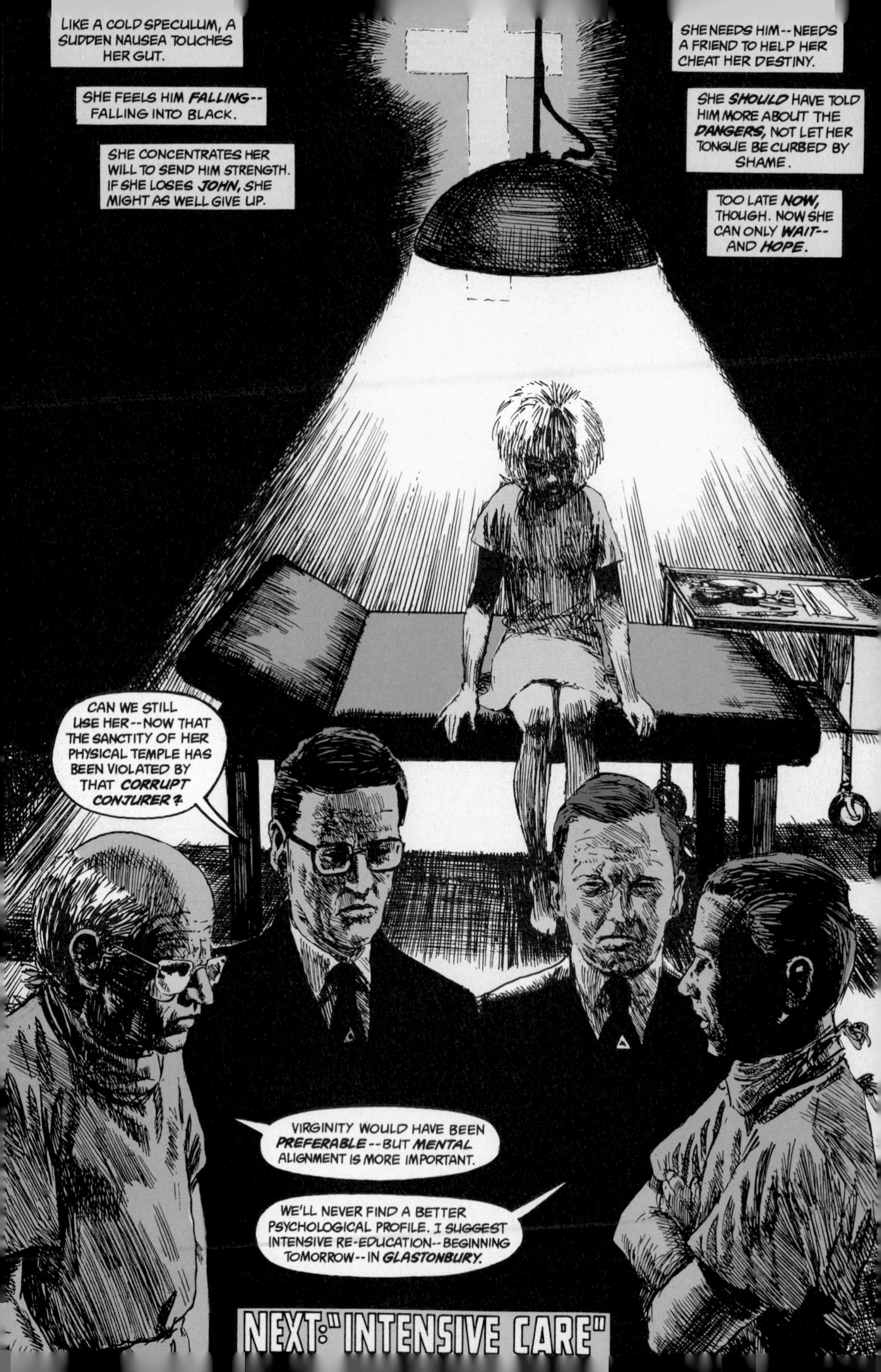

LIKE A COLD SPECULUM, A SUDDEN NAUSEA TOUCHES HER GUT.
SHE FEELS HIM FALLING-- FALLING INTO BLACK.
SHE CONCENTRATES HER WILL TO SEND HIM STRENGTH. IF SHE LOSES JOHN, SHE MIGHT AS WELL GIVE UP.
SHE NEEDS HIM--NEEDS A FRIEND TO HELP HER CHEAT HER DESTINY.
SHE SHOULD HAVE TOLD HIM MORE ABOUT THE DANGERS, NOT LET HER TONGUE BE CURBED BY SHAME.
TOO LATE NOW, THOUGH. NOW SHE CAN ONLY WAIT-- AND HOPE.
CAN WE STILL USE HER--NOW THAT THE SANCTITY OF HER PHYSICAL TEMPLE HAS BEEN VIOLATED BY THAT CORRUPT CONJURER?
VIRGINITY WOULD HAVE BEEN PREFERABLE--BUT MENTAL ALIGNMENT IS MORE IMPORTANT.
WE'LL NEVER FIND A BETTER PSYCHOLOGICAL PROFILE. I SUGGEST INTENSIVE RE-EDUCATION--BEGINNING TOMORROW--IN GLASTONBURY.
NEXT: "INTENSIVE CARE"

Extract C

Another *childhood* dream--about my sister, Cheryl.

It's a chilly early winter evening--must be a Saturday, the sports results are on the telly--be *DR WHO* soon. I'm in the yard, perched on the coalshed roof outside my sister's bedroom window. She can't see me--she's got the light on.

She's undressing--taking off the cheap, thin clothes she wears for her Saturday job at Woolworth's--pausing, breathtakingly naked, to kiss the pin-up picture of Paul McCartney thumb-tacked to her wall as she passes on the way to the wardrobe to fetch her makeup and 'going-out' clothes.

I've watched this many times before. I know them off by heart. The black stockings--the mini-skirt and sweater--the patent leather belt.

I'm fascinated by the way she dons her clothes, the faces she pulls in the mirror as she applies false eyelashes, like giant spiders and paints her face for the sexual tourney of the all-night disco in Leeds.

I watch her, breathing soothing coal-smoke, which wafts from geometric rows of red chimney pots, lost in the claustrophobic nostalgia of an urban, English evening.

I like to watch.

[Hmm, another one to keep away from the shrinks, else they'll be adding voyeurism and incest to my list of sins.

Cheryl, eh? 'Thought *she'd* have been to see me.

Still, poor kid's probably got her hands full. Last I heard she was pregnant and was going to marry that useless wanker Tony Masters--she'd be better off on her own.]

THE ABOVE REPRESENT RECONSTRUCTIONS MADE FROM CHARRED REMAINS OF LARGELY DESTROYED NOTEBOOK.

All evidence available attributes them to the above named patient.

RAVENSCAR SECURE HOSPITAL confidential file

PATIENT:--CONSTANTINE, John
D.H.S.S. No.:--YX 53 72 58 D
N.H.S. No.:--MPLQ 614
SUPERVISING DOCTOR:--Dr. Roger HUNTOON

ITEM:--Transcripts of hand-written notes found in the wastepaper bin of patients ward. File for ASSESSMENT/INFO

In my opinion, patient is currently on down-turn side of trauma cycle. Possibly DANGEROUS. Keep under CLOSE OBSERVATION and maintain STRICT REGIME.
This patient is possessed of a high IQ and an amoral intelligence!
DO NOT UNDERESTIMATE!
R.H.

Extract A

The bloody medication stops you DREAMING. I was so glad to be rid of the NIGHTMARES, it's taken me 'til now to realise. Christ, whacked into limbo by the *chemical cosh*, eh? So that's their game.

Well, sod 'em, from now on the pills go straight down the bloody toilet--ha, see them swirling in the vortex, rattling off around the bend and down the tubes--gurgling off to waste.

Wish I could follow them--pipe-dreams eh? Nah, *I'd* rather face the terrors on my own territory--with my own *magic*. I know a few tricks for fighting DEMONS--some of them even *work*.

Let the bastard nightmares come, bringing their threshing jaws to chew the quiet, peaceful night into bloody tatters--I'm a gambler, I'll take my chances on the Catherine Wheel of Fortune . . . . . *****

Extract B

Dreams last night, for the first time in what seems like months--probably is--time is condensed in this crazy bloody place.

I am in a waiting-room--a doctor's or dentist's--cold-leather, horsehair furniture--framed diploma on the wall--copies of *NATIONAL GEOGRAPHIC* and *COUNTRY LIFE* magazines on a glass table.

I'm waiting. I seem to have been waiting a very long time--but for what? I'm nervous and excited--there are faint, mysterious sounds in the distance--voices, machinery. Something important is happening--a secret ritual is taking place in the *SURGERY*. Soon it will by *my* turn.

I look at the cover of a *NATIONAL GEOGRAPHIC*. It shows a black woman, naked--pendulous breasts scarred with tribal markings. For some reason I am fascinated by this. I look down and am surprised to see bare and ink-stained knees--I am wearing short-trousers. I'm a schoolboy.

A girl--about thirteen comes into the waiting-room. She has a strange smile about her mouth. She comes and stands right in front of me--she smells warm.

"What's it like?" I ask her.

"I'm not supposed to tell you. It's a secret--for *adults*.

"Here, eat this."

She places a small, button-like lozenge in my mouth. It is pungent, aromatic--like my Grandma's gin--forbidden fruit.

There is laughter and, from the surgery, my name is called. It's my turn now to learn the secrets.

[well that's all pretty obvious--best not let the shrinks get their hands on any of these notes though. Let the bastards work for their keep.]

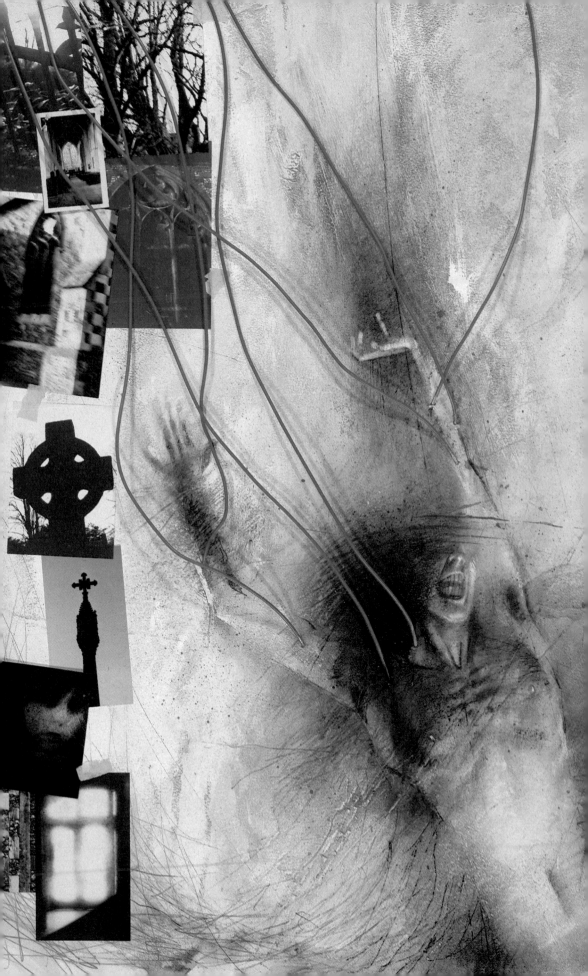

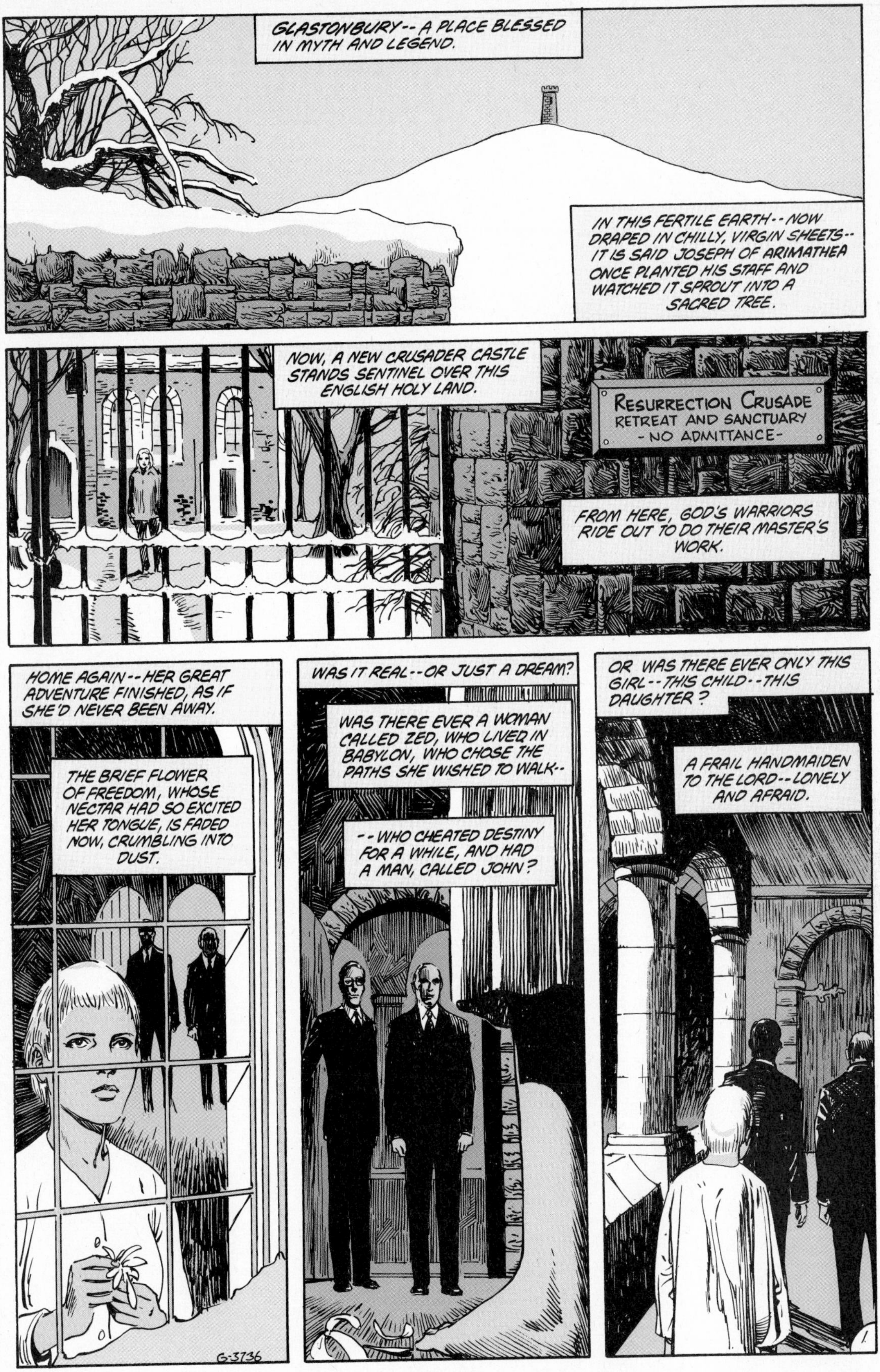

GLASTONBURY-- A PLACE BLESSED IN MYTH AND LEGEND.
IN THIS FERTILE EARTH-- NOW DRAPED IN CHILLY, VIRGIN SHEETS-- IT IS SAID JOSEPH OF ARIMATHEA ONCE PLANTED HIS STAFF AND WATCHED IT SPROUT INTO A SACRED TREE.
NOW, A NEW CRUSADER CASTLE STANDS SENTINEL OVER THIS ENGLISH HOLY LAND.
RESURRECTION CRUSADE
RETREAT AND SANCTUARY
-NO ADMITTANCE-
FROM HERE, GOD'S WARRIORS RIDE OUT TO DO THEIR MASTER'S WORK.
HOME AGAIN-- HER GREAT ADVENTURE FINISHED, AS IF SHE'D NEVER BEEN AWAY.
THE BRIEF FLOWER OF FREEDOM, WHOSE NECTAR HAD SO EXCITED HER TONGUE, IS FADED NOW, CRUMBLING INTO DUST.
G-3736
WAS IT REAL--OR JUST A DREAM?
WAS THERE EVER A WOMAN CALLED ZED, WHO LIVED IN BABYLON, WHO CHOSE THE PATHS SHE WISHED TO WALK--
--WHO CHEATED DESTINY FOR A WHILE, AND HAD A MAN, CALLED JOHN?
OR WAS THERE EVER ONLY THIS GIRL--THIS CHILD--THIS DAUGHTER?
A FRAIL HANDMAIDEN TO THE LORD--LONELY AND AFRAID.
1.

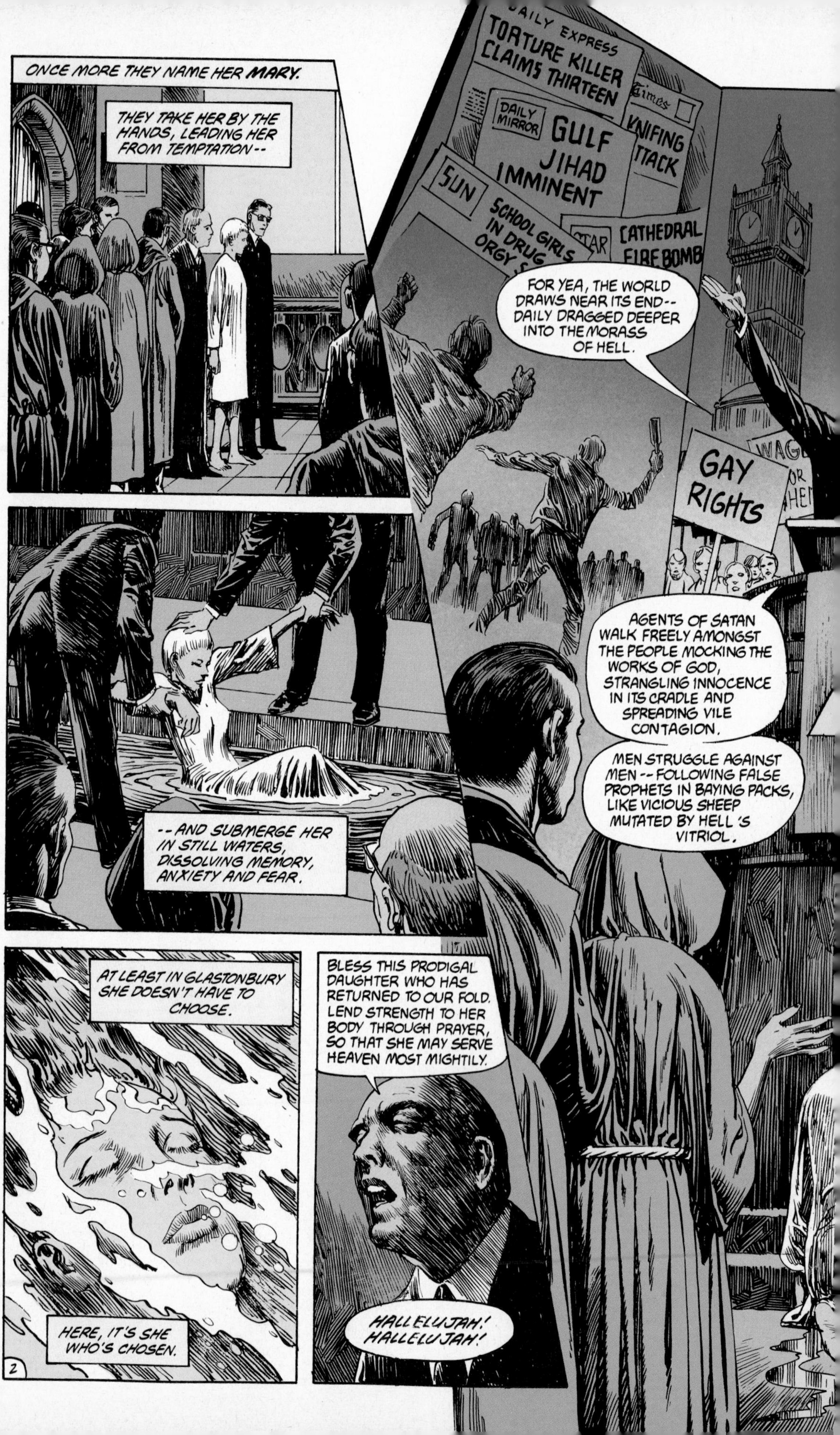

ONCE MORE THEY NAME HER MARY.
THEY TAKE HER BY THE HANDS, LEADING HER FROM TEMPTATION--
DAILY EXPRESS
TORTURE KILLER CLAIMS THIRTEEN
Times
KNIFING ATTACK
DAILY MIRROR
GULF JIHAD IMMINENT
SUN
SCHOOL GIRLS IN DRUG ORGY S
STAR
CATHEDRAL FIRE BOMB
FOR YEA, THE WORLD DRAWS NEAR ITS END-- DAILY DRAGGED DEEPER INTO THE MORASS OF HELL.
GAY RIGHTS
AGENTS OF SATAN WALK FREELY AMONGST THE PEOPLE MOCKING THE WORKS OF GOD, STRANGLING INNOCENCE IN ITS CRADLE AND SPREADING VILE CONTAGION.
MEN STRUGGLE AGAINST MEN -- FOLLOWING FALSE PROPHETS IN BAYING PACKS, LIKE VICIOUS SHEEP MUTATED BY HELL'S VITRIOL.
--AND SUBMERGE HER IN STILL WATERS, DISSOLVING MEMORY, ANXIETY AND FEAR.
AT LEAST IN GLASTONBURY SHE DOESN'T HAVE TO CHOOSE.
HERE, IT'S SHE WHO'S CHOSEN.
BLESS THIS PRODIGAL DAUGHTER WHO HAS RETURNED TO OUR FOLD. LEND STRENGTH TO HER BODY THROUGH PRAYER, SO THAT SHE MAY SERVE HEAVEN MOST MIGHTILY.
HALLELUJAH! HALLELUJAH!

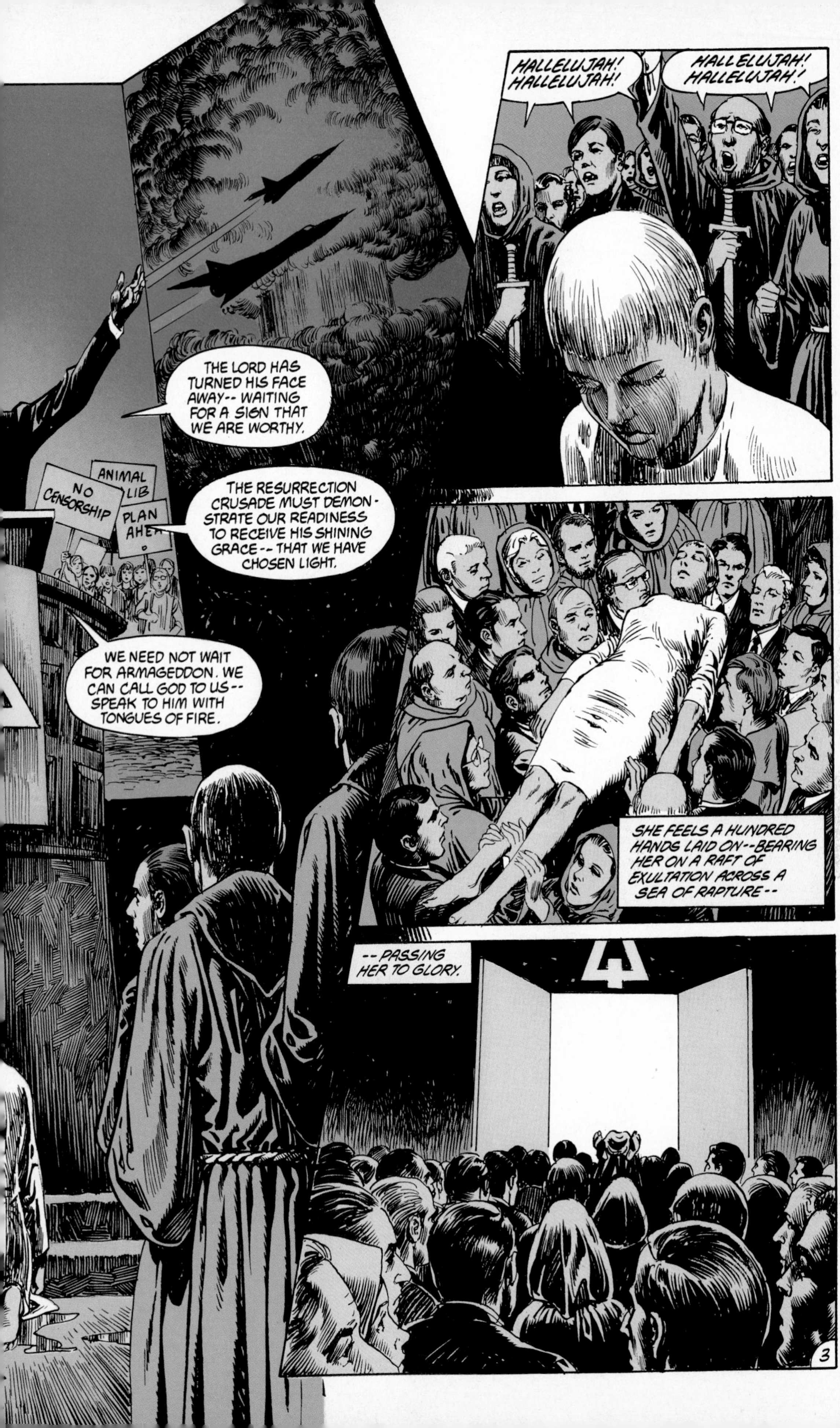
THE LORD HAS TURNED HIS FACE AWAY-- WAITING FOR A SIGN THAT WE ARE WORTHY.
NO CENSORSHIP
ANIMAL LIB
PLAN AHEAD
THE RESURRECTION CRUSADE MUST DEMON-STRATE OUR READINESS TO RECEIVE HIS SHINING GRACE-- THAT WE HAVE CHOSEN LIGHT.
WE NEED NOT WAIT FOR ARMAGEDDON. WE CAN CALL GOD TO US-- SPEAK TO HIM WITH TONGUES OF FIRE.
HALLELUJAH! HALLELUJAH!
HALLELUJAH! HALLELUJAH!
SHE FEELS A HUNDRED HANDS LAID ON--BEARING HER ON A RAFT OF EXULTATION ACROSS A SEA OF RAPTURE--
--PASSING HER TO GLORY.
3

THEY TAKE HER DOWN.

DOWN TO THE SANCTUM OF THE TONGUES OF FIRE.

IN THIS TEMPLE OF TECHNOLOGY THE LAST PROTESTS OF FREE WILL ARE SILENCED.

THE RE-INDOCTRINA-TION IS COMPLETE? SHE'S MENTALLY PREPARED NOW?

YES.

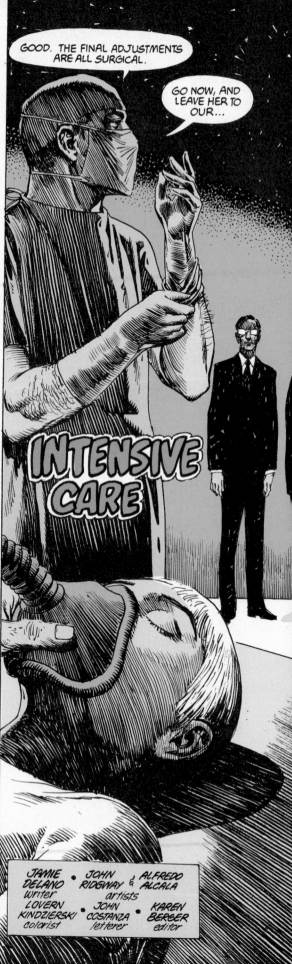

GOOD. THE FINAL ADJUSTMENTS ARE ALL SURGICAL.

GO NOW, AND LEAVE HER TO OUR...

INTENSIVE CARE

JAMIE DELANO writer • JOHN RIDGWAY & ALFREDO ALCALA artists • LOVERN KINDZIERSKI colorist • JOHN COSTANZA letterer • KAREN BERGER editor

SILENCE.

DARKNESS GRAYED BY SICK LIGHT.

FEAR.

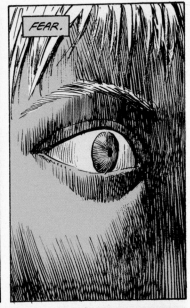

INSIDE ME, NAUSEA QUIVERS-- SOLID AND BLACK.

WHO AM I? WHERE AM I?

K-DOK K-DAK K-DOK K-DAK K-DON K-DAK SKUFF. SK-DON

OUT OF THE SILENCE FOOTSTEPS WALK--ECHOING AS IF THEY PACED A TOMB, OR PRISON.

SCHTANG CHANG SCHTUNNG

MY BODY ACHES AND TREMBLES.

WHY? WHY AM I HERE?

WHY AM I AFRAID OF THE LIGHT?

ALL RIGHT, CONSTANTINE, YOU FILTHY LITTLE PERVERT. GET ON YOUR BLEEDIN' FEET!

5

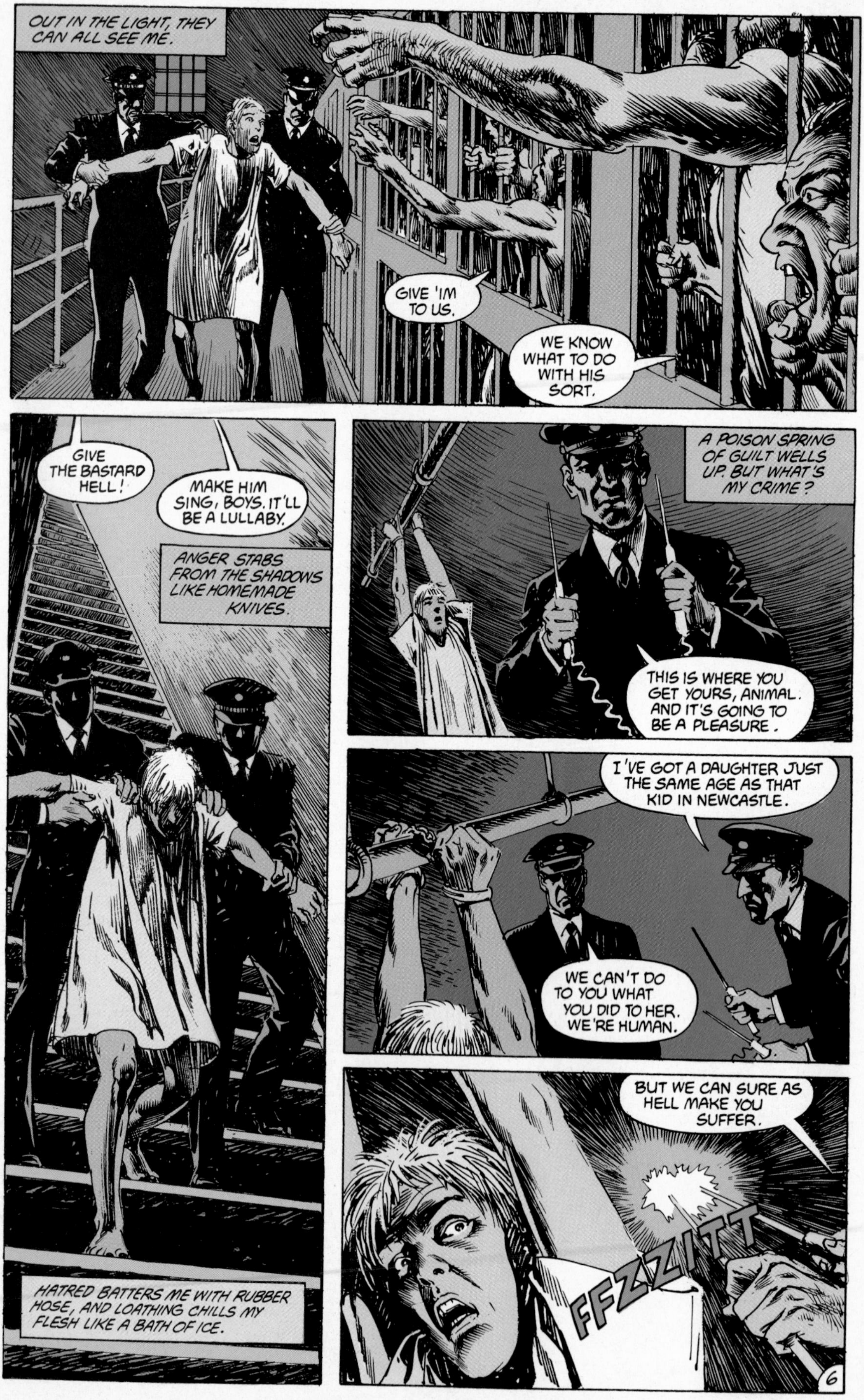
OUT IN THE LIGHT, THEY CAN ALL SEE ME.
GIVE 'IM TO US.
WE KNOW WHAT TO DO WITH HIS SORT.
GIVE THE BASTARD HELL!
MAKE HIM SING, BOYS. IT'LL BE A LULLABY.
ANGER STABS FROM THE SHADOWS LIKE HOMEMADE KNIVES.
HATRED BATTERS ME WITH RUBBER HOSE, AND LOATHING CHILLS MY FLESH LIKE A BATH OF ICE.
A POISON SPRING OF GUILT WELLS UP. BUT WHAT'S MY CRIME?
THIS IS WHERE YOU GET YOURS, ANIMAL. AND IT'S GOING TO BE A PLEASURE.
I'VE GOT A DAUGHTER JUST THE SAME AGE AS THAT KID IN NEWCASTLE.
WE CAN'T DO TO YOU WHAT YOU DID TO HER. WE'RE HUMAN.
BUT WE CAN SURE AS HELL MAKE YOU SUFFER.
FFZZITT
6

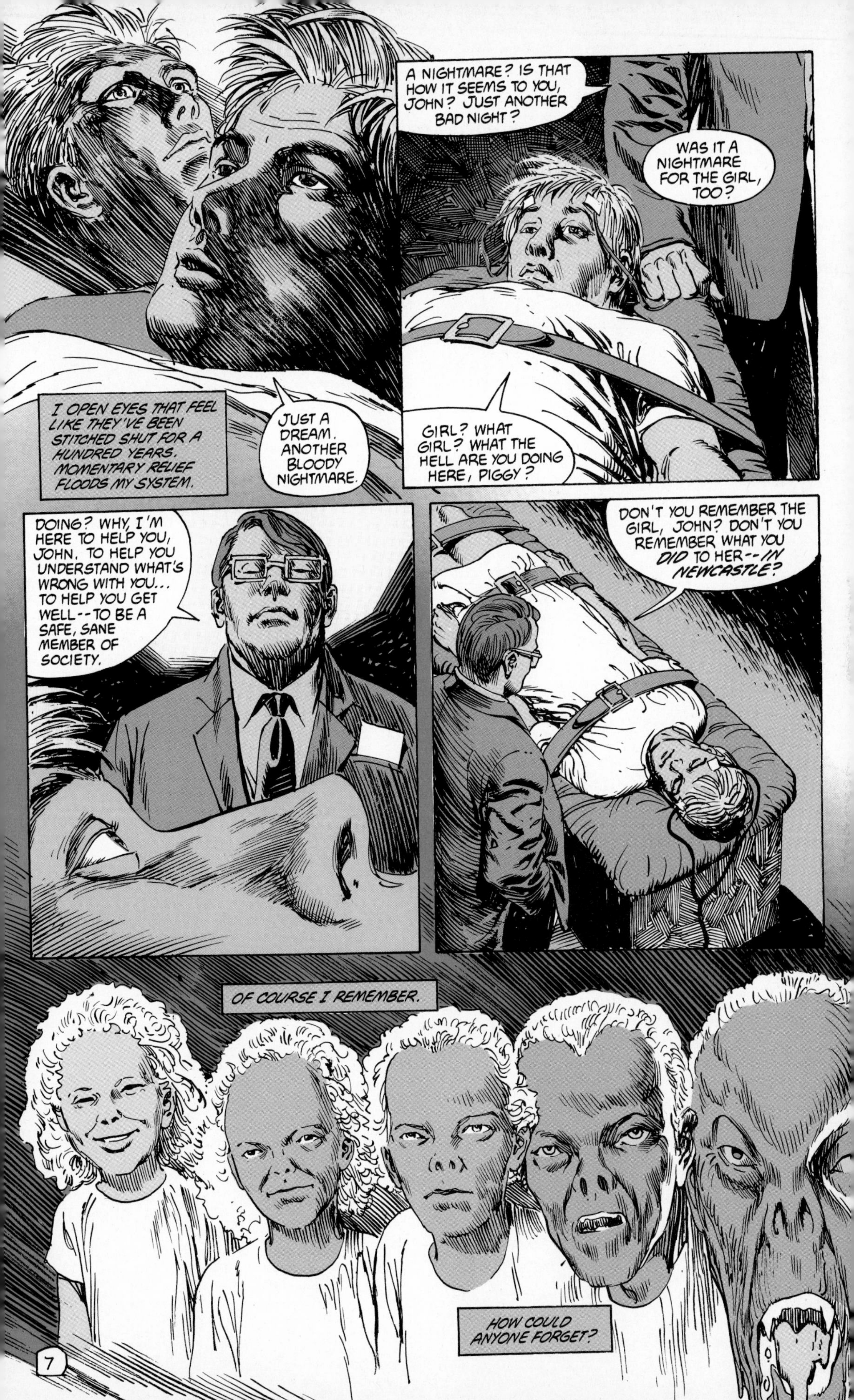
A NIGHTMARE? IS THAT HOW IT SEEMS TO YOU, JOHN? JUST ANOTHER BAD NIGHT?
WAS IT A NIGHTMARE FOR THE GIRL, TOO?
I OPEN EYES THAT FEEL LIKE THEY'VE BEEN STITCHED SHUT FOR A HUNDRED YEARS. MOMENTARY RELIEF FLOODS MY SYSTEM.
JUST A DREAM. ANOTHER BLOODY NIGHTMARE.
GIRL? WHAT GIRL? WHAT THE HELL ARE YOU DOING HERE, PIGGY?
DOING? WHY, I'M HERE TO HELP YOU, JOHN. TO HELP YOU UNDERSTAND WHAT'S WRONG WITH YOU... TO HELP YOU GET WELL--TO BE A SAFE, SANE MEMBER OF SOCIETY.
DON'T YOU REMEMBER THE GIRL, JOHN? DON'T YOU REMEMBER WHAT YOU DID TO HER--IN NEWCASTLE?
OF COURSE I REMEMBER.
HOW COULD ANYONE FORGET?

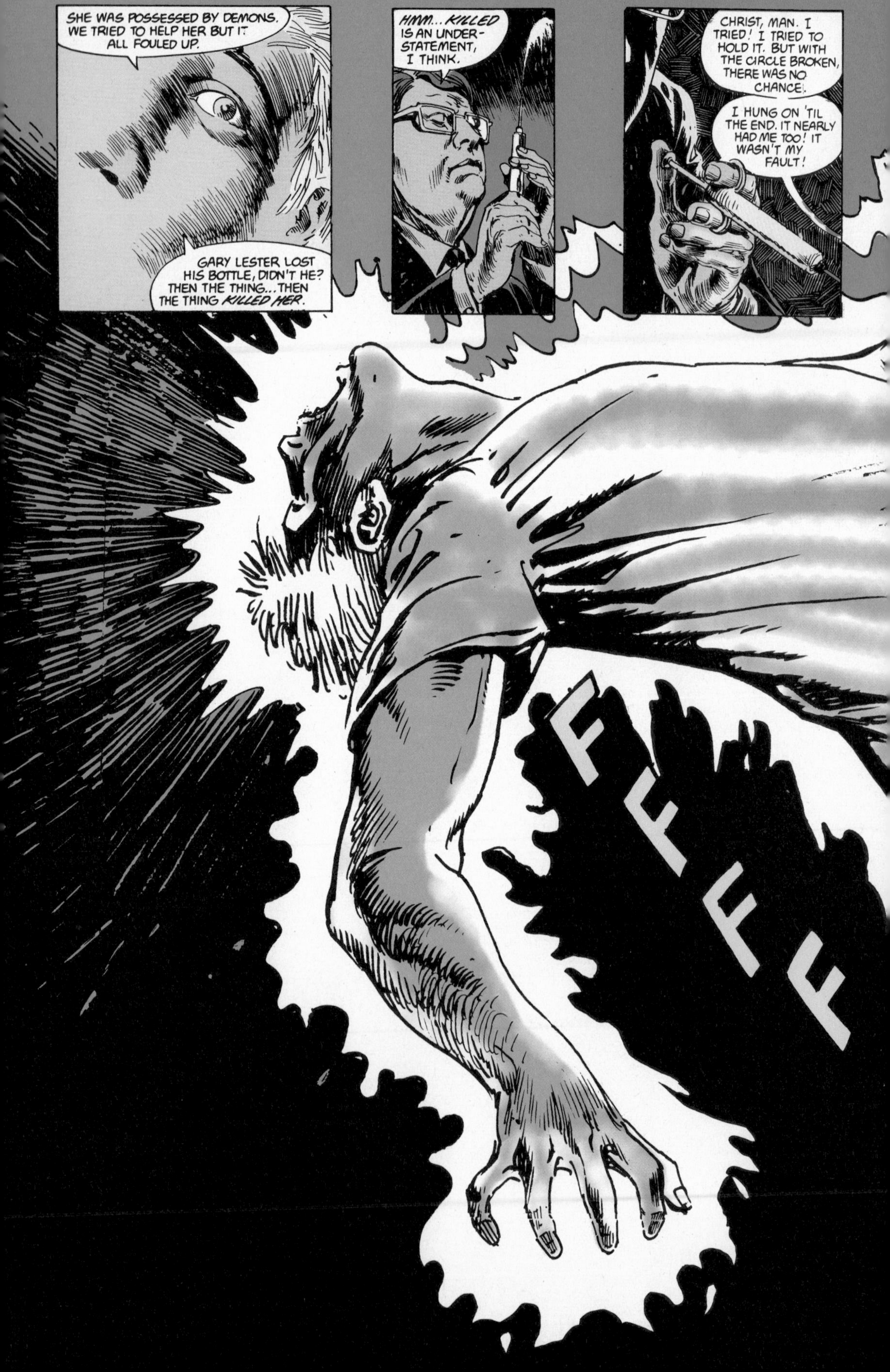
SHE WAS POSSESSED BY DEMONS. WE TRIED TO HELP HER BUT IT ALL FOULED UP.
GARY LESTER LOST HIS BOTTLE, DIDN'T HE? THEN THE THING... THEN THE THING KILLED HER.
HMM... KILLED IS AN UNDER-STATEMENT, I THINK.
CHRIST, MAN. I TRIED! I TRIED TO HOLD IT. BUT WITH THE CIRCLE BROKEN, THERE WAS NO CHANCE!
I HUNG ON 'TIL THE END. IT NEARLY HAD ME TOO! IT WASN'T MY FAULT!
FFFF

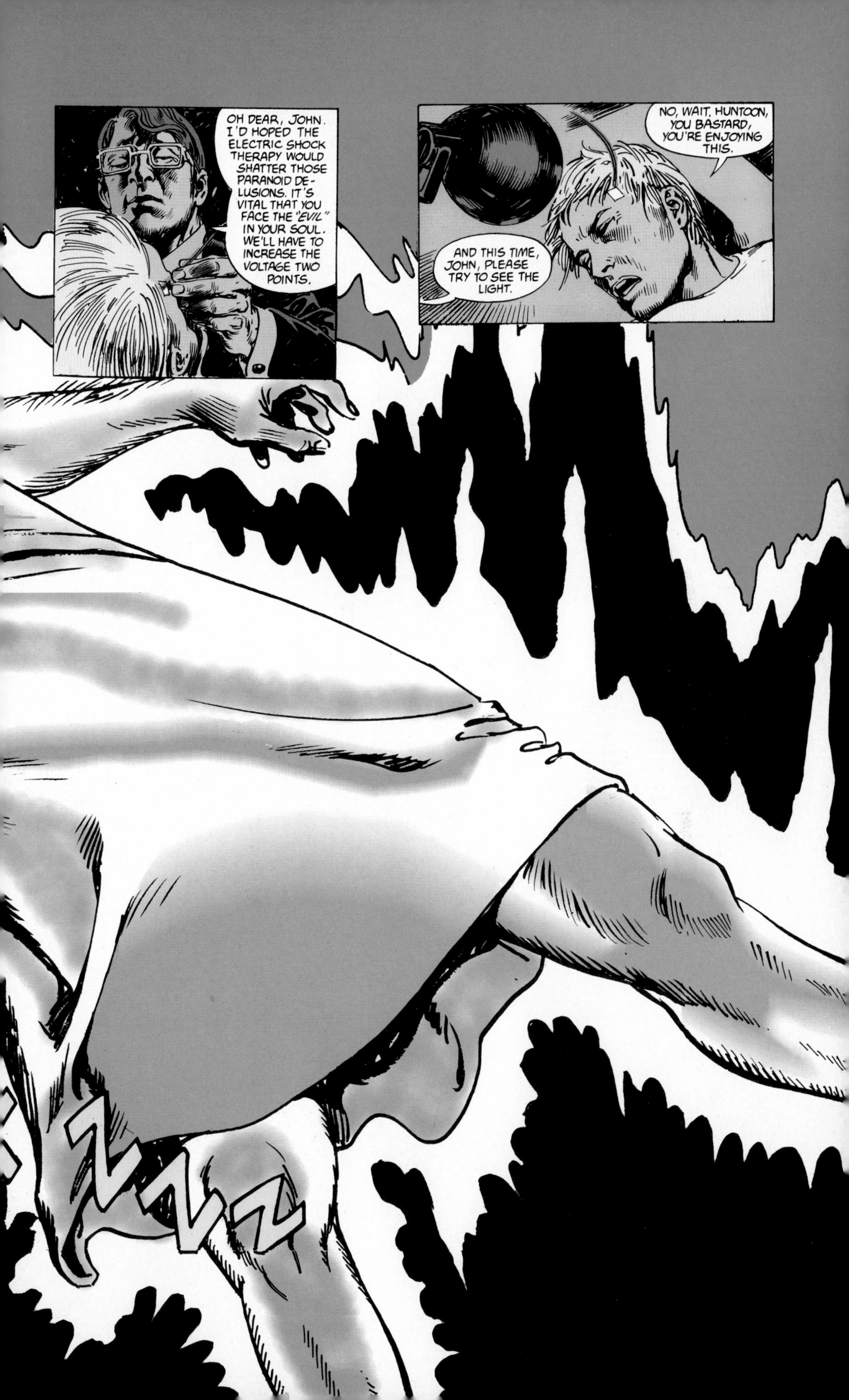
OH DEAR, JOHN. I'D HOPED THE ELECTRIC SHOCK THERAPY WOULD SHATTER THOSE PARANOID DE-LUSIONS. IT'S VITAL THAT YOU FACE THE "EVIL" IN YOUR SOUL. WE'LL HAVE TO INCREASE THE VOLTAGE TWO POINTS.
NO, WAIT, HUNTOON, YOU BASTARD, YOU'RE ENJOYING THIS.
AND THIS TIME, JOHN, PLEASE TRY TO SEE THE LIGHT.
ZZZZ

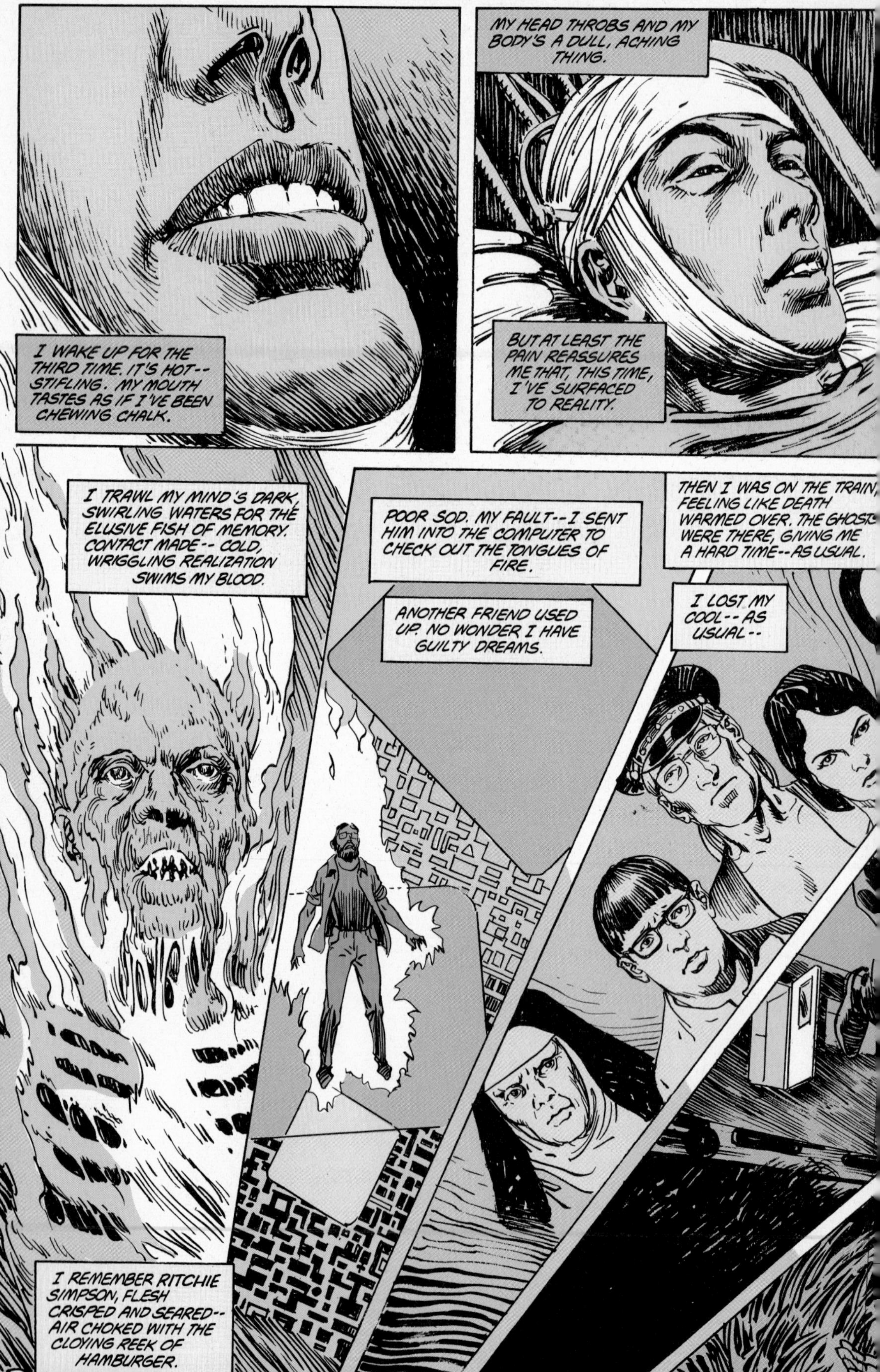

I WAKE UP FOR THE THIRD TIME. IT'S HOT-- STIFLING. MY MOUTH TASTES AS IF I'VE BEEN CHEWING CHALK.
MY HEAD THROBS AND MY BODY'S A DULL, ACHING THING.
BUT AT LEAST THE PAIN REASSURES ME THAT, THIS TIME, I'VE SURFACED TO REALITY.
I TRAWL MY MIND'S DARK, SWIRLING WATERS FOR THE ELUSIVE FISH OF MEMORY. CONTACT MADE-- COLD, WRIGGLING REALIZATION SWIMS MY BLOOD.
I REMEMBER RITCHIE SIMPSON, FLESH CRISPED AND SEARED-- AIR CHOKED WITH THE CLOYING REEK OF HAMBURGER.
POOR SOD. MY FAULT-- I SENT HIM INTO THE COMPUTER TO CHECK OUT THE TONGUES OF FIRE.
ANOTHER FRIEND USED UP. NO WONDER I HAVE GUILTY DREAMS.
THEN I WAS ON THE TRAIN, FEELING LIKE DEATH WARMED OVER. THE GHOSTS WERE THERE, GIVING ME A HARD TIME-- AS USUAL.
I LOST MY COOL-- AS USUAL--

WHERE, THOUGH? I'M NOT IN MY BED, NOR ZED'S.

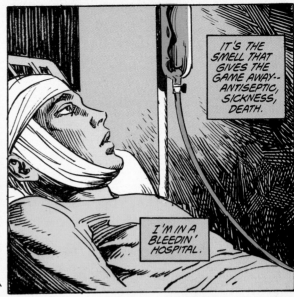

IT'S THE SMELL THAT GIVES THE GAME AWAY-- ANTISEPTIC, SICKNESS, DEATH.

I'M IN A BLEEDIN' HOSPITAL.

--AND STORMED OUT. FORGETTING THAT WE WERE RATTLING AT SIXTY MILES AN HOUR THROUGH THE NIGHT.

THEN PAIN-- A DEEP, MOSSY, WOODY SMELL-- AND ALL WAS BLACK.

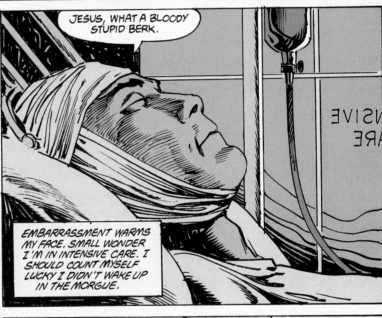

JESUS, WHAT A BLOODY STUPID BERK.

EMBARRASSMENT WARMS MY FACE. SMALL WONDER I'M IN INTENSIVE CARE. I SHOULD COUNT MYSELF LUCKY I DIDN'T WAKE UP IN THE MORGUE.

I'D BETTER SLOW DOWN-- START USING WHATEVER BRAINS ARE LEFT UNSCRAMBLED.

BUT FIRST I NEED TO KNOW HOW BADLY I'VE MANGLED THIS FRAIL, MORTAL FORM.

10

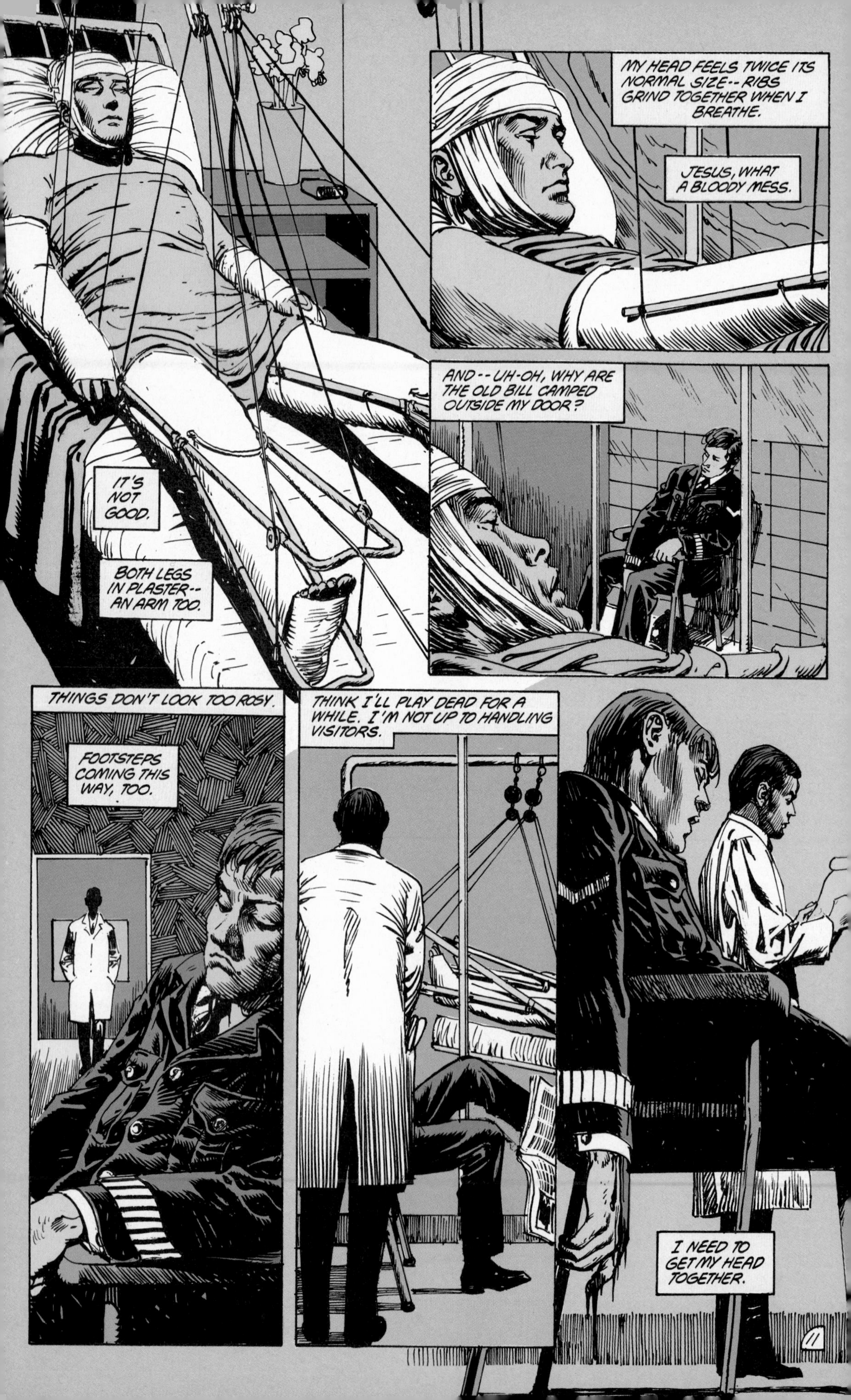
MY HEAD FEELS TWICE ITS NORMAL SIZE-- RIBS GRIND TOGETHER WHEN I BREATHE.
JESUS, WHAT A BLOODY MESS.
IT'S NOT GOOD.
BOTH LEGS IN PLASTER-- AN ARM TOO.
AND-- UH-OH, WHY ARE THE OLD BILL CAMPED OUTSIDE MY DOOR?
THINGS DON'T LOOK TOO ROSY.
FOOTSTEPS COMING THIS WAY, TOO.
THINK I'LL PLAY DEAD FOR A WHILE. I'M NOT UP TO HANDLING VISITORS.
I NEED TO GET MY HEAD TOGETHER.

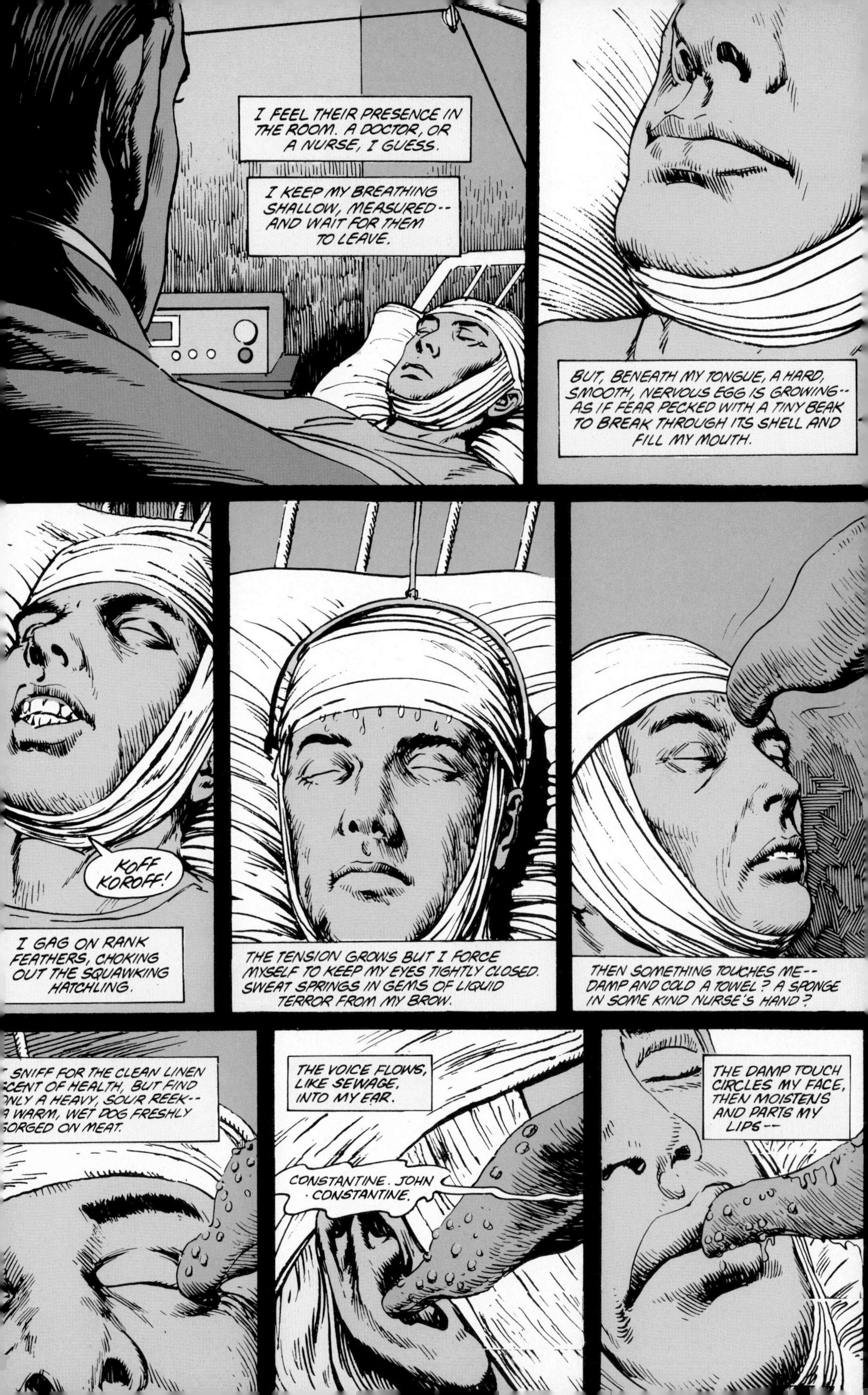
I FEEL THEIR PRESENCE IN THE ROOM. A DOCTOR, OR A NURSE, I GUESS.
I KEEP MY BREATHING SHALLOW, MEASURED-- AND WAIT FOR THEM TO LEAVE.
BUT, BENEATH MY TONGUE, A HARD, SMOOTH, NERVOUS EGG IS GROWING-- AS IF FEAR PECKED WITH A TINY BEAK TO BREAK THROUGH ITS SHELL AND FILL MY MOUTH.
KOFF KOROFF!
I GAG ON RANK FEATHERS, CHOKING OUT THE SQUAWKING HATCHLING.
THE TENSION GROWS BUT I FORCE MYSELF TO KEEP MY EYES TIGHTLY CLOSED. SWEAT SPRINGS IN GEMS OF LIQUID TERROR FROM MY BROW.
THEN SOMETHING TOUCHES ME-- DAMP AND COLD A TOWEL? A SPONGE IN SOME KIND NURSE'S HAND?
SNIFF FOR THE CLEAN LINEN SCENT OF HEALTH, BUT FIND ONLY A HEAVY, SOUR REEK-- A WARM, WET DOG FRESHLY GORGED ON MEAT.
THE VOICE FLOWS, LIKE SEWAGE, INTO MY EAR.
CONSTANTINE. JOHN CONSTANTINE.
THE DAMP TOUCH CIRCLES MY FACE, THEN MOISTENS AND PARTS MY LIPS--

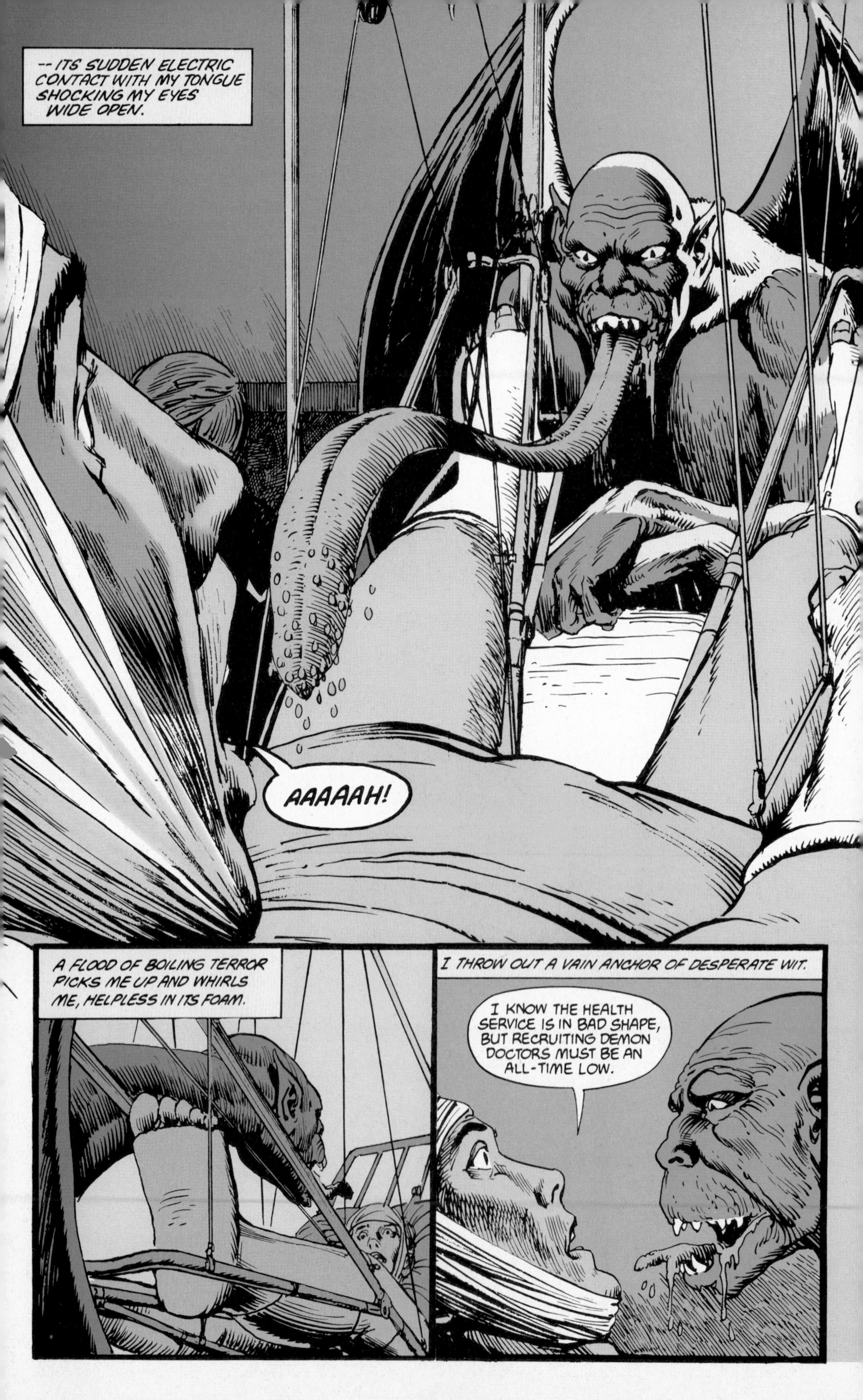

-- ITS SUDDEN ELECTRIC CONTACT WITH MY TONGUE SHOCKING MY EYES WIDE OPEN.
AAAAAH!
A FLOOD OF BOILING TERROR PICKS ME UP AND WHIRLS ME, HELPLESS IN ITS FOAM.
I THROW OUT A VAIN ANCHOR OF DESPERATE WIT.
I KNOW THE HEALTH SERVICE IS IN BAD SHAPE, BUT RECRUITING DEMON DOCTORS MUST BE AN ALL-TIME LOW.

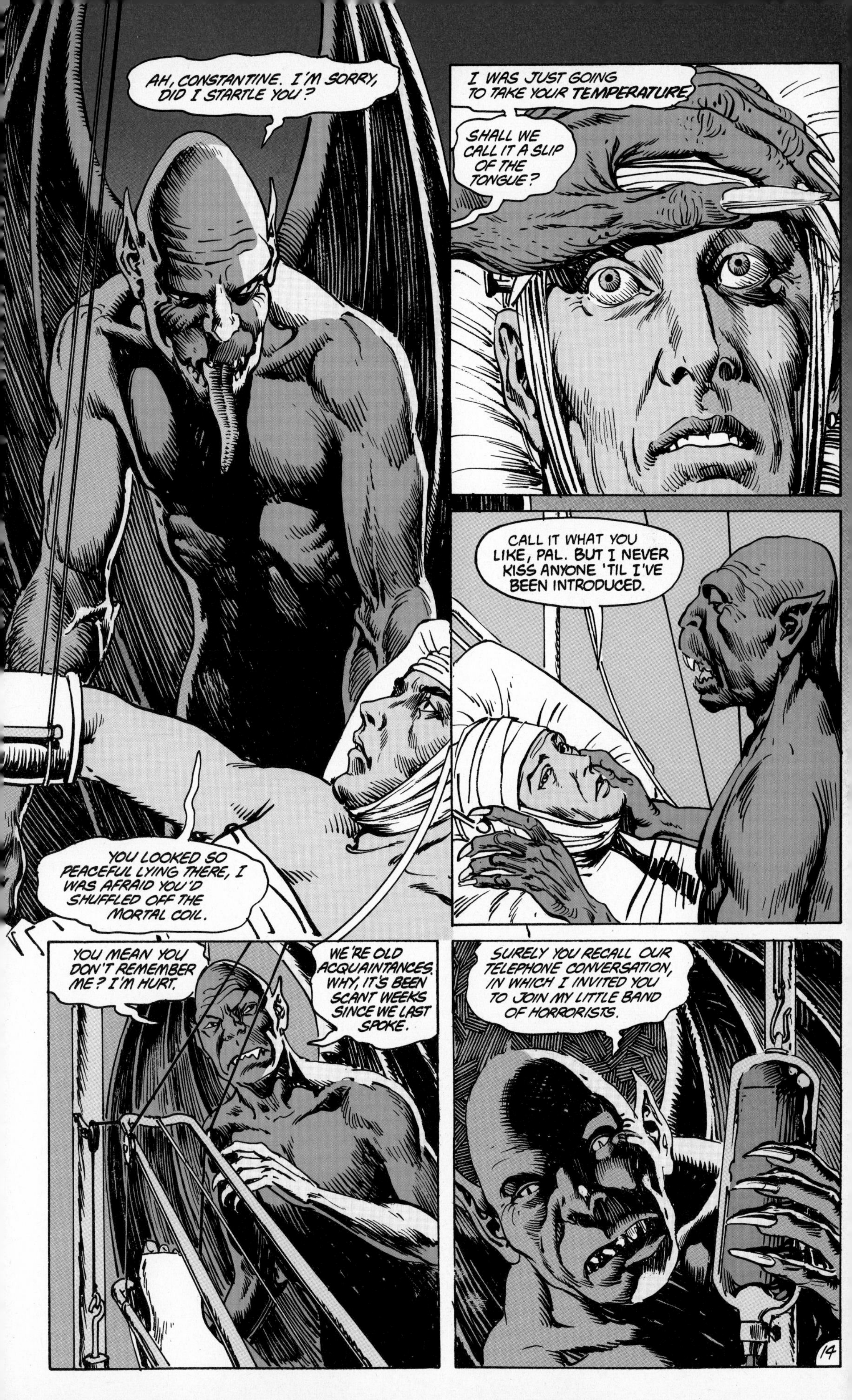
AH, CONSTANTINE. I'M SORRY, DID I STARTLE YOU?
I WAS JUST GOING TO TAKE YOUR TEMPERATURE.
SHALL WE CALL IT A SLIP OF THE TONGUE?
YOU LOOKED SO PEACEFUL LYING THERE, I WAS AFRAID YOU'D SHUFFLED OFF THE MORTAL COIL.
CALL IT WHAT YOU LIKE, PAL. BUT I NEVER KISS ANYONE 'TIL I'VE BEEN INTRODUCED.
YOU MEAN YOU DON'T REMEMBER ME? I'M HURT.
WE'RE OLD ACQUAINTANCES. WHY, IT'S BEEN SCANT WEEKS SINCE WE LAST SPOKE.
SURELY YOU RECALL OUR TELEPHONE CONVERSATION, IN WHICH I INVITED YOU TO JOIN MY LITTLE BAND OF HORRORISTS.
14

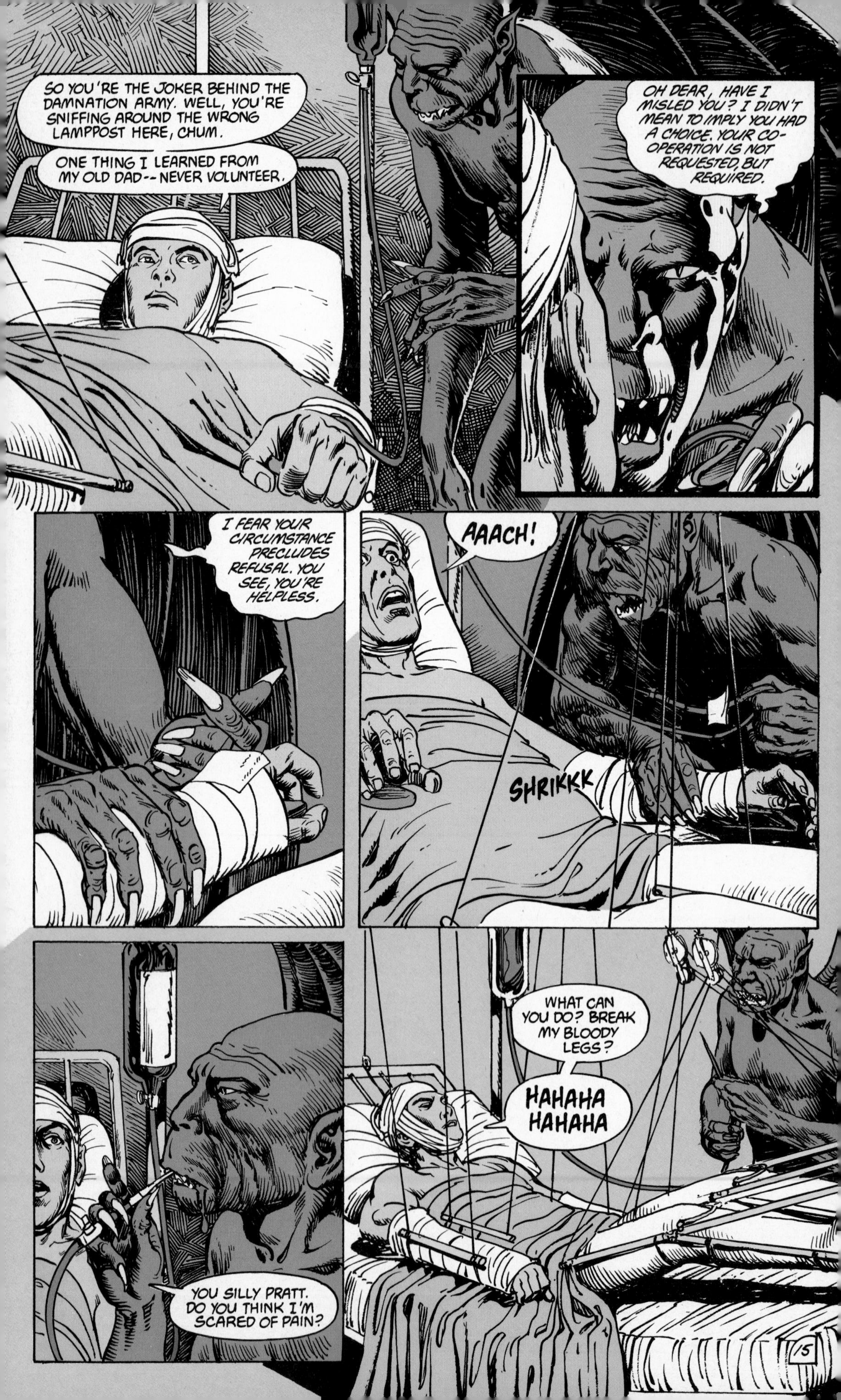
SO YOU'RE THE JOKER BEHIND THE DAMNATION ARMY. WELL, YOU'RE SNIFFING AROUND THE WRONG LAMPPOST HERE, CHUM.
ONE THING I LEARNED FROM MY OLD DAD--NEVER VOLUNTEER.
OH DEAR, HAVE I MISLED YOU? I DIDN'T MEAN TO IMPLY YOU HAD A CHOICE. YOUR CO-OPERATION IS NOT REQUESTED, BUT REQUIRED.
I FEAR YOUR CIRCUMSTANCE PRECLUDES REFUSAL. YOU SEE, YOU'RE HELPLESS.
AAACH!
SHRIKKK
YOU SILLY PRATT. DO YOU THINK I'M SCARED OF PAIN?
WHAT CAN YOU DO? BREAK MY BLOODY LEGS?
HAHAHA HAHAHA
15

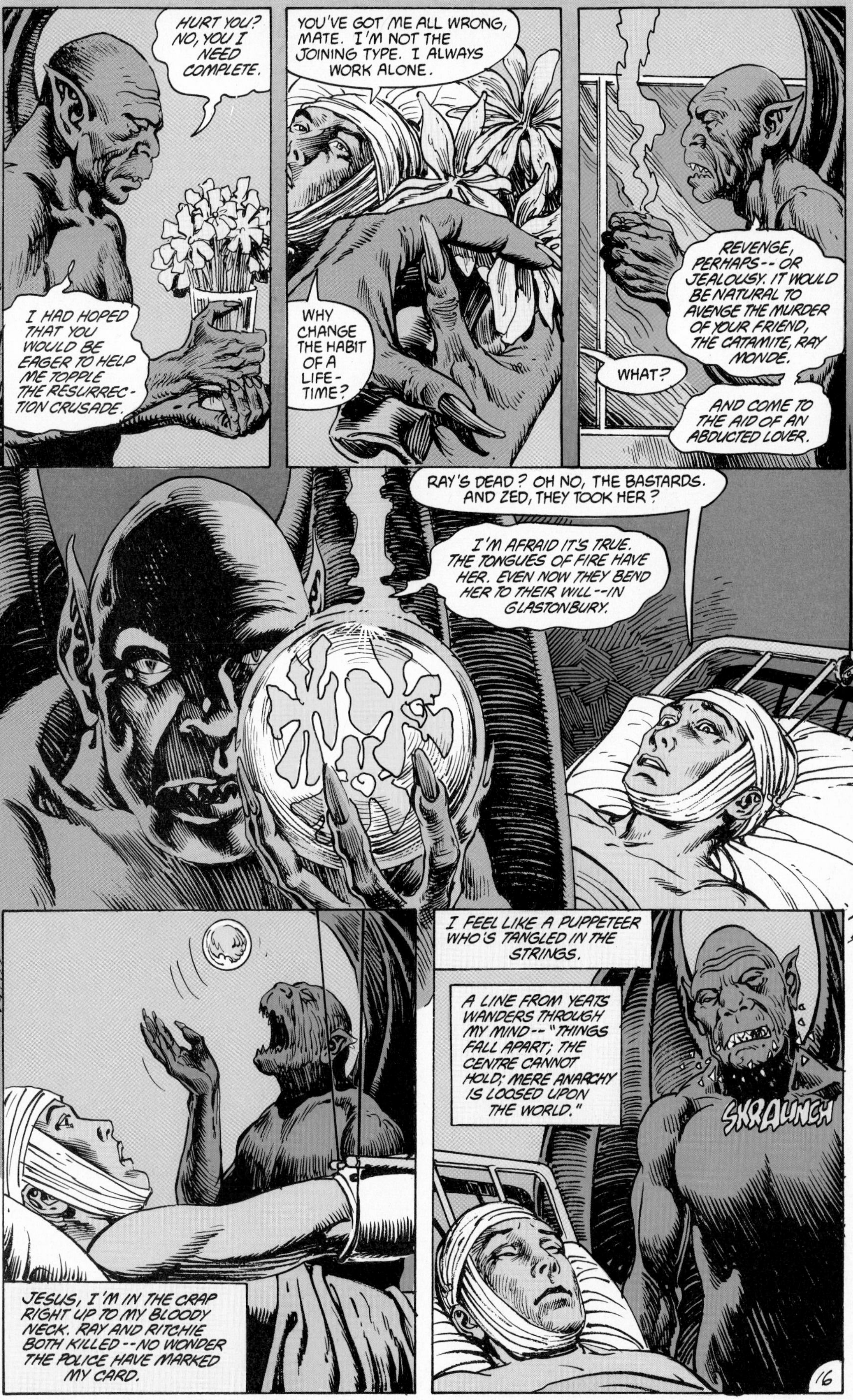
HURT YOU? NO, YOU I NEED COMPLETE.
I HAD HOPED THAT YOU WOULD BE EAGER TO HELP ME TOPPLE THE RESURRECTION CRUSADE.
YOU'VE GOT ME ALL WRONG, MATE. I'M NOT THE JOINING TYPE. I ALWAYS WORK ALONE.
WHY CHANGE THE HABIT OF A LIFETIME?
REVENGE, PERHAPS-- OR JEALOUSY. IT WOULD BE NATURAL TO AVENGE THE MURDER OF YOUR FRIEND, THE CATAMITE, RAY MONDE.
WHAT?
AND COME TO THE AID OF AN ABDUCTED LOVER.
RAY'S DEAD? OH NO, THE BASTARDS. AND ZED, THEY TOOK HER?
I'M AFRAID IT'S TRUE. THE TONGUES OF FIRE HAVE HER. EVEN NOW THEY BEND HER TO THEIR WILL--IN GLASTONBURY.
JESUS, I'M IN THE CRAP RIGHT UP TO MY BLOODY NECK. RAY AND RITCHIE BOTH KILLED--NO WONDER THE POLICE HAVE MARKED MY CARD.
I FEEL LIKE A PUPPETEER WHO'S TANGLED IN THE STRINGS.
A LINE FROM YEATS WANDERS THROUGH MY MIND--"THINGS FALL APART; THE CENTRE CANNOT HOLD; MERE ANARCHY IS LOOSED UPON THE WORLD."
SKRAUNCH

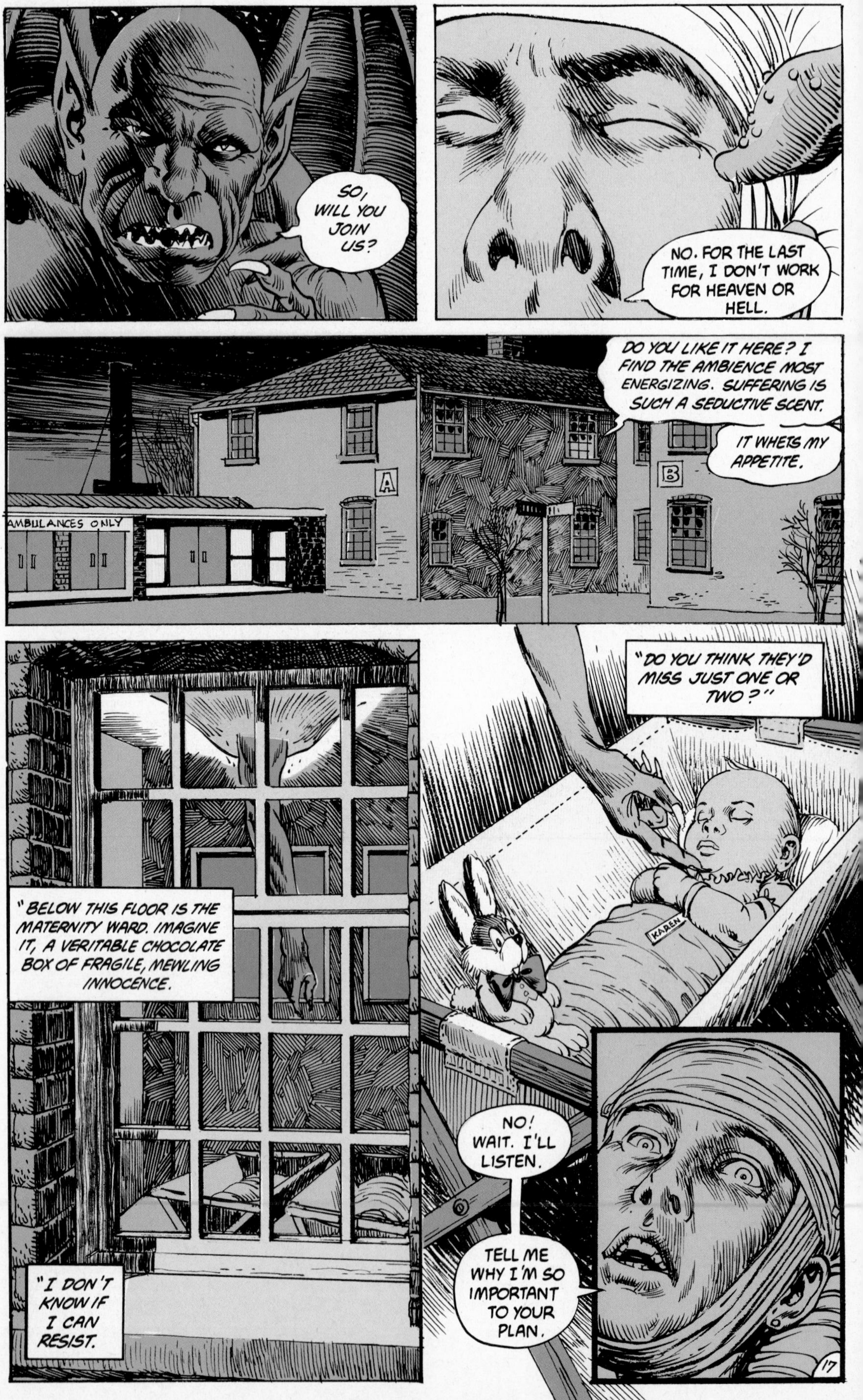
SO, WILL YOU JOIN US?
NO. FOR THE LAST TIME, I DON'T WORK FOR HEAVEN OR HELL.
DO YOU LIKE IT HERE? I FIND THE AMBIENCE MOST ENERGIZING. SUFFERING IS SUCH A SEDUCTIVE SCENT.
IT WHETS MY APPETITE.
A
B
AMBULANCES ONLY
"BELOW THIS FLOOR IS THE MATERNITY WARD. IMAGINE IT, A VERITABLE CHOCOLATE BOX OF FRAGILE, MEWLING INNOCENCE.
"I DON'T KNOW IF I CAN RESIST.
"DO YOU THINK THEY'D MISS JUST ONE OR TWO?"
KAREN
NO! WAIT. I'LL LISTEN.
TELL ME WHY I'M SO IMPORTANT TO YOUR PLAN.
17

YOU MEAN YOU DO NOT KNOW? YOU DISAPPOINT ME.

YEAH, WELL, I'VE GOT A LOT ON ME PLATE AT THE MOMENT.

THE BLOODY ELEMENTALS ARE ALL GOING LOOPY, Y'KNOW.

YES, EVEN THOSE PRIMITIVES ARE UNSETTLED BY THESE TROUBLED TIMES.

AN ERA IS PASSING, CONSTANTINE, FOR CENTURIES THE REALMS OF DARKNESS AND OF LIGHT HAVE SHARED THE BOUNTY OF THIS WORLD--

--GRAZING IN ROUGHLY EQUAL MEASURES THE VAST ROLLING PLAINS OF HUMAN SOULS.

"LIKE BISON, OCCASIONALLY LOCKING HORNS FOR PUSH AND SHOVE."

"BUT ALWAYS THE CONTEST WAS CIRCULAR--GROUND GAINED ON ONE FRONT WAS LOST ON ANOTHER."

ALL RIGHT, YOU CAN SKIP THE PRIMARY META-PHYSICS.

JUST GIVE ME THE DETAILS -- I'M OUT OF GRADE SCHOOL NOW.

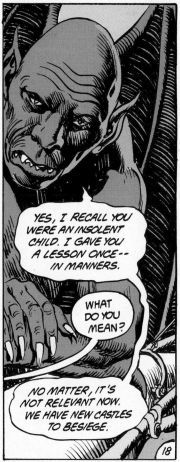

YES, I RECALL YOU WERE AN INSOLENT CHILD. I GAVE YOU A LESSON ONCE-- IN MANNERS.

WHAT DO YOU MEAN?

NO MATTER, IT'S NOT RELEVANT NOW. WE HAVE NEW CASTLES TO BESIEGE.

18

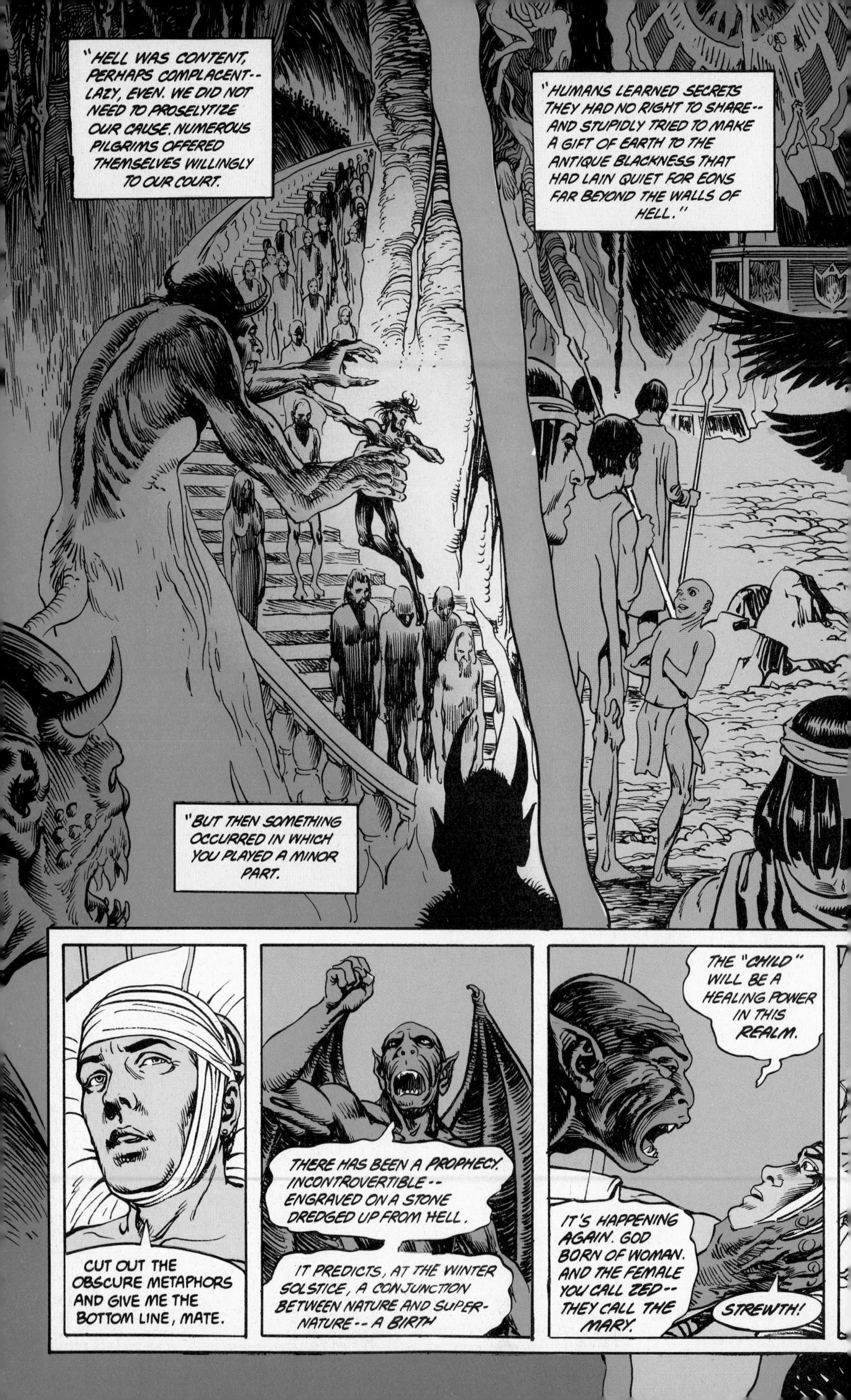
"HELL WAS CONTENT, PERHAPS COMPLACENT-- LAZY, EVEN. WE DID NOT NEED TO PROSELYTIZE OUR CAUSE. NUMEROUS PILGRIMS OFFERED THEMSELVES WILLINGLY TO OUR COURT.
"HUMANS LEARNED SECRETS THEY HAD NO RIGHT TO SHARE-- AND STUPIDLY TRIED TO MAKE A GIFT OF EARTH TO THE ANTIQUE BLACKNESS THAT HAD LAIN QUIET FOR EONS FAR BEYOND THE WALLS OF HELL."
"BUT THEN SOMETHING OCCURRED IN WHICH YOU PLAYED A MINOR PART.
CUT OUT THE OBSCURE METAPHORS AND GIVE ME THE BOTTOM LINE, MATE.
THERE HAS BEEN A PROPHECY. INCONTROVERTIBLE-- ENGRAVED ON A STONE DREDGED UP FROM HELL.
IT PREDICTS, AT THE WINTER SOLSTICE, A CONJUNCTION BETWEEN NATURE AND SUPER-NATURE-- A BIRTH
THE "CHILD" WILL BE A HEALING POWER IN THIS REALM.
IT'S HAPPENING AGAIN. GOD BORN OF WOMAN. AND THE FEMALE YOU CALL ZED-- THEY CALL THE MARY.
STREWTH!

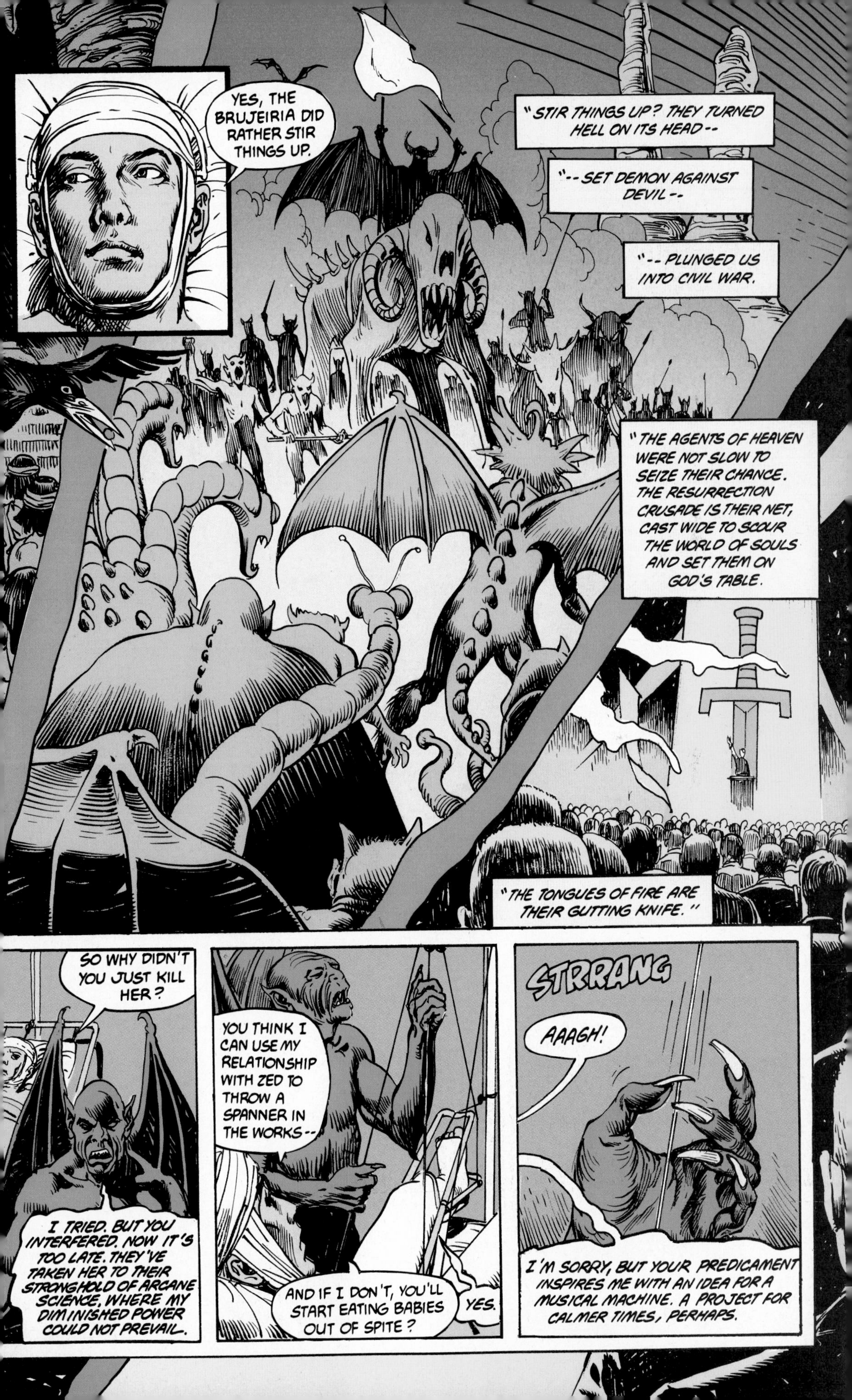
YES, THE BRUJEIRIA DID RATHER STIR THINGS UP.
"STIR THINGS UP? THEY TURNED HELL ON ITS HEAD--
"--SET DEMON AGAINST DEVIL--
"--PLUNGED US INTO CIVIL WAR.
"THE AGENTS OF HEAVEN WERE NOT SLOW TO SEIZE THEIR CHANCE. THE RESURRECTION CRUSADE IS THEIR NET, CAST WIDE TO SCOUR THE WORLD OF SOULS AND SET THEM ON GOD'S TABLE.
"THE TONGUES OF FIRE ARE THEIR GUTTING KNIFE."
SO WHY DIDN'T YOU JUST KILL HER?
I TRIED. BUT YOU INTERFERED. NOW IT'S TOO LATE. THEY'VE TAKEN HER TO THEIR STRONGHOLD OF ARCANE SCIENCE, WHERE MY DIMINISHED POWER COULD NOT PREVAIL.
YOU THINK I CAN USE MY RELATIONSHIP WITH ZED TO THROW A SPANNER IN THE WORKS--
AND IF I DON'T, YOU'LL START EATING BABIES OUT OF SPITE?
YES.
STRRANG
AAAGH!
I'M SORRY, BUT YOUR PREDICAMENT INSPIRES ME WITH AN IDEA FOR A MUSICAL MACHINE. A PROJECT FOR CALMER TIMES, PERHAPS.

YOUR ANSWER, NOW.

MY PATIENCE WEARS THIN.

SPIKED ON THE HORNS OF DILEMMA, EH? I'LL HAVE TO PLAY THIS HIS WAY--BUT HE NEEDS ME BADLY, THAT'S FOR SURE.

LET'S SEE WHAT HE'S PREPARED TO PAY.

OK, YOU WIN. I'LL HELP YOU.

THESE ARE MY TERMS.

TERMS?

FIRST, I NEED TIME TO TAKE CARE OF BUSINESS.

AGREED.

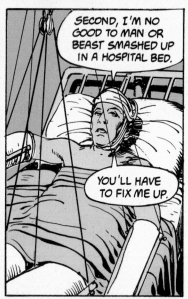

SECOND, I'M NO GOOD TO MAN OR BEAST SMASHED UP IN A HOSPITAL BED.

YOU'LL HAVE TO FIX ME UP.

VERY WELL. BUT BY THE SOLSTICE IT MUST BE DONE.

AND, BE WARNED, BETRAY ME AND YOU DIE-- AT LEAST A HUNDRED MILLION TIMES.

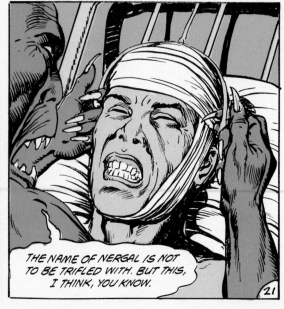

THE NAME OF NERGAL IS NOT TO BE TRIFLED WITH. BUT THIS, I THINK, YOU KNOW.

21

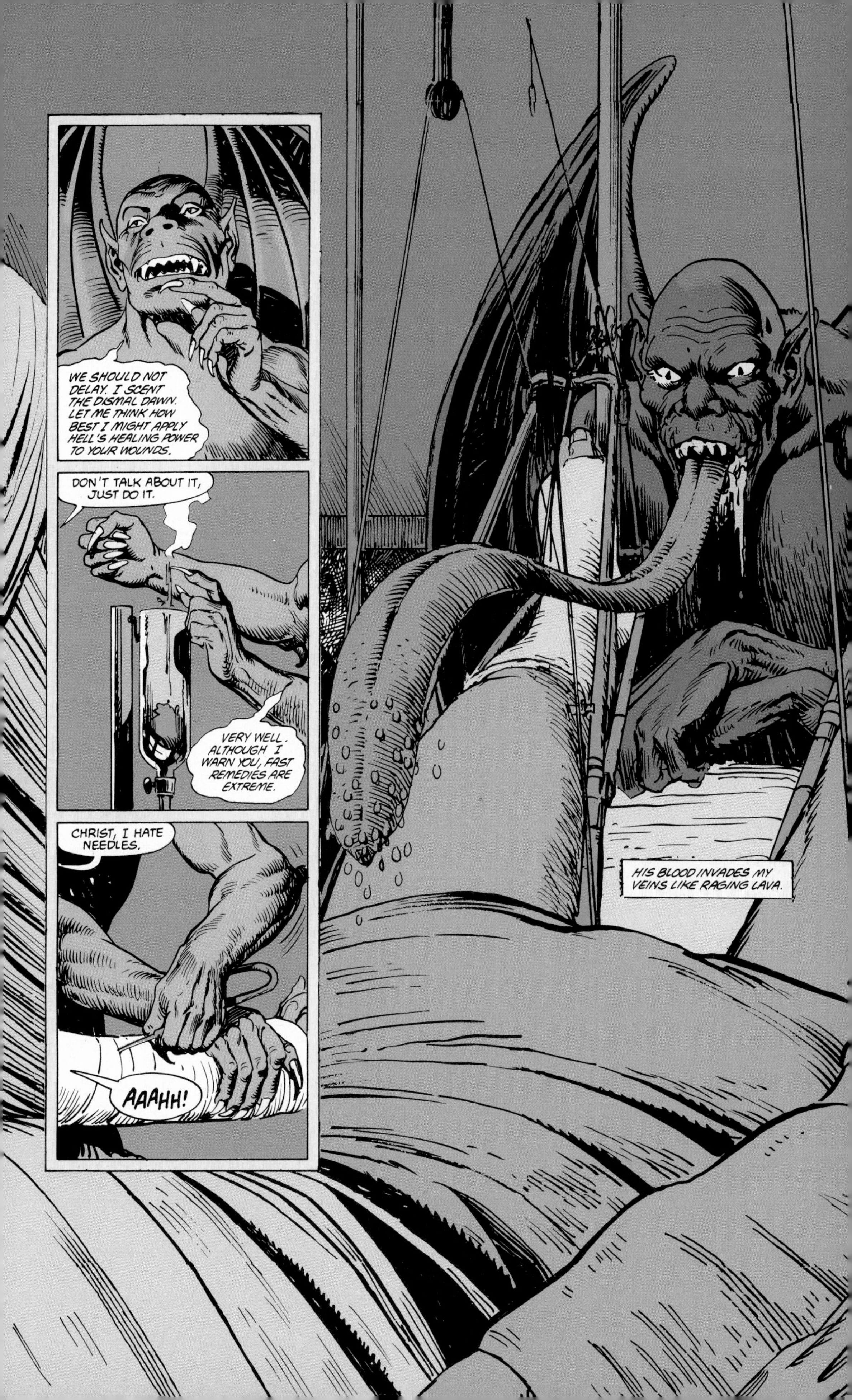
WE SHOULD NOT DELAY. I SCENT THE DISMAL DAWN. LET ME THINK HOW BEST I MIGHT APPLY HELL'S HEALING POWER TO YOUR WOUNDS.
DON'T TALK ABOUT IT, JUST DO IT.
VERY WELL. ALTHOUGH I WARN YOU, FAST REMEDIES ARE EXTREME.
CHRIST, I HATE NEEDLES.
AAAHH!
HIS BLOOD INVADES MY VEINS LIKE RAGING LAVA.

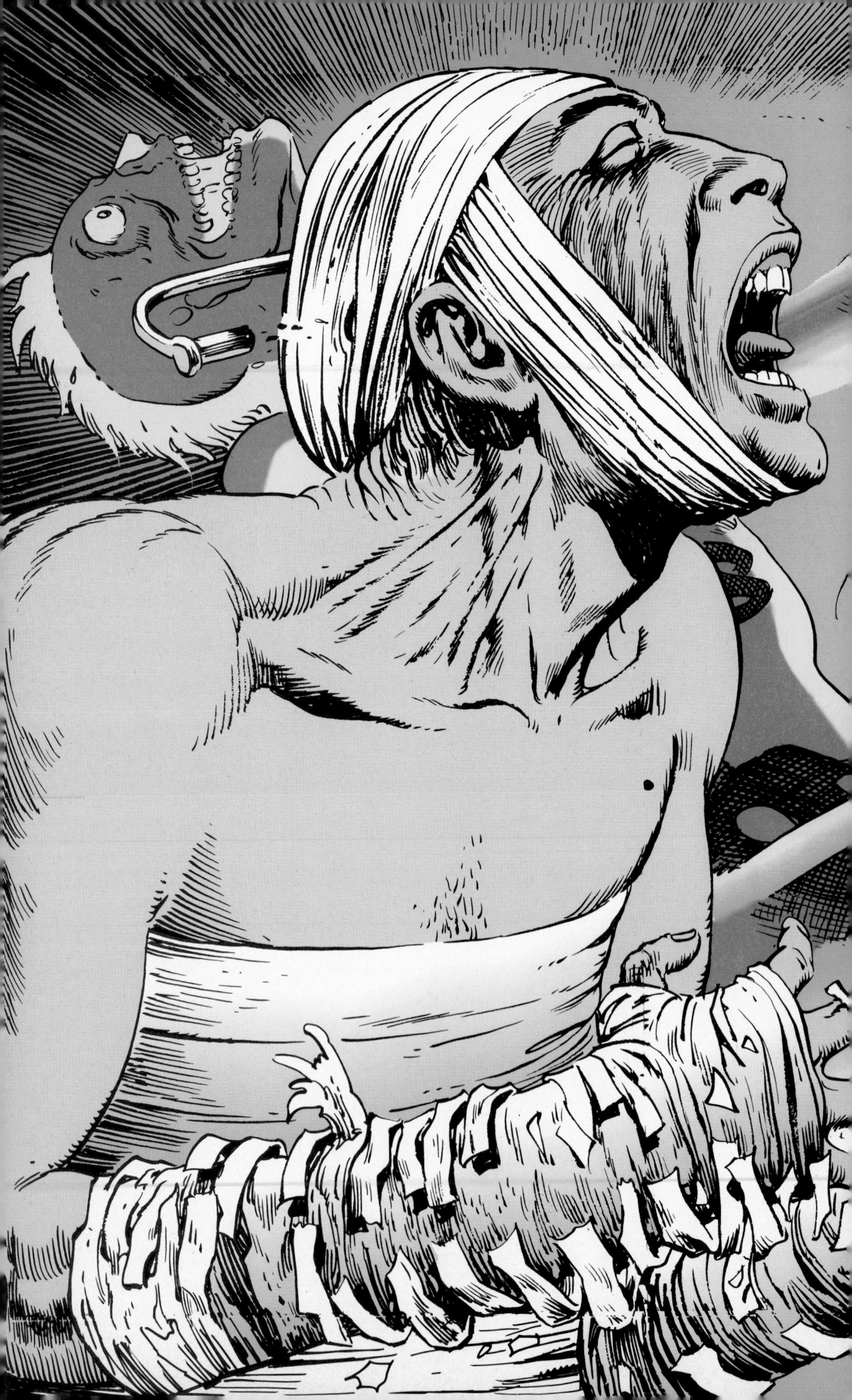

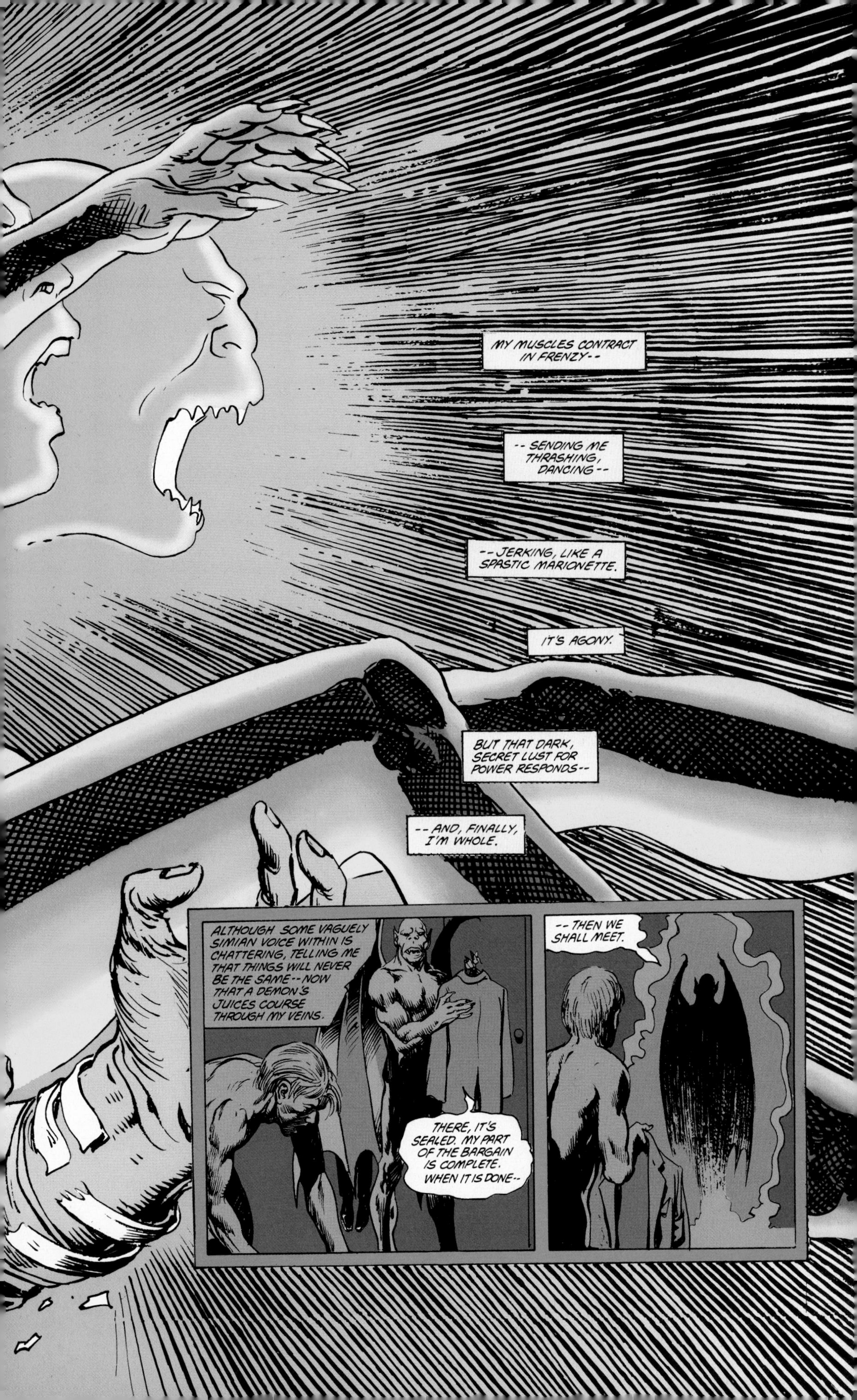
MY MUSCLES CONTRACT IN FRENZY--
--SENDING ME THRASHING, DANCING--
--JERKING, LIKE A SPASTIC MARIONETTE.
IT'S AGONY.
BUT THAT DARK, SECRET LUST FOR POWER RESPONDS--
--AND, FINALLY, I'M WHOLE.
ALTHOUGH SOME VAGUELY SIMIAN VOICE WITHIN IS CHATTERING, TELLING ME THAT THINGS WILL NEVER BE THE SAME--NOW THAT A DEMON'S JUICES COURSE THROUGH MY VEINS.
THERE, IT'S SEALED. MY PART OF THE BARGAIN IS COMPLETE. WHEN IT IS DONE--
--THEN WE SHALL MEET.

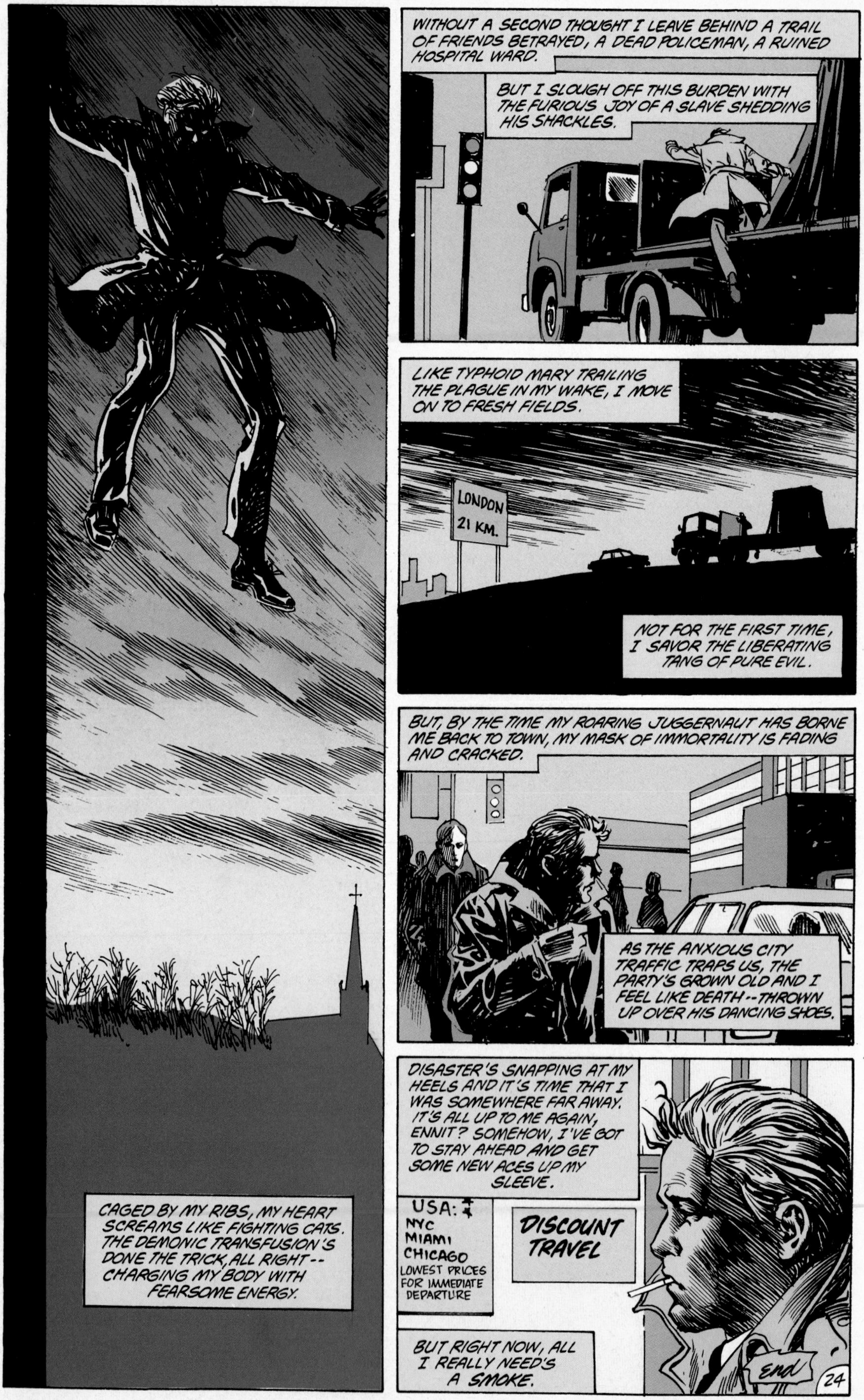
CAGED BY MY RIBS, MY HEART SCREAMS LIKE FIGHTING CATS. THE DEMONIC TRANSFUSION'S DONE THE TRICK, ALL RIGHT-- CHARGING MY BODY WITH FEARSOME ENERGY.
WITHOUT A SECOND THOUGHT I LEAVE BEHIND A TRAIL OF FRIENDS BETRAYED, A DEAD POLICEMAN, A RUINED HOSPITAL WARD.
BUT I SLOUGH OFF THIS BURDEN WITH THE FURIOUS JOY OF A SLAVE SHEDDING HIS SHACKLES.
LIKE TYPHOID MARY TRAILING THE PLAGUE IN MY WAKE, I MOVE ON TO FRESH FIELDS.
LONDON 21 KM.
NOT FOR THE FIRST TIME, I SAVOR THE LIBERATING TANG OF PURE EVIL.
BUT, BY THE TIME MY ROARING JUGGERNAUT HAS BORNE ME BACK TO TOWN, MY MASK OF IMMORTALITY IS FADING AND CRACKED.
AS THE ANXIOUS CITY TRAFFIC TRAPS US, THE PARTY'S GROWN OLD AND I FEEL LIKE DEATH --THROWN UP OVER HIS DANCING SHOES.
DISASTER'S SNAPPING AT MY HEELS AND IT'S TIME THAT I WAS SOMEWHERE FAR AWAY. IT'S ALL UP TO ME AGAIN, ENNIT? SOMEHOW, I'VE GOT TO STAY AHEAD AND GET SOME NEW ACES UP MY SLEEVE.
USA: NYC MIAMI CHICAGO LOWEST PRICES FOR IMMEDIATE DEPARTURE
DISCOUNT TRAVEL
BUT RIGHT NOW, ALL I REALLY NEED'S A SMOKE.
END
24

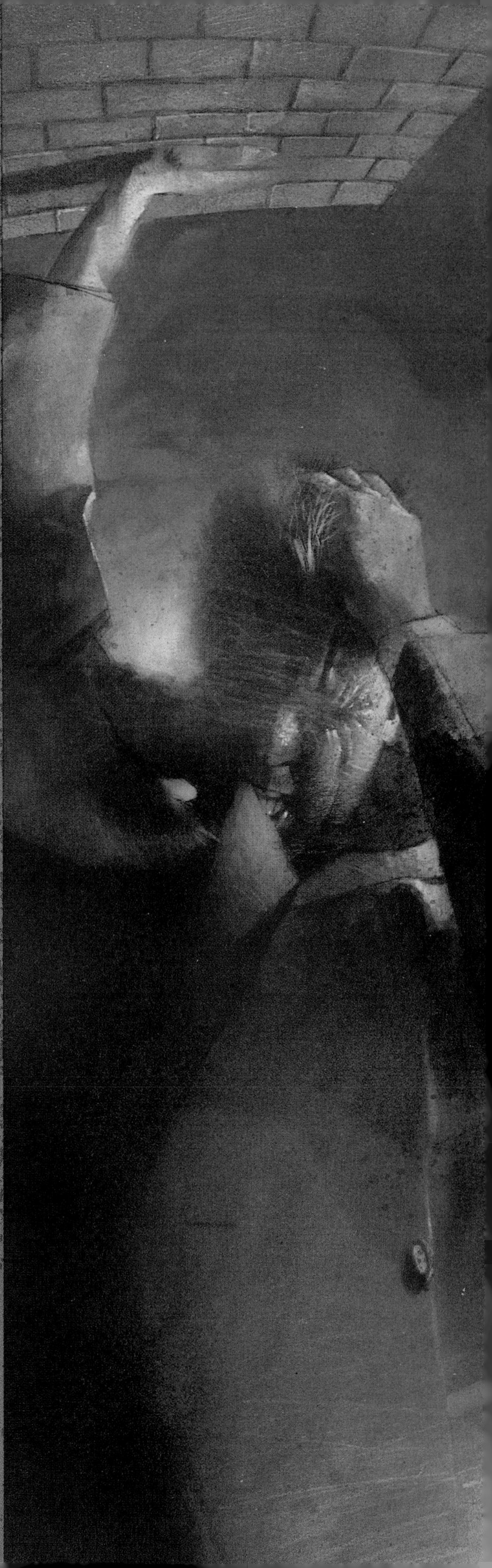

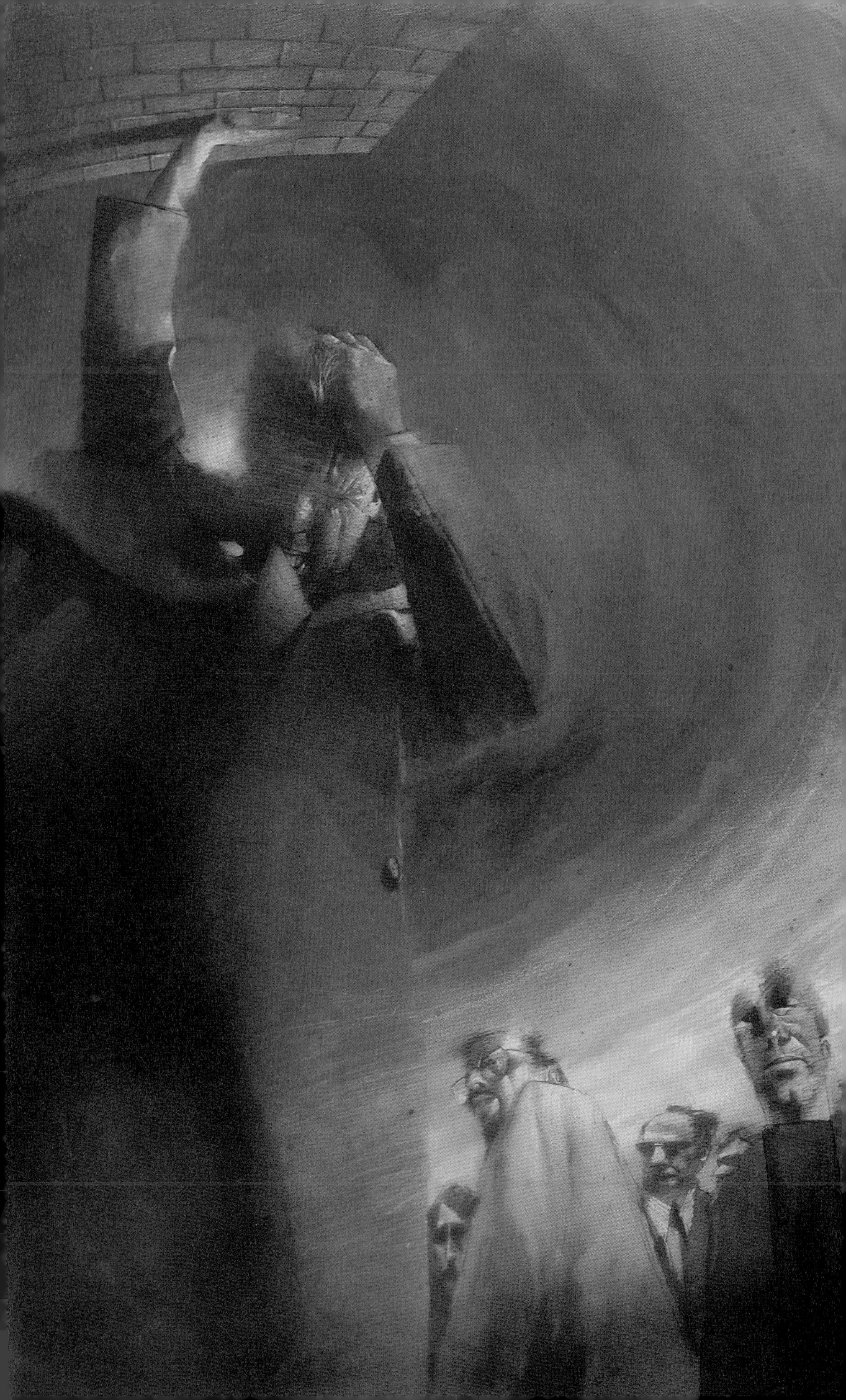

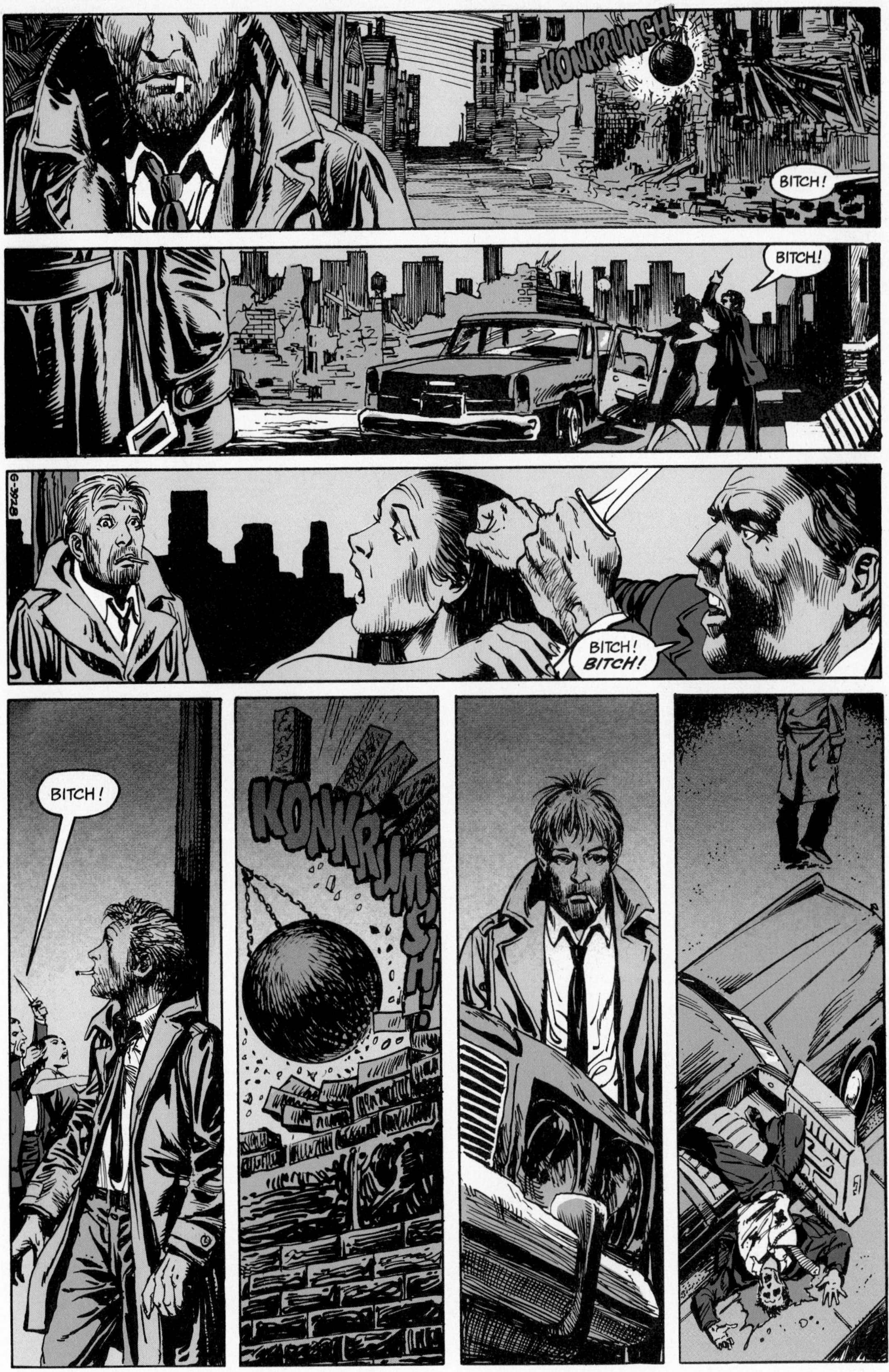
KONKRUMSH!
BITCH!
BITCH!
BITCH! BITCH!
BITCH!
KONKRUMSH!

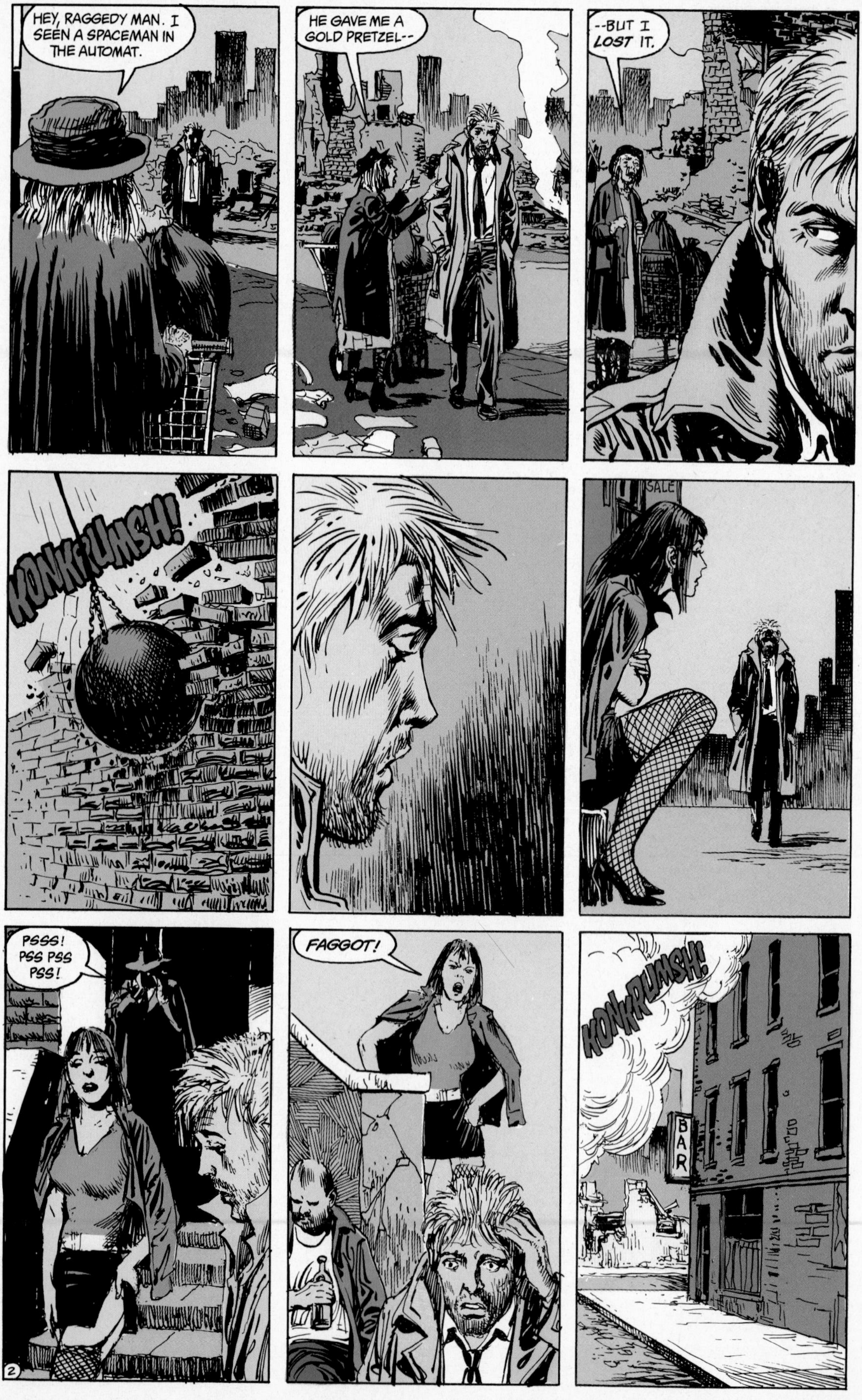

HEY, RAGGEDY MAN. I SEEN A SPACEMAN IN THE AUTOMAT.
HE GAVE ME A GOLD PRETZEL--
--BUT I LOST IT.
KONKRUMSH!
PSSS! PSS PSS PSS!
FAGGOT!
KONKRUMSH!
BAR

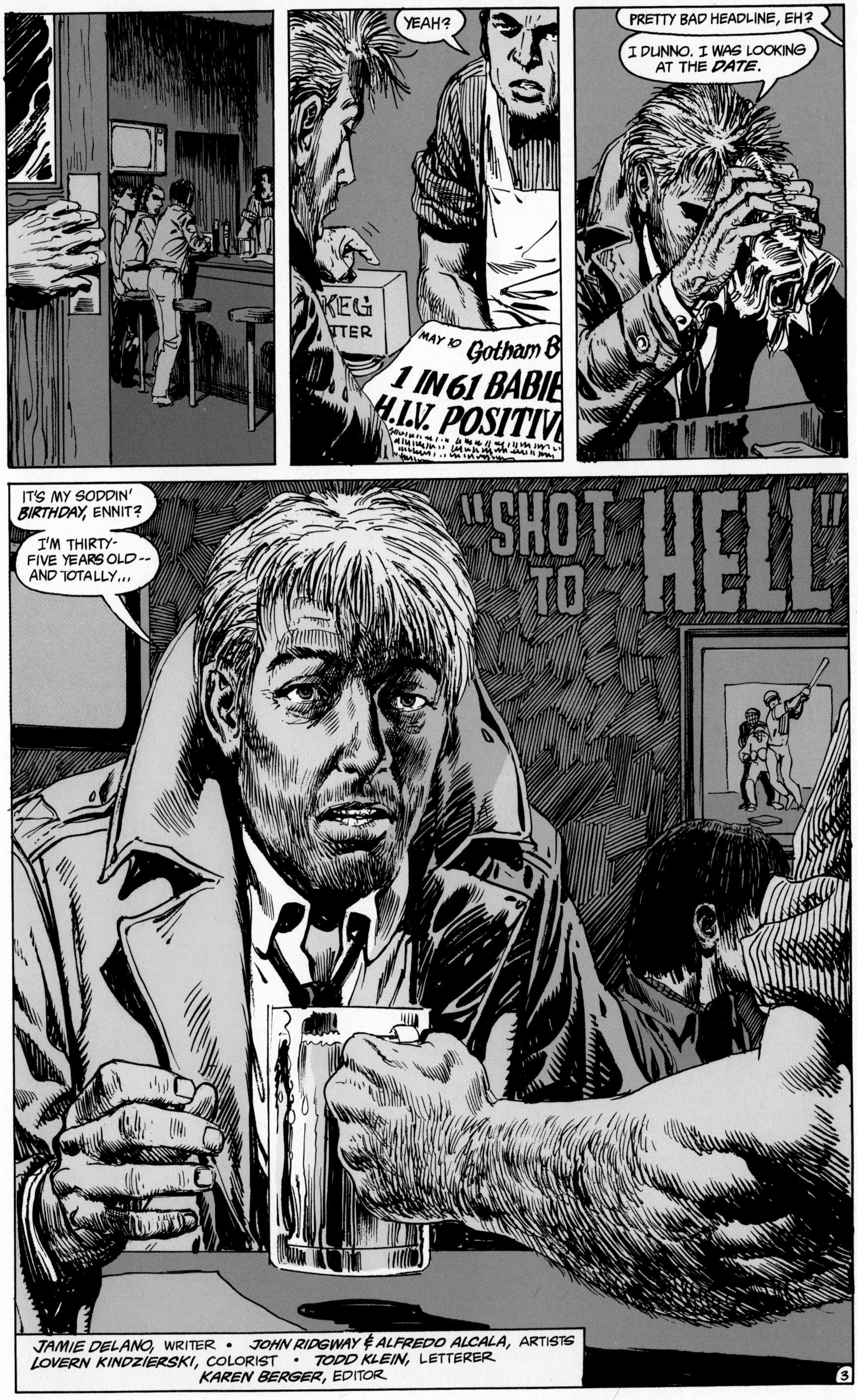
YEAH?
KEG
TTER
MAY 10 Gotham B
1 IN 61 BABIE
H.I.V. POSITIV
PRETTY BAD HEADLINE, EH?
I DUNNO. I WAS LOOKING AT THE *DATE*.
IT'S MY SODDIN' *BIRTHDAY*, ENNIT?
I'M THIRTY-FIVE YEARS OLD-- AND TOTALLY...
"SHOT TO HELL"
JAMIE DELANO, WRITER • JOHN RIDGWAY & ALFREDO ALCALA, ARTISTS
LOVERN KINDZIERSKI, COLORIST • TODD KLEIN, LETTERER
KAREN BERGER, EDITOR

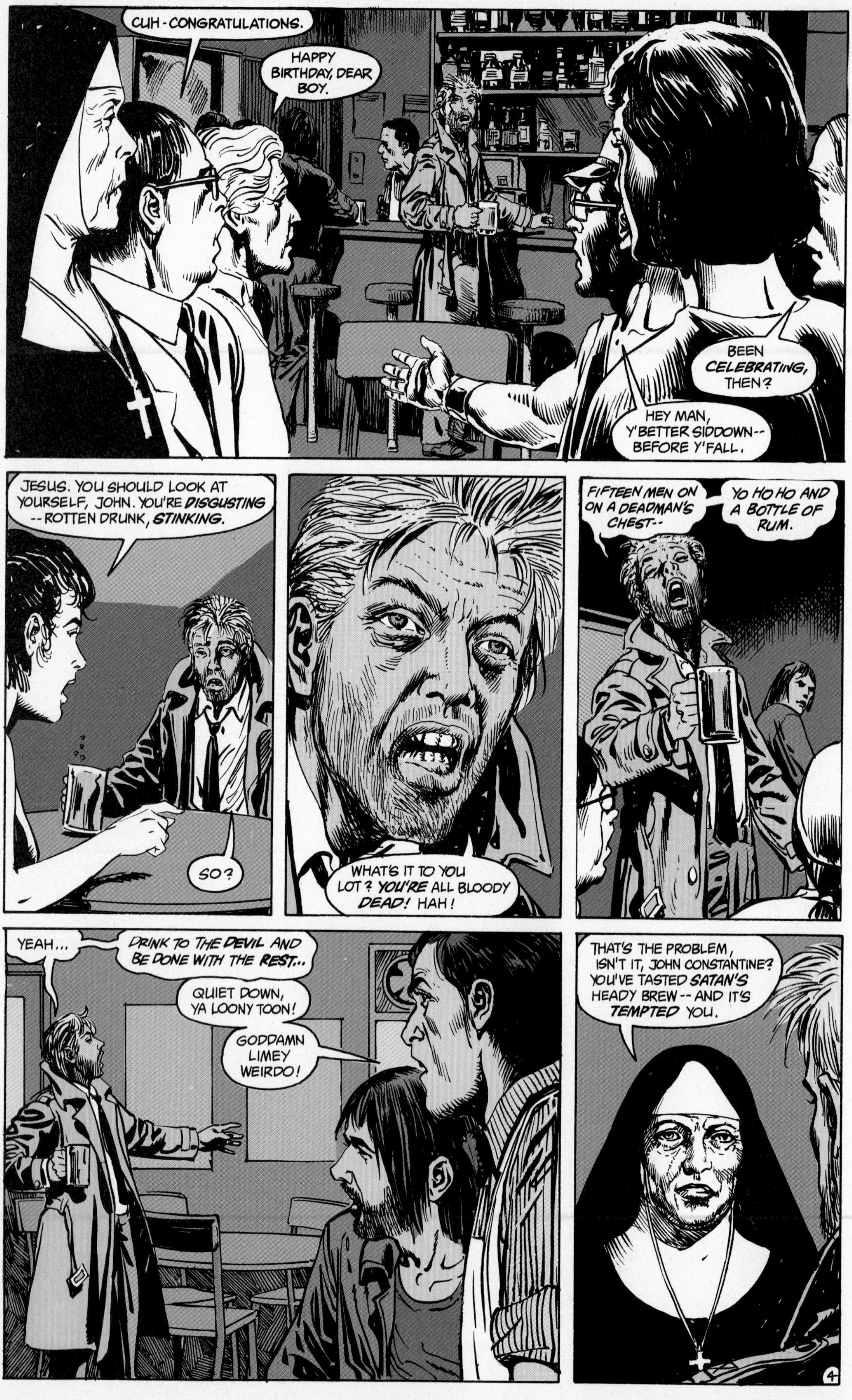

CUH - CONGRATULATIONS.
HAPPY BIRTHDAY, DEAR BOY.
BEEN CELEBRATING, THEN?
HEY MAN, Y'BETTER SIDDOWN-- BEFORE Y'FALL.
JESUS. YOU SHOULD LOOK AT YOURSELF, JOHN. YOU'RE DISGUSTING --ROTTEN DRUNK, STINKING.
SO?
WHAT'S IT TO YOU LOT? YOU'RE ALL BLOODY DEAD! HAH!
FIFTEEN MEN ON ON A DEADMAN'S CHEST--
YO HO HO AND A BOTTLE OF RUM.
YEAH...
DRINK TO THE DEVIL AND BE DONE WITH THE REST...
QUIET DOWN, YA LOONY TOON!
GODDAMN LIMEY WEIRDO!
THAT'S THE PROBLEM, ISN'T IT, JOHN CONSTANTINE? YOU'VE TASTED SATAN'S HEADY BREW -- AND IT'S TEMPTED YOU.
4

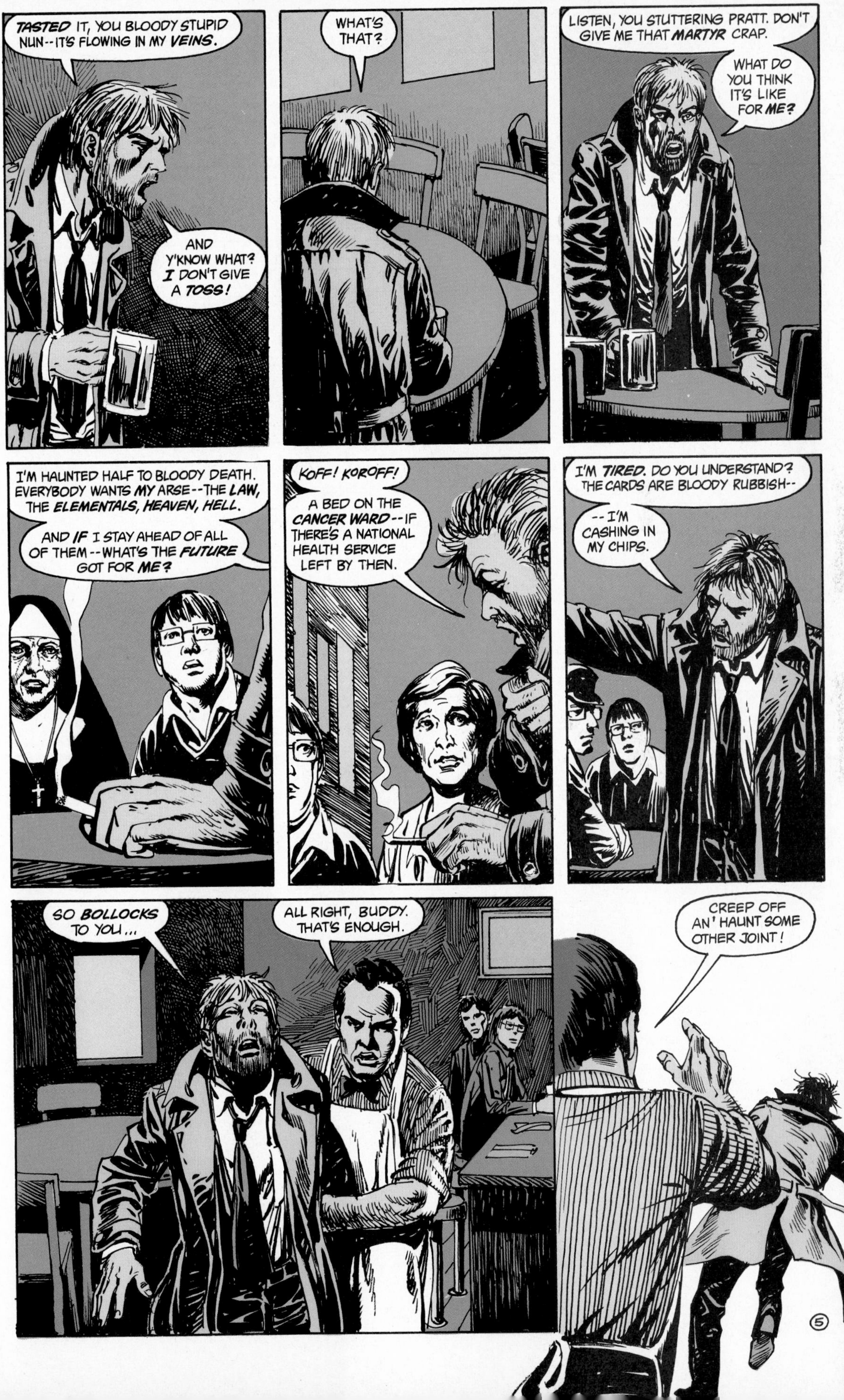

TASTED IT, YOU BLOODY STUPID NUN--IT'S FLOWING IN MY VEINS.
AND Y'KNOW WHAT? I DON'T GIVE A TOSS!
WHAT'S THAT?
LISTEN, YOU STUTTERING PRATT. DON'T GIVE ME THAT MARTYR CRAP.
WHAT DO YOU THINK IT'S LIKE FOR ME?
I'M HAUNTED HALF TO BLOODY DEATH. EVERYBODY WANTS MY ARSE--THE LAW, THE ELEMENTALS, HEAVEN, HELL.
AND IF I STAY AHEAD OF ALL OF THEM--WHAT'S THE FUTURE GOT FOR ME?
KOFF! KOROFF!
A BED ON THE CANCER WARD--IF THERE'S A NATIONAL HEALTH SERVICE LEFT BY THEN.
I'M TIRED. DO YOU UNDERSTAND? THE CARDS ARE BLOODY RUBBISH--
--I'M CASHING IN MY CHIPS.
SO BOLLOCKS TO YOU...
ALL RIGHT, BUDDY. THAT'S ENOUGH.
CREEP OFF AN' HAUNT SOME OTHER JOINT!

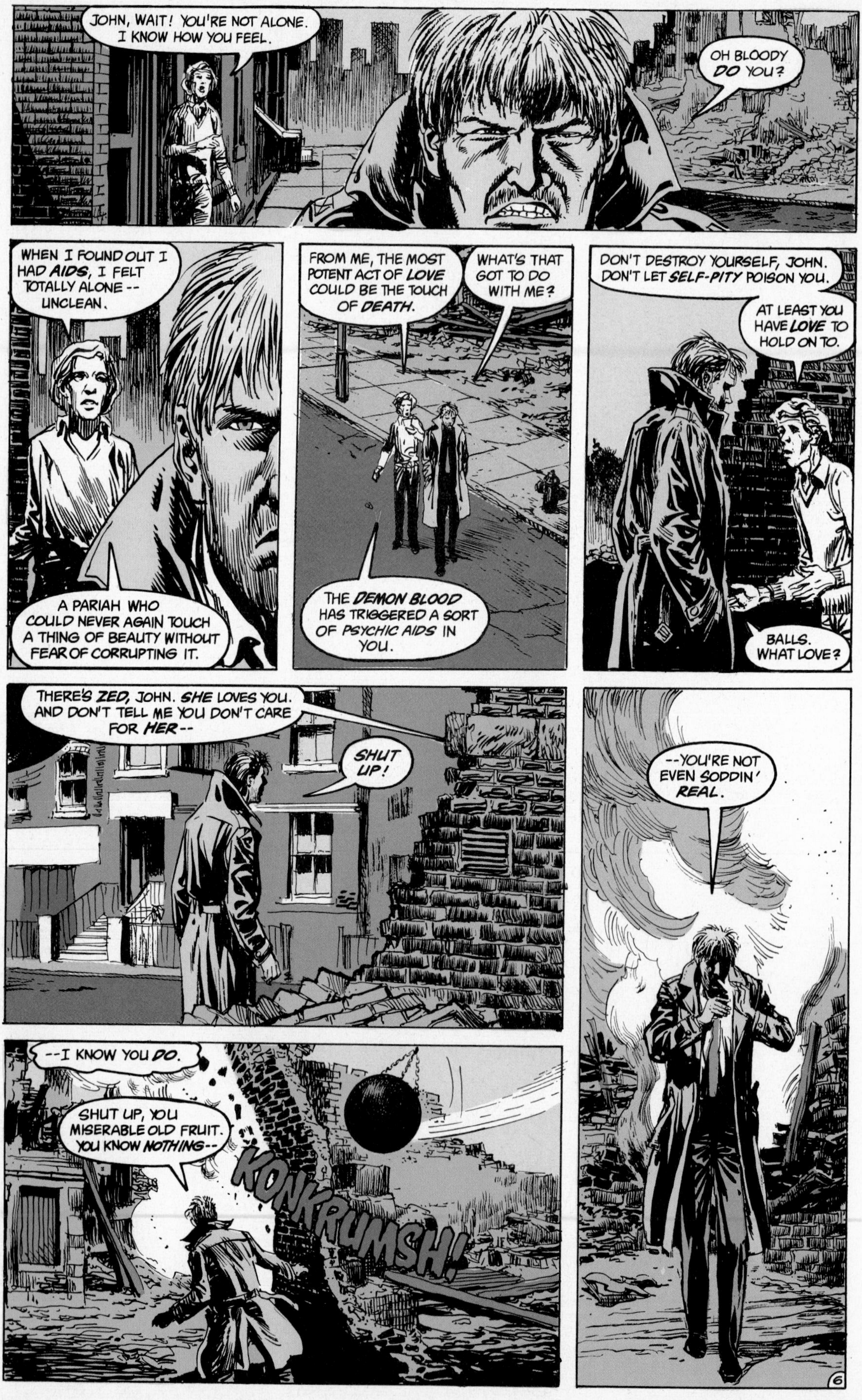
JOHN, WAIT! YOU'RE NOT ALONE. I KNOW HOW YOU FEEL.
OH BLOODY DO YOU?
WHEN I FOUND OUT I HAD AIDS, I FELT TOTALLY ALONE -- UNCLEAN.
A PARIAH WHO COULD NEVER AGAIN TOUCH A THING OF BEAUTY WITHOUT FEAR OF CORRUPTING IT.
FROM ME, THE MOST POTENT ACT OF LOVE COULD BE THE TOUCH OF DEATH.
WHAT'S THAT GOT TO DO WITH ME?
THE DEMON BLOOD HAS TRIGGERED A SORT OF PSYCHIC AIDS IN YOU.
DON'T DESTROY YOURSELF, JOHN. DON'T LET SELF-PITY POISON YOU.
AT LEAST YOU HAVE LOVE TO HOLD ON TO.
BALLS. WHAT LOVE?
THERE'S ZED, JOHN. SHE LOVES YOU. AND DON'T TELL ME YOU DON'T CARE FOR HER--
SHUT UP!
--I KNOW YOU DO.
SHUT UP, YOU MISERABLE OLD FRUIT. YOU KNOW NOTHING--
KONKRUMSH!
--YOU'RE NOT EVEN SODDIN' REAL.
6

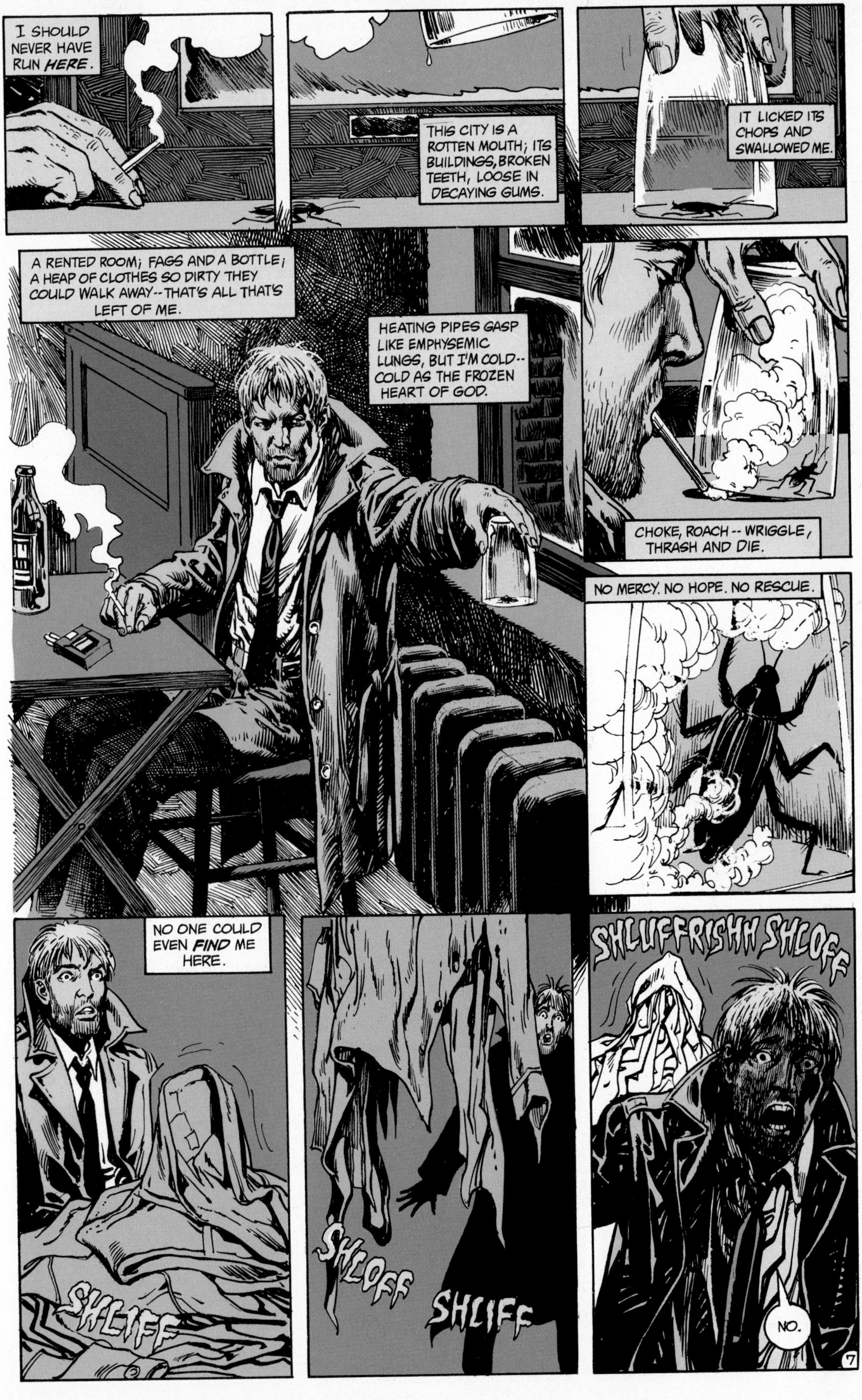
I SHOULD NEVER HAVE RUN HERE.
THIS CITY IS A ROTTEN MOUTH; ITS BUILDINGS, BROKEN TEETH, LOOSE IN DECAYING GUMS.
IT LICKED ITS CHOPS AND SWALLOWED ME.
A RENTED ROOM; FAGS AND A BOTTLE; A HEAP OF CLOTHES SO DIRTY THEY COULD WALK AWAY--THAT'S ALL THAT'S LEFT OF ME.
HEATING PIPES GASP LIKE EMPHYSEMIC LUNGS, BUT I'M COLD-- COLD AS THE FROZEN HEART OF GOD.
CHOKE, ROACH -- WRIGGLE, THRASH AND DIE.
NO MERCY. NO HOPE. NO RESCUE.
NO ONE COULD EVEN FIND ME HERE.
SHLIFF
SHLOFF
SHLIFF
SHLUFFRISHH SHLOFF
NO.
17

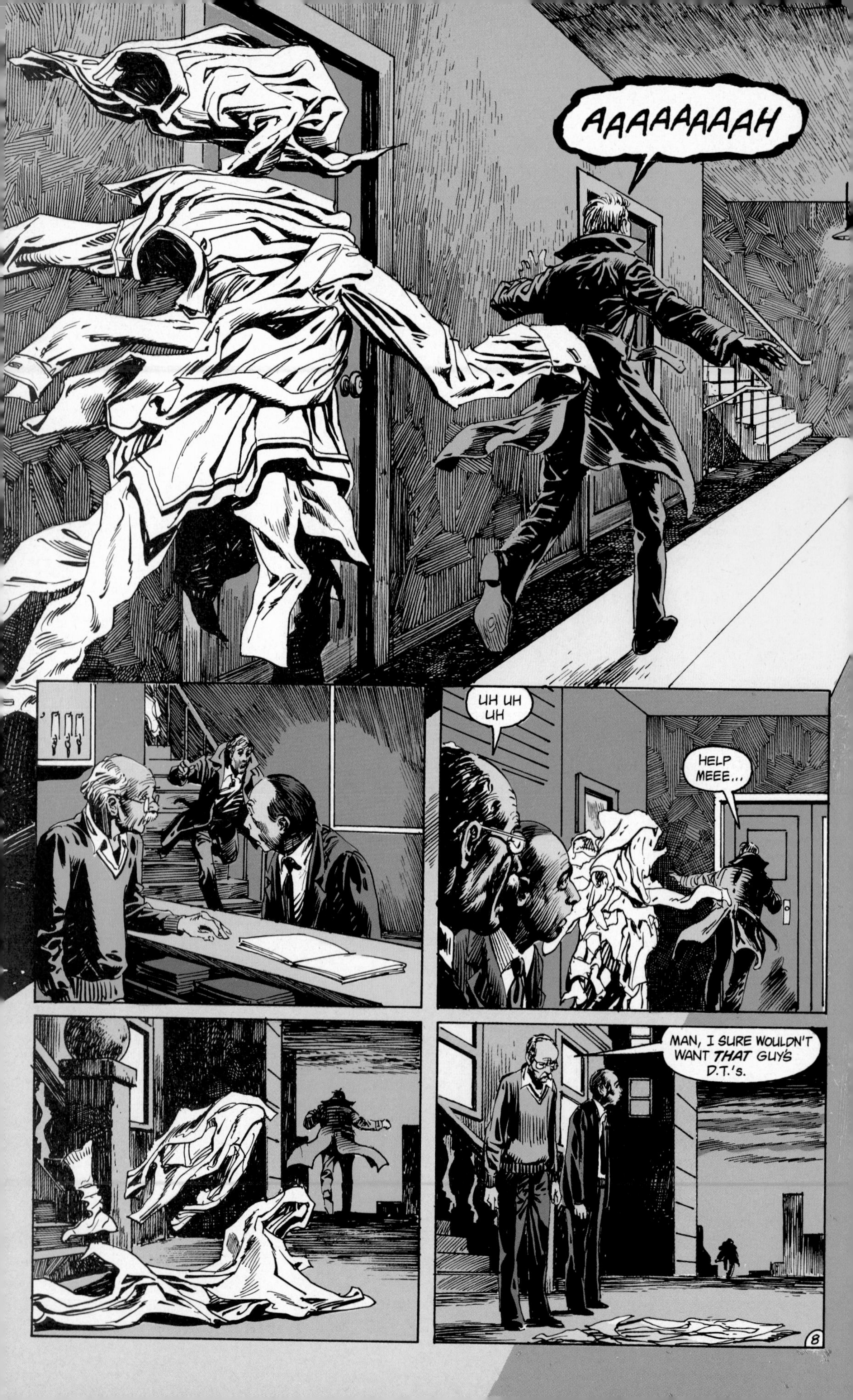
AAAAAAAAH
UH UH UH
HELP MEEE...
MAN, I SURE WOULDN'T WANT THAT GUY'S D.T.'s.
8

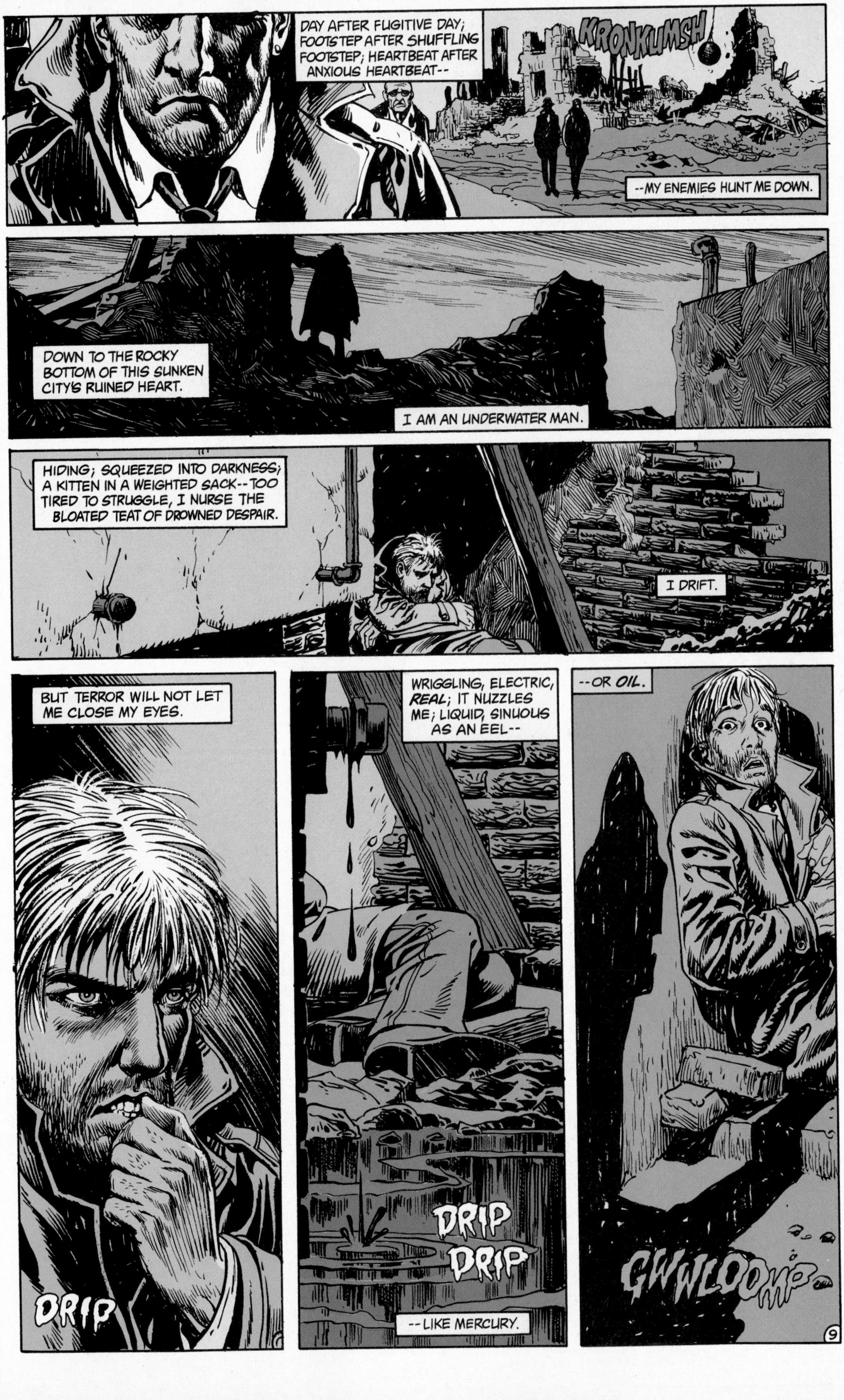
DAY AFTER FUGITIVE DAY; FOOTSTEP AFTER SHUFFLING FOOTSTEP; HEARTBEAT AFTER ANXIOUS HEARTBEAT--
KRONKLUMSH
--MY ENEMIES HUNT ME DOWN.
DOWN TO THE ROCKY BOTTOM OF THIS SUNKEN CITY'S RUINED HEART.
I AM AN UNDERWATER MAN.
HIDING; SQUEEZED INTO DARKNESS; A KITTEN IN A WEIGHTED SACK--TOO TIRED TO STRUGGLE, I NURSE THE BLOATED TEAT OF DROWNED DESPAIR.
I DRIFT.
BUT TERROR WILL NOT LET ME CLOSE MY EYES.
DRIP
WRIGGLING, ELECTRIC, REAL; IT NUZZLES ME; LIQUID, SINUOUS AS AN EEL--
DRIP
DRIP
--LIKE MERCURY.
--OR OIL.
GWWLOOMP
9

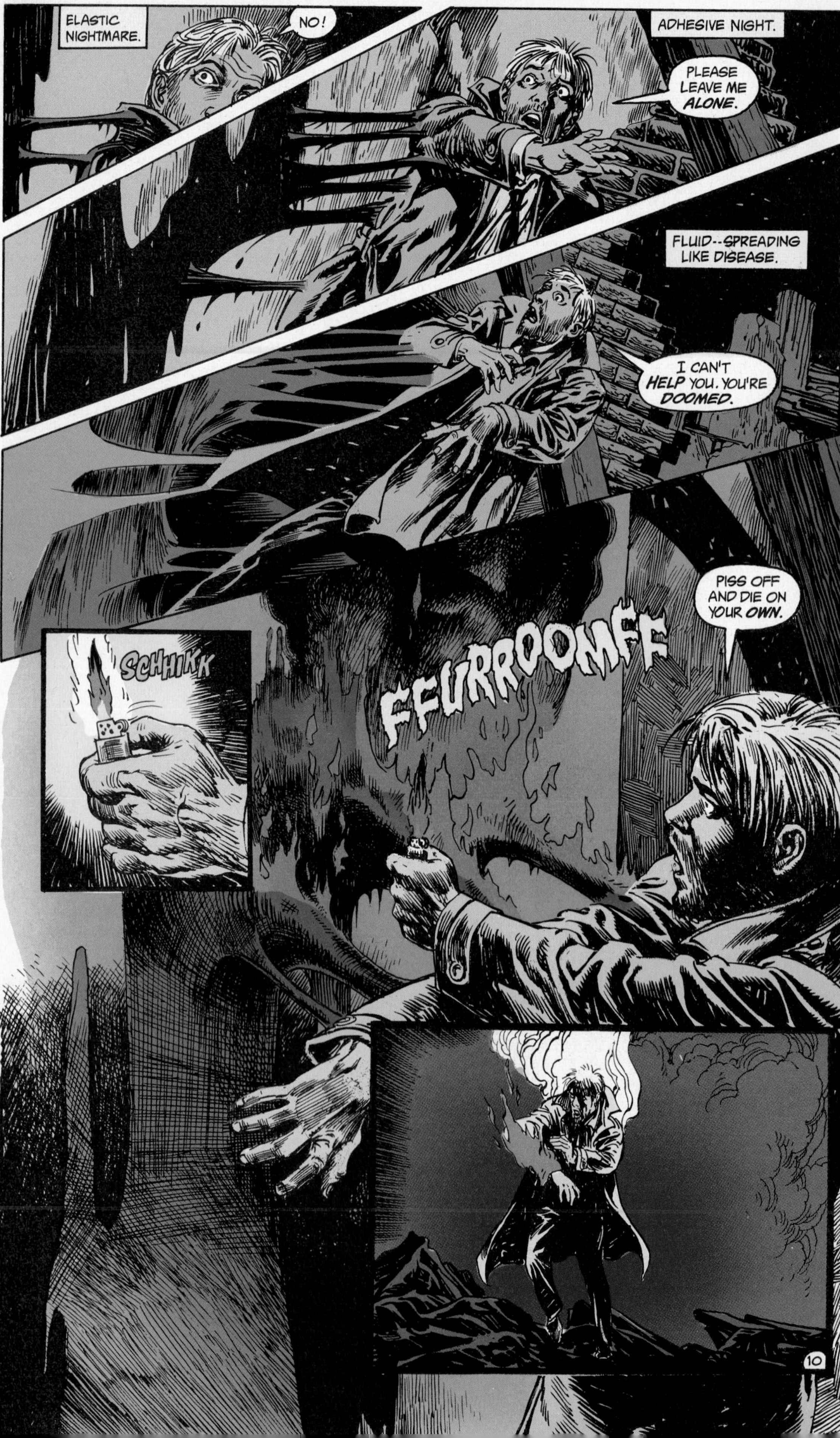

ELASTIC NIGHTMARE.
NO!
ADHESIVE NIGHT.
PLEASE LEAVE ME ALONE.
FLUID--SPREADING LIKE DISEASE.
I CAN'T HELP YOU. YOU'RE DOOMED.
SCHHIKK
PISS OFF AND DIE ON YOUR OWN.
FFURROOMFF

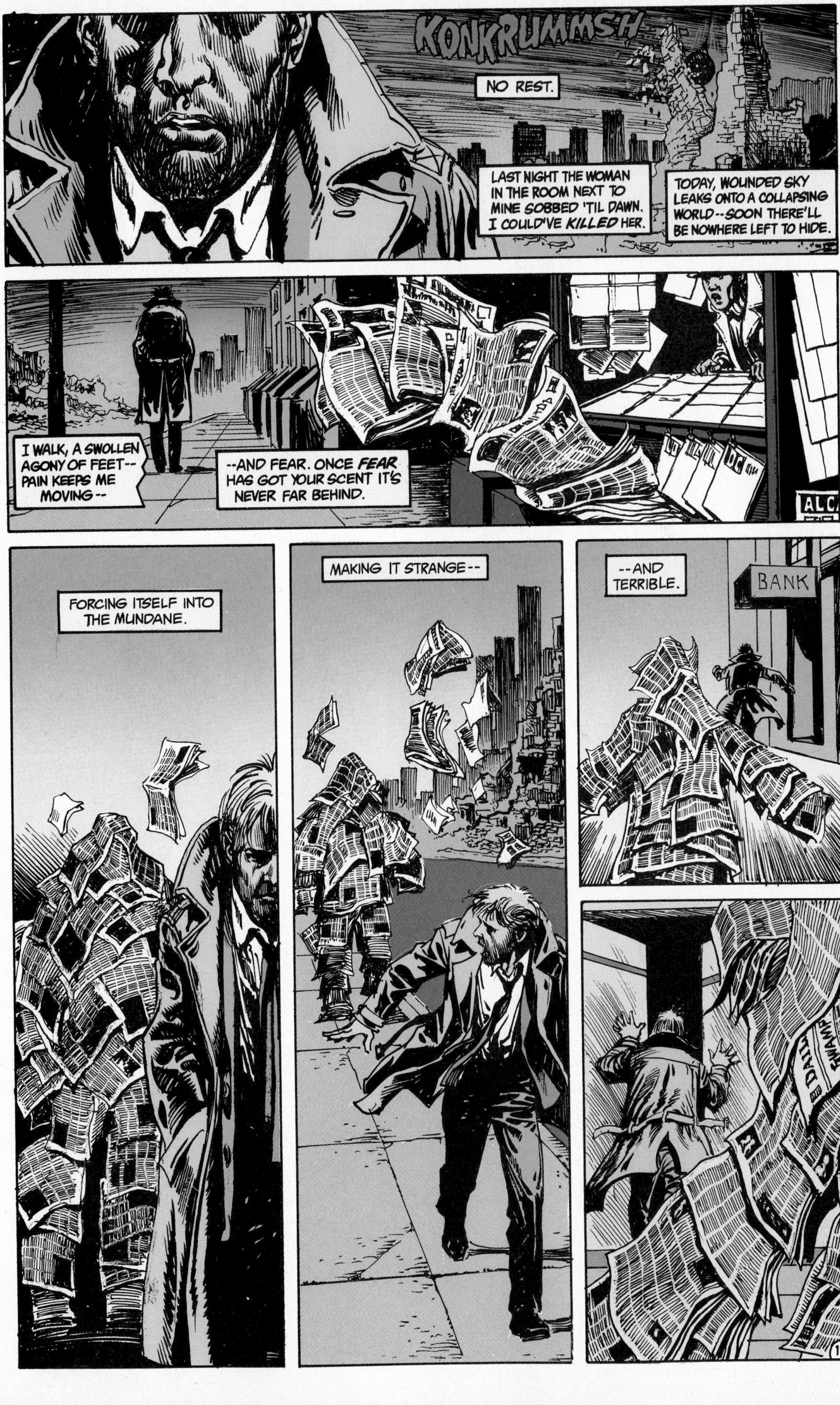
KONKRUMMSH
NO REST.
LAST NIGHT THE WOMAN IN THE ROOM NEXT TO MINE SOBBED 'TIL DAWN. I COULD'VE KILLED HER.
TODAY, WOUNDED SKY LEAKS ONTO A COLLAPSING WORLD--SOON THERE'LL BE NOWHERE LEFT TO HIDE.
I WALK, A SWOLLEN AGONY OF FEET--PAIN KEEPS ME MOVING--
--AND FEAR. ONCE FEAR HAS GOT YOUR SCENT IT'S NEVER FAR BEHIND.
FORCING ITSELF INTO THE MUNDANE.
MAKING IT STRANGE--
--AND TERRIBLE.
BANK

HE'S WEAK, AND *DESPERATE* TO TRAIL ME TO THIS DEAD PLACE.

BUT OF ALL THE ABANDONED GHOSTS THAT HAUNT ME --

EEEEEEEE

WHAT'S HAPPENING...?

PANIC EJECTS ME INTO A FROZEN WORLD --

--THAT'S QUICKLY THAWED BY JOYOUS GREED.

LOOK AT THE *MONEY*, MAN.

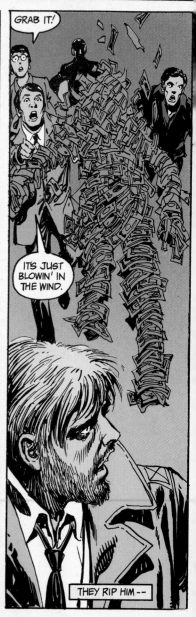

GRAB IT!

IT'S JUST BLOWIN' IN THE WIND.

THEY RIP HIM --

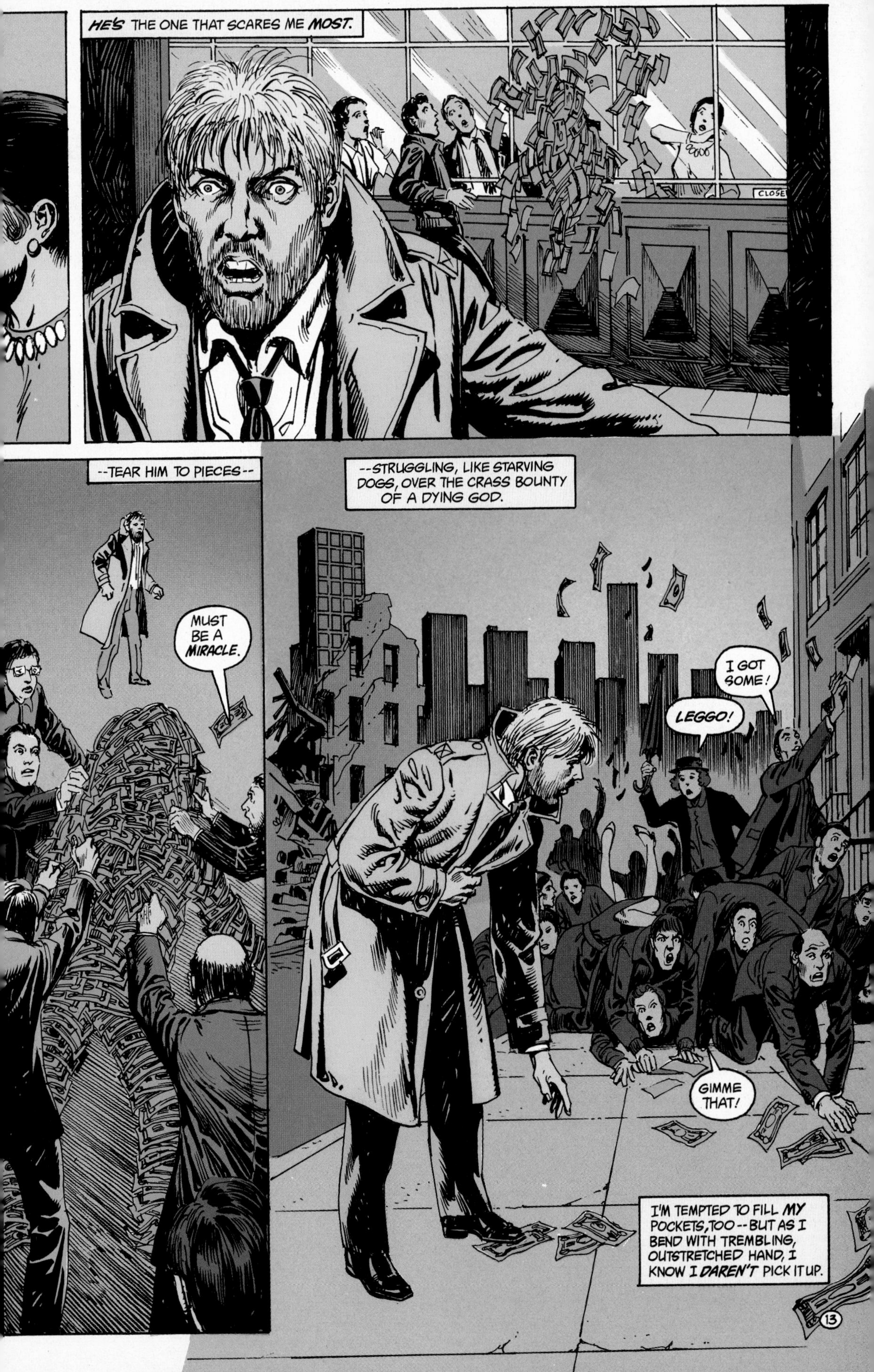
HE'S THE ONE THAT SCARES ME MOST.
CLOSE
--TEAR HIM TO PIECES--
MUST BE A MIRACLE.
--STRUGGLING, LIKE STARVING DOGS, OVER THE CRASS BOUNTY OF A DYING GOD.
I GOT SOME!
LEGGO!
GIMME THAT!
I'M TEMPTED TO FILL MY POCKETS, TOO -- BUT AS I BEND WITH TREMBLING, OUTSTRETCHED HAND, I KNOW I DAREN'T PICK IT UP.

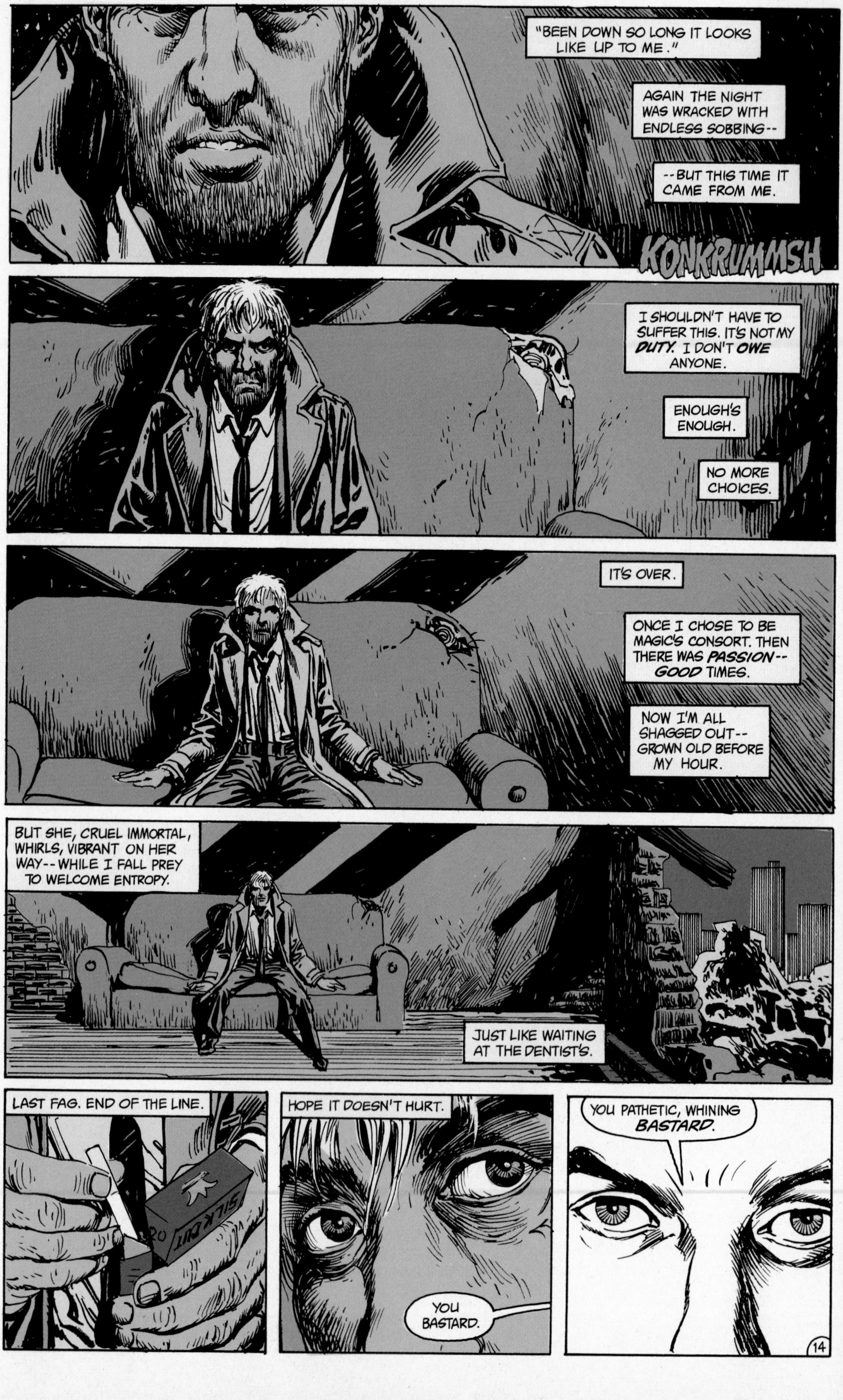
"BEEN DOWN SO LONG IT LOOKS LIKE UP TO ME."
AGAIN THE NIGHT WAS WRACKED WITH ENDLESS SOBBING--
--BUT THIS TIME IT CAME FROM ME.
KONKRUMMSH
I SHOULDN'T HAVE TO SUFFER THIS. IT'S NOT MY DUTY. I DON'T OWE ANYONE.
ENOUGH'S ENOUGH.
NO MORE CHOICES.
IT'S OVER.
ONCE I CHOSE TO BE MAGIC'S CONSORT. THEN THERE WAS PASSION-- GOOD TIMES.
NOW I'M ALL SHAGGED OUT-- GROWN OLD BEFORE MY HOUR.
BUT SHE, CRUEL IMMORTAL, WHIRLS, VIBRANT ON HER WAY-- WHILE I FALL PREY TO WELCOME ENTROPY.
JUST LIKE WAITING AT THE DENTIST'S.
LAST FAG. END OF THE LINE.
SILK CUT
20
HOPE IT DOESN'T HURT.
YOU BASTARD.
YOU PATHETIC, WHINING BASTARD.
14

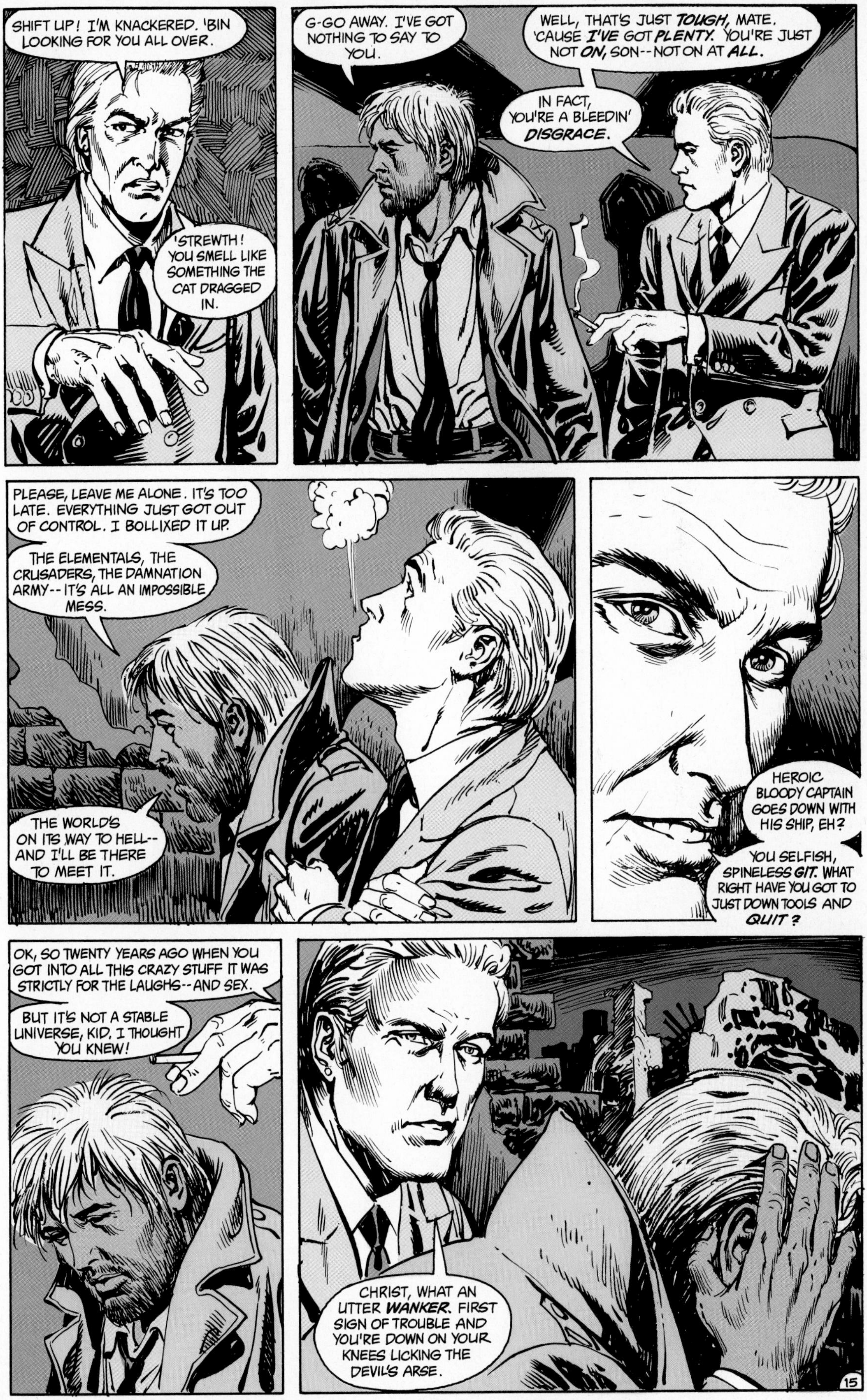
SHIFT UP! I'M KNACKERED. 'BIN LOOKING FOR YOU ALL OVER.
'STREWTH! YOU SMELL LIKE SOMETHING THE CAT DRAGGED IN.
G-GO AWAY. I'VE GOT NOTHING TO SAY TO YOU.
WELL, THAT'S JUST TOUGH, MATE. 'CAUSE I'VE GOT PLENTY. YOU'RE JUST NOT ON, SON--NOT ON AT ALL.
IN FACT, YOU'RE A BLEEDIN' DISGRACE.
PLEASE, LEAVE ME ALONE. IT'S TOO LATE. EVERYTHING JUST GOT OUT OF CONTROL. I BOLLIXED IT UP.
THE ELEMENTALS, THE CRUSADERS, THE DAMNATION ARMY--IT'S ALL AN IMPOSSIBLE MESS.
THE WORLD'S ON ITS WAY TO HELL--AND I'LL BE THERE TO MEET IT.
HEROIC BLOODY CAPTAIN GOES DOWN WITH HIS SHIP, EH?
YOU SELFISH, SPINELESS GIT. WHAT RIGHT HAVE YOU GOT TO JUST DOWN TOOLS AND QUIT?
OK, SO TWENTY YEARS AGO WHEN YOU GOT INTO ALL THIS CRAZY STUFF IT WAS STRICTLY FOR THE LAUGHS--AND SEX.
BUT IT'S NOT A STABLE UNIVERSE, KID. I THOUGHT YOU KNEW!
CHRIST, WHAT AN UTTER WANKER. FIRST SIGN OF TROUBLE AND YOU'RE DOWN ON YOUR KNEES LICKING THE DEVIL'S ARSE.
15

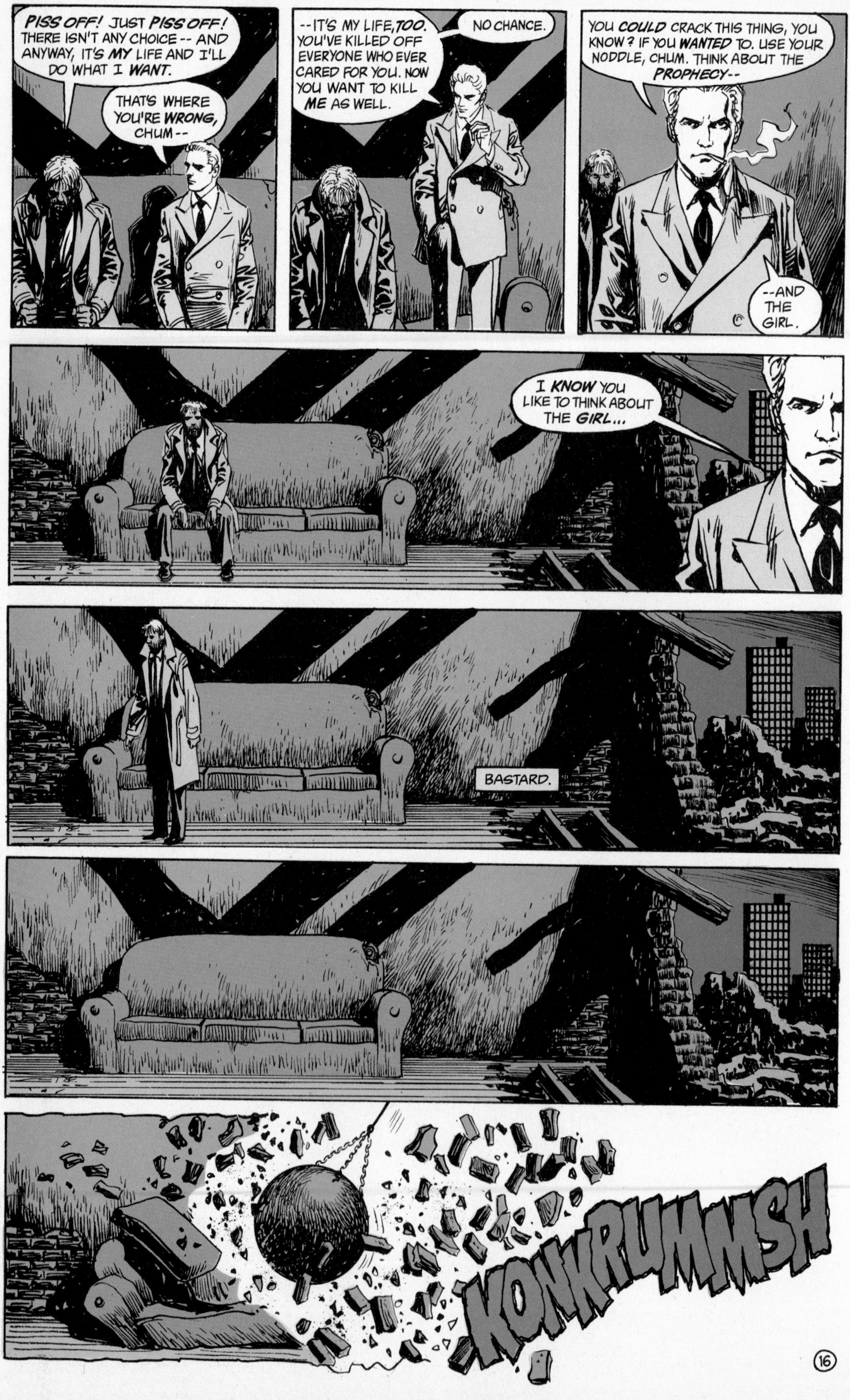

PISS OFF! JUST PISS OFF! THERE ISN'T ANY CHOICE -- AND ANYWAY, IT'S MY LIFE AND I'LL DO WHAT I WANT.
THAT'S WHERE YOU'RE WRONG, CHUM --
-- IT'S MY LIFE, TOO. YOU'VE KILLED OFF EVERYONE WHO EVER CARED FOR YOU. NOW YOU WANT TO KILL ME AS WELL.
NO CHANCE.
YOU COULD CRACK THIS THING, YOU KNOW? IF YOU WANTED TO. USE YOUR NODDLE, CHUM. THINK ABOUT THE PROPHECY--
--AND THE GIRL.
I KNOW YOU LIKE TO THINK ABOUT THE GIRL...
BASTARD.
KONKRUMMSH

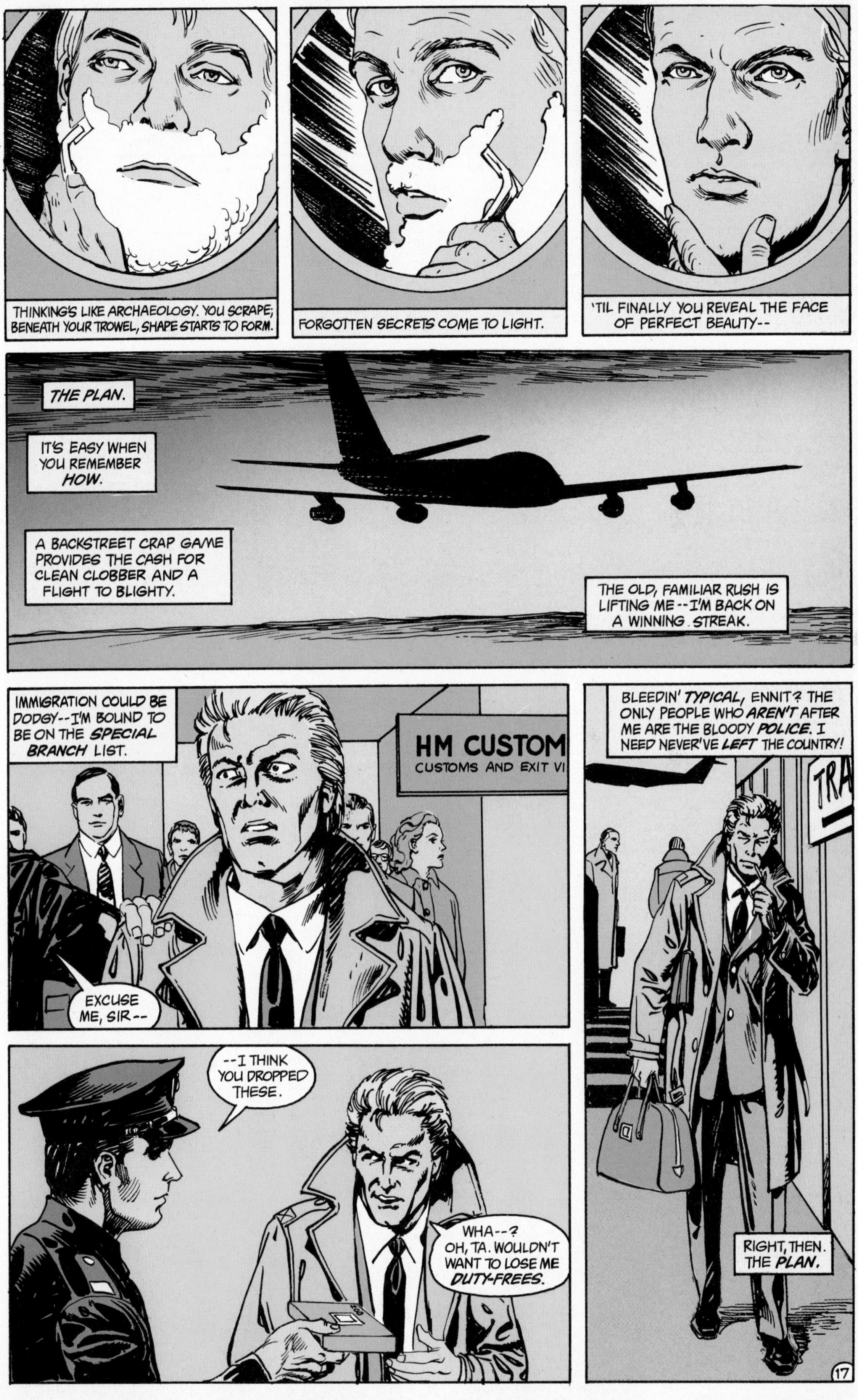
THINKING'S LIKE ARCHAEOLOGY. YOU SCRAPE; BENEATH YOUR TROWEL, SHAPE STARTS TO FORM.
FORGOTTEN SECRETS COME TO LIGHT.
'TIL FINALLY YOU REVEAL THE FACE OF PERFECT BEAUTY--
THE PLAN.
IT'S EASY WHEN YOU REMEMBER HOW.
A BACKSTREET CRAP GAME PROVIDES THE CASH FOR CLEAN CLOBBER AND A FLIGHT TO BLIGHTY.
THE OLD, FAMILIAR RUSH IS LIFTING ME--I'M BACK ON A WINNING STREAK.
IMMIGRATION COULD BE DODGY--I'M BOUND TO BE ON THE SPECIAL BRANCH LIST.
HM CUSTOM
CUSTOMS AND EXIT VI
EXCUSE ME, SIR--
--I THINK YOU DROPPED THESE.
WHA--? OH, TA. WOULDN'T WANT TO LOSE ME DUTY-FREES.
BLEEDIN' TYPICAL, ENNIT? THE ONLY PEOPLE WHO AREN'T AFTER ME ARE THE BLOODY POLICE. I NEED NEVER'VE LEFT THE COUNTRY!
RIGHT, THEN. THE PLAN.

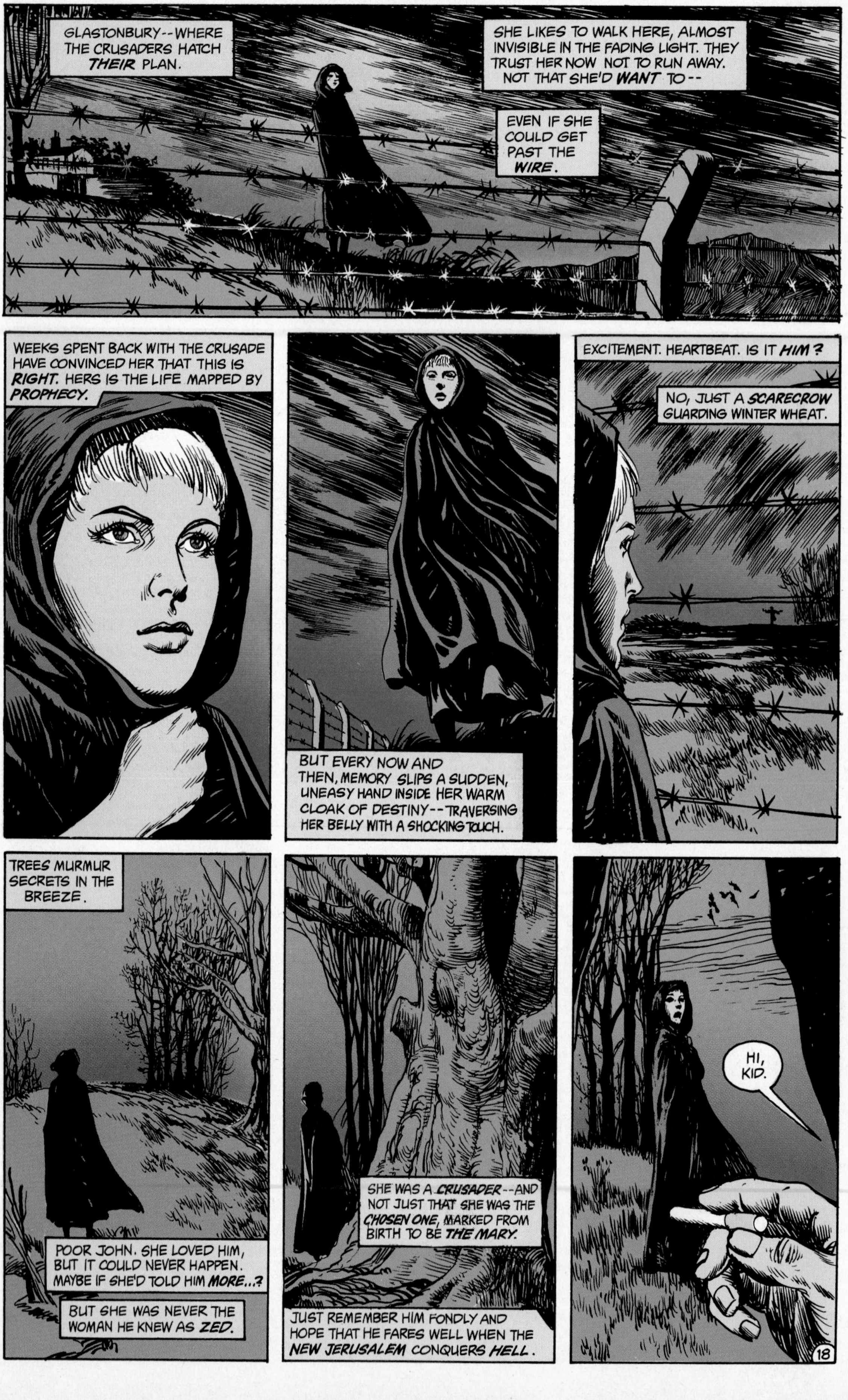
GLASTONBURY--WHERE THE CRUSADERS HATCH THEIR PLAN.
SHE LIKES TO WALK HERE, ALMOST INVISIBLE IN THE FADING LIGHT. THEY TRUST HER NOW NOT TO RUN AWAY. NOT THAT SHE'D WANT TO--
EVEN IF SHE COULD GET PAST THE WIRE.
WEEKS SPENT BACK WITH THE CRUSADE HAVE CONVINCED HER THAT THIS IS RIGHT. HERS IS THE LIFE MAPPED BY PROPHECY.
BUT EVERY NOW AND THEN, MEMORY SLIPS A SUDDEN, UNEASY HAND INSIDE HER WARM CLOAK OF DESTINY--TRAVERSING HER BELLY WITH A SHOCKING TOUCH.
EXCITEMENT. HEARTBEAT. IS IT HIM?
NO, JUST A SCARECROW GUARDING WINTER WHEAT.
TREES MURMUR SECRETS IN THE BREEZE.
POOR JOHN. SHE LOVED HIM, BUT IT COULD NEVER HAPPEN. MAYBE IF SHE'D TOLD HIM MORE...?
BUT SHE WAS NEVER THE WOMAN HE KNEW AS ZED.
SHE WAS A CRUSADER--AND NOT JUST THAT SHE WAS THE CHOSEN ONE, MARKED FROM BIRTH TO BE THE MARY.
JUST REMEMBER HIM FONDLY AND HOPE THAT HE FARES WELL WHEN THE NEW JERUSALEM CONQUERS HELL.
HI, KID.

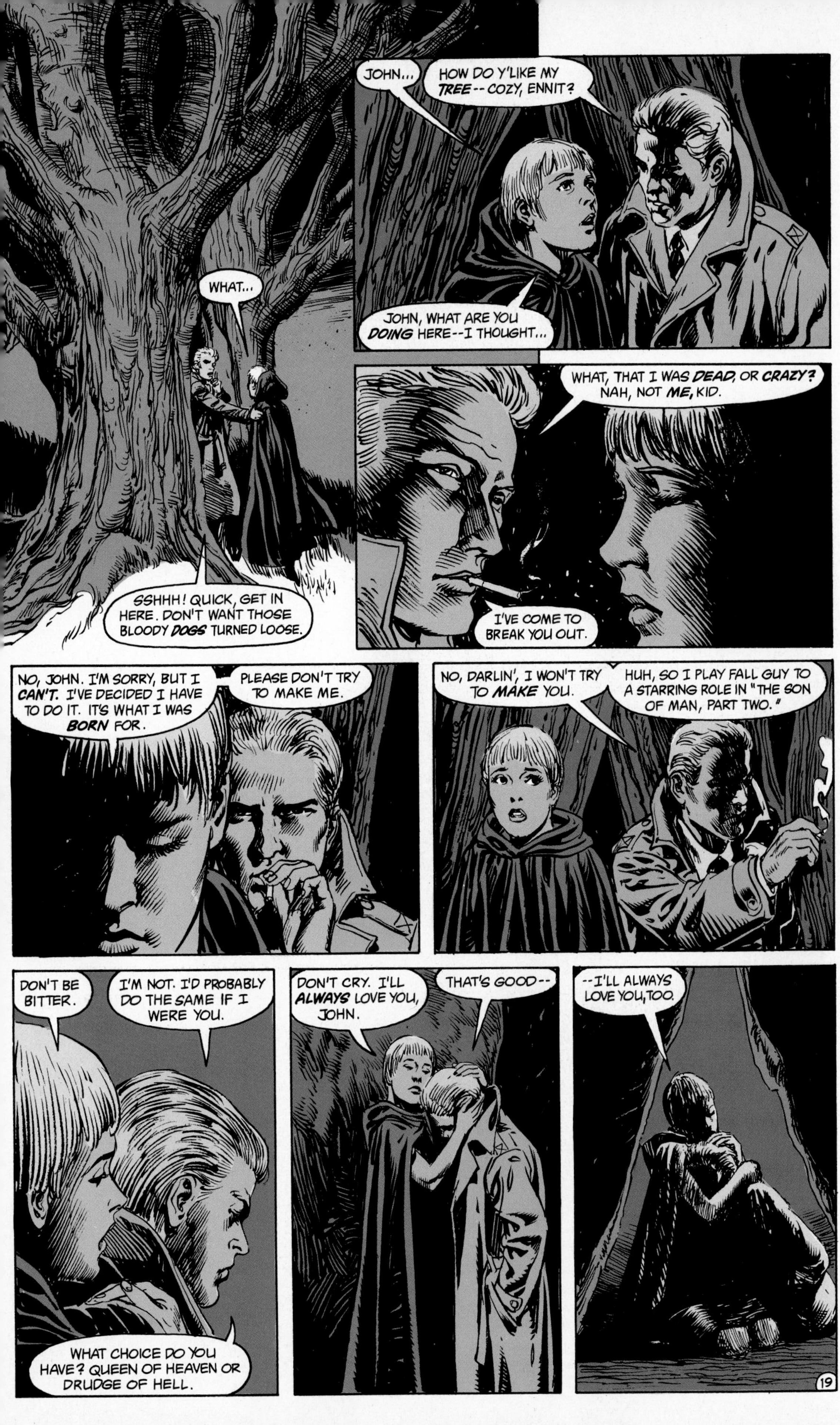

WHAT...
SSHHH! QUICK, GET IN HERE. DON'T WANT THOSE BLOODY DOGS TURNED LOOSE.
JOHN...
HOW DO Y'LIKE MY TREE -- COZY, ENNIT?
JOHN, WHAT ARE YOU DOING HERE--I THOUGHT...
WHAT, THAT I WAS DEAD, OR CRAZY? NAH, NOT ME, KID.
I'VE COME TO BREAK YOU OUT.
NO, JOHN. I'M SORRY, BUT I CAN'T. I'VE DECIDED I HAVE TO DO IT. IT'S WHAT I WAS BORN FOR.
PLEASE DON'T TRY TO MAKE ME.
NO, DARLIN', I WON'T TRY TO MAKE YOU.
HUH, SO I PLAY FALL GUY TO A STARRING ROLE IN "THE SON OF MAN, PART TWO."
DON'T BE BITTER.
I'M NOT. I'D PROBABLY DO THE SAME IF I WERE YOU.
WHAT CHOICE DO YOU HAVE? QUEEN OF HEAVEN OR DRUDGE OF HELL.
DON'T CRY. I'LL ALWAYS LOVE YOU, JOHN.
THAT'S GOOD--
--I'LL ALWAYS LOVE YOU, TOO.

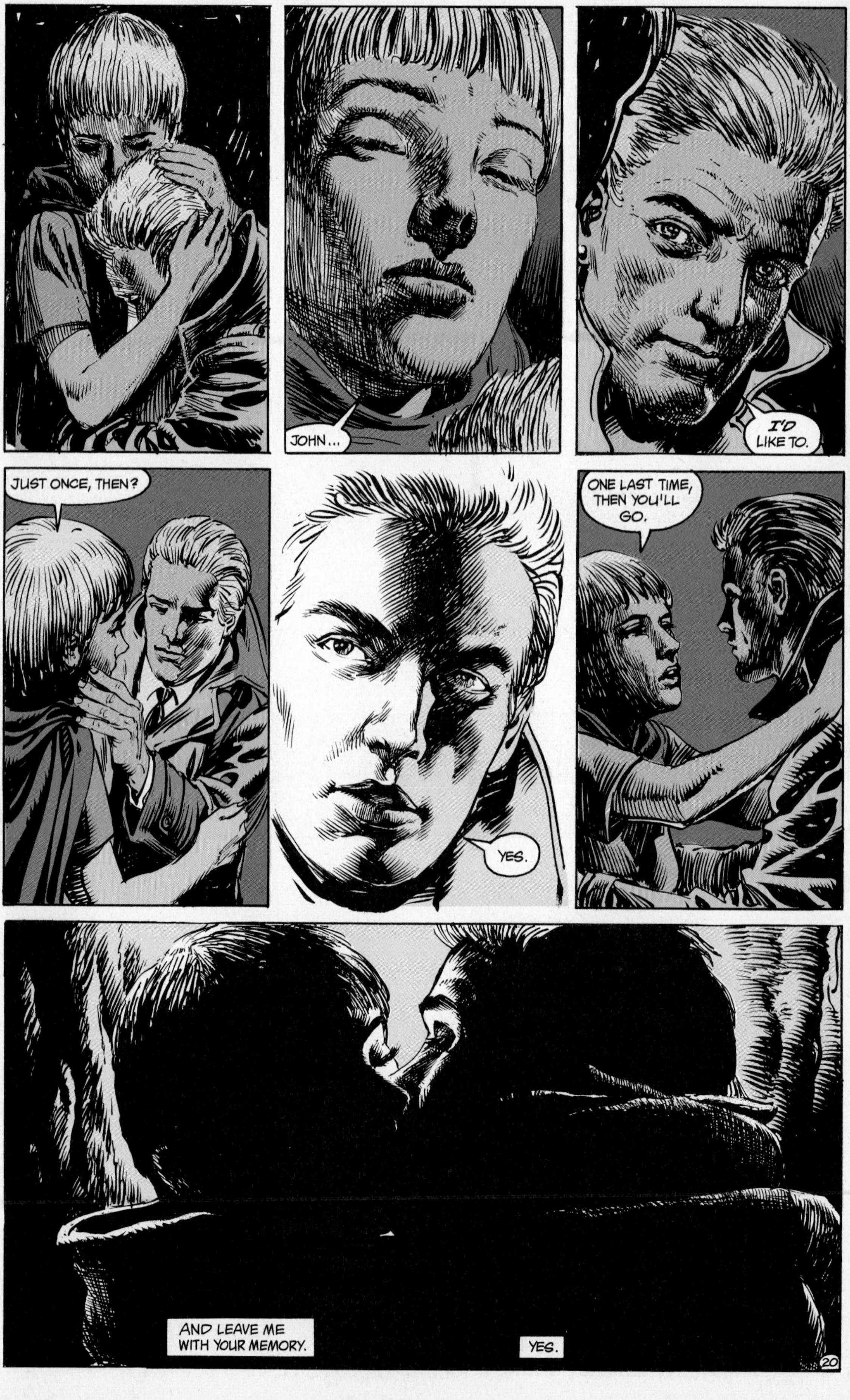
JOHN...
I'D LIKE TO.
JUST ONCE, THEN?
YES.
ONE LAST TIME, THEN YOU'LL GO.
AND LEAVE ME WITH YOUR MEMORY.
YES.

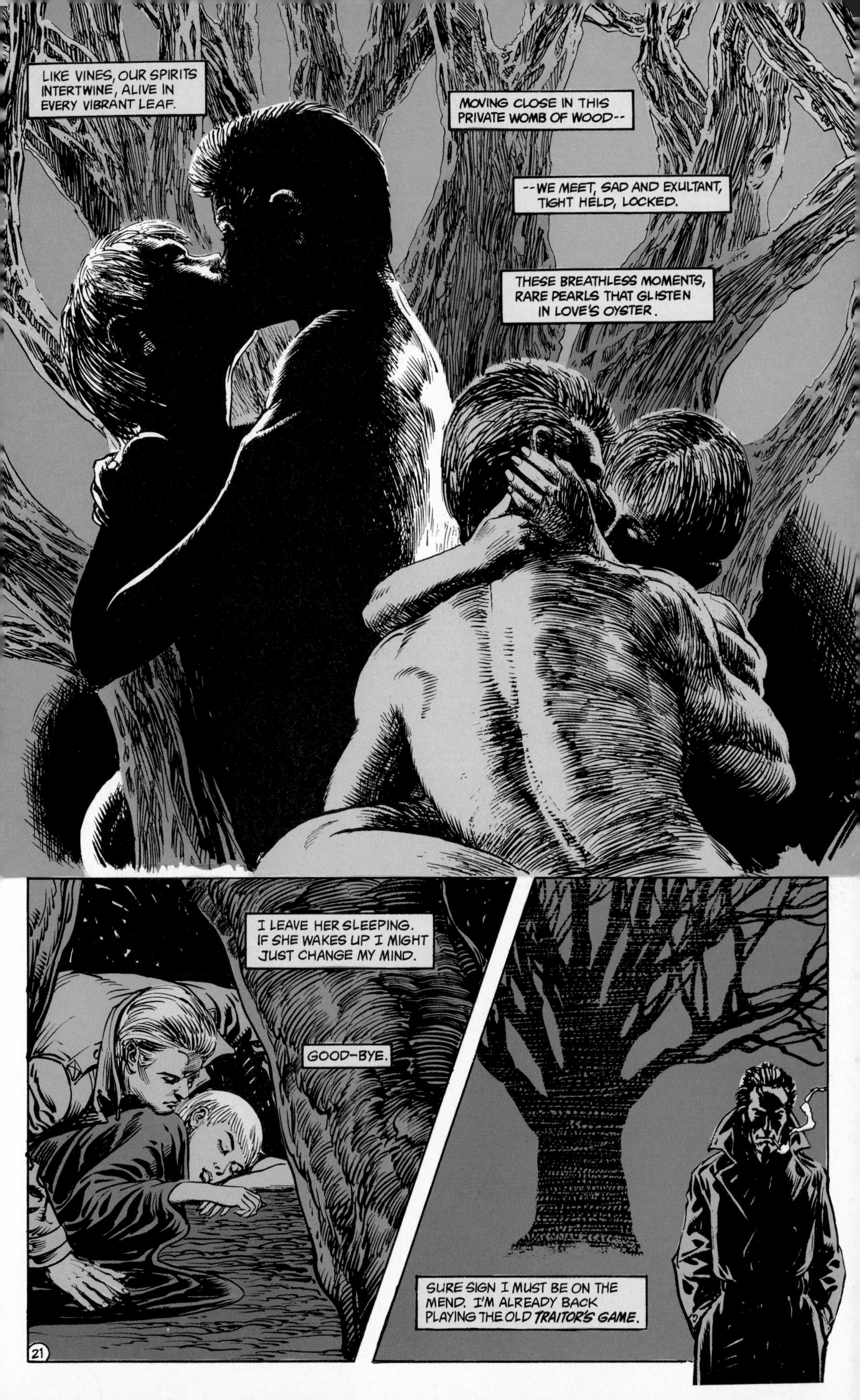
LIKE VINES, OUR SPIRITS INTERTWINE, ALIVE IN EVERY VIBRANT LEAF.
MOVING CLOSE IN THIS PRIVATE WOMB OF WOOD--
--WE MEET, SAD AND EXULTANT, TIGHT HELD, LOCKED.
THESE BREATHLESS MOMENTS, RARE PEARLS THAT GLISTEN IN LOVE'S OYSTER.
I LEAVE HER SLEEPING. IF SHE WAKES UP I MIGHT JUST CHANGE MY MIND.
GOOD-BYE.
SURE SIGN I MUST BE ON THE MEND. I'M ALREADY BACK PLAYING THE OLD *TRAITOR'S GAME*.

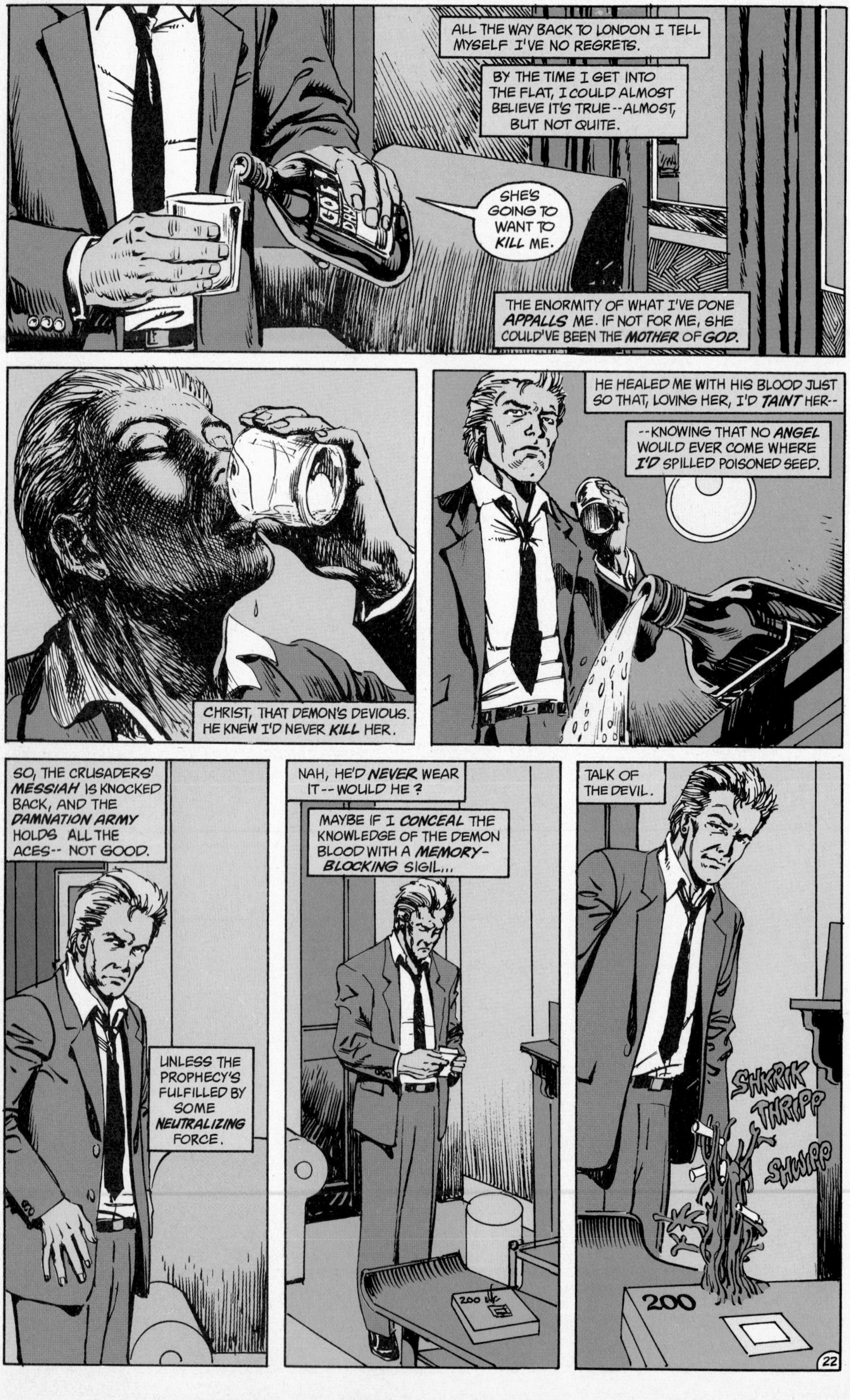
ALL THE WAY BACK TO LONDON I TELL MYSELF I'VE NO REGRETS.
BY THE TIME I GET INTO THE FLAT, I COULD ALMOST BELIEVE IT'S TRUE--ALMOST, BUT NOT QUITE.
SHE'S GOING TO WANT TO KILL ME.
THE ENORMITY OF WHAT I'VE DONE APPALLS ME. IF NOT FOR ME, SHE COULD'VE BEEN THE MOTHER OF GOD.
CHRIST, THAT DEMON'S DEVIOUS. HE KNEW I'D NEVER KILL HER.
HE HEALED ME WITH HIS BLOOD JUST SO THAT, LOVING HER, I'D TAINT HER--
--KNOWING THAT NO ANGEL WOULD EVER COME WHERE I'D SPILLED POISONED SEED.
SO, THE CRUSADERS' MESSIAH IS KNOCKED BACK, AND THE DAMNATION ARMY HOLDS ALL THE ACES-- NOT GOOD.
UNLESS THE PROPHECY'S FULFILLED BY SOME NEUTRALIZING FORCE.
NAH, HE'D NEVER WEAR IT--WOULD HE?
MAYBE IF I CONCEAL THE KNOWLEDGE OF THE DEMON BLOOD WITH A MEMORY-BLOCKING SIGIL...
TALK OF THE DEVIL.
SHKRRK
THRIPP
SHWIPP
200

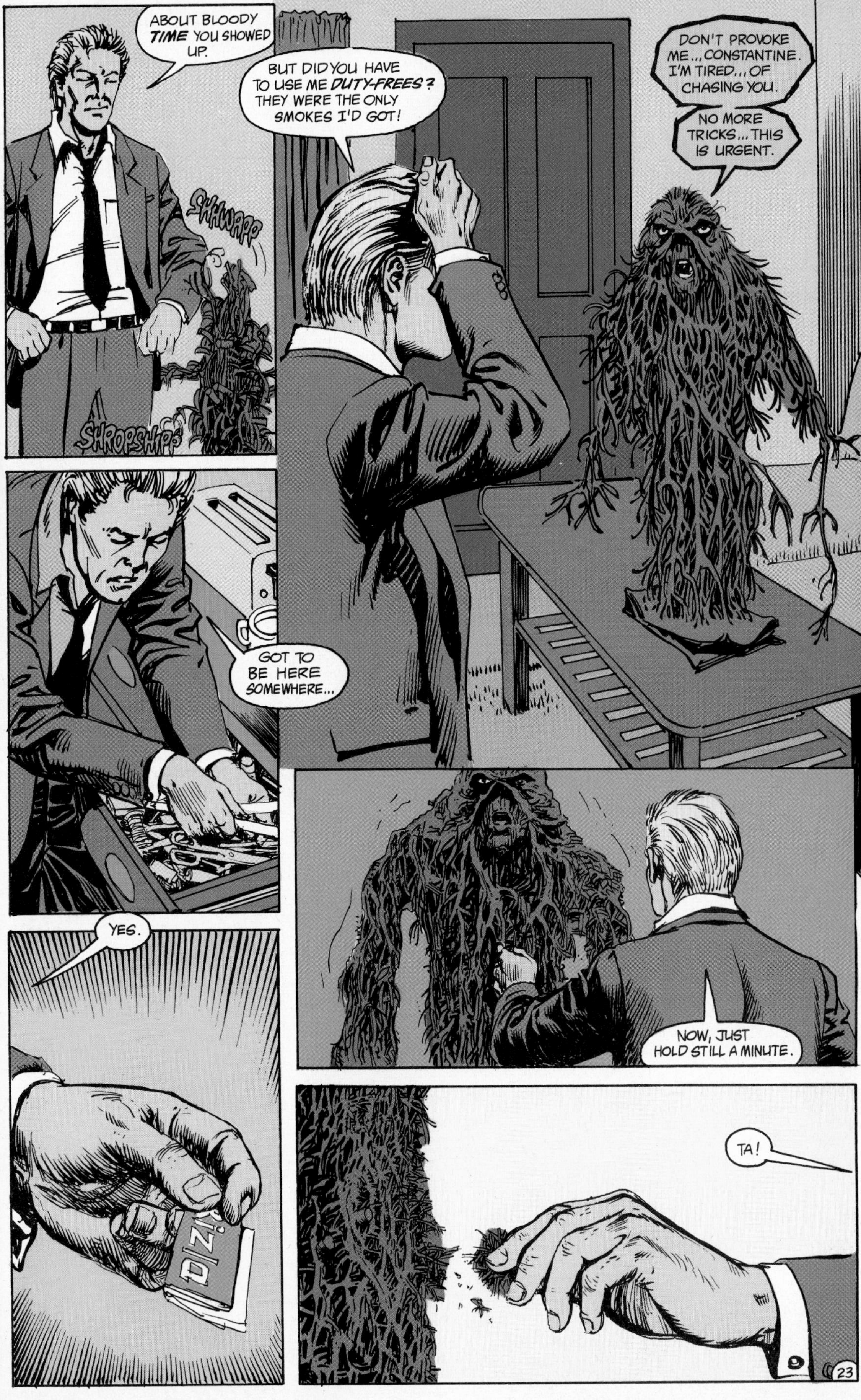
ABOUT BLOODY TIME YOU SHOWED UP.
SHHWAPP
SHROPSHIPP
BUT DID YOU HAVE TO USE ME DUTY-FREES? THEY WERE THE ONLY SMOKES I'D GOT!
DON'T PROVOKE ME... CONSTANTINE. I'M TIRED... OF CHASING YOU.
NO MORE TRICKS... THIS IS URGENT.
GOT TO BE HERE SOMEWHERE...
NOW, JUST HOLD STILL A MINUTE.
YES.
TA!
23

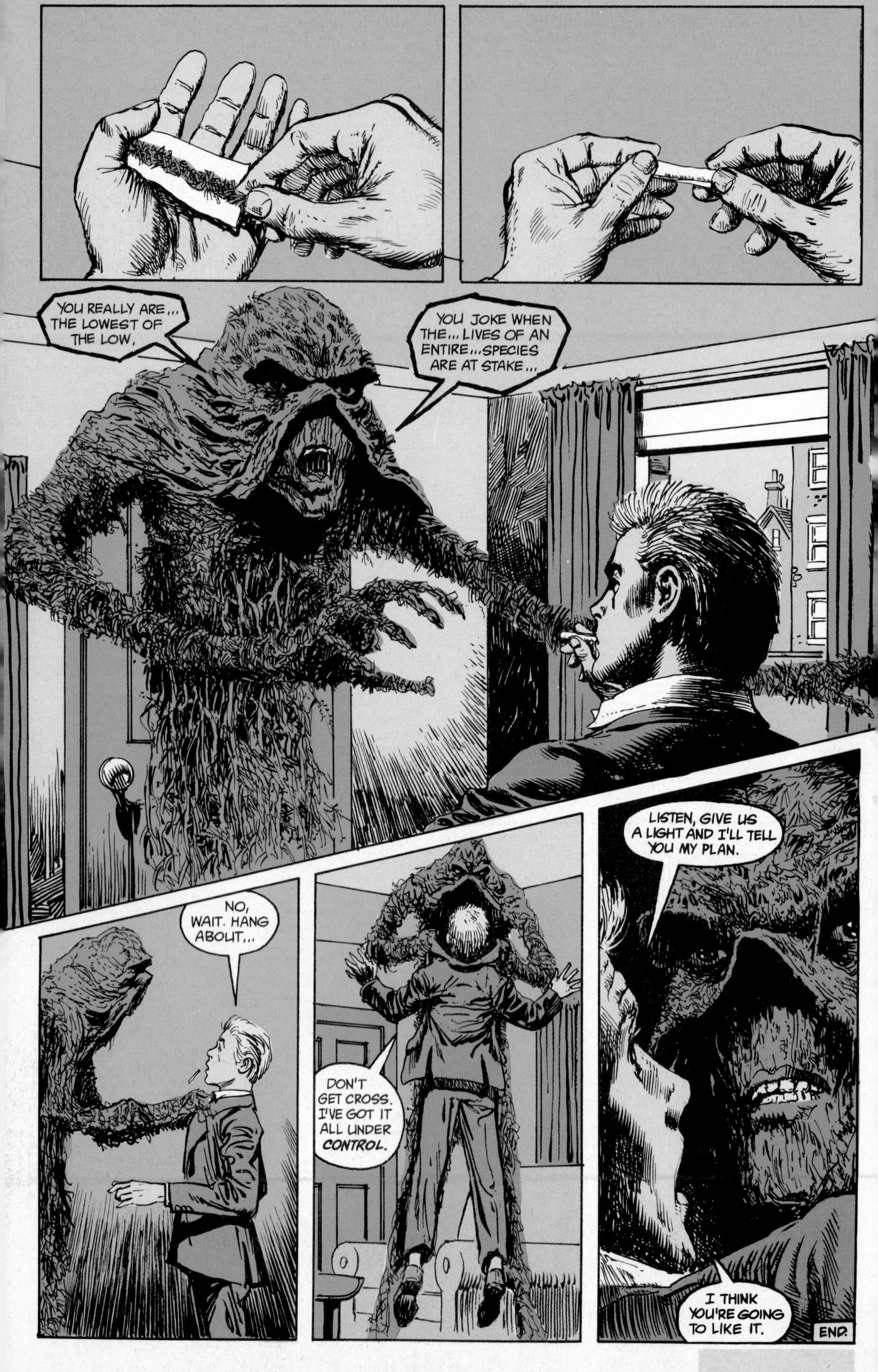
YOU REALLY ARE... THE LOWEST OF THE LOW.
YOU JOKE WHEN THE... LIVES OF AN ENTIRE... SPECIES ARE AT STAKE...
NO, WAIT. HANG ABOUT...
DON'T GET CROSS. I'VE GOT IT ALL UNDER CONTROL.
LISTEN, GIVE US A LIGHT AND I'LL TELL YOU MY PLAN.
I THINK YOU'RE GOING TO LIKE IT.
END.